# JUSTIFICATION AND EXCUSE IN INTERNATIONAL LAW

The defences available to an agent accused of wrongdoing can be considered as justifications (which render acts lawful) or excuses (which shield the agent from the legal consequences of the wrongful act). This distinction is familiar to many domestic legal systems, and tracks analogous notions in moral philosophy and ordinary language. Nevertheless, it remains contested in some domestic jurisdictions where it is often argued that the distinction is purely theoretical and has no consequences in practice. In international law too the distinction has been fraught with controversy, though there are increasing calls for its recognition. This book is the first to comprehensively and thoroughly examine the distinction and its relevance to the international legal order. Combining an analysis of State practice, historical, doctrinal and theoretical developments, the book shows that the distinction is not only possible in international law but that it is also one that would have important practical implications.

FEDERICA PADDEU is the John Tiley Fellow in Law at Queens' College and a fellow at the Lauterpacht Centre for International Law, Cambridge.

CAMBRIDGE STUDIES IN INTERNATIONAL
AND COMPARATIVE LAW: 130

Established in 1946, this series produces high quality, reflective and innovative scholarship in the field of public international law. It publishes works on international law that are of a theoretical, historical, cross-disciplinary or doctrinal nature. The series also welcomes books providing insights from private international law, comparative law and transnational studies which inform international legal thought and practice more generally.

The series seeks to publish views from diverse legal traditions and perspectives, and of any geographical origin. In this respect it invites studies offering regional perspectives on core *problématiques* of international law, and in the same vein, it appreciates contrasts and debates between diverging approaches. Accordingly, books offering new or less orthodox perspectives are very much welcome. Works of a generalist character are greatly valued and the Series is also open to studies on specific areas, institutions or problems. Translations of the most outstanding works published in other languages are also considered.

After 70 years, *Cambridge Studies in International and Comparative Law* remains the standard-setter for international legal scholarship and will continue to define the discipline as it evolves in the years to come.

*General Editors*

Larissa van den Herik
*Professor of Public International Law, Law School Leiden University*

Jean D'Aspremont
*Professor of Public International Law, Manchester International Law Centre, University of Manchester*

*A list of books in the series can be found at the end of this volume.*

# JUSTIFICATION AND EXCUSE IN INTERNATIONAL LAW

Concept and Theory of General Defences

FEDERICA PADDEU
*University of Cambridge*

# CAMBRIDGE
## UNIVERSITY PRESS

University Printing House, Cambridge CB2 8BS, United Kingdom

One Liberty Plaza, 20th Floor, New York, NY 10006, USA

477 Williamstown Road, Port Melbourne, VIC 3207, Australia

314-321, 3rd Floor, Plot 3, Splendor Forum, Jasola District Centre, New Delhi - 110025, India

79 Anson Road, #06-04/06, Singapore 079906

Cambridge University Press is part of the University of Cambridge.

It furthers the University's mission by disseminating knowledge in the pursuit of education, learning and research at the highest international levels of excellence.

www.cambridge.org
Information on this title: www.cambridge.org/9781107106208
DOI: 10.1017/9781316226841

© Federica Paddeu 2018

This publication is in copyright. Subject to statutory exception and to the provisions of relevant collective licensing agreements, no reproduction of any part may take place without the written permission of Cambridge University Press.

First published 2018
First paperback edition 2018

*A catalogue record for this publication is available from the British Library*

Library of Congress Cataloging in Publication data
Names: Paddeu, Federica, 1982– author.
Title: Justification and excuse in international law : concept and theory of general defences / Federica Paddeu.
Description: New York: Cambridge University Press, 2018. | Series: Cambridge studies in international and comparative law: 130 | Includes bibliographical references and index.
Identifiers: LCCN 2017001030 | ISBN 9781107106208 (hardback)
Subjects: LCSH: Government liability (International law) | International obligations. | Self-defense (International law) | Necessity (Law) | BISAC: LAW / International.
Classification: LCC KZ4080.P33 2017 | DDC 341.26–dc23
LC record available at https://lccn.loc.gov/2017001030

ISBN 978-1-107-10620-8 Hardback
ISBN 978-1-107-51399-0 Paperback

Cambridge University Press has no responsibility for the persistence or accuracy of URLs for external or third-party internet websites referred to in this publication, and does not guarantee that any content on such websites is, or will remain, accurate or appropriate.

*To my Plants*

CONTENTS

*Foreword    page* xix
*Acknowledgements    * xxiii
*Table of Cases    * xxv
*Select Table of Treaties and Other Documents    * xxxiii
*List of Abbreviations    * xxxix

Introduction    1

**PART I  Justification and Excuse in International Law**

1  Justification and Excuse in International Law    23
   1.1  Introduction    23
   1.2  A Primer on Justification and Excuse    27
   1.3  Justification and Excuse in the Law of State Responsibility    35
      1.3.1  The Distinction in Positive Law    35
      1.3.2  Reopening the Case: Justification and Excuse in the Articles on State Responsibility    37
         1.3.2.1  García-Amador: Total and Partial Excuse    38
         1.3.2.2  Ago: The Irrelevance of Excuses    40
            Ago's Report and Its Reception in the International Law Commission    40
            Missing Link: Off-the-Record Rejection of Excuses?    44
         1.3.2.3  Crawford: Justifications or Excuses    47
         1.3.2.4  The Position of the ILC: An Invitation for Further Development    49
      1.3.3  Defences in the World of Primary and Secondary Rules    52
         1.3.3.1  Primary and Secondary Rules in the Law of Responsibility    53
         1.3.3.2  Justification and Excuse: Primary or Secondary Rules?    57
   1.4  Interim Conclusion: Systemic Possibility of the Distinction in International Law    61

ix

## CONTENTS

2 Practical Consequences of the Distinction in International Law  63
 2.1 Introduction  63
 2.2 Effect on Reparation: The Problem of Satisfaction  63
 2.3 Responsibility of Accessories  66
 2.4 Reacting Against Wrongfulness  70
  2.4.1 Countermeasures Against Justified Conduct or Excused Actors  71
  2.4.2 Law of Treaties: Material Breach, Justification and Excuse  72
 2.5 Effect on Compensation for Material Loss  77
  2.5.1 Excuses and the Duty of Compensation  81
  2.5.2 Justifications and the Duty of Compensation  86
  2.5.3 Third Parties and the Duty of Compensation  92
  2.5.4 Conclusion on the Duty of Compensation  93
 2.6 Normative Considerations  94
 2.7 Interim Conclusion: A Distinction with a Difference  97

3 Classifying Defences into Justification and Excuse in International Law  98
 3.1 Introduction  98
 3.2 Concept and Theory of Justification  100
  3.2.1 Concept of Justification  101
   3.2.1.1 Defining Justifications  102
   3.2.1.2 Justifications as Permissions  102
   3.2.1.3 Justifications and the Breach of International Law  106
   3.2.1.4 Justified Conduct: Lawful or 'Non Wrongful'?  110
   3.2.1.5 Justifications: 'Deeds' or 'Reasons'?  113
  3.2.2 Theorising Justifications in International Law  115
 3.3 Concept and Theory of Excuse  117
  3.3.1 Concept of Excuse  118
   3.3.1.1 Defining Excuses in International Law  118
   3.3.1.2 Excuses and Corporate Entities  119
  3.3.2 Theorising Excuses in International Law  120
  3.3.3 Excuses and Fault  122
 3.4 Taxonomy of Defences: The Role of Concept and Theory  126
 3.5 General Conclusion to Part I  128

**PART II Classifying the Defences in the Articles on State Responsibility**

4 Consent  131
 4.1 Introduction  131
 4.2 Development of the Plea of Consent  134

4.2.1 A Brief History of the Plea of Consent
(1898–1979)   135
  4.2.1.1 Writings of Scholars   136
  4.2.1.2 State Practice   139
        Savarkar (1911)   139
        Russian Indemnity (1912)   143
  4.2.1.3 Interim Conclusions   144
4.2.2 Codification in the International Law
Commission   145
  4.2.2.1 First Reading of the ARS: The Adoption
        of Draft Article 29   146
        Ago's Report and the Debates at the
          International Law Commission   146
        Views of States in the General Assembly's
          Sixth Committee   149
  4.2.2.2 The Adoption of Article 20 on Second
        Reading   150
        Crawford's Report and the Debates at the
          International Law Commission   150
        Views of States in the Sixth Committee and
          Subsequent Practice   153
4.3 Consent as a Defence   154
  4.3.1 Three Objections to the Defence of Consent   156
    4.3.1.1 Consent as a Primary Rule   156
    4.3.1.2 The Temporal Logic of Consent   158
    4.3.1.3 Consent and Absolute Obligations   163
  4.3.2 Defending the Defence of Consent   165
4.4 Consent as a Justification   170
  4.4.1 Consent as the Renunciation of Legal Protection   170
  4.4.2 Renunciation, Absent Interest and Theories of
    Justification   172

5 Self-Defence   175
  5.1 Introduction   175
  5.2 Historical Premise: Armed Conflict during Peace   180
  5.3 Tracing the Development of Article 21 in the
    International Law Commission   184
    5.3.1 First Reading: Self-Defence and the Prohibition
      of Force   185
    5.3.2 Second Reading: Self-Defence Beyond the Prohibition
      of Force   189
  5.4 Self-Defence as a 'Circumstance Precluding
    Wrongfulness' in the Articles on State Responsibility   192
    5.4.1 A Justification for Forcible Measures Only   192
    5.4.2 Understanding the Scope of Article 21   193
      5.4.2.1 First Legal Relation: On the Legality
        of Resort to Force   193

              5.4.2.2  Second Set of Legal Relations: Other
                       Rights of the Aggressor State    197
              5.4.2.3  Third Set of Legal Relations: Obligations
                       of 'Total Restraint'    198
      5.4.3   Self-Defence and Other Obligations in Practice    199
              5.4.3.1  Territorial Sovereignty and
                       Non-Intervention    199
                       *Nicaragua v US* (1986)    199
                       *DRC v Uganda* (2005)    200
              5.4.3.2  Commercial Obligations    202
                       *Nicaragua v US* (1986)    202
                       *Oil Platforms* (2003)    203
  5.5  Justification for the Collateral Impairment
       of Other Obligations    205
      5.5.1   Consequentialist Theories    206
      5.5.2   Deontic Theories    210
              5.5.2.1  Preliminary Clarification: The Right
                       of Self-Defence as a Hohfeldian Liberty    210
              5.5.2.2  Unity of the Legal System    216
              5.5.2.3  Exercise of a Peremptory Right    217
              5.5.2.4  Forfeiture of Legal Protection    218
              5.5.2.5  The Acid Test: Compensation for
                       Material Loss    222
      5.5.3   Rights Forfeiture and the Justification of
              Self-Defence    223

6  Countermeasures    225
  6.1  Introduction    225
  6.2  Reprisals and the Origins of Countermeasures    228
      6.2.1   1800–1919: Classic Age of Reprisals    230
              6.2.1.1  Positive and Negative Reprisals    231
                       Positive Reprisals    232
                       Negative Reprisals    234
              6.2.1.2  What Limits on the Right to Reprisals?    237
      6.2.2   1919–1945: Period of Transition    238
              6.2.2.1  Outlawing Forcible Reprisals    239
              6.2.2.2  Regulating Non-Forcible Reprisals    242
      6.2.3   Interim Conclusions    244
              6.2.3.1  Reprisals as the Non-Performance of
                       the Law    246
              6.2.3.2  Function of Reprisals: Enforcement
                       of International Law    247
              6.2.3.3  Reprisals as Lawful Measures    249
  6.3  Countermeasures in Contemporary International Law    250
      6.3.1   The Dual Role of Countermeasures in the Law of
              Responsibility    252

## CONTENTS

        6.3.1.1   Incidental Function: A Circumstance Precluding Wrongfulness   253
        6.3.1.2   Primary Function: Implementation of State Responsibility   255
                First Reading: Countermeasures as Sanction   256
                Second Reading: Instrumental Countermeasures   259
    6.3.2   The Regime of Countermeasures in the Articles on State Responsibility   261
        6.3.2.1   Existence of a Wrongful Act   261
        6.3.2.2   Substantive Requirements   262
        6.3.2.3   Procedural Conditions   264
6.4   Countermeasures as Justifications   266
    6.4.1   Theorising the Legality of Countermeasures   267
        6.4.1.1   States as Organs of the International Community   267
        6.4.1.2   Consequentialist Theories   270
        6.4.1.3   Deontic Theories   272
                Preliminary Clarification: Countermeasures as Hohfeldian Liberties   273
                Unity of the Legal System   276
                Forfeiture Theory   276
        6.4.1.4   The Acid Test: Compensation for Material Loss   282
    6.4.2   Grounding the Justification of Countermeasures on Rights Forfeiture   284

7   *Force Majeure*   285
   7.1   Introduction   285
   7.2   Historical Notes on the Development of the Plea of *Force Majeure*   288
       7.2.1   The *Force Majeure* of Revolutions in the Nineteenth Century   289
       7.2.2   *Force Majeure* in Judicial and Arbitral Practice of the Early Twentieth Century   294
           7.2.2.1   *French Company of Venezuelan Railroads* (1904)   294
           7.2.2.2   *Russian Indemnity* (1912)   295
           7.2.2.3   *The SS Wimbledon* (1923)   297
           7.2.2.4   *Serbian* and *Brazilian Loans* (1929)   298
           7.2.2.5   *Société Commerciale de Belgique* (1939)   299
       7.2.3   An Assessment   300
           7.2.3.1   Changing Conceptions of *Force Majeure*   300
           7.2.3.2   What Rationale for the Plea?   303

7.3 *Force Majeure* in Contemporary International Law 306
   7.3.1 The ILC's Codification of Article 23 308
      7.3.1.1 First Reading: A Fault-Based Rationale for *Force Majeure*? 308
      7.3.1.2 Second Reading: Excluding Fault 313
   7.3.2 *Force Majeure* in the Practice of States since 1945 315
      7.3.2.1 States' Views in the Sixth Committee 315
      7.3.2.2 Arbitral and Judicial Practice 316
          Events of *Force Majeure*: *de Wytenhove* (1950) and *Ottoman Lighthouses* (1956) 316
          *Rights of US Nationals in Morocco* (1952) 317
          *Rainbow Warrior* (1990) 317
          *LAFICO v Burundi* (1991) 318
          *Gabčíkovo-Nagymaros* (1994) 318
          *Aucoven v Venezuela* (2003) 319
   7.3.3 A Postscript on the Standard of Material Impossibility 320
7.4 *Force Majeure* as an Excuse 323
   7.4.1 Explaining the Rationale 324
   7.4.2 *Force Majeure* as an Excuse 328
   7.4.3 Theorising the Excuse of *Force Majeure*: A Free Will Theory 330

# 8 State of Necessity 334
8.1 Introduction 334
8.2 State of Necessity in International Law: Historical Notes 339
   8.2.1 Seventeenth and Eighteenth Centuries: The Natural Right of Necessity 339
      8.2.1.1 The Early-Modern International Lawyers 339
      8.2.1.2 'Necessity' as Original Community in *The Neptune* 343
   8.2.2 The Long Nineteenth Century (1800–1914): Twilight of the General 'Right of Necessity' 345
      8.2.2.1 A Difficult Start: The Seizure of the Danish Fleet (1807) 345
      8.2.2.2 Necessity and the Fundamental Right of Self-Preservation 346
          The Fundamental Rights of States and the Right of Self-Preservation 346
          A Discrete Right: The Right of Necessity as a Corollary of the Right of Self-Preservation 349
          Inspiring Rights: The 'Necessity of Self-Defence and Self-Preservation' 350

## CONTENTS

- 8.2.2.3 Whither the Right of Necessity in International Law?   359
- 8.2.3 1914–1945: Towards State of Necessity in International Law   363
  - 8.2.3.1 A Doctrinal Development: State of Necessity in the Law of State Responsibility   363
    - New Frameworks: The Rule of Necessity and the Law of State Responsibility   364
    - New Conceptions: The Rule of Necessity as a Conflict of Interests   366
    - New Theories for the Rule of Necessity   368
  - 8.2.3.2 Fearing Anarchy and Chaos: Rejecting the Rule of Necessity   371
    - The 'Rape' of Belgium and Luxembourg   372
    - A Different Battlefield: The Intellectual Dispute over the Recognition of a Rule of Necessity   374
  - 8.2.3.3 Lagging Behind: Protection of Essential Interests in the Practice of States   377
    - The Defence of Necessity at the 1930 Hague Codification Conference   377
    - Essential Interests and *Force Majeure* in International Disputes   378
- 8.2.4 An Assessment: State of Necessity between Substance and Form   382
- 8.3 New Beginnings: Rehabilitating State of Necessity at the International Law Commission   386
  - 8.3.1 Codifying State of Necessity at the International Law Commission   387
    - 8.3.1.1 First Reading: The Inclusion of State of Necessity in the Draft Articles   388
      - Breaking Through: Ago's State of Necessity   388
      - The Commission's Views and the Adoption of Draft Article 33   390
    - 8.3.1.2 Second Reading and the Adoption of Article 25   394
      - Two Not So 'Minor' Changes: Taking Account of Community Interests   394
      - A Justification or an Excuse?   396
    - 8.3.1.3 Article 25 and the Commission's Commentary   397

        8.3.2    State of Necessity in the Practice of States since 1945    398
              8.3.2.1    Reactions to the Work of the International Law Commission on State of Necessity    398
              8.3.2.2    Invoking State of Necessity in Dispute Settlement    401
                    Protecting Environmental Interests: 'Ecological Necessity'    401
                    'Financial Necessity': State of Necessity in Investment Arbitration    404
                    Miscellaneous Cases: The Generality of the Defence of Necessity    410
        8.3.3    A Customary Defence?    414
    8.4    State of Necessity between Justification and Excuse    414
        8.4.1    Identifying the Rationale: Superiority of the Interest Safeguarded    415
        8.4.2    State of Necessity as a (Counterintuitive) Justification    418
        8.4.3    A Duty of Compensation?    421
        8.4.4    A Proposal for Excusing Necessity    426

9    Distress    430
    9.1    Introduction    430
    9.2    Historical Antecedents of the Defence of Distress    432
        9.2.1    The Law of the Sea and the Right of Entry in Distress    433
        9.2.2    Blockade Violations in Distress in the Long Nineteenth Century    435
        9.2.3    Distress and Humanitarian Considerations    440
    9.3    The Defence of Distress in Contemporary International Law    443
        9.3.1    First Reading: Formulating the Defence of Distress in the International Law Commission    443
              9.3.1.1    Ago's 'Relative Impossibility of Performance'    443
              9.3.1.2    Distress as a Discrete Defence: The Adoption of Draft Article 32 at the International Law Commission    446
        9.3.2    State Reactions and the *Rainbow Warrior* Affair (1979–1999)    447
              9.3.2.1    State Reactions to Draft Article 32    447
              9.3.2.2    Boosting the Defence: The *Rainbow Warrior* Arbitration    449
        9.3.3    Progressive Development and the Adoption of Article 24    453
        9.3.4    Customary Status Pending    456

9.4 Classifying Distress as Justification or Excuse   456
    9.4.1 Distress as an Excuse   456
    9.4.2 Distress as a Justification   459
    9.4.3 Justification or Excuse?   461

Conclusion   465

*Bibliography*   481
*Index*   525

# FOREWORD

J. L. Austin famously distinguished between two types of defence. One can admit that one did do the very thing one is accused of, but 'argue that it was a good thing, or the right or sensible thing, or a permissible thing to do'. Or one can admit that that very thing 'wasn't a good thing to have done, but ... argue that it is not quite fair or correct to say *baldly* "X did A" ... perhaps he was under somebody's influence, or was nudged ... it may have been partly accidental, or an unintentional slip.' In short, as Austin explained, 'In the one defence, briefly, we accept responsibility but deny that it was bad: in the other, we admit that it was bad but don't accept full, or even any, responsibility'.[1] The former defence constitutes a justification, the latter an excuse. The distinction between justification and excuse is an important one, if only because it tracks a societal and even moral intuition about the two forms of exoneration. If in both cases the result is that the agent does not suffer the legal consequences of responsibility, the reasons for this are quite distinct: in the one case, it is because the legal order permits the conduct; in the other, it is because the agent is not liable despite its conduct being impermissible.

The early common law distinguished between justified homicide and excused homicide; but by the end of the nineteenth century, the great English criminal lawyer Sir James Stephens declared this distinction to be one of pure 'historical interest'.[2] Yet, at around that same time, German criminal law theory was beginning to develop justification and excuse as concepts in the theory of crime. These concepts were subsequently adopted in German law and spread across many continental law jurisdictions, where they are still recognised and applied. Relegated to a historical peculiarity, justification and excuse exploded into the common law world with Austin's article. Indeed, since then, considerable effort has been put towards understanding and articulating the distinction between

---

[1] J. L. Austin, 'A Plea for Excuses' (1956–1957) 57 *Proc Arist Soc* 1, 2 (emphasis in original).
[2] Stephen, *History of the Criminal Law of England* (MacMillan, 1883) vol. 3, 11.

justification and excuse and towards assessing the merits, pragmatic or otherwise, of recognising it. The distinction is not recognised in all domestic legal orders, but even where it is not, as in the United Kingdom, the reasons for and against it have been carefully considered and weighed.

By contrast, the distinction between justification and excuse has so far received scant attention in international law. During the International Law Commission's codification of the Articles on State Responsibility, the distinction was put forward by some governments and by some Commission members. Ultimately, however, the Commission decided that no strict classifications should be drawn in the Articles themselves which, as a result, do not take a position on whether the distinction is recognised at international law or on the classification of the various circumstances as justifications or excuses. The matter was left open for subsequent development and, since the adoption of the Articles in 2001, there have been instances of engagement with the distinction in practice. Perhaps most prominently, the ICSID Annulment Committee in *CMS v Argentina* expressed, in no uncertain terms, that the plea of necessity operated as an excuse in international law.[3] Dr Federica Paddeu's book is therefore a welcome and timely examination of the notions of justification and excuse in international law.

In a thorough analysis, theoretically and historically informed, the author clarifies the meaning of these notions, as they are employed in general jurisprudential works and in domestic legal orders, and examines whether, and if so how, these concepts can be accommodated by the system of State responsibility. Dr Paddeu builds from the conceptual pillars of that system, premised on the distinction between the notions of wrongfulness and responsibility, to show that international law can accommodate defences which either preclude wrongfulness *or* preclude responsibility (but not wrongfulness). In this regard, Dr Paddeu's approach demonstrates a justified scepticism towards recurrent aprioristic arguments about these notions and their recognition in the international legal order. She argues against such positions, especially against those who maintain that the distinction has no place in international law because it is (primarily) used in domestic criminal law or because it is a distinction so 'fine as to be of pure ... theoretical interest'.[4] As the book shows, such *a priori* positions are rarely helpful. The concepts of justification and excuse were developed to

---

[3] *CMS Gas Transmission Company v Argentine Republic*, ICSID Case ARB/01/8, Annulment, 25 September 2007, [129–36].
[4] Franck, *Recourse to Force* (2002), 191.

perform specific functions in domestic legal orders, and the real question is whether these notions can perform equally useful functions, practical or normative, in the international legal order. She argues that the distinction would indeed have significant functions in relation to a number of issues, including the responses to unlawful acts, both in the law of responsibility (in the form of countermeasures) and the law of treaties (in the form of the termination or suspension of treaties due to material breach); the question of compensation in the event of the successful invocation of a defence; the issue of accessorial responsibility; and, finally, in relation to the normative implications on legal standards of the acceptance of a defence. Thus, for example, since the responsibility of accomplice States pursuant to Article 16 of the Articles on State Responsibility is derivative from the wrongfulness of the act of the principal, whether the principal's conduct is justified (permitted) or whether the principal is excused, affects the responsibility of the accomplice. Dr Paddeu is careful not to assert that, in respect of these issues, any particular implications follow, of necessity, from the distinction. But she explains that these are legal problems to which the distinction between justification and excuse can provide answers – answers which it is for the legal order to accept or reject. In her view, justification and excuse are, as a minimum, useful analytical tools through which to resolve real legal problems.

Dr Paddeu's study is the first comprehensive analysis of this important question of the law of responsibility. But its merits go much further than that: her work is thoroughly well researched, balanced in its views, and shows real depth of analysis. It is also rich in historical detail, especially in relation to the development of the six defences currently recognised in the ILC's Articles. Her consideration of certain historical incidents, including the *Caroline* incident and the *Savarkar* and *Russian Indemnities* cases, shows them in a new and often corrected light. This is a thoroughly original study, and a splendid first foray into the wilds of State responsibility.

James Crawford AC<br>Peace Palace, The Hague

ACKNOWLEDGEMENTS

This book is the culmination of many years of research, thinking and writing. It started out as the topic for my PhD dissertation (which I began in 2009), and it became clear within a few months of my doctoral studies that the three years of the usual PhD degree would be insufficient to complete the research. I was lucky enough to be awarded a Junior Research Fellowship, which gave me the luxury of focusing exclusively on this manuscript for a few additional years. Many people helped me along the way and I would like to express my gratitude to them all. A few, however, deserve special mention.

I am indebted, first of all, to my PhD supervisor, Judge James Crawford. He was an island of certainty in the sea of doctoral uncertainty. Professor Christine Gray was (and continues to be) a source of endless encouragement. Her comments on my project early on helped to focus and narrow the research question, and she had very helpful advice on the chapter on self-defence. Professor Vaughan Lowe patiently read as many as three different versions of an article I submitted on the defence of *force majeure* to the British Yearbook of International Law. His suggestions for that article have found their way into Chapter 7 of this book. Finally, Sarah Heathcote discussed with me, in Canberra, London and Cambridge, the many difficulties of the plea of necessity in international law. Her thoughts were central in developing my own ideas about this controversial defence.

My PhD examiners, Professor Christian Tams and Professor Malgosia Fitzmaurice, were tough but fair and, most importantly, kind. Their comments and questions on the dissertation forced me to reach deeper into the materials and the arguments, and to think about the themes of this study in a broader perspective. I am ever grateful to them for their engagement and their continuing support. This book would not have been the same without their input. Many colleagues and friends also discussed the various themes in this work with me. Among them, Lorand Bartels, Emma Bickerstaffe, Fernando Lusa Bordin, Daniel Costelloe, Luís Duarte d'Almeida, Mark D'Souza, Matt Dyson, James Goudkamp, Caroline Henckels, Jonathan Ketcheson, Randall Lesaffer, Nick McBride, Francesco Messineo, Odette Murray, Claire Nielsen, Roger O'Keefe, Brendan Plant, Kate Purcell, Surabhi Ranganathan, Cecily Rose, Ben Saul, Findlay Stark and Michael Waibel. My thanks go to all of them.

Special thanks go to Jan Morrison who allowed me to use her work as the cover image for this book. The mosaic depicting the Greenpeace vessel *Rainbow Warrior*, from a design by Vicki Worthington, was completed with the assistance of Claudia Pond Eyley for the thirtieth anniversary of Greenpeace in September 2001. My dear friend Claire Nielsen took her family to the Ports of Auckland on a rainy Saturday to take the picture that is in the cover of this book. I cannot thank her enough for this. At CUP, my deepest thanks go to Lisa Sinclair for her enthusiastic help with the cover image and, more generally, her assistance throughout the production stages of the book.

All of this work cannot, of course, happen without financial support. Girton College, where I was María Luisa de Sánchez scholar, and Cambridge European Trusts supported my PhD studies. Queens' College Cambridge gave me the privilege to spend three years as a Junior Research Fellow to devote entirely to this book. I am forever grateful to both Girton and Queens' for the financial support and for providing a rich, diverse, nurturing and friendly intellectual community within which to work. My law colleagues at Queens', Richard Fentiman, Martin Dixon and John Allison, were (and continue to be) a constant source of encouragement and support. Events in life are often connected in ways we cannot imagine. So it was that through Queens' alumni, I discovered the generosity of many Venezuelan families who supported the institution of scholarships for Venezuelan students in Cambridge, including the María Luisa de Sánchez scholarship at Girton whose donors I have now been able to thank personally. I hope that this book, alongside the achievements of other Venezuelan scholars that they have supported, will make them proud and hopeful that these dark times for our country have not extinguished the spirit of our *Bravo Pueblo*.

I also owe thanks to my multi-cultural family, now spread across four continents, and friends for their warm support and for reminding me, when the work got really stressful, of the things that matter in life. Lastly, I am most grateful to my husband, Brendan, without whose loving support this work would have never been completed.

TABLE OF CASES

Arbitral Awards

*Air Service Agreement of 27 March 1946 between the United States of America and France* (1978) 18 RIAA 417, 113–114, 225–226, 253n152, 263n219, 263n228, 271n272

*American Electric and Manufacturing Company Case (Damages to Property)* (1903–1905) 9 RIAA 145, 301n87

*Archer Daniels Midland Company and Tate & Lyle Ingredients Americas, Inc v Mexico*, ICSID Case No ARB/ (AF)/ 04/ 5, Award, 21 November 2007, 253n152, 279n303

*Autopista Concesionada de Venezuela v Bolivarian Republic of Venezuela* ICSID Case No ARB/ 00/ 5, Award, 23 September 2003, 319n185

*Bembelista Case* (1903) 10 RIAA 717, 301n87

*BG Group Plc v Argentina*, UNCITRAL Award, 24 December 2007, 89n116, 405–406, 424n587

*Brissot et al v Venezuela* (1898) 3 Moore Arbitrations 2949, 306n116

*Cargill, Inc v Mexico*, ICSID Case No ARB/ (AF)/ 05/ 2, Award, 18 September 2009, 253n152, 279n303

*Claim No 1, British Claims in the Spanish Zone of Morocco* (1924) 2 RIAA 639, 292–294

*CMS Gas Transmission Company v Argentine Republic*, ICSID Case ARB/ 01/ 8, Annulment, 25 September 2007, 12n42, 24, 70

*CMS Gas Transmission Company v Argentine Republic*, ICSID Case ARB/ 01/ 8, Award, 12 May 2005, 24, 70, 78, 406

*Continental Casualty Company v Argentine Republic*, ICSID Case ARB/ 03/ 9, Award, 5 September 2008, 253n152

*The Creole (United Kingdom/United States of America)* (1853) 4 Moore Arbitrations 4375, 434n19

*Cresceri Case (Italy/Peru)*, Case No 71 (1901) 15 RIAA 449, 306n116

*De Wytenhove Case (France/Italy)* (1950) 13 RIAA 228, 316–317

*The Dunn Case (Chile/UK) (1895), Reclamaciones presentadas al Tribunal Anglo-Chileno 1894–1896* (Santiago de Chile: Ercilla, 1896) vol. I, 537,   301n87

*EDF International SA, SAUR International SA and Leon Participaciones Argentinas SA v Argentine Republic,* ICSID Case ARB/ 03/ 23, Annulment, 5 February 2016,   90n121, 405–408, 422–423

*EDF International SA, SAUR International SA and Leon Participaciones Argentinas SA v Argentine Republic,* ICSID Case ARB/ 03/ 23, Award, 11 June 2012,   90n121, 405–408, 422–423

*El Paso Energy International Company v Argentine Republic,* ICSID Case ARB/ 03/ 15, Award, 31 October 2011,   24

*Enron Corporation and Ponderosa Assets LP v Argentine Republic,* ICSID Case ARB/ 01/ 3, Annulment, 30 July 2010,   405–408, 415n543, 422–423

*Enron Corporation and Ponderosa Assets LP v Argentine Republic,* ICSID Case ARB/ 01/ 3, Award, 22 May 2007,   405–408, 415n543, 422–423

*The Enterprise (United Kingdom/United States of America)* (1853) 4 Moore Arbitrations 4349,   434n19

*Faber Case* (1903) 10 RIAA 438,   335

*French Company of Venezuelan Railroads* (1904) 10 RIAA 285, 294–295, 304–305, 325, 378–379

*Fur Seals Arbitration* (1893) 1 Moore Arbitrations 755, 763,   350–351, 357–363, 410, 410n511

*General Company of the Orinoco* (1905) 10 RIAA 184,   422

*Georges Pinson (France) v United Mexican States* (1928) RIAA 324,   144n76

*Guyana v Suriname, Award, 17 September 2007,* UNCLOS Annex VII Tribunal,   183n45, 197n108

*The Hermosa (United Kingdom/United States of America)* (1853) 4 Moore Arbitrations 4374,   434n19

*Impregilo Spa v Argentine Republic,* ICSID Case No ARB/ 07/ 17, Award, 21 June 2011,   406–407

*Indus Waters Kishengaga Arbitration (Pakistan v India) PCA,* Partial Award, 18 February 2013,   334–335

*Kate A Hoff (The Rebecca) (USA v United Mexican States)* (1929) 4 RIAA 444,   434n19, 442n90

*Kummerow et al v Venezuela* (1903) 9 RIAA 369,   302n90

*Kuwait v American Independent Oil Company (Aminoil)* (1984) 66 ILR 518,   326

TABLE OF CASES                                           xxvii

*LG&E Energy Corp, LG&E Capital Corp, LG&E International Inc v Argentine Republic*, ICSID Case ARB/ 02/ 1, Liability, 3 October 2006,   78, 95–96, 406–408, 423
*Libyan Arab Foreign Investment Company (LAFICO) v Burundi* (1991) 96 ILR 279,   318
*Martini Case* (1903) 10 RIAA 644,   306n116
*Marvin Roy Feldman Karpa v United Mexican States*, ICSID Case ARB(AF)/ 99/ 1, Award, 16 December 2002,   168n181
*Metalpar SA and Buen Aire SA v Argentine Republic*, ICSID Case ARB/ 03/ 5, Award, 6 June 2008,   106n24, 406–408
*Michel Macri v Turkey*, Turco-Romanian Arbitral Tribunal, 19 January 1928, 7 TAM 981,   302n90
*National Grid Plc v Argentine Republic*, UNCITRAL Award, 3 November 2008,   97n138, 110, 168n181, 405–407
*North Atlantic Coast Fisheries Case (Great Britain/US)* (1910) 11 RIAA 167,   181n29, 248, 442
*Ottoman Empire Lighthouses Concession (France v Greece)* (1956) 12 RIAA 155,   317
*Petrocelli Case* (1903) 10 RIAA 591,   301n87
*Piola Case (Italy/Peru), Case No 63* (1901) 15 RIAA 444,   305n111
*Rainbow Warrior (New Zealand v France)* (1990) 20 RIAA 215,   1–5, 51, 75n57, 125, 313–314, 317–318, 394, 432, 443, 447–451, 453–457, 461, 473
*Russian Indemnity Case (Russia/Turkey)* (1912) Scott Hague Court Rep 297,   136, 143–145, 295–297, 301–304, 379–382
*Salvador Prats v United States* (1874) 3 Moore Arbitrations 2886,   305–306
*Sambiaggio Case* (1903) 10 RIAA 499,   305n109
*Savarkar Case (Great Britain, France)* (1911) 9 RIAA 243,   136, 139–143, 145, 170
*Sempra Energy International v Argentine Republic*, ICSID Case ARB/ 02/ 16, Annulment, 29 June 2010,   106n24, 404–408, 422–423
*Sempra Energy International v Argentine Republic*, ICSID Case ARB/ 02/ 16, Award, 29 September 2007,   106n24, 404–408, 422–423
*Southern Bluefin Tuna Case (Australia v Japan; New Zealand v Japan) (Jurisdiction and Admissibility)* (2000) 23 RIAA 1,   216–217
*Suez Sociedad General de Aguas de Barcelona SA and InterAgua Servicios Integrales del Agua SA v Argentine Republic [Suez (I)]*, ICSID Case ARB/ 03/ 17, Liability, 30 July 2010,   96–97, 406–408

*Suez Sociedad General de Aguas de Barcelona SA and Vivendi Universal SA v Argentine Republic [Suez (II)]*, ICSID Case ARB/ 03/ 19, Liability, 30 July 2010,   96–97, 406–408
*Total SA v Argentine Republic*, ICSID Case ARB/ 04/ 1, Liability, 27 December 2010,   95–96, 406–408
*von Pezold et al v Republic of Zimbabwe*, ICSID Case No ARB/ 10/ 15, Award, 28 July 2015,   37, 408–409, 424
*William Yeaton Case* (1885) 3 Moore Arbitrations 2944,   302n90

## Domestic Courts

### Canada

*Perka v The Queen* (1984) 2 SCR 232,   13n46, 99

### France

*La Caroline (1830)*, de Pistoye and Duverdy, *Traité de prises maritimes* (Durand, 1859), 381,   345, 351–360, 363, 410n511, 436n36
*La Louisa (1847)*, de Pistoye and Duverdy, *Traité de prises maritimes* (Durand, 1859), 382,   436n35
*La Marthe-Magdeleine* (year IX), de Pistoye and Duverdy, *Traité de prises maritimes* (Durand, 1859), 378,   436n34

### United Kingdom

*The Betsey* (1798) 1 C Rob 93   436n37
*The Charlotta* (1810) Edwards 252,   439–440
*The Columbia* (1798) 1 C Rob 154,   436n38
*The Courier* (1810) Edwards 249,   440n60
*The Eleanor* (1809) Edwards 135,   438–442
*The Elizabeth* (1810) 1 Edwards 198,   439n52
*The Fortuna* (1803) 5 C Rob 27,   440n65
*The Hurtige Hane* (1799) 2 C Rob 124,   440n65
*The James Cook* (1810) Edwards 261,   437n39
*The Mercurius* (1798) 1 C Rob 83,   436n31
*The Panaghia Rhomba* (1858) 2 Roscoe 635,   440n66, 442n89
*The Ringende Jacob* (1799) 1 C Rob 89,   437n40
*The Shepherdess* (1804) 5 C Rob 262,   439

TABLE OF CASES　　　　xxix

*United States*

*The Circassian* (1864) 69 US (2 Wall) 135,　436n38
*The Diana* (1868) 74 US 354,　438–440
*The Major Barbour* (1862) Blatchford 167,　439–440
*The New York* (1818) 16 US (3 Wheat) 59,　438n49, 442
*The Olinde Rodrigues* (1899) 174 US 510,　435n28
*The Rising Dawn* (1863) Blatchford 368,　440n61
*Vincent v Lake Erie Transportation Co* (1910) 109 Minn 456,　88, 424n597, 462–463

## International Court of Justice (ICJ)

*Accordance with International Law of the Unilateral Declaration of Independence in Respect of Kosovo* (2010) ICJ Rep 403,　111nn48–50
*Aerial Incident of 3 July 1988 (Iran v USA)*, Order of 22 February 1996 (1996) ICJ Rep 9,　183n40, 183n42, 197n107
*Aerial Incident of 10 August 1999 (India v Pakistan)*, Jurisdiction of the Court (2000) ICJ Rep 12,　182n38, 183n41
*Application of the Convention on the Prevention and Punishment of the Crime of Genocide, Order of 8 April 1993, Request for the Indication of Provisional Measures* (1993) ICJ Rep 3,　209n158
*Application of the Convention on the Prevention and Punishment of the Crime of Genocide (Croatia v Serbia)* ICJ, Judgment of 3 February 2015,　177–178
*Application of the Convention on the Prevention and Punishment of the Crime of Genocide (Bosnia and Herzegovina v Serbia and Montenegro)* (2007) ICJ Rep 43,　68n24
*Application of the Interim Accord of 13 September 1995 (FYR Macedonia v Greece)* (2011) ICJ Rep 644,　16, 108, 261n207, 262
*Armed Activities on the Territory of the Congo (New Application: 2002) (Democratic Republic of the Congo v Rwanda)*, Jurisdiction and Admissibility (2006) ICJ Rep 6,　182nn38–39
*Armed Activities on the Territory of the Congo (DRC v Burundi)* (2001) ICJ Rep 3,　182nn38–39
*Barcelona Traction, Light and Power Company, Limited, Judgment* (1970) ICJ Rep 3,　218n196
*Border and Transborder Armed Actions (Nicaragua v Costa Rica)*, Order of 19 August 1987 (1987), ICJ Rep 182,　182n38, 199

*Border and Transborder Armed Actions (Nicaragua v Honduras), Jurisdiction and Admissibility* (1988) ICJ Rep 69,   182n38, 199
*Case Concerning Armed Activities on the Territory of the Congo (DRC v Uganda)* (2005) ICJ Rep 168,   109n33, 161n155, 194n95, 199–202, 356n140
*Case Concerning Avena and other Mexican Nationals (Mexico v United States of America)* (2004) ICJ Rep 12,   107–108
*Case Concerning Rights of Nationals of the United States of America in Morocco (France v United States of America)* (1952) ICJ Rep 176,   317, 325
*Case Concerning the Temple of Preah Vihear (Cambodia v Thailand)* (1962) ICJ Rep 6,   327n227, 472n14
*Certain Activities Carried Out by Nicaragua in the Border Area (Costa Rica v Nicaragua); Construction of a Road in Costa Rica along the San Juan River (Nicaragua v Costa Rica),* ICJ, Counterclaims, Order of 18 April 2013 (unreported),   183, 197, 199
*Construction of a Road in Costa Rica along the San Juan River (Nicaragua v Costa Rica),* ICJ, Joinder of Proceedings, Order of 17 April 2013 (unreported),   183, 197, 199
*Corfu Channel (UK v Albania)* (1949) ICJ Rep 4,   123–124, 250n140
*Elettronica Sicula SpA (ELSI) (United States of America v Italy)* (1989) ICJ Rep 15,   6–7
*Gabčíkovo-Nagymaros Project (Hungary/Slovakia)* (1997) ICJ Rep 7, 51–52, 75n57, 110–111, 168n181, 253n152, 263n219, 271n272, 318–319, 321n197, 394, 401–402, 411, 416, 422–423
*Jurisdictional Immunities of the State (Germany v Italy: Greece intervening)* (2012) ICJ Rep 99,   171n197, 394n376
*Land and Maritime Boundary between Cameroon and Nigeria (Cameroon v Nigeria: Equatorial Guinea intervening)* (2002) ICJ Rep 303,   182n38
*Legal Consequences for States of the Continued Presence of South Africa in Namibia (South West Africa) Notwithstanding Security Council Resolution 276 (1970) (Advisory Opinion)* (1971) ICJ Rep 16,   73n47, 82n86
*Legal Consequences of the Construction of a Wall in the Occupied Palestinian Territory* (2004) ICJ Rep 136,   413–414
*Legality of the Threat or Use of Nuclear Weapons (Advisory Opinion)* (1996) ICJ Rep 226,   177n11
*Legality of the Use by a State of Nuclear Weapons in Armed Conflict (Advisory Opinion)* (1996) ICJ Rep 66,   181–182, 185, 190, 198–199

TABLE OF CASES                                    xxxi

*Legality of the Use of Force (Federal Republic of Yugoslavia v Belgium)*, Provisional Measures, Order of 2 June 1999 (1999) ICJ Rep 124,    412n528
*Legality of the Use of Force (Federal Republic of Yugoslavia v Belgium)* (2004) ICJ Rep 279,    182n38, 183n44
*Military and Paramilitary Activities in and against Nicaragua (Nicaragua v United States of America)* (1986) ICJ Rep 14,    51n141, 68n30, 108n31, 109, 184n53, 185, 199–200, 202–203, 253n152, 326, 356n140, 478n26
*Navigational and Related Rights (Costa Rica v Nicaragua) (2009)* ICJ Rep 213, 109,    133, 154–155
*North Sea Continental Shelf Cases (FR Germany/Denmark; FR Germany/Netherlands)* (1969) ICJ Rep 3,    64n5, 65n8, 387n322
*Oil Platforms (Islamic Republic of Iran v United States of America), Preliminary Objections* (1996) ICJ Rep 803,    36, 109n33, 110, 161n155, 183, 185, 190, 193n92, 195, 197–199, 203–205, 356n140
*Oil Platforms (Islamic Republic of Iran v United States of America)* (2003) ICJ Rep 161,    36, 109n33, 110, 160n153, 161n155, 183, 185, 190, 193n92, 195, 197–199, 203–205, 356n140
*United States Diplomatic and Consular Staff in Tehran* (1980) ICJ Rep 3,    253n152

### Iran–US Claims Tribunal

*RN Pomeroy v Iran* (1983) 2 Iran-US CTR 372,    168n181

### ITLOS

*M/ V Saiga (No 2) (St Vincent and the Grenadines v Guinea)* ITLOS, Judgment, 1 July 1999,    410–411, 416

### Permanent Court of International Justice (PCIJ)

*Case Concerning the Payment of Various Brazilian Loans Issued in France (France v Brazil)* (1929) PCIJ, Series A No. 20, 93,    298–299, 301–302
*Case Concerning the Payment of Various Serbian Loans Issued in France (France v Kingdom of the Serbs, Croats and Slovenes)* (1929) PCIJ, Series A No. 20, 5,    298–299, 301, 304, 325, 380, 386

*Customs Regime between Germany and Austria (Advisory Opinion)* (1931) PCIJ Series A/ B No 41, 37,   137n39
*Factory at Chorzów (Merits)* (1928) PCIJ, Series A No 17, 3,   123
*Oscar Chinn* (1934) PCIJ Series A/ B No 63, 65,   84n93
*Railway Traffic between Lithuania and Poland* (1931) PCIJ Series A/ B No 42, 108,   243–244, 247
*Société Commerciale de Belgique* (1939) PCIJ Series A/ B No 78, 160, 299–302, 325, 381, 385–386
*The SS 'Wimbledon'* (1923) PCIJ, Series A No 1,   15, 171, 297–298, 302n94, 325, 331–332, 380, 385–386

## World Trade Organization

*Chile – Price Band System* (Article 21.5 – Argentina), WT/ DS207/ AB/ RW,   168n181
*EC – Sardines,* WT/ DS231/ AB/ R,   168n181
*EC – Tariff Preferences,* WT/ DS246/ AB/ R,   168n181
*US – Gasoline,* WT/ DS2/ AB/ R, DSR 1996:I, 3,   168n181
*Wool Shirts and Blouses,* WT/ DS33/ AB/ R, 1,   168n181

SELECT TABLE OF TREATIES
AND OTHER DOCUMENTS

**Treaties**

Agreement on Prevention of Airspace Violations and for Permitting Over Flights and Landings by Military Aircraft (signed 6 April 1991, in force 19 August 1992), (1994) 1843 UNTS 60,   183n41

Convention on the Limitation of Employment of Force for Recovery of Contract Debts (The Hague, adopted 18 October 1907, in force 26 January 1910), 205 CTS 250,   237n68

Convention on the Prevention of Marine Pollution by Dumping of Wastes and Other Matter, (1972) 1046 UNTS 120,   445n104

Convention Relating to Intervention on the High Seas in Cases of Oil Pollution Casualties, (1969) 970 UNTS 211,   401n456

Declaration of Paris Respecting Maritime Law, 16 April 1856, 115 CTS 1,   435n27

General Act of Arbitration (Pacific Settlement of International Disputes) (signed 26 September 1928, in force 16 August 1929), 93 LNTS 343,   238n78

International Convention for the Prevention of Pollution of the Sea by Oil, (1954) 327 UNTS 8,   445n104

Iran–US Treaty of Amity, Economic Relations and Consular Rights (signed 15 August 1955, entered into force 16 June 1957), (1957) 284 UNTS 93,   183n40, 197n107, 203–205

Nicaragua–US Treaty of Friendship, Commerce and Navigation (signed 21 January 1956, entered into force 24 May 1958), (1960) 367 UNTS 3,   183n40, 202–205

Treaty between Belgium and the Netherlands Relating to the Separation of Their Respective Territories (signed at London 18 April 1839), 88 CTS 427,   372n233

Treaty for the Definitive Separation of Belgium from Holland between Austria, France, Great Britain, Prussia, Russia and Belgium (signed at London 15 November 1831), 82 CTS 255,   372n233

Treaty of Amity, Commerce and Navigation between His Britannick Majesty and the United States of America (Jay Treaty, signed at London 19 November 1794), 52 CTS 249,   344, 423, 433–434

Treaty of Peace between Russia and Sweden (signed at Friedrichshamn 17 September 1809), 60 CTS 457,   235n52

Treaty of Versailles (28 June 1919) 225 CTS 188, (1919) 13 AJIL Supp 151,   297–298, 373–374, 379–380

United Nations Convention on the Law of the Sea (UNCLOS) (adopted 10 December 1982, entered into force 16 November 1994), (1982) 1833 UNTS 397,   183n45, 197n108, 214n183, 410–411, 434, 453

US–China Immigration Treaty (signed in Peking 17 November 1880), 1 Malloy, 237,   235n55, 247

Vienna Convention on the Law of Treaties (VCLT) (adopted 23 May 1969, in force 27 January 1980), (1969) 1155 UNTS 331,   7n25, 72–77, 205, 254–255, 306, 315, 320–321, 446–447, 450n155, 458

## League of Nations Documents

Bases of Discussion for the Conference Drawn Up by the Preparatory Committee - Responsibility of States Damage Caused in Their Territory to the Person and Property of Foreigners, 15 May 1929, C.75.M.69.1929.V3,   54, 184, 242, 377

Réponses du Comité spécial de juristes visé par la Résolution du Conseil du 28 septembre 1923, Observations des gouvernements des Etats membres de la Société, 22 mars 1926, C.212.M.72.1926.V.12,   241n93

Report of the Commission of Enquiry on the Incidents on the Frontier between Bulgaria and Greece, Doc No C.727.M.270.1925.VII, (1926) 7 League of Nations Official Journal, 196,   385, 422

Special Committee of Jurists, 'Report: Interpretation of Certain Articles of the Covenant and Other Questions of International Law,' (1924) 5 League of Nations Official Journal 523,   241–245

## UN Documents

### General Assembly

Articles on Responsibility of States for Internationally Wrongful Acts, A/RES/56/83, 28 January 2002,   4–5, 8–12, 14–15, 24–25, 37–38, 48–57, 59–66, 77–88, 97, 117–118, 131–134, 145–154, 175–180, 187–205, 222–223, 250–251, 260–266, 307, 388–398, 425–432, 467–468

Articles on the Responsibility of International Organisations, A/RES/66/100, 9 December 2011,   17–18

Effects of Armed Conflicts on Treaties, A/RES/66/99, 9 December 2011, 182n35, 223

*Secretariat*

' "Force majeure" and "Fortuitous event" as Circumstances Precluding Wrongfulness: Survey of State Practice, International Judicial Decisions and Doctrine', UN Doc A/CN.4/315, ILC Yearbook 1978, vol. II(1), UN Doc A/CN.4/SER.A/1978/Add.1 (Part 1), 61, 4, 122–123, 286n6, 382n306

**International Law Commission Documents**

Draft Articles on the Responsibility of States for Internationally Wrongful Acts Adopted on First Reading and Commentaries, Report of the ILC on the work of its forty-eighth session, UN Doc A/51/10, ILC Yearbook 1996, vol. II(2), UN Doc A/CN.4/SER.A/1996/Add.1 (Part 2), 58, 5, 44–47, 49–52, 79, 144, 146–150, 171, 185–189, 201, 256–261, 307–315, 332n249, 387–393, 396–402, 410, 443–447, 450, 458, 468

Draft Article 1, 44–46
Draft Article 19, 260
Draft Article 29, 144, 146–150, 152–154, 217n95
Draft Article 30, 254
Draft Article 31, 311–315, 318, 321–322
Draft Article 32, 310–311, 432, 446–453
Draft Article 33, 390–396, 403–44, 411–413
Draft Article 34, 51n141, 185–189, 199–201
Draft Article 35, 79, 424

Articles on Responsibility of States for Internationally Wrongful Acts and Commentaries, Report of the ILC on the work of its fifty-third session, UN Doc A/56/10, ILC Yearbook 2001, vol. II(2), UN Doc A/CN.4/SER.A/2001/Add.1 (Part 2), 20, 3n13, 7n26, 44–47, 49–50, 67, 81–85, 93, 107, 124–125, 131, 144, 149, 170, 188–189, 192, 198, 311–315, 322, 324–325, 329–330, 391, 395–396, 477n24

Article 2, 106–107
Article 12, 106–107
Article 15, 223–224
Article 16, 60, 468
Article 17, 39
Article 18, 69–70, 327, 329

Article 20,   5, 131, 134, 136, 145, 150–154, 156, 170–171
Article 21,   5, 18, 114, 175–180, 184–193, 196–199, 202–206, 218, 220–223
Article 22,   5, 178, 225, 252–254
Article 23,   5, 286, 307–314, 320–325, 328, 390–394
Article 24,   430–432, 434–435, 442, 453–456, 458, 459–461
Article 25,   5, 17, 37, 84, 87, 106n24, 334–336, 340, 353n130, 394–398, 405, 408–409, 413–414, 419, 427–429
Article 26,   194, 264, 408–409, 410n509
Article 27,   5, 63, 77–82, 92, 222, 424
Article 29,   144, 146–154
Article 30,   210–213, 273, 275
Article 31,   205, 445–446
Article 32,   310–313, 446–449, 450–451
Article 33,   390–397, 410–411
Article 35,   79
Article 37,   64–65
Article 45,   144
Article 50,   263–264, 279n304
Article 51,   197–198, 261–263
Article 52,   264–265
Article 55,   204, 280

*Special Rapporteur Reports*

State Responsibility

Ago, R. Eighth Report on State Responsibility, UN Doc A/CN.4/318 and Add.1-4, ILC Yearbook 1979, vol. II(1), UN Doc A/CN.4/SER.A/1979/Add.1 (Part 1), 3,   4, 40–42, 44–46, 102, 118, 132n5, 136, 138, 144, 146–149, 253–258, 267, 307–313, 370, 384, 444–445, 457

Ago, R. Eighth Report on State Responsibility, UN Doc A/CN.4/318 and Add.5-7, ILC Yearbook 1980, vol. II(1), UN Doc A/CN.4/SER.A/1980/Add.1 (Part 1), 13,   4, 40–42, 44–46, 102, 118, 132n5, 136, 138, 144, 146–149, 180–186, 253–258, 267, 307–313, 337, 353, 362, 370, 384, 387–388, 389–390, 418–419, 444–445, 457

Ago, R. Fifth Report on State Responsibility, UN Doc A/CN.4/291 and Add.1 and 2, ILC Yearbook 1976, vol. II(1), UN Doc A/CN.4/SER.A/1976/Add.1 (Part 1), 3,   41–42, 187

Ago, R. First Report on State Responsibility, UN Doc A/CN.4/217 and Add.1, ILC Yearbook 1969, vol. II, UN Doc A/CN.4/SER.A/1970/Add.1, 177,   40–41, 44, 54

SELECT TABLE OF TREATIES AND OTHER DOCUMENTS    xxxvii

Ago, R. Second Report on State Responsibility, UN Doc A/CN.4/233, ILC Yearbook 1970, vol. II, UN Doc A/CN.4/SER.A/1969/Add.1,   125

Ago, R. Third Report on State Responsibility, UN Doc A/CN.4/246 and Add.1-3, ILC Yearbook 1971, vol. II(1), UN Doc A/CN.4/SER.A/1971/Add.1 (Part 1), 199,   256–258, 331

Ago, R. Working Paper, UN Doc A/CN.4/SC.1/WP.5, ILC Yearbook 1963, vol. II, UN Doc A/CN.4/SER.A/1963/Add.1, 251,   53–54, 56, 119

Arangio-Ruiz, G. Fourth Report on State Responsibility, UN Doc A/CN.4/444 and Add.1-3, ILC Yearbook 1992, vol. II(1), UN Doc A/CN.4/SER.A/1992/Add.1 (Part 1),   1, 246n123, 251n145, 255, 258, 279n304

Arangio-Ruiz, G. Preliminary Report on State Responsibility, UN Doc A/CN.4/416 and Add.1, ILC Yearbook 1988, vol. II(1), UN Doc A/CN.4/SER.A/1988/Add.1 (Part 1), 6

Arangio-Ruiz, G. Second Report on State Responsibility, UN Doc A/CN.4/425 and Add.1, ILC Yearbook 1989, vol. II(1), UN Doc A/CN.4/SER.A/1989/Add.1 (Part 1), 1,   124n103

Arangio-Ruiz, G. Third Report on State Responsibility, UN Doc A/CN.4/440 and Add.1, ILC Yearbook 1991, vol. II(1), UN Doc A/CN.4/SER.A/1991/Add.1 (Part 1), 1,   251n145, 258, 278

Crawford, J. First Report on State Responsibility, UN Doc A/CN.4/490 and Add.1– 7, ILC Yearbook 1998, vol. II(1), UN Doc A/CN.4/SER.A/1999/Add.1 (Part 1), 1,   56, 258

Crawford, J. Fourth Report on State Responsibility, UN Doc A/CN.4/517 and Add.1, ILC Yearbook 2001, vol. II(1), UN Doc A/CN.4/SER.A/2001/Add.1 (Part 1), 1,   264

Crawford, J. Second Report on State Responsibility, UN Doc A/CN.4/498 and Add.1– 4, ILC Yearbook 1999, vol. II(1), UN Doc A/CN.4/SER.A/1999/Add.1 (Part 1), 3,   5, 47–49, 107, 110–111, 151–153, 162–164, 178, 182, 188–191, 194–195, 201, 207, 255–256, 260–261, 313–314, 321, 394–396, 453–455

Crawford, J. Third Report on State Responsibility, UN Doc A/CN.4/507 and Add.1– 4, ILC Yearbook 2000, vol. II(1), UN Doc A/CN.4/SER.A/2000/Add.1 (Part 1), 3,   76, 255, 260–261, 278

García-Amador, F. First Report on International Responsibility, UN Doc A/CN.4/96, ILC Yearbook 1956, vol. II, UN Doc A/CN.4/Ser.A/1956/Add.1, 47,   38–40

García-Amador, F. Fourth Report on International Responsibility, UN Doc A/CN.4/119, ILC Yearbook 1959, vol. II, UN Doc A/CN.4/Ser.A/1959/Add.1, 2,   38–40

García-Amador, F. Sixth Report on International Responsibility, UN Doc A/CN.4/134 and Addendum, ILC Yearbook 1961, vol. II, UN Doc A/CN.4/Ser.A/1961/Add.1, 2,   38–40

García-Amador, F. Third Report on International Responsibility, UN Doc A/CN.4/111, ILC Yearbook 1958, vol. II, UN Doc A/CN.4/Ser.A/1958/Add.1, 47,   38–40

Riphagen, W. Fourth Report on the Content, Forms and Degrees of International Responsibility, UN Doc A/CN.4/366 and Add.1, Add.1/Corr.1, ILC Yearbook 1983, vol. II(1), UN Doc A/CN.4/SER.A/1983/Add.1 (Part 1), 3,   258, 278

Riphagen, W. Sixth Report on the Content, Forms and Degrees of International Responsibility, UN Doc A/CN.4/389 and Corr.1, Corr.2, ILC Yearbook 1985, vol. II(1), UN Doc A/CN.4/SER.A/1985/Add.1 (Part 1), 3,   255

*Others*

Fitzmaurice, G. Fourth Report on the Law of Treaties, UN Doc A/CN.4/120, ILC Yearbook 1959, vol. II, UN Doc A/CN.4/SER.A/1959/Add.1, 37,   191n83

Gaja, G. Fourth Report on Responsibility of International Organizations, UN Doc A/CN.4/564 and Add.1–2, ILC Yearbook 2006, vol. II(1), UN Doc A/CN.4/SER.A/2006/Add.1 (Part 1), 103,   58–60, 157

Thiam, D. Fourth Report on the Draft Code of Offences against the Peace and Security of Mankind, UN Doc A/CN.4/398, ILC Yearbook 1986, vol. II(1), UN Doc A/CN.4/SER.A/1986/Add.1 (Part 1), 53,   57

Waldock, H. Second Report on the Law of Treaties, UN Doc A/CN.4/156 and Add.1–3, ILC Yearbook 1963, vol. II, UN Doc A/CN.4/SER.A/1963/Add.1, 1,   73

**Institut de Droit International**

Déclaration concernant le blocus en dehors de l'état de guerre (1887–1888) 9 Annuaire IDI, 300,   237

Régime des représailles en temps de paix (1934) 38 Annuaire IDI 708,   70–71, 227–231, 241–244, 263–264

Réglement sur la responsabilité des Etats à raison des dommages soufferts par des étrangers en cas d'émeute, d'insurrection ou de guerre civile (1900) 18 Annuaire IDI, 254,   123, 291–293, 366–367

# ABBREVIATIONS

| | |
|---|---|
| AC | Appeals Cases (England & Wales) |
| AEDI | Anuario Español de derecho internacional |
| *Aegean Rev* | Aegean Review of the Law of the Sea and Maritime Law |
| AFDI | Annuaire Français de droit international |
| AJIL | American Journal of International Law |
| AJIL Supp | American Journal of International Law Supplement |
| *Alberta LR* | Alberta Law Review |
| All ER | All England Law Reports (England & Wales) |
| *Am Rev Int'l Arb* | American Review of International Arbitration |
| *Am J Comp L* | American Journal of Comparative Law |
| *Annuaire IDI* | Annuaire de l'Institut de droit international |
| *Anuario Argentino DI* | Anuario Argentino de derecho internacional |
| *Arab LQ* | Arab Law Quarterly |
| ARIEL | Austrian Review of International and European Law |
| ARS | Articles on the Responsibility of States for Internationally Wrongful Acts |
| *ASIL Proc* | Proceedings of the American Society of International Law |
| *Australian YIL* | Australian Yearbook of International Law |
| Blatchford | S Blatchford, *Reports of Cases in Prize: Argued and Determined in the Circuit and District Courts of the United States for the Southern District of New York* |
| *BU Int'l LJ* | Boston University International Law Journal |
| *Buffalo Crim LR* | Buffalo Criminal Law Review |
| Burr | Burrow's King's Bench Reports tempore Mansfield (England & Wales) |
| BYIL | British Yearbook of International Law |
| BYU LR | Brigham Young University Law Review |
| C Rob | *Reports of Cases Argued and Determined in the High Court of Admiralty*, vols 1–3 (Boston, 1853) |

| | |
|---|---|
| *California LR* | California Law Review |
| *Can J Phil* | Canadian Journal of Philosophy |
| *Canadian J of L & Juris* | Canadian Journal of Law & Jurisprudence |
| *Cardozo JICL* | Cardozo Journal of International & Comparative Law |
| *Cardozo LR* | Cardozo Law Review |
| *CJICL* | Cambridge Journal of International & Comparative Law |
| CLJ | Cambridge Law Journal |
| *CMI Yearbook* | Comité Maritime International Yearbook |
| Co Rep | Coke's King's Bench Reports (England & Wales) |
| *Columbia J Trans'l L* | Columbia Journal of Transnational Law |
| *Col LR* | Columbia Law Review |
| *Comm L Bull* | Commonwealth Law Bulletin |
| *Cornell ILJ* | Cornell International Law Journal |
| Cranch | Cranch's Supreme Court Reports (United States) |
| Crim App | Criminal Appeals Reports (England & Wales) |
| *Crim Just Ethics* | Criminal Justice Ethics |
| *Crim L & Phil* | Criminal Law & Philosophy |
| *Crim LR* | Criminal Law Review |
| *Croat Arb YB* | Croatian Arbitration Yearbook |
| CTS | Collected Treaty Series |
| *Denv J Int'l L & Pol'y* | Denver Journal of International Law & Policy |
| *Dick LR* | Dickinson Law Review |
| *Duke LJ* | Duke Law Journal |
| *Ecology LQ* | Ecology Law Quarterly |
| Edwards | *Reports of Cases Argued and Determined in the High Court of Admiralty*, vol. 4 (Boston, 1853) |
| EJIL | European Journal of International Law |
| ER | East's King's Bench Reports (England & Wales) |
| *Eur J Crime Crim L & Crim Justice* | European Journal of Crime, Criminal Law & Criminal Justice |
| EWCA Civ | Court of Appeals Civil Division (England & Wales) |
| Fam | Family (England & Wales) |
| GA | General Assembly |
| *Geo Wash LR* | George Washington Law Review |
| *Georgetown LJ* | Georgetown Law Journal |
| *Georgia J Int'l & Comp L* | Georgia Journal of International & Comparative Law |
| *Georgia LR* | Georgia Law Review |
| *Harv ILJ* | Harvard International Law Journal |
| *Harv LR* | Harvard Law Review |
| *Hist Pol Thought* | History of Political Thought |

| | |
|---|---|
| HL | House of Lords |
| ICJ | International Court of Justice |
| ICJ Rep | International Court of Justice Reports |
| ICLQ | International & Comparative Law Quarterly |
| ICSID | International Centre for the Settlement of Investment Disputes |
| IDI | Institut de Droit International |
| ILC | International Law Commission |
| ILM | International Legal Materials |
| ILR | International Law Reports |
| *Int'l Comm LR* | International Community Law Review |
| *Int'l J Marine & Coastal L* | International Journal of Marine & Coastal Law |
| Iowa | Iowa Reports (United States) |
| *Iowa LR* | Iowa Law Review |
| Iran-US CTR | Iran-US Claims Tribunal |
| *Israel LR* | Israel Law review |
| ITLOS | International Tribunal for the Law of the Sea |
| *J Comp Leg & Int'l L* | Journal of Comparative Legislation & International Law |
| *J Conflict & Security Law* | Journal of Conflict & Security Law |
| *J Crim L & Criminology* | Journal of Criminal Law & Criminology |
| *J Energy Nat Resour L* | Journal of Energy & Natural Resources Law |
| *J Int'l Arb* | Journal of International Arbitration |
| *J Legal Education* | Journal of Legal Education |
| *J Pacific History* | Journal of Pacific History |
| *J Soc Comp L* | Journal of the Society of Comparative Legislation |
| JDI | Journal du droit international |
| JICJ | Journal of International Criminal Justice |
| JIDS | Journal of International Dispute Settlement |
| JoMA | Journal of Maritime Affairs |
| JUFIL | Journal of the Use of Force in International Law |
| JWIT | Journal of World Investment and Trade |
| *King's College LJ* | King's College Law Journal |
| *Kobe Gakuin LJ* | Kobe Gakuin Law Journal |
| *Law & Bus Rev Am* | Law & Business Review of the Americas |
| *Law & Contemp Probs* | Law & Contemporary Problems |
| *Law Mag & Rev* | Law Magazine & Review |
| LJIL | Leiden Journal of International Law |
| LNOJ | League of Nations Official Journal |
| *Loy LA Int'l & Comp LJ* | Loyola of Los Angeles International & Comparative Law Journal |
| LPICT | Law & Practice of International Courts & Tribunals |

| | |
|---|---|
| LQR | Law Quarterly Review |
| LR-Ex | Law Reports, Exchequer Cases (England & Wales) |
| M J Law Reform | Michigan Journal of Law Reform |
| Manchester J Int'l Economic L | Manchester Journal of International Economic Law |
| Marquette LR | Marquette Law Review |
| McNair Intl L Op | A McNair, *International Law Opinions* (Cambridge, 1956), vols 1–3 |
| Melb Univ LR | Melbourne University Law Review |
| Mich JIL | Michigan Journal of International Law |
| Mont | Montana Reports (United States) |
| Moore Arbitrations | JB Moore, *History and Digest of the International Arbitrations to which the United States has been a Party*, vols 1–4 (Washington, 1898) |
| Naval LR | Naval Law Review |
| NCLR | North Carolina Law Review |
| NILR | Netherlands International Law Review |
| Nordic JIL | Nordic Journal of International Law |
| North American Rev | North American Review |
| Northwestern LR | Northwestern Law Review |
| Notre Dame LR | Notre Dame Law Review |
| NW | North Western Reporter (United States) |
| NYIL | Netherlands Yearbook of International Law |
| NYU J Int'l L & Pol | New York University Journal of International Law & Politics |
| ODIL | Ocean Development & International Law |
| Ohio State J Crim L | Ohio State Journal of Criminal Law |
| Ohio St LJ | Ohio State Law Journal |
| OJLS | Oxford Journal of Legal Studies |
| Ottawa LR | Ottawa Law Review |
| P.2d | Pacific Reporter, Second Series (United States) |
| PCIJ | Permanent Court of International Justice |
| Proc Arist Soc | Proceedings of the Aristotelian Society |
| QBD | Queen's Bench Division (England & Wales) |
| RBDI | Revue Belge de droit international |
| RDILC | Revue de droit international et législation comparée |
| Recueil | Recueil des cours de l'Académie de droit international |
| REDI | Revista Española de derecho internacional |
| Rev of Pol | Review of Politics |
| Rev de l'Arbitrage | Revue de l'arbitrage |
| RGDIP | Revue générale de droit international public |
| RIAA | Reports of International Arbitral Awards |

# ABBREVIATIONS

| | |
|---|---|
| Roscoe | ES Roscoe, *Reports of Prize Cases Determined in the High Court of Admiralty, Before the Lords Commissioners of Appeals in Prize Cases, and Before the Judicial Committee of the Privy Council* (London, 1905), 2 vols |
| RTD Civ | Revue Trimestrielle de Droit Civil |
| Rutgers LJ | Rutgers Law Journal |
| S Cal LR | Southern California Law Review |
| San Diego Int'l LJ | San Diego International Law Journal |
| San Diego LR | San Diego Law Review |
| SCOR | Security Council Official Records |
| Scott Hague Court Rep | JB Scott, *The Hague Court Reports* (Oxford, 1916) |
| SCR | Supreme Court Reports (Canada) |
| St John's LR | St John's Law Review |
| St Louis LR | St Louis Law Review |
| Stellenbosch LR | Stellenbosch Law Review |
| TAM | Recueil de la jurisprudence des tribunaux arbitraux mixtes créés par les traités de paix |
| TDM | Transnational Dispute Management |
| Texas Tech LR | Texas Tech Law Review |
| Tilburg Foreign LR | Tilburg Foreign Law Review |
| Toronto Fac LR | Toronto Faculty Law Review |
| Transactions Grot Soc | Transactions of the Grotian Society |
| Tulane Maritime LJ | Tulane Maritime Law Journal |
| Tulsa LR | Tulsa Law Review |
| U Chicago LR | University of Chicago Law Review |
| U Miami Inter-American LR | University of Miami Inter-American Law Review |
| UC Davis LR | University of California Davis Law Review |
| UCL J of L & Jur | University College London Journal of Law & Jurisprudence |
| UCLA LR | University of California in Los Angeles Law Review |
| UN | United Nations |
| UNCITRAL | United Nations Commission on International Trade Law |
| UNCLOS | United Nations Convention on the Law of the Sea |
| UNGA | United Nations General Assembly |
| UNSC | United Nations Security Council |
| UNSG | United Nations Secretary General |
| UNTS | United Nations Treaty Series |
| UTas LR | University of Tasmania Law Review |
| Utrecht LR | Utrecht Law Review |
| Va J Int'l L | Virginia Journal of International Law |

| | |
|---|---|
| *Vanderbilt J Transnat'l L* | Vanderbilt Journal of Transnational Law |
| VCLT | Vienna Convention on the Law of Treaties |
| *Virginia LR* | Virginia Law Review |
| *Wayne LR* | Wayne Law Review |
| Wheat | Wheaton's Supreme Court Reports |
| *Whittier LR* | Whittier Law Review |
| *Wisconsin ILJ* | Wisconsin International Law Journal |
| *Yale & Development LJ* | Yale Human Rights & Development Law Journal |
| *Yale LJ* | Yale Law Journal |
| ZaöRV | Zeitschrift für ausländisches öffentliches Recht und Völkerrecht |

## Note on Method of Citation

This study is divided into ten chapters, which form separate units with regard to footnote numbering. Citations to cases and doctrinal works (including the work of the ILC) are provided in full for the first citation, and then in abbreviated form for every other citation. Citations provide pages or paragraphs; when necessary, they provide both. Paragraphs are identified with brackets [].

The Articles on the Responsibility of States for Internationally Wrongful Acts adopted in 2001 are referred to as 'ARS' or 'Articles on State Responsibility'. The ILC's Commentary to this instrument is referred to throughout as 'Commentary'. Provisions adopted during the first reading of the ARS are indicated by means of the word 'draft', as in 'draft Article 33'. Likewise, the draft commentary is indicated by the word 'draft' or by the use of lower case in 'commentary'.

Debates on the ILC's Reports in the Sixth Committee of the General Assembly are identified with their UN Document number, for instance: Ukraine, A/C.6/35/SR.56, [34] (namely, Summary Records of the 56th meeting, of the 35th session of the Sixth Committee).

All translations, except where a source is specifically indicated, are the author's own.

# Introduction

On 10 July 1985, two bombs exploded at Auckland harbour.[1] The bombs had been placed on board the *Rainbow Warrior*,[2] a Greenpeace vessel that was taking part in protests against French nuclear testing in Mururoa atoll in the Pacific. Greenpeace's photographer, Fernando Pereira, who was on board the ship at the time, died when the ship sank. Within a few days of the incident, two French secret service agents, Captain Prieur and Major Mafart, were captured in Auckland. They were carrying fake Swiss passports. Criminal proceedings were instituted against the pair; they pleaded guilty to manslaughter and were sentenced to ten years' imprisonment each. France initially denied any involvement in the affair, but subsequently – thanks to the work of two journalists – documents were revealed showing that the attack had been ordered by high-ranking French officials, apparently with the knowledge of the minister of

---

[1] For a summary of the facts, see *UN Secretary-General: Ruling on the Rainbow Warrior Affair between France and New Zealand* (1987) 26 ILM 1346, 1349ff; *Rainbow Warrior (New Zealand v France)* (1990) 20 RIAA 215. For information on the background of the case, see Dickson, 'Bomb Scandal Highlights French Testing' (1985) 229 *Science* 948; Firth, 'The Nuclear Issue in the Pacific Islands' (1986) 21 *J Pacific History* 202; Sawyer, '*Rainbow Warrior*: Nuclear War in the Pacific' (1986) 8 *Third World Quarterly* 1325; Thakur, 'A Dispute of Many Colours: France, New Zealand and the "*Rainbow Warrior*" Affair' (1986) 42 *The World Today* 209. For legal analyses of the incident before the arbitral award of 1990, see Charpentier, 'L'affaire du *Rainbow Warrior*' (1985) 31 AFDI 210; Dickson, 'Bomb Scandal Highlights French Testing'; Charpentier, 'L'affaire du *Rainbow Warrior*: le règlement interétatique' (1986) 32 AFDI 873; Appolis, 'Le règlement de l'affaire du *Rainbow Warrior*' (1987) 91 RGDIP 9; Pugh, 'Legal Aspects of the *Rainbow Warrior* Affair' (1987) 36 ICLQ 655; Wexler, 'The *Rainbow Warrior* Affair: State and Agent Responsibility for Authorized Violations of International Law' (1987) 5 *BU Int'l LJ* 389; Palmer, 'Settlement of International Disputes: The *Rainbow Warrior* Affair' (1989) 15 *Comm L Bull* 585.

[2] The name of the Greenpeace vessel, as subsequently recounted by New Zealand's prime minister at the time of the arbitration, came from an American Indian legend: 'When the earth's creatures have been hunted almost to extinction a rainbow warrior will descend from the sky to protect them'; see Palmer, '*Rainbow Warrior*', 589.

defence.³ France eventually acknowledged having ordered the attacks; it maintained that, for this reason, its agents should not be held personally liable for the attack and demanded that New Zealand release the two agents.⁴

A serious diplomatic rift ensued, even leading France to restrict the importation of New Zealand products and threaten an economic embargo on New Zealand's exports to the European Community.⁵ The dispute was eventually settled by mediation of the UN Secretary-General. In his (binding) decision, the Secretary-General ordered that the French agents be transferred to French authorities. They were to spend three years in isolation in a French military base in Hao, French Polynesia. The agents were not to leave the island before the expiry of the three-year period, other than with the mutual consent of the two states. Within a year of the agents' arrival in Hao, France unilaterally repatriated Major Mafart, arguing that he needed urgent medical treatment not available in Hao. A few months later, it unilaterally repatriated Captain Prieur, first arguing that her pregnancy was risky and subsequently that she must see her terminally ill father in Paris. For New Zealand, which had not consented to either transfer, France was in breach of the Secretary-General's ruling.

The parties eventually agreed to submit their dispute concerning the fate of the French agents to an international tribunal. Before the arbitral Tribunal, France attempted to explain its conduct by reference to the defences in the law of responsibility. The parties' arguments on this point, at least as reported in the award,⁶ were, to say the least, confused and confusing. France, having initially referred to *force majeure* in the diplomatic

---

[3] The mission had been code-named 'Opération Satanique'. It is thought that more than ten French agents were involved, though only two were apprehended; Clark, 'State Terrorism: Some Lessons from the Sinking of the *Rainbow Warrior*' (1988) 20 *Rutgers LJ* 393, 397.

[4] For details on the apprehension of the French agents and the subsequent scandal in France (the so-called underwater gate), see Memorial of France, *Rainbow Warrior Ruling*, 1359–60; Charpentier, 'L'affaire' (1985) 210.

[5] The import restrictions on New Zealand products and the threat of an economic embargo led New Zealand to lodge a complaint before the OECD and, later, to initiate proceedings pursuant to the non-binding procedure of consultation under the GATT. The complaints were withdrawn prior to the agreement for submission of the dispute to the UN Secretary-General; see Memorial of New Zealand, *Rainbow Warrior Ruling*, 1355. France denied having adopted these measures in connection with the *Rainbow Warrior* dispute; see Memorial of France, *Rainbow Warrior Ruling*, 1367.

[6] The parties' pleadings and other documents relating to the arbitration remain confidential to this day.

correspondence with New Zealand,[7] later said before the Tribunal that it did not mean to invoke *force majeure* as a legal defence. Rather, France wished to rely on 'the whole theory of special circumstances that exclude or "attenuate" illegality'.[8] On the facts, France emphasised the 'very special' nature of the circumstances of the two agents,[9] pleaded 'obvious' humanitarian considerations[10] and referred to the extreme urgency of the agents' position;[11] but at no point did France provide a specific legal basis for its actions. New Zealand opined that France's claims could plausibly come under the pleas of *force majeure* or distress – neither of which were, in any event, met on the facts. Crucially, however, New Zealand argued that the defences in the law of responsibility were *not* applicable to the breach of conventional obligations, such as those deriving from the Secretary-General's ruling. A party to a treaty, New Zealand said, is 'not entitled to set aside the specific grounds for termination or suspension of a treaty'.[12] In other words, the non-performance of treaty obligations could only be justified by reference to the grounds of suspension and termination in the law of treaties itself.

The Tribunal was thus presented, for the first time in contemporary international law, with the opportunity to address the 'circumstances precluding wrongfulness' as a discrete category of the law of responsibility. The award was significant for many reasons,[13] but specifically in respect of the defences, the Tribunal made two fundamental contributions. First,

[7] Note from the French ambassador in Wellington to the New Zealand Ministry of Foreign Affairs, 14 December 1987, quoted at *Rainbow Warrior*, [24] ('In carrying out their duty to protect the health of their agents, the French authorities, in this case of force majeure, are forced to proceed, without any further delay, with the French officer's health-related repatriation'). See also ibid., [76].
[8] *Rainbow Warrior*, [76].
[9] Ibid., [66].
[10] Ibid., [70].
[11] Ibid., [71].
[12] Ibid., [73].
[13] For legal analyses of the award and its significance, see Charpentier, 'L'affaire du *Rainbow Warrior*: la sentence arbitrale du 30 avril 1990 (Nouvelle Zélande c. France)' (1990) 36 AFDI 395; Marks, 'Treaties, State Responsibility and Remedies' (1990) 49 CLJ 387; Palmisano, 'Sulla decisione arbitrale relativa alla seconda fase del caso *Rainbow Warrior*' (1990) 73 Rivista di diritto internazionale 874; Pinto, 'L'affaire du Rainbow Warrior: à propos de la sentence du 30 avril 1990, Nouvelle-Zélande c/France' (1990) 117 JDI 841; Davidson, 'The *Rainbow Warrior* Arbitration Concerning the Treatment of the French Agents Mafart and Prieur' (1991) 40 ICLQ 446; Chatterjee, 'The *Rainbow Warrior* Arbitration between New Zealand and France' (1992) 9 J Int'l Arb 17; Migliorino, 'Sur la déclaration d'illicéité comme forme de satisfaction: à propos de la sentence arbitrale du 30 avril 1990 dans l'affaire du *Rainbow Warrior*' (1992) 96 RGDIP 61; Guillaume, 'L'affaire du *Rainbow Warrior* et son règlement' in Guillaume (ed.), *Les grandes crises internationales et le droit* (1994), 219. As reported by Daillier, the award is the second most referred to in the Commentary to the

the Tribunal clarified that the defences in the law of responsibility were applicable *also* to treaty breaches – thus endorsing a unitary system of international responsibility, one applicable regardless of the conventional or customary origins of the obligation allegedly breached. When similar issues came up before the ICJ some years later, in *Gabčíkovo-Nagymaros*, the Court did not hesitate to endorse this position, despite the invitation from one of the parties to find that, on this point, *Rainbow Warrior* had been incorrectly decided.[14] Second, in considering the 'whole theory' of defences invoked by France, the Tribunal turned to the ILC's draft Articles on 'circumstances precluding wrongfulness' that had been adopted on first reading in 1979–80. The draft Articles adopted by the Commission on that occasion constituted the first compilation of circumstances exonerating from responsibility. The ILC's adoption of these six provisions took place over two sessions, during which the Commission (and states) examined two reports by Roberto Ago and a comprehensive memorandum by the UN Secretariat.[15] Of these rules, the Tribunal thought three were relevant to France's case: *force majeure*, distress and state of necessity. In its assessment, the Tribunal relied heavily on the Commission's work to explain the defences, their requirements, conditions and differences, and its findings will be discussed in the relevant chapters of this book. With the exception of state of necessity, the Tribunal unhesitatingly endorsed the customary status of these rules.[16] The *Rainbow Warrior* award thus provided some welcome conceptual clarifications about the defences and their role in international law and gave a stamp of approval to the Commission's *démarche* on this issue. The award moreover contributed to the perceived authority of the ILC's work on responsibility, at the very least, in respect of its work on the defences.

Since then, most tribunals faced with questions concerning the defences simply rely on the Articles on the Responsibility of States for

---

ARS: Daillier, 'The Development of the Law of Responsibility through the Case Law' in Crawford et al. (eds), *The Law of International Responsibility* (2010), 43.

[14] Slovakia initially invited the Court to find that *Rainbow Warrior* had incorrectly stated the relationship between treaty law and the law of responsibility: Memorial of Slovakia, 315 [8.16]. But it subsequently changed its position: statement of Slovakia, CR 1997/8, 25 March 1997, 48–9 [2].

[15] UN Secretariat, '"*Force Majeure*" and "Fortuitous Event" as Circumstances Precluding Wrongfulness: Survey of State Practice, International Judicial Decisions and Doctrine', ILC Yearbook 1978, vol. II(1), 61; Ago, Eighth Report on State Responsibility, ILC Yearbook 1979, vol. II(1), 3; Ago, Eighth Report on State Responsibility, ILC Yearbook 1980, vol. II(1), 13.

[16] *Rainbow Warrior*, 252–5.

INTRODUCTION 5

Internationally Wrongful Acts (ARS),[17] often uncritically, and do not look any further. Yet, despite the welcome clarifications and endorsement in *Rainbow Warrior*, there is much that remains unsettled around these circumstances. The list of defences produced on first reading remained unchanged during the second reading of the ARS, despite Special Rapporteur Crawford's attempt to expand it.[18] Chapter V of Part One of the ARS lists as 'circumstances precluding wrongfulness': consent (Article 20), self-defence (Article 21), countermeasures (Article 22), *force majeure* (Article 23), distress (Article 24) and necessity (Article 25). During the second-reading process, some disputed aspects were clarified and improved, as will be seen in Part II of this book. Nevertheless, uncertainties remain. As recently as 2006, Ian Brownlie (who as a member of the ILC participated in the second reading of the ARS) remarked during a meeting of the Commission:

> With hindsight, it was clear that in the context of the draft articles on responsibility of States for internationally wrongful acts, the question of justifications had never been properly worked out. With every new case that came before the ICJ and every new arbitration, it became increasingly clear that the subject was immature, yet the Commission had adopted an 'emperor's new clothes' policy, so that it now had a splendid set of draft articles relating to justifications in the context of responsibility of States, which were very difficult to apply.[19]

These difficulties concern several aspects of the defences. On a practical level, there are uncertainties in respect of specific elements of each defence. To name but a few: that of the organ (or organs) authorised to give consent on behalf of the state; the scope (and recognition) of self-defence as a defence for the collateral infringement of 'other' obligations by measures of self-defence; the proportionality test in relation to countermeasures; whether the 'material impossibility' required for *force majeure* is absolute or may include instances of (extreme) difficulty of performance; the recognition, at customary law, of the defence of distress; and what constitutes an 'essential interest' for the purposes of state of necessity, or what does the 'only way' condition entail. More generally, the obligation referred to in Article 27(b) to compensate for 'material loss' in the event of the successful invocation of a defence remains a mystery: in respect of

---

[17] Articles on Responsibility of States for Internationally Wrongful Acts, annexed to UNGA Res 56/83 (28 January 2002) UN Doc A/RES/56/83.
[18] Crawford, Second Report on State Responsibility, ILC Yearbook 1999, vol. II(1).
[19] Brownlie, 2877th meeting, ILC Yearbook 2006, vol. I, 70 [18].

which circumstances is it applicable, when does it arise, and what is its legal basis? There are also other conceptual and theoretical uncertainties. Given the obvious differences between the various defences included in the ARS, most pressing is the question whether they all operate in the same way, or whether they can be classified into different categories. At its core, this difficulty relates to an important issue: that of the explanation of how defences operate, how they go about performing their exonerating effect. The ARS provide no explanation on this point, and neither does the case-law of international tribunals. Tellingly, it has been suggested that their operation is shrouded in mystery such that the most that can be said is that they work like 'optical illusions': now you see wrongfulness and responsibility, and now you do not.[20]

Defences are a fundamental part of any legal order. Legal orders regulate the relations between their subjects (mostly) through general and abstract rules.[21] Moreover, and this is especially the case in respect of orders based on customary law, they regulate for the future on the basis of past experience. And yet, every legal order must cater to, or accommodate, the exceptional, the uncertain, the unforeseen. Indeed, international life, like life in general, does not always follow an uninterrupted and undisturbed path. It is possible that in any given situation where it appears that a rule has been broken there are other factors, not necessarily explicit in that rule, which may cast a different light on the conduct in question. In this different light, it may appear, for example, that the application of the rule to the relevant conduct is unfair, inequitable, unjust or undesirable; it may be that the application of the rule to the relevant conduct undermines other policies or goals of the legal order. Indeed, as explained by Chile in the Sixth Committee of the General Assembly, 'the requirements of elementary justice [call] for certain exceptions to the normal rule'.[22] By way of example, a Chamber of the ICJ held in the *ELSI* case that '[e]very system of law must provide ... for interferences with the normal exercise of rights during public emergencies and the like'.[23] Exceptional circumstances disturb normal legal relations in multiple ways, and legal orders thus provide for

---

[20] Christakis, 'Les "circonstances excluant l'illicéité": une illusion optique?' in Corten et al. (eds), *Droit du pouvoir, pouvoir du droit: Mélanges offerts à Jean Salmon* (2007), 223.
[21] On the generality of rules, see Schauer, *Playing by the Rules: A Philosophical Examination of Rule-Based Decision-Making in Law and in Life* (1993), ch. 2.
[22] A/C.6/35/SR.47, [7].
[23] *Elettronica Sicula SpA (ELSI)* (1989) ICJ Rep 15, [74].

various accommodation mechanisms. There is a paradox in the a priori regulation, through general and abstract rules, of the exceptional and unforeseen. But the alternative – to leave it up to decision-makers to assess, on a case-by-case basis, potential exceptional circumstances in which the 'normal' rules do not apply[24] – could result in a disturbing arbitrariness, contrary to the conduct-guiding function of law and the certainty of legal relations. This is all the more so in a decentralised order like the international one in which there exist no mandatory judicial authorities. A casuistic approach to exceptions in international law would result in a veritable law between Schmittian-sovereigns: each entitled to decide on the exception – if such a legal order is at all possible. In international law, mechanisms for the accommodation of exceptional situations include, for example, the grounds for the suspension or termination of treaties by reason of supervening impossibility or fundamental change of circumstances.[25] They also include the defences in the law of state responsibility.[26] Given how crucial defences are to

---

[24] A phenomenon that domestic law theorists refer to as the defeasibility of legal rules, on which see Ferrer Beltrán and Ratti, 'Defeasibility and Legality: A Survey' in Ferrer Beltrán and Ratti (eds), *The Logic of Legal Requirements: Essays on Defeasibility* (2012), 11. Note, however, that there are also broader understandings of legal defeasibility. See, e.g., Hage, *Studies in Legal Logic* (2005), ch. 1.

[25] Especially Article 60 (material breach of treaty), Article 61 (supervening impossibility of performance) and Article 62 (fundamental change of circumstances) in the Vienna Convention on the Law of Treaties (adopted 23 May 1969, in force 27 January 1980), (1969), (1969) 1155 UNTS 331.

[26] The book cannot address the difficult jurisprudential question of defining the concept of 'defence' – and providing a basis upon which to distinguish defences from rule elements (what the ARS calls 'constituent requirements of obligations': Commentary to Chapter V of Part I, [7]), if such a distinction is at all possible. Rather, the book will take as a starting point the assumption made in the ARS that the defences are *distinct* from obligations. This assumption is not an uncontroversial proposition as a matter of legal theory, and many works in domestic law have been devoted to examining it. See, among others, Williams, 'Offences and Defences' (1982) 2 *Legal Studies* 233; Campbell, 'Offence and Defence' in Dennis (ed.), *Criminal Law and Justice* (1987); Finkelstein, 'When the Rule Swallows the Exception' in Meyer (ed.), *Rules and Reasoning: Essays in Honour of Frederick Schauer* (1999), 147; Fletcher, *Rethinking Criminal Law* (2000); Gardner, 'Fletcher on Offences and Defences' (2003–4) 39 *Tulsa LR* 817; Gardner, 'In Defence of Defences' in Gardner (ed.), *Offences and Defences: Selected Essays in the Philosophy of Criminal Law* (2007), 77; Duarte d'Almeida, *Allowing for Exceptions: A Theory of Defences and Defeasibility in Law* (2015). International lawyers and theorists have yet to address this issue. While theoretically controversial, as a matter of positive law it seems to be the case that states, international tribunals and international lawyers think of and treat defences as distinct from obligations. Note, however, that this assumption caused some difficulties in respect of the plea consent, which will be addressed in Chapter 4.

any legal order, it is surprising that they, as a category, have received such minimal attention in the international legal literature, which has so far not engaged in a deep and sustained manner with the analysis and understanding of the function and operation of defences and with the clarification of the conceptual, theoretical and practical difficulties posed by them.

The aim of this book is not to examine or clarify every lingering uncertainty about defences in the law of state responsibility, for the topic is a very broad one. Moreover, as Brownlie observed, it is also a topic that may still be immature to allow the resolution of every one of these difficulties. The immaturity that Brownlie referred to results from both a paucity of practice and a scarcity of legal-theoretical development. Practically, this is because the provisions relate to circumstances of such exceptionality that, by definition, they will occur only rarely. In the absence of more practice (especially judicial or arbitral practice, where the defences are more likely to be considered in depth), very little can be said in respect of the various practical problems mentioned earlier. Elucidation of these problems will require further experience with the defences, and this may take some time. This book will therefore focus on conceptual and theoretical difficulties instead. It is possible that the 'ripening' of the defences from a theoretical standpoint may illuminate (and even guide) the resolution of practical difficulties if and when these may emerge. Indeed, as argued by Roger O'Keefe:

> Explicitly or effectively explanatory theory can serve to elucidate what the hidden sense – over and above any rationale or rationales offered by the system itself or its actors – of a specific rule of international law might be, lending a purposiveness or deeper purposiveness to what may appear an arbitrary or at least unconvincingly rational normative arrangement. The elaboration of a plausible 'thick' rationale for an applicable positive rule may in turn have an implicitly prescriptive import.[27]

The book will thus hone in on the question of the operation of the defences – in particular, whether they all produce their effects in the same way (do they all preclude wrongfulness?) or whether they can be classified into two different typologies: circumstances that preclude wrongfulness (justifications) and circumstances that preclude responsibility (excuses). Its aim will be primarily that of presenting an explanatory theoretical account of the law and practice of defences. Incidentally, as will be seen,

---

[27] O'Keefe, 'Theory and the Doctrinal International Lawyer' (2015) 4 *UCL J of L & Jur*, sec. E.

these explanatory theories may also involve normative or prescriptive elements, in that they may enlighten previously obscure aspects or they may even guide the development of the law where the law is uncertain.[28]

The defences in the ARS, as becomes evident from a quick glance at the text of Chapter V of Part One, address very different exceptional circumstances ranging from the breach of obligations, to the use of force, to the occurrence of natural disasters. Such are the differences among them that Chapter V of Part One has been described – not without a tinge of criticism – as a 'grab bag'[29] of rules. Is it possible to account for some of the variations among them by distinguishing different typologies among the circumstances? In domestic legal orders, which often recognise a much larger collection of disparate defences, scholars and theorists have elaborated different taxonomies in an effort to organise and systematise them.[30] Justification and excuse are the most common and well-known concepts used in this regard.[31] These are not exclusively legal concepts. They exist in theology and moral philosophy,[32] and are part of ordinary language as well.[33] As Vaughan Lowe has observed, 'no dramatist, no novelist would confuse [these concepts]. No philosopher or theologian would conflate them.'[34] In the legal field, the development of justification and excuse as concepts relevant to the classification of exceptional circumstances began in the early twentieth century, primarily in the context of criminal law. Since then, aside from some enduring fuzzy edges,[35] it is now no longer disputed that there is a conceptual distinction between justifications and excuses and that these notions, and their difference,

---

[28] On the role of theory in legal argument, see Mills, 'Rethinking Jurisdiction in International Law' (2013) 84 BYIL 187, 237.
[29] Rosenstock, 'The ILC and State Responsibility' (2002) 96 AJIL 792, 794.
[30] For an impressive example of such an exercise in the context of US criminal law, see Robinson, *Criminal Law Defences* (1984).
[31] Robinson, cited earlier, identified as many as four different types of defences. For an argument in favour of these additional typologies (at least in the criminal law) see Husak, 'Beyond the Justification/Excuse Dichotomy' in Cruft et al. (eds), *Crime, Punishment, and Responsibility: The Jurisprudence of Antony Duff* (2011), 141.
[32] Greenawalt, 'The Perplexing Borders of Justification and Excuse' (1984) 84 *Col LR* 1897, 1903.
[33] See the *Oxford English Dictionary* definitions of both words: justification is '[t]he action of justifying or showing something to be just, right, or proper; vindication of oneself or another' (3), and excuse is the 'attempt to clear (a person) wholly or partially from blame, without denying or justifying his imputed action' (I.1.a).
[34] Lowe, 'Precluding Wrongfulness or Responsibility: A Plea for Excuses?' (1999) 10 EJIL 405, 406.
[35] On which see Greenawalt, 'Perplexing'.

are legally relevant. The criminal law philosopher Douglas Husak has summarised the consensus on these notions as follows:

> Justifications are defenses that arise from properties or characteristics of acts; excuses are defenses that arise from properties or characteristics of actors. A defendant is justified when his *conduct* is not legally wrongful, even though it apparently violates a criminal law. A defendant is excused when *he* is not blameworthy or responsible for his conduct, even though it ... violates the criminal law.[36]

Note, however, that even if conceptually distinct, not all legal orders actually employ these notions in their criminal (or private) law to systematise the defences recognised in the legal order.

Moreover, there are also voices (an admittedly dwindling number) who contend that the distinction has no significance in practice, that this is, in short, a distinction without a difference. But this criticism is overstated. A number of practical implications can be derived from the distinction between justification and excuse. Since justifications concern the legal qualification of an act, if the act is justified and, as such, in accordance with the legal order, this qualification has a universalising tendency. Namely, it can affect the liability of accessories and the availability of rights of reaction. Moreover, if invoked against a criminal charge, it can have an impact on the liability of the invoking party for civil damages. Excuses, in turn, concern the actor and are, for this reason, individualised. They have a relative effect only: they cannot be enjoyed by accessories, they do not affect rights of reaction and, if invoked in criminal settings, they have no bearing on liability for civil damages. These are, of course, only logical implications of the distinction and need not be, and in fact are not, all followed in the domestic legal orders which distinguish between these two typologies of defences. That these consequences follow from the distinction does not entail that they must, therefore, be binding in the domestic legal orders

---

[36] Husak, 'Justifications and the Criminal Liability of Accessories' (1989–90) 80 *J Crim L & Criminology* 491, 496 (emphasis in original, footnotes omitted). The quotation elides Husak's statement that excuses concern conduct that 'apparently' violates the criminal law. Husak's statement in this regard appears related to his view that there exists no logical priority between justification and excuse: Husak, 'The Serial View of Criminal Law Defences' (1992) 3 *Criminal Law Forum* 369; Husak, 'On the Supposed Priority of Justification to Excuse' (2005) 24 *Law & Philosophy* 557. But note that his view is not widely shared, see, e.g., Baron, 'Is Justification (Somehow) Prior to Excuse? A Reply to Douglas Husak' (2005) 24 *Law & Philosophy* 595, and the references cited therein. These definitions represent the core of the consensus, but note that there are still differences of opinion on the margins; for a useful review of these differences see Ferzan, 'Justification and Excuse' in Deigh and Dolinko (eds), *The Oxford Handbook of Philosophy of Criminal Law* (2011), 239.

that employ the distinction. To assert the opposite would amount to nothing more than what the American legal philosopher Felix Cohen dubbed in the interwar years 'transcendental nonsense',[37] it would be an exercise in conceptualist jurisprudence ill-suited to formal and positivist legal orders. This is not to say, however, that legal concepts have no role to play in the law. As observed by Jeremy Waldron, Cohen's critique of 'technical legal vocabulary and its blunt rejection of the idea that the manipulation of concepts has any important role to play in legal problem-solving' is overstated.[38] Legal concepts have remained a feature of legal discourse, they are crucial for the internal coherence and systematicity of the law, and are 'affirmatively indispensable for policy analysis in a legal context'.[39] Thus, elaborating the concepts of justification and excuse, and understanding the implications of the distinction in the international legal order is important and useful because it may pinpoint problems not previously identified, highlight areas requiring regulation, and provide some solutions to (or guidance as to the solution of) practical problems of the law. The two concepts are juristic tools that may be relied upon in legal orders for the pursuit of policies and goals. Moreover, the distinction is a helpful analytical tool, enabling a decision-maker to unpack complex factual scenarios and ultimately facilitating the rational application of the law.[40] Ultimately, justification and excuse will have the relevance that legal orders assign to them. But if for nothing else, the distinction plays a fundamental role in the systematization of the legal order.

This book argues that the distinction between justification and excuse is both possible and desirable in the international legal order. Justification and excuse are not unknown concepts in the international law of state responsibility. The expressions 'circumstances precluding wrongfulness' and 'circumstances precluding responsibility' used by the ILC during its work on the ARS are, essentially, references to these two notions. In international law too, as the ILC's work suggests, 'circumstances precluding wrongfulness' concern the legality of the state's conduct, and 'circumstances precluding responsibility' concern the set of consequences that arise for states from the commission of a wrongful act (the legal relations that constitute the 'content of state responsibility' in the language of the ARS).[41] But in contrast to the flourishing literature on justification and

---

[37] Cohen, 'Transcendental Nonsense and the Functional Approach' (1935) 35 *Col LR* 809.
[38] Waldron, '"Transcendental Nonsense" and System in the Law' (2000) 100 *Col LR* 16, 16.
[39] Ibid., 17.
[40] Bacigalupo, *Manual de derecho penal (Parte general)* (1996), 67.
[41] To use the language of the title of Part II of the ARS: 'Content of the International Responsibility of a State'.

excuse in domestic law settings, the topic is still underexplored in international law. While practice and literature occasionally (although with increasing regularity) appeal to them,[42] those are still mostly superficial references – the distinction between justification and excuse in the law of state responsibility is far from being 'mature' (to borrow Brownlie's words). Moreover, in international law too there are those who doubt the practical significance of the distinction. Thomas Franck has issued the most damning critique yet: the distinction, in his view, 'is so fine as to be of pure (yet also considerable) theoretical interest'.[43] But this critique, just as its domestic law counterpart, is somewhat short-sighted. Arguing against Franck's view, this book will show that there are practical problems of international law which may be revealed and/or resolved by the distinction. These will be explored in some detail in Chapter 2, but for now it may be noted that the distinction may have an impact on the responsibility of accessories, on the availability of the entitlement to suspend or terminate a treaty if the defence relates to a treaty breach, on the duty to make compensation for material loss, and on the normative pull of rules. For these reasons, the distinction between these two notions which, as will be seen, is conceptually possible in the contemporary system of responsibility, is also a (practically) desirable one.

How then to classify the existing defences into the two typologies? Each defence is not inherently a justification or an excuse; indeed, most defences can take either form. This is most obvious with the plea of necessity which many legal systems recognise in both its justifying and excusing type. The same is true of any other defence.[44] In domestic legal orders criminal codes or other legislation can contain classifications of the defences. Legislatures may choose, for policy, moral or other normative reasons, to classify one defence as a justification or an excuse. Nevertheless, it need not (and arguably should not) be the case that legislatures perform the classification themselves.[45] When the law does not classify the defences, courts may be required to do so at the point of

---

[42] See, e.g., *CMS Gas Transmission Company v Argentine Republic*, ICSID Case ARB/01/8, Annulment, 25 September 2007, [129]. For the views of states and scholarship see, generally, Chapter 1.

[43] Franck, *Recourse to Force* (2002), 191.

[44] For an example concerning self-defence, see Fletcher and Ohlin, *Defending Humanity: When Is Force Justified and Why?* (2013), 57–8.

[45] On which see Gur-Aye, 'Should a Criminal Code Distinguish between Justification and Excuse?' (1992) 5 *Can JL & Juris* 215; Simester et al., *Criminal Law: Theory and Doctrine* (4th edn, 2010), 661–9.

application.[46] How is a court to make this decision, in the absence of guidance from the legislature? A court may rely, to this end, on scholarly writing, frequently engaged in the elaboration of taxonomies of defences or in the examination of a given defence's character as a justification or an excuse.[47] To rely on scholarly work, however, simply displaces the problem: for scholars too must provide (or at least possess) some method, approach, or principle upon which to base their classifications. An overview of the literature shows that there are competing approaches to be followed in this regard. Kimberley Kessler Ferzan identifies two main approaches, which will be discussed in more detail in Chapter 3. It is possible to work from the top-down: one could start from the premise that this or that defence constitutes a justification or an excuse. Then, by reference to theories of justification or excuse, which serve to explain *why* a given defence justifies or excuses, determine how the defence ought to be formulated. It is also possible to take a bottom-up approach: one could start from the formulation of the defence, identify a theory that can explain the defence's exonerating effect and finally consider whether that is a theory of justification or excuse.[48] There is some circularity in both approaches, in that they presume that theories of justification or excuse have been developed in the legal order. Indeed, these theories are either the starting point or the end-point of the reasoning.

In international law the 'legislators' do not show agreement on the proper classification of (most) defences. Moreover, the scholarship has yet to elaborate theories of justification and excuse; namely those theories that serve to explain *why* each type of defence produces the effect it does. There is thus a fundamental obstacle to the adoption of either of the two approaches mentioned. Whichever is chosen will require some modifications to account for this absence. As will be explained in Chapter 3, this book will opt for a bottom-up approach to the classification as this seems most in keeping with the voluntarist foundation of international law. The analysis of the classification of each defence will thus start with a thorough examination of the formulation and the rationale of each defence, as these have been accepted by states, and then consider the theory that best explains the exonerating effect of that particular

---

[46] The Canadian Supreme Court in *Perka* was faced with the question whether the plea of necessity should be classified as a justification or an excuse, see *Perka v The Queen* (1984) 2 SCR 232.
[47] In the criminal law, see Robinson, *Criminal Law Defences*. For a taxonomy of tort law defences, see Goudkamp, *Tort Law Defences* (2013).
[48] Ferzan, 'Justification and Excuse', 253.

circumstance. For example, after considering the formulation of countermeasures as the non-performance of an obligation owed to the responsible state, and identifying its rationale as relating to the enforcement of international law, the book will query *why* it is the case that the countermeasure (despite taking the form of non-performance of an obligation) is nevertheless lawful.[49] Once the theory is identified (in the case of countermeasures, a rights forfeiture theory), the book will consider whether that theory should be construed as a theory of justification or excuse. This analysis will take into account multiple factors including the views and practice of states, the formulation of the defence, its rationale, potential implications of the theory and other policy concerns, and the equivalent theories elaborated by (domestic) legal theorists. This approach may require some top-down qualifications, either to account for the fact that practice may be clear as to the effect of some defences or because the classification may require reasoning from the definitions of justification and excuse. A by-product of this analysis will be the elaboration of theories of justification and excuse for international law. The theories will be both descriptive, insofar as they describe the phenomenon of exoneration, and prescriptive, insofar as the classification of each defence (may) involve certain practical implications.

The argument in this book is presented in two steps. In Part I, the book will make the conceptual and theoretical case for the distinction between justification and excuse in international law. Chapter 1 will consider the question whether the distinction is already recognised and, if not, whether it *can* be recognised – namely, whether the international legal order and, in particular, the system of state responsibility are capable of accommodating the distinction. Chapter 2 then queries whether, if possible, the distinction *should* be recognised. To this end, it will assess the potential practical implications of the distinction and, having found that the distinction involves certain consequences which may aid in the resolution of practical problems of the law, it will argue that it is indeed desirable to distinguish between justification and excuse. If it is possible and desirable, then how to proceed to the classification? Chapter 3 answers this question by elaborating the concept and theory of justification and excuse and proposing a methodological approach to the classification of the defences currently recognised in international law.

---

[49] See Chapter 6.

In Part II the book will then set out to apply this approach to the defences included in the ARS with a view to classifying them into justifications and excuses. Each of the six defences included in the ARS, consent (Chapter 4), self-defence (Chapter 5), countermeasures (Chapter 6), *force majeure* (Chapter 7), state of necessity (Chapter 8) and distress (Chapter 9), will be considered against the conceptual and theoretical framework developed in Part I. All six chapters concerning the individual defences (Chapters 4–9) follow a similar structure. After introductory remarks on each defence, formulation in the ARS and explanation in the ILC's Commentary, each chapter will examine their development in historical perspective. The starting point of this historical analysis will be, in most cases, the nineteenth century,[50] since it was in this century that the contemporary law of responsibility began to take shape.[51] In this review, no attempt is made to discover universally accepted, even Platonic, concepts; rather, care is taken to portray, as faithfully as possible, the textual and contextual understanding of each defence in the sources analysed. The chapters will then review the codification of each defence at the ILC and the corresponding reactions of states and their practice. This analysis will not be centred on the customary recognition of each defence (though this may be incidentally remarked upon), but rather on identifying as clearly as possible the formulation and rationale of each defence as well as to glean possible views as to the character of each defence as a justification or an excuse. In the last section, each chapter will discuss the classification of the defence as a justification or excuse.

The conceptual and theoretical aims of this book demand clarity and consistency in the use of terminology. If a distinction is to be drawn between justification and excuse or, in the language of the ARS, between circumstances precluding wrongfulness and circumstances precluding responsibility, among the provisions in Chapter V of Part One, the question then arises as to what the chapter as a whole may be called given that, as will be seen in Chapter 1, the expression 'circumstance precluding wrongfulness' was introduced in the ARS as a synonym of 'justification'.

---

[50] Where necessary, the analysis will take into account developments before this period (see, e.g., Chapter 8 on state of necessity). Equally, in some instances, the analysis will begin in later periods (see, e.g., Chapter 4 on consent).

[51] See Crawford et al., 'Towards an International Law of Responsibility: Early Doctrine' in De Chazournes and Kohen (eds), *International Law and the Quest for Its Implementation: Liber Amicorum Vera Gowlland-Debbas* (2010), 377; and the later, updated version of this paper in Crawford, *State Responsibility: The General Part* (2013), ch. 1.

There is no unified terminology in this regard in domestic law. Some continental legal systems use the term 'exception';[52] whereas in the common law the expression 'defence' is preferred.[53] In international law too usage is inconsistent. The text of ARS speaks of 'circumstances precluding wrongfulness', and its Commentary uses the terms 'justification', 'excuse' and 'defences'.[54] The ICJ in *FYR Macedonia v Greece*, for example, used the terms 'justification' and 'defence' when referring to countermeasures.[55] Among all these terms, there are agreed differences between the concepts of justification and excuse, as already noted. But the same is not true of the terms 'defence' and 'exception'. These are often used as synonyms,[56] with the term 'defence' prevailing in discussions about responsibility or liability in the English language. The term 'defence', moreover, is often assigned a much broader meaning, to refer to the set of arguments presented in response to a claim by a respondent (on the substance). In its broad sense, the term 'defence' would include substantive defences, procedural arguments, and arguments about admissibility or statutes of limitation.[57]

This book will use the terms justification and excuse to refer to international law's 'circumstances precluding wrongfulness' and 'circumstances precluding responsibility', respectively. Furthermore, this book will use the expression 'defence' to refer to the collection of rules included in Chapter V of Part One.[58] The term defence will thus be used in a narrow

---

[52] Grando, *Evidence, Proof, and Fact-Finding in WTO Dispute Settlement* (2009), 188 (fn. 171).
[53] See, e.g., Robinson, *Criminal Law Defences*; Goudkamp, *Tort Law Defences*.
[54] Not, as is often noted, out of confusion as to the meaning of these terms. Rather as explained in Chapter 1, the Commission knew very well the meaning of these terms and used them in this context for a clear purpose.
[55] *Application of the Interim Accord of 13 September 1995 (FYR Macedonia v Greece)* (2011) ICJ Rep 644, 682 [120].
[56] See, e.g., the use of these terms by Williams, 'Offences and Defences'; Williams, 'The Logic of "Exceptions"' (1988) 47 CLJ 261.
[57] On this point, see Duarte d'Almeida, *Allowing for Exceptions*, 32–3. As an aside, note that a respondent in the substance need not correspond to the procedural respondent. In international law, this is particularly the case where disputes are brought before tribunals by special agreement and in the case of counterclaims (in which the procedural applicant is a respondent on the substance of the counterclaim).
[58] The term 'defence' can be reserved to the circumstances recognised at customary law and applicable as a matter of the general law of responsibility; namely, applicable (in principle) to all obligations, regardless of their content and their source. In international scholarship and practice the term 'exception' is often used to refer to specific circumstances provided for in treaties, such as the 'essential security interests exception' of various Bilateral Investment Treaties, e.g., Newcombe and Paradell, *Law and Practice of Investment*

sense: only to refer to substantive arguments invoked by a respondent, and which are intended to defeat a claim on the merits.[59] This term is preferable to the expression 'circumstances precluding wrongfulness' insofar as it is agnostic as to the characterisation of each circumstance in this section of the ARS as either a justification or an excuse. It will thus avoid the nonsense of saying that certain 'circumstances precluding wrongfulness' operate as excuses – or, what is the same, that certain justifications are excuses, which is plainly wrong. Thus, the terminology employed in this book is at variance with the language of the ARS. This need not be problematic. As authoritative as the ARS are, they are not a treaty and the language employed in that instrument is therefore neither definitive nor dispositive. Lastly, the term 'exoneration' is used as a generic term to refer to the practical effect of the operation of defences: to get the state 'off the hook', in colloquial terms, irrespective of the reasons for this result (by preclusion of wrongfulness or responsibility).

The book will also modify the terminology employed by the ARS in respect of the defence in Article 25. The English language text of the ARS labels this defence 'necessity', whereas the French and Spanish version speak of 'state of necessity' (*état de nécessité* and *estado de necesidad*, respectively). The notion of necessity (as an ordinary, or non-legal, concept) plays many different roles in the law, as will be explained in Chapter 8. The defence of state of necessity is linked to (in the sense that it is inspired by) the ordinary concept of necessity. To avoid conflating these two notions, necessity as an ordinary concept and 'necessity' as a defence, it is best to refer to them with different terms. This book will thus follow the linguistic choice of the French and Spanish versions of the ARS by referring to the rule as 'state of necessity'. Indeed, 'necessity' is not a legal term of art, 'state of necessity' is.

The book will also alter, in one place, the order in which the defences appear in the ARS. Since the defence of distress too is a rule inspired by necessity,[60] and its examination would benefit from an understanding of

---

*Treaties: Standards of Treatment* (2009), ch. 10 (reserving the term 'exception' for treaty-based provisions). There are good reasons to use separate terms to refer to the (general) customary and the (specific) conventional circumstances: factors relevant to the latter may be irrelevant to the former. Indeed, the scope, operation and interaction between treaty rules and treaty grounds of exoneration may be affected by the language, policies and goals of the treaty itself.

[59] This usage excludes from the scope of the term other defensive arguments, such as jurisdictional and admissibility objections, statutes of limitation, immunities, and so on.

[60] E.g. Scalese, *La rilevanza delle scusanti nella teoria dell'illecito internazionale* (2008), 148–9.

the relation between ordinary necessity and the law, the chapter on state of necessity (Chapter 8) will precede that on distress (Chapter 9). This is an alteration of the listing of the circumstances in Chapter V of Part One, which places state of necessity last, in an effort to convey that state of necessity is a defence of last resort. The concern with discouraging reliance on state of necessity poses no logical or substantive impediment to, nor is it defeated or undermined by, addressing state of necessity and distress in an alternative order in this book.

Finally, three caveats are necessary. First, on the scope of this work. The book is focused on the law of state responsibility only, and it will not consider individual criminal responsibility under international law[61] or the responsibility of international organisations.[62] By the same token, the book will not consider substantive rules of international law: making use of the ILC's helpful heuristic device, the book does not discuss 'primary' rules of international law. In particular, it will not discuss the substance of the right of self-defence in the chapter on ARS Article 21 (Chapter 5), nor will it consider military reprisals during armed conflict (Chapter 6), discuss the principle of necessity pursuant to international humanitarian law (Chapter 8) or the right of refuge for ships in distress (Chapter 9).

Second, the book will focus on the 'general defences', namely those defences recognised at, or claimed to belong to, customary law and which are applicable across the whole range of international legal relations (save where specifically excluded). Treaty-based exceptions are, therefore, excluded from the scope of this work. The reasons for this are both pragmatic and conceptual. The variation among treaty exceptions is (and can be) 'infinite', to use again Baxter's expression.[63] This is not only in terms of their content, but also in terms of the form that they take. Moreover, as they are embedded in a particular treaty they are likely to respond to the particular goals and policies of *that* treaty and these issues can affect the way in which they are interpreted and applied. Generalisations about these treaty exceptions are therefore rather difficult to make or, if at all possible, they would be at such high level of abstraction as to be virtually meaningless. This said, it is of course possible that treaty exceptions be classified by the treaty parties (expressly in the treaty or in the *travaux préparatoires*) as either justifications or excuses. To the extent that these

---

[61] On which see, generally, O'Keefe, *International Criminal Law* (2015), chaps 5 and 6; Knoops, *Defenses in Contemporary International Criminal Law* (2008).

[62] On which see Articles on the Responsibility of International Organisations, A/RES/66/100, 9 December 2011.

[63] Baxter, 'International Law in "Her Infinite Variety"' (1980) 29 ICLQ 549.

classifications are clear from the treaty, then (some of) the findings of this book may be applicable to those treaty exceptions as well. Thus, the treaty exception can operate as a justification (that is, rendering conduct lawful) or an excuse and, if this is the case, the findings of this book will be relevant.[64] Likewise, the practical consequences of the distinction between the two will also apply (at least, to the extent that these are not excluded by the parties). For example, as between treaty parties, conduct justified by a treaty exception will not attract countermeasures. Whether the theories of justification and excuse explained in this book are also applicable to treaty exceptions is an unexplored question, which this study, regrettably, cannot answer. It may be argued that excluding these topics from the scope of this book renders this study somewhat narrow. This may be the case. But this choice was made necessary by the embryonic stage of development of the international law of defences, which more than justifies the exclusive attention paid to the question of the classification of the six circumstances included in the ARS.

Finally, in developing and explaining the argument in this book, references will inevitably be made to equivalent notions in domestic law. These references will predominantly be made to domestic criminal law and criminal law theory, insofar as the notions of justification and excuse were developed in this field. Nevertheless, where this is helpful, references will also be made to domestic tort law or other forms of delictual responsibility. In either case, it should be clear that the book is not engaging in the transposition of domestic (criminal or tort) law notions to international law as such. This approach would be inadequate and fruitless for, as is well known, responsibility in international law is 'neither civil nor criminal'.[65] This notwithstanding, it is undeniable that the law of state responsibility shares many concepts with domestic law systems of responsibility and liability, both civil and criminal. An illustration of this is the notions of complicity in the law of responsibility, as well as the distinctions between the instantaneous, complex, or continuous violations of international obligations.[66] The examination of equivalent concepts in domestic law will simply serve to gain a greater conceptual and theoretical awareness that can illuminate the enquiry in this book.

---

[64] This is the position endorsed in the *CMS (Annulment)* decision; see [132–6].
[65] Pellet, 'The Definition of Responsibility in International Law' in Crawford et al. (eds), *The Law of International Responsibility* (2010), 12.
[66] See Distefano, 'Fait continu, fait composé et fait complexe dans le droit de la responsabilité' (2006) 52 AFDI 1.

# PART I

Justification and Excuse in International Law

# 1

# Justification and Excuse in International Law

## 1.1 Introduction

There is conduct that is unlawful, there is conduct that is justified, and there is conduct for which, despite being unlawful, the actor is excused.[1] This paraphrase of Vaughan Lowe's words captures the distinction between justifications and excuses: justifications exclude the wrongfulness of conduct; excuses preclude the responsibility of an actor for wrongful conduct. The former concern the conduct, the latter the actor. The distinction between the two, also according to Lowe, is 'the very stuff of classical tragedy': 'no dramatist, no novelist would confuse them. No philosopher or theologian would conflate them.'[2] In international law, the distinction is tracked in the clear, although clumsy, expressions 'circumstances precluding wrongfulness' and 'circumstances precluding responsibility'. But behind this apparent terminological clarity, there is very little certainty about these two notions. There has been very little exploration and, therefore, very little agreement on the concept, theory and effect of justification and excuse in the international law of state responsibility. As a result, it has been difficult to provide a classification of the defences included in the Articles on the Responsibility of States for Internationally Wrongful Acts (ARS) into these two categories.[3] And yet, there are increasing calls

---

[1] To paraphrase Lowe, 'Precluding Wrongfulness or Responsibility: A Plea for Excuses?' (1999) 10 EJIL 405, 406. In turn, borrowing from J. L. Austin's famous 'Plea for Excuses' (1956–7) 57 *Proc Arist Soc* 1.
[2] Lowe, 'Plea', 406.
[3] In addition to Lowe's article cited above, other notable exceptions include: Malanczuk, 'Countermeasures and Self-Defence as Circumstances Precluding Wrongfulness in the ILC Draft Articles on State Responsibility' (1983) 43 *ZaöRV* 705, 711–15; Johnstone, 'The Plea of "Necessity" in International Legal Discourse: Humanitarian Intervention and Counter-terrorism' (2005) 43 *Columbia J Trans'l L* 337, 349–57; Christakis, 'Les "circonstances excluant l'illicéité": une illusion optique?' in Corten et al. (eds), *Droit du pouvoir, pouvoir du droit: Mélanges offerts à Jean Salmon* (2007), 223; Scalese, *La rilevanza delle scusanti nella teoria dell'illecito internazionale* (2008); Sloane, 'On the Use and Abuse of Necessity in the Law of State Responsibility' (2012) 106 AJIL 447; Crawford, *State Responsibility: The General Part*

for, and endorsements of, the distinction in international law; and not just in scholarly commentary.[4] Several states endorsed the distinction in the Sixth Committee of the General Assembly,[5] and the *CMS v Argentina* Annulment Committee also relied upon it.[6]

It seems that there are two main reasons why the topic has remained underexplored in international law. First is the view that the distinction is not possible in international law. There are two versions of this view: in one view excuses are not possible in international law; in the other it is justifications that are not possible in international law. The former view is based on an assumption that the ARS exclude the possibility of excuses in international law altogether. Indeed, Special Rapporteur Ago expressly denied that excuses had any role in international law, and Special Rapporteur Crawford, albeit more sympathetic to the distinction, ultimately opted not to distinguish between the justification and excuse in the ARS. This assumption is further enhanced by the ARS's choice of terminology in this regard. Both the title of Chapter V of Part One, as well as (most of) the provisions in that part of the ARS, use the language of 'preclusion of wrongfulness'; that is, the language of justification. The latter view is based on a misunderstanding of the primary/secondary rule distinction and its function in the field of state responsibility. Unlike the previous assumption, this misunderstanding has led scholars to exclude the possibility of justifications in the law of state responsibility. The law of responsibility, goes this argument, is limited to secondary rules. Justifications are 'part of the framework within which'[7] the obligations of states operate; in other

---

(2013), ch. 9; Aust, 'Circumstances Precluding Wrongfulness and Shared Responsibility' in Nollkaemper and Plakokefalos (eds), *Principles of Shared Responsibility* (2014), 169; Paddeu, 'Circumstances Precluding Wrongfulness' in Wolfrum (ed.), MPEPIL (2015). Most of these pieces, at any rate, contain only superficial discussions of the distinction.

[4] Among scholars, see Malanczuk, 'Countermeasures', 711–15; Lowe, 'Plea'; Johnstone, 'Necessity'; Viñuales, *Foreign Investment and the Environment in International Law* (2012), 366; Crawford, *General Part*, ch. 9; Sloane, 'Necessity', 482–6; Aust, 'Circumstances Precluding Wrongfulness'. Contra Szurek, 'The Notion of Circumstances Precluding Wrongfulness' in Crawford et al. (eds), *The Law of International Responsibility* (2010), 435–7.

[5] See Section 1.3.1.

[6] *CMS Gas Transmission Company v Argentine Republic*, ICSID Case ARB/01/8, Annulment, 25 September 2007, [129]. See also *Continental Casualty Company v Argentine Republic*, ICSID Case ARB/03/9, Award, 5 September 2008, at fn. 236; *El Paso Energy International Company v Argentine Republic*, ICSID Case ARB/03/15, Award, 31 October 2011, [553].

[7] Crawford, 'The International Court of Justice and the Law of State Responsibility' in Tams and Sloane (eds), *The Development of International Law by the International Court of Justice* (2013), 75.

## 1.1 INTRODUCTION

words, they concern the conduct of states. Indeed, as will be seen, justifications constitute permissions of the legal order and, as a result, they are primary in character. In contrast, excuses concern the legal consequences of wrongfulness and can therefore be classified as secondary rules. If the law of responsibility is composed of secondary rules *only*, it follows that the only types of defence that can be part of the law of responsibility are excuses. The second reason is the widely held perception that the distinction between justification and excuse, as put by Thomas Franck, 'is so fine as to be of pure (yet also considerable) theoretical interest'.[8] In short, the view that a distinction between these two categories of defences would carry no practical consequences. The first question goes, therefore, to the possibility of the distinction (whether it can be drawn), and the second to its usefulness and, as such, its desirability (whether it should be drawn).

The first two chapters of this study will be dedicated to challenging these views. Chapter 1 will tackle the question of the possibility of the classification and argue that, although not presently recognised in positive law, the distinction *can* be recognised. Chapter 2 will then consider whether drawing the distinction has any practical consequences. It will show that there are indeed potential practical implications of the distinction or, better put, that there exist practical problems of international law which can be solved, or at the very least analysed, by means of the distinction between justification and excuse. Having clarified in Chapters 1 and 2 that the distinction is both possible and desirable, Chapter 3 then develops the concept and theory of justification and excuse for international law and, by way of conclusion of Part I of this study, it will propose a methodological approach to the classification of the defences in the ARS into each of these categories. These three chapters, which form Part I of this study, thus focus on what may be called the 'general part' of the law of defences. The 'special part', namely the classification of each individual defence, is the subject of Part II.[9]

Turning to the substance of this chapter: can the distinction be made in international law? This chapter will argue that it can – that the distinction between justification and excuse is, in other words, systemically possible. It will begin in Section 1.2 with some introductory remarks on the notions of justification and excuse, as these have been developed by legal theorists. Given the relatively modest developments on this point in international law, the chapter will take as a starting point the notions

---

[8] Franck, *Recourse to Force* (2002), 191.
[9] I am grateful to Roger O'Keefe for his suggestion to frame the issue in this way.

as they have developed in domestic law – primarily in criminal law. As already emphasised in the Introduction to this study, this is not an attempt at transposition of domestic criminal law into international law. Nevertheless, an examination of the criminal law notions may provide useful guidance in studying and devising the development of equivalent notions for the international law of state responsibility. Besides, this is not an unknown approach in the law of responsibility, since many of its institutions and concepts, such as the notions of instantaneous, complex or continuous wrongful acts, have been developed by reference to their domestic criminal law counterparts.[10]

In Section 1.3, the chapter then turns to international law. This section begins with a consideration of the current recognition of excuses in international law (Section 1.3.1). It will show that, at present, the practice of states and their *opinio juris* is limited and it is, at best, inconclusive. Thus, the starting point of this work is that the distinction has not yet been recognised as a matter of positive law. Nevertheless, this does not mean that the distinction cannot be recognised. Indeed, contrary to the view that the ILC has excluded the distinction by opting to classify all its defences as circumstances precluding wrongfulness (or justifications), Section 1.3.2 will show that despite the language used in Chapter V of Part One of the ARS, the ILC did not intend to be dispositive on this point. The references to 'excuse' scattered throughout the Commentary of the ARS, far from showing a Commission mistakenly using the terms 'justification' and 'excuse' as synonyms, show a Commission intent on leaving the door open for the development and (potential) recognition of these notions as part of the system of state responsibility. At any rate, the law of responsibility can certainly develop beyond the ARS so that, in the ultimate analysis, whatever the ILC's position may have been in 2001 it is not the final word on this question. Section 1.3.3 will then address the objections based on the primary and secondary rule distinction and will show that, even though justifications possess primary character, this is not enough to disqualify them from the law of state responsibility. As will be seen, this objection is too dogmatic and is premised on a strict and formalist approach to the distinction between primary and secondary rules which is untenable, unwarranted and unsupported in the ILC's work. Moreover, it fundamentally ignores the reality that the distinction between primary

---

[10] On which see, e.g., Distefano, 'Fait continu, fait composé et fait complexe dans le droit de la responsabilité' (2006) 52 AFDI 1. For a different view, see: Cassese, 'On the Use of Criminal Law Notions in Determining State Responsibility for Genocide' (2007) 5 JICJ 875.

and secondary rules was adopted for mere pragmatic purposes. The distinction was intended as a legislative technique, rather than a jurisprudential position on the character of rules in the international legal order. The law of responsibility can and does include primary rules so that it is perfectly possible for certain defences to concern wrongfulness rather than responsibility. By way of conclusion, Section 1.4 will argue that international law is systemically capable of accommodating a distinction between justifications and excuses, insofar as the law of responsibility is built upon the conceptual distinction between the notions of the 'internationally wrongful act' and 'responsibility' (in the sense of the legal consequences arising from the wrongful act). Justifications can thus be understood as defences that concern the wrongfulness of the act, and excuses as defences that concern the responsibility of the actor.

## 1.2 A Primer on Justification and Excuse

The distinction between the notions of justification and excuse appears to be old.[11] Early common law, for instance, distinguished justified and excused homicide. The former resulted in acquittal 'as if the finding had been that [the accused] did not do the killing'; the latter in the imposition of the same sentence for homicide (death and forfeiture of all goods), but the excused defendant was entitled to plead for discretionary remission of punishment by the Crown.[12] The distinction was not, however, made on the basis of defined abstract categories of justification and excuse. Indeed, the technical legal distinction between the two notions was only formulated in the late nineteenth and early twentieth centuries.[13]

The elaboration of the concepts of justification and excuse accompanied important (parallel) developments in the theory of crime, originating primarily in Germany.[14] At least since the early twentieth century,

---

[11] See the historical account in Milhizer, 'Justification and Excuse: What They Were, What They Are and What They Ought to Be' (2004) 78 *St John's LR* 725.

[12] Horowitz, 'Justification and Excuse in the Program of the Criminal Law' (1986) 49 *Law & Contemp Probs* 109, 112ff.

[13] Eser, 'Justification and Excuse: A Key Issue in the Concept of Crime' in Eser (ed.), *Justification and Excuse: Comparative Perspectives* (1987), 34ff.

[14] For an account of the development of criminal law theories in this period (and subsequently), see, e.g., Padovani, *Diritto penale* (9th edn, 2008), 98–102; Fletcher, *The Grammar of Criminal Law* (2007), 43ff; Ambos, 'Toward a Universal System of Crime: Comments on George Fletcher's *Grammar of Criminal Law*' (2006-7) 28 *Cardozo LR* 2647; Marinucci and Dolcini, *Manuale di diritto penale* (2nd edn, 2006), 141–53; Roxin, *Derecho penal. Parte general* (1997) vol. 1, 196ff; Eser, 'Key Issue'; Eser, 'Justification and Excuse' (1976) 24 *Am J Comp L* 621.

German criminal law has recognised a 'structured' notion of crime. This notion is composed of three different elements: definition of the offence (the *Tatbestand*), the unlawfulness of the act (*Rechtswidrigkeit*), and the blameworthiness of the actor (*Schuld*).[15] These elements are analysed in successive evaluative stages to establish criminal responsibility: a judge must first determine whether the elements of the definition of the offence are met in the case, then determine whether the conduct is wrongful, and, finally, whether the actor is blameworthy for his actions.[16] The difference between the elements of the offence is not one of degree, but one of kind and a single category of defences would not have been adequate for this structured system. So criminal law theorists elaborated defences attendant to each evaluative stage in this structure: at the first evaluative stage the defendant can deny the elements of the offence, in the second he can invoke a justification to deny the unlawfulness of his act and, in the third evaluative stage, he can invoke an excuse to deny his blameworthiness. Albin Eser's metaphor of the multistorey house usefully depicts this approach, in which:

> one must, in order to reach full punishability, ascend floor by floor to reach the highest level. In this model, each floor has an outside exit from liability in the form of defenses.[17]

The structured system was subsequently adopted by other continental law jurisdictions, in Europe and beyond,[18] and by some common law jurisdictions as well.[19] There are significant variations in the 'structure' of criminal liability across these various legal orders. For instance, alongside the 'tripartite' structure just mentioned, some jurisdictions recognise a 'bipartite' structure (encompassing unlawfulness and blameworthiness) or even a 'quadripartite' one (capacity, conduct, unlawfulness and blameworthiness).[20] All of these multilevel conceptions of criminal responsibility can accommodate different categories of defences; as many as conceptual elements there may be. So long as the ascertainment of responsibility can be

---

[15] See the 'Brief Introduction' in Bohlander, *The German Criminal Code: A Modern English Translation* (2008), 5–6. In general, see Bohlander, *Principles of German Criminal Law* (2009).
[16] See the useful table 2 in Ambos, 'Universal System', 2651.
[17] Eser, 'Key Issue', 23.
[18] E.g., Austria, Germany, Spain and Switzerland in Europe, most of Latin American states, and Korea, Japan and Taiwan, cited in Eser, 'Key Issue', 20 (fn. 4); Pradel, *Droit pénal comparé* (2nd edn, 2002), 325.
[19] Model Penal Code and Commentaries, sec. 3-02.
[20] On which see, generally, Fletcher, *Grammar*, 43–58.

structured around different conceptual categories, different typologies of defences can be similarly distinguished to match those categories.[21]

The 'structured' notion of criminal responsibility is contrasted with what has been called a 'flat' or 'holistic' notion in which defences all operate at the same level, as it were. Eser, resorting again to the house metaphor, compares these 'flat' or 'holistic' notions to a 'one-story bungalow with two main entrances in the form of "*actus reus*" and "*mens rea*" and many exits constituting (equally ranked) defenses'. The consequence of this approach, he says, is that for a finding of not guilty, it 'does not matter too much whether this entrance is barred or that exit open'.[22] In such a system, therefore, there is little use in distinguishing between justification and excuse. While it could be said that justifications deny the *actus reus* and excuses deny *mens rea*, the point is that in either case, the successful invocation of a defence results in a verdict of acquittal pure and simple.

The notions of justification and excuse have been the subject of an engaged debate among criminal lawyers and theorists. Initially of interest to continental legal scholars primarily, the debate eventually spread to the common law world as well: beginning with the now famous 'plea for excuses' made by Oxford linguistic philosopher J. L. Austin,[23] ever more Anglo-Saxon criminal lawyers and legal philosophers have addressed the topic. Despite the assertion by the English criminal lawyer James Stephen in the late nineteenth century that the distinction between justification and excuse was one of mere 'historical significance',[24] since the mid-twentieth century, the writings of H. L. A. Hart[25] and Glanville Williams[26] in England and, perhaps more influentially, those of George Fletcher[27] and Paul

---

[21] Husak, 'Beyond the Justification/Excuse Dichotomy' in Cruft et al. (eds), *Crime, Punishment, and Responsibility: The Jurisprudence of Antony Duff* (2011), 141. For an example of a four-fold classification of criminal defences, see Robinson, *Criminal Law Defences* (1984).
[22] Eser, 'Key Issue', 23.
[23] Austin, 'A Plea for Excuses' (1956–7) 57 *Proc Arist Soc* 1.
[24] Stephen, *History of the Criminal Law of England* (MacMillan, 1883), vol. 3, 11.
[25] Hart, *Punishment and Responsibility* (1968), 13–24, 28–53.
[26] Williams, 'Offences and Defences' (1982) 2 *Legal Studies* 233.
[27] See, e.g., Fletcher, 'Fairness and Utility in Tort Theory' (1972) 85 *Harv LR* 537; Fletcher, 'Proportionality and the Psychotic Aggressor: A Vignette in Comparative Criminal Theory' (1973) 8 *Israel LR* 367; Fletcher, 'The Individualization of Excusing Conditions' (1973–4) 47 *S Cal LR* 1269; Fletcher, 'The Right Deed for the Wrong Reason: A Reply to Mr. Robinson' (1975–6) 23 *UCLA LR* 293; Fletcher, *Rethinking Criminal Law* (1978); Fletcher, 'Should Intolerable Prison Conditions Generate a Justification or an Excuse for Escape' (1978–9) 26 *UCLA LR* 1355.

Robinson[28] in the United States, prompted a renewed interest in the distinction. The literature is now flourishing, and the academic debate which ensued has been so fruitful that some have acclaimed its success: by the early twenty-first century, during a meeting of the Criminal Law Section of the American Association of Law Schools, Joshua Dressler invoked as an example of successful criminal law theory the 'resolution' of the conceptual debate between justification and excuse.[29] Indeed, scholars no longer dispute that justification and excuse are distinct and relevant legal categories.[30] Moreover, there is also a broad consensus in respect of the definitions of these two notions.[31] Douglas Husak's definition, quoted in the Introduction, encapsulates this consensus. It may be useful to recall it here:

> Justifications are defenses that arise from properties or characteristics of acts; excuses are defenses that arise from properties or characteristics of actors. A defendant is justified when his *conduct* is not legally wrongful, even though it apparently violates a criminal law. A defendant is excused when *he* is not blameworthy or responsible for his conduct, even though it ... violates the criminal law.[32]

This definition (slightly modified here)[33] represents the minimum consensus among scholars, and indeed significant issues remain.[34] To begin

---

[28] Who proposed a German-style 'structured' analysis of criminal offences, in Robinson, 'Criminal Law Defences: A Systematic Analysis' (1982) 82 *Col LR* 199; and subsequently in Robinson, *Criminal Law Defences*.

[29] Cited in Berman, 'Justification and Excuse, Law and Morality' (2003) 53 *Duke LJ* 1, 4.

[30] Horder, *Excusing Crime* (2007), 7.

[31] This meaning largely follows that of ordinary language. See in this respect, the *Oxford English Dictionary* definitions of both words: justification is '[t]he action of justifying or showing something to be just, right, or proper; vindication of oneself or another' (3), and excuse is the 'attempt to clear (a person) wholly or partially from blame, without denying or justifying his imputed action' (I.1.a).

[32] Husak, 'Justifications and the Criminal Liability of Accessories', (1989–90) 80 *J Crim L & Criminology* 491, 496 (emphasis in original, footnotes omitted).

[33] As already noted, the quotation elides Husak's statement that excuses concern conduct that 'apparently' violates the criminal law. This statement relates to Husak's view that justification and excuse are not serially ordered: Husak, 'The Serial View of Criminal Law Defences' (1992) 3 *Criminal Law Forum* 369; Husak, 'On the Supposed Priority of Justification to Excuse' (2005) 24 *Law & Philosophy* 557. In essence, a court could decide on a defendant's excuse *without* having considered if he or she possesses justifications with the result that the court may not have reached the conclusion that the conduct violates the criminal law. The view is not widely shared, as the overwhelming majority of scholars agree that excuses presume the existence of a wrongful act (or, in short, they presume that justifications are unavailable). On this point see the rebuttal by Baron, 'Is Justification (Somehow) Prior to Excuse? A Reply to Douglas Husak' (2005) 24 *Law & Philosophy* 595, and references cited there.

[34] For a useful overview of these issues, see Ferzan, 'Justification and Excuse' in Deigh and Dolinko (eds), *The Oxford Handbook of Philosophy of Criminal Law* (2011), 239.

## 1.2 A PRIMER ON JUSTIFICATION AND EXCUSE

with, it is difficult to determine whether certain facts are relevant to the act or the actor and, at any rate, most defences – be it justification or excuse – refer to a combination of both. In respect of justifications, moreover, is it enough that the conduct be permissible or is it the case that the conduct ought to be morally praiseworthy as well?[35] Must the justifying circumstances actually exist, is it enough that the actor reasonably and in good faith believes those circumstances to exist, or both?[36] In respect of excuses, is blameworthiness a subjective or a normative concept; that is, does it concern the agent's fault or does it refer to the situation in which it is not reasonable to expect an actor to comply with the law?[37] Is it the case that an excuse is a denial of responsibility or is it, rather, an assertion of responsibility?[38] These issues need not (and cannot) be resolved here. But it is useful to highlight these questions since, as will be seen throughout this book, similar issues have arisen in international law as well.

Criminal law scholars mostly agree that the distinction between justification and excuse is also important from a practical standpoint. Certain implications flow from this distinction which may affect practical problems of the law. Justifications, centring on the character of the

---

[35] On justified conduct as permissible, see Husak, 'Justifications and the Criminal Liability' 499–500; Dressler, 'New Thoughts about the Concept of Justification on the Criminal Law: A Critique of Fletcher's Thinking and Rethinking' (1984–5) 32 UCLA LR 61, 77. On justified conduct as morally praiseworthy, see Greenawalt, 'The Perplexing Borders of Justification and Excuse' (1984) 84 *Col LR* 1897, 1927; Greenawalt, 'Distinguishing between Justification and Excuse' (1986) 49 *Law & Contemp Probs* 89; Robinson, 'A Theory of Justification: Societal Harm as a Prerequisite for Criminal Liability' (1975–6) 23 UCLA LR 266, 274; Byrd, 'Wrongdoing and Attribution: Implications beyond the Justification-Excuse Distinction' (1986–7) 33 *Wayne LR* 1289, 1293; Baron, 'Justifications and Excuses' (2005) 2 *Ohio State J Crim L* 387.

[36] On the disagreements between the 'deeds' theory and the 'reasons' theory of justifications, as these are referred to in the literature, see Robinson, 'Theory of Justification'; Fletcher, 'The Right Deed for the Wrong Reason: A Reply to Mr. Robinson'; Robinson, 'Competing Theories of Justification: Deeds versus Reasons' in Simester and Smith (eds), *Harm and Culpability* (1996), 45; Robinson, 'Objective versus Subjective Justification: A Case Study in Function and Form in Constructing a System of Criminal Law Theory' in Robinson et al. (eds), *Criminal Law Conversations* (2011), 343.

[37] For a summary of the differing theories of blameworthiness: Roxin, *Derecho penal*, 799ff. For the development and critique of the normative notion of blameworthiness see Jescheck, 'Evolución del concepto jurídico de la culpabilidad en Alemania y Austria' (2003) 05(1) *Revista Electrónica de Ciencia Penal y Criminología*; Roxin, *Derecho penal*, 788ff; Velásquez, 'La culpabilidad y el principio de culpabilidad' (1993) 50 *Revista de Derecho y Ciencias Políticas*, 283.

[38] Contrast, e.g., Austin, 'Plea'; Gardner, 'In Defence of Defences' in Gardner (ed.), *Offences and Defences: Selected Essays in the Philosophy of Criminal Law* (2007), 83–4.

act, have a universal tendency in that they (may) produce effects beyond the individual case.[39] For example, accessories to the offence can benefit from the principal's justification.[40] If Helper aids Victim to forcibly repel an unjust attack launched by Aggressor, Helper will not be responsible towards Aggressor since Helper aided Victim to engage in lawful behaviour.[41] In contrast, excuses are personal to the actor only and may not be extended to accessories. Thus a defence of duress does not extend to the coercing agent: if Coerced is excused for harming Victim as a result of duress, the coercing agent cannot benefit from the excuse.[42] Similarly, the reach of justifications can extend to the entire legal order: a justification in crime will, therefore, be valid also as against civil remedies against the individual invoking the defence. A criminal law excuse, in contrast, does not produce such collateral effects.[43] Finally, a finding of justification by a court produces normative consequences beyond the particular case: every other subject of the law, in the same circumstances, ought to be able to successfully invoke the justification in question. Excuses carry the opposite implication; although the actor is excused because of individual circumstances, the conduct is unlawful and others should avoid engaging in it.[44] Thus, justifications are said to be 'universal' and excuses only 'relative'.[45]

These are, of course, only implications of the distinction, and as such only potentially relevant in practice. No one would (and does) suggest that they are binding as such or that the recognition of the distinction

---

[39] Note, however, that the universality of justification is only possible if the justifying circumstances actually exist and not if they depend on the reasonable beliefs of the actor, see Ferzan, 'Justification and Excuse', 244–5.
[40] Radbruch, 'Jurisprudence in the Criminal Law' (1936) 18 *J Comp Leg & Int'l L* 218, 218. Similarly Robinson, 'Systematic Analysis', 279–80; Hassemer, 'Justification and Excuse in Criminal Law: Theses and Comments' (1986) BYULR 573, 603–4; Eser, 'Key Issue', 33–4.
[41] This is a simple representation, which assumes that Helper had no individual intention or motive for attacking Aggressor and used Aggressor's unjust aggression against Victim as a pretext.
[42] This is, again, a simple representation and there may be complicating factors.
[43] See, e.g., by reference to Italian law: Marinucci and Dolcini, *Manuale*, 197; Mantovani, *Principi di diritto penale* (2nd edn, 2007), 100. This said, whether civil liability is due for criminal conduct is, itself, a controversial question in many legal orders. See, e.g., Spencer, 'Civil Liability for Crimes' in Dyson (ed.), *Unravelling Tort and Crime* (2014), 304.
[44] Mousourakis, 'Justification and Excuse' (1998–9) 7 *Tilburg Foreign LR* 35, 44. Similarly, Sangero, *Self-Defence in Criminal Law* (2006), 15; Dressler, 'Justifications and Excuses: A Brief Review of the Concepts and the Literature' (1986–7) 33 *Wayne LR* 1155, 1169; Horowitz, 'Justification', 116.
[45] Fletcher, *Rethinking*, 761–2.

in any given legal order demands the acceptance of these consequences. Domestic legal orders often regulate these practical problems in ways different from those implied by the notions of justification and excuse. For instance, whether an accessory is responsible in any case where justification or excuse is successfully pleaded depends, ultimately, on the paradigm of responsibility accepted in each legal order. Where the accessory is responsible for his own actions, the principal's defences (whatever they may be) will not reach; but where the accessory's responsibility is derivative from the illegality of the principal's conduct, the latter's justification or excuse may affect the former's responsibility.[46] Moreover, answers to these practical problems may be found in principles or concepts *other* than those of justification and excuse.[47] The variation among legal orders in the recognition of these various potential consequences is such that it is very difficult to pinpoint practical implications of the distinction that are generally accepted.

Arguably because of the difficulty of generalising the practical consequences of the distinction, critics remain who contend that, while conceptually distinct, justification and excuse are irrelevant in practice.[48] Scepticism towards the distinction tends to come from common law jurisdictions (especially the United Kingdom), with scholars echoing Sir James Stephen's claim over a century ago that the distinction had 'historical significance' but involved 'no legal consequences' in the common law.[49] English and Welsh law's disregard for these notions derives, among others, from the perception that this is a distinction without a difference.[50]

The practical irrelevance critique is, nevertheless, short-sighted. Justification and excuse are doctrinal concepts, juristic tools, that legal systems may employ in the ordering of legal and social relations, the

---

[46] Dressler, 'New Thoughts', 95. As examples, see the thorough analysis of German and Italian law on this point in, respectively, Schreiber, 'Problems of Justification and Excuse in the Setting of Accessorial Conduct' (1986) BYULR 611; McAuley, 'Theory of Justification and Excuse: Some Italian Lessons' (1987) 35 *Am J Comp L* 359, 375ff.

[47] The distinction between justification and excuse is arguably not the only answer to these practical problems. For example, Hassemer notes that legal systems must provide an answer to the question of accessorial liability in case of justified/excused defendant, whether or not this is through the distinction between justification and excuse itself or through other means, Hassemer, 'Justification', 603.

[48] E.g., Hall, 'Comment on Justification and Excuse' (1976) 24 *Am J Comp L* 638; Colvin, 'Exculpatory Defences in Criminal Law' (1990) 10 OJLS 381; Chin, 'Unjustified: The Practical Irrelevance of the Justification/Excuse Distinction' (2009) 43 *UM J Law Reform* 79.

[49] Stephen, *History of the Criminal Law of England* (1883), vol. 3, 11.

[50] See, e.g., Herring, *Criminal Law: Texts, Cases, and Materials* (6th edn, 2014), 718.

expression of policies and the attainment of goals. The review of the various doctrinal debates on these notions, as well as an overview of their regulation in domestic legal orders, shows that justification and excuse are flexible concepts which may be adapted to differing frameworks and systems of responsibility. It is possible that some legal orders do not need these notions or that they only need them in some fields and not others; it is also possible that pre-existing institutional structures prevent these notions from acquiring relevance. In England, for example, the institutional setup of criminal trials, which are decided by a jury in binary guilty/not-guilty verdicts, precludes (or complicates, at the very least) findings that the actor's conduct is justified or that the actor is excused.[51] Besides, even if justification and excuse may not always resolve, in a complete and automatic way, practical problems faced by the law, the classification of defences into these two categories provides at the very least an analytical tool that may help identify these problems and, potentially, to address them.[52]

Ultimately, justification and excuse are abstract and doctrinally elaborated categories aimed at the organisation and systematisation of defences in the law. The defences recognised in domestic legal orders developed mostly haphazardly and not as the product of systematic thinking by legislators and judges.[53] The categories 'justification' and 'excuse' thus constitute legal theorists' attempts to bring coherence and consistency to this miscellany of defences and, more broadly, to the law.[54] Systematising the defences is not simply an aesthetic exercise, but one that facilitates the rational application of the law to what are often very complex factual situations.[55] As observed by George Mousourakis, the distinction has 'enabled courts and legislatures to achieve a greater measure of consistency in the criminal law', and both legislation and courts should continue to be guided by it.[56] Even if the distinction may not generate specific and discernible practical consequences, or definitely and definitively resolve practical problems in the law, the classification of the casuistic collection of general defences into distinct categories furthers the coherence and consistency of legal systems, a goal worth pursuing in itself.[57]

---

[51] Greenawalt, 'Perplexing', 1898.
[52] See, e.g., Sangero, *Self-Defence*, 16–17.
[53] Robinson, 'Systematic Analysis', 201.
[54] Greenawalt, 'Perplexing', 1900–1.
[55] Bacigalupo, *Manual de derecho penal (Parte general)* (1996), 67.
[56] Mousourakis, 'Distinguishing between Justifications and Excuses in the Criminal Law' (1998) 9 *Stellenbosch LR* 165, 180.
[57] Greenawalt, 'Perplexing', 1927.

## 1.3 Justification and Excuse in the Law of State Responsibility

Is this distinction recognised in international law or, at any rate, can it be recognised? The question is occasionally raised, but rarely is it considered or discussed in any depth. At present, the state practice seems to be insufficient to assert that the distinction between justification and excuse is recognised in the international legal order. Nevertheless, as said above, there are increasing calls for its adoption – from states, tribunals and scholars alike. And indeed, as the next chapter will show, there are good reasons why the distinction should be recognised in this legal system.

The introduction to this chapter hypothesised that one of the reasons why the question whether the distinction is recognised in international law has remained, so far, underexplored is the assumption that, given the current articulation of the law of responsibility, the distinction cannot be made. This assumption takes one of two forms: first, that the possibility of the distinction was foreclosed by the ILC and, second, that the secondary character of the rules of state responsibility prevents the distinction.[58] After considering the status of the distinction in positive law, this section will tackle both versions of this assumption to show that the ILC did not intend to dispose of this question and that the primary/secondary rule distinction is not a bar to the recognition of a distinction between justification and excuse.

### *1.3.1 The Distinction in Positive Law*

Does international law recognise the distinction between justification and excuse? This is a difficult question to answer in the abstract. Justification and excuse are legal concepts and are not, as such, susceptible of recognition in customary law. At any rate, insofar as state practice and *opinio juris* are concerned, states rarely have had occasion to state their views in respect of the distinction other than in relation to the ILC's work on the ARS. Very few states expressed their views in this context: the distinction did not give rise to much debate in the Sixth Committee. Among those who expressed their views, there was a tendency to be favourable towards drawing the distinction. France,[59]

---

[58] These views are not attributable to any scholar in particular. The two hypotheses are the articulation of perceptions gleaned from general readings on this topic and discussions with sceptics of the distinction.

[59] Comments and observations received by Governments, A/CN.4/488 and Add.1–3, ILC Yearbook 1998, vol. II(1), 130, 133.

India,[60] Japan,[61] Mexico,[62] Morocco,[63] Russia,[64] Slovakia,[65] and the United Kingdom,[66] all favoured distinguishing between justification and excuse in the ARS. Burkina Faso,[67] France[68] and Switzerland,[69] for their part, considered that the draft should only refer to excuses, insofar as it was limited to the codification of secondary rules; a position which assumed that defences could be distinguished between the two. Only Ethiopia objected to this distinction, specifically by way of rejecting the possibility of excuses in international law.[70] In addition, the United States also objected to the distinction in its pleadings before the ICJ in the *Oil Platforms* case.[71]

The concepts of justification and excuse could potentially be recognised by means of general principles of the law. While this is plausible in respect of justifications, it is not clear that the notion of excuse has been generally accepted in domestic legal orders. As Section 1.2 noted, the notion of excuse is primarily recognised in Civil law jurisdictions, but it is absent from, and often actively resisted in, many Common law jurisdictions. It thus seems difficult to conclude that both these concepts and, implicitly, their difference is recognised as a matter of general principles of the law.

Another way of testing the recognition of the distinction is by reference to individual defences: states may have expressed their views in respect of the character of particular defences as justifications or excuses. If there were evidence of agreement in the sense that a given defence is a justification, and another one is an excuse, then this would imply that

---

[60] A/C.6/54/SR.23, [33].
[61] Comments and observations received from Governments, A/CN.4/492, ILC Yearbook 1999, vol. II(1), 107 (a distinction must be drawn between circumstances which 'precluded wrongfulness' and circumstances which did 'not preclude wrongfulness but render[ed] it non-existent').
[62] A/C.6/54/SR.23, [11].
[63] A/C.6/34/SR.48, [31].
[64] A/C.6/55/SR.18, [53].
[65] A/C.6/54/SR.22, [54].
[66] A/CN.4/488, 130.
[67] A/C.6/54/SR.26, [43]. See also A/C.6/55/SR.24, [54].
[68] A/C.6/56/SR.11, [70]. Ultimately, however, France was happy to accept Chapter V as finally approved: Comments and observations received from Governments, A/CN.4/515 and Add.1–3, ILC Yearbook 2001, vol. II(1), 54.
[69] A/C.6/54/SR.27, [32].
[70] A/C.6/34/SR.43, [18] (agreeing with Ago that 'it was difficult to conceive that international law could characterize an act as wrongful without attaching to it disadvantageous consequences for its author').
[71] United States: oral statement, *Oil Platforms (Islamic Republic of Iran v United States of America)* (2003) ICJ Rep 161, at CR 2003/12 (translation), 23 February 2003, [17.16]

## 1.3 LAW OF STATE RESPONSIBILITY

states recognise the distinction in international law. As will be seen in Chapter 5, states overwhelmingly accept that countermeasures constitute justifications. But in respect of none of the other defences is there evidence (of the required consistency, generality and uniformity) that states consider them to act as excuses. The only defence in respect of which states have made clear statements as to its classification as an excuse is the plea of necessity, codified in ARS Article 25. But even here, it is only a handful of states that have made such assertions. In the context of discussing the ILC's codification of ARS Article 25, Britain,[72] France,[73] India,[74] Japan[75] and Russia,[76] expressed the view that state of necessity is an excuse. Brazil and Thailand, instead, opined that the defence is a justification.[77] Moreover, since the adoption of the ARS in 2001, Argentina and Zimbabwe have both pleaded state of necessity as a justification before investment tribunals.[78]

It can thus be concluded that, as a matter of positive law, the distinction has yet to be recognised in international law. States, it seems, are familiar with it, for otherwise there would be no point insisting that countermeasures are a justification or that the plea of necessity is an excuse. Nevertheless, the practice and the views of states in this regard are still relatively few. This paucity of practice may be due to the lack of clarity regarding the position of the ARS in respect of this distinction. And it is to this question that this chapter now turns.

### 1.3.2 Reopening the Case: Justification and Excuse in the Articles on State Responsibility

The first of the two assumptions mentioned holds that all defences in the ARS constitute justifications because the ILC rejected the possibility of excuses and that, at any rate, such a distinction cannot be accommodated by the system of responsibility codified in the ARS. In essence, this assumption simply relies on what its supporters perceive to be the

---

('these are circumstances which preclude wrongfulness and thus responsibility ... they are not circumstances whose effect is merely to exonerate from responsibility while leaving wrongfulness to subsist').

[72] A/CN.4/488, 130.
[73] A/CN.4/488, 130, 133.
[74] A/C.6/54/SR.23, [33].
[75] Comments and Observations Received from Governments, A/CN.4/492, ILC Yearbook 1999, vol. II(1), 101, at 107.
[76] A/C.6/55/SR.18, [53].
[77] Brazil: A/C.6/35/SR.47, [23]; Thailand: A/C.6/35/SR.56, [48].
[78] See Section 8.3.2.2 on 'Financial Necessity'.

position of the ILC on this question. But what the ILC's position is (or was) on this point is not easy to ascertain.

As will be seen, the ILC's position on the subject of defences, throughout its decades-long work on responsibility, was far from being consistent or constant. Among the three Special Rapporteurs to have considered this question, there exists a quite wide range of views. From Francisco García-Amador's recognition of excuses only, to Roberto Ago's recognition of justifications only, to James Crawford's openness to the distinction between the two. Of this range of views, it is Ago's that has proven the most enduring, so much so that the text of Chapter V of Part One and the wording of the provisions bear the marks of his approach. Nevertheless, as a collective body, the Commission was much less assertive on this question than is often assumed. Even at the time of Ago's tenure as Special Rapporteur, Commission members expressed their doubts and disagreements about his unflinching position against excuses. The position of the ILC on this matter, as reflected in the ARS, is far from being as conclusive as some scholars suggest. Rather, as this section will show, the Commission did not take an exclusionary stance in respect of the distinction between justification and excuse, thereby showing preference for justifications only. A better interpretation of the Commission's position is that, aware of the distinction, it simply left the matter for subsequent resolution.

This section traces the Commission's consideration of the question of justification and excuse, by reviewing the Special Rapporteurs' positions and the reactions of the members of the Commission. States' views on this aspect of the Commission's work have already been noted earlier, so they will not be re-stated here.

### 1.3.2.1 García-Amador: Total and Partial Excuse

The first Special Rapporteur on state responsibility, García-Amador, who worked on this topic from 1956 to 1961, recognised a distinction between exonerating and extenuating circumstances. This distinction, he said, was 'by no means simple', but it could not be ignored since it was evident in the practice of states.[79] Acknowledging that the practice was not uniform, García-Amador suggested that the distinction between exoneration and attenuation of responsibility was evident at the very

---

[79] García-Amador, First Report on International Responsibility, ILC Yearbook 1956, vol. II, [160].

least in respect of fault-based wrongful acts – that is, wrongful acts incorporating a requirement of fault.[80] For this reason he addressed the two types of defences in different reports: exonerating circumstances in connection with the wrongful act,[81] and extenuating circumstances in connection with reparations.[82] Exoneration, he said, concerned circumstances 'unconnected with the state's volition' which, since the state was not therefore at fault, allowed it to 'deny responsibility'.[83] However, the conduct in question remained 'illegal and unjustified'.[84] Attenuation, in turn, concerned situations in which it was 'possible to consider that the responsibility is not of the same degree as that which would have been imputable to the State had that circumstance not been present'.[85]

Rather than distinguishing justification from excuse, García-Amador's approach distinguished between total and partial excuses. In both cases, the act remained wrongful and only responsibility was affected by either (total) exoneration or (partial) extenuation. This was not a distinction of kind, but one of degree, as is evident from the language of the draft Article proposed:

> Article 17. Exonerating and extenuating circumstances
>
> 4. *Force majeure*, state of necessity and the fault imputable to the alien, if not admissible as grounds for exoneration from responsibility, shall operate as extenuating circumstances …[86]

Under this provision, the same defence could provide total exoneration if it passed an (undetermined) threshold and, if insufficient to that effect, it would provide only partial exoneration. García-Amador did not, however, specify the threshold above which the defence would entail total exoneration and below which it would only afford extenuation. At any rate, the draft Article proposed in this regard, which was not discussed by the Commission, was eventually set aside.

---

[80] Ibid., [191].
[81] García-Amador, Third Report on International Responsibility, ILC Yearbook 1958, vol. II, 50ff.
[82] García-Amador, Sixth Report on International Responsibility, ILC Yearbook 1961, vol. II, 43ff.
[83] García-Amador, Third Report, [1].
[84] Id.
[85] Ibid., [2]. García-Amador addressed the 'extenuating' circumstances again only briefly in the sixth report: García-Amador, Sixth Report, 43ff.
[86] García-Amador, Sixth Report, 48.

#### 1.3.2.2  Ago: The Irrelevance of Excuses

**Ago's Report and Its Reception in the International Law Commission**   The second Special Rapporteur on state responsibility, Roberto Ago, who worked in this capacity from 1969 to 1980, put forward complex views on the defences, which were tied to his conceptualisation of the notions of 'wrongfulness' and 'responsibility' and to his vision of the system of responsibility in international law. It is thus necessary to say something about these subjects, before examining his views on the character of the defences and his antagonistic stance towards excuses.

Ago is now mostly remembered as the mastermind behind the ILC's ingenious proposal to distinguish between so-called primary and secondary rules, a distinction which will be considered in some more detail later. This proposal, as is well known, helped the Commission overcome the usual stalemate of every attempt of codification of the law of responsibility until then, that is to codify the responsibility of states for damages to aliens (an approach followed also by first Special Rapporteur García-Amador), and, eventually, successfully to complete the ARS. But the real genius of Ago's framework for the responsibility project concerned the conceptual differentiation between the notions of 'wrongfulness' and 'responsibility'.[87] The 'essence of wrongfulness', he said, lay in the contrast between the conduct of the state and what was required of it by an international obligation binding upon it.[88] Wrongfulness, in short, amounted to the breach of an international obligation: the 'internationally wrongful act' was the act which *breached* that obligation. In turn, the concept of 'responsibility' concerned the different legal consequences entailed by wrongfulness; that is, the consequences entailed by the internationally wrongful act.[89] For Ago, then, the notion of wrongfulness was not defined by its legal consequences (i.e., responsibility), though responsibility (i.e., the legal consequences) required the existence of wrongfulness. Wrongfulness was the source of responsibility, but not the same as responsibility. Responsibility depended on wrongfulness, but not the other way around. It was this conceptual distinction which allowed the elaboration of a unitary system of responsibility applicable,

---

[87] Ago, Eighth Report on State Responsibility, ILC Yearbook 1979, vol. II(1), [50].
[88] Ago, Second Report on State Responsibility, ILC Yearbook 1970, vol. II, [41].
[89] Which vary depending on the character and content of the obligation and the breach in question; see Ago, Second Report, [14].

in principle and in a residual manner, to the breach of all international obligations.[90]

According to Ago, the wrongful act could give rise to at least two sets of legal relations: an obligation of reparation for the wrongdoer and the faculty to impose a sanction for the injured state. Ago criticised conceptions of responsibility that contemplated only one of these two consequences, to wit the 'classical' view, according to which the sole consequence of wrongfulness is the duty to make reparation, and the Kelsenian view, according to which law is concerned with sanctions for unlawfulness. Indeed, for Ago, wrongfulness could entail both reparations and sanctions and the choice between them would depend on the specific obligation breached.[91] Since the content of responsibility varied depending on the obligation breached, the only way to ensure that the system would be unitary (not criminal, delictual or contractual) was to detach the notion of wrongfulness from its consequences. Unity was ensured through a fixed, so to speak, notion of wrongfulness combined with a modular set of consequences applicable depending on the obligation breached. This understanding, accepted by the Commission, ultimately determined the structure of the project and of the ARS themselves: wrongfulness became the subject of Part One of the ARS, and responsibility that of Part Two.[92] The unity of the system was the basis for its application to diverse obligations; unity was, paradoxically, at the basis of diversity.[93]

This conceptual distinction between wrongfulness and responsibility which Ago espoused in the Commission during the 1970s, was a departure from the position Ago had maintained in his previous scholarly work. In 'Le délit international', published in 1939, Ago had defined the wrongful

---

[90] Ago, Second Report, [24]. Generally Ago, Fifth Report, ILC Yearbook 1976, vol. II(1), 3. Including both bilateral and multilateral obligations, see Dominicé, 'The International Responsibility of States for Breach of Multilateral Obligations' (1999) 10 EJIL 353.

[91] Ago, Second Report, [18–21].

[92] Indeed, the Commission upheld the conceptual distinction between wrongfulness and responsibility, see ILC Report, thirty-first session, ILC Yearbook 1979, vol. II(2), 107 [3].

[93] On which see Tams, 'Unity and Diversity in the Law of State Responsibility' in Zimmerman and Hofmann (eds), *Unity and Diversity in International Law* (2005), 435. This unitary system was, according to Paul Reuter, one of the most important achievements of international law: Reuter, 'Principes de droit international public' (1961) 103 *Recueil* 425, 585. This unity concerned the regime of responsibility for wrongfulness only. Other regimes of responsibility for non-wrongful conduct were later developed and studied by the ILC itself. However, the development of these regimes did not affect the unity of the system of responsibility arising out of wrongfulness. On the 'unity' and 'fragmentation' of the theory of state responsibility (including liability for lawful activities), see Dupuy, 'The International Law of State Responsibility: Revolution or Evolution' (1989–90) 11 *Mich JIL* 105.

act by means of the legal consequences that derived from it: the wrongful act was a 'legal fact' which was characterised by the generation of the legal consequence of responsibility and not by its incompatibility with an international obligation.[94] One of the consequences of this definition of the internationally wrongful act was that all defences necessarily acted like justifications. If a defence precluded responsibility, and responsibility was a part of the definition of wrongfulness, then of necessity defences precluded wrongfulness.[95] As a result, the idea of preclusion of responsibility, at the time supported by, among others, Dionisio Anzilotti,[96] was for Ago a 'grave nonsense'. Ago's system of responsibility of 1939 was incapable of accommodating excuses.

But the new conceptions of wrongfulness and responsibility presented to the Commission in the 1970s no longer implied, logically, the rejection of excuses. On the contrary, the new understanding was capable of accommodating this notion insofar as 'wrongfulness' was a concept independent from 'responsibility'; wrongfulness could, in short, exist without responsibility. As a result, there could be defences which while leaving intact the wrongfulness of an act nevertheless precluded responsibility. Yet, throughout his reports to the ILC, Ago insisted that *all* defences operated in the manner of justifications.[97] This was reasserted most emphatically in Ago's analytical explanation of the operation of circumstances precluding wrongfulness, contained in his Eighth Report of 1979: the circumstances operated by temporarily suspending the obligation allegedly breached, thereby preventing the commission of a wrongful act by the state.[98] To be sure, Ago accepted the 'theoretical' possibility of circumstances that precluded responsibility, since this possibility followed from the conceptual distinction between wrongfulness and responsibility which he had presented to the ILC.[99] But he maintained that while 'any circumstance precluding the wrongfulness of an act necessarily has the effect of also precluding responsibility', the 'converse', namely that a circumstance may preclude responsibility without affecting the wrongfulness of the

---

[94] Ago, 'Le délit international' (1939) 68 Recueil 415, 425–6.
[95] Ibid., 532–3.
[96] 'É generalmente ammesso che vi sono dei casi in cui un atto, di per sè illecito ... non produce le conseguenze proprie dei fatti illeciti', Anzilotti, 'Corso di diritto internazionale' in *Opere di Dionisio Anzilotti* (reprint of 3rd edn originally published in 1927, 1955), 413.
[97] E.g., Ago, First Report on State Responsibility, ILC Yearbook 1969, vol. II, [91]; Ago, 1204th meeting, ILC Yearbook 1973, vol. I, 14 [11]; Ago, Eighth Report, 27ff; Ago, 1537th meeting, ILC Yearbook 1979, vol. I, 32 [27].
[98] Ago, Eighth Report, [55].
[99] Ibid., [53].

## 1.3 LAW OF STATE RESPONSIBILITY

conduct, did not apply 'with the same ineluctable logic'.[100] Ago backed this claim with a multi-layered argument.

First, he adduced the practice of states which, he said, did not evidence that states recognised the notion of 'excuse'. Indeed, in all the instances surveyed, states always invoked defences *as* justifications. And if on some occasions states used the term 'excuse' and the language of 'preclusion of responsibility', they did not actually mean what they said.[101] Ago exemplified this by reference to self-defence, relying in particular on the comments made by states in the process leading to, and during, the 1930 Hague Codification Conference. Norway, for example, had said that 'only an act, performed in the defence of the rights of the State, that is authorized by international law should involve exemption from responsibility; but then the act would not be an "act contrary to international law"'.[102] But the examples cited were self-serving. They all referred to circumstances in which the states claimed to be 'authorised' to act in a certain way by the legal order, and thus to be acting lawfully. What is more, the instances of practice cited all concerned the use of force at a period (the late 1920s, early 1930s) when the prohibition of force had yet to crystallise in customary law.[103] At any rate, that states upheld these entitlements as instances of lawful conduct does not mean, as a general matter, that they excluded that other types of circumstances may be classified as excuses.

Second, Ago added that the notion of wrongfulness without responsibility was contrary to the structure of international law and to the systemic coherence of the responsibility project. He maintained that structurally the international legal system, a system whose 'dominant characteristic' was that of effectivity, could not possibly accept the idea of wrongfulness-without-consequences:

> Imposing an obligation while at the same time attaching no legal consequences to breaches of it would in fact amount to not imposing the obligation in question at all. And to conceive of such a situation precisely in relation to a legal order so imbued with effectivity as the international

---

[100] Ibid., [51].
[101] Ibid., [53].
[102] Rosenne, *Committee of Experts for the Progressive Codification of International Law (1925–1928)* (1972) vol. 2, 203.
[103] When the prohibition of force crystallised as a rule of customary international law is a matter still debated in the scholarship. The earliest possible time is that identified by Brownlie who, after an extensive survey of the relevant practice, concluded that the prohibition of force had crystallised in customary law by the early 1940s: Brownlie, *International Law and the Use of Force by States* (1963), 110–11.

order seems to us to be in glaring contradiction with one of the dominant characteristics of that system of law.[104]

Systemically, moreover, justifications were the only type of defences consistent with the basic principle in draft Article 1, namely that 'every internationally wrongful act of the State engages' its responsibility, a principle which admitted of no exception.[105] But these arguments were tantamount to defining wrongfulness by its consequences: the breach of an international obligation was no longer the 'essence of wrongfulness',[106] for its 'essence' consisted in the consequences that followed from it. With this argument, Ago collapsed the notion of wrongfulness into that of responsibility, bringing him closer to the views he had expressed in 1939 than to those he had presented to the Commission throughout the 1970s. However valid these arguments may have been in 1939, they fundamentally undermined the system of responsibility that Ago had presented to the Commission by doing away with one of its core tenets: the conceptual separation of wrongfulness and responsibility.

The distinction between justification and excuse and Ago's rejection of excuses received scant attention in the ILC discussions of his 1979 report.[107] Only Stephen Verosta insisted that a clear distinction should be maintained between justification and excuse, which were 'entirely different concepts'.[108] Ago ignored Verosta's suggestion. Eventually, the opinions Ago had expressed in his Eight Report of 1979 were reproduced almost verbatim in the first reading commentary to Chapter V.[109] Yet, it is far from clear that the Commission as a whole supported Ago's position on excuses, as shown next.

**Missing Link: Off-the-Record Rejection of Excuses?** The Commission's commentary to Chapter V of Part One, adopted on first reading, indicated that:

---

[104] Ago, Eighth Report, [52].
[105] Ago, 1204th meeting, 14 [11].
[106] Ago, Second Report, [41].
[107] Only a few members commented on it, e.g., Pinto, 1538th meeting, ILC Yearbook 1979, vol. I, 37 [35]. It had, however, been raised during the meetings of the sub-committee in 1963, see De Luna, Summary Records of the Sub-Committee on State Responsibility, ILC Yearbook 1963, vol. II, 229, 235.
[108] Verosta, 1572nd meeting, ILC Yearbook 1979, vol. I, 205 [22]; Verosta, 1614th meeting, ILC Yearbook 1980, vol. I, 164 [28].
[109] ILC Report, thirty-first session, 106ff.

The Commission has already had occasion to state its view that the true effect of the presence of such circumstances is not, at least in the normal case, to preclude responsibility that would otherwise result from an act wrongful in itself, but rather to preclude the characterization of the conduct of the State in one of those circumstances as wrongful.[110]

The passage, which is a word-for-word reproduction of the views expressed by Ago in his Eighth Report,[111] has a certain finality to it: the matter, it suggests, has been considered and decided upon. Indeed, the passage referred to the views 'already' stated by the Commission in 1973. This was a reference to views expressed in the Commission in the context of discussing draft Article 1.

The verbatim records of the ILC's 1973 session, during which the Commission considered Ago's third report, show that the question of the character of the defences was discussed by the Drafting Committee, during the review of the proposed commentary to draft Article 1. The draft commentary stated that the Commission had 'felt bound to reject' the possibility of excuses in international law, since the principle in the draft Article, that 'every internationally wrongful act of the State entails its responsibility', admitted no exceptions. In the Drafting Committee, some members voiced concern about this statement. Thus, Richard Kearney objected to the assertion that the Commission had 'felt bound to reject' the possibility of excuses. Kearney 'hesitated to accept [that] conclusion ... because he did not think that the matter had ever been discussed by the Commission.'[112] This remark gave rise to a disagreement among members of the Drafting Committee as to whether the matter had indeed been discussed by the Commission. Ago asserted that the Commission 'had discussed that point at length',[113] Doudou Thiam thought it 'had not discussed the question thoroughly'[114] and Mustafa Yasseen said that 'it had been agreed in the Commission that the circumstances in question precluded wrongfulness, not responsibility.'[115] Given these widely divergent views, and to avoid entering into the substance of the question at such late stage in the Commission's session, members of the Drafting Committee agreed to leave the question open for later consideration.[116] To reflect this consensus,

---

[110] ILC Report, thirty-first session, 106 [2].
[111] Ago, Eighth Report, [49].
[112] Kearney, 1244th meeting, ILC Yearbook 1973, vol. I, 216 [60].
[113] Ago, 1244th meeting, ILC Yearbook 1973, vol. I, 216 [61].
[114] Thiam, 1244th meeting, ILC Yearbook 1973, vol. I, 216 [62].
[115] Yasseen, 1244th meeting, ILC Yearbook 1973, vol. I, 216 [63].
[116] See the comments by Thiam, 1244th meeting, 216 [62]; Ago, 1244th meeting, 216 [64]; Ushakov, 1244th meeting, ILC Yearbook 1973, vol. I, 217 [70].

the paragraph containing the disputed observation was accepted by the Drafting Committee with some changes: it now stated that only 'some members' were of the view that excuses must be rejected and that '*[f]or the time being*, in the Commission's view, it [was] only necessary to say that the true effect of the presence of such circumstances is not, at least in the normal case, to preclude responsibility ... but rather to preclude [wrongfulness]'.[117] It can be added that, a review of the verbatim records of the 1973 meetings of the Commission shows no evidence that the discussion which led to the 'conclusion' included in the proposed draft commentary had taken place.[118]

The commentary to draft Article 1 adopted in 1973 thus stated that 'only some members' of the Commission thought that excuses should be excluded, and then, that this view was adopted by the Commission only 'for the time being'. Somehow, by 1979, the partial and provisional character of this passage had become total and permanent. When Ago referred to the 1973 discussion and consensus in his Eighth Report, and quoted from the commentary to draft Article 1, he omitted the 'some members' and 'for the time being' disclaimers. On the contrary, he introduced the paragraph as evidence of the Commission's final view on the matter: the Commission, he said, had 'already had occasion to state its view' that excuses ought to be rejected.[119] Despite the requests made in 1973 to discuss and examine the point at a later stage and despite Verosta's unheeded observation in 1979, the assertion made by Ago in the Eighth Report made its way, unchanged, onto the draft commentary to Chapter V of Part One. And so was the language of justification used by Ago in his reports and in his proposed articles: the title of Chapter V of Part One

---

[117] Ago, 1245th meeting, ILC Yearbook 1973, vol. I, 217 [2] (emphasis added). The text was adopted as [12] of the commentary to draft art. 1: ILC Report, twenty-fifth session, ILC Yearbook 1973, vol. II, 176.

[118] An observation by the Chairman of the Drafting Committee, Yasseen, suggests that the discussion may have occurred in the Drafting Committee rather than during a plenary meeting of the Commission. Yasseen stated, 'The Committee thought the commentary should explain that the principle stated in article 1 suffered no exception. It was true that justifying circumstances might be an obstacle to the attribution of international responsibility, and some provisions of the draft would be devoted to such circumstances. But justifying circumstances did not constitute exceptions; they divested the act of the State of its wrongful character. Thus, where there was justification, there was no internationally wrongful act and the conduct of the State did not fall within the scope of article 1': 1225th meeting, ILC Yearbook 1973, vol. I, 118 [51]. This might explain why there are no records of it happening. Indeed, as explained by Giorgio Gaja, a former member of the ILC, '[n]o verbatim or summary records are made in the drafting committee': Gaja, 'Interpreting Articles Adopted by the International Law Commission' (2014) 85 BYIL 10, at 15.

[119] Ago, Eighth Report, [49].

described these as 'circumstances precluding wrongfulness', and this language was reflected in the text of the articles themselves.

It is difficult from this review not to conclude that for Ago the matter had never been one open for discussion. The defences, for him, *all* precluded wrongfulness. But it is difficult to draw the same conclusion about the Commission as a whole. On the contrary, the discussions in both the plenary and the Drafting Committee show a Commission hesitant to go along with Ago on this point. Unable to discuss the point further, the ILC managed to leave the door open to the possibility that some defences may operate as excuses. Thus, in the commentary to Chapter V adopted on first reading, the Commission stated that defences precluded wrongfulness 'at least in the normal case'.[120] In other words, defences need not preclude wrongfulness in *every* case. Could they, sometimes, preclude responsibility?[121]

### 1.3.2.3 Crawford: Justifications or Excuses

Crawford, the last Special Rapporteur on state responsibility, submitted his report on the defences in 1999, exactly twenty years after the Commission had considered Ago's reports on the matter. Crawford began his report on the 'concept of circumstances precluding wrongfulness' with a quotation from the commentary adopted on first reading: that the defences precluded wrongfulness 'in the normal case'. But what was the 'normal case'? Crawford noted that not all of the circumstances in Chapter V 'operate in the same way and to the same extent'.[122] It seemed that 'some (for example, self-defence and consent) render the conduct in question lawful; in other words, they preclude wrongfulness', but 'the position with such circumstances as distress and necessity' was less clear.[123] In their written observations to the ILC, Japan, France and the United Kingdom had also maintained that 'conceptual differences' existed between the defences listed in Chapter V and that while some may preclude wrongfulness, others precluded responsibility.[124]

---

[120] ILC Report, thirty-first session, 106 [2].
[121] Reference to the 'normal case' is misleading, insofar as it suggests that preclusion of wrongfulness is, somehow, the default position and that preclusion of responsibility might be exceptional. Nor is it the case that in 'normal' situations a defence will preclude wrongfulness and that in 'abnormal' cases that same defence will preclude responsibility. There is no presumption that defences 'normally' preclude wrongfulness: the character of particular defences as either category depends on a number of other factors, as explained in Chapter 3. Nonetheless, this statement is important in that it shows that excuses were not rejected definitely and definitively.
[122] Crawford, Second Report on State Responsibility, ILC Yearbook 1999, vol. II(1), [230].
[123] Id.
[124] Ibid., [218–20].

Crawford thus wondered whether the text of the draft articles on *force majeure*, distress and state of necessity might be changed to reflect their character as excuses. However, 'on balance' the Special Rapporteur was 'not persuaded that a categorical distinction need[ed] to be made as between the circumstances to be covered by Chapter V'.[125] There was 'in truth a range of cases, and a clear and simple example of distress or even necessity may be more convincing as a circumstance precluding wrongfulness than a marginal case of self-defence'.[126] This range was too broad to allow for categorical distinctions, so all defences should be dealt with 'under the existing general rubric of Chapter V'.[127]

Crawford's position seems to be based on the understanding that the listed defences can function both as justifications *and* excuses depending on the merits of each case (perhaps depending on the 'normality' of the case?). Such a view was tantamount to establishing two-tier defences: if the defence is very convincing, then it is a justification, if it is less convincing then it is an excuse.[128] However, as explained in Section 1.2, the distinction between justification and excuse is not one of degree, but one of kind. Both types of defence ought to be equally convincingly proven – whatever the standard of proof may be in any given case[129] – but they affect different elements of the analysis of wrongfulness and responsibility. This notwithstanding, Crawford's suggestion not to specify whether the defences constituted justifications or excuses in the ARS themselves was arguably a wise one. Individual defences, as noted earlier, are not inherently justifications or excuses and whether to classify them as one or the other may respond to particular policies or goals, which may change over time. It was best, then, not to set these classifications and leave them open to subsequent development and change.

The Commission chose to discuss Crawford's report article by article, so that no general discussion on the 'circumstances precluding wrongfulness' took place.[130] As such, there were no views expressed on this point. Implicitly, however, the Commission accepted Crawford's suggestion not to engage in a classification of the defences in the ARS themselves. Since the question was not discussed by the Commission, it did not have

---

[125] Ibid., [355].
[126] Id.
[127] Id.
[128] This appears to have been the opinion of the special rapporteur, see id.
[129] On the standard of proof, see Riddell and Plant, *Evidence before the International Court of Justice* (2009), 123–37.
[130] See Crawford, 2587th meeting, ILC Yearbook 1999, vol. I, 140 [2].

a chance to reconsider the wording used in the text of the ARS on this point. Thus, the ARS as finally adopted refer to 'preclusion of wrongfulness', both in the title to Chapter V and in the text of the articles on defences. Yet, scattered through the various pages of the Commentary to Chapter V and its articles are references to 'justification' and 'excuse'.[131]

### 1.3.2.4 The Position of the ILC: An Invitation for Further Development

Against the backdrop of the Commission's consideration of the question during the first reading of the ARS, the disagreements that arose on that occasion, and of Crawford's recognition of the distinction and suggestion not to engage in a classification in the ARS themselves, it is difficult to conclude that the ILC's position on the distinction between justification and excuse and its preference for justifications was in any way categorical.

The very premises of the work of the Commission, upon which the ARS are built, attest to the very possibility of accommodating the distinction in international law.[132] As was seen, the law of responsibility is built upon the conceptual distinction between wrongfulness and responsibility. The former relates to the breach of an international obligation, by virtue of the incompatibility between a state's conduct and what is required of it by international law. The latter, to the legal relations arising between the wrongdoing state and the injured state, namely the obligations of cessation and reparation, as a result of the wrongful act. It is this conceptual distinction which ensures the unity of the system of responsibility in international law: a fixed notion of wrongfulness combined with a modular set of consequences applicable depending on the obligation breached. Indeed, the very title of Chapter V and its 'basic idea' derived from the distinction

> between the idea of 'wrongfulness' indicating the fact that certain conduct by a State conflicts with an obligation imposed on that State by a 'primary' rule of international law, and the idea of 'responsibility', indicating the legal consequences which another ('secondary') rule of international law attaches to the act of the State constituted by such conduct.[133]

If this premise is accepted, then it must follow that, at least conceptually, there may be defences that negate the wrongfulness of an act *and* defences

---

[131] Commentary to Chapter V of Part One, [2], [4], [7–8]; ARS Commentary art. 23, [10]; ARS Commentary art. 24, [10]; ARS Commentary art. 25, [2].
[132] See also Christakis, 'Illusion', 229.
[133] ILC Report, thirty-first session, 107 [3].

that negate the legal relations of responsibility arising from a wrongful act. In short, it must be accepted that it is possible to distinguish between justifications, as circumstances precluding wrongfulness, and excuses, as circumstances precluding responsibility.

The language of the ARS is no more conclusive or dispositive in this regard. While the title of Chapter V of Part One and the text of Articles 20–25 refer to preclusion of wrongfulness, the Commentary to these various provisions refers to both justification and excuse. What may be inferred from this use of terminology? Some scholars have put emphasis on the text of the ARS themselves (to the exclusion of the Commentary) and on this basis argued that the Commission's position is that all defences operate as justifications and that, therefore, excuses were excluded by the ILC.[134] But this approach to the interpretation of ILC Articles is unsuitable. The ARS are not a treaty and their interpretation is not limited to the text of the articles themselves. As stated by former ILC member David Caron, the interpretation of the ARS (as of all other documents produced by the Commission) requires '[tracing] every step of the development' of any particular article.[135] That is, it requires careful consideration of the reports and discussions leading to the adoption of each article.

Taking stock of the ILC work on the classification of defences reviewed earlier, it is reasonable to conclude that the title 'circumstances precluding wrongfulness' in the text of the ARS does not entail that the listed defences all operate as justifications.[136] Nor does it suggest that the ILC rejected altogether the possibility of excuses in international law. Indeed, the use of the terms 'justification' and 'excuse' in the Commentary is not, as suggested by some,[137] the result of the Commission's confusion as to the meaning of these terms and its use of them as synonyms. On the contrary, Commission members knew very well the difference between these terms, as the discussions suggest. The use of both terms in the

---

[134] For an argument along these lines, see, Wittich, 'The International Law Commission's Articles on the Responsibility of States for Internationally Wrongful Acts Adopted on Second Reading' (2002) 15 LJIL 891, 898; Szurek, 'The Notion', 427; Klabbers, *International Law* (2013), 130.

[135] Caron, 'The ILC Articles on State Responsibility: The Paradoxical Relationship between Form and Authority' (2002) 96 AJIL 857, 868.

[136] Gaja suggests that where there exist discrepancies between the text of an article and its Commentary, 'one element to be taken into account is the summary record of the discussion in the plenary when the commentary was adopted. Should it result that the ILC was aware of a possible discrepancy, but nevertheless adopted the commentary, this would strengthen the conclusion that the latter prevails': Gaja, 'Interpreting Articles', 20.

[137] As argued by some: Sloane, 'Necessity', 483.

Commentary seems to have been deliberate, and not the result of confusion: the Commission was attempting to convey the unresolved character of the classification of the recognised defences; it was an invitation to further develop this aspect of the law of responsibility. What is more, it can be seen as the introduction of a 'degree of flexibility' into the ARS allowing 'further refinement of the principles by international tribunals and in State practice'.[138] To be sure, the choice to retain the (cumbersome) title 'circumstances precluding wrongfulness' for Chapter V of Part One is certainly perplexing. This choice could be attributed to the last Special Rapporteur's and the Commission's minimalist approach to the modification of the wording of the draft articles where modification was not strictly necessary.[139] Militating against the modification of the text – unless this was made necessary by a change in the law – was the fact that many of the draft articles had already been referred to in judicial proceedings and in the practice of states even before the ILC had finalised its work.[140] This was certainly the case with Chapter V of Part One: the articles on defences had been invoked in two high-profile international proceedings, the *Rainbow Warrior* arbitration and in the ICJ's *Gabčíkovo-Nagymaros* case.[141] While an understandable policy, it would have been preferable for the Commission to adopt neutral language in these provisions, replacing the expression 'circumstances precluding wrongfulness' with the term 'defence', as suggested in this work, or some generic term capable of encompassing both justifications and excuses. The upshot is that the labelling of the ARS defences as 'circumstances precluding wrongfulness' need not constitute a bar to the characterisation of some defences as excuses. Beneath the linguistic surface of the 'circumstances precluding wrongfulness', it is clear that the ILC not only acknowledged, but accepted, the possibility that the international law defences included in the ARS can operate as justifications or excuses as made clear by its use

---

[138] As was suggested by the United Kingdom during the second reading of the articles; with respect to the articles as a whole: see A/CN.4/488, 99 [8].

[139] On the modification of the wording of provisions adopted on first reading during the second reading of the ARS, see the plenary discussion relating to the provision on self-defence at 2589th meeting, ILC Yearbook 1999, vol. I, 157–161.

[140] *Difference Relating to Immunity from Legal Process of a Special Rapporteur of the Commission on Human Rights* (1999) ICJ Rep 62, [62].

[141] *Rainbow Warrior (New Zealand v France)* (1990) 20 RIAA 217; *Gabčíkovo-Nagymaros Project (Hungary/Slovakia)* (1997) ICJ Rep 7. Moreover, the parties referred to draft Article 34 in their arguments in *Military and Paramilitary Activities in and Against Nicaragua (Nicaragua v United States of America)* (1986) ICJ Rep 14. See, e.g., ICJ Pleadings, vol. IV, Memorial, 30 April 1985, 112 [427]; ICJ Pleadings, vol. V, Oral arguments, 190 [4].

of both these terms in the Commentary.[142] In the ultimate analysis, whatever the language of the ARS or position of the ILC in this regard, neither is or can constitute an impediment to the continued development of the law of responsibility in customary law: the distinction between justification and excuse can certainly develop beyond the ARS.

### 1.3.3 Defences in the World of Primary and Secondary Rules

The second (perceived) obstacle to the distinction between justification and excuse in international law is the 'secondary' character of the rules on state responsibility. As was said earlier, some scholars have argued that the circumstances included in Chapter V of Part One of the ARS must be classified as excuses *because* they are secondary rules. Since the ARS are a codification of secondary rules, and the defences are included in the ARS, it follows that the defences too are secondary rules. Further, since secondary rules concern the responsibility of states, therefore *all* defences in the ARS must be classified as excuses. This conclusion, it is said, follows from the 'logic' of the ARS. Unlike the obstacle considered in the previous section – which posited that *all* defences in the ARS were justifications – the present one posits that *all* defences in the ARS are excuses. This position does not exclude that justifications may exist, it nevertheless asserts that these are not 'properly' rules that belong to the law of responsibility. Indeed, since justifications concern the wrongfulness of conduct, then they constitute primary rules and cannot, therefore, properly be included in the law of state responsibility.

As will be explained here, however, this view is mistaken and stems from a misunderstanding about the primary/secondary rule distinction and its use by the ILC in the codification of the ARS. So before tackling the argument that all defences in the ARS are excuses because the ARS are a codification of secondary rules, it is necessary to take a step back

---

[142] Gaja has observed that this 'distinction ... has not been made in the articles on State responsibility': 'Primary and Secondary Rules in the International Law of State Responsibility' (2014) 97 *Rivista di diritto internazionale* 981, 986. The distinction was certainly not made textually. However, as noted the Commission, following Special Rapporteur Crawford's advice, decided not to distinguish between the two categories in the ARS themselves. This is not to say, however, that the ARS do not recognise the distinction or that the ILC rejected it. As already noted, the use of both the terms 'justification' and 'excuse' in the Commentary, in full knowledge and understanding of the distinction between both concepts, is telling.

and explain the distinction between primary and secondary rules and its function in the law of state responsibility.

### 1.3.3.1 Primary and Secondary Rules in the Law of Responsibility

The distinction between primary and secondary rules is one of the key organising ideas of contemporary thinking about the law of state responsibility.[143] This distinction is today most frequently associated with Ago, the ILC's second Special Rapporteur on state responsibility and the architect of the current structure and system of the ARS. Yet by the time it was adopted by the ILC, this idea was not new – it can be traced back at least to Anzilotti's *Teoria generale della responsabilità internazionale* published in 1902.[144] In the context of the Commission's work on state responsibility, this key organising idea crystallised during the work of the sub-committee on state responsibility which had been created in 1962 to consider a new approach for the codification of this topic after the false start made by the first Special Rapporteur,[145] whose term had come to an end in 1961. The sub-committee proposed that the ILC should limit its work to the rules on state responsibility, to the exclusion of what it called the 'substantive' rules of international law.[146] That is, the codification should be limited to the rules concerning the violation of 'primary rules' and the consequences arising from that violation.[147] Indeed, as Ago had noted in a working paper presented to the sub-committee, the substantive rules of international law and the general rules of responsibility were 'intrinsically separate'.[148] According to Ago, this realisation had been the most valuable methodological lesson learnt from past codificatory efforts.[149] The Commission accepted the sub-committee's proposal to limit the project in this way, and it set out to codify only the general rules on responsibility.[150]

---

[143] Crawford, *General Part*, 64–6. On this distinction, see David, 'Primary and Secondary Rules' in Crawford et al. (eds), *The Law of International Responsibility* (2010), 29; and Gaja, 'Primary and Secondary Rules'.

[144] Anzilotti, *Teoria*, Prefazione at v (explaining the focus on 'fundamental principles' of responsibility).

[145] Crawford, 'Revising', 436.

[146] See Ago, Working Paper, ILC Yearbook 1963, vol. II, 253. See also ILC, Sub-Committee on State Responsibility, comments by de Luna at 232, Gros at 233–4, Ago at 234.

[147] See Ago, Working Paper, 253. See also comments within the sub-committee: ILC, Sub-Committee on State Responsibility, comments by de Luna at 232, Gros at 233–4, Ago at 234.

[148] Ago, Working Paper, 252.

[149] Ago, First Report, [6].

[150] Report of the ILC on the work of its fifteenth session, ILC Yearbook 1963, vol. II, 223–4.

In time, the substantive rules of international law came to be known as 'primary', whereas the rules of responsibility as 'secondary'. But this terminological choice was not made until 1969, when the Commission discussed Ago's first report. In this report, Ago referred to the 'substantive' rules as 'primary',[151] and during the debates, Arnold Tammes made the following suggestion:

> For want of a better terminology, the distinction which was being adopted could be described as a distinction between primary, material or substantive rules of international law, on the one hand, and secondary or functional rules on the other. Primary rules were intended to influence the conduct of States directly; secondary rules, which were those of State responsibility proper, were intended to promote the practical realization of the substance of international law contained in the primary rules.[152]

The terminology was adopted by Ago in his second report to the Commission,[153] and from then onwards it became the standard terminology used in this regard.

Notwithstanding the avowed importance of the distinction, the Commission put little or no effort into defining primary and secondary rules and clearly demarcating the boundaries between the two. Primary rules were roughly defined as rules concerning the conduct of states, they were 'substantive' rules; secondary rules instead concerned the determination of the breach of primary rules and responsibility for that breach. The superficial treatment of the primary/secondary rule distinction was a cause for concern, both within and without the Commission. Within the Commission,[154] this was expressed most clearly by Constantin Eustathiades. Commenting on Ago's first report, Eustathiades agreed in principle with the idea of limiting the Commission's work to the 'secondary' rules of responsibility, but he noted that (some) rules about responsibility were substantive in character. For example, state of necessity and self-defence, which 'were involved in the subject-matter of responsibility',

---

[151] Ago, 1011th meeting, ILC Yearbook 1969, vol. I, 104–5 [3]. Ago's use of the expression 'primary rules' was likely influenced by an observation made by Sir Herbert Briggs at a meeting of the sub-committee in 1962, when he referred to state responsibility as a 'secondary obligation, having its source in the non-observance of a primary obligation under international law', see ILC, Sub-Committee on State Responsibility, 231. Briggs' use of the terms referred, in turn, to the terminology used by Borchard in 'Harvard Draft on the Law of Responsibility of States for Damage Done in Their Territory to the Person or Property of Foreigners' (1929) 23 AJIL Spec Supp 131, 141.
[152] Tammes, 1012th meeting, ILC Yearbook 1969, vol. I, 109 [5].
[153] Ago, Second Report, 179 [11].
[154] See also Tammes, 1075th meeting, ILC Yearbook 1970, vol. I, 185 [38].

were substantive rules.[155] Outside the Commission, the Italian scholar Rolando Quadri argued that the distinction between primary and secondary rules should be rejected entirely since it confused 'the structure and functioning of the legal order and a legislative technique or scientific convenience'.[156] Among States, moreover, Egypt observed that '[t]he distinction between "primary" and "secondary" rules was imperfect and sometimes difficult to draw'.[157]

These remarks were on point. Some rules of responsibility can, indeed, be characterised as substantive. This is the case with the rules on reparations[158] and the rules on aid and assistance,[159] since both impose obligations on states and, as such, guide their conduct. It is also the case, as will be seen later, of justifications insofar as these too guide the behaviour of states. But these remarks also missed the fact that the distinction was not developed as a conceptual one,[160] and it was only intended to serve a pragmatic purpose:[161] to aid the Commission in delimiting the scope of its work and, in so doing, avoid the obstacles encountered by previous codification efforts which had focused on the responsibility of states for damages to aliens and had, on every occasion, stalled when states could not agree on the standard of treatment due to aliens.[162] Indeed, warnings against the strict application of the distinction to the codification of the law of responsibility were common throughout the drafting of the ARS. Early on in his tenure as Special Rapporteur, Ago had noted that the distinction should not be pushed too far, as there was otherwise a real risk of 'sterilizing' the topic of state responsibility and rendering it too academic.[163] He also said that the distinction between primary and secondary rules 'must be understood rather loosely'[164] and that the Commission should not ignore the primary rules the breach of which gave rise to responsibility.[165] The final Special Rapporteur, Crawford, also endorsed

---

[155] Eustathiades, 1013th meeting, ILC Yearbook 1969, vol. I, 114 [9].
[156] Quadri, 'Cours général de droit international public' (1964) 113 *Recueil* 237, 455.
[157] A/C.6/54/SR.27, [29]. See also comments by Germany, A/CN.4/488, 102 [2].
[158] ARS arts 35-7.
[159] ARS art. 16 and Commentary at [10].
[160] E.g., Nollkaemper and Jacobs, 'Shared Responsibility in International Law: A Concept Paper' (2013) 34 *Mich JIL* 359, 408–12.
[161] Malanczuk, 'Countermeasures', 708–9.
[162] Crawford, *The International Law Commission's Articles on State Responsibility* (2002), Introduction, 15.
[163] Ago, 1036th meeting, ILC Yearbook 1969, vol. I, 241 [19].
[164] Ago, 1013th meeting, ILC Yearbook 1969, vol. I, 117 [33].
[165] Ago, Working Paper, 253.

this understanding,[166] and some of its members urged the Commission to avoid becoming a 'prisoner of its own dialectic'.[167] The ILC indeed acknowledged that the distinction was not watertight,[168] and it approached the distinction pragmatically and not dogmatically. The Commission thus included in the ARS rules which, although guiding state behaviour, were necessary in a comprehensive codification of the law of responsibility. The primary/secondary rule dichotomy and its imperfections did not impede the elaboration of an integrated and coherent system of responsibility, including provisions on the defences.[169]

To be sure, and as was later observed by John Dugard in his reports on Diplomatic Protection, the distinction between primary and secondary rules rests on 'unclear jurisprudential grounds'.[170] Indeed, as judged through the primary/secondary rule distinction prism, it often seems that the choice as to what is included in the ARS (and what is excluded) is somewhat arbitrary. For there are indeed rules properly characterised as primary in the ARS such as those on reparations and aid and assistance, as already noted. Perhaps a better way of characterising the rules of state responsibility, as argued by Daniel Bodansky and John Crook, is not as 'secondary', but rather as general:

> [w]hat defines the scope of the [ARS] is not their 'secondary' status but their generality: the [ARS] represent those areas where the ILC could identify and reach consensus on general propositions that can be applied more or less comprehensively across the entire range of international law.[171]

Of course, this too will be an imperfect solution for some rules may be general and yet not about responsibility, and other rules may be about responsibility and yet not general (such as the rules on serious violations of peremptory rules) – it seems that most organising principles will be imperfect in some or other way. But at the very least, to think about the law of responsibility as concerned with general propositions applicable to the issue of responsibility 'across the entire range of international law' may help overcome certain formalist arguments, which do not help our understanding of the law of responsibility and could, most importantly,

---

[166] Crawford, First Report on State Responsibility, ILC Yearbook 1998, vol. II(1), [14–18].
[167] Rosenne, 1080th meeting, ILC Yearbook 1970, vol. I, 220 [58].
[168] ILC Report, thirty-first session, 88 [63].
[169] See also Gaja, 'Primary and Secondary Rules', 990–1.
[170] Dugard, Second Report on Diplomatic Protection, ILC Yearbook 2001, vol. II(1), [7].
[171] Bodansky and Crook, 'Symposium: The ILC's State Responsibility Articles: Introduction and Overview' (2002) 96 AJIL 773, 780–1.

lead to the incorrect application of the relevant legal principles. In particular, these are arguments to the extent that certain rules are not part of the law of responsibility because they are primary or that certain rules are secondary because they are included in the law of responsibility,[172] both arguments that have been made in respect of justifications and excuses.

### 1.3.3.2 Justification and Excuse: Primary or Secondary Rules?

What, then, is the character of the rules on defences in the ARS? During the drafting of the ARS, the Commission was aware that the defences were secondary rules only in a 'loose' sense.[173] Eustathiades himself had summoned up two of the defences (self-defence and state of necessity) to make his point that some rules on responsibility were substantive in character.[174] Other Commission members also noted that, insofar as they affected the characterisation of conduct as wrongful, these rules would more appropriately be located 'upstream' within the realm of primary rules.[175] States too remarked on the character of the rules included in Chapter V of Part One. In the Sixth Committee, Burkina Faso commented that '[t]he lawfulness or otherwise of acts was determined primarily by other rules of international treaty law or customary law, before the rules on responsibility came into play';[176] the defences could not affect this finding of unlawfulness only precluding, at most, responsibility from arising.[177] A similar concern was expressed by France, which stated that it 'would have preferred the title of Part One, Chapter V to be "Circumstances precluding responsibility", as a means of indicating that the draft articles dealt only with secondary rules'.[178] Notwithstanding doubts as to the characterisation of the defences as primary or secondary, it was clear to states and to the Commission that no project on the law of responsibility would be complete without rules on defences.[179] Ian

---

[172] On which see, Gaja, 'Primary and Secondary Rules', 990–1.
[173] To use Ago's terminology: Ago, 1013th meeting, 117 [33].
[174] Eustathiades, 1013th meeting, 114 [9].
[175] See, e.g., Riphagen, 1538th meeting, ILC Yearbook 1979, vol. I, 34 [11]; Reuter, 1538th meeting, ILC Yearbook 1979, vol. I, 35 [17]. This view was also expressed by Doudou Thiam in his Fourth Report on the Draft Code of Offences against the Peace and Security of Mankind, ILC Yearbook 1986, vol. II(1), [178]. The term 'upstream' is taken from: David, 'Primary', 29.
[176] A/C.6/55/SR.24, [54].
[177] A/C.6/54/SR.26, [43].
[178] A/C.6/56/SR.11, [70].
[179] David, 'Primary', 32. See also Italy: A/C.6/54/SR.22, [54].

58    JUSTIFICATION AND EXCUSE IN INTERNATIONAL LAW

Brownlie thus urged the Commission not to succumb to the 'purist and slightly esoteric view [that] chapter V consisted of a series of formulations of conditions for the legality of State conduct that could be represented – albeit in a rather academic way – as primary rules. In that case, chapter V would fall.' This was an 'unhelpful view' that the Commission was now 'estopped' from taking.[180]

These remarks highlighted an important point: that the distinction between primary and secondary rules broke down in the defences.[181] The breaking point, however, exists *solely* in respect of justifications. Excuses neatly fit in the definition of secondary rules: they serve to determine the content of a state's responsibility, following the breach of an international obligation.[182] Justifications, instead, are substantive in character: they guide state behaviour by indicating what a state can or cannot do in specified circumstances. In this sense, they can therefore be seen as primary rules. Indeed, as will be explained in Chapter 3, justifications like self-defence or countermeasures constitute permissions of the legal order to engage in certain conduct. In its justification variant, state of necessity too has primary rule features: it too grants a permission to engage in certain conduct.[183] So do they belong in the law of responsibility?

Similar difficulties in respect of the classification of rules on defences have arisen in domestic law, where theorists have used the notions of conduct rules and decision rules to explain or resolve these difficulties. Especially illuminating in this regard is Meir Dan-Cohen's thought experiment on 'acoustic separation' in the law. According to Dan-Cohen, law is a 'set of normative messages' in which conduct rules are 'directed at the general public and provide guidelines for conduct' and decision rules

---

[180] Brownlie, 2589th meeting, ILC Yearbook 1999, vol. I, 169 [158].

[181] David, 'Primary', 29. See also Díaz Barrado, *El consentimiento, causa de exclusión de la ilicitud del uso de la fuerza en Derecho Internacional* (1989), 106–9.

[182] Though it has been observed that excuses too 'affect the scope of the obligation' since 'in the presence of an excuse, compliance with the obligation is not required.' In short, that excuses too have primary rule characteristics. See Gaja, 'Primary and Secondary Rules', 986–7. This is not strictly speaking correct: compliance with the obligation in question is required (and this is why the conduct is wrongful). What is not required is compliance with the obligations of responsibility – namely the obligations of cessation and reparation.

[183] This is potentially a weaker permission than that afforded by self-defence and countermeasures. On strong and weak permissions, see Uniacke, *Permissible Killing: The Self-Defence Justification of Homicide* (1994), 26–8.

are 'directed at the officials and provide guidelines for their decisions'.[184] However, a legal system cannot function if there is an 'acoustic separation' between citizens and officials, in which citizens only hear conduct rules and officials only hear decision rules. Indeed, the behaviour of the law's subjects is equally influenced by conduct *and* decision rules and, likewise, decision-makers cannot apply decision rules in a vacuum – these must be applied in the context of the conduct rules. Dan-Cohen thus argues that all provisions in a given legal system are of three kinds: either conduct rules, decision rules, or both.[185] While excuses are usually characterised as decision rules, justifications fall in the third mixed category presenting both features of conduct rules and of decision rules. Thus, justifications 'tell persons that they may engage in the described conduct even though such conduct would be a violation of the rule absent the justification',[186] but they are formulated as defences,[187] thus being of concern to judges in their assessment of criminal responsibility. Excuses, instead, 'govern the evaluative decisions of courts. They are not designed as levers for channelling conduct in particular directions'.[188] Or put in the words of Joachim Hruschka, excuses '[tell] one who judges what to do when the law has been violated. Namely, it tells us when not to impute blame to an individual who has failed to follow the rules of conduct imposed upon him'.[189]

This argument can be transposed to international law, where the notions of primary and secondary rules have the same meaning and function as, respectively, the notions of conduct and decision rules. Thus, following Dan-Cohen's explanation, it can be said that while excuses are secondary rules only (they are decision rules), justifications have mixed character: they are both conduct and decision rules, both primary and secondary rules. As such, despite being substantive in character, they are rules that belong in the law of responsibility. And indeed, as stated by

---

[184] Dan-Cohen, 'Decision Rules and Conduct Rules: On Acoustic Separation in Law' (1985) 97 *Harv LR* 625, 630. For a similar argument, Alldridge, 'Rules for Courts and Rules for Citizens' (1990) 10 OJLS 487.
[185] Dan-Cohen, 'Acoustic Separation', 631.
[186] Robinson, 'Rules of Conduct', 741.
[187] Ibid., 742.
[188] Fletcher, 'Rights and Excuses' (1984) 3 *Criminal Justice Ethics* 19.
[189] Hruschka, 'On the History of Justification and Excuse in Cases of Necessity' in Byrd and Hruschka (eds), *Kant and Law* (2006), 335.

Italy in the Sixth Committee and as argued by Eric David, no project on responsibility would have been complete without these rules.[190]

It follows from the above that arguments to the effect that *because* the ARS constitute secondary rules *therefore* all defences ought to be classified as excuses or that *because* justifications constitute primary rules *therefore* they do not properly belong to the law of responsibility must be rejected.[191] There are, as has been noted, several other provisions which may be classified as primary rules in the ARS. A clear example of this is the provision in Article 16 in relation to aid and assistance in the wrongful act of another state, an Article which, as acknowledged in the Commentary, actually imposes on states an obligation *not* to aid and assist in the wrongful conduct of another state.[192] A formalist and dogmatic view of the concept of secondary rules (one which, it must be recalled, the Commission never took and never advocated) would require the exclusion of this important provision from the scope of the law of responsibility or the artificial re-characterisation of this rule as secondary (perhaps, and contrary to the Commission's view in this regard as explained in Chapter 2, as a form of 'indirect' responsibility, in which a state is responsible for the wrongful act of another?). The same could be said of the provisions on reparation, which impose obligations on states to make restitution, compensation or provide satisfaction. Could the law of responsibility function without these rules? Certainly not. The omission of any rule from the ARS because it has primary rule features, as has been clearly explained by Giorgio Gaja, would not be 'based on solid ground'.[193] The same must be true of the forced characterisation of certain rules as secondary merely as a result of their inclusion in the ARS. For indeed, it is not the primary or secondary character of a given defence which determines its classification as a justification or an excuse, but the other way around: it is the classification of a defence as a justification or an excuse – a complex task taking into account a number of different factors as explained in Chapter 3 – which determines its character as a primary or secondary rule. In consequence, defences included in the

---

[190] See, Italy: A/C.6/54/SR.22, [54]; David, 'Primary', 32.
[191] For an example of this mistaken view, see the comments by France, cited at Section 1.3.1, and the argument put forward by Tsagourias, 'Self-Defence Against Non-State Actors: The Interaction between Self-Defence as a Primary Rule and Self-Defence as a Secondary Rule' (2016) 29 LJIL 801, 823–4.
[192] ARS Commentary art. 16, [9] (speaking of the 'obligation not to provide aid or assistance to facilitate the commission of an internationally wrongful act by another State ...').
[193] Gaja, 'Primary and Secondary Rules', 990–1.

ARS may be either justifications or excuses and their character as one or the other – as will be seen in Chapter 3 – cannot be determined by their primary or secondary rule characteristics.

## 1.4 Interim Conclusion: Systemic Possibility of the Distinction in International Law

In his famous article 'Precluding Wrongfulness or Responsibility: A Plea for Excuses?', Lowe noted that the distinction between justification and excuse is the 'very stuff of classical tragedy'. It would be far-fetched to describe the ILC's engagement with the distinction between justification and excuse as a 'tragedy', but the analysis made in this chapter between the views expressed in the scholarly commentary and the Commission's work and the conclusions reached, do give the impression of a sense of restoration of, or reversal of fortunes for, the distinction. The Commission at no point expressed a definite and definitive view on the question – and yet, scholars were ready to attribute to the Commission strong and exclusionary views on the basis of a partial analysis of its work: the language of the ARS or the primary/secondary rule dichotomy that it employed in the codification of the law of responsibility. A comprehensive and in-depth consideration of the work of the Commission on defences, as well as of the structure and system of the law of responsibility, has nevertheless restored the possibility of the distinction between justification and excuse in the law of responsibility.

The possibility of the distinction in contemporary international law follows from the very premises of the system of state responsibility. As was seen, the ARS are grounded upon the distinction between the notion of wrongfulness (the breach of international law) and the notion of responsibility (the legal consequences that follow from the breach). Given this conceptual distinction, it is thus feasible to conceive of defences which affect the wrongfulness of conduct (exclude that there is a breach of international law) and defences which affect responsibility (exclude the legal consequences that follow from the breach).

This possibility is not, in any way, ruled out by the language employed in the ARS. The text of the ARS does indeed use the language of preclusion of wrongfulness, but the Commentary also employs the term 'excuse' and the language of preclusion of responsibility. The Commission did not clearly articulate its position, so the use of this heterogeneous terminology may, at first glance, be considered as an inconsistency. This chapter, however, has put forward an alternative interpretation. On the basis of a holistic assessment of the work of the ILC on defences, it suggests that the use of the terms 'justification' and 'excuse' in the Commentary to the ARS, and of the language of preclusion of wrongfulness and preclusion of responsibility during the work on the responsibility project, show that the Commission understood and acknowledged the distinction. Indeed, there is no evidence in the Commission's work that it, at any point, took a conclusive position in favour of justifications to the exclusion of excuses, but rather that it left the matter open for subsequent development and resolution. At any rate, even if the Commission had taken a conclusive position this would have been unable to bar the subsequent development of the distinction – the law of responsibility can develop beyond the ARS.

Finally, the primary/secondary rule distinction, used as the key organising idea of the law of responsibility, is not an obstacle to the recognition of the distinction between justifications and excuses in international law. The primary/secondary rule dichotomy was only ever intended to be a practical one, and it was employed by the ILC as a heuristic device to delimit the scope of its work. The ILC did not take the distinction formally and dogmatically and did not exclude certain provisions from the scope of the draft *because* they were primary in character. If the rules were essential to a complete and coherent statement of the law of responsibility, they were included in the draft. The ARS thus include provisions which may be classified as secondary as well as provisions which may be classified as primary. By the same token, if the ARS include both primary and secondary rules, then it is not necessary to recast all rules included in the ARS as secondary. Consequently, defences included in the ARS may have primary or secondary character; they may, therefore, be justifications or excuses.

The distinction can, therefore, be drawn. But should it be drawn? Is it a desirable distinction? Answering this question requires understanding what implications the distinction may have in the international legal order – to which the next chapter turns.

# 2

# Practical Consequences of the Distinction in International Law

## 2.1 Introduction

The distinction, as Chapter 1 showed, can be drawn in international law. But should it be drawn; is it in any way desirable to distinguish between justification and excuse in the international legal order? This question is related to that of the practical consequences of the distinction. On this point, there is a not uncommon perception that the distinction would have no practical implications in international law, perhaps best summed up in Franck's view that the distinction is of 'pure ... theoretical interest'.[1] But is this so?

This chapter will home in on the question whether it would be practically relevant to distinguish justification and excuse in international law. If it were, then there would be a good reason to distinguish between the two types of defence in the international legal order. This question is examined here by reference to five potential practical consequences: (i) the effects on reparation; (ii) the responsibility of accessories; (iii) rights of reaction against wrongful acts; (iv) the effect of the distinction on the duty to make compensation for material loss, as per ARS Article 27(b); and (v) the normative implications of both types of defence. Each of these practical consequences is addressed in turn in Sections 2.2 through to 2.5, before providing some concluding remarks in Section 2.6.

## 2.2 Effect on Reparation: The Problem of Satisfaction

The first thing to consider is whether there are differences between justification and excuse from the standpoint of the legal relations of responsibility. A state responsible for an internationally wrongful act is subject to two sets of legal relations vis-à-vis the injured state. First, as established in ARS Article 31, is the obligation to make reparation for the injury caused by its

---

[1] Franck, *Recourse to Force* (2002), 191.

wrongful act. Reparation, can take one of three forms: restitution (ARS Article 35), compensation (ARS Article 36) or satisfaction (ARS Article 37). In addition, as set out in ARS Article 30, states are also under an obligation to cease the wrongful act if it is continuing and are (potentially) under an obligation to provide assurances and guarantees of non-repetition.

In principle there is no distinction between justification and excuse in respect of the consequences that arise for the invoking state. Justifications exonerate the state by excluding that the act is wrongful, and excuses by excluding the legal relations entailed by the wrongful act (at least insofar as excuses provide total exoneration). Both in the case of justification and of excuse, the invoking state is not liable to obligations of cessation and is not obliged to provide reparation, in any of its forms, to the claimant state. It is also unlikely that obligations to provide guarantees of non-repetition would arise.[2] In the case of justification, this is because states cannot offer a guarantee not to engage in permissible conduct. In the case of excuse, this is because the excusing circumstance, which is usually exceptional and unforeseen and irresistible, coerces or compels the state to act in a way not compliant with the law, so how can a state guarantee it will not be coerced by such circumstances? Moreover, in both cases states remain bound by the obligations owed to the state affected by their conduct (be it lawfully or unlawfully), and are therefore required to return to compliance with that obligation as soon as the cause of justification or excuse ceases.[3]

Nevertheless, a potential difference may arise in respect of satisfaction, one of the possible forms of reparation recognised in ARS Article 37. According to this provision, satisfaction 'may consist in an acknowledgment of the breach' or any other 'appropriate modality',[4] including a judicial declaration of illegality,[5] so long as the relevant means is not disproportionate and humiliating for the responsible state.[6] This is an exceptional form of reparation which the ARS allow only where the damage cannot be made good by restitution or compensation.[7] Since the

---

[2] On guarantees of non-repetition, see the thorough analysis by Londoño Lázaro, *Las garantías de no repetición en la jurisprudencia Interamericana. Derecho Internacional y cambios estructurales del Estado* (2014).

[3] ARS art. 27(a).

[4] ARS art. 37(2).

[5] See, e.g., *North Sea Continental Shelf Cases (FR Germany/Denmark; FR Germany/Netherlands)* (1969) ICJ Rep 3, 53–4.

[6] ARS art. 37(3).

[7] ARS art. 37(1) and Commentary, [1]. Though note that there are serious doubts as to the logical priority between the various forms of reparation. See Kerbrat, 'Interaction between

ascertainment of an excuse requires, as a prior step, an express finding of the wrongfulness of the excused actor's conduct, or it may even imply an acknowledgment of that wrongfulness, a question arises as to whether excuses can ever exclude this form of reparation or if, on the contrary, excuses can only provide partial exoneration (from obligations of cessation, and restitution and compensation as forms of reparation). If so, this would be a practical difference between justification and excuse: the former would provide total exoneration since the act is not wrongful, and the latter only partial exoneration since an ascertainment of the wrongfulness (a potential form of satisfaction) of the act will normally precede a finding of excuse. But this is only an apparent difference, for the mere ascertainment of wrongfulness is insufficient to constitute satisfaction.

Where a plea of excuse is raised before a tribunal, the tribunal may be required to ascertain, as a preliminary step, that the conduct of the invoking state is a breach of one of its obligations. Judicial declarations of breach can be a form of satisfaction and have indeed been afforded to claimant states on a number of occasions by both the PCIJ and the ICJ.[8] But, crucially, judicial declarations do not always constitute the remedy of satisfaction. Thus the ARS Commentary explains that the text of Article 37 omits a reference to judicial declarations precisely because 'any court or tribunal which has jurisdiction over a dispute has the authority to determine the lawfulness of conduct in question and make a declaration of its findings, as a necessary part of the process of determining the case.'[9] Indeed, a 'declaration may be made by a court or tribunal merely as a preliminary step on the way to its decision on the appropriate form of reparation, even if it decides that no further remedy is necessary.'[10] Judicial declarations of illegality are, therefore, not 'intrinsically associated with the remedy of satisfaction'.[11] To constitute satisfaction the determination of illegality must be included in the operative paragraphs or *dispositif* of the judgment or award; but so long as the finding of illegality is included in the tribunal's reasons it will not constitute a remedy.[12] Consequently, the determination of illegality made by a tribunal in the

---

the Forms of Reparation' in Crawford et al. (eds), *The Law of International Responsibility* (2010), 574.

[8] See, e.g., *North Sea Continental Shelf Cases (FR Germany/Denmark; FR Germany/Netherlands)* (1969) ICJ Rep 3, 53–4.

[9] ARS Commentary art. 37, [6].

[10] Crawford, *State Responsibility: The General Part* (2013), 529.

[11] ARS Commentary art. 37, [6].

[12] Kolb, *The International Court of Justice* (2013), 757.

course of ascertaining a plea of excuse does not constitute satisfaction so long as this determination is included in the reasons of the decision only.[13] The *dispositif* could then hold that the respondent state is excused from responsibility, without containing declarations of the conduct's illegality.

Matters are slightly different where the dispute is resolved bilaterally (or even multilaterally) through negotiation. In these settings, it is possible that the invocation and acceptance of an excuse may imply an acknowledgment of wrongfulness committed by the invoking party. Since the modality of satisfaction is dependent on the circumstances of each case,[14] the acceptance of the excuse plea may be seen as an appropriate form of satisfaction. Nevertheless, it could be argued that if a tribunal's finding of illegality in its reasons is not an appropriate form of satisfaction, a non-judicial determination in the context of political negotiations may not constitute satisfaction either. *A fortiori* this will be the case where the wrongfulness of the conduct is merely implied from an invocation of a plea of excuse. To be sure, the explicit or implicit acknowledgment of illegality (be it by a tribunal or by the parties) may have significant normative, moral or political weight, but it does not, as such, constitute a form of reparation.

In principle, therefore, there will be no difference between justification and excuse in respect of satisfaction since both types of defence exclude this legal relation from arising. Nevertheless, it remains necessary to exercise caution in the drafting of decisions and negotiated settlements in which excuses have been successfully invoked so as to avoid either the inclusion of declarations of illegality in the dispositif of the award or judgment or the express acknowledgment of illegality in the negotiated settlement, for either of these expressions may constitute the remedy of satisfaction.

## 2.3 Responsibility of Accessories

Next is the question of the effect of justification and excuse on the responsibility of accessories. This is one of the practical effects of the distinction frequently mentioned in the domestic law literature.[15] However, this

---

[13] But see Christakis, 'Les "circonstances excluant l'illicéité": une illusion optique?' in Corten et al. (eds), *Droit du pouvoir, pouvoir du droit: Mélanges offerts à Jean Salmon* (2007), 243.

[14] ARS Commentary art. 37(1), [5].

[15] See, e.g., Radbruch, 'Jurisprudence in the Criminal Law' (1936) 18 *J Comp Leg & Int'l L* 218, 218. Similarly Robinson, 'Criminal Law Defences: A Systematic Analysis' (1982) 82 *Col LR* 199, 279–80; Hassemer, 'Justification and Excuse in Criminal Law: Theses

practical consequence is not unanimously adopted across legal systems. In practice, different legal systems resolve the question of accessorial liability differently;[16] even more so, they may resolve it differently in different fields such as criminal law and tort law.[17] It is thus not possible to say that this is a generally recognised consequence of the distinction between justification and excuse. As a general observation, however, it can be said that whether the effect of justification and excuse can reach beyond the principal, and also affect the accessory, ultimately depends on the paradigm of responsibility existing in any given legal system. Insofar as the accessory's responsibility is in some way or other derivative from the illegality of the principal actor's conduct, then whether the principal has a justification or an excuse can affect the responsibility of the accessory.[18]

In international law, responsibility is premised on the principle of independent responsibility,[19] meaning that responsibility is specific to the state which has engaged in a wrongful act. As Crawford has observed, however, states 'rarely operate in isolation',[20] preferring, instead, to 'hunt in packs' be it in conjunction with other states or with other non-state entities.[21] In these cases, states will as a rule be responsible for their own conduct; or, in cases of multiple attribution, the same conduct may implicate the responsibility of more than one state.[22] Exceptionally,

---

and Comments' (1986) BYU LR 573, 603–4; Eser, 'Justification and Excuse: A Key Issue in the Concept of Crime' in Eser (ed.), *Justification and Excuse: Comparative Perspectives* (1987), 33–4.

[16] Under Italian law, for example, questions of accessorial responsibility will depend on the type of participation in the offence and on the defence argued: McAuley, 'Theory of Justification and Excuse: Some Italian Lessons' (1987) 35 *Am J Comp L*, 375ff. The reach of justification and excuse to accessories is even more remote under English law: Smith, *Justification and Excuse in the Criminal Law* (1989), 27–8.

[17] For example, English tort law addresses the responsibility of accessories to torts for which the principal has a defence through a solution which is peculiar to tort law. On this, see: Dietrich, 'Accessorial Liability in the Law of Tort' (2011) 31 *Legal Studies* 23; Davies, 'Defences and Third Parties: Justifying Participation' in Dyson et al. (eds), *Defences in Tort* (2015), 107.

[18] A similar conclusion is reached by Schreiber after an examination of the German law on the matter: Schreiber, 'Problems of Justification and Excuse in the Setting of Accessorial Conduct' (1986) BYU LR 611.

[19] Commentary to Chapter IV of Part One, [1].

[20] Crawford, *General Part*, 325.

[21] As quoted by Aust, *Complicity and the Law of State Responsibility* (2011), 2 (citing Crawford).

[22] On which see Dominicé, 'Attribution of Conduct to Multiple States and the Implication of a State in the Conduct of Another State' in Crawford et al. (eds), *The Law of International Responsibility* (2010), 281; Messineo, 'Multiple Attribution of Conduct' in Nollkaemper and Plakokefalos (eds), *Principles of Shared Responsibility* (2014), 60.

however, there are circumstances in which 'one State should assume responsibility for the internationally wrongful act of another.'[23] These circumstances include the aid and assistance[24] in, and the direction[25] or coercion[26] of, another state's wrongful act. The responsibility of the aiding, directing or coercing states is said to be 'derivative' in that it originates in the wrongful act of another state. Crawford has explained this situation with a hypothetical scenario. If State A participates in the commission of a wrongful act by State B:

> it is state B which has committed the wrongful act, and state A's responsibility is derived from that of state B on account of its contribution to the commission of the act, even though its own conduct taken independently may not actually amount to a breach of its international obligations.[27]

The factual situations envisaged in the rules on participation in the wrongful act of another state in the ARS are complex, and it is helpful to distinguish between two different scenarios: aid and assistance, on the one hand, and direction and coercion, on the other. In the former case, State A is responsible for its *own* conduct (the aid or assistance) and not for the conduct of State B.[28] In the second case, State A is responsible for the wrongful act of State B.[29] In all cases, however, State A's conduct (whether aid and assistance, direction or coercion) would not normally be wrongful;[30] rather, it is rendered wrongful *because* it constitutes a

---

[23] Commentary to Chapter IV of Part One, [5]. On which see, generally, Padelletti, *Pluralità di stati nel fatto illecito internazionale* (1990).
[24] ARS art. 16. On complicity, see Quigley, 'Complicity in International Law: A New Direction in the Law of State Responsibility' (1986) 57 BYIL 77; Graefrath, 'Complicity in the Law of International Responsibility' (1996) 29 RBDI 370; Aust, *Complicity*; Lanovoy, 'Complicity in an Internationally Wrongful Act' in Nollkaemper and Plakokefalos (eds), *Principles of Shared Responsibility* (2014); Jackson, *Complicity in International Law* (2015), ch. 7. This provision was recognised as part of customary law by the ICJ in *Application of the Convention on the Prevention and Punishment of the Crime of Genocide (Bosnia and Herzegovina v Serbia and Montenegro)* (2007) ICJ Rep 43.
[25] ARS art. 17.
[26] ARS art. 18. On which see Fry, 'Coercion, Causation, and the Fictional Elements of Indirect Responsibility' (2007) 40 *Vanderbilt J Transnat'l L* 611.
[27] Crawford, *General Part*, 336.
[28] ARS Commentary art. 16, [10].
[29] ARS Commentary art. 17, [1]; ARS Commentary art. 18, [1].
[30] Of course, State B would be responsible if its conduct vis-à-vis State A were itself prohibited by international law, for example where the coercion amounts to a threat of the use of force or an intervention. For an example of unlawful coercion, see *Military and Paramilitary Activities in and Against Nicaragua (Nicaragua v United States of America)* (1986) ICJ Rep 14, [205].

## 2.3 RESPONSIBILITY OF ACCESSORIES

form of participation in the wrongful act of another, of State B. It is in this sense that responsibility is derivative: it originates in the wrongful act of the principal actor. Thus, if State B's conduct is *lawful* then State A would have participated in a lawful act and would not, therefore, be responsible.

In these circumstances, whether the principal actor's conduct is justified or the principal actor has an excuse will affect the derivative responsibility of the accessory. A state's aid or assistance in a lawful act cannot, in principle,[31] involve its responsibility. Thus, the United Kingdom argued, in response to Libya's claim that it had acted wrongfully in allowing its territory to be used by the United States as a launch pad for attacks in Tripoli and Benghazi in 1986,[32] that its action was lawful because it constituted assistance in the United States' lawful exercise of self-defence.[33] Similarly, a state's aid or assistance in the *justified* conduct of another is lawful. Take the following example: State X takes a countermeasure against State Y in the form of a restriction of dairy product imports from Y. State X depends, to a high degree, on State Y's dairy to provide for its national consumption. State Z agrees to export some of its dairy to X to make up for the shortages of dairy for as long as the countermeasure against Y is in place. The three states are parties to a free trade agreement covering dairy products. State Z's assistance to State X, without which X could not effectively take the envisaged countermeasure against Y, is lawful as it involves participation in conduct that while incompatible with the free trade agreement (it is a trade-restrictive measure), is nevertheless justified as a countermeasure.

But matters may be different in the case of excuses. Derivative responsibility is still possible in these circumstances, as the principal actor's conduct is wrongful even though the principal may be exonerated from the legal consequences of its wrongful act. The case of coercion of another state provides a good illustration of this. Pursuant to ARS Article 18, the coercing state is responsible so long as the coerced state's act is wrongful. In principle, the coerced state is also responsible for the conduct even though it was merely an 'instrument' of the coercing state for the commission of the relevant wrongful act. Now, there is no general defence of coercion or duress in international law, but the coerced state may benefit from the defence of *force majeure* if the coercion is such that it eliminates the

---

[31] Unless its own conduct constitutes the breach of an obligation binding upon it.
[32] Statement of the Libyan representative to the Security Council, Doc S/PV.2674, 11.
[33] Statement of the UK representative to the Security Council, Doc S/PV.2679, 26–8.

coerced state's volition or free will.[34] If this is the case, depending on how *force majeure* is classified, its successful invocation may have an impact on the coercing state's responsibility as well. If *force majeure* were a justification and the coerced state benefitted from it, its conduct would be lawful. As such, the coercing state would also derivatively benefit from it: if its conduct does not itself constitute an unlawful form of coercion, it would have coerced the commission of a lawful act for which, consequently, it can bear no responsibility. In contrast, if *force majeure* were an excuse, then the coerced state may be relieved of responsibility for its wrongful act and the coercing state could still be derivatively responsible for that act.[35]

In international law, then, it seems that justification and excuse can have an impact on the responsibility of accessories: justifications affect the responsibility of accessories to it and, in this sense, they have a universalist tendency; excuses, in contrast, are individualist in tendency, insofar as they attach only to the invoking state.

## 2.4 Reacting Against Wrongfulness

Third is the question whether justification and excuse differently impact on the availability of reactions against wrongful acts. Under international law, states injured by the breach of an obligation owed to them can resort to a great variety of reactions.[36] Of these, two are particularly relevant here: countermeasures[37] and, if the breach concerns a treaty obligation and it constitutes a 'material breach' thereof, the possibility to suspend or terminate that treaty.[38] Are either of these reactions affected if the relevant conduct is justified or if the wrongdoer possesses an excuse? It seems intuitive to assert that these reactions are excluded in the case of justified conduct; since justified conduct is lawful, then the necessary precondition for the adoption of these reactions (a wrongful act) is missing. By the same token, it seems intuitive that if the actor is only excused, the state injured by its conduct be entitled to react against it. Nevertheless, matters are slightly more complex than this, as will be seen.

---

[34] ARS Commentary art. 18, [6].
[35] See also Aust, 'Circumstances Precluding Wrongfulness and Shared Responsibility' in Nollkaemper and Plakokefalos (eds), *Principles of Shared Responsibility* (2014), 193–4.
[36] As explained by Simma and Tams in 'Reacting against Treaty Breaches' in Hollis (ed.), *The Oxford Guide to Treaties* (2012), 578.
[37] See ARS art. 22 and Chapter II of Part Three.
[38] See VCLT art. 60.

## 2.4.1 Countermeasures Against Justified Conduct or Excused Actors

Countermeasures can only be taken against a prior wrongful act. It follows that countermeasures cannot be taken against justified conduct, since justified conduct does not involve the breach of an international obligation and, as such, does not amount to a wrongful act. A particular corollary of this principle is that there can be no countermeasures against countermeasures.[39] This is an especially important corollary, as it constitutes the closure point of what would otherwise amount to a logically possible, and legally permissible, circle of wrongfulness. Countermeasures are themselves justified behaviour, so that if countermeasures were allowed against justified behaviour, then a state target of countermeasures could take counter-countermeasures, and so on, *ad infinitum*. Likewise, an aggressor state cannot take countermeasures against a state legitimately exercising self-defence.[40] The corollary is applicable in general to all entitlements that contain, as a precondition, the existence of a wrongful act. Thus, just as there can be no countermeasures against countermeasures, there can be no self-defence against self-defence.[41]

The corollary does not, however, exclude that countermeasures may be adopted against an excused actor. In these circumstances there is a wrongful act, so the triggering condition of the entitlement to take countermeasures would be met.[42] Thus, for example, if the plea of necessity were classified as an excuse, then it would seem intuitively possible that the (innocent) state whose rights are impaired by another state in a situation of necessity may take countermeasures against a state excused

---

[39] *US v Ohlendorf (Einsatzgruppen trial)* (1949) 4 NMT 1, 493–4: 'Under international law, as in domestic law, there can be no reprisal against reprisal. The assassin who is being repulsed by his intended victim may not slay him and then, in turn, plead self-defence.' In the literature, see the observation by Strupp at 'Le régime des représailles en temps de paix. Observations des Membres de la Commision' (1934) 41 *Annuaire IDI* 89, 138; Darcy, 'The Evolution of the Law of Belligerent Reprisals' (2003) 175 *Mil L Rev* 184, 191: 'The prohibition of counter-reprisals, as such, is not a legal norm, but a mere consequence of strict observance of the law of belligerent reprisals.'

[40] Politis, 'Le régime des représailles en temps de paix. Rapport et projets de résolution et de règlement' (1934) 38 *Annuaire IDI* 1, 49.

[41] For judicial statements of this corollary, see *The Maria* (1799) 1 *C Rob* 340, 361 ('it is a wild conceit, that wherever force is used, it may be lawfully resisted. A lawful force cannot be lawfully resisted'); *United States v von Weizsaecker et al (Ministries trial)* (1949) 14 NMT 314, 329. In the literature, see Dinstein, *War, Aggression and Self-Defence* (5th edn, 2012), 190; de Hoogh, 'Restrictivist Reasoning on the *Ratione Personae* Dimension of Armed Attacks in the Post 9/11 World' (2016) 29 LJIL 19, 22.

[42] In favour of this position, see Christakis, 'Illusion', 243–4.

under the plea of necessity.[43] After all, if this were the case, the conduct of the state invoking necessity would constitute a breach of the injured state's rights. Nevertheless, countermeasures are only permissible if adopted with the purpose of inducing a responsible state to comply with its obligations of cessation or reparation. They are not a sanction against wrongfulness, but an instrument of enforcement.[44] Now, excuses operate precisely to exclude the legal relations of cessation and reparation arising from a wrongful act. Consequently, a countermeasure taken against an excused actor would fail the purpose test: since the excused actor does not owe these obligations, the injured state cannot induce their performance by way of countermeasures.

In practice, then, both justified conduct and excused states are not liable to countermeasures. In either case, however, the analytic explanation why this is so differs, and this may be relevant if the possibility of partial excuses, namely excuses that exclude only some of the legal consequences of the wrongful act, was accepted. Indeed, in this case, a state could still adopt countermeasures to induce the performance of the legal relations of responsibility that are *not* precluded by the excuse.

### 2.4.2   Law of Treaties: Material Breach, Justification and Excuse

States are also entitled to request the suspension or termination of a treaty as a result of the non-performance of that treaty by another treaty-party. This entitlement is codified in VCLT Article 60, which provides that in the case of 'material breach' of a treaty by a treaty-party, other specified treaty-parties (depending on the bilateral or multilateral character of the treaty, and of the obligations within it) may request the suspension or termination of that treaty in whole or in part.[45] Can this entitlement be

---

[43] This assertion is premised on the characterisation of state of necessity as an excuse, on which see Chapter 8, Section 8.4.4.
[44] On which see Chapter 6.
[45] Pursuant to VCLT art. 60:

1. A material breach of a bilateral treaty by one of the parties entitles the other to invoke the breach as a ground for terminating the treaty or suspending its operation in whole or in part.
2. A material breach of a multilateral treaty by one of the parties entitles:
   (a) the other parties by unanimous agreement to suspend the operation of the treaty in whole or in part or to terminate it either:
      (i) in the relations between themselves and the defaulting State; or
      (ii) as between all the parties;

## 2.4 REACTING AGAINST WRONGFULNESS

exercised when the 'material breach' is justified or when the state committing the material breach is excused?

A 'material breach', for the purposes of the VCLT, can take one of two forms. First, it can take the form of a 'repudiation of the treaty not sanctioned by the present Convention'.[46] Repudiation refers to 'all means by which a party intends to relieve itself from its obligations under the treaty'.[47] Second, it can take the form of a 'violation of a provision essential to the accomplishment of the object and purpose of the treaty'.[48] This second form has given rise to some controversy, especially in respect of the adjective 'material': does it concern the degree of the breach, does it relate to the quality of the obligation breached, or both? There is some basis in the drafting history of this provision for a reading of 'material' requiring a substantial breach of an essential provision.[49] But the textual interpretation of Article 60(3) leads in the opposite direction: what matters is the obligation breached, not the intensity of its breach. In short, 'material' is a qualitative criterion only. Thus, even a trivial breach may be 'material' if it affects an 'essential provision' of the treaty.[50]

> (b) a party specially affected by the breach to invoke it as a ground for suspending the operation of the treaty in whole or in part in the relations between itself and the defaulting State;
> (c) any party other than the defaulting State to invoke the breach as a ground for suspending the operation of the treaty in whole or in part with respect to itself if the treaty is of such a character that a material breach of its provisions by one party radically changes the position of every party with respect to the further performance of its obligations under the treaty.
> 3. A material breach of a treaty, for the purposes of this article, consists in:
>    (a) a repudiation of the treaty not sanctioned by the present Convention; or
>    (b) the violation of a provision essential to the accomplishment of the object or purpose of the treaty.
> 4. The foregoing paragraphs are without prejudice to any provision in the treaty applicable in the event of a breach.
> 5. Paragraphs 1 to 3 do not apply to provisions relating to the protection of the human person contained in treaties of a humanitarian character, in particular to provisions prohibiting any form of reprisals against persons protected by such treaties.

---

[46] VCLT art. 60(3)(a).
[47] Simma and Tams, 'Article 60 (1969)' in Corten and Klein (eds), *The Vienna Convention on the Law of Treaties: A Commentary* (2011), 1358. For an example, see *Legal Consequences for States of the Continued Presence of South Africa in Namibia (South West Africa) Notwithstanding Security Council Resolution 276 (1970) (Advisory Opinion)* (1971) ICJ Rep 16, [95].
[48] VCLT art. 60(3)(b).
[49] See, e.g., Waldock, Second Report on the Law of Treaties, ILC Yearbook 1963, vol. II, 73ff.
[50] Simma and Tams, 'Article 60 (1969)', 1359. Cf. Kirgis, 'Some Lingering Questions about Article 60 of the Vienna Convention on the Law of Treaties' (1989) 22 *Cornell ILJ* 549, 550–5.

The availability of the entitlement in Article 60 in response to justified conduct or excused actors raises two fundamental questions: first, whether the 'material breach' must be wrongful and, second, whether the entitlement to suspend or terminate the treaty can be classified as belonging to the concept of 'responsibility', namely as one of the legal relations arising from wrongfulness within the framework of the law of responsibility. The first question relates to the availability of the entitlement in the case of justified conduct; the second, its availability in the case of excused actors. Each of these will be examined separately.

Although Article 60 does not expressly indicate that the 'material breach' must constitute an internationally wrongful act, that this breach must be wrongful is implicit in the wording of this provision.[51] Article 60(3)(a) states that the repudiation of the treaty must not 'be sanctioned' by the VCLT itself. Thus, if a state repudiates a treaty by basing itself on one of the grounds of invalidity,[52] suspension or termination contained in the VCLT,[53] then its conduct will not amount to a material breach. By implication, then, the repudiation will constitute a material breach when it is not based on any of these grounds. And when it is not based on any of these grounds, as the ICJ found in *Gabčíkovo-Nagymaros*,[54] then it is wrongful. So repudiation must be wrongful to amount to a material breach and to bring the entitlement in Article 60 into operation.

Article 60(3)(b), on the violation of an essential provision of the treaty, does not contain a similar qualification: it does not qualify 'violations' by reference to their being 'sanctioned' or not by the VCLT. From this, it has been concluded that whether the violation is wrongful or justified is irrelevant for the determination of the 'material breach'. So long as a state does not perform an essential provision in a treaty, there will be a 'material breach' for the purposes of suspension or termination of that treaty under Article 60.[55] But this conclusion is at odds with the language of paragraph (b) and the relation between the law of treaties and the law of

---

[51] The concept of 'breach' in the law of responsibility, as will be explained in Chapter 3, entails wrongfulness. That is, a breach is always wrongful. However, it could be the case that this same concept may have a different meaning in the law of treaties. It is thus necessary to explain why in the law of treaties as well the notion of 'material breach' entails wrongfulness.

[52] See VCLT arts 46–53.

[53] See VCLT arts 54–64.

[54] *Gabčíkovo-Nagymaros Project (Hungary/Slovakia)* (1997) ICJ Rep 7, [46–7].

[55] Lefeber, 'Case Analysis: The *Gabčíkovo-Nagymaros Project* and the Law of State Responsibility' (1998) 11 LJIL 609, 611–12.

responsibility. As to the language of the provision, paragraph (b) speaks of a 'violation' of an essential provision of the treaty. The term 'violation' is one that connotes wrongfulness,[56] so it would have been redundant to add that 'violations' must not be 'sanctioned' by the VCLT. Besides, the VCLT does not govern questions of non-performance of treaty obligations, a matter reserved by VCLT Article 73 to the law of responsibility. Indeed, on this front, there is a 'functional separation' between the law of treaties and the law of responsibility. The law of treaties determines the validity, suspension or termination of treaties, whereas the law of responsibility determines whether treaty (and other) obligations have been breached.[57] The existence of a 'material breach' of the treaty which triggers the entitlement under Article 60 must therefore be assessed by reference to the law of responsibility. Now, under the law of responsibility, the determination of the existence of a breach of international law requires both that there is an act which is not in conformity with what is required by an international obligation *and* that the conduct in question is not covered by a justification.[58] Therefore, there will be a breach only where there is no justification available. It thus seems clear that the 'material breach' to give rise to the entitlement in Article 60 must be a wrongful act[59] and that, by implication, if the non-performance is justified under the law of responsibility, it will not constitute a material breach entailing the right to suspend or terminate the treaty.[60]

What if the state author of the material breach is excused; is the entitlement in Article 60 triggered anyway? In this case there would still be a wrongful act, but one which does not generate the legal relations of responsibility for its author. Whether Article 60 is triggered in

---

[56] On which see Forlati, *Diritto dei trattati e responsabilità internazionale* (2005), 67. Also Rosenne, *Breach of Treaty* (1985), 6–7.

[57] On which see *Rainbow Warrior*, [75]; *Gabčíkovo-Nagymaros Project*, [47–8].

[58] See ARS art. 12 and Commentary, at para 1 ('In order to conclude that there is a breach of an international obligation in any specific case, it will be necessary to take account of ... the provisions of chapter V dealing with circumstances which may preclude the wrongfulness of an act of a State'). This will be explained in more detail in Chapter 3. On this issue see further Duarte d'Almeida, 'Defences in the Law of State Responsibility: A View from Jurisprudence' and Paddeu, 'Explaining the Concept of Circumstances Precluding Wrongfulness (Justifications) in International Law', both in Paddeu and Bartels (eds), *Exceptions and Defences in International Law* (2018) (forthcoming).

[59] Simma, 'Reflections on Article 60 of the Vienna Convention on the Law of Treaties and Its Background in General International Law' (1970) 20 *Österreichische Zeitschrift für öffentliches Recht* 5, 38; Gomaa, *Suspension or Termination of Treaties on Grounds of Breach* (1996), 36; Forlati, *Diritto dei trattati*, 67–9.

[60] Simma, 'Reflections', 60 (fn. 250); Gomaa, *Suspension or Termination*, 43–4.

these circumstances thus depends on how one classifies the entitlement provided therein, namely whether it is one included in the concept of responsibility or not. If the entitlement is included within the concept of responsibility, then an excuse precludes the entitlement to suspend or terminate the relevant treaty. If, on the contrary, the entitlement to suspend or terminate a treaty due to material breach is not included in the concept of responsibility, then the excuse will not have the effect of precluding it. In this regard, some scholars have argued that the right to suspend or terminate a treaty following a material breach fits 'into the concept of international responsibility'.[61] This argument is based on two related assumptions. First, that the concept of responsibility includes, as Ago had stated in his reports to the ILC,[62] two types of legal relations arising from the wrongful act: a set of obligations for the wrongdoer (cessation and reparation) *and* a legal faculty for the injured party to impose a sanction on the wrongdoer (countermeasures). Second, that the entitlement in Article 60 is (like countermeasures) a form of sanction. By implication, if a wrongdoing state benefits from an excuse, the excuse will *also* preclude (at least in principle) the entitlement in Article 60. Nevertheless, both of the assumptions upon which this view rests were rejected by the ILC and states, as will be discussed in the chapter concerning countermeasures.[63] Indeed, responsibility does not entail a faculty to impose sanctions; it is limited to the obligations of cessation and reparation. In any event, as clarified by Special Rapporteur Crawford:

> Within the field of State responsibility, there do not seem to be any other general legal consequences of the commission of an internationally wrongful act than those referred to in present part two – viz. cessation, restitution, compensation, satisfaction and the possible liability to countermeasures in the event that a State fails to comply with these secondary obligations.[64]

Thus, even if the entitlement in Article 60 were a sanction, then it would be excluded from the concept of responsibility. Moreover, the entitlement

---

[61] Pisillo Mazzeschi, 'Termination and Suspension of Treaties for Breach in the ILC Works on State Responsibility' in Spinedi and Simma (eds), *United Nations Codification of State Responsibility* (1987), 89 (the expression quoted is from p. 68).

[62] See Chapter 1, Section 1.3.2.2.

[63] See Chapter 6.

[64] Crawford, Third Report on State Responsibility, ILC Yearbook 2000, vol. II(1), [68]. Crawford includes here countermeasures, but crucially not in terms of a faculty of the injured state arising from the wrongful act itself – but rather as a 'possible liability' of the wrongdoer and then only if the wrongdoer fails to comply with its obligations of cessation and reparation. It is not, in short, a consequence of the wrongful act itself.

## 2.5 EFFECT ON COMPENSATION FOR MATERIAL LOSS

in Article 60 has, as Crawford noted, 'nothing to do with responsibility'.[65] Unlike the legal relations arising from the wrongful act, which are intended to restore the injured state to the situation it would have been in had the wrongful act not occurred, the purpose of entitlement in Article 60 is to remedy the balance of rights and obligations between treaty-parties which is disturbed by the material breach.[66] As a result, insofar as excuses preclude the legal relations encompassed by the notion of responsibility *only*, they cannot exclude the entitlement in Article 60. Consequently, the entitlement in Article 60 can be invoked where the wrongdoing state is excused for its material breach of the treaty.[67]

### 2.5 Effect on Compensation for Material Loss

Fourth is the question of the duty of compensation for material loss referred to in ARS Article 27(b). Pursuant to this provision:

> Article 27. Consequences of invoking a circumstance precluding wrongfulness
>
> The invocation of a circumstance precluding wrongfulness in accordance with this chapter is without prejudice to ...
>
> (b) the question of compensation for any material loss caused by the act in question.

Article 27(b) does not itself impose a general obligation of compensation where 'circumstances precluding wrongfulness' have been successfully invoked.[68] It merely notes that such a duty may exist, and the ARS

---

[65] Ibid., [60]. See also Fitzmaurice and Olufemi, *Contemporary Issues in the Law of Treaties* (2005), 133–5.

[66] Simma, 'Reflections', 20–1; Capotorti, 'L'extinction et la suspension des traités' (1971) 134 *Recueil* 417, 548–9; Simma and Tams, 'Treaty Breaches', 582.

[67] Equally, as was seen in Section 2.3.1, excuses do not exclude countermeasures *as such*; excuses simply undercut the very object of countermeasures, by precluding the obligations of cessation and reparation, rendering them inapplicable. A not dissimilar conclusion, although on the basis of different reasoning, was reached by Simma in his 1970s work 'Reflections'. For Simma, a 'material breach' is an internationally wrongful act, in that it is both objectively contrary to a treaty obligation and includes an element of *culpa*. Nevertheless, there could be 'less substantial' violations that were objectively contrary to the treaty but were not accompanied by *culpa*, because the actor benefitted from an excuse (excusable mistake or excuse of necessity). In these cases, he thought that the injured party was entitled *only* to suspend the treaty, as a way to re-establish the balance between the parties, but it was not entitled to take reprisals or to terminate the treaty. See ibid., 38.

[68] ARS Commentary art. 27, [1].

are without prejudice to such a possibility. It is often stated in the literature that the duty arises only in respect of excuses, but not in the case of justifications. As will be seen, however, matters are much more complex than this.

The possibility of a duty of compensation in circumstances in which a defence is available has been considered (and has troubled) international lawyers for many centuries.[69] To be sure, as pointed out by some scholars, there are good policy reasons in support of this duty: '[w]ithout such a provision a state might be tempted to use a [defence] as against another state to shift the burden of defending its own interests on to another state.'[70] And yet, positive law has remained rather uncertain on the point. Indeed, not much can be inferred from the existing state practice, international case-law or domestic law. Historically, states often paid gratuitous compensation for damage even in cases where they had been exonerated by reference to *force majeure*. But they did so on the basis of equitable considerations,[71] and not as a matter of obligation. Most recently, the question has come up in the context of Argentina's invocation of the plea of necessity in disputes arising out of its financial crisis of the early 2000s. But again, not much can be made of the resulting case-law: tribunals have taken radically different approaches to this question in their decisions.[72] Domestic legal orders, albeit often containing provisions on civil compensation in the case of criminal exoneration, vary too greatly to allow the identification of any general principles. For example, under Italian law, civil remedies may be due in the case of criminal behaviour where the actor is excused, but not when he is justified.[73] The criminal codes

---

[69] See, e.g., Grotius, *De jure belli ac pacis [1625]* (2005), II.2.§vii–ix; Pufendorf, *De jure naturae et gentium [1688]* (1934), II.6.§vi.

[70] Crawford, *General Part*, 318.

[71] See, e.g., the French decree of 1848 on indemnities for the February 1848 revolution, granting indemnities on an equitable basis, cited by Calvo, *Le droit international théorique et pratique* (3rd edn, 1880) vol. 1, 443. See also Laurent, 'State Responsibility: A Possible Historic Precedent to the Calvo Clause' (1966) 15 ICLQ 395, 420–1 (on equitable compensation granted to foreigners following Belgian insurrection of 1830).

[72] Contrast the tribunals' approaches in *CMS Gas Transmission Company v Argentine Republic*, ICSID Case ARB/01/8, Award, 12 May 2005, [338]; *LG&E Energy Corp, LG&E Capital Corp, LG&E International Inc. v Argentine Republic*, ICSID Case ARB/02/1, Liability, 3 October 2006, [260–4]; and later the clarification in *CMS (Annulment)*, [147]. In the literature, see Christakis, 'Quel remède à l'éclatement de la jurisprudence CIRDI sur les investissement en Argentine? La décision du comité ad hoc dans l'affaire *CMS c. Argentine*' (2007) 111 RGDIP 879, 888–90; Schill, 'International Investment Law and the Host State's Power to Handle Economic Crises' (2007) 24 *J Int'l Arb* 265, 281ff.

[73] Marinucci and Dolcini, *Manuale di diritto penale* (2nd edn, 2006), 197; Mantovani, *Principi di diritto penale* (2nd edn, 2007), 100.

## 2.5 EFFECT ON COMPENSATION FOR MATERIAL LOSS 79

of Alabama and New Jersey, instead, state that neither justification nor excuse 'abolish or impair' possible civil remedies due.[74] The positive law recognition of this duty is uncertain at best.

In addition to the doubts on its recognition at customary law, the duty of compensation referred to in Article 27(b) is also afflicted by two related uncertainties: first, the identification of the defences in respect of which the duty of compensation may arise; and, second, the legal basis of the duty.[75] The ILC discussed both of these uncertainties during the codification of the ARS, considering several proposals and ultimately endorsing none. With respect to the first one, draft Article 35 adopted on first reading (perhaps reflecting historical practice) limited its application to *force majeure*, state of necessity, distress and consent.[76] On second reading, however, the provision was broadened and made applicable to all the defences. This modification was explained as a measure to protect third parties whose interests may be affected, for example, in the course of self-defensive action or by countermeasures.[77] Arguably a justified policy choice, this decision did nothing to clarify the circumstances in which the duty would be relevant.[78] As to the second, on the identification of a legal basis for this duty,[79] the Commission considered two possible legal bases for the duty in Article 27(b): that this compensation may be a case of international liability for conduct not prohibited by international law;[80]

---

[74] Alabama Code, sec. 13A-3-21(c) (2011); New Jersey Code, sec. 2C:31(b) (2011).
[75] Forteau, 'Reparation in the Event of a Circumstance Precluding Wrongfulness' in Crawford et al. (eds), *The Law of International Responsibility* (2010), 888.
[76] Draft art. 35(2)(b), ILC Report, forty-eighth session, ILC Yearbook 1996, vol. II(2), 58.
[77] ILC Report, fifty-first session, ILC Yearbook 1999, vol. II(2), 85 [407]. See, e.g., Economides, 2591st meeting, ILC Yearbook 1999, vol. I, 174 [47]; Pellet, 2591st meeting, ILC Yearbook 1999, vol. I, 175 [55]. Japan endorsed this expansion, though suggested that cases in which ARS art. 27(b) was not applicable should be identified in the Commentary, see A/CN.4/515, 56–7.
[78] For it is recognised that it does not apply in all cases: Yamada, 'Revisiting the International Law Commission's Draft Articles on State Responsibility' in Ragazzi (ed.), *International Responsibility Today: Essays in Memory of Oscar Schachter* (2005), 122–3.
[79] Historically, the legal basis of this duty constituted one of the main differences between Grotius' and Pufendorf's concepts of necessity; on which see Swanson, 'The Medieval Foundations of John Locke's Theory of Natural Rights: Rights of Subsistence and the Principle of Extreme Necessity' (1997) 18 *Hist Pol Thought* 399, 431; Salter, 'Grotius and Pufendorf on the Right of Necessity' (2005) 26 *Hist Pol Thought* 285.
[80] Quentin-Baxter and Barboza, who later became Special Rapporteurs on the topic of liability arising out of acts not prohibited by international law, upheld this view: Quentin-Baxter, 1615th meeting, ILC Yearbook 1980, vol. I, 168 [16]; Barboza, 1617th meeting, ILC Yearbook 1980, vol. I, 176 [27]. It was also popular with legal scholars, e.g., Cahier, 'Changements et continuité du droit international' (1985) 195 *Recueil* 9, 304; Sucharitkul, 'State Responsibility and International Liability under International Law' (1995–6) 18

or that the duty applied to excuses (but not to justifications),[81] thus basing the duty on the wrongfulness of the excused state's conduct. The former explanation was rejected by the Commission;[82] the latter was neither endorsed nor rejected, and is not mentioned in the ARS Commentary.

Scholarship has tended to be persuaded by this latter rationale, since it would be capable of resolving both uncertainties at once. If the duty of compensation were determined along the justification/excuse divide then it would be possible to narrow down the circumstances in which the duty does (or could) arise. Thus, only excuses would generate a duty of compensation. Additionally, this solution would also solve the riddle of the legal basis of this duty: the duty would be based on the wrongfulness of the conduct of the excused actor. Seemingly, therefore, the distinction can actually resolve both of the uncertainties of Article 27(b). Indeed, the resolution of these uncertainties has often been championed as one of the practical benefits of distinguishing between justification and excuse in the law of state responsibility.[83] But the claim has been dismissed by others. For example, Crawford has argued that it is doubtful whether a state invoking *force majeure*, which he understands to act as an excuse, may be required to provide compensation: a state victim of *force majeure* is, in the circumstances, just as innocent as the state injured by its conduct. For Crawford, the question of compensation for material loss is a more complex problem, and it is one that cannot be resolved merely by reference to the particular defence's characterisation as a justification or excuse.[84]

So, can the distinction help solve the riddles of Article 27(b)? While the simplicity of the solution makes it intuitively appealing, a number of

---

Loy LA Int'l & Comp LJ 821, 833; Tomuschat, 'International Law: Ensuring the Survival of Mankind on the Eve of a New Century' (1999) 281 *Recueil* 9, 288–9.

[81] At least not those justifications which rely on the previous wrongful act of the injured State (e.g., self-defence and countermeasures): ILC Report, fifty-first session, 85 [408]. This explanation was endorsed, in the Sixth Committee, by Slovakia: A/C.6/54/SR.22, [57]; and Russia: A/C.6/55/SR.18, [53].

[82] This rationale did not have 'sufficient basis in international law', ILC Report, fifty-first session, 85 [406]. Also arguing against this possibility in the literature, see: Song, 'Between Scylla and Charybdis: Can a Plea of Necessity Offer Safe Passage to States in Responding to an Economic Crisis without Incurring Liability to Foreign Investors?' (2008) 19 *Am Rev Int'l Arb* 235, 262–3.

[83] See, e.g., Lowe, 'Precluding Wrongfulness or Responsibility: A Plea for Excuses?' (1999) 10 EJIL 410; Johnstone, 'The Plea of "Necessity" in International Legal Discourse: Humanitarian Intervention and Counter-terrorism' (2005) 43 *Columbia J Trans'l L*, 353–4; Christakis, 'Illusion', 235–40.

[84] Crawford, *General Part*, 319.

more or less powerful objections can be raised against it. The argument and its objections will be considered in respect of excuses, justifications, and third parties respectively. Given the complexity of the question, this section will include interim conclusions on the duty of compensation. As will be said there, to assert that the distinction between justification and excuse resolves the riddles of the duty of compensation is an overstatement. And yet the distinction between justification and excuse may still be relevant to the determination of the existence of a duty of compensation and of its legal basis – at least where the two parties in the responsibility relation are concerned. Indeed, the distinction between justification and excuse is irrelevant in respect of the potential compensation due to third parties, when their rights are affected by a state invoking a defence.

### 2.5.1 Excuses and the Duty of Compensation

The duty to make compensation for material loss could be limited to defences classified as excuses. As was said earlier, if this solution were taken, then the two related uncertainties of the duty referred to in Article 27(b) would be resolved at once: only excuses generate it, and its legal basis would be the wrongfulness of the conduct in question. Two sets of objections may be raised against this argument: that it collapses compensation for material loss into compensation as a form of reparation and that it cannot resolve the problem highlighted by Crawford in respect of *force majeure*. As will be seen neither of these objections is fatal to the possibility of attaching compensation for material loss to excuses – indeed, excuses could be understood as providing only partial exoneration leaving open the possibility of compensation.

The first set of objections stems from wrongfulness as the legal basis of the duty of compensation. The first thing to note here is that to accept this legal basis essentially elides the distinction between the duty of compensation for material loss (in ARS Article 27(b)) and compensation as a form of reparation (in ARS Articles 34 and 36). For what would be the difference between paying compensation for material loss caused by a wrongful act, and providing reparation through compensation for damage caused by a wrongful act? This elision would be contrary to the views expressed by the Commission in the Commentary to the ARS.[85] Nevertheless, inconsistency with the view stated by the ILC in the Commentary is not fatal

---

[85] ARS Commentary art. 27, [4].

to the argument, for whatever the position taken by the Commission in the ARS, this cannot be an impediment to the refinement and further development of the law of responsibility. Indeed, the ARS are not a binding instrument and the customary source of the rules embodied therein makes them susceptible to subsequent developments through state practice.[86] This is all the more so in an area in which the ARS do not actually take a clear stance (recall that Article 27(b) is merely a without prejudice clause) and in which the positive law is largely uncertain and undeveloped. There is wide scope for the development of the law in this area beyond the position stated in the ARS. It is therefore possible to accept that excuses generate a duty of compensation, and that this duty has its legal basis in the wrongfulness of the conduct.

However, accepting this position means *also* accepting the implication that the duty of compensation is subsumed within the wider notion of compensation as a form of reparation. And this is more problematic to the argument. The subsumption of the duty of compensation within the notion of reparation paves the ground for the exclusion of the duty precisely in the cases in which this argument asserts the duty to be applicable. For if the duty to compensate material loss is nothing other than compensation as a form of reparation, then its very possibility is undercut by the notion of excuse as a defence that precludes the obligation of reparation arising from the wrongful act. This objection can be overcome by recognising that excuses may only afford partial exoneration.[87] Partial defences are recognised in many domestic legal orders. As explained by Douglas Husak, partial defences are a kind of mitigating circumstance, in that they 'alleviate, abate or diminish the severity of a punishment imposed by law'.[88] In international law, a partial excuse, about which more will be said later, could be a defence which excludes some but not all consequences of the wrongful act. The duty to pay compensation may thus be seen as a consequence not excluded by the partial excuse.

---

[86] To be sure, treaties too may be modified by the subsequent practice of the treaty-parties. See, e.g., *Legal Consequences for States of the Continued Presence of South Africa in Namibia (South West Africa) Notwithstanding Security Council Resolution 276 (1970) (Advisory Opinion)* (1971) ICJ Rep 16, in relation to the voting procedures of the Security Council, as established in the UN Charter and as practised by UN members.

[87] As argued by, among others, Schwebel, 1614th meeting, ILC Yearbook 1980, vol. I, 163 [20]. Some states endorsed this view in the Sixth Committee, e.g., Spain: A/C.6/34/SR.44, [5].

[88] Husak, 'Partial Defenses' (1998) 11 *Canadian J of L & Juris* 167, 168.

## 2.5 EFFECT ON COMPENSATION FOR MATERIAL LOSS 83

The second objection relates to the circumstances in which the duty will arise. In essence, to attach a duty of compensation to all excuses does not allow to make some important distinctions between different types of circumstances. After all, in all cases of excuse the state's conduct is wrongful; and if the conduct produces a material loss, then the invoking state will be under a duty to make compensation. This lack of nuance was at the heart of Crawford's observation about *force majeure* noted earlier. In his view, to accept that all excuses generate a duty of compensation would lead to the conclusion that compensation would follow from an invocation of *force majeure* whenever there is material loss, since this defence (as Chapter 7 of this book corroborates) is an excuse. But this conclusion is unfair, he thinks, for in such a case both the invoking state and the injured state are equally innocent – both are, in a sense, victims of the supervening event which causes the material impossibility to perform the obligation.[89] Indeed, if the rationale of the duty of compensation is based on notion of fairness, then how to explain the apportionment of the duty to compensate on the state benefitting from the defence instead of simply letting the damage fall where it lies?

A potential retort to this objection relies on the notion of partial excuse.[90] As was said earlier, even though the conduct of excused states is wrongful it is possible that excuses provide complete exoneration or only partial exoneration from responsibility. And the determination of when an excuse is complete or partial *need not* (and indeed should not for such an approach would simply beg the question) depend on the existence of material loss for the injured state. But then, on what does the complete or partial degree of the excuse depend? This determination is no easy task – and it is indeed a matter that has troubled criminal law theorists for a long time. So one uncertainty (which defences entail a duty of compensation?) is replaced by another (when do excuses provide a complete defence and when a partial defence?). Admittedly, this is a more circumscribed uncertainty: at the very least, it applies in respect of a narrower group of defences.

Crawford's observation about *force majeure* is grounded upon the intuition that not all excuses are the same – and it seems that there are indeed good reasons to treat the various excuse defences differently when

---

[89] Crawford, *General Part*, 319.
[90] Some ILC members suggested that compensation should be applicable where the circumstances attenuated responsibility, e.g., Schwebel, 1614th meeting, ILC Yearbook 1980, vol. I, 163 [20]. Some states endorsed this view in the Sixth Committee, e.g., Spain: A/C.6/34/SR.44, [5].

it comes to assessing whether compensation may be due. As evidenced from the Commentary to the ARS, and as borne out by this book, there are significant differences between the various defences that can be classified as excuses. The ARS do not provide a classification of defences; but this study will argue that *force majeure* is an excuse,[91] that distress can be an excuse[92] and that state of necessity may be reformulated as an excuse (currently, it is formulated as a justification).[93] Theoretically, all these excuses can be explained by reference to free will rationales, in the sense that they afford exoneration because the invoking state acted in circumstances in which its capacity to choose its conduct was restricted or compelled by factors external to it. But although all of these defences excuse as a result of a restriction of the state's free will, in each case the degree of restriction of that will varies. The ARS Commentary expresses this difference by reference to the voluntary or involuntary nature of the conduct at issue. In the case of *force majeure*, the conduct in question is involuntary since the state has no choice but to fail to perform its obligation.[94] In state of necessity, the state's freedom to choose has been restricted to a binary choice: either to protect its essential interests *or* to comply with its international obligations. Crucially, as ARS Article 25 states, the breach of the international obligation must be the 'only way' to protect the essential interest.[95] Given this choice, the Commission notes that the conduct in these circumstances is 'not involuntary'.[96] In the case of distress, the state organ's freedom to choose is also reduced: he either saves life (his own or that of individuals entrusted to his care) or he complies with the state's obligations. But the choice is not binary: acting in a manner incompatible with the state's obligations must not be the *only way* to save life, but simply the only reasonable way to save life. This suggests that there may be other, albeit unreasonable, ways to protect life which would not require the breach of the state's obligations. Here too the ARS describe the conduct as 'not involuntary'.[97]

---

[91] See Chapter 7, Section 7.4.
[92] See Chapter 9, Section 9.4.
[93] See Chapter 8, Section 8.4.4.
[94] ARS Commentary art. 23, [1].
[95] As stated by Judge Anzilotti in the *Oscar Chinn* case: 'the plea of necessity ... by definition implies the impossibility of proceeding by any other method than the one contrary to law', see *Oscar Chinn* (1934) PCIJ Series A/B No 63, sep op Anzilotti, 114.
[96] ARS Commentary art. 25, [1].
[97] ARS Commentary art. 24, [1].

## 2.5 EFFECT ON COMPENSATION FOR MATERIAL LOSS

It would be possible to argue that involuntary conduct (*force majeure*) affords a complete defence and 'not involuntary' conduct (distress and potentially the excuse of necessity) affords only a partial defence. By implication, *force majeure* would not entail a duty of compensation whereas distress and the (potential) excuse of necessity would. But this conclusion may still be too strong and lacking in nuance, for there may be cases in which, for example, it would be unfair to impose a duty of compensation on a state acting in a situation of distress – even if its conduct is voluntary. Say that the captain of a public vessel of a developing country carrying refugees rescued at sea takes shelter from a storm in the military port of a developed state without the latter's consent. In entering the port, the captain, to avoid a big wave, takes a turn and collides with a wharf causing damage. Financially, the amount of the damage is insignificant for the coastal state but would be considerable for the flag state. Should the flag state be required to pay compensation for the material loss? It may be unfair to expect as much. Similarly, the possibility that compensation may arise following a successful invocation of distress may discourage a state organ from, for example, acting to protect the lives of those entrusted to his care – such as the refugees in the hypothetical just formulated – and this may be an undesirable outcome. It may be that the voluntariness of the conduct is not an adequate criterion, and that a different principle is necessary to determine the complete or partial degree of exoneration afforded by an excuse; at this point, however, no such principle could be discerned from the practice of states, the work of the ILC or the writings of international law scholars.

Given the objections noted, the most that can be said at this time is that excuses may allow the possibility of a duty of compensation for material loss, since the material loss was caused by a wrongful act and that, when they do so, excuses will only afford partial exoneration. The question of the degree of exoneration (complete or partial) is not one dependent only on the specific excuse at issue and its rationale (*force majeure*, state of necessity or distress), but potentially also on the specific circumstances in which it is invoked. Nevertheless, this is a question which requires further theoretical development and, most importantly, the recognition of states in their practice.

The absence of practical and theoretical development on this issue should not, in any event, suggest that at present the notion of excuses (and the classification of certain defences as excuses) will be an irrelevant consideration to the determination of whether compensation may be due. As proposed by the Commentary to the ARS, '[i]t will be for the

State invoking a circumstance precluding wrongfulness to agree with any affected States on the possibility and extent of compensation payable in a given case',[98] or perhaps a tribunal may be tasked with deciding the issue. In determining whether a duty of compensation arises, the parties in a negotiation or a tribunal in its decision may take into account factors such as the wrongfulness of the conduct in question or the voluntary or involuntary character of the act that caused the loss, two factors that are highlighted and supported by the characterisation of a given defence as an excuse.

### 2.5.2 Justifications and the Duty of Compensation

A much more complex question is whether justifications can generate a duty of compensation. If the question were considered solely from the standpoint of the justification/excuse distinction, then the conclusion would be that justifications do *not* entail a duty of compensation. Indeed, the conduct engaged in is lawful, the state had permission to act in the way it did, and therefore there is no legal basis for a duty to compensate material loss.

This conclusion is certainly in accordance with the practice (and possibly the general intuition) in relation to self-defence, countermeasures and consent. Indeed, in no judicial or arbitral dispute in which self-defence, countermeasures or consent have been invoked as a defence have the parties requested or even considered a potential duty of compensation. The exclusion of a duty of compensation in these instances may be said to follow from two legal maxims: *ex injuria jus non oritur*, excluding compensation in cases of self-defence and countermeasures (both of which are triggered by the prior wrongful act of the target state), and *volenti non fit injuria*, excluding compensation in the case of consent (since the consenting state may be said to have assumed the risk of the damage).[99] Equally, the theoretical explanations underlying these defences (rights forfeiture and absent interest), which will be explained in Chapters 4–6, can account in a principled manner for the exclusion of compensation. Pursuant to these theories, the state invoking the defence possesses a permission of the legal order to act in a manner incompatible with an obligation which ordinarily binds it to the target state. By the same token, the target state's rights are not impaired because it has

---

[98] ARS Commentary art. 27, [6].
[99] At least to the extent that the damage is foreseeable.

## 2.5 EFFECT ON COMPENSATION FOR MATERIAL LOSS

forfeited the protection that the law affords to its interests through its conduct (self-defence and countermeasures) or because it has voluntarily renounced that protection (consent).

More difficult is the question whether the plea of necessity gives rise to a duty of compensation. As will be argued in Chapter 8, state of necessity as currently formulated in ARS Article 25 constitutes a justification. This conclusion is supported by the majority of the existing state practice, although there are some dissenting voices who would rather see it as an excuse.[100] The justification of state of necessity is significantly different from the justifications of self-defence, countermeasures and consent. In the case of state of necessity, there is no prior action (wrongful or lawful as it may be) of the state against which the defence is invoked, namely of the state who is affected by the invocation of the defence. Unlike self-defence, countermeasures and consent, all of which are usually explained on the basis of deontic rationales,[101] state of necessity is a consequentialist defence: it affords justification because the action in question produces a net benefit since it protects an interest that is deemed to be superior in the circumstances; indeed, the defence is only available for the protection of an essential interest to the detriment of an interest which in the circumstances is deemed to be inferior. Since state of necessity affords a justification, then the state that acts in these circumstances has permission so to act. But, unlike the other justifications, the party affected by the necessitated act has not forfeited (either through conduct or expressly) the legal protection of its rights. Thus, an action in necessity, while lawful, will impair a right of the state against which it is invoked. Must the state invoking necessity be obliged to pay compensation to the state affected by its actions?

The dilemma is thus set: a state has a permission to act in necessity, but another state's rights are impaired by that action. It is for this reason that considerations about the existence of a duty of compensation have been most prominent precisely in respect of this plea.[102] The majority of scholars who have considered this issue seem to favour a duty of compensation.[103] In practice, the parties and the ICJ considered this possibility in *Gabčíkovo-Nagymaros*[104] and the issue has featured in investment

---

[100] On which see Section 8.4.4.
[101] Though they need not be, as will be seen in Chapters 4–6.
[102] See Section 8.4.3.
[103] See Reinisch and Binder, 'Debts and State of Necessity' in Boholavsky and Cernic (eds), *Making Sovereign Financing and Human Rights Work* (2014), 225 and references cited there.
[104] *Gabčíkovo-Nagymaros*, [48].

arbitration in the disputes arising out of Argentina's financial crisis of the early 2000s.[105] But the existing practice is inadequate and insufficient to evidence a customary rule in this regard, as will be shown in Chapter 8.[106] Similarly, it is unlikely that a duty to make compensation in cases of necessity may be a general principle of law. Domestic legal orders take widely different views on this question. For example, whereas Germany stipulates a duty to make compensation in these cases,[107] the laws of the United Kingdom and France do not make provision for such a duty.[108] Moreover, even in those orders in which compensation is due, the legal basis for such a duty remains a matter of contention. By way of example, one need only read doctrinal consideration of the *Vincent v Lake Erie* case, decided by the Supreme Court of Minnesota in 1910.[109] The steamship *Reynolds* was moored on the claimant's dock when a storm developed. The captain kept fast to the dock, while the wind and waves, continually hitting the ship, pushed it against the dock resulting in its damage. The owner of the dock sued the owners of the vessel for the damage. In a brief judgment, the Court decided that the *Reynolds* had been justified in not leaving the dock during the storm, but nevertheless awarded compensation to the owner of the dock.[110] Subsequent doctrinal commentary has discussed at length the potential legal basis for such a duty – given that the judgment failed to point to one – but none of the explanations or theories proposed to explain or reject the court's decision has received general assent.[111] Positive international law does not therefore currently recognise a duty to make compensation for material loss caused by conduct adopted in a situation of necessity, either as a matter of customary law or of general principles.

---

[105] On which see Ripinsky, 'State of Necessity: Effect on Compensation' (2007) 4(6) TDM.
[106] Section 8.4.3.
[107] On which see Bücheler, *Proportionality in Investor-State Arbitration* (2015), ch. 8.
[108] On which see Christie, 'The Unwarranted Conclusions Drawn from *Vincent v Lake Erie Transportation Co* Concerning the Defence of Necessity' (2005) 5 *Issues in Legal Scholarship* 7, at 7–9 (esp. fn. 72–3).
[109] *Vincent v Lake Erie Transportation Co* (1910) 109 Minn 456.
[110] Ibid., 460 (per O'Brien J.; Lewis J. and Jaggard J. dissenting, at 460–1).
[111] See, e.g., the symposium on this case in (2005) 5(2) *Issues in Legal Scholarship*, available at www.degruyter.com/view/j/ils.2005.5.issue-2/issue-files/ils.2005.5.issue-2.xml. Further references can be found in the various contributions to the symposium. A comprehensive and illustrative overview of the various legal and moral arguments on the point can be found in Sugarman, 'The "Necessity" Defense and the Failure of Tort Theory: The Case against Strict Liability for Damages Caused while Exercising Self-Help in an Emergency' (2005) *Issues in Legal Scholarship*, Article 1.

## 2.5 EFFECT ON COMPENSATION FOR MATERIAL LOSS 89

A separate question is whether positive law *should* recognise such a duty in cases of necessity and, if so, what could be its legal basis. The first thing to note in this regard is that there is no inconsistency between the exercise of a right and an obligation to make compensation for that exercise. That is, compensation is not inherently linked to, nor is it proof of, wrongfulness.[112] Indeed, legal orders often recognise forms of strict liability and international law is no exception. Thus, expropriation for public purposes is permitted under international law and it requires compensation. Similarly, a state's warship can interfere with a foreign merchant ship on the high seas when there is reasonable suspicion that, among others, that ship is engaged in piracy or the slave trade; but if the suspicions turn out to be unjustified, the flag state of the warship must pay compensation for any loss caused by the interference.[113] The ILC's Principles on the Allocation of Loss in the Case of Transboundary Harm Arising Out of Hazardous Activities are another example.[114] These regimes are usually exceptional and tend to respond to specific aims and policies; for instance, in respect of the ILC Principles the imposition of compensation results from transboundary risk creation by ultra-hazardous activities.[115] Is there a specific aim or policy that might support a duty of compensation in situations of necessity? Scholars have relied on broad notions of fairness to justify this duty.[116] The argument is, in short, that it would be unfair for an innocent party to bear the burden of the loss in the circumstances. The ARS propose a similar rationale. According to the Commentary, the duty of compensation is intended to discourage states from shifting

---

[112] Sugarman, '"Necessity" Defense', 88.
[113] Art. 110, United Nations Convention on the Law of the Sea (adopted 10 December 1982, entered into force 16 November 1994), (1982) 1833 UNTS 397.
[114] Principles on the Allocation of Loss in the Case of Transboundary Harm Arising out of Hazardous Activities, ILC Yearbook 2006, vol. II(2), 56ff. The Principles were noted by the General Assembly in Res 61/36 (18 December 2006). For a commentary (and further references), see Boyle, 'Liability for Injurious Consequences of Acts Not Prohibited by International Law' in Crawford et al. (eds), *The Law of International Responsibility* (2010), 95.
[115] Commentaries to the Principles on Allocation of Loss, Principle 1, [2].
[116] Grounding the duty on notions of fairness see Ripinsky, 'State of Necessity: Effect on Compensation', 14; Viñuales, *Foreign Investment and the Environment in International Law* (2012), 390. Arguing against the duty, also on the basis of a fairness argument, see *BG Group v Argentina*, UNCITRAL Award, 24 December 2007, at [398]: 'it would make no sense to accept that the State acted in a state of necessity, protecting its essential interests, and to demand reparation, thus risking the very essential interests that the State intended to protect'.

'the burden of defending [their] own interests on to another state'[117] – a rationale which seems particularly apt in relation to the plea of necessity.

The situation was best summarised by Michael Akehurst, for whom 'whether compensation is payable *de lege lata* is open to doubt. *De lege ferenda*, however, acts of necessity ought always to be accompanied by compensation.'[118] If so, then what could be its legal basis? Given that justified conduct is lawful, the duty cannot be grounded – as in the case of excuses – on the illegality of the conduct. But there exist other legal doctrines which could provide a legal basis to this duty. The duty could, for example, be anchored to the right of the affected state. As mentioned earlier and as will be explored in more detail in Chapter 8,[119] state of necessity is formulated as a choice of evils in which the invoking state's interest is made to prevail over the affected state's right. But the affected state's right is not, unlike in the case of the other justifications, forfeited or renounced: that state retains the legal protection afforded to its interest by the legal order. So while the invoking state is acting in a lawful manner, it is still impairing the rights of another state. Indeed, this other state retains its right that the invoking state *not* act in a way detrimental to its rights. To capture this, moral philosophers have drawn a distinction between the violation and the infringement of rights, where the violation of a right is the combination of infringement plus wrongfulness.[120] The state invoking state of necessity does not violate the right of the affected state, but it nevertheless infringes it. And it is for this reason that compensation is due. Indeed, according to some scholars, in the absence of compensation the infringement of the right becomes a violation thereof.[121] Alternatively, compensation may be

[117] ARS Commentary art. 27, [5]. See also Crawford, *General Part*, 318.
[118] Akehurst, 'International Liability for Injurious Consequences Arising Out of Acts Not Prohibited by International Law' (1985) 16 NYIL 3, 12.
[119] See Section 8.4.
[120] See, especially, Feinberg, 'Voluntary Euthanasia and the Inalienable Right to Life (Tanner Lecture)' (1978) 7 *Philosophy and Public Affairs* 93; Thomson, 'Rights and Compensation' (1980) 14 *Noûs* 3. For further developments (and critiques) on this view, see Montague, 'Rights and Duties of Compensation' (1984) 13 *Philosophy & Public Affairs* 79; Davis, 'Rights, Permission, and Compensation' (1985) 14 *Philosophy & Public Affairs* 374; Westen, 'Comment on Montague's "Rights and Duties of Compensation"' (1985) 14 *Philosophy & Public Affairs* 385; Montague, 'Davis and Westen on Rights and Compensation' (1985) 14 *Philosophy & Public Affairs* 390; Coleman, *Risks and Wrongs* (2002), 299ff; Oberdiek, 'Lost in Moral Space: On the Infringing/Violating Distinction and Its Place in the Theory of Rights' (2004) 23 *Law & Philosophy* 325; Wigley, 'Disappearing Without a Moral Trace? Rights and Compensation during Times of Emergency' (2009) 28 *Law & Philosophy* 617.
[121] See, e.g., Coleman, *Risks and Wrongs*, 300–1; Feinberg, 'Voluntary Euthanasia', 102. A similar version of this position was maintained by the tribunal in *EDF v Argentina*,

## 2.5 EFFECT ON COMPENSATION FOR MATERIAL LOSS

grounded on the doctrine of unjust enrichment.[122] In situations of necessity, the state invoking the defence obtains a benefit to the detriment of the affected state, in the form of the protection of its own interests. But the affected state is not obliged to bear the burden of the protection of the invoking state's interests. The benefit derived by the invoking state from its behaviour, while lawfully obtained (it was obtained in the exercise of a permission granted by the justification of necessity), is not just and, for this reason, may require compensation. As explained by Akehurst, '[a] State which commits an act of necessity expropriates the right of another State in order to safeguard its own essential interest. Such expropriation constitutes unjust enrichment unless it is accompanied by compensation'.[123] Note that the choice of either of these approaches may affect the estimation of the amount of compensation due. In the former approach, the quantum of compensation is assessed from the standpoint of the affected state – that is, it refers to the extent of the infringement of the affected state's right.[124] In the latter approach, instead, the quantum is assessed from the standpoint of the invoking state and it refers to the extent of the benefit that this state has derived from its conduct.

Lastly, compensation for situations of necessity could be ensured by recasting state of necessity as an excuse, a possibility discussed in Chapter 8.[125] This reformulation is in keeping with the policy aim of restricting the invocation of necessity as much as possible, given the risk that this defence may

---

who asserted that 'the invoking State is required to 'return to the pre-necessity status quo when possible, or compensate Claimants for damage suffered as a result of the relevant measures'. That is, state of necessity will only be lawful if compensation is paid. See: *EDF International SA, SAUR International SA and Leon Participaciones Argentinas SA v Argentine Republic*, ICSID Case ARB/03/23, Award, 11 June 2012, [1171], [1177]. Argentina instituted annulment proceedings against the award partly on the basis that the Tribunal had 'invented' this requirement of the plea of necessity. The Annulment Committee rejected this ground because the Tribunal's reasoning on this point reflected 'what is inherent in the very concept of necessity'. See: *EDF International SA, SAUR International SA and Leon Participaciones Argentinas SA v Argentine Republic*, ICSID Case ARB/03/23, Annulment, 5 February 2016, [291] and [325] for Argentina's claim and [330] for the Committee's decision.

[122] On unjust enrichment in international law see Binder and Schreuer, 'Unjust Enrichment' (2013) MPEPIL. In domestic law, this argument has been made by Gordley, 'Damages Under the Necessity Doctrine' (2005) 5 *Issues in Legal Scholarship*, Article 2.

[123] Akehurst, 'International Liability', 12–13.

[124] In this sense, it would appear to be more in keeping with the approach to compensation taken by the ILC in art. 27(b), since the provision and the Commentary refer to the 'material loss' suffered by the affected state rather than the extent of the benefit derived by the invoking state.

[125] See Section 8.4.4.

be abused.[126] Indeed, this policy aim is difficult to attain if the defence is formulated as a consequentialist-based justification; after all, why would the law discourage the safeguarding of superior interests threatened by grave and imminent perils at the cost of inferior interests? To advance what will be said in Chapter 8,[127] if reformulated as an excuse, the focus of the plea would not be on the net benefit gained by the conduct adopted in the situation of necessity, but rather on the pressures suffered by the state which forced it to act in a manner incompatible with its obligations. If considered as an excuse, as noted earlier, compensation would be grounded on the wrongfulness of the conduct in question. (Of course the difficulty of identifying and theorising when excuses, including the plea of necessity, operate to provide only partial exoneration would remain.)

As this overview shows, the question remains open: some justifications seem not to attract a duty of compensation, others potentially may. At present it can only be said that there is no one-size-fits-all answer. For the time being, the optimal solution will still be that proposed by the ARS: a negotiated solution between the parties or, it may be added, a decision by an international tribunal where this is possible. In weighing the equities of the case, the parties may consider factors such as the legality of the conduct in question, the character of the interest protected (is it collective or individual?) and the interest impaired, and whether it is desirable to encourage (other) states to act in a similar way or whether they should be discouraged from so doing – all factors that, as with excuses above, are brought to the fore and highlighted by the classification of the defence as a justification (rather than an excuse).

### 2.5.3   Third Parties and the Duty of Compensation

A different and separate question is whether third parties are entitled to compensation when their rights are affected by the conduct of a state which benefits from a defence. In an increasingly interdependent world it is plausible that conduct in relation to which a state invokes a defence may affect third parties. It was precisely for this reason that the ILC opted to enlarge the scope of Article 27(b), which had been initially limited to some defences only.[128] It is possible to envisage a scenario where conduct in relation to which a state has a defence has an impact on third parties. Think, for

---

[126] On which see Chapter 8.
[127] See Section 8.4.4.
[128] ILC Report, fifty-first session, ILC Yearbook 1999, vol. II(2), 85 [407]. See, e.g., Economides, 2591st meeting, ILC Yearbook 1999, vol. I, 174 [47]; Pellet, 2591st meeting,

## 2.5 EFFECT ON COMPENSATION FOR MATERIAL LOSS

example, of the case where State A acting in self-defence targets a legitimate military objective of State B and causes collateral damage to property owned by State C. Or the situation where State A freezes assets of the responsible State B as a countermeasure and, as a result of this action, State B lacks the funds to pay a debt it owes to a third State C. Or even, where an earthquake destroys an iron mine in State A and that State is therefore unable to hand over, as it is conventionally obliged to do, the iron to State B. This impossibility, in turn, affects the delivery by State B of steel construction materials it is conventionally obliged to hand over to a third State C. Are these third states entitled to compensation from State A in the circumstances?

As already advanced, the answer to this question cannot be found in the distinction between justification and excuse. Whether in the circumstances the conduct is justified or the state is excused is an assessment which affects exclusively the bilateral relations between the state invoking the defence and the state against which the defence is invoked, namely the relations between State A and State B in the examples above. Thus, between the state acting in self-defence and the aggressor, between the state taking countermeasures and the responsible state, or between the state who suffers the impossibility to perform and its treaty-party. Any analysis of possible compensation owed to State C will require consideration of State C's relations with both States A and B. But these two sets of relations are separate and distinct from those existing between State A and State B, which are the only ones affected by the justification or excuse that State A invokes. There is very little development on this point in international case-law and literature so far, so not much can be said with any certainty. The matter exceeds the scope of this study, so no more will be said about it. At any rate, the inability of justification and excuse to address the question of compensation towards third parties should not detract from the relevance that this distinction may have in the relations between the state invoking the defence and the state against which the defence is invoked (so A–B relations in the examples above).

### 2.5.4 Conclusion on the Duty of Compensation

To summarise what has been said so far, in the bilateral relations between the state invoking the defence and the claimant state, whether a duty of compensation exists is a matter not currently resolved by positive

---

ILC Yearbook 1999, vol. I, 175 [55]. Japan endorsed this expansion, though suggested that cases in which ARS art. 27(b) was not applicable should be identified in the Commentary, see A/CN.4/515, 56–7.

international law. The distinction between justification and excuse cannot provide a complete answer to the many difficulties posed by this duty. The best solution, for the time being, remains that suggested by the ILC in the Commentary to the ARS: the question should be decided, through negotiations, by the parties. It may be added that, where available, the decision could be made by an international tribunal. In the absence of any positive law, such a determination will be made on an equitable basis and a number of factors can be relevant in weighing the equities of the case. These may include whether the conduct in question is lawful or unlawful, whether the claimant state is entitled to the legal protection of its rights, whether that state has itself triggered (either by its wrongful act or by its consent) the situation, whether the conduct was voluntary or involuntary; all of which are factors that are highlighted and, therefore, implicate the distinction between justification and excuse. As can be seen, while unable to definitively resolve the question of when compensation for material loss is due, the distinction is nevertheless relevant to its consideration.

This matter will be reprised in some of the chapters to follow, but it will not be addressed in a discrete manner in each one. It will be addressed only where it has been specifically raised (as in the case of state of necessity) or where it is relevant to the analysis and evaluation of a specific defence (for example, in explaining the difference between two theoretical approaches to the same defence as in the case of self-defence and countermeasures).

## 2.6 Normative Considerations

Finally, the distinction between justification and excuse may produce normative consequences beyond the individual case. In considering this question, domestic legal theorists have advanced that justifications have a universalist tendency insofar as a finding of justification by a court is said to produce normative consequences beyond the particular case: every other subject of the law, in the same circumstances, ought to be able to successfully invoke the justification in question. Excuses, instead, do not produce such consequences beyond the particular case. This normative function of justification and excuse is said to reinforce the law and clarify the 'message of the … law' by distinguishing conduct which is permissible and conduct that the law prohibits.[129]

---

[129] Mousourakis, 'Justification and Excuse' (1998–9) 7 *Tilburg Foreign LR*, 44. Similarly, Sangero, *Self-Defence in Criminal Law* (2006), 15; Dressler, 'Justifications and Excuses: A

## 2.6 NORMATIVE CONSIDERATIONS

In international law, this argument was made by Lowe in his article 'A Plea for Excuses'. For Lowe there is 'a real question whether exculpation may weaken the pull to compliance exercised by a rule to a greater extent than excuse would'.[130] Rules of law are intended to influence behaviour, and 'different formulations of a rule may have different degrees of success in securing compliance' with that rule.[131] If state of necessity were a justification, then all states would know that acts of necessity are lawful, regardless of the obligations they might affect. Or, what is the same, they would know that all of their obligations are applicable only insofar as the circumstances are normal, or unexceptional. Given this effect, as a matter of policy, for Lowe all the defences in the ARS should have been characterised as excuses which 'might in practice strengthen the normative pull of rules'.[132]

The effect of justifications on the normative pull of the relevant obligations can be observed in relation to Argentina's invocation of the plea of necessity in investment disputes arising out of its crisis of the early 2000s.[133] The parties and the tribunals, notwithstanding the occasional

---

Brief Review of the Concepts and the Literature' (1986–7) 33 *Wayne LR*, 1169; Horowitz, 'Justification and Excuse in the Program of the Criminal Law' (1986) 49 *Law & Contemp Probs*, 116.

[130] Lowe, 'Plea', 410. Note that he uses the term 'exculpation' here to refer to justification.
[131] Ibid., 409.
[132] Ibid., abstract.
[133] A significant amount of literature exists on these disputes. See, e.g., Bjorklund, 'Emergency Exceptions: State of Necessity and *Force Majeure*' in Muchlinski and Ortino (eds), *Oxford Handbook of International Investment Law* (2007), 459; Fouret, '"*CMS c/ LG&E*" ou l'état de nécessité en question' (2007) 2 *Rev de l'Arbitrage* 249; Kentin, 'Economic Crisis and Investment Arbitration: The Argentine Cases' in Kahn and Wälde (eds), *New Aspects of International Investment Law* (2007), 629; Reinisch, 'Necessity in International Investment Arbitration – An Unnecessary Split of Opinions in Recent ICSID Cases?' (2007) 8 JWIT 191; Samra, 'Five Years Later: The CMS Award Placed in the Context of the Argentine Financial Crisis and the ICSID Arbitration Boom' (2007) 38 *U Miami Inter-American LR* 667; Alvarez-Jiménez, 'New Approaches to the State of Necessity in Customary International Law: Insights from WTO Law and Foreign Investment Law' (2008) 19 *Am Rev Int'l Arb* 463; Valenti, 'Lo stato di necessità nei procedimenti arbitrali ICSID contro l'Argentina' (2008) 91 *Rivista di diritto internazionale* 114; Binder, 'Changed Circumstances in International Investment Law: Interfaces between the Law of Treaties and the Law of State Responsibility with a Special Focus on the Argentine Crisis' in Binder et al. (eds), *International Investment Law in the 21st Century: Essays in Honour of Christoph Schreuer* (2009), 608; Gazzini, 'Foreign Investment and Measures Adopted on Grounds of Necessity: Toward a Common Understanding' (2010) 7(1) TDM; Kasenetz, 'Desperate Times Call for Desperate Measures' (2010) 41 *Geo Wash LR* 709; Reinisch, 'Necessity in Investment Arbitration' (2010) 41 NYIL 137; Martin, 'Investment Disputes after Argentina's Economic Crisis: Interpreting BIT Non-precluded Measures

use of 'excuse' language, approached the defence of necessity as a justification for Argentina's conduct.[134] The awards in these disputes evidence that tribunals were often concerned about the possible impact of their decision regarding the plea on the standards of investment protection worldwide. Upholding the plea was seen as a stamp of approval of Argentina's conduct, permitting or encouraging similar conduct by other crisis-stricken states. This preoccupation was not misplaced. After the *LG&E* decision, the first to uphold Argentina's state of necessity plea, a comment highlighted the decision's significance for acknowledging 'the sovereign right of a (developing) State to take action in times of necessity to manage its economy and socio-political environment, even if such action breached certain obligations previously agreed by the State'.[135] The tribunal's upholding of the defence in an individual case was transformed into a general right of states. At the same time David Foster asked whether this decision had opened the door to abuse:

> An investment treaty is, after all, intended to afford to a foreign investor the minimum level of protection he is entitled to expect under international law. If these protections are suspended in times of economic hardship, which is when most acts of expropriation or unfair/inequitable treatment tend to occur, this will inevitably render such treaties less effective.[136]

Later awards restated Foster's concern. The *Suez (I)* Tribunal, for instance, maintained that:

> The severity of a crisis, no matter the degree, is not sufficient to allow a plea of necessity to relieve a state of its treaty obligations ... The reason of course is that given the frequency of crises and emergencies that nations, large and small, face from time to time, to allow them to escape their treaty obligations would threaten the very fabric of international law and indeed the stability of the system of international relations.[137]

---

and the Doctrine of Necessity under Customary International Law' (2012) 29 *J Int'l Arb* 49; Subramanian, 'Too Similar or Too Different: State of Necessity as a Defence under Customary International Law and the Bilateral Investment Treaty and Their Relationship' (2012) 9 *Manchester J Int'l Economic L* 68.

[134] See, e.g., *LG&E*, referring to 'excuse from liability' at [201], and 'exclusion of wrongfulness' at [249]; *Total SA v Argentine Republic*, ICSID Case ARB/04/1, Liability, 27 December 2010, referring to 'excuse [for] an otherwise wrongful act' and to 'necessity as a justification for non-compliance', both at [221].

[135] Falkof, '"State of Necessity" Defence Accepted in *LG&E v Argentina* ICSID Tribunal' (2006) 3(5) TDM, sec. E (text accompanying fn. 52).

[136] Foster, 'Necessity Knows No Law! *LG&E v Argentina*' (2006) 9 *Int'l Arb LR* 149, 155.

[137] *Suez Sociedad General de Aguas de Barcelona SA and InterAgua Servicios Integrales del Agua SA v Argentine Republic [Suez (I)]*, ICSID Case ARB/03/17, Liability, 30 July

## 2.7 Interim Conclusion: A Distinction with a Difference 97

Given these concerns, it may be wondered whether tribunals would have approached the argument with less scepticism had Argentina pleaded state of necessity as an excuse. Some tribunals, while denying the plea and thus showing a reluctance to endorse a justification of necessity, were indeed willing to consider that the situation of necessity could be taken into account in determining the quantum of damages.[138] As suggested by Lowe, such an approach would not diminish in any way the normative pull of the rule: the breach is upheld, and along with it, so is the obligation. Counterfactual reasoning is, of course, fraught, but on the evidence of these awards it seems that – at least in respect of concerns about the normative implications of upholding the defence – tribunals may have been less sceptical about the defence.

### 2.7 Interim Conclusion: A Distinction with a Difference

The foregoing sections have shown that the distinction has potentially important practical implications in a variety of areas, including the responsibility accessories, responses to breaches of the law, the enigma of the duty of compensation for material loss and wider normative effects of the invocation of any given defence. While on the basis of the state practice available, it is difficult to assert that the distinction is currently recognised as a matter of positive law, it nevertheless seems that there are important reasons why recognising the distinction is desirable.

If the distinction is desirable, the next question is how to determine which of the recognised defences belong to which category. In short, how to classify the defences into justifications and excuses? The next chapter will endeavour to answer this question.

---

2010, [236]. See also *Suez Sociedad General de Aguas de Barcelona SA and Vivendi Universal SA v Argentine Republic [Suez (II)]*, ICSID Case ARB/03/19, Liability, 30 July 2010, [258].

[138] See, e.g., *National Grid Plc v Argentine Republic*, UNCITRAL Award, 3 November 2008, [274].

# 3

# Classifying Defences into Justification and Excuse in International Law

## 3.1 Introduction

The previous two chapters showed that the distinction is both possible and desirable in international law. The next step is, therefore, that of providing a taxonomy of the recognised defences which distinguishes between justifications and excuses. No clear taxonomy emerges from either the views of states, or the opinions of tribunals and scholars. As noted in Chapter 1, moreover, the ILC opted not to provide a classification in the ARS themselves.

Providing a classification of the defences is, to be sure, no simple task. The defences recognised in any legal order are not inherently justifications or excuses. Intuitively, some appear to be obvious candidates for one or the other. For example, in domestic law self-defence is usually classified as a justification. In international law, the same can be said of countermeasures. For other defences, the intuitions are not as strong. This is typically the case of the plea of necessity. Aside from these intuitions, however, any defence can be formulated to reflect a justification or an excuse. This is especially clear in the case of the plea of necessity: in some legal systems it is a justification, in some it is an excuse, in some still it can be both.[1] But it could also be true of any of the other defences. Take self-defence. This is a defence that is frequently characterised as a justification: a victim is entitled to use force against an aggressor. The victim, therefore, has the permission of the legal order to engage in such conduct (as will be seen in Chapter 5, this permission takes the form of a Hohfeldian privilege or

---

[1] See, e.g., Germany, which recognises a justification and an excuse of necessity in its Criminal Code, at secs 34 and 35 respectively. For the text of these provisions, see Bernsmann, 'Private Self-Defence and Necessity in German Penal Law and in the Penal Law Proposal – Some Remarks' (1996) 30 *Israel LR* 171, at 180 and 184, respectively. Bohlander refers to excusing necessity in sec. 35 as 'duress' in his English translation of the German Criminal Code: Bohlander, *The German Criminal Code: A Modern English Translation* (2008), 44–5. For an overview, see Heathcote, 'State of Necessity and International Law', unpublished thesis, Graduate Institute of International and Development Studies, 2005, chaps 10 and 11.

liberty).² But a decision could be made in the legal order that the prohibition of force embodies collective values and interests that are superior to all others, be they collective or individual. In an effort to discourage unilateral resorts to force (to uphold these superior values), self-defence could be formulated as an excuse. Indeed, although it cannot be expected of a victim to tolerate the aggression, it would be preferable if the victim resorted to multilateral rather than unilateral means, and this preference can be expressed by retaining the illegal character of defensive force and excluding the consequences of the wrongful act for the victim.³

How, then, to determine whether a defence constitutes a justification or an excuse? The answer is not straightforward. In domestic legal orders a combination of approaches is used in this regard, as will be seen later. In most cases, however, this determination involves consideration of a number of elements, including the formulation and rationale of each individual defence, the concepts of justification and excuse, and theories of justification and excuse. In addition, policy considerations may also be relevant. For example, if the same defence can be formulated as both a justification and an excuse, it will be necessary to inquire into the potential normative and policy implications of that characterisation. A hypothetical example was given above in relation to self-defence. A good illustration from practice is given by the *Perka v Queen* case in the Supreme Court of Canada. The case concerned the offloading of a cargo of drugs on Canadian soil by a ship which had entered Canadian waters following mechanical issues and deteriorating weather conditions. The captain of the ship invoked the plea of necessity as a defence to a charge of drug trafficking. The Court had to decide whether the plea of necessity was a justification or an excuse. It thus considered two formulations of the plea, as justification and as excuse, examined their rationales, and then decided between the two on policy grounds. For the Court excusing necessity arose from a situation of moral involuntariness, where external circumstances essentially coerced the individual to act in a manner incompatible with the law, and justifying necessity involved conflicting duties requiring the defendant to choose which of the two duties to comply with, on the basis of a utilitarian (lesser evils) calculus. According to Dickson J, speaking for the majority, justifying necessity would import

---

² Hohfeld, 'Some Fundamental Legal Conceptions as Applied in Judicial Reasoning' (1913) 23 *Yale LJ* 16.
³ On self-defence as a justification or an excuse, see Fletcher and Ohlin, *Defending Humanity: When Is Force Justified and Why* (2013), 57–60.

'undue subjectivity to the criminal law' as it would 'invite the courts to second-guess the legislature and to assess the relative merits of social policies underlying criminal prohibitions' every time they had to consider a plea of necessity.[4] But this was not a 'role which fits well with the judicial function.'[5] Excusing necessity, in contrast, was more acceptable for it rested on a 'realistic assessment of human weakness, recognizing that a liberal and humane criminal law cannot hold people to the strict obedience of laws in emergency situations where normal human instincts, whether of self-preservation or of altruism, overwhelmingly impel disobedience.' This approach preserved the 'objectivity of the criminal law.'[6] It was the preferable approach, according to the Court, since it was compatible with the '[Canadian] traditional legal, moral and philosophic views as to what sorts of acts and what sorts of actors ought to be punished.'[7]

Providing a taxonomy of defences in international law is especially difficult given that there are significant disagreements – and also some degree of confusion – on the definitions and theories of justification and excuse. Moreover, it is not always clear what the rationale of each of the recognised defences is. The classification of each of the defences included in the ARS is the subject of Part II (Chapters 4–9) of this book. This chapter will provide the groundwork for that analysis. Over the next three sections, this chapter will explore and develop for the international legal order the concept and theory of justification, the concept and theory of excuse, and then conclude by considering the different approaches for the classification of defences identified in domestic law and by proposing an approach for the classification of defences in international law.

## 3.2 Concept and Theory of Justification

The case-law and literature on 'circumstances precluding wrongfulness' or justifications is confusing, to say the least. Indeed, the language used to describe, explain and apply this concept in international law is considerably inconsistent and equivocal. For example, justified conduct is oftentimes described as 'lawful' and other times as 'non wrongful' or as 'unlawful with precluded wrongfulness'. Likewise, justifications are sometimes said to involve a breach of an international obligation, and other

---

[4] *Perka v The Queen* (1984) 2 SCR 232, 248.
[5] Id.
[6] Id.
[7] Ibid., 250.

times to merely be incompatible with that obligation. These may seem like banal linguistic differences. And yet, they have potentially important implications. Thus, if countermeasures are not available against lawful conduct, as said in Chapter 2, can they be taken against 'non-wrongful' conduct; or can a treaty be terminated on the ground of a material breach where that breach is 'non-wrongful' or 'unlawful with precluded wrongfulness'? Likewise, if accessorial responsibility derives from the wrongfulness of the principal's conduct, what is to be made of their potential responsibility where the principal's conduct is 'non-wrongful' or 'unlawful with precluded wrongfulness'? More generally, the certainty and stability of legal relations may be affected by the use of inconsistent and imprecise language. What does it mean to say that justified conduct is non-wrongful, is it the same as saying that it is lawful or is it different? And if so, what are the practical consequences of this difference? This section will focus on the concept and theory of justification in international law, with a view to providing a clear definition of this concept, a coherent explanation of its operation, and an analysis of certain of its more important characteristics.

### 3.2.1  Concept of Justification

How are justifications conceptualised in international law? State practice, case-law and the work of the ILC all suggest that justifications are defences which exclude the wrongfulness of an act. However, this simplistic definition leaves unaddressed and unresolved a number of important questions concerning justifications, some of which were highlighted in Chapter 1 while reviewing the domestic law developments on this notion. It should be no wonder, then, that as the following analysis will show, the very language used to describe and explain this notion and its operation by states, international tribunals, and scholars, is so inconsistent and equivocal.

The analysis of the concept of justification in international law will be undertaken here in five steps. First, this section will provide a definition of justification in international law. Second, it will clarify that justifications constitute permissions of the legal order to engage in certain conduct. Third, it will explain the relation between the concepts of justification, breach and non-performance of obligations. Fourth, this section will clarify that justified conduct is *lawful* and not, as some have stated, 'non-wrongful' or 'unlawful with precluded wrongfulness'. Fifth, it will consider whether justifications in international law may be invoked when the circumstances triggering them actually exist or whether it is enough for the invoking state to reasonably believe that they exist; in short, whether international law adopts a 'deeds' or 'reasons' conception of justification. While some of these issues will clarify the concept of justification, others will allow us to begin delineating the *conception* of justifications recognised in (or at the very least, best suited to) international law.

### 3.2.1.1   Defining Justifications

Summarising the consensus in criminal law theory and practice, Husak defined justifications as: 'defenses that arise from properties or characteristics of acts ... A defendant is justified when his *conduct* is not legally wrongful, even though it apparently violates a criminal law'.[8] This definition is not dissimilar from the ILC's understanding of 'circumstances precluding wrongfulness' as circumstances in which an act, which would otherwise be a breach of an obligation of the state, is exceptionally not an 'internationally wrongful act'.[9] A justification, then, can be defined as a defence that relates to properties or characteristics of the conduct of a state which render that conduct lawful even though it is apparently in breach of an international obligation of that state.

### 3.2.1.2   Justifications as Permissions

What deontic modality do justifications take? This question is rarely considered in international law, and yet it is crucial for a proper understanding of the function and operation of justifications in the legal order. Domestic legal theorists agree that justifications constitute permissions of the legal order to do or not to do something that is prohibited or required by another norm of that legal order.[10] But not all justifications constitute the same type of permission. Indeed, a distinction can be drawn between justifications that can be analysed in terms of rights and justifications that cannot be so reduced. The latter are sometimes referred to as 'real' justifications;[11]

---

[8] Husak, 'Justifications and the Criminal Liability of Accessories' (1989–90) 80 *J Crim L & Criminology*, 496 (emphasis in original, footnotes omitted).
[9] As had been explained by Ago, and subsequently endorsed by the ILC: Ago, Eighth Report, 28–30; ILC Report, thirty-first session, 106–7 [2]. The current Commentary is not explicit on this point, arguably because of the possibility that some of the 'circumstances precluding wrongfulness' included in the ARS might actually operate as excuses.
[10] Berman, 'Justification and Excuse, Law and Morality' (2003) 53 *Duke LJ* 1, 29.
[11] Contrast, e.g., Thorburn, 'Justifications, Powers and Authority' (2008) 117 *Yale LJ* 1070; Gur-Aye, 'Justifying the Distinction between Justifications and Power (Justification vs Power)' (2011) 5 *Criminal Law & Philosophy* 293. The expression 'real justification' is taken from Gur-Aye's paper.

however, this terminology is perhaps misleading in that it creates the impression that there are real and 'fake' justifications, so it will not be used here. All these rules amount to justifications – but their internal logical structure differs. Hohfeld's scheme of legal relations is fundamental to understand this difference and, since this scheme will also be employed in the analysis of the defences in Part II, this is a good point at which to introduce it.

The US legal philosopher Wesley Newcomb Hohfeld, writing in 1913, argued that the term 'right' in legal discourse was used to mean different types of legal situations, and identified a number of 'jural conceptions' which described these different types of legal situations. These conceptions were, in his view, fundamental in that they could not be reduced to any more primitive notions. Of relevance, here, are what are known as the first-order fundamental conceptions: claim-rights,[12] privileges,[13] duties and no-rights. He did not define these jural conceptions, other than by reference to the logical relations existing between them. Hohfeld identified two different types of legal relations between these conceptions: jural correlation and jural opposition. As explained by David Rodin, '[j]ural correlates are logical equivalents with different subjects. Jural opposites are logical contradictories with the same subject.'[14] Correlation exists, for example, between claim-right and duty. A claim-right refers to the position of a subject of the law X who can claim that another subject Y do (or not do) a certain thing. In this relation, Y's duty to do (or not to do) a certain thing is the correlative to X's claim-right that Y do or not do that very thing. Likewise, a privilege or liberty is the entitlement of X to do or not to do a certain thing. Its correlative is a position which Hohfeld describes as one of no-rights: that is, Y (the other subject in the jural relation) does not have a right that X do or not do that very thing. In a sense, correlatives describe the same position viewed from different angles. Thus, the sentences 'X has a claim-right that Y do a certain thing' or 'Y has a duty to X to do a certain thing' have the same meaning. The other jural relation identified by Hohfeld is that of jural opposition. This relation describes

---

[12] Hohfeld called these 'rights', as distinct from privileges. However, the term claim-right, as employed by J. L. Mackie, will be used here to describe this typology of legal relation, see *Ethics: Inventing Right and Wrong* (1977), 173–4.

[13] Contemporary scholarship often uses the term 'liberty' to refer to Hohfeld's 'privilege'. For an exploration of Hohfeldian privileges as liberties see: Williams, 'The Concept of Legal Liberty' (1956) 56 *Col LR* 1129. In this work, both terms privilege and liberty will be used in this regard.

[14] Rodin, *War and Self-Defense* (Oxford: Clarendon Press, 2002), 18.

the position of a subject by means of its contradictory. To illustrate, X has a claim-right that Y do a certain thing. The jural opposite of this situation (viewed from X's angle) is that of no-right: under this position, X would have a no-right that Y do that very thing. The opposite of a privilege or liberty is what Hohfeld calls a position of no-duty. If X has a privilege or liberty to do a certain thing, in the opposite position it would have a no-duty not to do that very thing.[15]

As will be seen, self-defence and countermeasures, although traditionally referred to as 'rights' in international law, may be analysed in the Hohfeldian scheme as privileges or liberty rights. So, State A has a privilege to engage in self-defence (or take countermeasures) against State B. Given this characterisation, these justifications are capable of explanation by means of deontic theories of justification. And indeed, as will be argued in Chapters 5 and 6, respectively, it is a deontic theory, that of rights forfeiture, which possesses the most persuasive explanatory power of the justifying effect of these defences.[16] Under this theory, through its (wrongful) conduct, State B forfeits the protection of its claim-rights vis-à-vis State A and thereby places itself in a position of no-rights, the correlative jural position to State A's liberty. Moreover, since State B loses the protection of its claim-rights vis-à-vis State A, the latter State finds itself in a situation of no-duty towards B: it not only has a liberty to act as it does, but also has no duty to respect the (forfeited) claim-rights of State B.

As already advanced, however, not all justifications can be analysed as Hohfeldian privileges. This is precisely because the jural position of the entity affected by the justified conduct cannot always be characterised as one of no-rights. This is typically the case of justifications based on consequentialist considerations. The point is well explained by Rodin, so it may be worth quoting the relevant passage in full:

> A classic example of a consequentialist justification, is the case of the farmer who burns his neighbour's field to prevent a wild fire from engulfing a town. The neighbour has a right not to have his field destroyed, but the farmer's action is justified in the circumstances because it is

---

[15] Hohfeld summarises these relations by means of two tables, one for jural correlatives and one for jural opposites. See, Hohfeld, 'Fundamental Legal Conceptions', 30:

| Jural Opposites | rights | privilege | power | immunity |
|---|---|---|---|---|
| | no-rights | duty | disability | liability |

| Jural Correlatives | right | privilege | power | immunity |
|---|---|---|---|---|
| | duty | no-right | liability | disability |

[16] Chapter 5, Section 5.5, and Chapter 6, Section 6.4.1.

## 3.2 CONCEPT AND THEORY OF JUSTIFICATION

> overwhelmingly the lesser evil. What is distinctive about this case, however, is that the farmer does not have a simple Hohfeldian liberty to burn the field, since the neighbour's claim-right against having his property destroyed does not disappear in the face of the justification ... What this implies is that justifications arising from consequentialist considerations (in particular 'lesser evil' justifications) are not reducible to a simple Hohfeldian relation.[17]

The state of necessity can be (and indeed, in international law is) formulated as a lesser evils defence. Now, to say that a state has a privilege to act in a situation of necessity implies that the state affected by the act of necessity is in a situation of no-rights in that regard since, it will be recalled, these are correlative positions. By way of example, say State A, in a situation of necessity, forgoes its payment of debts towards State B to attend to its own essential interests. For A to have a privilege to do so would require that B has a *no-right* to the payment of its credit. And this is at the very least doubtful. There exist theories that support B's no-right in the circumstances, such as the early modern natural lawyers' theory of revival of the original community of goods.[18] According to this theory, the right of B to its property would be extinguished in the situation of necessity since, in these circumstances, all property becomes common again. But this is not the current theoretical explanation of the plea of necessity, nor has it been since at least the late eighteenth century, as will be seen in Chapter 8.[19] The state affected by the act of necessity does retain its rights (it does not forfeit them in any way, be it through its consent or through its conduct), and so state of necessity cannot be characterised as a privilege. This is not to say that state of necessity may not be a justification – it simply means that the theory needed to explain the justifying effect of state of necessity is different. It is, as Rodin notes, a consequentialist theory, and not a deontic one.

This difference does not affect the premise that all justifications constitute permissions, it simply goes to the question of the 'strength of the permission involved' in each case.[20] Suzanne Uniacke has thus proposed a distinction between 'weak' and 'strong' justifications to account for this difference. In her view, strong justifications rely on a *positive right* on the part of the agent to act as he or she does, so that someone whose interests are damaged by the wrong is *not thereby wronged*.[21] Weak justifications,

---

[17] Rodin, *Self-Defence*, 28.
[18] On which see Chapter 8, Section 8.2.1.
[19] See Chapter 8, Section 8.2.1.2.
[20] Uniacke, *Permissible Killing: The Self-Defence Justification of Homicide* (1994), 26.
[21] Ibid., 27 (emphasis in original).

instead, 'arise when an act which is normally wrong because (say) it infringes someone else's right, is chosen as the lesser evil'.[22] This difference, in addition to requiring different theoretical explanations, can also have important consequences in practice. For example, as advanced in Chapter 2, it may affect the question of compensation for justified conduct. A duty of compensation could, for example, be grounded on the right of the victim state which is infringed (but not violated) by the justification. In this case, compensation would arise only in favour of those affected states which possess a right and only when the invoking state possesses a weak justification.

### 3.2.1.3 Justifications and the Breach of International Law

Another important aspect of justifications concerns their relation with the notions of non-performance and of breach of an international obligation. A perusal of the relevant case-law and legal scholarship shows that the relations between these concepts are not often understood. Thus, it is not unusual to read that justified conduct amounts to a 'non wrongful breach' of international law,[23] or that it is a violation of an obligation, or to find explanations of the operation of justifications as consisting in 'erasing' the wrongfulness of a breach of the law.[24] The assumption underlying these statements is that conduct covered by a justification, while permitted, is nevertheless a breach of an international obligation.

Such descriptions of justified conduct are, however, based on a misunderstanding of the relation between the concepts of justification, breach and non-performance of (or non-conformity with) an obligation.[25] This

---

[22] Ibid., 26.
[23] See, e.g., Reinisch, 'Necessity in Investment Arbitration' (2010) 41 NYIL 148–9.
[24] In the literature, see Bannelier and Christakis, '*Volenti non fit injuria*? Les effets du consentement à l'intervention militaire' (2004) 50 AFDI 102. By way of example: *Sempra Energy International v Argentine Republic*, ICSID Case ARB/02/16, Annulment, 29 June 2010, at [200] ('Article 25 presupposes that an act has been committed that is incompatible with the State's international obligations and is therefore "wrongful" '); *Continental*, Award, [166] ('an act otherwise in breach of an international obligation ("not in conformity" with it) is not considered wrongful, and does not therefore entail the secondary obligations attached to an illicit act, thanks to the "exceptional" presence of one of the conditions that under international law preclude wrongfulness, here necessity'); *Metalpar SA and Buen Aire SA v Argentine Republic* ICSID Case ARB/03/5, Award, 6 June 2008, [213] (state of necessity is only relevant if 'it is shown that the conduct of the State violates' the right of another party).
[25] On this point, see Duarte d'Almeida, 'Defences in the Law of State Responsibility: A View from Jurisprudence' in Paddeu and Bartels (eds), *Exceptions and Defences in International Law* (forthcoming), section 3.3 (on file with author).

## 3.2 CONCEPT AND THEORY OF JUSTIFICATION

misunderstanding is potentially derived from the manner in which the 'breach' of international law is expressed in the text of Articles 2 and 12 of the ARS. According to Article 2, the internationally wrongful act is a 'breach of an international obligation'[26] which is attributable to the state.[27] The 'breach' of an international obligation is then defined in Article 12, which adds that a breach exists when 'an act of that State is not in conformity with what is required of it by that obligation'. The conclusion that follows from these two premises is that there is an internationally wrongful act *whenever* there is an act of the state 'not in conformity' with what is required by an international obligation. In practice, it is often the case that the ascertainment that a given act of State A is not in conformity with what is required of that State by an international obligation is sufficient to establish that a breach of the obligation (and therefore an internationally wrongful act) has been committed. A good illustration of this is the *Avena* case before the ICJ.[28] The case concerned the obligation to notify foreign nationals of their right to consular assistance, established in the Vienna Convention on Consular Relations (VCCR).[29] The Court found that, by failing to notify Mexican nationals of their right to consular assistance, the United States had acted in a manner incompatible with its obligation under VCCR. The Court thus concluded that there was a breach of the relevant treaty provision and, as such, the United States had committed an internationally wrongful act.

Such an understanding of the notion of breach, however, elides some important distinctions. The first one is that the term 'breach' and the expression 'not in conformity with an obligation' are not synonymous, despite the latter having been used to define the former in the ARS. Indeed, although the text of Article 12 describes the breach as conduct incompatible with an obligation, the Commentary to this provision makes the following important clarification:

> In order to conclude that there is a breach of an international obligation in any specific case, it will be necessary to take account of ... the provisions of chapter V dealing with circumstances which may preclude the wrongfulness of an act of a State.[30]

---

[26] ARS art. 2(b).
[27] The discussion here assumes the attributability of the relevant conduct to the state.
[28] See *Case Concerning Avena and other Mexican Nationals (Mexico v United States of America)* (2004) ICJ Rep 12.
[29] Art. 36(2), Vienna Convention on Consular Relations, (1963) 596 UNTS 261.
[30] ARS art. 12 Commentary, [12]. See also: Crawford, Second Report on State Responsibility, ILC Yearbook 1999, vol. II(1), 12–13.

To establish a breach of an international obligation, then, something *more* than non-conformity between conduct and obligation is required: the conduct must, in addition, not be covered by a justification. The relations between these three concepts are thus becoming clear: non-conformity with an obligation and absence of justification are the ingredients of the breach. For any non-conformity with an international obligation, where there is no justification, there will be a breach of the obligation. By the same token, where there is a justification, then the non-conformity will not give rise to a breach of the obligation. As a result, it is mistaken to describe justified conduct as amounting to a 'breach' of international law, and whatever adjectives are added to the term breach (e.g., 'non-wrongful' or 'justified') cannot change this conclusion.

The above should not be interpreted to mean that a tribunal or other decision-maker will need to ascertain, in every case, that none of the recognised justifications under international law are present to establish that a breach of international law exists. Rather, it will only need to do so when prompted by the respondent[31] and, in this case, no conclusion as to breach can be reached until the tribunal has considered the justification. The practice of international courts and tribunals supports this conclusion. Thus, in *Avena* the ICJ did not have to ascertain that there was no consent, no self-defence and so on, in order to reach its conclusion as to the existence of a breach since none of these justifications was raised by the United States. In turn, in *Interim Agreement*, the Court considered only whether the justifications raised by Greece against the Federal Yugoslav Republic of Macedonia's claim were met.[32] Usually, where a respondent invokes a justification, a tribunal or other decision-maker will follow a two-step process to determine the existence of the breach of obligation. First it will consider whether the conduct is incompatible with the relevant obligation. If it finds that the conduct is indeed incompatible with that obligation, it will then move on to assess, in a second step, whether a

---

[31] There are certain situations in which a tribunal may be required to do this, for example, in cases of non-appearance of the respondent State. See, e.g., art. 53(2) of the ICJ Statute, which mandates the Court to 'satisfy itself, not only that it has jurisdiction in accordance with Articles 36 and 37, but also that the claim is well founded in fact and law.' The Court has interpreted this mandate as a requirement to *also* consider possible defences. See, e.g., the *Nicaragua* case in which the Court considered (if briefly) the (potential) plea of countermeasures on behalf of the United States: *Military and Paramilitary Activities in and Against Nicaragua (Nicaragua v United States of America)* (1986) ICJ Rep 14, at [249] and [252].

[32] *Application of the Interim Accord of 13 September 1995 (FYR Macedonia v Greece)* (2011) ICJ Rep 644.

## 3.2 CONCEPT AND THEORY OF JUSTIFICATION

justification is applicable.[33] A good example of this way of proceeding is the ICJ's judgment in *Nicaragua*. There the Court explained that:

> In so far as acts of the Respondent may *appear* to constitute violations of the relevant rules of law, the Court will then have to determine whether there are present any circumstances excluding unlawfulness, or whether any such acts may be justified upon any other ground.[34]

Thus, once the Court (preliminarily) concluded that 'the activities of the United States in relation to the activities of the contras in Nicaragua constitute *prima facie* acts of intervention', it then moved on to 'consider whether they may nevertheless be justified on some legal ground.'[35] At the end of the first step, then, the tribunal has only reached a preliminary conclusion as to the existence of a breach of international law, which still requires the second step (analysis of justifications) to be confirmed or rejected. It is only at the end of the second step that the tribunal will be able to confirm that the conduct in question is a breach of international law (that it constitutes an internationally wrongful act) if the justification is not met; or, if the justification is met, that there is no breach of international law. While the reasoning is taken in separate steps, these steps should not imply temporally distinct moments but merely the performance of conceptually distinct legal operations. It is not the case that, after the first step, a breach or a wrongful act 'already exists' as suggested by some part of the literature.[36] Indeed, tribunals are careful to convey this preliminary conclusion in their reasoning by means of the expressions '*prima facie*' or 'apparent' breach.[37] It is important to emphasise that a

---

[33] This order is not demanded by logic, but is often followed for reasons of judicial economy. Indeed, judicial economy may often demand that the order be altered. See, e.g., *Case Concerning Armed Activities on the Territory of the Congo (DRC v Uganda)* (2005) ICJ Rep 168; *Continental*, Award, [161] (the Tribunal explained the reasons supporting its decision to discuss the Argentine pleas before the claims of breach as follows: 'The pervasive nature of these general exceptions, which Argentina raises against all claims of Continental, might be such as to absolve Argentina, in whole or in part, from the alleged breaches and from the ensuing responsibility to pay damages'). The ICJ's decision in *Oil Platforms*, in which the order of analysis of claims and defences was altered, was criticised not so much because of the reversal of analysis per se but because in the circumstances this was not warranted by judicial economy. See, e.g., *Oil Platforms*, decl Ranjeva, 220–2; sep op Higgins, 230–1 [23], 231–2; sep op Parra-Aranguren, 244 [14]; sep op Kooijmans, 252–7.
[34] *Nicaragua*, [226] (emphasis added).
[35] Ibid., [246].
[36] Bannelier and Christakis, 'Volenti', 107.
[37] Note that the expression '*prima facie* wrong' is used by domestic law theorists in different ways: Gardner, 'In Defence of Defences' in Gardner (ed.), *Offences and Defences: Selected Essays in the Philosophy of Criminal Law* (2007), 77–8; Duarte d'Almeida, *Allowing for*

*prima facie* or apparent breach is *not* a breach of international law. These expressions represent merely a step in the tribunal's reasoning, a reasoning that still needs to consider whether the justification is met.[38] It is possible that the sources noted earlier intended to convey precisely this when describing justified conduct as a 'non-wrongful breach' and so on, but if this is the case then these tribunals and scholars have inappropriately used the relevant terminology to express this idea.

### 3.2.1.4   Justified Conduct: Lawful or 'Non Wrongful'?

The next question concerns the legal qualification of justified conduct. The previous two sections explained that justified conduct is permitted and that it does not amount to a breach of international law. How, then, legally to characterise justified conduct? Many different descriptions of justified conduct can be found in the case-law and the literature. For example, Argentina has referred to its necessity-based conduct as 'licit' in various international arbitrations,[39] and in *Oil Platforms* the United States asserted that: '[t]he action taken under [a circumstance precluding wrongfulness] is not an internationally wrongful act; it is an internationally lawful act.'[40] But in *Gabčíkovo-Nagymaros* the ICJ held that the defence of necessity could not permit 'the conclusion that [Hungary] had acted in accordance with its obligations'.[41] Special Rapporteur Crawford spoke alternatively of 'conduct the wrongfulness of which is precluded',[42] 'lawful conduct'[43] and of conduct that is 'not "in conformity" with the primary obligation' but that does not constitute a breach of that

---

*Exceptions: A Theory of Defences and Defeasibility in Law* (2015), 259–66. In this book, this expression is used in an evidential sense; namely, to indicate a situation which at first blush seems to be the case but that, after a complete analysis of the evidence, turns out not to be the case. It is in this sense that the ICJ used the expression in the *Nicaragua* case.

[38] This clarification will become relevant in Chapter 4 on consent, Section 4.3.1.2.

[39] See, e.g., *National Grid*, [205]; *Continental*, [160] (the state of necessity would render Argentina's conduct 'entirely lawful').

[40] US oral statement, *Oil Platforms*, CR 2003/12 (translation), 23 February 2003, [17.16].

[41] *Gabčíkovo-Nagymaros*, [48]. Though note the Court's subsequent statement that this defence 'would only permit the affirmation that, under the circumstances, Hungary would not incur international responsibility by acting as it did', which suggests that for the Court the plea may have been an excuse rather than a justification.

[42] Crawford, Second Report, [228]. In subsequent scholarly work, Crawford has referred to justifications as defences that 'seemingly render an act lawful': Crawford, *State Responsibility: The General Part* (2013), 278.

[43] Crawford, Second Report, [238].

## 3.2 CONCEPT AND THEORY OF JUSTIFICATION 111

obligation.[44] Moreover a distinction is often made between lawful conduct and 'unlawful conduct with precluded wrongfulness',[45] or between 'perfectly lawful' conduct and 'non-wrongful' conduct.[46]

Whether there exist juridically meaningful differences between these various expressions or whether they are simply different semantic ways of describing the same state of affairs depends, ultimately, on differing views as to the deontic modalities recognised in the international legal order. On the traditional view, international law operates on a bivalent deontic modality, in which permission and prohibition exhaust the normative field. In this legal order, therefore, conduct is either permitted (in which case it will be lawful) or prohibited (in which case it will be unlawful).[47] Indeed, it is precisely this understanding that underpinned the ICJ's recent decision in *Kosovo*, in which the Court was asked whether a unilateral declaration of independence was in accordance with international law and the Court responded that it was not prohibited.[48] So, on this view, to say that conduct is non-wrongful is the same as saying that it is lawful. Nevertheless, some scholars have questioned whether permissibility and prohibition are sufficient deontic modalities to exhaust the normative field of international law, arguing that the legal order should recognise what Judge Simma called 'intermediate categories' such as toleration, legal neutrality and non-prohibition.[49] If this latter view were accepted, then non-wrongfulness could not be equated with legality for the absence of a prohibition will not necessarily correspond to the existence of permission. Indeed, it is possible that in the absence of prohibition conduct be classified as legally neutral.[50] This is a complex and important debate

---

[44] Id.
[45] See, e.g., Paparinskis, 'Circumstances Precluding Wrongfulness in International Investment Law' (2016) 31 *ICSID Review* 484, 491 ('Use of force falling under self-defence is plainly lawful, rather than unlawful with precluded wrongfulness'); Reinisch, 'Necessity in Investment Arbitration' (2010) 41 NYIL 137, 148–9 ('Treaty clauses are primary rules; if their preconditions are fulfilled there is no treaty violation. A state of necessity excludes the unlawfulness of a treaty violation').
[46] Crawford, Second Report, [239].
[47] Kammerhofer, 'Gaps, the Nuclear Weapons Advisory Opinion and the Structure of International Legal Argument Between Theory and Practice' (2010) 80 BYIL 333, 337.
[48] *Accordance with International Law of the Unilateral Declaration of Independence in Respect of Kosovo* (2010) ICJ Rep 403, 425 [56].
[49] *Kosovo*, decl Simma, 480–1 [8–9].
[50] The point is that not all behaviours are (or need to be) regulated by the legal order. For example, the killing of a mosquito. It is not prohibited by the legal order, but it is strange to derive from this that the law *permits* the killing of mosquitoes and that, therefore, one has a

which exceeds the scope of this book, so no more will be said about it. In what concerns the topic under consideration, at any rate, it is unnecessary to take sides in the debate. Indeed, as already explained, justifications are express permissions of the legal order with the result that conduct adopted in pursuance of such permissions will be classified as lawful. From a legal standpoint, then, to say that justified conduct is non-wrongful is the same as saying that it is lawful.

This is not to say that there is no significance to the frequent descriptions of justified conduct as 'non-wrongful' and the like. The qualifier 'non-wrongful' (as well as its analogues) is, however, better seen as relating to a moral, political or other normative evaluation of the conduct in question. Indeed, the assertion that justified conduct is 'non-wrongful' may have some rhetorical value, in that it may signal the disapproval of the legal order towards such conduct because, for example, it is morally the wrong thing to do or because it is politically undesirable in the circumstances. Whether conduct is lawful and whether it is the morally right (or wrong) thing to do in the circumstances involve evaluations on different planes. It is possible that conduct be lawful, on the juridical plane, and still be the wrong thing to do in the circumstances on the moral plane. A creditor state may lawfully demand the service of its debt from a developing state that is on the brink of bankruptcy and that, at the time, may have been hit by a natural catastrophe which is causing a humanitarian crisis. It may be morally wrong to demand payment in such circumstances, when clearly the state's resources should be spent on assisting its population, but it is nevertheless lawful to do so. In a similar vein, the description of countermeasures as 'intrinsically wrongful' acts may be seen as having a similar function: it channels the undesirability of resort to unilateral action. The opposite is also true: conduct may be unlawful and yet be the right thing to do. Think of the situation of distress. It may be unlawful for a state organ to break into the diplomatic mission of a foreign state in an effort to seek a secure place for a minority

---

right to kill a mosquito. Some of the arguments presented before the ICJ in the *Kosovo* case supported the legal neutrality of unilateral declarations of independence (UDIs) under international law: there is no right to secede (outside of self-determination) and secession is not prohibited as such or by the principle of territorial integrity (which is applicable only as between States). See, e.g., the argument of the United Kingdom: *Kosovo*, Written Statement of the United Kingdom, 17 April 2009, ch. 5. As the United Kingdom argued: 'it is one thing to say that there is no right to secede in international law and another to say that secession is contrary to international law', at [5.17]; and 'international law neither authorises nor prohibits secession', at [5.61].

group being persecuted by an angry mob.[51] But it seems like the morally right thing to do in the circumstances. The upshot is that justified conduct is lawful – even though it may be morally, politically or otherwise normatively desirable or undesirable.

### 3.2.1.5 Justifications: 'Deeds' or 'Reasons'?

One final issue concerning the concept (or better, the conception) of justifications is whether the invocation of a justification requires that the circumstances triggering it must actually exist, or whether it is enough that the party invoking it believed, in good faith, that those circumstances existed. This is the debate between what domestic legal theorists call the 'deeds' and 'reasons' conceptions of justification.[52] The classic example of the difference between these theories is the Bomb Thief scenario, in which an individual stole an unattended backpack from a beach and, having inspected the contents and found a terrorist's bomb inside, took it to the police who proceeded to disarm the bomb. The thief saved many lives, but at the time of stealing the backpack he did not know this. Can he benefit from a lesser-evils justification, such as necessity? The thief would be justified under a deeds conception of justification, insofar as the material conditions of justification existed at the time of his conduct. But he would not be justified under a reasons conception, for he did not know at the time of his actions that the backpack contained a bomb.[53]

In international law, the question arose in the *Air Service Agreement* dispute between the United States and France. In its explanation of the institution of countermeasures, the Tribunal seemed to accept that the belief that a prior wrongful act had been committed was enough for the taking of these measures. According to the Tribunal:

> Under the rules of present-day international law, and unless the contrary results from special obligations arising under particular treaties, notably from mechanisms created within the framework of international organisations, each State establishes for itself its legal situation vis-à-vis other States. If a situation arises which, *in one State's view*, results in the

---

[51] As will be seen in Chapter 9, the plea of distress can be classified as an excuse (the relevant conduct would, therefore, be wrongful).
[52] See Chapter 1, Section 1.2.
[53] This is, admittedly, a simple statement of the facts of the case and a reductionist explanation of the implications of the two conceptions of justification. For a thorough explanation of the issue, see: Robinson, 'The Bomb Thief and the Theory of Justification Defences' (1997) 8 *Criminal Law Forum* 387.

> violation of an international obligation by another State, the first State is entitled, within the limits set by the general rules of international law pertaining to the use of armed force, to affirm its rights through 'counter-measures'.[54]

But this approach was subsequently rejected by the ILC, with the support of states in the Sixth Committee.[55] Countermeasures, to produce their exonerating effect, must be based on an actual prior wrongful act. This means that since countermeasures are unilaterally adopted, the invoking state does so at its own risk for it may turn out to be the case, on subsequent analysis, that no prior wrongful act existed.[56] In this way, the ILC had opted for a 'deeds' conception of justification in respect of countermeasures.

Without explicitly framing the issue in these terms, the ARS take a deeds conception also in respect of the other defences. Thus, consent 'must be actually expressed by the State rather than merely presumed on the basis that the State would have consented if it had been asked.'[57] In the case of Article 21, too, this defence will be applicable in the same circumstances in which self-defence under Article 51 of the UN Charter is available, namely 'if an armed attack occurs'.[58] The same holds true for the justification of state of necessity. In this case, the state invoking it must be able to prove the existence of an impending threat to one of its essential interests at the time of the adoption of the necessitated act. Of course, this cannot be proven with absolute certainty, since by definition the peril concerned is in the future. According to the ARS Commentary, 'a measure of uncertainty about the future does not necessarily disqualify a State from invoking necessity'; so long as the 'peril is clearly established on the basis of the evidence reasonably available at the time' the defence will be available.[59] This is not simply the establishment of the peril as it reasonably appears to

---

[54] *Air Service Agreement of 27 March 1946 between the United States and France* (1978) 18 RIAA 417, [81] (emphasis added).
[55] See Section 6.3.2.1.
[56] ARS Commentary art. 49, [3].
[57] ARS Commentary art. 21, [6].
[58] This is corroborated by the case-law of the ICJ on self-defence. In every case in which self-defence has been invoked, the argument was rejected by the Court because on an analysis of the facts an armed attack had not actually taken place before the resort to the alleged self-defensive force. For a review of these cases, see Chapter 5. It should be noted that acceptance of a doctrine of anticipatory self-defence, in the case of imminent attacks, does not alter this conclusion. There must be proof that the attack is imminent, and mere belief that it is so will not be enough.
[59] ARS Commentary art. 25, [16].

the invoking state at the time; rather the peril must be established in fact as far as this is possible in the circumstances.[60]

There are indeed good policy reasons mitigating in favour of a 'deeds' approach to justifications in international law. Given the decentralised character of international law, in which states act on the basis of unilateral appreciations not subjected to mandatory oversight by tribunals, it seems preferable to insist on the actual existence of circumstances triggering justifications rather than relying on the good faith appreciation of the state which is the potential beneficiary of the defence.

### 3.2.2 Theorising Justifications in International Law

Finally, something should be said about the theory of justification in international law. A theory of justification answers the question *why* justifications justify, namely why one subject's justification prevails over another subject's (claim-)rights against the former.[61] Theories of justification have been referred to throughout Part I of this study, and will be developed more fully in the various chapters of Part II. It is, however, important to provide here a brief summary of the main theories so far developed in domestic legal contexts, and to consider the equivalent developments (or lack thereof) in international law.

Three main groups of theories of justification can be identified in the domestic law literature. These are, first, deontological theories. These include the rights theory, explaining justifications as an 'affirmative legal right to protect a particular moral interest' in pursuance of which the actor can cause an 'otherwise socially unacceptable result',[62] and the moral forfeiture theory, pursuant to which the wrongful conduct is justified because the victim, by his act, has placed himself outside the protection of the law.[63] Second are consequentialist theories. There are two versions of consequentialist theories: lesser evils, pursuant to which conduct is justified if it causes a lesser harm or avoids a greater evil;[64] and public benefit,

---

[60] *Gabčíkovo-Nagymaros*, [51].
[61] For an overview, see Dressler, *Understanding Criminal Law* (1987), 180–3.
[62] Dressler, 'Justifications and Excuses: A Brief Review of the Concepts and the Literature' (1986–7) 33 *Wayne LR* 1163.
[63] Id.
[64] E.g., Fletcher, 'Rights and Excuses' (1984) 3 *Criminal Justice Ethics* 17; Bettiol and Pettoello-Mantovani, *Diritto penale parte generale* (12th edn, 1988), 379; Alexander, 'A Unified Excuse of Preemptive Self-Protection' (1999) 74 *Notre Dame LR* 1475, 1499.

a variant of lesser evils, pursuant to which conduct is justified when its performance, despite being contrary to law, benefits society.[65] The former may be called 'private' lesser evils (for it concerns the protection of individual interests), the latter may be seen as a 'public' version of the same theory (for it concerns the protection of collective interests). Last is the theory of absent interest, pursuant to which conduct is not wrongful because the interest protected by the provision allegedly breached has been waived by the interest holder.[66]

One question that has troubled domestic law theorists is that of finding a unified theory of justification – that is one theory that is capable of providing an explanation for all justifications recognised in a legal order. However, attempts to agree on a unitary theory of justification have been mostly unsuccessful, for not all recognised justification defences in any given legal order can be rationalised under one of these theories,[67] or can only be so rationalised by either straining the formulation of the defences in question or of the theory. For example, state of necessity, which usually concerns harm done to an innocent victim, cannot be considered a justification under the theory of moral forfeiture (for the victim has not committed a wrong which would entail forfeiture). Certain formulations of the plea of necessity may be considered justifications under the lesser evils and public benefit theories.[68] The burning of a house to prevent a fire from spreading may be considered a justification under these two theories. But self-defence, a paradigmatic justification, can hardly be thought of in terms of greater or lesser evils, since arguably both interests at stake (physical integrity and life) are of the same value. For this reason, self-defence tends to be grounded on deontic theories, such as moral forfeiture.[69] Indeed, in most legal orders justifications are grounded on a number of different theories.

---

[65] Dressler, 'Brief Review', 1163.
[66] E.g., Lenckner, 'The Principle of Interest Balancing as a General Basis of Justification' (1986) BYULR 645, 655; Eser, 'Justification and Excuse: A Key Issue in the Concept of Crime' in Eser (ed.), *Justification and Excuse: Comparative Perspectives* (1987), 47.
[67] Dressler, *Understanding Criminal Law*, 180.
[68] See, e.g., Arnolds and Garland, 'The Defence of Necessity in Criminal Law: The Right to Choose a Lesser Evil' (1974) 65 *J Crim L & Criminology* 289; Alexander, 'Lesser Evils: A Closer Look at the Paradigmatic Justification' (2005) 24 *Law & Philosophy* 611; Simons, 'Exploring the Intricacies of the Lesser Evils Defense' (2005) 24 *Law & Philosophy* 645; Berman, 'Lesser Evils and Justification: A Less Close Look' (2005) 24 *Law & Philosophy* 681.
[69] Dressler, *Understanding Criminal Law*, 181. For an extensive analysis of this theory, see Leverick, *Killing in Self-Defence* (2006). For a critique, see Grabczynska and Ferzan, 'Justifying *Killing in Self-Defence*' (2007) 99 *J Crim L & Criminology* 235.

What theory or theories underpin justifications in international law? Very little has been written about this issue. There are scattered references and theoretical explanations in respect of specific justifications in the literature. For example, Hans Kelsen devoted considerable attention to theoretically explaining the legality of countermeasures. He developed a theory of countermeasures as sanctions executed by states acting as organs of the international community which was based on an analogy with the institution of vendetta in primitive societies, as will be seen in Chapter 6. But there has been, thus far, no comprehensive consideration of the theory or theories that might explain the effect of justifications in international law. As will be seen in the chapters that follow, just as in domestic law, in international law different justifications are also best explained through different theories. Thus, deontic theories best explain the exonerating effect of self-defence and countermeasures (rights forfeiture), consequentialist theories best explain the effect of state of necessity (lesser evils), and absent interest underpins the defence of consent. The development of these theories *for* international law will be undertaken in subsequent chapters in Part II, in connection with the defence(s) for which they are most relevant. In each case, the various potential theories will be identified and, where necessary, developed as much as is possible, and they will be critically evaluated. On the basis of this analysis, the book will then propose which of the theories possesses the best explanatory power for any given justification. Given the scant attention this issue has received in international law scholarship up until now, the analysis in this book constitutes only an initial exploration of the question. Much work on this issue remains to be done.

## 3.3 Concept and Theory of Excuse

Even less developed than the concept of justification is the concept of excuse in international law. Mirroring the previous section, this section will consider both the definition and theory of excuse. A difficult question concerns the role of fault in relation to excuses: is it the case, as some international lawyers have argued, that excuses relate to the element of fault? This is an issue which affects both the definition and theory of excuse. Rather than addressing it first, it seems that the best way of explaining the relation between excuses and fault is to start by defining excuses, considering potential theories of excuse, and then assess the place of fault. This section will therefore conclude with a consideration of the relevance of fault to the definition and theory of excuse.

### 3.3.1 Concept of Excuse

#### 3.3.1.1 Defining Excuses in International Law

In Husak's consensus definition, excuses 'are defenses that arise from properties or characteristics of actors.' Thus, a 'defendant is excused when he is not blameworthy or responsible for his conduct, even though it ... violates the criminal law.'[70] The concept of 'circumstances precluding responsibility' used in international legal literature roughly mirrors this definition. Anzilotti, for example, maintained that 'it is generally acknowledged that there exist cases in which an act, wrongful in itself ... does not produce the normal consequences of wrongfulness.'[71] This is also how Giuseppe Sperduti[72] and Ago understood these circumstances.[73] Furthermore, since the adoption of the ARS, Helmut Aust has stated that excuses 'concern the particular situation in which the state ... that acted found itself when the relevant conduct was committed.'[74] It is thus plausible to define excuses in international law as circumstances that focus on the properties or characteristics of the invoking state that, if successful, exclude that state's responsibility for its wrongful conduct. Insofar as it is a defence that focuses on the actor and its situation, domestic law scholars have described excuses as 'individualised' defences.[75]

A state's responsibility is constituted by the legal relations arising as a result of the commission of an internationally wrongful act. Part Two of the ARS specifies two such legal relations: an obligation of cessation, if the conduct is continuing, and an obligation to provide reparation in adequate form, be it through restitution, compensation or satisfaction (or a combination thereof). A potential third relation is the obligation to provide assurances and guarantees of non-repetition, though it is still unclear whether this obligation is recognised as a matter of customary

---

[70] Husak, 'Justifications', 496 (footnotes omitted).
[71] 'É generalmente ammesso che vi sono dei casi in cui un atto, di per sè illecito ... non produce le conseguenze proprie dei fatti illeciti', Anzilotti, 'Corso di diritto internazionale' *Opere di Dionisio Anzilotti* (1955 reprint of 3rd edn originally published in 1927), 413.
[72] Sperduti, 'Introduzione allo studio delle funzioni della necessitá nel diritto internazionale' (1943) 22 *Rivista di diritto internazionale* 19, 20.
[73] Ago, Eighth Report, [51].
[74] Aust, 'Circumstances Precluding Wrongfulness and Shared Responsibility' in Nollkaemper and Plakokefalos (eds), *Principles of Shared Responsibility* (2014), 204.
[75] Fletcher, 'The Individualization of Excusing Conditions' (1973–4) 47 *S Cal LR* 1269.

law.[76] Excuses, by 'precluding responsibility', prevent these obligations from arising: the wrongdoing state will not be under obligations of cessation and reparation or under the (potential) obligation to provide assurances and guarantees of non-repetition.

Nevertheless, excuses cannot foreclose other legal consequences of wrongfulness from arising. For example, insofar as countermeasures do not form part of the content of responsibility, they cannot be excluded by an excuse. Nevertheless, as mentioned earlier, since countermeasures must be aimed at enforcing the obligations of cessation and reparation, they will be devoid of an object against an excused actor. Likewise, the entitlement to suspend or terminate treaties as a result of material breach is also not included in the concept of responsibility, so excuses cannot preclude this entitlement. In principle, therefore, excuses preclude, borrowing Ago's words, the 'whole of responsibility, and nothing but responsibility'.[77]

### 3.3.1.2 Excuses and Corporate Entities

One difficult aspect of the notion of excuse is the possibility of employing this concept in respect of corporate entities. It could be argued that since excuses are afforded in recognition of human frailty and they relate to questions of blame and the morality of human actions, the concept is inapposite for international law – at least insofar as the concept is to be applied in respect of states. But there is a powerful counter-argument. As argued by Andrew Simester, the attribution of excuses to corporate entities is possible under doctrines of identification. Under these doctrines, 'the corporation is imputed with a package comprising some designated (senior) individual's conduct and culpability.' In particular, he says, 'at international law, analogous doctrines of identification are required to recognise the state as an agent, and in principle such doctrines could also impute excuses. More generally, there seems no reason to exclude the possibility of excuses within any legal system where the state is itself

---

[76] On which see Barbier, 'Assurances and Guarantees of Non-Repetition' in Crawford et al. (eds), *The Law of International Responsibility* (2010), 551. For an extended analysis, focusing on the Inter-American human rights system, see: Londoño Lázaro, *Las garantías de no repetición en la jurisprudencia Interamericana. Derecho Internacional y cambios estructurales del Estado* (2014).

[77] Ago, Working Paper, ILC Yearbook 1963, vol. II, 253. It is possible, as mentioned in the previous chapter, that excuses afford only partial exoneration thus excluding only some part of the legal relations of responsibility.

a subject.'[78] Indeed, in international law, the responsibility of states results from the acts (and omissions) of certain individuals who, for the purposes of international law, are considered as agents of the state. These are either the state's organs (be they de jure or de facto), or private individuals whose conduct is exceptionally attributed to the state.[79]

At any rate, this critique is not one directed at the concept of excuse but at a particular conception of excuse as one concerned with an individual's blameworthiness. But this need not be the only conception of excuse. It is indeed possible to develop a conception of excuse (as evidenced in Husak's definition given earlier) as a defence concerned with responsibility instead of with an individual's blameworthiness.

### 3.3.2 Theorising Excuses in International Law

As with justifications, theories of excuse provide an explanation for the exclusion of an actor's responsibility despite his having committed an unlawful act. Again, criminal law theorists do not agree on a unitary theory of excuse, capable of explaining all the circumstances in which the law does not consider that a person is blameworthy for his unlawful behaviour.[80] It is widely agreed that utilitarian theories are mostly unable to explain this type of defence. Jeremy Bentham's view that excuses may be afforded to the insane, the coerced, and so on, for they are undeterrable and punishing them would therefore be inefficacious,[81] was described by H. L. A Hart as the 'most spectacular *non-sequitur*'.[82] In Hart's view, the opposite is true. Thus, the utilitarian value of conformity with the law may be enhanced by the punishment of the undeterrable: punishment becomes the consequence of choice, the choice to act in conformity with, or contrary to, the law. The recognition of excuses for those who are undeterrable, in this account, maximises the satisfaction derived by individuals from the knowledge that they have avoided punishment because they

---

[78] Simester, 'Necessity, Torture and the Rule of Law' in Ramraj (ed.), *Emergencies and the Limits of Legality* (2008), 302.
[79] See, ARS art. 4–7 (on state organs) and arts. 8–11 (on attribution of conduct of private individuals).
[80] Dressler, *Understanding Criminal Law*, 183.
[81] Bentham, *An Introduction to the Principles of Morals and Legislation* (1823, J. H. Burns and H. L. A. Hart, eds, 1996), 160–2. For more recent restatements of this view, see Eser, 'Key Issue', 58; Padovani, *Diritto penale* (9th edn, 2008), 237.
[82] Hart, *Punishment and Responsibility: Essays in the Philosophy of Law* (2nd edn, 2008), 19. For the same criticism, see Fletcher, *Rethinking Criminal Law* (2000), 814–17; Kadish, 'Excusing Crime' (1987) 75 *California LR* 257, 263.

have so chosen.[83] Other, non-utilitarian, theories of excuse include the causation, character and personhood theories. Causation theory holds that an individual is excused if his conduct was caused by circumstances over which the individual had no control; for example, an insane defendant cannot be blamed since he has no control over his insanity.[84] Under the character theory, an individual is excused if his 'bad act' does not reflect his possession of a 'bad character'.[85] Finally, the personhood theory grounds excuse on the unique essential feature of personhood: 'rational free choice-making'.[86] That is, individuals are not punishable when their conduct is not free and has been involuntarily adopted, where 'involuntariness' is understood in a normative (and not physical) sense. This is involuntariness in an Aristotelian sense: as action which is compelled by external circumstances, insofar as in such circumstances 'nobody would choose' to behave differently.[87] For Aristotle, this is different from the situation in which 'a voyager [is] conveyed somewhere by the wind'.[88] Normative involuntariness is, in other words, involuntariness due to lack of choice. And this is precisely how contemporary legal scholarship understands this notion. Thus, according to Fletcher, an act is involuntary in this sense when extreme circumstances affect the actor's capacity to make decisions.[89] This is the theory that was the basis of Austin's *Plea for Excuses*,[90] and has subsequently found support in a number of writers in the common law.[91]

As far as international law is concerned, only Giancarlo Scalese has put forward a (unified) theory of excuse which would explain, in his view,

---

[83] Hart, 'Legal Responsibility and Excuses' in Hart (ed.), *Punishment and Responsibility*, 40–4.
[84] Dressler, 'Brief Review', 1166.
[85] For a refutation of this theory, see Gardner, 'The Gist of Excuses' in Gardner (ed.), *Offences and Defences: Selected Essays in the Philosophy of Criminal Law* (2007), 122–3.
[86] Dressler, *Understanding Criminal Law*, 185. On this theory see, generally, Horder, *Excusing Crime* (2007), 30–7.
[87] Aristotle, *Nicomachean Ethics*, iii, 1109b30-1110a16, cited in Horder, *Excusing*, 31.
[88] Aristotle, *Nicomachean Ethics*, iii, 1110a17-b7, cited in Horder, *Excusing*, 31.
[89] Fletcher, *Rethinking*, 803. See further, Bronaugh, 'Freedom as the Absence of an Excuse' (1964) 74 *Ethics* 161 (freedom as precondition of moral responsibility); Fletcher, 'The Individualization of Excusing Conditions' (1973–4) 47 *S Cal L R*, 1271; Fletcher, *Rethinking*, 802–7; Horowitz, 'Justification and Excuse in the Program of the Criminal Law' (1986) 49 *Law & Contemp Probs*, 118; Kadish, 'Excusing'; Simester, 'Necessity, Torture and the Rule of Law', 289.
[90] Austin, 'Plea'. For a critique see Holdcroft, 'A Plea for Excuses?' (1969) 44 *Philosophy* 314.
[91] For example, Bronaugh, 'Freedom as the Absence of an Excuse', 161 (freedom as precondition of moral responsibility); Fletcher, 'Individualization', 1271; Fletcher, *Rethinking*, 802–7; Horowitz, 'Justification', 118; Kadish, 'Excusing'.

the excusatory effect of *force majeure*, distress and state of necessity.[92] Scalese grounds these three defences on a free will theory: in all three cases, an external event, beyond the state's control, places that state in a situation in which it is not able to exercise its will freely, that is a situation in which the state is compelled, by the circumstances, to act in breach of its obligations. It may be advanced here that the analysis of some of the recognised defences in international law, in particular *force majeure* and distress, points towards a free will theory of excuses as argued by Scalese. Pursuant to this theory, as will be argued, the state is granted an excuse because its free will was constrained by circumstances beyond its control: in a sense, the circumstances compel the state to act as it does. Put another way, the circumstances limit the range of choice available to the state in respect of compliance with its obligations. That the state's will can be constrained by external circumstances is uncontroversial in international law, and it is an idea which is already catered to in other rules of the legal order, such as the invalidity of treaties concluded under the threat of the use of force.

Theoretically, as will be seen, this suggests that the concept of responsibility in international law is premised on the idea of state will: if responsibility is based on state will, then the absence or coercion of that will precludes responsibility from arising. But Scalese, while proposing a theory of free will, does not draw this conclusion. Instead, he correlates free will with fault: where the state's free will is constrained, its actions reveal no fault and for this reason the state cannot be held responsible. This view is incorrect, and to understand why it will be necessary to clarify the relation between excuses and fault.

### 3.3.3 Excuses and Fault

It is not an uncommon view among international scholars that excuses are defences that negate the fault of the invoking state. This was the view held by Ago, before his time in the ILC, in respect of *force majeure*,[93] and

---

[92] See, generally, Scalese, *La rilevanza delle scusanti nella teoria dell'illecito internazionale* (2008).

[93] Ago, 'La colpa nell'illecito internazionale' in 1 *Scritti sulla responsabilità internazionale degli Stati* (1979, first published 1939), 286, 299ff. As Palmisano explains, however, Ago's own understanding of fault reduces this notion to the idea of will: it is because the act is willed that it can be imputed to the organ, and not because of any psychological relation between the organ and the act. In his conception of fault, therefore, the statement 'the organ acted with fault' is the same as saying that 'the act is an act of the organ'. For

it was the conclusion arrived at by the UN Secretariat's memorandum on *force majeure* and fortuitous event.[94] Scholars have derived two different consequences from this premise. On the one hand, scholars like Andrea Gattini and Scalese have relied on the fault-negating aspect of *force majeure* (and fortuitous event) to argue in favour of the inclusion, in the law of responsibility, of a general requirement of fault. On this view, fault would constitute a 'negative' requirement of responsibility, one that falls to the respondent to disprove by invoking *force majeure* (or fortuitous event).[95] Arguing in the other direction, Karl Zemanek and Rosalyn Higgins have argued that, since these defences negate fault and fault is not a general requirement of responsibility, they have no place in the ARS.[96]

The place of fault in the law of state responsibility is an old and vexed question, which has been extensively dealt with in the literature. While early writers and practice based the responsibility of the state on fault,[97] from the early 1900s onwards international law began to move away from fault-based responsibility.[98] Early in their history, both the PCIJ, in *Chorzów Factory*,[99] and the ICJ, in *Corfu Channel*,[100] maintained that international responsibility was engaged by a violation of international law *only* – without requiring that the violation be the consequence of the

---

this reason, Ago could accept that *force majeure*, a situation which excludes the will of the actor, was a defence 'excluding fault'. See Palmisano, 'Colpa dell'organo e colpa dello Stato nella responsabilità internazionale: Spunti critici di teoria e di prassi' (1992) 19–20 *Comunicazioni e Studi* 623, 657–8.

[94] UN Secretariat, '"*Force Majeure*" and "Fortuitous Event" as Circumstances Precluding Wrongfulness: Survey of State Practice, International Judicial Decisions and Doctrine', ILC Yearbook 1978, vol. II(1), 67 [7], 69 [15].

[95] Gattini, 'Smoking/No Smoking: Some Remarks on the Current Place of Fault in the ILC Draft Articles on State Responsibility' (1999) 10 EJIL 397; Gattini, 'La notion de la faute à la lumière du projet de convention de la Commission du droit international sur la responsabilité internationale' (1992) 3 EJIL 253.

[96] Higgins, *Problems and Process: International Law and How We Use It* (1994), 161; Zemanek, 'The Legal Foundations of the International System' (1997) 266 *Recueil* 9, 264–5. Similarly, Cassella, *La nécessité en droit international* (2011), 411.

[97] For a review of early doctrine and practice, see Ago, 'Le délit international' (1939) 68 *Recueil des cours de l'Académie de droit international*, 476ff.

[98] See, primarily, Anzilotti, *Teoria generale della responsabilità dello stato nel diritto internazionale* (1902); Anzilotti, 'La responsabilité internationale des Etats à raison des dommages soufferts par des étrangers' (1906) 13 RGDIP 5, 5–29, 285–309. For the enduring impact of Anzilotti's theory of 'objective responsibility' in international law, see Passero, *Dionisio Anzilotti e la dottrina internazionalistica tra Otto e Novecento* (2010), 246–61.

[99] *Factory at Chorzów (Merits)* (1928) PCIJ, Series A No 17, 3, 29.

[100] *Corfu Channel (UK v Albania)* (1949) ICJ Rep 4, 22–3.

state or its organ's fault. This was not a rejection of the relevance of fault to a finding of international responsibility.[101] It was simply an acknowledgment of the fact that nothing general could be said about the place of fault in the system of state responsibility.[102] Whether fault is necessary in any given case will depend on the specific obligation in question; namely, on whether the obligation's definition contains fault (in whatever form) as a constituent requirement.[103] This is not a unique approach to the location, so to speak, of the element of fault in the theory of responsibility. Some domestic legal systems include fault (as a psychological element) in the definition of the offence: thus, fault may form part of the *Tatbestand* (in German) or *tipo* (in Italian and Spanish) in the theory of crime. An analogous position is currently enshrined in the ARS, the Commentary to which specifies that, in accordance with the practice of states, fault is not generally necessary for international responsibility to arise.[104] Whether it is necessary depends on the definition of the obligation in question. Fault is thus not excluded from the law of responsibility, but neither is it generally required.

It is of course conceivable that *force majeure*, distress, and other excuses be construed as circumstances in which the state's fault is excluded. If fault is incorporated into the obligation's definition, then these circumstances will constitute facts relevant to the *proof* (or, better, disproof) of the state's fault. Take the example of due diligence obligations. These obligations require the state to adopt (or maintain) a certain course of conduct, but they do not require of the state to achieve a given result. In respect of that conduct, the state is only bound to act diligently. To breach the obligation, therefore, it is necessary to demonstrate that the state did not use the required diligence or that, in other words, it acted negligently. A situation of impossibility caused by an external event, for example, would negate that the state acted negligently. Absent proof of negligence, the state's

---

[101] On which see Dupuy, 'Le fait générateur de la responsabilité des Etats' (1984) 188 *Recueil des cours de l'Académie de droit international*, 33–5.

[102] Crawford, 'Revising the Draft Articles on State Responsibility' (1999) 10 EJIL 435, 438; Crawford, *General Part*, 49, 60–1.

[103] See further, Brownlie, *State Responsibility* (1983), 45; Dupuy, 'Fait générateur', 37; Conforti, 'Cours général de droit international public' (1988) 212 Recueil 9, 173. Some authors, though maintaining that fault is necessary, ultimately reach this same conclusion, e.g., Quadri, *Diritto internazionale pubblico* (5th edn, 1968), 588ff; Arangio-Ruiz, Second Report on State Responsibility, ILC Yearbook 1989, vol. II(1), [179].

[104] ARS Commentary art. 2, [2].

conduct is not incompatible with its obligation.[105] The *Rainbow Warrior* Tribunal's treatment of distress, explained in Section 9.3.2.2 of Chapter 9, is a good illustration of this situation. It is important to highlight that in these cases it is not the defence which cancels the element of fault as such. Analytically, what happens is that the *factual* circumstances which would normally give rise to the defence (e.g., a supervening event such as an earthquake affecting the state's ability to perform its obligations) provide evidence of the state's diligence.

At any rate, it is not necessary to construe *force majeure*, distress and other (potential) excuses as defences negating fault. In his study of fault in international law, Giuseppe Palmisano noted the distinction between the notion of fault, as a subjective concept relating to the psychological relation of a state agent towards his conduct or towards a desired result, and the notion of *suitas*, defined as the 'sphere of voluntariness and freedom of choice' within which each state operates.[106] Excuses can be construed as circumstances relating to the concept of *suitas*; namely, as circumstances in which the state's freedom to choose whether to comply with its obligations has been restricted, namely, as circumstances which compel a state to act in a manner contrary to its obligations.[107] Thus, in the absence of a free act no responsibility can ensue. This construction assumes that a state's freedom of choice is relevant to an evaluation of its responsibility; even more, it assumes that the very concept of responsibility is premised on the notions of free will and voluntary acts – a point which was advanced in the previous section and which will be elaborated upon in Chapter 7 on *force majeure*.

The distinction between fault and *suitas* will be of crucial importance in reframing state of necessity as an excuse, as will be seen in Chapter 8.[108] The ARS distinguish state of necessity from *force majeure* on the basis that state of necessity involves 'voluntary' conduct: the state, to protect one of its essential interests, voluntarily acts in a manner incompatible with its obligation towards a third state.[109] If excuses negated the element

---

[105] Zegveld, *Accountability of Armed Opposition Groups in International Law* (2002), 217; Lozano Contreras, *La noción de debida diligencia en derecho internacional público* (2007), 220–8.
[106] Palmisano, 'Fault' in Wolfrum (ed.), *Max Planck Encyclopedia of Public International Law* (2007–), [19]. See more broadly Palmisano, 'Colpa dell'organo'.
[107] Palmisano, 'Fault', [19].
[108] See Chapter 6, Section 6.4.4.
[109] ARS Commentary art. 25, [2].

of 'fault', the plea of necessity could not be formulated as an excuse: the act in necessity is, by definition, an intended one.[110] However, if excuses concerned the free will of the state then it might be possible to recast state of necessity as an excuse: it is not the intention to engage in the act that is relevant to the defence, but whether the state had a choice to act otherwise to protect its interests in the circumstances.

## 3.4 Taxonomy of Defences: The Role of Concept and Theory

The classification of justification and excuse in domestic law is, as noted earlier, a complex operation, involving consideration of multiple elements: the definitions of justification and excuse, the theory (or theories) underlying the defence and whether they constitute theories of justification or of excuse, the definition and rationale of each individual defence and other policy considerations. This exercise usually involves one of two forms of analysis: top-down or bottom-up.[111] To work top-down would require first to develop a general theory of justification or excuse and then to formulate (or reformulate, as the case may be) a defence so as to ensure that it reflects a logic of justification or of excuse. For example, one could start from the premise that state of necessity is a justification and then, by reference to the chosen theory of justification (e.g., lesser evil), determine how it ought to be formulated and what its conditions and requirements ought to be. A drawback of this approach is that, as explained by Kimberley Kessler Ferzan, it 'means that our understandings of particular defenses will ultimately be hostage to the theorist's underlying theory of justification.'[112] Alternatively, one can start from an analysis of each defence and work upwards towards a theory that might explain its justifying or excusing effect. The starting point here is the formulation of the defence, followed by an assessment of what theory might be able to explain this defence and account for its various conditions and requirements. This approach, as Ferzan notes, maintains 'the structure of the defense constant, but depending on the net social benefit (or some other such calculation), the defense may or may not fit within the theory of justification'[113] or, as the case may be, the theory of excuse.

---

[110] On first reading, the commentary to draft art. 33 indicated that the conduct was 'deliberate': ILC Report, thirty-second session, ILC Yearbook 1980, vol. II(2), 34 [3].
[111] Ferzan, 'Justification and Excuse' in Deigh and Dolinko (eds), *The Oxford Handbook of Philosophy of Criminal Law* (2011), 253.
[112] Ibid., 255.
[113] Ibid., 253.

As was just seen, international law has yet to develop theories of justification or excuse. It would thus be possible to elaborate theories of both justification and excuse and then, taking a top-down approach, classify the defences as one or the other. The risk of such an approach is the imposition of a certain characterisation to defences, even though positive law may point in the opposite direction. This deductive approach seems also ill-suited to the inductive method of law-creation and law-ascertainment of international law.[114] It is thus preferable to work in the other direction, and elaborate theories that are capable of describing adequately the accepted formulation of each defence and the practice of states. This book will therefore take a primarily bottom-up approach to the classification of the defences, for if the classification is to serve any useful purpose it must be grounded in the actual practice concerning the particular defences.[115] It will do so only 'primarily' because, as will be seen, on account of the still limited developments in this field in international law some elements of top-down reasoning will be necessary.

In respect of some defences there is clear evidence, in the practice of states, that they constitute justifications. In these cases, a combination of the two approaches is both helpful and warranted. For instance, there is no doubt that countermeasures constitute justifications and that, therefore, the conduct of the state resorting to these measures (if compliant with the relevant conditions and requirements) is lawful. Whatever the theory underpinning this defence (which will be discovered in a bottom-up analysis), it will be a theory of justification (a top-down conclusion). However, there is no agreement on the classification of many other defences. In these cases, the analysis will begin with an examination of the formulation and rationale of each defence and then consider what theory or theories can explain the defence's exonerating effect. When more than one theory is available, it will be necessary to assess which theory possesses the most persuasive explanatory power. This will be done by testing how well the theory can accommodate the existing conditions and requirements of the defence, as well as by testing the limits that the theory may impose on the defence (for example, can the theory sustain a duty of compensation for material loss?). Finally – given that the positive law is not clear on the classification of these defences as justifications or excuses –

---

[114] Cf. Schwarzenberger, 'The Inductive Approach to International Law' (1947) 60 *Harv LR* 539; Talmon, 'Determining Customary International Law: The ICJ's Methodology between Induction, Deduction and Assertion' (2015) 26 EJIL 417.
[115] Similarly, Horowitz, 'Justification', 112.

it will be indispensable to inquire whether that theory is more suitable as a theory of justification or a theory of excuse. This suitability will be determined by reference to the formulation of the defence, as well as systemic, normative and policy considerations. It is here that some top-down elements may appear: for example, the definitions of justification and excuse as defences concerning, respectively, the act or the actor, may be relied upon. As an illustration, *force majeure* affords a defence because in the circumstances, where there is a material impossibility to perform an obligation resulting from an unforeseen or irresistible event beyond the control of the state, the state was compelled to act in a manner incompatible with its obligations. The defence is focused on the actor (its situation following the supervening event); moreover, its rationale points to a theory of free will: the defence is given because the state's capacity to choose whether to comply with its obligation is eliminated or coerced by the circumstances. Free will, it will be concluded, constitutes a theory of excuse because it focuses on the actor (what was the situation of the state in the circumstances?) and also for policy reasons, in particular the need to hold coercing states responsible towards the injured state for the acts of the coerced state.

## 3.5 General Conclusion to Part I

To summarise, the distinction between justification and excuse can be accommodated by the current system of state responsibility, codified in the ARS. It is, therefore, a possible distinction as argued in Chapter 1. It is, moreover, also a desirable one for it is a distinction capable of providing answers to practical problems of the law, as shown in Chapter 2. This final chapter of Part I thus elaborated conceptions of justification and excuse *for* international law and briefly considered potential theories of justification and excuse. These conceptions and theories are crucial to the classification of individual defences as either justifications or excuses, and this chapter concluded by proposing a methodological approach to the classification. This theoretical framework will now be applied, in Part II, to each of the defences with the aim of classifying them between the two categories of defences. As will be seen, this book will argue that consent, self-defence, countermeasures and state of necessity constitute, in their current formulation, justifications, that *force majeure* constitutes an excuse and that distress can be classified as an excuse.

# PART II

Classifying the Defences in the Articles
on State Responsibility

# 4

# Consent

## 4.1 Introduction

In domestic law, it is said that the consent of a potential victim 'turns a rape into love-making, a kidnapping into a Sunday drive, a battery into a football tackle, a theft into a gift, and a trespass into a dinner party'.[1] The same holds true in international law. Thus, it is the consent of the territorial state that turns an intervention into aid[2] and an exercise of extraterritorial jurisdiction into cooperation.[3] To reflect this, the ILC included a defence of consent in Article 20 of the ARS in the following terms:

> Valid consent by a State to the commission of a given act by another State precludes the wrongfulness of that act in relation to the former State to the extent that the act remains within the limits of that consent.

The Commentary to this provision explains that states 'may dispense with the performance of an obligation owed to them individually, or generally to permit conduct to occur which (absent such permission) would be unlawful so far as they are concerned.'[4] This dispensation does not affect the underlying obligation: it is not a renunciation of the right itself, but only of the performance of that right in a given case. Consent in this sense is different from consent to the underlying obligation. For example, in 'the case of a bilateral treaty, the States parties can at any time agree to terminate or suspend the treaty, in which case obligations arising from the

---

[1] Hurd, 'Blaming the Victim: A Response to the Proposal That Criminal Law Recognize a General Defense of Contributory Responsibility' (2005) 8 *Buffalo Crim LR* 503, 504.
[2] See, e.g., Woolsey, *Introduction to the Study of International Law* (1860), 89: 'there is nothing in the law of nations which forbids one nation to render assistance to the established government in such case of revolt, if its assistance is invoked. This aid is no interference, and is given to keep up the present order of things, which international law takes under its protection.'
[3] E.g., agreements on hot pursuit on land in Europe, on which see Daman, 'Cross-Border Hot Pursuit in the EU' (2008) 16 *Eur J Crime Crim L & Crim Justice* 171.
[4] ARS art. 20 Commentary, [2].

treaty will be terminated or suspended accordingly.'[5] Moreover, insofar as consent excludes the breach of an obligation, it must also be distinguished from a waiver of claim. Indeed, in the case of waiver there exists a wrongful act and the injured state solely renounces its right to invoke the wrongdoing state's responsibility.[6] Consent, to produce its effect as a defence, has to be validly expressed, namely it must be given by an entity authorised to do so on behalf of the state and it must be free from vitiating factors including coercion. Who may give consent on behalf of the state in any given situation may depend on the obligation in question.[7] Finally, there are no formal requirements: consent need not be in writing (it can be implied from the state's conduct),[8] and it may take the form of a unilateral act or an ad hoc agreement between two states.[9]

The defence of consent has been controversially received in the literature – though not so by states.[10] Among scholars, some have argued that the Commission made an error in separating two different functions of consent in international law: first, as a means for the creation of obligations and, second, as a defence. On the contrary, it is said, the Commission should have upheld a single, unified function for consent as a source of law.[11] But this is a short-sighted critique. The phenomenon of state consent is translated into a variety of different rules in the international legal order.[12] Thus, state consent may create obligations (through, for example, treaties) but it may also grant jurisdiction to international courts and tribunals.[13] These are certainly two different functions of consent, and

---

[5] Id. The legal nature of consent as an agreement between consenting and acting state was the subject of heated debate during the ILC work. Ago's report suggested that consent created an agreement through which the parties suspended, for the specific case, the underlying obligation. There being no obligation binding the parties, the conduct of the state could not infringe the rights of the consenting State: Ago, Eighth Report on State Responsibility, ILC Yearbook 1979, vol. II(1). This point will be addressed in Section 4.4.1.

[6] ARS art. 20 Commentary, [3].

[7] Ibid., [5–6].

[8] Ibid., [4].

[9] Though this is not indicated in the Commentary, it is inferred from the Commission's work, as will be seen later. It should be emphasised at this point that the agreement in question is an ad hoc agreement for the specific circumstances, and not one intended to modify for the future the relations between the parties.

[10] See Section 4.2.2.

[11] This is the gist of Farhang's argument in 'The Notion of Consent in Part One of the Draft Articles on State Responsibility' (2014) 27 LJIL 55.

[12] The same is true of domestic law, see Ferzan, 'Clarifying Consent: Peter Westen's The Logic of Consent' (2006) 25 *Law & Philosophy* 193, 195.

[13] Crawford, 'Sovereignty as a Legal Value' in Crawford and Koskenniemi (eds), *Cambridge Companion to International Law* (2013), 124–5.

## 4.1 INTRODUCTION

there is no principled reason why a third function – as a defence to responsibility – may not be recognised. Moreover, there is a fundamentally important difference between consent to the non-performance of a right in an individual case and consent creating (or modifying) rights and obligations. For example, in the *Navigational Rights in the San Juan River* case, Nicaragua's acquiescence to subsistence fishing by Costa Rican nationals in the San Juan River was general and, over time, generated bilateral customary rights between the two parties which it can no longer unilaterally withdraw from.[14] This is certainly different to consent granted to, say, the inhabitants of a specific riparian village to fish in the river for a limited period: in this case, the consent is unlikely to generate rights and obligations of indefinite duration and may, as a result, be withdrawn unilaterally.

The question that has most divided scholars relates to whether consent constitutes a defence at all. Without dismissing the effects that consent can have in this role, a considerable number of scholars – including James Crawford, the last Special Rapporteur on state responsibility – have rejected the idea that the plea of consent may constitute a defence in international law, in the same way as countermeasures or *force majeure* constitute defences. In their view, consent (or rather non-consent) is better seen as a constituent requirement of the definition of states' obligations or, what is the same, as a negative rule-element. On this view, every international obligation would contain, as part of its definition, an element of non-consent.[15] Consent is, therefore, not a question of defences; but a matter of the definition of states' obligations. As a result, the argument goes, it has no place in the law of state responsibility. This chapter disputes this view: as will be seen later, while consent *may* be a negative rule-element in relation to certain obligations, there is nothing preventing the possibility that consent *may* constitute a defence in relation to other obligations. And where it constitutes a defence, consent is classified as a justification.

The chapter explains this argument in three steps. To begin with, Section 4.2 will provide an overview of the historical development of this plea. This review is divided into two parts. First, this section will cover developments in the period between 1898 and 1979, namely the period between the earliest found reference to consent as a defence in the law of state responsibility and the year of Special Rapporteur Roberto Ago's report on consent to the ILC. From 1979 onwards, developments on this

---

[14] See *Navigational and Related Rights (Costa Rica v Nicaragua)* (2009) ICJ Rep 213.
[15] See Section 4.3.

notion have been shaped by the Commission's work, so the second part of this section will consider the work of the ILC in the formulation of Article 20. As will be seen, while states were on the whole favourable to Article 20, the question of whether consent was a defence or a negative rule-element divided the Commission which, unable to reach a consensus on this point, simply agreed to disagree. Section 4.3 considers the scholarly arguments put forward against the defence of consent, and will show that these arguments, singly or in combination, are unable to exclude the conceptual (and practical) possibility that consent be classified as a defence in international law. Finally, Section 4.4 will discuss the characterisation of the defence of consent as a justification or an excuse. As will be said, the plea of consent involves the renunciation by a state of the legal protection afforded by law to its interests. In these circumstances, there is no reason for the law to protect that interest with the result that the conduct in question does not breach international law. Consent, that is, operates as a justification.

## 4.2 Development of the Plea of Consent

While the principle *volenti non fit injuria* dates back to at least the Digest,[16] the idea that consent may act as a defence to responsibility is a relatively recent development in both domestic[17] and, as this review will show, international law.[18] The historical development of the plea of consent will be divided into two parts: (i) the period between 1898 and 1979 and (ii) from 1979 onwards. The dividing point between these two periods is Ago's presentation of his report on consent to the ILC, with the subsequent adoption by the Commission and discussion in the Sixth Committee of a defence of consent. Since 1979, much of the scholarly debate on Article 20 has been shaped by the Commission's work and its choices.

As will be seen, while states have on the whole been favourable to a defence of consent, the question of its place vis-à-vis state obligations divided the Commission which was unable to reach an agreement on this issue.

---

[16] Palazzo, *Corso di diritto penale. Parte generale* (2008), 268.
[17] On domestic law, see Soler, *Derecho penal argentino* (1945), 370.
[18] Until Ago's report in 1979, no codification of state responsibility had included a defence of consent: Díaz Barrado, *El consentimiento, causa de exclusión de la ilicitud del uso de la fuerza en Derecho Internacional* (1989), 87.

### 4.2.1 A Brief History of the Plea of Consent (1898-1979)

In international law, the plea of consent began appearing in scholarly works in the context of responsibility only at the turn of the twentieth century.[19] The earliest reference found is in Franz von Liszt's *Das Völkerrecht*, published in 1898.[20] Since then, the few scholars who have addressed consent as a defence to responsibility – whose works will be examined later – have done so only cursorily, dedicating to it no more than a few superficial observations. Thus in 1986, Natalino Ronzitti observed that, with the notable exception of consent to the use of force discussed time and again since the mid-nineteenth century,[21] '[u]ntil recently, the subject of consent as a circumstance precluding wrongfulness was dealt with by few writers'.[22] This situation has not significantly changed since Ronzitti's statement. Contemporary scholarship rarely engages with consent as a general notion of the law of responsibility, with textbooks frequently restating, uncritically, the views of the ILC on the matter.[23]

In terms of state practice, the majority of instances in which an ad hoc consent was given to relieve a state from performing an obligation involve the use of force or, relatedly, the presence of foreign military forces in a

---

[19] Ago remarked in 1939 that scholarship 'glisse en général sur une telle situation', citing von Liszt and Strupp as the 'only' scholars to have addressed consent as a defence to responsibility: Ago, 'Le délit international' (1939) 68 *Recueil* 415, 533 and fn. 1.

[20] von Liszt, *Das Völkerrecht: systematisch Dargestellt* (1898), 128.

[21] For general works examining the relevant literature of the nineteenth century, see Flöckher, *De l'intervention en droit international* (1896); Hodges, *Doctrine of Intervention* (1915); Stowell, *Intervention in International Law* (1921); Winfield, 'The History of Intervention in International Law' (1922-3) 3 BYIL 130; Winfield, 'Grounds of Intervention in International Law' (1924) 5 BYIL 149. Intervention with the consent of the territorial state remains a controversial question in contemporary international law; see Gray, *International Law and the Use of Force* (3rd edn, 2008), ch. 3; Fox, 'Intervention by Invitation' in Weller (ed.), *Oxford Handbook on the Use of Force* (2015), 816.

[22] Ronzitti, 'Use of Force, *Jus Cogens* and State Consent' in Cassese (ed.), *The Current Legal Regulation of the Use of Force* (1986), 148.

[23] See, e.g., Gutiérrez-Espada, *El hecho ilícito internacional* (2005), 114–16; Shaw, *International Law* (7th edn, 2014), 577; Crawford and Olleson, 'The Character and Forms of International Responsibility' in Evans (ed.), *International Law* (4th edn, 2014), 465. There are notable exceptions: Alaimo, 'La natura del consenso nell'illecito internazionale' (1982), *Rivista di diritto internazionale* 257; Bannelier and Christakis, '*Volenti non fit injuria*? Les effets du consentement à l'intervention militaire' (2004) 50 AFDI 102; Abass, 'Consent Precluding State Responsibility: A Critical Analysis' (2004) 53 ICLQ 211; Ben Mansour, 'Consent' in Crawford et al. (eds), *The Law of International Responsibility* (2010), 439; Farhang, 'The Notion of Consent in Part One of the Draft Articles on State Responsibility'. The views expressed by these scholars will be discussed throughout this chapter where they are relevant.

state's territory. Ago's report to the Commission on the plea of consent relied heavily on this practice from which he distilled the various elements ultimately included in Article 20.[24] Nevertheless, this practice will not be considered here because it has been discussed expansively in the literature and because of the peculiar circumstances surrounding these instances of consent.[25] This section will instead focus on two international arbitrations in which consent was discussed in relation to the non-performance of international obligations other than the prohibition of force: the *Savarkar* and *Russian Indemnities* cases.

#### 4.2.1.1 Writings of Scholars

A relatively small number of scholars discussed consent as a defence to responsibility throughout this period.[26] Of these, the majority were favourable to its recognition. Many, including Paul Fauchille,[27] Antoine Favre,[28] Alf Ross,[29] Riccardo Monaco,[30] Angelo Sereni,[31] Gaetano Morelli[32] and Eduardo Jiménez de Aréchaga,[33] simply asserted that consent constituted a defence to responsibility, without elaborating on either conceptual aspects or specific requirements.[34]

A handful of scholars, however, elaborated in more detail the formulation of this defence as well as its rationale. According to von Liszt, who was the first scholar to discuss consent as a defence to responsibility, the recognition of the defence followed logically from the sovereignty of

---

[24] See, generally, Ago, Eighth Report, 30–8.
[25] See, e.g., Díaz Barrado, *Consentimiento* (for a comprehensive review of practice and literature); Doswald-Beck, 'The Legal Validity of Military Intervention by Invitation of the Government' (1985) 56 BYIL 189, and references cited therein.
[26] Compare, for example, with the rich literature on reprisals or state of necessity, on which see Chapters 6 and 8 respectively.
[27] Fauchille, *Traité de droit international public (Paix)* (8th edn, 1922) vol. 1, part 1, 533. Fauchille's *Traité* was a substantial revision of Henry Bonfils' *Manuel de droit international public*, first published in 1894. Note that consent was Fauchille's own addition of 1922. Previous editions of Bonfils' *Manuel* (even those updated by Fauchille) contained sections on state responsibility without including consent as a defence (or any other defence, for that matter): see Bonfils, *Manuel de droit international public* (1894), 167–72; through to Bonfils, *Manuel de droit international public* (Fauchille ed., 7th edn, 1914), 207–14.
[28] Favre, 'Fault as an Element of the Illicit Act' (1964) 52 *Georgetown LJ* 566, 565.
[29] Ross, *A Textbook on International Law* (1947), 243.
[30] Monaco, *Manuale di diritto internazionale pubblico* (1960), 378.
[31] Sereni, *Diritto internazionale* (1962) vol. 3, 1523.
[32] Morelli, *Nozioni di diritto internazionale* (7th edn, 1967), 351.
[33] Jiménez de Aréchaga, 'International Responsibility' in Sørensen (ed.), *Manual of Public International Law* (1968), 541.
[34] For additional references, see Ago's Eighth Report, 30–8.

states. Indeed, if international rights and obligations were recognised for the protection of state interests, then, he thought, the state had the option to renounce that protection for an individual case.[35] This possibility was almost unlimited – its sole exception being when the right was established for the protection of a collective interest. The neutralisation of Belgium provided a good example of this situation. Since the neutralisation was established in the general interest,[36] Belgium could not consent to the occupation of its territory by a foreign power.[37]

Karl Wolff also recognised consent as a defence to responsibility. Wolff explained that to be valid, and therefore to exonerate the other state from the performance of an obligation towards the consenting state, consent must be given for the specific act and it must be given by the sovereign or by an authorised organ of the state.[38] Wolff explained that consent entailed the renunciation of the protection afforded by international law to one of the state's interests. According to this author, the state could renounce the protection of *any* of its rights: this possibility was, unlike for von Liszt, virtually unlimited. Wolff noted that the state could go as far as renouncing its own existence and self-preservation,[39] protected by the cardinal right of self-preservation which, in his system of international law, served as the source of all other state rights.[40] It followed from this, *argumentum*

---

[35] von Liszt, *Le droit international: Exposé systématique* (translation of 1913, 9th edn, 1927), 201. Similarly, Balladore-Pallieri, *Diritto internazionale pubblico* (7th edn, 1956), 216.

[36] Belgium had been 'neutralised' by the treaties of 15 November 1831 and 19 April 1839. This neutralisation served both the individual interest of the state as well as a collective interest – at the very least the interest of the guarantors of the neutralised state. As explained by de Visscher, neutralisation (in contrast with neutrality) is '[f]ounded on an international agreement, and generally inspired by considerations due to the balance of power' and it 'aims definitely at sheltering from all danger of armed conflict a state, of which the independent existence and territorial integrity are considered to be to the common interest of several Powers', at de Visscher, *Belgium's Case: A Juridical Enquiry* (1916), 2.

[37] von Liszt, *Droit*, 201.

[38] Wolff, 'Les principes généraux du droit applicables dans les rapports internationaux' (1931) 36 *Recueil* 479, 523.

[39] Wolff, 'Principes', 522; see also ibid., 504–5. The possibility for a state to renounce its own existence was also endorsed in Judge Anzilotti's separate opinion in *Customs Regime between Germany and Austria (Advisory Opinion)* (1931) PCIJ Series A/B No 41, 37, 58–9, where he states that: 'admitted that this quality [independence] ceases to exist by the will of the State itself when the latter agrees to renounce it in favour of another State, for example, by becoming absorbed in the latter or placing itself under the latter's authority … According to ordinary international law, every country is free to renounce its independence and even its existence'. In that case, however, Austria's independence was a matter of interest to other European states and, therefore, Austria could not renounce it – at least not in favour of Germany.

[40] Wolff, 'Principes', 504.

*a maiori*, that the state could renounce the legal protection of every one of its rights.[41]

Possibly the most extensive discussion of consent in the context of state responsibility appeared in Ago's work *Le délit international*. His views differed considerably from those of von Liszt and Wolff. In common with these two scholars, Ago explained that consent could be express or tacit but never presumed, that it must exist at the time the conduct is adopted and that it must be valid. As to the limits of consent, Ago argued that in international law the state's power to consent to the non-performance of obligations was more extensive than in domestic law. Moreover, Ago added that a consented act may be lawful in respect of one state and unlawful in respect of another: this was, for example, the situation of a state which consented to the presence of foreign troops in its territory even though it had a commitment to a third state not to allow this (a scenario which recalls that of Belgium discussed by von Liszt).[42] However, Ago explained the operation of this defence in different terms from von Liszt's and Wolff's. It was not a question of renunciation of protection or absent interest, rather, for Ago consent precluded the wrongfulness of state conduct because the presence of that consent 'suspend[ed], in relation to the concrete situation to which it applies, the effect (*jeu*) of the legal obligation binding on the State which performs the act'.[43] In these circumstances, the wrongful act was not constituted because the conduct was not in breach of any obligation binding on the state.

Finally, few scholars argued against the recognition of a plea of consent. Paul Guggenheim's remarks are representative of these views. For Guggenheim, in the case of consent there was no question of preclusion of wrongfulness: 'the acts in question are perfectly in accordance with the law'.[44] In essence, Guggenheim was expressing the view that consent was not a defence but rather a negative rule-element included in the definition of all states' obligations – a view which would later be considered by the ILC during the second reading of the ARS. Guggenheim (or any of the other scholars arguing against a defence of consent) did not, however, offer an explanation of his position.

---

[41] Ibid., 522.

[42] Ago, 'Délit', 534–6. Note that Ago drew extensively from domestic criminal law in the exposition of this defence.

[43] Ibid., 534.

[44] Guggenheim, *Traité de droit international public* (1954) vol. 2, 57. A similar view was also held by Strupp and Steineger, both cited in Ago, Eighth Report, [67] (fn. 152).

## 4.2.1.2  State Practice

***Savarkar* (1911)**  Vinayak Damodar Savarkar, a law student at Gray's Inn in London, was an Indian pro-independence activist. He was accused of political offences in India and, having been arrested in London, he had been extradited.[45] Savarkar undertook his journey to India on the British merchantman *Morea* which was due to make a stop, among others, in Marseilles. Aware of the presence of Indian revolutionaries in the continent, on 29 June 1910, a few days before the *Morea*'s departure, the British Chief of Police notified the Ministry of Interior in Paris of Savarkar's presence in the vessel and requested the French police to assist in securing Savarkar's safety.[46] In compliance with the request, instructions were duly sent to the local police in Marseilles to provide assistance with Savarkar's safety during the ship's stay.[47] The *Morea* departed London on 1 July and arrived in Marseilles on 7 July.

On the morning of 8 July, Savarkar escaped from the vessel and swam ashore to the port of Marseilles. Two Indian constables on board the *Morea* saw Savarkar in the water and, while screaming to draw attention to him, began running towards the port. A French brigadier of the Maritime Gendarmerie, alerted by the screams, saw Savarkar running on land, chased him and captured him a few minutes later. The French brigadier was then joined by the Indian constables who grabbed Savarkar by his free arm (his other arm being under the hold of the French brigadier), and together walked towards the ship. Throughout this time, the brigadier did not 'relax his hold' on Savarkar and handed him over to the British officers on board the *Morea* in the 'half deck of the vessel'.[48] The *Morea* departed from Marseilles the next day, 9 July. Until that time, no disclaimers were presented to the *Morea*'s crew as to the brigadier's conduct by his superiors in the French Maritime Gendarmerie.[49] On that same day, the director of the Sûreté Nationale in Paris informed the British Chief of Police that, in accordance with his request of 29 June, instructions

---

[45] See the warrant of arrest (28 February 1910) and the warrant of the Secretary of State for Home Affairs for the return of Savarkar to India (29 June 1910), in PCA, *Savarkar Arbitration. Case Presented on Behalf of the Government of His Britannic Majesty* (1910) ('*UK Case*'), Annexes 4 and 5, respectively.

[46] See letter from Sir E. Henry to M. Hennion (Communicated by Home Office), 29 June 1910, in *UK Case, Savarkar Arbitration*, Annex 6.

[47] *Savarkar Case (Great Britain, France)* (1911) 9 RIAA 243, 254.

[48] Ibid., 253–4.

[49] Ibid., 254.

in relation to Savarkar had been issued.[50] Over a week later, on 18 July, the French ambassador in London informed the British government that Savarkar had been irregularly surrendered to the British authorities since he should have been considered an asylee once he reached French soil, and requested that Savarkar be restored to France.[51] The British refused the request[52] and, unable to find a diplomatic solution, the two parties agreed to submit the dispute to arbitration.[53]

There were three interrelated points of contention before the Tribunal. First, France claimed that it had a right of asylum and that Savarkar, upon reaching French soil, had become an asylee in France.[54] The right of asylum could be refused by a state in one of two ways only: expulsion, a unilateral act; or extradition, a bilateral act.[55] Savarkar's irregular surrender to the British authorities, not corresponding to either of these two ways, violated France's right of asylum. Second, Savarkar's surrender should be classed as an extradition since it entailed a bilateral relation. As such, it should have followed the procedures established in the 1876 Anglo-French Extradition Treaty. Since the extradition failed to follow these formalities, the suspect's surrender was incompatible with the treaty.[56] Third, the conduct of the Indian constables constituted a violation of France's territorial sovereignty insofar as, in apprehending Savarkar, they had exercised (enforcement) jurisdiction within French soil.[57] The United Kingdom contested all three claims. First, it maintained that France had renounced the right of asylum in respect of Savarkar when it accepted the request

---

[50] Letter from M. Hennion to Sir Henry, 9 July 1910, in PCA, *Affaire Savarkar. Contre-mémoire présenté par le Gourvenement de la République Française* (1911) ('*France Contre-mémoire*'), Annex VII.

[51] See note communicated by M. Cambon (18 July 1910), letter from M. Cambon to Sir Edward Grey (23 July 1910) and Letter from M. Daeschner to Sir Edward Grey (2 August 1910), in *UK Case, Savarkar Arbitration*, Annexes 12–14, respectively.

[52] Letter from Sir Edward Grey to M. Daeschner, 24 September 1910, *UK Case, Savarkar Arbitration*, Annex 20.

[53] Letter from M. Cambon to Sir Edward Grey (3 October 1910) and letter from Sir Edward Grey to M. Cambon (4 October 1910), in *UK Case, Savarkar Arbitration*, Annexes 21 and 22, respectively.

[54] Note by M. Cambon, 18 July 1910, *UK Case, Savarkar Arbitration*, Annex 12.

[55] Statement of France, *France Contre-mémoire, Affaire Savarkar*, 7; *Affaire Savarkar. Protocole des séances et sentence* (1911) ('*Protocole*'), 17.

[56] M. Cambon to Sir Edward Grey, *UK Case, Savarkar Arbitration*, Annex 13; *France Contre-mémoire, Affaire Savarkar*, 26–9.

[57] M. Daeschner to Sir Edward Grey, *UK Case, Savarkar Arbitration*, Annex 14. See further *France Contre-mémoire, Affaire Savarkar*, 20, 29.

## 4.2 DEVELOPMENT OF THE PLEA OF CONSENT 141

formulated by the chief of the British Police.[58] Second, the exchange of letters between the UK and French officials evidenced a special arrangement between the two in relation to Savarkar's case, pursuant to which France had undertaken to assist to prevent Savarkar's escape. This commitment entailed an obligation to return Savarkar in case he attempted to flee. While an extradition treaty existed between the two states, the two could agree to alternative arrangements and this was not a violation of the treaty.[59] Third, the British officers did not capture Savarkar on French soil: they merely assisted the French brigadier. Not having exercised any enforcement authority in France, their conduct was not a violation of France's territorial sovereignty.[60]

The Tribunal resolved the dispute in a succinct decision (a short three pages),[61] in which it held that the British officers had reason to 'believe that they could count on the assistance of the French police' in relation to Savarkar; that the rendition of Savarkar had been 'irregular', but that there was no rule of international law imposing on the United Kingdom an obligation to restore Savarkar to the French authorities; and that there had been 'nothing in the nature of a violation of the sovereignty of France' since the Indian constables only had a secondary role in the arrest.[62]

*Savarkar* is often cited as an example of the exercise of extraterritorial enforcement with the consent of the territorial state: the French brigadier is seen as having consented to the capture of Savarkar by the Indian constables on French soil.[63] This does not, however, reflect the views of the parties or the decision of the Tribunal. France had initially claimed that the apprehension of Savarkar had been carried out by the Indian

---

[58] *Savarkar Arbitration. Reply Presented on Behalf of the Government of His Britannic Majesty* (1911) ('*UK Reply*'), 3.

[59] *Savarkar Arbitration. Counter-case Presented on Behalf of the Government of His Britannic Majesty* (1911) ('*UK Counter-case*'), 18–20; *UK Reply, Savarkar Arbitration*, 9–22.

[60] Sir Edward Grey to M. Daeschner, *UK Case, Savarkar Arbitration*, Annex 20. See further *UK Case, Savarkar Arbitration*, 14; *UK Counter-case, Savarkar Arbitration*, 11–12; *UK Reply, Savarkar Arbitration*, 4–9.

[61] For a critique of the award's brevity, see van Hamel, 'Les principes du droit d'extradition et leur application dans l'affaire Savarkar' (1911) 13 RDILC 370, 376–7.

[62] *Savarkar*, 254.

[63] This is how the ARS Commentary refers to this case: art. 20 Commentary, [8]. See also, during the first reading of the ARS, the following observations: Ago, Eighth Report, [63]; Francis, 1543rd meeting, ILC Yearbook 1979, vol. I, 53 [17]; Ago, 1543rd meeting, ILC Yearbook 1979, vol. I, 54 [23]. On second reading, see Goco, 2588th meeting, ILC Yearbook 1999, vol. I, 151 [41]; Pellet, 2588th meeting, ILC Yearbook 1999, vol. I, 151 [44]. In the literature, see Cassese, *International Law* (2nd edn, 2005), 253; Ben Mansour, 'Consent', 442; Crawford and Olleson, 'Character and Forms', 463.

constables in violation of its sovereignty. However, as the case proceeded, evidence was presented to the effect that the capture was carried out by the French brigadier – there was simply no question of an extraterritorial enforcement by the Indian constables and, even less, of France's consent to this conduct. This conclusion was confirmed by the Tribunal, as seen earlier.

The parties did discuss the role of consent in relation to the claims of the case, just not in relation to Savarkar's apprehension on French soil. Consent, and whether France had given it, was a relevant consideration in relation to the surrender of Savarkar to the United Kingdom after his apprehension by the French brigadier. France had claimed that the surrender was in violation of its right of asylum and, at any rate, that it failed to comply with the requirements of the extradition treaty. As to the former, the United Kingdom insisted that France, by acceding to British requests in relation to Savarkar, had renounced its right of asylum in respect of that individual. Therefore, France could not now claim that it had granted refuge to Savarkar and, consequently, the United Kingdom was under no obligation to return him. France responded that the renunciation of this right was a serious matter and could not arbitrarily be presumed.[64] In respect of extradition, the United Kingdom argued that there existed an arrangement, as evidenced by the exchange of letters between the British and French officials, in which France had undertaken the obligation to assist in the custody of Savarkar and return him to his custodians should he escape.[65] But France denied having assented to any such agreement: there was no 'certain and conscious' consent,[66] it said, and in any event consent to such an arrangement could only be expressed by its Foreign Minister and not by any other state official.[67] On both grounds, the legality of Savarkar's surrender turned on the consent of France: either to renounce its right of asylum vis-à-vis Savarkar or to the special arrangement for his rendition.

The Tribunal did not address either point in its award; it merely stated that there was no basis in international law for the restitution required by France. While the Tribunal did not state this, it can be inferred from its conclusion that the surrender was lawful. Indeed, if restitution is a

---

[64] Statement of France, *Protocole des séances, Affaire Savarkar*, 17.
[65] UK statement, PCA, *Protocole des séances, Affaire Savarkar*, 30.
[66] *Affaire Savarkar. Réplique du Gouvernement de la République Française* (1911) ('*France Réplique*'), 14.
[67] *Affaire Savarkar. Mémoire présenté par le Gouvernement de la République Française* (1911), 22–3; *Réplique Française, Affaire Savarkar*, 15–16.

form of reparation which follows from the breach of international law,[68] then the surrender of Savarkar, 'irregular' as it may have been, was not a breach of international law. As the award explains, the surrender had taken place either under instructions of superiors or had (subsequently) been approved by those superiors. A plausible argument could thus be made that the Tribunal understood the conduct of France, through the various organs which intervened, as signalling its assent to the renunciation of the right of asylum and to the application of special arrangements outside the extradition treaty to Savarkar.

The parties' arguments in the case show that they both accepted that through consent, unilateral or bilateral as it may be, a state could renounce its rights in respect of an individual case.

***Russian Indemnity* (1912)** The *Russian Indemnity* case concerned the payment of war indemnities by the Ottoman Empire to Russian citizens for injuries suffered during the Turco-Russian war of 1877–8. Internal revolts and insurrections in the Ottoman Empire had a negative impact on the Empire's finances, resulting in delays in the service of its debt to Russia.[69] A dispute ensued as to whether the Empire owed 'interest-damages' to Russia arising out of the delayed payments,[70] which was submitted for resolution to an arbitral tribunal. The Tribunal ruled that under the principle of state responsibility interest-damages were due on late payments.[71] The dispute then turned to whether the Ottoman Empire, in this case, was obliged to pay those interests to Russia.[72] The Ottoman Empire argued that Russia had (tacitly) consented to the non-payment of the interests by way of the Russian embassy's acceptance of payments of the

---

[68] Restitution was a recognised form of reparation at the time, even though it was (and continues to be) rarely awarded. The PCIJ endorsed it as a 'principle of international law' some 10 years after *Savarkar* in *Factory at Chorzów (Merits)* (1928) PCIJ, Series A No 17, 3, at 47. For a review of historical arbitral practice see Gray, *Judicial Remedies in International Law* (1987), 12–16.
[69] For a historical account of the Ottoman debts in general, see Waibel, *Sovereign Defaults before International Courts and Tribunals* (2011), 89.
[70] Note that the award uses the expression 'interest-damages' in view of a controversy between the parties in respect of the character of the damages sought and in respect of the obligation to pay those damages, *Russian Indemnity Case (Russia/Turkey)* (1912) Scott Hague Court Rep 297, 312–13.
[71] *Russian Indemnity*, 315. For the continued relevance of this principle, see Waibel, *Sovereign Defaults*, 94.
[72] Questions of *force majeure* and state of necessity also arose in this connection, and they will be discussed in Chapters 7 and 8, respectively.

principal (net of interest) without reservation.[73] The Tribunal agreed that this constituted a 'renunciation' or a 'relinquishment' by Russia of its right to interest.[74] The Tribunal reached this conclusion by analogy from the 'principles of private law' applicable to pecuniary debts[75] – an approach criticised by later tribunals[76] – and not by application of an international legal rule recognising that consent may act as a defence for a claim of breach.

Fauchille and Ago both considered the *Russian Indemnity* award as an example of consent as a defence to responsibility.[77] But contemporary legal commentary has (correctly) tended to see the *Russian Indemnity* award as an example of waiver of claims,[78] since the Russian consent to the non-payment by the Ottoman Empire was given *after* the interest-damages were already due, namely after the breach of the Empire's legal obligation had been constituted by way of its late payment. Indeed, the ILC itself removed the reference to this case from the commentary to draft Article 29 on the defence of consent adopted on first reading,[79] and relocated it to the current Commentary to Article 45 on waiver of claims.[80]

### 4.2.1.3   Interim Conclusions

Aside from the practice relating to consent to foreign military intervention, which as noted earlier was common, developments on consent as a defence to the breach of international law more generally were limited. Both the practice on, and the and scholarly engagement with, the defence of consent throughout this period were certainly scant and mostly superficial. And yet, it is possible to identify in these early materials the contours of the defence as it was later formulated: among others, consent must be valid, it must be prior to the act in question, and it need not be formally or even expressly given.

---

[73] *Contre-Mémoire présenté au nom du Gouvernement de l'Empire Ottoman* (1911), 54–70.
[74] *Russian Indemnity*, 322–3.
[75] Ibid., 322.
[76] *Georges Pinson (France) v United Mexican States* (1928) RIAA 324, 448.
[77] Fauchille, 1 *Traité*, part 1, 533; Ago, Eighth Report, [65].
[78] See, e.g., Beknazar, 'Russian Indemnity Arbitration' in Wolfrum (ed.), *Max Planck Encyclopaedia of Public International Law* (2009–, available at www.mpepil.com), [17]; Tams, 'Waiver, Acquiescence and Extinctive Prescription' in Crawford et al. (eds), *The Law of International Responsibility* (2010), 1037; Crawford, *State Responsibility: The General Part* (2013), 559.
[79] ILC Report, thirty-first session, ILC Yearbook 1979, vol. II(2), 111 [9].
[80] ARS art. 20 Commentary, [3].

For the purposes of this chapter, there are two notable aspects of the developments of this period. First, both in the practice and the scholarship, the operation of consent as a defence to responsibility was described as a *renunciation* by a state of the legal protection afforded to one of its interests; a renunciation which was ad hoc and did not affect the legal status of the relevant rule as such. This can be seen in the works of von Liszt, Wolff and Ago, and also in the pleadings and decisions in *Savarkar* and *Russian Indemnities*. This power of renunciation, as explained by von Liszt, was a logical implication of the concept of state sovereignty. Second, Guggenheim's work contained the seeds of what would later become one of the thorniest questions in relation to the plea of consent: that of whether consent was a defence or whether it was a negative rule-element, implicit in all of the international obligations of states.

### 4.2.2 Codification in the International Law Commission

By the time Special Rapporteur Ago addressed the defence of consent in his report of 1979 to the ILC, consent as a defence to responsibility was at best in embryonic form. Both during the first and second readings of the ARS, Commission members expressed (more or less insistent) doubts on, and objections to, the inclusion of consent as a defence in the ARS. These critiques, albeit for different reasons, all boiled down to the same issue: could consent, really, be classified as a defence or was it rather the case that it was a negative rule-element implicit in all international obligations? If the latter, then it had no place in the ARS as these were a codification of 'secondary rules only'. This challenge raised an immensely difficult theoretical question, one which has been considered at multiple times by domestic lawyers, and one which remains without a generally acceptable answer – at least, an acceptable *principled* answer. Ultimately, the Commission, after some heated exchanges among its members, desisted from solving this theoretical question and opted for the practical way out: to leave the defence in the ARS in view of states' general support for it.

This section summarises the developments leading to the adoption of Article 20 by the Commission, focusing on the debates and disagreements around the place of consent vis-à-vis states' obligations, namely whether it is a defence or it is better seen as a negative rule-element. These debates will only be highlighted in this overview of the ILC's work leading to the adoption of Article 20. As will be seen, members of the Commission presented different views as to the role of consent in this context, but they did not provide fully articulated arguments in support of such views. The task of reconstructing the arguments in support of these views and of their critical analysis will be carried out later, in Section 4.3.

### 4.2.2.1 First Reading of the ARS: The Adoption of Draft Article 29

**Ago's Report and the Debates at the International Law Commission** Special Rapporteur Ago introduced the defence of consent in his Eighth Report to the ILC submitted in 1979. According to the report, there existed 'in international law a firmly established principle whereby consent of the State' precludes the wrongfulness of conduct.[81] This was evidenced by the practice of states,[82] which also showed that consent precluded wrongfulness only when certain conditions were met. First, consent had to be 'validly expressed'; it could be express or tacit so long as it was clearly established.[83] Second, consent must be prior to, or contemporaneous with, the conduct in question.[84] Finally, a state may not consent to the non-performance of a peremptory rule of international law.[85] Ago explained that consent precluded wrongfulness through 'the formation of an agreement between the two subjects whereby the international obligation ceases to have effect as between [them] or, at least, is suspended in relation to the particular case involved.'[86] The obligation having lost its effect or having been suspended, the acting state was no longer obliged to act in accordance with its terms with the result that its conduct could not infringe that obligation.[87]

Ago also noted in the report that some scholars objected to the conceptualisation of consent as a defence. The report explained that this objection was based on the fact that to present consent as a circumstance precluding wrongfulness 'presupposed the existence of a wrongful act which, by way of exception, becomes lawful'.[88] And yet, continued the critics, conduct adopted with the consent of the target state was lawful as

---

[81] Ago, Eighth Report, [68].
[82] Reviewed ibid. at 31–4. See also Ago, 1537th meeting, ILC Yearbook 1979, vol. I, 32 [29].
[83] Ago, Eighth Report, [69]. Also Ago, 1537th meeting, 30 [32].
[84] Ago, Eighth Report, [72]. Also Ago, 1537th meeting, 30 [35].
[85] Ago, Eighth Report, [75]. Also Ago, 1537th meeting, 30 [36].
[86] Ago, Eighth Report, [57]. That consent operates through the formation of an agreement was supported in the literature as well: Alaimo, 'Natura del consenso'; Salmon, 'Les circonstances excluant l'illicéité' in Zemanek and Salmon (eds), *La responsabilité internationale* (1987), 95; Kamto, 'La volonté de l'Etat en droit international' (2004) 310 *Recueil* 9, 370–6.
[87] Ago, Eighth Report, [68]. Recall that according to Ago, all circumstances precluding wrongfulness operated in this manner: ibid., [55].
[88] Ibid., [67].

## 4.2 DEVELOPMENT OF THE PLEA OF CONSENT

a matter of the 'application of the general rule and not as an exception to it'.[89] In essence, these critiques challenged the idea that rule and defence were distinct: that conduct was lawful in situations where consent had been given was simply the result of the application of the (single) 'general rule'. Implicit in these critiques was the understanding that consent constituted a negative element of the rule in question. In response to these critics, Ago retorted (tautologically, it must be said) that the exceptionality of the conduct's lawfulness in the presence of consent was due to the fact that while that conduct would generally be wrongful, by virtue of the presence of consent, it was exceptionally lawful.[90] That is, it was an exceptional case, because it was not the general case. Ago's report missed the gist of these critiques (he would miss it again during the ILC debate), and his response asserted rather than explained his position.

At the Commission, Ago's colleagues were on the whole favourable to the draft article on consent.[91] However, Ago's explanation that consent operated by way of an agreement to suspend the operation of the underlying obligation was inconsistently received. Some Commission members accepted Ago's explanation.[92] But others challenged it. Thus, Nikolai Ushakov and Robert Quentin-Baxter both argued that if consent operated by creating an agreement between the relevant parties, then it really was a question of the existence of obligations rather than preclusion of wrongfulness.[93] As Quentin-Baxter put it, consent lay 'at the very root of the existence of international obligations, and it was very difficult, from a strictly theoretical point of view, to fit the concept of consent into the patterns of a mere exception'.[94] Others still, while agreeing with Ago's

---

[89] Id.
[90] Id.
[91] E.g., Jagota, 1538th meeting, ILC Yearbook 1979, vol. I, 36 [24]; but see his subsequent doubts at: Jagota, 1540th meeting, ILC Yearbook 1979, vol. I, 43 [30–1]; Thiam, 1538th meeting, ILC Yearbook 1979, vol. I, 37 [30–2]; Schwebel, 1538th meeting, ILC Yearbook 1979, vol. I, 37 [33]; Tsuruoka, 1540th meeting, ILC Yearbook 1979, vol. I, [1]; Francis, 1540th meeting, ILC Yearbook 1979, vol. I, 39 [5]; Sucharitkul, 1542nd meeting, ILC Yearbook 1979, vol. I, 45 [6]. There were some difficulties with the text of the article, especially the reference to the 'injured State'. It was correctly noted that the consenting state was not injured, see Reuter, 1538th meeting, ILC Yearbook 1979, vol. I, 35 [16]; Thiam, 1538th meeting, 37 [30]; Verosta, 1540th meeting, ILC Yearbook 1979, vol. I, 40 [14]; Quentin-Baxter, 1540th meeting, ILC Yearbook 1979, vol. I, 43 [26].
[92] Verosta, 1540th meeting, 41 [16].
[93] Ushakov, 1538th meeting, ILC Yearbook 1979, vol. I, 33 [2–3]; Ushakov, 1542nd meeting, ILC Yearbook 1979, vol. I, 46 [17–18], [34]. On this basis, Ushakov favoured deleting the provision.
[94] Quentin-Baxter, 1540th meeting, 42 [22].

position that consent operated by way of an agreement to suspend the underlying obligation, added that consent could also operate as a unilateral act.[95] For Willem Riphagen, always an acute conceptual observer, the members of the Commission were confounding three different scenarios in their remarks on this question: (i) an oral or written agreement suspending or ending an obligation between the parties; (ii) a 'type of conduct by so-called victim State B which might preclude the responsibility of the so-called wrongdoing State A'; and (iii) a waiver by the injured state of its right to invoke the wrongdoing state's responsibility. The plea of consent, in his view, concerned exclusively scenario (ii)[96] – what Special Rapporteur Crawford would later refer to as the 'middle case'.[97]

In response to these observations, Ago clarified his position on the operation of the defence. While consent precluded wrongfulness through the creation of an agreement between the parties concerned, Ago warned that 'one should not go too far in that direction'.[98] The agreement was only about the commission or omission of a specific act, and it had no effect on the relevant (primary) obligation: that obligation remained unchanged. The consenting state was consenting only to the 'non-application' of the rule, and not to its modification.[99] It was simply a matter of 'releasing' the obliged state from the performance of its obligation in the specific case.[100] This view, which was later included in the draft commentary adopted on first reading,[101] contradicted Ago's explanation of the operation of the 'circumstances precluding wrongfulness': it was not the case that consent suspended the obligation (as the report stated), but of it setting aside the application of the obligation for the time being.

The question of whether consent constituted a defence at all, or whether it was better seen as a negative rule-element, was raised only by Francis Vallat. Vallat noted that the exclusion of consent in respect of breaches of peremptory rules conflicted with the accepted practice of consent to the use of force, since the prohibition of force had peremptory character. He argued that it was possible that consent related to obligations in different ways: it could be that it was incorporated in some obligations like the prohibition of force (as a negative rule-element), and that it was a defence

---

[95] Reuter, 1538th meeting, 35 [18]; Jagota, 1540th meeting, 43 [32]; Schwebel, 1542nd meeting, ILC Yearbook 1979, vol. I, 47 [21]; Riphagen, 1542nd meeting, ILC Yearbook 1979, vol. I, 48 [36].
[96] Riphagen, 1542nd meeting, 48 [36].
[97] Crawford, 2588th meeting, ILC Yearbook 1999, vol. I, 153 [60].
[98] Ago, 1543rd meeting, 50 [2].
[99] Ibid., 50 [3].
[100] Id.
[101] ILC Report, thirty-first session, 109 [2].

## 4.2 DEVELOPMENT OF THE PLEA OF CONSENT

in respect of others. It was thus necessary to consider and examine 'very carefully' the way in which 'the concept of consent was expressed' in the articles on responsibility.[102] This lucid observation went unremarked in the first reading Commission and elicited no direct response from Ago.

The Commission adopted draft Article 29 in 1979 pursuant to which (in relevant part):

> 1. The consent validly given by a State to the commission by another State of a specified act not in conformity with an obligation of the latter State towards the former State precludes the wrongfulness of the act in relation to that State to the extent that the act remains within the limits of that consent.

The Commission's commentary to this provision largely followed Ago's report, with the added clarification that the agreement created through consent was solely directed at the non-application of an obligation, rather than its modification. The agreement, as the commentary put it, merely suspended the 'operation' of the obligation without having any effect on the obligation itself.[103] The draft commentary excluded the possibility that consent might operate through a unilateral act.

**Views of States in the General Assembly's Sixth Committee**  Draft Article 29 did not give rise to many disagreements among states. Indeed, the majority of states which commented on this provision were favourable to its inclusion in the ARS and agreed with the text as adopted. These included, in alphabetical order, Algeria, Argentina, Australia, Austria, Bangladesh, Byelorussia, Chile, Cyprus, Egypt, India, Italy, Japan, Jordan, Mali, Mexico, Mongolia, Syria, Thailand, Tunisia, Ukraine, the United Kingdom, the United States, Uruguay and Venezuela (on behalf of the Andean Pact countries),[104] although some had difficulty with the wording

---

[102] Vallat, 1538th meeting, ILC Yearbook 1979, vol. I, 38 [38].
[103] ILC Report, thirty-first session, 109 [2].
[104] See Algeria: A/C.6/34/SR.49, [35]; Argentina: A/C.6/34/SR.46, [52]; Australia: A/C.6/34/SR.47, [34]; Austria: A/C.6/34/SR.47, [61]; Bangladesh: A/C.6/34/SR.50, [32]; Byelorussia: A/C.6/34/SR.44, [22]; Chile: A/C.6/34/SR.48, [45]; Cyprus: A/C.6/34/SR.44, [45]; Egypt: A/C.6/34/SR.51, [23]; India: A/C.6/34/SR.51, [63]; Italy: A/C.6/34/SR.47, [22–3]; Japan: A/C.6/34/SR.42, [3]; Jordan: A/C.6/34/SR.51, [56]; Mali: A/C.6/34/SR.47, [54]; Mexico: A/C.6/34/SR.41, [46]; Mongolia: A/C.6/34/SR.50, [38]; Syria: A/C.6/34/SR.51, [13]; Thailand: A/C.6/34/SR.40, [43]; Tunisia: A/C.6/34/SR.51, [41]; Ukraine: A/C.6/34/SR.47, [46]; United Kingdom: A/C.6/34/SR.47, [12]; United States: A/C.6/34/SR.45, [3]; Uruguay: A/C.6/34/SR.50, [48]; and, Venezuela (on behalf of Andean Pact countries) A/C.6/34/SR.44, [16] (the Cartagena Agreement on Andean Sub-regional Integration, signed at Bogotá, 26 May 1969, (1969) 8 ILM 910, instituted the Andean Community of Nations, originally composed of Bolivia, Chile, Colombia, Ecuador and Peru. Chile withdrew from membership, and became an observer state

of the provision.[105] Only a few objected to the provision: Sweden thought it was too general a provision to be effective in practice;[106] the United Kingdom thought it may be abused in practice;[107] and Kenya, recalling the history of abusive interventions in Africa, argued that it was best if the provision was deleted from the draft.[108]

Only two states remarked on the explanation of consent as an agreement between the parties. Chile articulated a position similar to Riphagen's second scenario: the agreement created by consent did not modify or derogate from the rule, it simply 'precluded the enforcement of an obligation in a particular case'.[109] For Czechoslovakia, instead, if there was an agreement between the parties then 'there could be no question in such cases of an internationally wrongful act or, consequently, of responsibility for it.'[110] No state directly argued that consent should be excluded from the draft on the grounds that it constituted a negative rule-element and that, by implication, it was not a defence. Czechoslovakia's remark was the closest to such an objection, but it could also be seen as a targeted criticism of the explanation that consent operated by way of an agreement and not as an overall rejection of the plea on this basis.

#### 4.2.2.2 The Adoption of Article 20 on Second Reading

**Crawford's Report and the Debates at the International Law Commission** Special Rapporteur Crawford's report, presented to the Commission in 1999, began by questioning the place of consent as a defence in the draft as there were 'deep' problems with it. Crawford accepted that consent related to the 'middle case' between an agreement giving rise to an obligation and a waiver of claims.[111] But he had difficulty explaining what this 'middle case' was. In view of this difficulty,

---

in 1976. Venezuela became a member in 1973 and withdrew from the Community in 2006. See www.comunidadandina.org/ingles/quienes/brief.html.

[105] See comments by Austria, France and the United Kingdom, in: Comments by Governments on all the Draft Articles, A/CN.4/488, ILC Yearbook 1998, vol. II(1), 130–1.

[106] A/C.6/34/SR.43, [45]. See further comments of governments on part one of the draft articles on state responsibility for internationally wrongful acts, ILC Yearbook 1981, A/CN.4/342 and Add.1–4, vol. II(1), 77.

[107] A/C.6/34/SR.47, [12].

[108] A/C.6/34/SR.43, [3].

[109] A/C.6/34/SR.48, [45].

[110] A/C.6/34/SR.48, [54]. Also comments and observations of governments on part I of the draft articles on state responsibility for internationally wrongful acts, A/CN.4/362, ILC Yearbook 1983, vol. II(1), 1 [3].

[111] Crawford, 2588th meeting, 153 [60].

## 4.2 DEVELOPMENT OF THE PLEA OF CONSENT

Crawford criticised the idea that consent was a defence, and presented a multilayered argument against it. For present purposes, it is sufficient to summarise his position and review the reactions of the Commission and of states in the Sixth Committee. The many layers of this critique, which have since been repeated in the scholarly commentary, will be examined in detail in Section 4.3.

Crawford began his report by wondering whether it was possible to distinguish between:

> on the one hand, the issue of consent as an element in the application of a rule (which is accordingly a part of the *definition* of the relevant obligation) and, on the other hand, the issue of consent as a basis for precluding the wrongfulness of conduct inconsistent with the obligation.[112]

In his view, if 'consent must be given in advance, if it is only validly given in some cases and not in others, and if authority to consent varies with the rule in question', then it could be asked 'whether the element of consent should not be seen as incorporated in the different primary rules, possibly in different terms in different rules.'[113] That consent was, indeed, an element incorporated in the different primary rules was confirmed by the fact that when consent was given there was not even a *prima facie* breach of the relevant obligation: the consented-to conduct was 'perfectly lawful'.[114] This was a notable difference between consent and the other circumstances precluding wrongfulness, in which there was *prima facie* wrongfulness or at least a situation which required 'some explanation and some justification'.[115] For Crawford, in summary, consent related to the existence of the obligation and not to the question of justification for non-performance.[116] He later added – during his presentation of the report to the ILC – that in cases of consent there was no question of breach of the relevant obligation, rather there 'was simply a question of the application of the primary rule'.[117] For all these reasons, he was of the opinion that draft Article 29 on consent should be deleted from the project.[118]

---

[112] Crawford, Second Report on State Responsibility, ILC Yearbook 1999, vol. II(1), [238] (emphasis in original).
[113] Id.
[114] Id.
[115] Ibid., [240].
[116] Ibid., [238], [241].
[117] Crawford, 2587th meeting, ILC Yearbook 1999, vol. I, 138 [12].
[118] Crawford, Second Report, [243]. Also Crawford, 2587th meeting, 138 [14]: consent was a 'specific tailor-made component of each primary rule in respect of those cases where consent could properly be given'.

This issue elicited an 'intense' debate in the Commission, to use Enrique Candioti's words.[119] The records of the debate show that there was a real cleavage between critics and supporters of draft Article 29. Among the critics, Dugard noted that for historical reasons domestic legal systems recognised that consent was sometimes an element of the definition of an offence, and other times it was a defence. The Commission now had the choice whether 'to preserve the muddiness of domestic waters' or to adopt 'the logic advocated by' Crawford in his report. For his part, he preferred the 'clarity of jurisprudence' and considered that the absence of consent was better viewed as an 'intrinsic condition of wrongfulness', and not as a defence.[120] Other Commission members also supported Crawford's view. They argued – echoing Crawford's report – that consent was a primary rule,[121] that it dealt with the existence of obligations (it rendered them non-existent) rather than the existence of wrongfulness,[122] and that in the case of consent conduct was 'perfectly lawful' at the time of its occurrence.[123]

For their part, supporters of draft Article 29 also relied on a variety of arguments. Some proceeded from practical arguments: whether or not the article was retained, the phenomenon it reflected would continue to occur in practice.[124] Others argued that it was not clear that all primary rules included an element of (non-)consent.[125] From a theoretical standpoint, moreover, Pellet found it difficult to understand why consent was included in the primary rule.[126] Further, if consent was indeed a primary rule and, for this reason, was incorporated in the definition of states' obligations, could the same not be said about the other defences? As Gaja remarked:

> one could go along with the Special Rapporteur and say that the rule of international law prohibiting overflights was one that prohibited them but for consent. In the same vein one could say – although the Special Rapporteur would probably disagree – that a rule prohibited overflights save in the case

---

[119] As Candioti explained to the GA Sixth Committee in his presentation of the Commission's report: A/C.6/54/SR.21, 2 [8].
[120] Dugard, 2588th meeting, ILC Yearbook 1999, vol. I, 152 [50].
[121] Rosenstock, 2587th meeting, ILC Yearbook 1999, vol. I, 143 [48].
[122] Melescanu, 2587th meeting, ILC Yearbook 1999, vol. I, 145 [62]; Simma, 2588th meeting, ILC Yearbook 1999, vol. I, 147 [12].
[123] Kabatsi, 2588th meeting, ILC Yearbook 1999, vol. I, 146 [3].
[124] Lukashuk, 2588th meeting, ILC Yearbook 1999, vol. I, 149 [30]; Brownlie, 2588th meeting, ILC Yearbook 1999, vol. I, 149 [31].
[125] He, 2588th meeting, ILC Yearbook 1999, vol. I, 149 [29].
[126] Pellet, 2588th meeting, 150 [33].

of distress, or of self-defence, both of which were circumstances precluding wrongfulness.[127]

Brownlie was also puzzled by the position taken by Crawford and his supporters, for it was certainly possible to consider that consent did not affect the primary rule (which remained in force) and still operate as a defence.[128]

The records of the meeting give the impression of a rather frustrating debate. Also, they evidence that the debate was frustrated by the Commission's approach to the question: Commission members insisted on framing the issue as one about the primary or secondary character of consent (and of the other defences), and as one about the boundary between primary and secondary rules. As was already advanced in Chapter 1, and as will be seen further later, this choice of approach created an impasse which the Commission was unable to overcome: the question could simply *not be resolved* through this approach. In the event, the Commission decided to retain the provision in view of the general assent it had received from states, agreeing to disagree on the theoretical question.

**Views of States in the Sixth Committee and Subsequent Practice** States commenting on the draft provision in the Sixth Committee were favourable to the inclusion of consent as a defence. Some states engaged directly with the main challenge to the provision mounted by the Special Rapporteur. Among others, Germany found the Special Rapporteur's views 'unconvincing' and wished to retain the article on consent,[129] and for Italy, deletion was too radical since the importance of consent as a defence was 'undeniable'.[130] Spain[131] and Austria[132] agreed with the Special Rapporteur's view about consent as an intrinsic condition of obligations from a doctrinal standpoint. However, they added, it was both practical and wise to retain the article in the project. In a similar practical vein, Russia wished to retain the draft article and added that the 'much debated question of primary and secondary norms, their permissibility and their relevance to the draft articles on State responsibility should not have a decisive influence on consideration of the text'.[133] Other states, including Mexico, India, Slovakia and Tunisia, also agreed that consent should

---

[127] Gaja, 2587th meeting, ILC Yearbook 1999, vol. I, 144 [54].
[128] Brownlie, 2588th meeting, 149 [31].
[129] A/C.6/54/SR.23, [4].
[130] A/C.6/54/SR.24, [24].
[131] A/C.6/54/SR.21, [18].
[132] A/C.6/54/SR.22, [12].
[133] A/C.6/54/SR.23, [70].

remain in the ARS, though they requested that the Commission clarify its conditions and requirements of application.[134]

Outside of the context of the ILC's codification, the plea of consent was endorsed by the parties in *DRC v Uganda* before the ICJ. The case concerned the presence of Ugandan troops in the DRC's territory. The DRC claimed that Uganda had thus breached the prohibition on the use of force, principles of territorial sovereignty, and the principle of non-intervention. Uganda, in response, argued that its forces were present in the DRC's territory, and had used force there, with the consent of the DRC. While the parties endorsed Article 20 of the ARS in their pleadings, the Court's decision, which partially upheld the DRC's argument (it only accepted it in respect of certain time-periods), does not mention this provision.[135] This case involved precisely one of the rules in respect of which it is frequently stated that consent constitutes a negative rule-element: the prohibition of force. Is consent a negative rule-element only in respect of this rule; or is it a negative rule-element in respect of several, many or even all rules of international law?

### 4.3  Consent as a Defence

It seems clear from the practice, scholarship and ILC codification, that there exists a 'middle case' between an agreement creating (or permanently modifying) rights and obligations between two states, and the waiver of the right to invoke the responsibility of a state. This difference is not only conceptual, but also practically important. In respect of the creation or modification of rights and obligations, the difference is important since, as evidenced in the example of *Navigational Rights* mentioned in the introduction to this chapter, it may affect the possibility of unilateral withdrawal of the consent given. As to the waiver of claims, the difference may be relevant where multiple parties are involved: if consent precludes wrongfulness, this effect is universal; whereas the waiver of a claim is only personal, in that it need not affect the position of other parties in respect of the wrongful act. Take the example of an obligation owed by State A to States B and C jointly. States B and C can consent to the non-performance

---

[134] In alphabetical order: Mexico: A/C.6/54/SR.23, [16]; India: A/C.6/54/SR.23, [33]; Slovakia: A/C.6/54/SR.22, [52]; Tunisia: A/C.6/54/SR.25, [28].

[135] See the following references in the written pleadings of *DRC v Uganda*: Memorial of the DRC, 6 July 2000, 210–11 [5.38] (referring to draft Article 29); Reply of the DRC, 29 May 2002, 255–6; Rejoinder of Uganda, 6 December 2002, 128 [307]. In the oral pleadings, see Statement of Uganda, 19 April 2005, CR 2005/8, 9 [6] (original).

### 4.3 CONSENT AS A DEFENCE

of the obligation by A, in which case there will be no breach of the obligation with respect to either B *or* C. But if A breaches the obligation owed to both B and C, and B waives its right to claim compensation as against A, this does not affect C's right to claim on its own account.[136]

Although conceptually distinct from these two cases, the difficulty remains of legally representing this 'middle case'. The Commission discussed two possible options: either to conceptualise consent as a defence, or to understand (non-)consent as a negative rule-element implicit in the definition of all the international obligations of states, excepting those derived from peremptory rules and those specifically excluding the availability of consent.[137] As was seen, the Commission did not take a position on this matter: it simply agreed to disagree. Part of the difficulty faced by the Commission was its insistence on treating the question of consent in absolute terms. Plausibly in an effort to steer clear of what Dugard had called the 'muddiness' of domestic law,[138] the Commission's debate was pervaded by an all-or-nothing disposition: consent was *either* a negative rule-element of all international obligations, *or* it was a defence with respect to all international obligations. But as will be argued here, such an absolutistic approach ultimately led to distortion and artificiality: on the one hand, not all rules of the international legal order require an element of non-consent to represent a complete and coherent conduct-guiding message; on the other, some rules may result in absurd statements without the element of non-consent. A single, conceptually coherent, approach to the place of consent vis-à-vis states' obligations would thus come at the cost of the ability adequately to represent legal reality.

There seem to be no principled objections to the possibility of non-consent being incorporated into the definition of states' obligations; that is, of consent constituting a negative rule-element. If states so wish, an element of non-consent can be, and has in fact been, incorporated into the definition of certain obligations. The following discussion will therefore take for granted that this is both acceptable in theory and, as discussed

---

[136] Pursuant to ARS art 46: 'Where several States are injured by the same internationally wrongful act, each injured State may separately invoke the responsibility of the State which has committed the internationally wrongful act.' This is a separate question to that of the quantum of compensation which may be due to each of the beneficiaries of the obligation, namely States B and C in the hypothetical contained in the text.

[137] Domestic legal systems face similar difficulties in the classification of consent as an element of the offence or a defence. For an examination of the question in the field of tort, see Goudkamp, *Tort Law Defences* (2013), 65–8, 113–14. In the criminal law, see the overview in Fletcher, *Rethinking Criminal Law* (2000), 566.

[138] Dugard, 2588th meeting, 152 [50].

later, also observable in practice. The focus will therefore be on the more controversial of the two possibilities, namely that consent may constitute a defence. The purpose is not to argue that consent is (or must be) always a defence, but rather that it *can also* be construed as a defence to claims of breach of international law.

Throughout the work of the ILC and in the scholarly literature, three main objections have been raised to the recognition of consent as a defence. First, it has been argued that consent is not a defence because it is a primary, instead of a secondary, rule. Second, it has been argued that non-consent ought to be an (implicit) element of the definition of all international obligations of states because these obligations are not 'absolute'. Third, it has been argued that consent is not a defence because its 'temporal logic' differs from that of the other defences: while consent results in *ab initio* legality, the other defences require *prima facie* wrongfulness. It follows that consent must be located 'upstream', to use Eric David's metaphor, within the definition of the relevant obligation.[139] These three objections are distilled from the various observations made by Commission members during the discussions on Article 20 as well as critiques made in the literature. They are examined and refuted in Section 4.3.1. As will be seen, individually or jointly, these arguments are insufficient to exclude that consent may constitute a defence in international law. Subsection 4.3.2 then argues that, just as in domestic law, in international law too consent can be both a negative rule-element or a defence – depending on the underlying obligation at issue.

### 4.3.1 Three Objections to the Defence of Consent

#### 4.3.1.1 Consent as a Primary Rule

While drafting Article 20, the Commission seemed to work under the assumption that defences were secondary rules and that states' obligations were primary rules. When it came to consider the role of consent in the law of state responsibility, therefore, the Commission described its task as one concerned with determining the 'boundary between primary and secondary rules'.[140] After all, the question under consideration was whether or not consent was a defence: if consent could be classed as a secondary rule, then it would constitute a defence; in turn, if it was classed

---

[139] David, 'Primary and Secondary Rules' in Crawford et al. (eds), *The Law of International Responsibility* (2010), 29.
[140] Crawford, 2588th meeting, 151 [46].

as a primary rule, then it would constitute a negative rule-element. The battle-lines drawn in this way, most of the debate within the ILC (and also beyond it) centred on the primary or secondary rule character of consent. According to Special Rapporteur Crawford and several other Commission members, consent is a 'primary rule' insofar as it concerns state behaviour. As such, consent must be located upstream, with the primary rule itself.[141] *Therefore*, the argument continued, consent ought to be a negative rule-element incorporated into the definition of states' international obligations.

While it is correct to say that consent directs or guides the conduct of states and that, in this sense, it can be characterised as a primary rule, it does not follow from this that consent is not a defence. Indeed, as was explained in Chapter 1, justifications possess both primary and secondary rule characteristics.[142] They are primary in that they serve to guide the behaviour of states, by essentially indicating what they have permission to do. But they are also secondary, insofar as they are relevant to the determination of a state's responsibility for the breach of international law. And this holds true for consent as much as for other justifications, such as countermeasures and self-defence. If the conclusion were drawn from its primary rule character that consent is a negative rule-element, then must this conclusion not follow for other defences that are conduct-guiding as well, such as self-defence and countermeasures?[143] The Commission, scholars or states, did not draw this conclusion in respect of either of these defences. So why should it be different for consent? Moreover, as Judge Gaja has clearly demonstrated in his scholarly work, many rules in the ARS are more properly classified as 'primary' (in the sense that they are conduct-guiding) than secondary – and yet, they are present in the ARS and are essential to a comprehensive statement of the law of responsibility. The bottom-line is that whatever the characterisation given to these rules as either primary or secondary rules, these are all rules that 'contribute to determine whether a State is responsible or not'.[144] For this reason:

> criticisms of particular articles on State responsibility to the effect that they should be omitted because they state rules which should be considered to be primary rather than secondary are not based on solid ground.[145]

---

[141] David, 'Primary', 29.
[142] Section 1.5.
[143] Gaja, 2587th meeting, 144 [54].
[144] Gaja, 'Primary and Secondary Rules in the International Law of State Responsibility' (2014) 97 *Rivista di diritto internazionale*, 990.
[145] Ibid., 990–1.

The challenge to the classification of consent as a defence based on its primary rule characteristics must, therefore, fail.

#### 4.3.1.2  The Temporal Logic of Consent

The role of consent as a negative rule-element has also been grounded on what may be termed its 'temporal logic'. In essence, the argument runs as follows. Consent must be prior to, or at the very least contemporaneous with, the act in question if it is to preclude that act's wrongfulness.[146] Given this temporal logic, it is impossible to conclude that at the time of its occurrence the consented act is unlawful. What is more, the act in question does not violate international law at all: the act is 'perfectly lawful' and it is lawful '*ab initio*'. If this is the case, then it must follow that consent is a negative rule-element, so that its presence prevents the constitution of the internationally wrongful act. The argument (or at least its essence) was put forward by several members of the ILC, including Special Rapporteur Crawford, and in the scholarly literature by Karine Bannelier and Théodore Christakis. Though Bannelier and Christakis's argument is not, by their own admission, intended to resolve the question of the classification of consent as a negative rule-element or a defence in a general manner, it will nevertheless be used here as it is the clearest and most detailed exposition of the temporal logic argument.

Bannelier and Christakis note that consent has to be given prior to, or at the same time as, the conduct in question. The consequence of this, they say, is that when the conduct occurs it is lawful. They then contrast this with the temporal logic of the other circumstances precluding wrongfulness. By the time the other circumstances 'intervene', they say, the wrongful act 'already exists' and the defence intervenes only subsequently to 'erase' that wrongfulness.[147] This is why, they explain, the ILC used the cumbersome expression 'acts the wrongfulness of which is precluded' instead of 'lawful acts' in respect of conduct justified by one of the defences. While the time-frame of consent precedes the wrongful act, the time-frame of the other defences is only ever ex post. They illustrate this difference with a vignette about the operation of consent:

> This absence of wrongfulness at the time the [consented-to] conduct occurs has the curious effect of depriving us of any objective measure to qualify the phenomenon which unfolds before our eyes. Certain witnesses can maintain that they have seen a secondary rule whose application has

---

[146] ARS art. 20 Commentary, [3].
[147] Bannelier and Christakis, '*Volenti*', 107.

## 4.3 CONSENT AS A DEFENCE 159

miraculously prevented the certain and inevitable violation of a primary rule. Others can, in contrast, swear that no secondary rule was present at the place and that no crime has been committed at all. They can add that consent allowed the formation of an agreement between two subjects of the law, and that only primary rules were pertinent in the circumstances, rules which incorporate consent, permitting a State to consent in advance to facts which, in the absence of such consent (and *only* in the absence of such consent) would be qualified as unlawful.[148]

In their view, these different temporal logics signal a fundamental distinction between consent and the other defences: that the other defences are properly a matter of secondary rules whereas consent is a matter of the relevant primary rule. Ultimately, these authors come to the conclusion that consent is a negative rule-element because of three, interrelated, reasons. First, consent must exist before or at the time that the act is performed, whereas the other defences come into play only after the act has been performed. Second, in the case of consent the conduct is lawful *ab initio*, whereas 'wrongfulness *already exists*' at the time of the defences.[149] Lastly, this difference is, in their view, backed by the language of the ARS, which uses the expression 'acts the wrongfulness of which is precluded' in the context of the defences. But the argument is unconvincing, on all three grounds.

To begin with, the premise of the argument, that consent operates on a different temporal logic to the other defences, is a misunderstanding (or misrepresentation) of the other defences. The same temporal logic is required of *all* defences included in the ARS. Just as consent must be prior to, or at the very least contemporaneous with, the consented-to conduct, so must the circumstances giving rise to all the other defences be prior to, or contemporaneous with, the conduct sought to be justified (or excused). Self-defence requires, to be validly invoked, that the armed attack has already occurred (or is in the process of occurring, to those who accept that self-defence may be anticipatory) at the time the injured state uses

---

[148] Ibid., 108 (emphasis in original). The original text in French states as follows: 'Cette absence d'illicéité au moment où le fait intervient a pour curieux effet de nous priver de toute mesure objective nous permettant de qualifier le phénomène qui se produit sous nos yeux. Certains témoins peuvent prétendre qu'ils ont vu une règle secondaire dont l'application a empêché miraculeusement la violation certaine et inévitable d'une règle primaire. D'autres peuvent au contraire jurer qu'aucune règle secondaire n'était présente sur les lieux et qu'aucun crime n'a failli y être commis. Ils peuvent ajouter que le consentement a permis la formation d'un accord de volontés entre deux sujets du droit, et que seules des règles primaires étaient pertinentes en l'espèce, des règles qui intègrent le consentement, permettant à un État de consentir à l'avance à des faits qui, en l'absence de ce consentement (et seulement en l'absence de ce consentement) seraient qualifiés d'illicites.'

[149] Ibid., 107 (emphasis in original).

force against its aggressor. Countermeasures, in turn, can only be invoked as a reaction to a *previous* breach of international law by the target state. For *force majeure* to operate the situation of material impossibility of performance must exist at the time the failure to perform occurs: the failure to perform must 'be due'[150] to that material impossibility, implying a temporal precedence of the impossibility with respect to the relevant conduct. Similarly, the situation of necessity must exist at the time a state acts to protect its essential interest from a grave and imminent peril. Finally, in relation to distress, the threat to the life of the state organ or individuals entrusted to his care must also exist, or must be thought to exist on a reasonable assessment of the situation at the relevant time, namely at the time the organ in question makes the decision to act in a manner incompatible with the international obligations of his or her state. Just like consent, the circumstances triggering the other defences too must exist at the time the relevant conduct occurs. This holds true regardless of the timing of the invocation of the defence by the state which performs the relevant conduct: the point is that, to preclude wrongfulness (or responsibility), the circumstance must exist before, or at the same time as, the conduct in question occurs. Besides, the requirement of prior consent was not intended to demarcate this defence from the other defences. Rather this requirement was intended to distinguish the defence from a waiver of responsibility in which consent is given ex post, after the wrongful act has been ascertained.[151]

Second, the authors' reference to the 'existence' of wrongfulness at the time the defences intervene is incorrect. As explained in Chapter 3,[152] whether conduct is wrongful is a legal conclusion that can only be arrived at once it has been determined that no justifications are available.[153] Indeed, the whole point of raising a justification is to question that the conduct is wrongful *at all*. Perhaps what the authors have in mind is a notion of *prima facie* wrongfulness, namely an assessment that, on a first glance of the matter, the conduct is contrary to what was required of that state by an international obligation. But this is merely a preliminary assessment of the situation, one that precedes the evaluation of the applicability of the defence to the case and, as such, one that precedes a conclusion as to the

---

[150] ARS art. 23.
[151] A possibility envisaged in ARS art. 45.
[152] See Chapter 3, Section 3.2.1.3.
[153] In this sense see *Oil Platforms (Islamic Republic of Iran v United States of America)* (2003) ICJ Rep 161, sep op Higgins, 226–7 [7].

## 4.3 CONSENT AS A DEFENCE

wrongfulness of the conduct.[154] To arrive at the conclusion that the conduct is wrongful, a judge (or other law-applier) will usually consider first whether the conduct is incompatible with an obligation and then consider whether the conduct is covered by a defence.[155] In legal terms, however, no wrongful act 'exists' until after a consideration of the circumstances relevant to the defence.

Finally, no more helpful to these authors' conclusion is the fact that the ILC used the expression 'acts the wrongfulness of which is precluded' instead of 'lawful acts' in these provisions. The Commission used the expression 'preclusion of wrongfulness' *also* in respect of consent,[156] so not much can be derived for these purposes from this linguistic usage. At any rate, it is unclear whether the expressions 'act the wrongfulness of which is precluded' and 'lawful act' are indeed different in international law or whether they are just two ways of stating the same: that the conduct does not breach an international legal obligation of the state.[157] As explained in Chapter 3, there is no legal difference between these two characterisations. Whether or not international law possesses deontic modalities beyond permission and prohibition – a matter which exceeds

---

[154] Legal theorists accept the possibility that justified conduct be, nevertheless, wrong: in these cases *there is a wrong*, and only because there is a wrong, the defendant offers a justification. Note that this is a *wrong* in a moral and not legal sense: it is conduct which, albeit permissible, there are nevertheless good reasons not to perform. For an enlightening analysis of justified wrongs, see Gardner, 'In Defence of Defences' in Gardner (ed.), *Offences and Defences: Selected Essays in the Philosophy of Criminal Law* (2007), 77. Now this does not seem to be the sense in which Bannelier and Christakis speak of 'wrongfulness already existing', nor is it the way in which states and the ARS understand the concept of justification.

[155] Note that this order is not demanded by logic, but is often followed for reasons of judicial economy. Indeed, judicial economy may often demand that the order be altered. See, e.g., *Case Concerning Armed Activities on the Territory of the Congo (DRC v Uganda)* (2005) ICJ Rep 168; *Continental Casualty Company v Argentine Republic*, ICSID Case ARB/03/9, Award, 5 September 2008, [161] (the Tribunal explained the reasons supporting its decision to discuss the Argentine pleas before the claims of breach as follows: 'The pervasive nature of these general exceptions, which Argentina raises against all claims of Continental, might be such as to absolve Argentina, in whole or in part, from the alleged breaches and from the ensuing responsibility to pay damages'). Note, as well, that the ICJ's decision in *Oil Platforms*, in which the order of analysis of claims and defences was altered, was criticised not so much because of the reversal of analysis per se but because in the circumstances this was not warranted by judicial economy. See, e.g., *Oil Platforms*, decl Ranjeva, 220–2; sep op Higgins, 230–1 [23], 231–2; sep op Parra-Aranguren, 244 [14]; sep op Kooijmans, 252–7.

[156] The text of ARS art. 20 speaks of consent precluding 'the wrongfulness of that act'. See also ARS art. 20 Commentary, [1].

[157] On this point see Chapter 3, Section 3.2.1.2.

the scope of this study – insofar as justifications are concerned, these constitute permissions of the legal order to engage in certain conduct. As a result, conduct adopted in accordance with these permissions is lawful. In this context, therefore, to say that the wrongfulness of certain conduct is precluded (that conduct is 'not wrongful'), is just to say that that conduct is lawful. In consequence, nothing meaningful can be inferred about the difference between consent and the other defences from the choice of this expression (instead of the expression 'lawful acts') in the ARS.

A similar argument, based on the temporal logic of consent, may be found in Crawford's report to the ILC.[158] Crawford explained to the Commission that it was possible to speak of consented-to conduct as being 'perfectly lawful', whereas 'one is not inclined to say' the same about 'conduct excused on grounds such as necessity, force majeure or distress'.[159] Moreover, he added that 'even in the case of self-defence or countermeasures, where the conduct may be lawful in the circumstances, at least there is a situation which requires some explanation and some justification.'[160] There is certainly a difference between consent and state of necessity, *force majeure* or distress: as will be seen in the chapters relating to each of those defences, those three defences are the most clear examples of (potential) excuses in international law. There is therefore a clear legal basis for the 'inclination' not to treat conduct covered by these defences in the same manner as conduct covered by consent: the conduct of an excused actor is unlawful. Self-defence and countermeasures are, in contrast, clear examples of justifications. So what is the difference between conduct covered by these defences and consented-to conduct? Crawford does not state this in so many words, but the gist of his argument relies on an assumed distinction between conduct being 'perfectly lawful' or being 'lawful' *tout court*. In both cases, the conduct will be lawful; whether it is 'perfectly' or 'imperfectly' so is not a question of legality but at most of morality ('perfect' and 'imperfect' are not relevant legal properties of conduct), in the same way that the description of conduct as non-wrongful is a question of morality (or other such normative considerations) as explained in Chapter 3. At any rate, it is not the case that consented-to conduct does *not* call for explanation: there was much that Uganda was called to explain in *DRC v Uganda*, where the parties debated at length whether the DRC had consented to Ugandan military presence

---

[158] For a similar view, Kabatsi, 2588th meeting, 146 [3].
[159] Crawford, Second Report, [239].
[160] Id.

in its territory and the extent of that consent.[161] Similarly, Russia's claim that Mr Yanukovych, the (ousted) Ukrainian president, had requested the deployment of Russian troops in Ukrainian territory was met with questions about the legitimacy of Mr Yanukovych.[162] In the case of consent too there may be conduct that calls for explanation and justification.

### 4.3.1.3 Consent and Absolute Obligations

Finally, the view that consent cannot be a defence, but that it rather must be a negative rule-element of the relevant obligation, has been based on the absolute or dispositive character of obligations. Since international obligations are not 'absolute' (save for some peremptory rules), then they must implicitly include an element of (non-)consent. For Crawford, who presented this argument at the ILC, a defence of consent would make sense only if it were possible to 'envisage cases where an obligation is properly formulated in absolute terms (i.e. without any condition or qualification relating to consent), but nonetheless the consent of the State concerned precludes the wrongfulness of conduct.'[163] While this was possible in theory, the Special Rapporteur was 'not aware of any such case' in practice.[164] Indeed, all the examples of practice identified by the Commission

---

[161] See, e.g., Memorial of the DRC, at 210–15 and Reply, 247–63; Counter-Memorial of Uganda, 161–79, and Rejoinder, 127–35.

[162] Russia argued that it had been invited to deploy troops in Ukrainian territory by (ousted) President Yanukovych during a meeting of the Security Council: S/PV.7124, 1 March 2014, at 5. The United States, the United Kingdom and France challenged the Russian statement calling its presence in Ukraine 'illegal': ibid. at 6–7. See also Russia's argument of consent (extended to include an invitation by the Prime Minister of Crimea) at S/PV.7125, 3 March 2014, at 3–4, and the specific objections to the argument of consent proffered by the United States (at 5–6), the United Kingdom (at 7), Ukraine (15). Other states present at the meeting questioned the legality of the Russian action (thus implicitly questioning the argument of consent): France, Lithuania, Rwanda, Jordan, Australia, Chile, Argentina, Korea and Luxembourg, in that order.

[163] Crawford, Second Report, [240].

[164] Id. Crawford has restated this view in subsequent scholarly work: Crawford, *General Part*, 288. Bannelier and Christakis would add that the purpose of formulating an obligation in absolute terms is precisely to avoid a state consenting to its non-performance. Since a defence of consent would apply generally so long as the obligation is not of a *jus cogens* character (see ARS arts 12 and 26), then a state could rely on this defence to override the absolute obligation. Indeed, unlike art. 25 on state of necessity, art. 20 does not contain a safeguard clause in respect of obligations which preclude the invocation of consent. In their view, the only way to ensure that absolute obligations are immune from consented-to non-performance is to incorporate an implicit condition of (non-)consent in the statement of all dispositive obligations: if the obligation does not possess one such condition, then the state cannot consent to its non-performance. See Bannelier

concerned obligations which were not couched in absolute terms but which 'allow[ed] that the conduct in question may be validly consented to by the target State',[165] such as the 'non-exercise of foreign jurisdiction on the territory of a State; non-use of force against it; non-intervention in its internal affairs'.[166] On this view, there are only two possibilities in this context: either the obligation is absolute, in which case consent cannot be given; or it is 'dispositive', in which case the question of preclusion of wrongfulness does not arise at all (for non-consent is internalised by the rule).

But the argument does not succeed in excluding the possibility that consent be a defence instead of a negative rule-element. To begin with, the current lack of practical examples and the lack of imagination as to potential or hypothetical examples cannot in itself be a bar to the conceptual point that consent can be a defence. Moreover, the absolute or dispositive character of an obligation simply goes to the question whether it can (or cannot) be set aside. This displacement can be achieved through different means, either by way of conditions implicit in the obligation (e.g., a hypothetical non-consent rule-element) or by way of elements external to it (e.g., an agreement to do things differently). Both of these means are underpinned by state consent: but they take different forms and, therefore, have different implications.[167] Absolute or dispositive character, therefore, goes to the amenability of an obligation to being set aside through consent. The form that that consent must take for these purposes is, however, a separate question. The obligation may be set aside by, as was said, conditions

and Christakis, '*Volenti*', 108–9. Regrettably, this is only a false security. To begin with, international obligations – as formulated – do not always contain an element of (non-)consent. This condition either has to be read into them, or implied in them. This means that potentially every obligation is subject to one such condition and it would have to be argued, on a case by case basis, whether consensual non-performance was possible or not with respect to that specific rule. As far as conduct guidance and stability of relations are concerned, this strategy is far from ensuring that states clearly perceive which obligations are absolute (and therefore not amenable to consensual non-performance) and which dispositive. At any rate, *ex* art. 55, the rules in the ARS are applicable only insofar as they are not excluded by the relevant obligations. So if an obligation was intended to be absolute, then it would exclude the application of the plea of consent despite the absence of a savings clause to this effect in ARS Art 20.

[165] Crawford, Second Report, [240].
[166] Id.
[167] Thus an agreement between two states could set aside the general rule permanently; whereas consent implicit in the obligation may be temporary, or even just a one-off. The former scenario involves the sources of international law, and the application of norm conflict rules (in particular the *lex specialis* principle); the latter scenario, instead, concerns the scope and application of the rule itself.

implicit in it or by way of agreement. Most importantly for present purposes, it could also take the form of a defence. Indeed, there is nothing in the argument based on the absolute or dispositive character of obligations to suggest that the last alternative is not conceptually possible or that it is undesirable. For this reason, this argument too must fail.

### 4.3.2 Defending the Defence of Consent

None of the three objections reviewed earlier exclude the theoretical (and certainly the practical) possibility that consent may constitute a defence and not a negative rule-element. This is not to say that consent is *always* a defence. As advanced earlier, what rendered the Commission's consideration of this question so fraught was the absolutist attitude adopted by its members, which argued under the assumption that consent must always and only constitute a defence or always and only a negative rule-element. Subsequent doctrinal works too have taken this absolutist stance. What seems to be missing from the discussion both within and beyond the ILC is the acknowledgment that neither of these two positions can claim to be a complete and accurate description of legal reality.[168] In domestic law, certain legal rules embody normative messages that require an element of (non-)consent. The classic example in this case is rape: without the element of (non-)consent, the offence definition would relate to sexual intercourse – yet it seems obvious that societies do not condemn sexual intercourse per se.[169] They condemn non-consensual intercourse. The same is not true of the crime of battery: even without an element of (non-)consent, the crime of battery embodies a complete normative message accepted by a society. Indeed, it may be the case that *some* rules incorporate an element of (non-)consent and that some do not. And yet, it is possible that, in respect of the latter, consent can nevertheless act as a defence.[170] In German law, for instance, these two roles of consent are clearly communicated through the use of two different terms: *'Einwilligung'* (referring to consent as a defence) and *'Einverständnis'* (referring to consent as

---

[168] For the analogous argument in domestic law, see Finkelstein, 'When the Rule Swallows the Exception' in Meyer (ed.), *Rules and Reasoning: Essays in Honour of Frederick Schauer* (1999), 147; Fletcher, *Rethinking Criminal Law* (2000), 566.

[169] But see Dempsey and Herring, 'Why Sexual Penetration Requires Justification' (2007) 27 OJLS 467.

[170] A defence of consent in respect of rules containing an element of non-consent would be redundant.

a negative element of the *Tatbestand*, or definition of the offence).[171] This is not the prevalence of 'muddiness' over the 'clarity of jurisprudence', as Dugard would have it, but merely the attempt by the law to reflect and accommodate different normative purposes, goals, and messages, and different societal understandings about what is harmful and what is permissible.[172] To impose a single approach to this complicated reality is artificial and risks oversimplifying and, very often, distorting that reality.

In international law too there exist rules that incorporate an element of non-consent. An example, cited by the ARS,[173] is the prohibition of force. As stated in Article 2(4) of the UN Charter, this rule bans the use of force '*against* another State'.[174] Presumably, then, when there is consent of the target state the force is not *against* it.[175] But not all obligations in international law are formulated as containing one such requirement. If one wanted to maintain that non-consent was incorporated into all obligations, then an element of non-consent would have to be implied or read into each one of these rules. This would mean, in turn, that in every case a state claiming that there is a breach of that obligation would have to prove, alongside the positive rule-elements, that there was no consent to the act in question (the negative rule-element). Yet, practice (and scholarly writings, for that matter) do not seem to reflect this approach: it is not the case that *every* time a state claims one of its rights has been breached, it has to prove that it did not consent to that breach. So it may just be that in international law, like in domestic law, consent has a dual role: it can act as a negative rule-element in relation to some obligations, and as a defence in relation to others.

To be sure, this is not an exclusive characteristic of consent. Other defences (or, more correctly, the facts that enliven those defences) are sometimes incorporated as rule-elements in the definition of the obligation in question. This phenomenon was explained by Nigeria in

---

[171] Bohlander, *Principles of German Criminal Law* (2009), 77.

[172] On the varying roles of consent vis-à-vis crimes in domestic law, see Malawi: see Bande, Suppl. 45, 97; Netherlands: see Lensing, Suppl. 10, 72; Portugal: see Faria, Suppl. 48, 79; Singapore: see Koh and Tan, Suppl. 5, 71; Spain: see Bachmaier Winter and del Moral García, Suppl. 46, 101; England and Wales: see Leigh and Hall Williams, 59; all in *International Encyclopaedia of Laws (Criminal Law)* (multiple dates).

[173] ARS art. 26 Commentary, [6].

[174] Emphasis added.

[175] See Díaz Barrado, *Consentimiento*, 77. This is not to say that all consensual uses of force are permissible under international law. But in those cases in which consensual force is permissible, it will be so by operation of the rule itself, as explained by Crawford in the ILC (Crawford, 2587th meeting, 138 [12]), and not by application of a defence.

## 4.3 CONSENT AS A DEFENCE

its pleadings in the case of *Cameroon v Nigeria*. According to Nigerian counsel:

> In some cases what may usually be seen as a defence may in fact be one of the constituent elements of the substantive rule the breach of which is in question. Defences are thus, on analysis, not absolute concepts, but relative to the primary obligation in question.[176]

Among scholars, it has also been endorsed by Phoebe Okowa, according to whom: 'many substantive rules clearly provide for specific defences as part of the definition of the content of the relevant obligation'.[177] To put it more precisely, it is the facts and circumstances which give rise to the defence that are incorporated into the definition of the relevant rules and not, as the examples above imply, the defence itself. Due diligence obligations provide a good example of this situation. Due diligence obligations are limited by possibility: states are not required to do the impossible to conform with their obligation, but only what is possible so long as they act diligently. Due diligence obligations require states to behave in a specified way (diligently), independently of the result of such behaviour.[178] These obligations therefore require the state to maintain a certain standard of diligence; a standard which is relative to the circumstances. If a supervening event beyond the state's control prevents the state from exercising the same degree of diligence that it displays in normal circumstances, then the state does not act incompatibly with its due diligence obligations: in the circumstances, the state displayed the standard of diligence it was able (or not able) to exercise.[179] As a result of this impossibility, the state will not have breached its obligation. Impossibility of performance, the fact which enlivens the defence of *force majeure*, is here incorporated into the very definition of the obligation. It is thus possible that the facts that enliven defences be incorporated as in the definition of the obligations of states.

But a difficulty nonetheless remains: how to know in which case consent is a negative rule-element and in which case is it a defence? One

---

[176] Oral statement of Nigeria, *Cameroon v Nigeria*, 15 March 2002, CR 2002/20, 28–9.

[177] Okowa, 'Defences in the Jurisprudence of International Tribunals' in Goodwin-Gill and Talmon (eds), *The Reality of International Law: Essays in Honour of Ian Brownlie* (1999), 391.

[178] Pisillo Mazzeschi, 'Responsabilité de l'état pour violation des obligations positives relatives aux droits de l'homme' (2008) 333 *Recueil* 175, 284. See generally Pisillo Mazzeschi, *Due diligence e responsabilità internazionale degli Stati* (1989).

[179] Zegveld, *Accountability of Armed Opposition Groups in International Law* (2002), 217; Lozano Contreras, *La noción de debida diligencia en derecho internacional público* (2007), 220–8.

criterion that can be used in this regard is the burden of proof in relation to the relevant facts. So, it may be said that if the applicant is required to prove non-consent to make out its claim then consent will be a negative rule-element; if, on the contrary, it is the respondent who must prove that there is consent, then it will be a defence.[180] This seems a relatively simple way of dealing with the question, after all international law too accepts the principle that the burden of proving the claim (including negative rule-elements) falls on the claimant, and the burden of proof of defences falls on the respondents.[181] But there are nevertheless certain objections to it. For one, some have criticised this criterion for putting the cart before the horse: the burden of proof is a consequence of the character of any given fact as belonging to the claim or the defence, and not the other way around.[182] Moreover, its application to international law may run into some difficulties. The clearest example is the burden of proof in respect of consent to the use of force. As noted earlier, it is often claimed that consent is a negative rule-element of the prohibition of force. Indeed, it seems that consent can *only* be a negative rule-element in relation to the prohibition since the prohibition is accepted and recognised by states as a peremptory rule. As such, pursuant to Article 26 ARS, consent could not operate as a defence to acts involving the use of force.[183] Yet, it would seem that the burden of proof in relation to this consent falls on the respondent

---

[180] This argument is elaborated, at length, by Duarte d'Almeida, *Allowing for Exceptions: A Theory of Defences and Defeasibility in Law* (2015).

[181] This corollary has been accepted by numerous international courts and tribunals. For the ICJ, see, e.g., *Gabčíkovo-Nagymaros Project (Hungary/Slovakia)* (1997) ICJ Rep 7, 41–5; WTO: *US - Gasoline*, WT/DS2/AB/R, DSR 1996: I, 3 at 21; *Wool Shirts and Blouses*, WT/DS33/AB/R, 14; *EC - Sardines*, WT/DS231/AB/R, [275]; *Chile - Price Band System* (Article 21.5 - Argentina), WT/DS207/AB/RW, [134–6]; *EC - Tariff Preferences*, WT/DS246/AB/R, [88, 90]; Iran–US CTR: *RN Pomeroy v Iran* (1983) 2 Iran–US CTR 372, 382; in international investment tribunals, see *Feldman v Mexico* (AF) Award, 16 December 2002, [177]; for a specific example see *National Grid Plc v Argentine Republic*, UNCITRAL Award, 3 November 2008, [260] (failure to prove the requirements of state of necessity, leading to rejection of the plea). For scholarly support, see Kazazi, *Burden of Proof and Related Issues: A Study on Evidence before International Tribunals* (1996), 111–12; Pauwelyn, 'Evidence, Proof and Persuasion in WTO Dispute Settlement: Who Bears the Burden?' (1998) 1 JIEL 227, 232, 235; Amerasinghe, *Evidence in International Litigation* (Leiden: Martinus Nijhoff, 2005); Riddell and Plant, *Evidence before the International Court of Justice* (2009), 87; Foster, *Science*, 209–10. Cf. Grando, *Evidence, Proof, and Fact-Finding in WTO Dispute Settlement* (2009), 187–9.

[182] For this criticism, see: Goudkamp, *Tort Law Defences* (2013), 41.

[183] ARS art 26 states that: 'Nothing in this chapter precludes the wrongfulness of any act of a State which is not in conformity with an obligation arising under a peremptory norm of general international law.'

(and not the applicant). This is indeed what can be inferred from the ICJ's judgment in *Congo v Uganda*. The parties disagreed on this question,[184] yet the Court (in usual form) did not clearly specify the allocation of the evidentiary burdens in its judgment. If the burden of proof were used as a means of determining when any given fact is an element of the rule or a defence, then it must be concluded that in relation to the prohibition of force consent is a defence. But if this is the case and if, as states accept, the prohibition is a peremptory rule, then consent would not be a valid defence for uses of force. Alternatively, if this is the case and consent is a valid defence, then the prohibition of force is not a peremptory rule.

Legal theorists who have engaged with this question have so far failed to agree on a single criterion which can be used to determine when a certain fact is an element of the rule or a defence.[185] George Fletcher has gone as far as to say that the answer to this question cannot be found in the law or in 'logical or abstract theories', but rather it ought to be found in other considerations: policy, moral, and so on.[186] In the absence of any such principle, a case-by-case analysis may be necessary; namely, that the role of consent may need to be determined in relation to the relevant obligation. The formulation of international legal norms may often clarify the point, as is potentially the case for the prohibition of force which bans the use of force *against* a state. Other factors may also be helpful in this analysis. Among others, it may be queried whether the statement of the rule reflects a clear and coherent normative message; what the rationale of the rule is and, whether, non-consent is part of the essence of the rule; whether the absence of consent is necessary to a finding that the rule has been breached (in which case the claimant has proven this absence), or whether consent results in a finding that the rule has not been breached (in which case, it acts as a defence to be proven by the respondent).

---

[184] The DRC, claimant in the case, argued in its Reply of 29 May 2002 that it fell on Uganda to prove that the DRC had given consent to the presence of its troops in DRC territory, at 356. In its Rejoinder, Uganda noted that the DRC presented 'no evidence to refute the existence of such consent', see Rejoinder of 6 December 2002, 128.

[185] See, on this issue, Stone, 'Burden of Proof and the Judicial Process' (1944) 60 LQR 262; Schauer, 'Exceptions' (1991) 58 *U Chicago LR* 871; Husak, *Philosophy of Criminal Law* (1987), 190–2; Finkelstein, 'When the Rule Swallows the Exception'; Fletcher, *Rethinking Criminal Law* (2000), 566; Gardner, 'In Defence of Defences' in Gardner (ed.), *Offences and Defences: Selected Essays in the Philosophy of Criminal Law* (2007), 77; Horder, *Excusing Crime* (2007), 254ff. A concise overview of the main arguments can be found in Goudkamp, *Tort Law Defences*, ch 2.

[186] Fletcher, *Rethinking Criminal Law* (2000), 566.

## 4.4 Consent as a Justification

The question that remains to be considered is whether the defence of consent operates to preclude wrongfulness or whether it precludes responsibility. The point may seem a bit trite – after all, the references to the 'perfect' legality of consented-to conduct imply that consent acts as a justification. Nevertheless, in the interests of analytical clarity, it is important to examine how this effect is achieved and what theory may explain it.

### 4.4.1 Consent as the Renunciation of Legal Protection

The Commentary to Article 20 explains consent as the 'dispensation' by a state of 'the performance of an obligation owed to [it] individually'.[187] The state consents to the non-application of one of its rights in a particular case;[188] or, to put it another way, through its consent the state renounces the protection that the law affords to one of its rights in a specific set of circumstances.[189] This dispensation does not entail a renunciation of the right as such, a renunciation leading to the extinction of the relevant right.[190] The 'primary rule', says the Commission, 'continues to govern the relations between the two States.'[191] For example, ad hoc waivers of immunity constitute dispensations of performance in the individual case, which do not entail a waiver of the right as such.[192] Equally, the United Kingdom's argument in relation to France's right of asylum vis-à-vis Savarkar was one of renunciation in the individual case: through its conduct, the United Kingdom argued, France had renounced its right to give him asylum.[193]

That states can consent to this dispensation is, as von Liszt had maintained in the late nineteenth century,[194] a logical implication of state

---

[187] ARS art. 20 Commentary, [2].
[188] As clarified by the Commission in its Report, thirty-first session, 130 [2]. In the literature, see Díaz Barrado, *Consentimiento*, 128.
[189] See, e.g., von Liszt, *Droit*, 201; Wolff, 'Principes', 522–3; Balladore-Pallieri, *Diritto internazionale pubblico*, 216; Riphagen, 1542nd meeting, [36]; Ben Mansour, 'Consent', 445–6.
[190] Venturini, 'La portée et les effets juridiques des attitudes et des actes unilatéraux des Etats' (1964) 112 *Recueil* 363, 394. Of course, states may renounce rights definitively, see Venturini, i 394, 405, 415–16.
[191] ARS art. 20 Commentary, [2].
[192] ILC Report, sixty-third session, 2011, [177] (not yet published).
[193] *UK Reply, Savarkar Arbitration*, 3.
[194] von Liszt, *Droit*, 201.

sovereignty.[195] It is because they are sovereigns, that states can enter into international obligations, as the PCIJ recognised in *Wimbledon*.[196] Likewise, it is because they are sovereigns that they can set aside the application of obligations through agreements or special customary rules; and it is because they are sovereigns that they can waive the right to invoke the responsibility of a wrongdoing State.[197] It seems logical that it is also because they are sovereigns that States can consent to the non-performance of their rights.

There are no requirements as to the way in which this consent ought to be expressed, so long as it can be inferred clearly and definitively from either the conduct or the statements of a state.[198] This means that Ago's insistence, during the first reading of the Article, that consent operated through the creation of an agreement is beside the point. Most certainly states can enter into ad hoc agreements (oral or in writing) envisaging the non-performance of an obligation existing between them in respect of a concrete case. But this can also be achieved through a unilateral act.[199] The Commentary does not exclude either possibility; on the contrary, its recognition that no formalities are required is further evidence that consent may be given through agreement or unilateral act. Note, however, that the manner chosen to express that consent may have an impact on the manner of its withdrawal, as discussed by the parties in the *DRC v Uganda* case.[200]

Moreover, it may be useful to clarify that when consent takes the form of an agreement this is an ad hoc agreement intended to operate in the specific circumstances only. Indeed, if the agreement were intended to exclude or modify some right or obligation existing between the parties on a permanent basis, then that would affect the underlying obligation. Such

---

[195] For recent statements of this view, see: Alaimo, 'Natura del consenso', 258; Abass, 'Consent', 225; Aust, 'Circumstances Precluding Wrongfulness and Shared Responsibility' in Nollkaemper and Plakokefalos (eds), *Principles of Shared Responsibility* (2014), 180.

[196] *The SS 'Wimbledon'* (1923) PCIJ, Series A No 01, 15, 25.

[197] For an example of a waiver of claims, see the treaties at issue in *Jurisdictional Immunities of the State (Germany v Italy: Greece intervening)* (2012) ICJ Rep 99.

[198] ARS art. 20 Commentary, [6].

[199] This view was expressed by several ILC members throughout the Commission's work; see Section 4.2.2. See further Gaja, '*Jus Cogens*. Beyond the Vienna Convention' (1981) 172 *Recueil* 271, 295. But see Alaimo, 'Natura del consenso'; Díaz Barrado, *Consentimiento*, ch. 6.

[200] See, e.g., statement of the DRC, 13 April 2005, CR 2005/4, 14–15 (original); statement of Uganda, 19 April 2005, CR 2005/8, 14–15 (original). The Court accepted that informal consent may be informally withdrawn, but remained silent on the withdrawal of consent expressed formally: *DRC v Uganda*, [50].

an agreement would no longer belong to the 'middle case', in Crawford's taxonomy. While this distinction may seem somewhat formalistic, it has substantive effects in that it affects the continued validity of the underlying obligation as between the parties which would either no longer exist as between them or exist with modified content.

The power of renunciation is, of course, limited to those rights held individually by the consenting state. An (individual) state could not, however, renounce the performance (or consent to the non-performance) of a right established for the collective interest.[201] In von Liszt's example, Belgium could not consent to the passage of German troops over its territory since its neutralisation had been established for the collective interest of European states (as a guarantee for the maintenance of the balance of power).[202] For a contemporary example, one could think of consent to vessel-source pollution within a state's EEZ: such a consent would affect a rule established in the collective interest, so an individual state could not renounce its performance in an individual case.[203]

### 4.4.2 Renunciation, Absent Interest and Theories of Justification

Theorists disagree, however, on why this renunciation provides a basis for justification. The issue has been developed mostly in domestic law settings – international lawyers have only made rather superficial remarks on this issue. One of the theories put forward by domestic law theorists states that underpinning the defence of consent is a balancing of interests, in which the superior interest is made to prevail. This is a well-known theory of justification, also known as 'lesser-evil' or 'choice of evils', which will be discussed again in respect of self-defence, countermeasures and state of necessity, in Chapters 5, 6 and 8, respectively. In respect of consent, the theory explains its justifying effect as follows. Where an individual renounces the protection of the criminal law (or private law, for that matter) to one of its interests, there arises a clash between two interests:

---

[201] Villalpando, *L'émergence de la communauté internationale dans la responsabilité des Etats* (2005), 260–1. This was also a concern which emerged during the discussions in the ILC on Article 20. See, e.g., Reuter, 1537th meeting, ILC Yearbook 1979, vol. I, 33 [38]; Quentin-Baxter, 1540th meeting, 43 [28]; Riphagen, 1538th meeting, ILC Yearbook 1979, vol. I, 34 [12]; Hafner, 2587th meeting, ILC Yearbook 1999, vol. I, 145 [59]; Crawford, 2587th meeting, 145 [60]. Among States commenting on ARS art. 20 and its predecessor draft art. 29, see India: A/C.6/54/SR.23, [33].

[202] von Liszt, *Droit*, 201.

[203] For further remarks on this issue, see Gaja, '*Jus Cogens*', 293–6.

## 4.4 CONSENT AS A JUSTIFICATION

on the one hand, the interest protected by the rule establishing the crime (or delict) and, on the other, the consenting individual's autonomy allowing him to dispose – within certain limits – of his rights. In this clash of interests, it is the individual's autonomy which prevails and, as result, his consent can set aside the rule establishing the crime or offence.[204] The 'interest-balancing' theory of justification can accommodate the limitations usually recognised to this defence; thus, crimes established for the public interest cannot be renounced by the individual, since his autonomy cannot prevail over the public interest of the law. But the thesis is not without critiques. Authors have suggested that the explanation of consent as a clash of interests is a (stretched) attempt to make consent fall within the broader theory of justification of lesser evils. Indeed, as will be seen later on in this book, unlike in other justifications, the clash of interests in the situation of consent 'takes place within the owner's private mind when he is faced with the question whether it is worthwhile for him to sacrifice his' interests.[205] The individual has to consider two of *his own* interests: *his* interest in legal protection and *his* autonomy. But after he consents, there is nothing more to be balanced. This is different from the clash of interests contemplated by other defences in which the balancing occurs between the interests of two different subjects: to take the example of state of necessity, these are the interests of the individual acting in necessity and the individual injured by that act.[206] The theory can be reframed to concern states and their interests. In any case where consent is at issue, there is a clash between two state interests: its sovereign power to renounce the legal protection offered by international law and the specific interest protected by the rule renounced. Nevertheless, as in domestic law, it seems that the difference with the usual formulation of the lesser-evil theory is such as to distort that theory for the sole purpose of extending it to cover the plea of consent.

An alternative theory explains the effect of consent as an *absence* of a legally protected interest. If through consent a state releases another from the performance of an obligation owed to it, it follows that conduct adopted within the limits of that consent does not breach the law since

---

[204] E.g., Merle and Vitu, *Traité de droit criminel: Droit pénal général* (6th edn, 1988), 528; Koh and Tan, 'Singapore', *International Encyclopaedia of Laws (Criminal Law: Suppl. 5)* (1995), 71; de Francesco, *Diritto penale. I fondamenti* (2008), 311; Padovani, *Diritto penale* (9th edn, 2008), 147.

[205] Lenckner, 'The Principle of Interest Balancing as a General Basis of Justification' (1986) BYU LR 645, 656.

[206] See Chapter 8.

the relevant legal protection has been renounced.[207] Theodore Lenckner, writing in the context of the domestic criminal law defence of consent, has explained that in these circumstances '[t]he point is that there is no reason for the law to protect an interest from a particular intrusion when the possessor of that interest does not wish to be protected against the violation in that particular situation.'[208] Applying this to international law, it can be said that the in *absence* of a legally protected interest, there can be no breach of international law. This theory is also able to account for some of the limitations of the defence of consent in a principled manner. Thus, as explained earlier, a state cannot renounce an interest that is protected for the benefit of the collectivity – in the exercise of its autonomy (its sovereignty) it can only renounce the protection of its own individual interests. A state could not, in other words, renounce the protection afforded by peremptory rules.[209]

So which theory provides a better explanation of consent in international law? There are elements both in favour and against each of these theories. The theory of interest balancing, or lesser evils, would have the benefit of (potentially) providing a unified theory of justification capable of explaining all justifications. But, as was seen, it can do so only when stretched to an artificial point. Absent interest, instead, while posing an obstacle to the identification of a unitary theory of justification, has the benefit of providing a more elegant explanation of the operation of this defence. In the absence of any practical difference between the two, the choice between the two may turn on which value is to be preferred: the identification of a unitary theory of justification, or the elaboration of theories capable of accurately describing the phenomenon studied. Here, as with the absolutist arguments about consent's position as a negative rule-element or a defence, ensuring a unitary theory of justification comes at the cost of an accurate depiction of legal reality. Given the inability of theory of demonstrating why a unitary theory of justification is a goal worth pursuing, it seems that the absent interest theory ought to be preferred.

---

[207] E.g., Eser, 'Justification and Excuse' (1976) 24 *Am J Comp L* 621, 630; di Amato, *Criminal Law in Italy* (2011), 92; Bachmaier Winter and del Moral García, 'Spain', *International Encyclopaedia of Laws (Criminal Law: Suppl. 46)* (2012), 93.
[208] Lenckner, 'Interest Balancing', 655.
[209] See ARS art. 26.

# 5

## Self-Defence

### 5.1 Introduction

Pursuant to Article 21 of the ARS:

> The wrongfulness of an act of a State is precluded if the act constitutes a lawful measure of self-defence taken in conformity with the Charter of the United Nations.

As indicated in the Commentary, this provision does not concern the relationship between the right of self-defence and the prohibition of force. That is, Article 21 does not provide a justification (or excuse) for action incompatible with the prohibition of force.[1] Rather, Article 21 looks to *other* obligations that are potentially infringed by a state that uses force in self-defence. In the course of self-defence a state may, for example, use force in the territory of the aggressor resulting in an impairment of the latter's territorial sovereignty, or its actions may impair the principle of non-intervention. It is these and other similar impairments that are justified by Article 21.[2] The Commentary clarifies, however, that Article 21 cannot justify (or excuse) the impairment of *any* and *every* right by self-defensive force. On the authority of the *Nuclear Weapons* opinion, the Commentary excludes from the material scope of this provision the so-called 'obligations of total restraint' – namely, obligations intended to impose definitive restrictions on state conduct in times of conflict. Among others, these include humanitarian law, certain basic human rights and certain environmental rules.[3] The Commentary also limits Article 21 to the relations between the states involved in the armed conflict; it does not, however, take a position in respect of third parties potentially affected by the use of force.[4] Finally, a necessary condition for the operation of Article 21 is

---

[1] ARS art. 21 Commentary, [1].
[2] Ibid., [2].
[3] Ibid., [3–4].
[4] Ibid., [5].

that the use of force in question be 'lawful' in that it must comply with the relevant *jus ad bellum*.[5]

This provision of the ARS is infrequently discussed in the literature.[6] Most general works on international law that address it simply discuss the right of self-defence, codified in Article 51 of the UN Charter, rather than the circumstance precluding wrongfulness codified in ARS Article 21.[7] This same approach can also be observed in some specialised works on state responsibility.[8] A few of the works that discuss Article 21 in its own right argue that the provision is redundant since its intended scope is already covered by the right of self-defence and countermeasures, and that for this reason it is useless.[9] This chapter will show that these views are based on a misunderstanding of the scope and function of Article 21 in the international legal system.

When a state resorts to force against another state, that resort to arms may infringe the prohibition of force, but it may also encroach upon the target state's territory, it may affect its freedom to conduct its affairs without external interference and, depending on the object targeted, it could even impair the enjoyment of (conventionally protected) commercial or trade rights. These few examples clearly show that the use of force may affect a number of legal relations existing between the states in conflict.

---

[5] Ibid., [6].

[6] For exceptions, see Christakis and Bannelier, 'La légitime défense en tant que "circonstance excluant l'illicéité"' in Kherad (ed.), *Légitimes défenses* (2007), 247ff; Christakis and Bannelier, 'La légitime défense a-t-elle sa place dans un code sur la responsabilité internationale?' in Constantinides and Zaikos (eds), *The Diversity of International Law: Essays in Honour of Professor Kalliopi K Koufa* (2009); Thouvenin, 'Self-Defence' in Crawford et al. (eds), *The Law of International Responsibility* (2010), 455; van Steenberghe, *La légitime défense en droit international public* (2012), 128; Crawford, *State Responsibility: The General Part* (2013), 289–92; Paddeu, 'Self-Defence as a Circumstance Precluding Wrongfulness: Understanding Article 21 of the Articles on State Responsibility' (2014) 85 BYIL 90; Paddeu, 'Use of Force Against Non-State Actors and the Circumstance Precluding Wrongfulness of Self-Defence' (2017) 30 LJIL 93.

[7] See, e.g., Cassese, *International Law* (2nd edn, 2005), 254; Daillier et al., *Droit international public* (8th edn, 2009), 875–6; de Oliveira Mazzuoli, *Curso de direito internacional público* (6th edn, 2012), 591–2; Klabbers, *International Law* (2013), 130; Shaw, *International Law* (7th edn, 2014), 577.

[8] E.g., Gutiérrez-Espada, *El hecho ilícito internacional* (2005), 125–8; Farhang, 'Mapping the Approaches to the Question of Exemption from International Responsibility' (2013) 60 NILR 93; Farhang, 'Self-Defence as a Circumstance Precluding the Wrongfulness of the Use of Force' (2015) 11 *Utrecht LR* 1. These three works all address the right of self-defence (Article 51 UN Charter) in the context of analyses of ARS art. 21.

[9] Christakis and Bannelier, 'Légitime défense', 247ff; Christakis and Bannelier, 'La légitime défense a-t-elle sa place'; van Steenberghe, *Légitime défense*, 128.

## 5.1 INTRODUCTION

As explained in Section 5.4.1, to understand the role of Article 21 it is essential to classify these various legal relations into three categories. First is the legal relation arising under the (conventional and customary) rule prohibiting force in international relations. Second is the set of legal relations arising under other rules of international law, be they customary or conventional, the performance of which may be collaterally impaired by the use of force. These comprise an 'infinite variety'[10] and include the rights of territorial sovereignty and non-intervention, trade and commercial rights, treaties for the exchange of technology, and so on. Third is the category of legal relations which impose 'obligations of total restraint';[11] the impairment of these cannot be justified even in self-defence, so they are excluded from the scope of Article 21.

A state which resorts to force in self-defence does not thereby infringe, or act in a manner incompatible with, the prohibition of force[12] – the first legal relation mentioned. Nevertheless, the fact that the use of force in self-defence is lawful by reference to the prohibition of force does not entail that it is also lawful under the second set of legal relations. The use of force in the territory of the aggressor state could be lawful under the prohibition of force, but unlawful under, for example, the right of territorial sovereignty. Indeed, it is well known that international law often 'looks at the same act in two different ways',[13] in many different ways even. As a result, conduct may be lawful under one rule and unlawful by reference to another – a phenomenon that is at the core of the fragmentation debate.[14] In the words of the ICJ in *Croatia v Serbia*: '[t]here can be no doubt that, as a general rule, a particular act may be perfectly lawful under one body of legal rules and unlawful under another.'[15] That self-defence is lawful under the prohibition of force has, on its own, no bearing on the issue of the legality of that same conduct under the second set of legal relations. These obligations are all conceptually distinct, so that their breach

---

[10] The expression is taken from Baxter, 'International Law in "Her Infinite Variety"' (1980) 29 ICLQ 549.
[11] ARS art. 21 Commentary, [4]. The expression is the ICJ's: *Legality of the Threat or Use of Nuclear Weapons (Advisory Opinion)* (1996) ICJ Rep 226, [30].
[12] Of course, when the conditions and requirements for the exercise of this right are met. This chapter's consideration of self-defence will assume that these requirements are met.
[13] To use Shapiro's words: Shapiro, 'Ralph Nader's Tort Museum', *The New Yorker*, 28 September 2015, www.newyorker.com/culture/culture-desk/ralph-naders-tort-museum.
[14] For a useful summary of the main points in the debate, see Crawford, 'Chance, Order, Change: The Course of International Law' (2013) 365 *Recueil* 9, ch. 9.
[15] *Application of the Convention on the Prevention and Punishment of the Crime of Genocide (Croatia v Serbia)*, ICJ, Judgment of 3 February 2015, [474] (not yet reported).

need not be justified 'by the sole fact of the existence of a right of self-defence'.[16] The distinction between the effect of self-defence on the prohibition of force and on *other* obligations is often blurred in practice when self-defence is exercised between two states. But the distinction is patently clear (and indeed, has been the cause of much difficulty) in arguments about the use of force against non-state actors: while a state may be justified by self-defence to use force against a non-state actor (and thereby, act compatibly with the prohibition of force), insofar as those non-state actors are located in the territory of a third state self-defensive force in the latter's territory will impair that state's territorial sovereignty.[17] Article 21 is concerned precisely with the justification of the impairment caused by the self-defensive force on the rights belonging to the second set of legal relations; with what may be called the collateral impairment of these rights by lawful self-defensive action.

Article 21 may be seen as an *incidental* function of the (lawful) exercise of the right of self-defence under international law. In this sense, Article 21 is not dissimilar from ARS Article 22 on countermeasures. As will be explained in Chapter 6, countermeasures constitute a means of implementing state responsibility, which takes the form of the non-performance of an obligation owed by the injured state to the responsible state. Countermeasures, as is often remarked, are 'intrinsically'[18] wrongful acts which are justified *because* they are intended to induce the state to comply with its obligations of responsibility. The justification of the non-performance of the obligations owed to the target state is ancillary or incidental to countermeasures' main function of implementation of responsibility.[19] Analogously, the right of self-defence is concerned, primarily, with the warding off of an armed attack.[20] Incidental to this,

---

[16] Thouvenin, 'Self-Defence', 461.

[17] See, e.g., Ruys and Verhoeven, 'Attacks by Private Actors and the Right of Self-Defence' (2005) 10 *J Conflict & Security Law* 289, 310. For an argument about the application of Article 21 to the scenario of use of force against non-state actors, see Paddeu, 'Use of Force Against Non-State Actors'.

[18] Alland, 'The Definition of Countermeasures' in Crawford et al. (eds), *The Law of International Responsibility* (2010), 1131–2.

[19] This is what emerges from the ARS's bifurcated regulation of countermeasures, in art. 22 of Chapter V of Part One and, later, on Chapter II of Part Three. As explained by Crawford, 'the main focus of countermeasures should be on their instrumental purpose in relation to cessation and reparation, rather than their incidental effect as circumstances precluding wrongfulness': Crawford, Second Report on State Responsibility, ILC Yearbook 1999, vol. II(1), [393].

[20] On the protective function of self-defence, see Tams, *Enforcing Obligations Erga Omnes in International Law* (2005), 22.

## 5.1 INTRODUCTION

the lawful exercise of this right in international law will also justify the impairment of other rights of the aggressor state caused by that defensive force. Schematically, these two functions are represented by Article 51 of the UN Charter and ARS Article 21.

This chapter will explain the intended scope of Article 21 by reference to developments in the ILC and state practice. The practice, as will be seen, is relatively scarce, but insofar as it exists it is supportive of the principle embodied in Article 21. The analysis will be divided into four parts. Section 5.2 begins with some brief historical notes on the developments which rendered a provision like Article 21 possible (if not necessary). Section 5.3 then moves on to review how Article 21 evolved in the work of the ILC and Section 5.4 turns to Article 21 itself: by reference to the available state practice, this section will attempt to illuminate the scope of this defence. Finally, Section 5.5 will consider the plea of self-defence pursuant to Article 21 as a justification or an excuse. As will be seen, the practice in relation to Article 21 supports the proposition that the impairment of these rights is justified (rather than excused). After a review of different theories of justification, this chapter will argue that the most persuasive theoretical explanation of the justifying effect of self-defence relies on a theory of forfeiture of legal protection by the aggressor.

Before turning to this analysis, some clarifications on the terminology used and on the scope of this chapter are necessary. As to terminology, the chapter will use the expression 'right of self-defence' to refer to the entitlement under customary and conventional international law to resort to force when an 'armed attack occurs', which is codified in Article 51 of the UN Charter; and to 'justification' or 'circumstance precluding wrongfulness' of self-defence to refer to the provision of Article 21. For ease of reference, it will use the expression 'collateral impairment' to refer to the encroachment upon the second set of legal relations by the use of self-defensive force. As to scope, this chapter does not contain an analysis of the historical development of self-defence in international law. The history of this right (and of the *jus ad bellum* generally) has been well charted in the scholarship and not much can be added here.[21] Only

---

[21] See, e.g., Waldock, 'The Regulation of the Use of Force by Individual States in International Law' (1952) 81 *Recueil* 451; Bowett, *Self-Defence in International Law* (1958); Brownlie, *International Law and the Use of Force by States* (1963); Lamberti-Zanardi, *La legittima difesa nel diritto internazionale* (1972); Alexandrov, *Self-Defense Against the Use of Force in International Law* (1996), chaps 1–3; Grewe, *The Epochs of International Law* (2000); Neff, *War and the Law of Nations* (2005); Kolb, 'La légitime défense des Etats au XIXième siècle et pendant l'époque de la Société de Nations' in Kherad (ed.), *Légitimes défenses*

limited historical remarks will be made in Section 5.2 in relation to the continued relevance of the 'state of war' as a legal institution. For the same reason, this chapter will not discuss the requirements and conditions of the right of self-defence in international law.[22] Finally, the analysis will be limited to the effect of Article 21 on the relations between the aggressor and defending (or victim) state: what the Commentary refers to as the 'essential' effect of this provision.[23] The chapter will thus exclude from its consideration the effects of the exercise of self-defence on third parties, a matter 'left open' by the ILC.[24]

## 5.2 Historical Premise: Armed Conflict during Peace

The formulation of (and the need for) the function of self-defence as a justification for the collateral impairment of the aggressor's rights must be understood in historical perspective.[25] Until 1945 the institution of the state of war governed all of the legal relations existing between the belligerent states.[26] The state of war 'wholly excluded' the law of peace, and replaced it with the law of war in the relations between belligerents.[27] In addition, the state of war also produced effects in respect of treaty commitments between belligerent states. Until the end of the nineteenth century it was accepted that the state of war extinguished all treaty relations between belligerents, as evidenced by the fact that peace treaties usually

---

(2007), 67; van Steenberghe, *Légitime défense*; Lesaffer, 'Too Much History: From War as Sanction to the Sanctioning of War' in Weller (ed.), *Oxford Handbook of the Use of Force in International Law* (2015), 35.

[22] Many scholarly works consider the conditions of the right of self-defence. See, e.g., Franck, *Recourse to Force* (2002), chaps 3–7; Gazzini, *The Changing Rules on the Use of Force in International Law* (2005), chaps 4–5; Ruys, '*Armed Attack' and Article 51 of the UN Charter* (2010); Lubell, *Extraterritorial Use of Force Against Non-State Actors* (2010), chaps 1–3; Gardam, *Necessity, Proportionality and the Use of Force by States* (2010); Gray, *International Law and the Use of Force* (4th edn, 2012), chaps 4–6; Dinstein, *War, Aggression and Self-Defence* (5th edn, 2012), chaps 7–9; van Steenberghe, *Légitime défense*, 446–84; Corten, *Le droit contre la guerre* (2nd edn, 2014), ch. 7. There are, in addition, numerous journal articles concerning this question. References can be found in these general works.

[23] ARS art. 21 Commentary, [5].

[24] According to the Commentary, this issue is governed by the law of neutrality and the right of self-defence itself, see id. For some developments on this point, see Paddeu, 'Use of Force Against Non-State Actors'.

[25] Crawford, *General Part*, 290.

[26] The state of war consisted of the situation, condition or status during which the extraordinary law of war substituted the law of peace in the regulation of the relations between the parties to the conflict, see Wright, 'When Does War Exist?' (1932) 26 AJIL 362, 363.

[27] Neff, *War*, 177.

## 5.2 HISTORICAL PREMISE 181

included clauses for the revival of those instruments.[28] This extreme effect of war on treaties was subsequently softened, and from the early twentieth century onwards it was thought that the state of war merely suspended treaties between belligerents.[29] Whether treaties were terminated or suspended, the point is that the state of war set aside the normal (peaceful) relations between states, be they customary or conventional, and replaced the law of peace wholly with the law of war as the normative order governing the relations between belligerents. In these circumstances, in which the law of peace and treaty relations were displaced, there was no risk that a state's armed measures during war might constitute a violation of its (peacetime) obligations towards the enemy.

The legal institution of war is of little practical relevance in contemporary international law. Scholarly debates remain as to its compatibility with the UN Charter collective security system,[30] and save for a few instances of declared formal war, states engaged in armed conflict do not usually consider themselves to be in a state of war.[31] The existence of war as a legal status is no longer a precondition for the application of the law of armed conflict, which is now triggered by the actual existence of armed hostilities.[32] The application of the law of armed conflict, furthermore, does not have the effect of displacing the normal, peacetime, legal relations existing between the states in conflict. As stated by the ICJ in *Nuclear Weapons*, the law of armed conflict constitutes a *lex specialis* in the situation of armed conflict,[33] a statement which implies that the *lex generalis* – the normal legal relations existing between states – remains in the background.[34] Treaties too are no longer considered as '*ipso facto*', to

---

[28] Mancini, *Stato di guerra e conflitto armato nel diritto internazionale* (2009), 44; Mancini, 'The Effects of a State of War or Armed Conflict' in Weller (ed.), *Oxford Handbook of the Use of Force in International Law* (2015), 988–1013.

[29] See, e.g., *North Atlantic Coast Fisheries Case (Great Britain/US)* (1910) 11 RIAA 167, 181 ('International law in its modern development recognises that a great number of Treaty obligations are not annulled by war, but at most suspended by it'). The doubts surrounding this question in the early twentieth century were described by Hurst, 'The Effect of War on Treaties' (1921) 2 BYIL 37.

[30] For a summary of the scholarly debate, see Neff, *War*, 335–40.

[31] See the exhaustive review of practice in Mancini, *Stato di guerra*, ch. 4. See also, for practice related to commercial and economic relations, Silingardi, *Gli effetti giuridici della guerra sui rapporti economici e commerciali* (2012).

[32] Greenwood, 'The Concept of War in Modern International Law' (1987) 36 ICLQ 283, 295.

[33] *Nuclear Weapons*, [25].

[34] Thus, the Court found that obligations of 'total restraint' in human rights law and environmental law ought to be taken into account in the assessment of the necessity and proportionality of armed force, see *Nuclear Weapons*, [30]. Admittedly, the characterisation of international humanitarian law (IHL) as *lex specialis* has been criticised in the scholarship,

use the ILC's terminology, terminated or suspended by virtue of the existence of armed hostilities.[35] While states may wish to suspend treaty relations with the other parties to a conflict, this suspension does not occur by operation of law upon the commencement of armed action.[36] In contemporary conditions, states engaged in armed conflict remain 'formally at "peace"'.[37]

The use of force in contemporary international law thus occurs against the background of the complex web of legal relations binding the states involved in the conflict. In this state of affairs, it is not implausible that such uses of force may infringe other obligations existing between these states. Thus states have claimed before international courts and tribunals that, through the use of force, other states had breached their right of territorial sovereignty,[38] their right of non-intervention,[39]

---

see, e.g., Milanović, 'The Lost Origins of *Lex Specialis*: Rethinking the Relationship between Human Rights and International Humanitarian Law' in Ohlin (ed.), *Theoretical Boundaries of Armed Conflict and Human Rights* (2016), 45. Aside from the existence of a normative conflict between IHL and other areas of international law, the underlying point made by the Court is fundamental: that even if there exists an armed conflict the 'peaceful' relations between the states parties to it are not automatically set aside.

[35] Articles on the Effects of Armed Conflicts on Treaties, annexed to General Assembly Res 66/99 of 9 December 2011, art. 3 and Commentary, in ILC Report, sixty-third session (26 April–3 June and 4 July–12 August 2011), A/66/10, 173ff. The Report will appear in ILC Yearbook 2011, vol. II(2) (not yet published).

[36] See, on this matter, the ILC's Articles on the Effects of Armed Conflict on Treaties, with Commentaries, Report of the ILC on the work of its sixty-third session, Supp No. 10 (A/66/10), (2011).

[37] ARS art. 21 Commentary, [2]. See also Crawford, Second Report, [299].

[38] *Nicaragua*, Memorial of Nicaragua, 30 April 1985, ICJ Pleadings, vol. IV, 115; *Border and Transborder Armed Actions (Nicaragua v Honduras)*, ICJ, Application instituting proceedings, 28 July 1986, 5–7; *Border and Transborder Armed Actions (Nicaragua v Costa Rica)*, ICJ, Memorial of Nicaragua, 19 August 1987, 109; *Armed Activities on the Territory of the Congo (DRC v Burundi)*, ICJ, Application instituting proceedings, 23 June 1999, 15–19; *Armed Activities on the Territory of the Congo (DRC v Rwanda)*, ICJ, Application instituting proceedings, 23 June 1999, 16–19; *Aerial Incident of 10 August 1999 (India v Pakistan)*, ICJ, Application instituting proceedings, 21 September 1999, section II; *Land and Maritime Boundary between Cameroon and Nigeria (Cameroon v Nigeria: Equatorial Guinea intervening)*, ICJ, Cameroon statement, 26 February 2002, CR 2002/7, 36 [7]; *Legality of the Use of Force (Federal Republic of Yugoslavia v Belgium)* (2004) ICJ Rep 279, [1]; *Certain Activities Carried Out by Nicaragua in the Border Area (Costa Rica v Nicaragua)*, ICJ, Application instituting proceedings, 18 November 2010, 4.

[39] *Nicaragua*, Memorial of Nicaragua, 120; *Nicaragua v Honduras*, Application instituting proceedings, 5–7; *Cameroon v Nigeria*, CR 2002/7, 36 [7]; *DRC v Burundi*, Application instituting proceedings, 15–19; *DRC v Rwanda*, Application instituting proceedings, 16–19; *Certain Activities (Nicaragua v Costa Rica)*, Memorial of Nicaragua, 55ff.

rights under bilateral commercial treaties,[40] bilateral aviation agreements,[41] the Chicago Convention on Civil Aviation,[42] freedom of navigation at sea,[43] freedom of navigation in international rivers,[44] and the obligation to settle disputes peacefully.[45] Indeed, as clarified by the ICJ in *Oil Platforms*, all international obligations can be breached through forcible means:

> Any action by [a State] that is incompatible with those obligations is unlawful, regardless of the means by which it is brought about. A violation of the rights of one party under the Treaty [or any customary obligation] by means of the use of force is as unlawful as would be a violation by administrative decision or by any other means.[46]

When a state resorts to force in self-defence it may, therefore, affect or impair a multiplicity of legal relations (other than the prohibition of force) binding it to the aggressor state.[47] Could the impairment of these other obligations by a lawful resort to self-defence be justified; or would these impairments remain unlawful regardless of the legality of the resort to force? This is the question which presented itself to the ILC, when it was embarking upon the second reading of the ARS, as will be seen next.

---

[40] Nicaragua claimed the breach of the Nicaragua–US Treaty of Friendship, Commerce and Navigation (signed 21 January 1956, entered into force 24 May 1958), (1960) 367 UNTS 3, in *Nicaragua*, Memorial of Nicaragua, 110–11. Similarly, Iran claimed breaches of the Iran–US Treaty of Amity, Economic Relations and Consular Rights (signed 15 August 1955, entered into force 16 June 1957), (1957) 284 UNTS 93, by the use of force of the United States in *Aerial Incident of 3 July 1988 (Iran v USA)*, ICJ, Memorial of Iran, 24 July 1990, 146, 238, and in *Oil Platforms*, Application instituting proceedings, 2 November 1992.

[41] *Aerial Incident (India v Pakistan)*, Application instituting proceedings, section II, claiming the violation of the Agreement on Prevention of Airspace Violations and for Permitting Over Flights and Landings by Military Aircraft (signed 6 April 1991, in force 19 August 1992), (1994) 1843 UNTS 60.

[42] *Aerial Incident (Iran v US)*, Memorial of Iran, 182, 238.

[43] See *Certain Activities Carried Out by Nicaragua in the Border Area (Costa Rica v Nicaragua)*; *Construction of a Road in Costa Rica Along the San Juan River (Nicaragua v Costa Rica)*, Counterclaims, Order of 18 April 2013, 5–6 (unreported).

[44] *Legality of the Use of Force (FRY v Belgium)*, [1].

[45] *Guyana v Suriname*, UNCLOS Annex VII Tribunal, Memorial of Guyana, 22 February 2005, 125–8 and Reply, 1 April 2006, 139ff, claim under art. 279 UNCLOS.

[46] *Oil Platforms (Islamic Republic of Iran v United States of America)*, Preliminary Objections (1996) ICJ Rep 803, [21].

[47] The rights of third parties may also be affected; see ARS art. 21 Commentary, [5].

## 5.3 Tracing the Development of Article 21 in the International Law Commission

Self-defence first appeared in codifications of the law of responsibility in the framework of the 1930 Hague Codification Conference. José Gustavo Guerrero, rapporteur on state responsibility to the Committee of Experts set up by the League of Nations in preparation for the Conference, included the 'defence of the rights of the State' as a circumstance in which the state could 'disclaim responsibility' for the violation of obligations owed to foreigners.[48] The proposed defence was criticised for its vagueness, and Guerrero explained that the 'defence of the rights of the State' included situations such as the requisitioning of foreign property by a belligerent state when this was necessary for the defence of its rights during war.[49] To reflect Guerrero's thinking, the defence was formulated as 'self-defence against an aggressor State' but it was eventually excluded from the Bases of Discussion prepared for the Codification Conference, since the Conference had not been called upon to deal with the law of war.[50]

Between the 1930 Codification Conference and the next time self-defence would be included in a project on state responsibility – at the ILC – the very notion of self-defence underwent a significant change. In the interwar years, the right of self-defence, until then an institution of the law of peace which permitted states to resort to force (as a measure short of war) for the defence of their rights,[51] was attached to the then evolving prohibition of force as an exceptional circumstance.[52] This development was later included in the UN Charter, in the form of a general prohibition of force in Article 2(4) and its exception in Article 51, provisions which are now accepted to reflect customary law.[53] In this new regime, the

---

[48] League of Nations, Committee of Experts for the Progressive Codification of International Law, Report to the Council of the League of Nations, Doc C.196.M.79.1927.V [C.P.D.I.95(2)], Geneva, 20 April 1927, Conclusion 3(b).

[49] League of Nations, Committee of Experts for the Progressive Codification of International Law, Minutes of the First Session, held at Geneva, 1–8 April 1925, C.P.D.I. 1st Session/P.V., Geneva, 7 May 1925, 96.

[50] League of Nations, Conference for the Codification of International Law, Bases of Discussion for the Conference Drawn up by the Preparatory Committee, Doc C.75.M.69.1929.V, vol. III (Responsibility of States for Damage Caused in Their Territory to the Person and Property of Foreigners), 127 (Observations).

[51] On this point, see, generally, Lesaffer, 'Too Much History', 46–7.

[52] See Neff, *War*, 303–4.

[53] See, e.g., *Military and Paramilitary Activities in and Against Nicaragua (Nicaragua v United States of America)* (1986) ICJ Rep 14, 97ff.

right of self-defence was only available as against a use of force, and not in response to the breach of any other of the rights of the victim state.[54] In parallel to this development, as was highlighted earlier, the significance of war as a legal institution diminished to the point that the continued relevance of war as a legal status is, to say the least, doubtful.

Roberto Ago, the Commission's second Special Rapporteur on state responsibility, first included self-defence as one of the circumstances precluding wrongfulness in the ILC's codification project in the late 1970s. Ago's report focused exclusively on self-defence in its function as an exception to the prohibition of force, and the Article adopted on first reading (draft Article 34) reflected this focus. However, a few years after the adoption of draft Article 34 in 1980, the *Nicaragua* case, the jurisdiction judgment in *Oil Platforms* and the *Nuclear Weapons* Advisory Opinion highlighted some important phenomena associated with the use of force and self-defence in international relations which the ILC's draft had overlooked. In particular, these cases highlighted that force may breach more than one obligation at a time and that self-defence could act as a justification in relation to these breaches as well. These developments were incorporated in the draft by the final Special Rapporteur, James Crawford, during the second reading of the draft and are now reflected in the ARS.

### 5.3.1  First Reading: Self-Defence and the Prohibition of Force

Ago included self-defence as a circumstance precluding wrongfulness in his final report to the ILC in 1980, in the following terms:

> The wrongfulness of an act of a State not in conformity with an international obligation to another State is precluded if the State committed the act in order to defend itself or another State against armed attack as provided for in Article 51 of the Charter of the United Nations.[55]

Ago explained that self-defence was not a 'subjective right' (in the sense of a Hohfeldian claim-right).[56] In his view, self-defence could not be characterised as a 'subjective right' because it was not possible to identify a

---

[54] Although some part of the literature continued to argue that it was applicable also when certain rights of the victim state were infringed. See, most notably, Bowett, *Self-Defence in International Law* (1958).

[55] Ago, Eighth Report on State Responsibility – Add.5–7, ILC Yearbook 1980, vol. II(1), [124].

[56] Hohfeld, 'Some Fundamental Legal Conceptions as Applied in Judicial Reasoning' (1913) 23 *Yale LJ* 16. Hohfeld called these 'rights', as distinct from privileges (on which see Chapter 3, Section 3.2.1.2). However, the term claim-right, as employed by J. L. Mackie,

correlative obligation to this right: an aggressor state was not under a duty to tolerate the defensive forcible action of the attacked state.[57] The invocation of self-defence by the attacked state did not, therefore, entail the formulation of a legal claim requiring a specific performance (to tolerate the defensive force) from the aggressor state. In consequence, self-defence could not properly be characterised as a right. Instead, according to Ago, through the invocation of self-defence, a state was simply attempting to 'justify' its denial of a 'legitimate legal claim' that could be formulated against it. That is, the invocation of self-defence constituted a denial of the 'legitimate legal claim' of the aggressor state that the self-defensive measure against it was contrary to the prohibition on the use of force.[58] Thus Ago preferred to speak of a *faculté* to act in self-defence.[59]

To justify the inclusion of self-defence among the circumstances precluding wrongfulness, Ago emphasised what he thought were commonalities between them. He argued that self-defence was a 'situation of *de facto* conditions',[60] and that in this situation the relevant primary rule was suspended.[61] The reports do not explain what Ago meant by 'situation of *de facto* conditions'; it is likely that it meant simply that the action in self-defence was triggered by the mere existence of factual circumstances (e.g., the existence of an armed attack). In this connection, Ago drew a parallel with the state of necessity (a set of factual circumstances of imminent threat to an essential interest), but the same can be said about, for example, *force majeure*: it is a set of factual circumstances (external event with certain characteristics) which creates an impossibility to perform an obligation.[62] With these parallels, Ago was attempting to smooth the

---

will be used here to describe this typology of legal relation, see *Ethics: Inventing Right and Wrong* (1977), 173–4.

[57] This is the correlative duty of the right of self-defence as identified by some scholars, e.g., Čepelka, 'Les conséquences juridiques du délit en droit international contemporain', *Acta Universitatis Carolinae, Iuridica, Monographia* (1965), vol. 3, 44–6. See also Sicilianos, *Les réactions décentralisées à l'illicite. Des contre-mesures à la légitime défense* (1990), 46–7.

[58] Analogous views were held by some contemporaneous literature, see, e.g., Moursi Badr, 'The Exculpatory Effect of Self-Defence in State Responsibility' (1980) 10 *Georgia J Int'l & Comp L* 1, 1; Sicilianos, *Réactions décentralisées*, 40–7. For an earlier statement of a similar view, see Bowett, *Self-Defence*, 8–9, also cited by Ago in Eighth Report – Add.5–7, 53 (fn. 208).

[59] Ago, Eighth Report – Add.5–7, [87].

[60] Id. For Ago's conception of 'subjective rights', see ibid. [9].

[61] Generally, Ago, Eighth Report on State Responsibility, ILC Yearbook 1979, vol. II(1), [55]; Ago, 1629th meeting, ILC Yearbook 1980, vol. I, 235–6 [4–5]. Specifically, in respect of self-defence, see Ago, 1629th meeting, 238 [17].

[62] See, generally, Paddeu, 'A Genealogy of *Force Majeure* in International Law' (2011) 82 BYIL 381.

acceptance of the draft article on self-defence as part of the circumstances precluding wrongfulness and, by extension, as a relevant notion of the law of responsibility rather than as a notion belonging to the law on the use of force. Indeed, for Ago, there was no doubt that self-defence was a notion that belonged to the law of responsibility; in his view it was the 'circumstance *par excellence* which precluded wrongfulness'. So 'it simply could not go unmentioned in chapter V of the draft' on state responsibility.[63] He was not alone in conceptualising self-defence in this way. For instance, Gamal Moursi Badr, writing in 1980, explained that:

> In the new world legal order, self-defense has become merely a defense against responsibility for the violation of the obligation to refrain from use of force; therefore, its role as an exculpatory factor calls for a more precise definition.[64]

This was not, however, a widely shared view. At least two ILC members, Stephan Verosta and Nikolai Ushakov, vigorously opposed Ago's approach, emphasising that self-defence was not a concept which belonged to the law of responsibility.[65]

Despite the commonalities emphasised by Ago, draft Article 34 was also different from the rest of the circumstances precluding wrongfulness in one crucial respect: its narrow effect. Ago's proposed article on self-defence used broad language: it spoke of preclusion of wrongfulness of acts 'not in conformity with *an* international obligation',[66] the indefinite article 'an' suggesting that self-defence could operate as a justification in respect of any and all international obligations. Yet, Ago's report focused on preclusion of wrongfulness in respect of one international obligation only: the prohibition of force. The report thus limited the effect of self-defence as a circumstance precluding wrongfulness to the potential breach of the obligation not to use force in international relations *only*. In this sense, self-defence stood apart from the other defences included in the ARS (and from the ARS as a whole)[67]: those defences were

---

[63] Ago, 1629th meeting, 239 [31].
[64] Moursi Badr, 'Exculpatory Effect', 1.
[65] Ushakov, 1620th meeting, ILC Yearbook 1980, vol. I, 190 [16–17]; and later at Ushakov, 1635th meeting, ILC Yearbook 1980, vol. I, 272 [55]; Verosta, 1628th meeting, ILC Yearbook 1980, 229 [10]. Verosta eventually accepted the Special Rapporteur's proposal, but Ushakov maintained his objection which was recorded in the commentary to draft art. 34, see ILC Report, thirty-second session, ILC Yearbook 1980, vol. II(2), 60–1 [27].
[66] Ago, Eighth Report – Add.5–7, [124] (emphasis added).
[67] The rules on responsibility, as Ago's Fifth Report had extensively demonstrated, were applicable to the breach of any international obligation, regardless of source and content. They

of general application, applicable as against any and all obligations in international law.

Following the emphasis in Ago's report, the Commission's discussion on draft Article 34 focused exclusively on the effect of self-defence on the prohibition of force. Very little attention was paid to the effect of self-defensive measures on other obligations binding the defending state to its aggressor. The matter was only alluded to, and obliquely at that, in an observation by Willem Riphagen. Riphagen stated that self-defence could not justify the breach of *jus cogens* obligations. Surely, he said, rules concerning human rights in armed conflict 'remained valid even in the relationship with an aggressor State'.[68] The observation was brief, but it was conceptually a very astute one. It raised the question of the (uncertain) status of treaties during armed conflict, and contained an acknowledgment that defensive force could produce effects on other 'relationships' binding between the defending and aggressor states beyond the obligation not to use force. The remark went mostly unnoticed in the Commission, and indeed it is not clear from the records of the meeting that his colleagues grasped the issue at all.[69]

The majority of the Commission was happy to accept Ago's proposals in respect of self-defence,[70] and draft Article 34 was adopted with minimal changes.[71] In its commentary to the draft Article, the Commission also limited the scope of self-defence to preclusion of wrongfulness in relation to the prohibition of force; namely it considered the notion of

---

were, as such, of general application. See Ago, Fifth Report on State Responsibility, ILC Yearbook 1976, vol. II(1) 6ff, and the current ARS art. 12 and its Commentary.

[68] Riphagen, 1620th meeting, ILC Yearbook 1980, vol. I, 189 [5].

[69] Note, however, that at the suggestion of Riphagen and Vallat the ILC excluded the application of draft art. 34 to the breach of obligations owed to third states: ILC Report, thirty-second session, 61 [28]. For the comments of these two members of the Commission, see Riphagen, 1620th meeting, ILC Yearbook 1980, vol. I, 189 [7] (emphasis in original); Vallat, 1621st meeting, ILC Yearbook 1980, vol. I, 194 [22].

[70] Reuter, 1620th meeting, 191 [24]; Schwebel, 1621st meeting, ILC Yearbook 1980, vol. I, 191 [1]; Vallat, 1621st meeting, 194 [20]; Tsuruoka, 1627th meeting, ILC Yearbook 1980, vol. I, 220 [1]; Díaz-González, 1627th meeting, ILC Yearbook 1980, vol. I, 221 [9]; Barboza, 1627th meeting, ILC Yearbook 1980, vol. I, 222 [14]; Quentin-Baxter, 1627th meeting, ILC Yearbook 1980, vol. I, 222 [16–17]; Pinto, 1627th meeting, ILC Yearbook 1980, vol. I, 222 [18]; Sucharitkul, 1628th meeting, ILC Yearbook 1980, vol. I, 231 [28]. Note also that some members suggested giving the draft article on self-defence a 'special place' within the ARS, see, e.g., Tabibi, 1628th meeting, ILC Yearbook 1980, vol. I, 230 [21].

[71] Draft art. 34 reads as follows: 'The wrongfulness of an act of a State not in conformity with an international obligation of that State is precluded if the act constitutes a lawful measure of self-defence taken in conformity with the Charter of the United Nations'; see ILC Report, thirty-second session, 52.

self-defence exclusively in its relation to the obligation not to resort to force in international relations. Arguably to pre-emptively deflect criticisms that self-defence did not belong in the responsibility project, the commentary to draft Article 34 also states that, by including self-defence in the responsibility project, the ILC was simply drawing 'the inevitable inferences regarding preclusion of the wrongfulness of acts of the State involving such recourse under the conditions that constitute a situation of self-defence.'[72] But the Commission failed to note that the 'inevitable inferences' extended beyond the effect of self-defence on the prohibition on the use of force.

### 5.3.2 Second Reading: Self-Defence Beyond the Prohibition of Force

The final Special Rapporteur to the ILC on state responsibility, James Crawford, took issue with the understanding of the draft article on self-defence which emerged from the first reading of the ARS. To begin with, he argued that self-defence was not a circumstance precluding wrongfulness in relation to the prohibition of force. Under the UN Charter, in accordance with which the ARS must be interpreted,[73] self-defence was a condition internal to the prohibition of force: it was an exceptional right which formed part of the definition of the rule itself. Indeed, this was corroborated by the fact that in practice, as had been suggested by numerous states in the Sixth Committee,[74] when a state acts in self-defence there is not 'even potentially' a breach of the obligation not to use force.[75] This aspect of self-defence was *not* what the ARS should be concerned with: the right of self-defence belonged to the primary rules of international law and, as the mantra had by then become, the ARS were limited to the secondary rules of international law only.[76] In this sense at least, self-defence was not a notion that belonged to the law of state responsibility.

While the role that self-defence plays in relation to the prohibition of force was excluded from the draft, Crawford thought that a provision on

---

[72] ILC Report, thirty-second session, 52 [1]; see also at 60 [23]. Echoing Ago's final remarks to the Commission: Ago, 1629th meeting, 239 [31].
[73] See ARS art. 59 Commentary, [2].
[74] See, e.g., Byelorussia (as it then was): A/C.6/35/SR.57, [42]; Ethiopia: A/C.6/35/SR.51, [46]; France: A/C.6/35/SR.50, [43]; Hungary: A/C.6/35/SR.55, [45]; Mongolia: A/C.6/35/SR.53, [29–30]; Spain: A/C.6/35/SR.55, [11]; Trinidad and Tobago: A/C.6/35/SR.56, [26]; and USSR (as it then was): A/C.6/35/SR.52, [63].
[75] Crawford, Second Report, [298].
[76] On the primary or secondary rule character of the defences, see Chapter 1, Section 1.3.3.

self-defence in the ARS nevertheless remained necessary to deal with the type of situation that *Nicaragua*, *Oil Platforms* and *Nuclear Weapons* had exposed: that self-defensive force could violate other obligations binding on the parties to an armed conflict.[77] In both *Nicaragua* and *Oil Platforms*, as will be explained in more detail later, the Court was concerned with the question whether the forcible impairment of rights under bilateral treaties of friendship and commerce could be justified if, as the respondent claimed, the use of force under scrutiny had been adopted in self-defence.[78] In *Nuclear Weapons*, instead, the Court was called to consider the effect that the use of nuclear weapons on self-defence would have on *other* rules of international law – thereby implying that the exercise of self-defence could involve the impairment of other obligations in the international legal order.[79] For Crawford, these cases had to be understood in historical perspective: they were the consequence of the contemporary irrelevance of the legal institution of war (formal war). In modern conditions, states acting in self-defence were 'formally at peace' with their aggressor. Self-defensive action took place in a context in which all of the 'normal' legal relations which bound the defending state to the aggressor state remained in force.[80] In practice this meant that in the course of self-defence a state may violate other obligations towards the aggressor. For example, it 'may trespass on its territory, interfere in its internal affairs, disrupt its trade

---

[77] Crawford, Second Report, 75 (fn. 592).
[78] See Section 3.4.2.
[79] Some of the states making submissions before the Court argued that nuclear weapons, so long as their use was necessary and proportionate, were lawful when employed in self-defence: written statement, 20 September 1994, *Nuclear Weapons* (WHO request), 77–81; written statement, 16 June 1995, *Nuclear Weapons* (GA request), 37–9. France: written statement, *Nuclear Weapons* (WHO request), June 1994, 23–4; oral statement, *Nuclear Weapons*, CR 95/23, 65–7 [36–7]. All the statements, written and oral, can be found at www.icj-cij.org. In particular, the United Kingdom stated that it was 'impossible to argue that this fundamental, inherent right [of self-defence] has been limited or abandoned on the basis of mere inferences drawn from other rules, whether conventional or customary': oral statement, *Nuclear Weapons*, CR 95/45, 33. For other states, however, the legality of nuclear weapons under *jus ad bellum* rules said nothing as to the possible effect of their use on other rules of international law. For New Zealand, for instance, 'the right of self-defence cannot be exercised in isolation from other applicable rules and principles of international law', such that even if lawfully used in self-defence nuclear weapons may still breach other rules of international law: oral statement, *Nuclear Weapons*, CR 95/28, 42. The Solomon Islands queried 'what use [was] there in justifying behavior by reference to one category of rules where that behavior would violate another category of rules?': Written comments of the Government of Solomon Islands, 19 June 1995, *Nuclear Weapons* (GA request), [4.73–4].
[80] Crawford, Second Report, [299].

## 5.3 ARTICLE 21 IN THE ILC

contrary to the provisions of a commercial treaty, etc.'[81] And this was the real question: did self-defence constitute a 'justification or an excuse ... in relation to breaches of [these] other obligations'?[82] Crawford thought it did. So he proposed to modify the draft Article on self-defence to address these types of situation: the self-defending state was thus exonerated for the breach of *other* obligations so long as the breach was 'related' to its defensive action and that defensive action was in accordance with the UN Charter.[83]

Crawford also added that self-defence could not justify the breach of *every* obligation. On the authority of the ICJ's Opinion in *Nuclear Weapons*, the Special Rapporteur proposed to exclude from the scope of the justification obligations of so-called total restraint.[84] Namely, obligations like those of international humanitarian law and certain international human rights which are 'expressed or intended to apply as a definitive constraint even to States in armed conflict'.[85] The Commission rejected a proposal to state this in the text of the article itself,[86] but agreed to refer to the commentary the explanation that the availability of self-defence as a circumstance precluding wrongfulness depended on compliance with the rules of the *jus ad bellum* and the obligations of 'total restraint'.[87]

The Commission was generally in agreement with the approach chosen by the Special Rapporteur, and it agreed to adopt what became Article 21, in the terms quoted at the beginning of this chapter.

---

[81] Id.
[82] Crawford, 2589th meeting, ILC Yearbook 1999, vol. I, 159–60 [53–4].
[83] The idea was not new. It had already been articulated, albeit with different requirements, by Sir Gerald Fitzmaurice in his Fourth Report on the Law of Treaties: he had envisaged a justification for the non-performance of treaty obligations on the ground of 'legitimate self-defence'. Fitzmaurice's draft article, which was not discussed by the Commission and was eventually left out (together with all other articles concerning performance) of the draft convention on the law of treaties, was limited to the non-performance of obligations owed by the state acting in self-defence towards third states. See Fitzmaurice, Fourth Report on the Law of Treaties, ILC Yearbook 1959, vol. II, 64–5.
[84] This language is borrowed from the ICJ's opinion in *Nuclear Weapons*, [30].
[85] Crawford, Second Report, [301].
[86] Galicki, 2589th meeting, ILC Yearbook 1999, vol. I, 161 [65]. For the proposal, see Crawford, Second Report, [304]; see also his remarks to the plenary of the Commission: Crawford, 2587th meeting, ILC Yearbook 1999, vol. I, 141 [32]; he later accepted to delete the proposed paragraph, so long as the Commission authorised him to explain that the word 'lawful' covered both the *jus ad bellum* and the obligations of total restraint: Crawford, 2589th meeting, 160 [54].
[87] ARS art. 21 Commentary, [6].

## 5.4 Self-Defence as a 'Circumstance Precluding Wrongfulness' in the Articles on State Responsibility

In accepting the proposals of the Special Rapporteur, the ILC thus distinguished between two functions of self-defence in international law. The first, principal, function of self-defence is that of permitting a state to fend off an unlawful armed attack against it by forceful means. When a state is the victim of an armed attack, it can resort to defensive force lawfully. Incidentally, self-defence can also constitute a defence in respect of the breach of other obligations owed by the defending to the aggressor state, which are impaired by the defensive force used to fend off the armed attack. These two functions are, of course, not independent from each other: the role of self-defence as a defence is merely incidental to its role as an exceptional right to use force in international relations. Therefore, to exonerate the breach of other obligations, self-defence must have been lawfully exercised to begin with.

This section explains the intended role of Article 21 – thus demonstrating, contrary to the views of some part of the literature, that this provision is 'useless' – and then considers some examples from the practice of states.

### 5.4.1 A Justification for Forcible Measures Only

The first thing to clarify in this regard is that Article 21 only operates in respect of breaches of other obligations brought about by force. According to the Commentary to Article 21:

> Self-defence may justify non-performance of certain obligations other than that under Article 2, paragraph 4, of the Charter of the United Nations, *provided that such non-performance is related to the breach of that provision*.[88]

The choice of words here is certainly infelicitous. If a state acting in (lawful) self-defence does not 'not even potentially' breach the prohibition of force, how can there be 'non-performance related to the breach' of the prohibition? Wording aside, the gist of this statement is that the non-performance in question must have been the consequence of a use of force. The prohibition of force can only be breached through the use of force (small-scale or grave, direct or indirect), so that a non-performance 'related to' that breach must also have been caused by a use of force. Thus,

---

[88] ARS art. 21 Commentary, [2] (emphasis added).

excluded from the scope of Article 21 are non-military measures that a state may adopt to accompany its self-defence campaign.[89]

### 5.4.2 Understanding the Scope of Article 21

To understand the function and scope of Article 21 it is useful to separate the legal relations existing between the states involved in an armed conflict into three categories. First is the relation governed by the prohibition of force and its exception, the right of self-defence. Second are all the other legal relations (conventional or customary) existing between those states. These comprise an 'infinite variety' and include the rights of territorial sovereignty and non-intervention, trade and commercial rights, treaties for the exchange of technology, and so on. Third is the category of legal relations which impose 'obligations of total restraint',[90] including (some) rules of international humanitarian law and human rights law. As will be explained in what follows, the customary right of self-defence provides a legal ground of justification for the breach of the first and second sets of legal relations. These effects are codified in separate provisions: the legality of force under the first legal relation is addressed by Article 51, the legality of the impairment by (defensive) force of the second set of legal relations is addressed by Article 21.[91] The third set of legal relations *cannot* be impaired *even* when acting in self-defence.

#### 5.4.2.1 First Legal Relation: On the Legality of Resort to Force

States are bound, under international law, by an obligation not to use force against one another. The prohibition, codified in Article 2(4) of the UN Charter, is widely regarded as one of *jus cogens*.[92] This obligation not

---

[89] On which see, generally, Paddeu, 'Self-Defence'. But see Christakis and Bannelier, 'Légitime défense', 233; Christakis and Bannelier, 'La légitime défense a-t-elle sa place', 519, who understand the only role of Article 21 to be that of justifying the impairment of aggressor state rights by the defending State's non-forcible measures.

[90] ARS art. 21 Commentary, at [4].

[91] It may be worthwhile to recall that, as clarified by the ICJ in *Nicaragua*, Article 51 is not a complete statement of the law of self-defence as this exists in customary law. Customary law (to which a *renvoi* is made by Article 51's reference to the 'inherent right') complements the Charter provision. See *Nicaragua*, [176].

[92] For a thorough review of the relevant practice, see Corten, *Droit contre la guerre*, 341–59. A significant number of judges and scholars support the peremptory status of the prohibition of force: *Nicaragua*, sep op Singh, 153; sep op Sette-Camara, 199; *Oil Platforms (Islamic Republic of Iran v United States of America)* (2003) ICJ Rep 161, sep op Kooijmans, 260

to use force possesses (at least) one exception in the form of a right of self-defence.[93]

The relation between the prohibition of force and the right of self-defence is a tricky question. The scholarship has proposed at least two main ways of conceptualising it: either self-defence is a negative rule-element of the prohibition of force, or self-defence is independent from the prohibition of force. The question as to the relation between these two norms of the legal order may seem a matter of pure academic concern; but how one construes this relationship may have effects in practice in relation, among others, to the burden of proof and the peremptory status of the prohibition. In respect of the burden of proof, following the principle *actori incumbit probatio*, it falls on the claimant to prove all elements of its claim – including negative elements. If self-defence were a negative rule-element of the prohibition of force, then it would fall on the claimant to prove it. As a corollary of the principle *actori incumbit probatio*, it is the respondent who must prove its defences. So, if self-defence were a defence, then it would fall on the respondent to prove it. Turning to the peremptory status of the prohibition of force, as is well known, peremptory rules cannot be set aside by any other rule including, as stated in ARS Article 26,[94] defences. But peremptory rules may be subject to internal qualifications, limiting their scope. In short, it is not of their essence to be absolute.[95] States accept that the prohibition of force is a peremptory rule, so that whether one sees self-defence as a negative rule-element, qualifying the scope of the prohibition, or as a defence may affect its availability as against the prohibition of force.

Following Special Rapporteur Crawford's proposal, the ILC construed the prohibition of force and its exception of self-defence as both constituting a single norm.[96] The prohibition of force and the right of self-defence,

---

[46]; diss op Elaraby, 291; sep op Simma, 327, [6]; *Legal Consequences of the Construction of a Wall in the Occupied Palestinian Territory* (2004) ICJ Rep 136, sep op Elaraby, 254; Ruys, *Armed Attack*, 27; Dörr and Randelzhofer, 'Article 2(4)' in Simma et al. (eds), *The Charter of the United Nations: A Commentary* (2012) vol. 1, 231; van Steenberghe, *Légitime défense*, 137–40.

[93] There are other exceptions too, see Helmersen, 'The Prohibition of the Use of Force as *Jus Cogens*: Explaining Apparent Derogations' (2014) 61 NILR 167.

[94] Pursuant to ARS art. 26: 'Nothing in this chapter precludes the wrongfulness of any act of a State which is not in conformity with an obligation arising under a peremptory norm of general international law.'

[95] Orakhelashvili, *Peremptory Rules in International Law* (2009), 68.

[96] ARS art. 21 Commentary, [1]. This reading was endorsed by Judge Tomka in *Case Concerning Armed Activities on the Territory of the Congo (DRC v Uganda)* (2005) ICJ Rep 168, declaration Tomka, 353–4.

in other words, are two segments of an overarching norm which can be restated, in simplified but relevant part, as follows: 'the use of force is prohibited except in self-defence against an armed attack'. In this statement of the rule, self-defence would constitute a negative rule-element. In conceptualising the norm in this way, the ILC was accommodating the opinions of states according to whom the use of force in self-defence is not inconsistent with the prohibition of force.[97] In this understanding, the exception of self-defence constitutes a limit on the material scope of the prohibition. Thus, the prohibition of force would be applicable only if there were a non-defensive use of force and defensive force would fall wholly outside of the prohibition's scope of application.[98] The ILC's approach thus ensures the availability of self-defence as against the prohibition of force, all the while maintaining the peremptory character of the prohibition.

The ILC's approach is, to be sure, not uncontested or unproblematic. To begin with, it is incompatible with the allocation of the burden of proof in relation to self-defence. Indeed, according to the ICJ in *Oil Platforms* it is not the claimant who must prove absence of self-defence (as would be required by the ILC's approach), but the respondent.[99] Moreover, the approach has been criticised for its artificiality.[100] Scholars have thus proposed construing the relation between self-defence and the prohibition of force differently, in a way that upholds the independence of the right of self-defence from the prohibition; that is, in a way that does not reduce the right of self-defence to a mere negative rule-element of the prohibition of force. In this construction there would be two rules, the prohibition *and* the right, both applicable to the same set of facts: the use of defensive force would be banned under the prohibition of force and permitted by the right of self-defence. The two rules would, therefore,

---

[97] See, e.g., Ethiopia: A/C.6/35/SR.51, [46]; Hungary: A/C.6/35/SR.55, [45]; Mongolia: A/C.6/35/SR.53, [29–30]; Spain: A/C.6/35/SR.55, [11]; Trinidad and Tobago: A/C.6/35/SR.56, [26]; (the then) USSR: A/C.6/35/SR.52, [63]. On this point, see Crawford, Second Report, 74–5.

[98] Kammerhofer describes this approach as a 'gap' in the prohibition of force: Kammerhofer, *Uncertainty in International Law: A Kelsenian Perspective* (2011), 9.

[99] *Oil Platforms*, [61], [72].

[100] E.g., Fragmentation of International Law: Difficulties Arising from the Diversification and Expansion of International Law, Report of the Study Group of the International Law Commission, UN Doc A/CN.4/L.682, 13 April 2006, 52–3 [95]; Green, 'Questioning the Peremptory Status of the Prohibition of the Use of Force' (2011) 32 Mich J Int'l L 215; de Hoogh, 'Jus Cogens and the Use of Armed Force' in Weller (ed.), *Oxford Handbook of the Use of Force in International Law* (2015), 1172–5.

be in a normative conflict. To conclude in favour of the legality of self-defence, the right of self-defence must be able to set aside the application of the prohibition. This construction of the relation between the prohibition and the right, while compatible with the allocation of the burden of proof, runs into an obvious obstacle: the prohibition's peremptory status. As a *jus cogens* rule, the prohibition cannot be set aside,[101] and the conflict would be resolved by the *lex superior* principle: the prohibition would prevail over the right, with the result that defensive force is unlawful. This is a paradoxical conclusion, in utter contradiction of the practice of states. The paradox can be overcome in one of two ways. First, by 'elevating', so to speak, the right of self-defence to a peremptory rule. In this case, the conflict would arise between two peremptory rules and could potentially be resolved by application of the *lex specialis* principle.[102] Since self-defence is the most factually specific of the two rules, it would set aside the prohibition of force in the circumstances. Alternatively, it could be argued that only the prohibition of aggression possesses peremptory status. The resulting conflict between self-defence and the prohibition of force would be a conflict between 'ordinary' rules, in which self-defence would again prevail as the factually most specific rule. Both solutions, however, lack grounding in positive law: states do not accept the *jus cogens* status of the right of self-defence,[103] and they do uphold the *jus cogens* status of the prohibition as a whole.[104]

As the review above shows, the conceptualisation of the right of self-defence and the prohibition of force is quite complex, both as a matter of theory and of practice. At any rate, ARS Article 21 is not premised on either of the two constructions of this relation. Indeed, in whatever way this relation is construed, the point is that the right of self-defence

---

[101] As confirmed by ARS art. 26: 'The wrongfulness of any act of a State which is not in conformity with an obligation arising under a peremptory norm of general international law.'

[102] Note, at any rate, that it is not clear how conflicts between peremptory rules would be resolved. According to the Report of the ILC's Study Group on Fragmentation, 'it cannot be presumed that the doctrine of *jus cogens* could itself resolve such conflicts: there is no hierarchy between *jus cogens* norms *inter se*': Fragmentation of International Law, 185 [367]. Conflict between peremptory norms is a severely understudied topic. Some analysis of the issue can be found in Kolb, 'Conflits entre normes de *jus cogens*' in Corten et al. (eds), *Droit du pouvoir, pouvoir du droit: Mélanges offerts à Jean Salmon* (2007), 481; Kolb, *Peremptory International Law – Jus Cogens: A General Inventory* (2015), ch. 7.

[103] van Steenberghe, *Légitime défense*, 118.

[104] See references supra, at note 92. It may be added that distinguishing 'aggression' from 'force' is not a simple task either in theory or in practice, on which see Díaz Barrado, *El consentimiento, causa de exclusión de la ilicitud del uso de la fuerza en derecho internacional* (1989), 74–5.

constitutes an authorisation to use force where force would otherwise be banned. To put it in symbolic terms, Article 51 of the Charter authorises conduct otherwise prohibited by Article 2(4). When a state resorts to force in self-defence, Article 51 in a sense 'takes care' of the inconsistency existing between that force and Article 2(4): either by limiting the prohibition's scope or by setting aside its application in the circumstances. Crucially, however, the right of self-defence (even as a self-standing norm of the legal order), as codified in Article 51, is not an authorisation to impair all other rights of the aggressor state.[105]

### 5.4.2.2 Second Set of Legal Relations: Other Rights of the Aggressor State

The victim and aggressor states are also bound by a more or less wide set of other rights and obligations, of both customary and conventional origins. All of these other legal relations can potentially be impaired by military measures. The case-law of the ICJ and other international tribunals shows the great variety of rules of international law potentially impaired by the use of force: commercial obligations under bilateral treaties,[106] aviation agreements,[107] the obligation to settle disputes peacefully[108] and so on. Indeed, as the ICJ made clear in the *Oil Platforms* case, international obligations may be breached by whatever means: by the decision of a court, by an act of Parliament, or by the use of force.[109]

The question thus emerges whether the impairment of these obligations through defensive force is unlawful, or whether these impairments

---

[105] From the standpoint of Charter law, it could be argued that the language of art. 51 does indeed authorise the impairment of other Charter rights of the aggressor State. Thus, art. 51 states that 'nothing in the present Charter shall impair ...' Nevertheless, art. 51 cannot authorise the impairment of customary rights. It could be counter-argued that, pursuant to Article 103 of the UN Charter, rights arising under the Charter take priority over all other treaty and customary commitments. But art. 103 of the Charter is not helpful in this regard. To begin with, it is expressly limited to other conventional rights – though it seems logical that it may extend to customary rights as well. At any rate, art. 103 gives priority to obligations arising under the Charter and not to *rights* arising under it.

[106] See, e.g., Nicaragua's claims at Memorial of Nicaragua, *Nicaragua*, ICJ Pleadings, vol. IV, 110–11, and oral statement, ICJ Pleadings, vol. V, 210–12. For Iran's claims, see *Oil Platforms*, 166 [1]; also 176 [26].

[107] See, e.g., Memorial of Iran, *Aerial Incident of 3 July 1988 (Iran v USA)*, at 146 (breach of the Chicago Convention), 182 (breach of the Treaty of Amity), 238 (both).

[108] See, e.g., *Guyana v Suriname*, Award, 17 September 2007, UNCLOS Annex VII Tribunal, at 147, para. 445, and dispositif at 165, para. 2, on the obligation to solve disputes peacefully contained in art. 279 of the 1982 UN Convention on the Law of the Sea, 1833 UNTS 397.

[109] *Oil Platforms, Preliminary Objections*, [21].

may be justified if the military force was resorted to in self-defence. Of course, it is perfectly plausible that these interferences are unlawful even if the state using force was acting in self-defence. Thus, self-defence may be lawful in relation to the prohibition of force and be unlawful in relation to, for example, the right of territorial sovereignty. That is to say, a use of force may be compatible with the first legal relation mentioned earlier, but incompatible with the second set of legal relations. But if these impairments are (or should be) justified, the legal basis for such justification cannot be self-defence in its guise as an authorisation to use force, namely in its function codified in Article 51 of the Charter. As explained earlier, this is an authorisation to use force, where force would otherwise be banned. It is not an authorisation to lawfully impair every other right of the aggressor state.

Article 21 is concerned precisely with the justification of what may be termed the collateral, impairment of the aggressor state's rights caused by (lawful) self-defensive force. Article 21 reflects this additional function of the right of self-defence in the international legal order. It is worth pointing out that this is not an additional norm in the legal order, capable of going beyond the right of self-defence. Simply put, Article 51 and Article 21 codify different effects of the exercise of the customary right of self-defence in the legal order. Article 51 concerns its effect on the prohibition of force, and Article 21 the effects of that exercise on other legal relations.

### 5.4.2.3 Third Set of Legal Relations: Obligations of 'Total Restraint'

Self-defence, however, cannot justify the collateral impairment brought about through force of all obligations of the victim state (or rights of the aggressor state). The Commentary to Article 21 expressly excludes from the scope of this provision what it termed, following the ICJ's advisory opinion in *Nuclear Weapons*,[110] the 'obligations of total restraint'.[111] By these are meant those obligations 'expressed or intended to apply as a definitive constraint even to States in armed conflict', including non-derogable human rights, the 'intransgressible'[112] principles of international humanitarian law and other obligations designed to place a limit on the conduct of hostilities.[113] This exclusion was accepted by Iran in *Oil Platforms*,[114]

---

[110] *Nuclear Weapons*, [30].
[111] ARS art. 21 Commentary, [4].
[112] The term is, once again, taken from the ICJ's judgment in *Nuclear Weapons*, [30].
[113] ARS art. 21 Commentary, [4].
[114] Iran statement, *Oil Platforms*, 17 February 2003, CR 2003/5, 41 [29] (references omitted).

and by Uganda in *DRC v Uganda*, whose memorial explicitly stated that self-defence may in no circumstances justify breaches of human rights and humanitarian law.[115] Since the impairment of these obligations may not be justified by self-defence, no more will be said about them in this chapter.

### 5.4.3 Self-Defence and Other Obligations in Practice

There is relatively scant practice explicitly supporting Article 21 of the ARS. Nevertheless, the recognition of the principle reflected in Article 21 can be deduced from practice and international case-law. This section will consider the effects of self-defence as a justification for the collateral impairment of the rights to territorial sovereignty and non-intervention, and of conventional commercial obligations. This is, of course, only a sample of the 'infinite variety' of obligations belonging to the second set of legal relations that may be impaired by self-defensive force. The choice of these obligations, among the many that bind states in international law, is warranted for two reasons. First, because they represent examples from both treaty law and customary law. Second, because these obligations were at the core of three cases before the ICJ: *Nicaragua*, *Oil Platforms* and *DRC v Uganda*. The parties to these cases invoked Article 21 (and its predecessor draft Article 34) and, to a greater or lesser extent, they elaborated on the scope, operation and recognition of this rule. They thus provide a good sample to test whether and how self-defence justifies the collateral impairment of other rights of the aggressor state. For ease of analysis, the rights to territorial sovereignty and non-intervention are addressed together, since they are usually invoked as a pair by states claiming to have been the victim of unlawful uses of force by another state.

#### 5.4.3.1 Territorial Sovereignty and Non-Intervention

*Nicaragua v US* **(1986)** Nicaragua claimed that the United States had violated its sovereignty through forcible measures of trespass into its territory, including the mining of, and attacks on, Nicaraguan ports.[116] In its pleadings, Nicaragua explained that the violation of a state's sovereignty could take place through both forcible and non-forcible means so long as there was trespass on the state's territory. In the instant case, the breach of

---

[115] Uganda Memorial, *DRC v Uganda*, 232–3 [5.93–4].
[116] Memorial of Nicaragua, *Nicaragua*, 115 (territorial sovereignty); 117 (use of force); 120 (non-intervention).

territorial sovereignty had been brought about through measures involving the use of force,[117] including armed attacks against its territory by land, sea and air.[118] Nicaragua clarified that, 'although the claim based upon violations of sovereignty overlap[ped] with other causes of action relating to the use of force' it did not 'simply coincide with those other causes of action and consequently plays a significant independent role.'[119] Similarly, in relation to the principle of non-intervention, Nicaragua claimed that these same acts also constituted infringements of this principle and that 'although the relevant evidentiary materials may be identical, it cannot be said that the principle of non-intervention has no autonomous role to play as a basis of claim.'[120]

In its judgment, the Court accepted Nicaragua's claim. The measures complained of, in addition to being acts contrary to the prohibition of force, also constituted breaches of Nicaragua's territorial sovereignty and of the principle of non-intervention.[121] The Court likewise rejected that self-defence precluded the wrongfulness of these breaches because on the facts of the case the United States did not have a right of self-defence.[122] The Court's reasoning implied, *a contrario*, that if self-defence had been exercised lawfully there would have been no breach of these obligations either. This position of principle was also explicitly endorsed by some judges in their individual opinions. Thus, Judge Jennings stated that the plea of self-defence was 'obviously a possible justification of intervention',[123] and Judge Schwebel noted that '[w]here a State is charged with an unlawful use of force, but actually has employed force in self-defence, that State is absolved of any breach of its international responsibility', such that the plea of self-defence would constitute a complete 'defence to virtually all Nicaraguan claims'.[124]

***DRC v Uganda* (2005)** In *DRC v Uganda*, the Court considered claims about the violation of the principles of territorial sovereignty and non-intervention through the use of military force and a plea of self-defence.

---

[117] Ibid., 116 [441]: 'Many of the violations of sovereignty covered by Nicaragua's claim, and probably the majority of instances, involve the use of armed force.'
[118] Ibid., 115 [438].
[119] Ibid., 116 [441].
[120] Ibid., 120 [463].
[121] *Nicaragua*, [251].
[122] Ibid., [252].
[123] Ibid., diss op Jennings, 535.
[124] Ibid., diss op Schwebel, 377.

## 5.4 SELF-DEFENCE IN THE ARS

The parties' pleadings in this case do not expressly identify self-defence as a justification for the breach of each of these obligations. Nevertheless, that this was the case is implicit in the arguments made by both parties.

The DRC claimed that through forcible measures, including the continued presence of armed forces in the DRC, Uganda had breached the principle of territorial sovereignty and non-intervention.[125] Anticipating Uganda's response, the DRC's Memorial of July 2000 examined (and rejected) a potential plea of self-defence. In this connection, the DRC cited draft Article 34 adopted on first reading in 1980[126] and referred to self-defence as the 'only' exception to the prohibition of force.[127] The Memorial also contained several references to Crawford's Second Report on state responsibility in which, as discussed earlier, he recast the draft provision on self-defence as one concerned with legal relations *other* than the prohibition of force.[128] Furthermore, tracing the ILC's work on the matter, the DRC also explicitly excluded that self-defence could justify the breach of certain obligations deriving from human rights law and humanitarian law (the obligations of 'total restraint').[129] This express exclusion implies an acknowledgment that the plea could justify the infringement of other obligations, in particular those of territorial sovereignty and non-intervention invoked by the DRC.

Uganda, in turn, invoked self-defence in response to the DRC's claim.[130] Uganda's written pleadings did not pair the various breaches alleged by the DRC with specific defences, so it must have assumed that its plea of self-defence was valid in respect of these allegations too. Indeed, if this were not the case then, even if the plea of self-defence was found to be successful and thus excluded a breach of the prohibition of force, Uganda would still have been found in breach of the DRC's territorial sovereignty and its right of non-intervention. The respondent would surely have

---

[125] Memorial of the DRC, *DRC v Uganda*, 160–93, esp. 182–5 (non-intervention) and 185–6 (territorial sovereignty), 273. In the first round of oral arguments, the DRC did not discuss the principle of territorial sovereignty as an individual head of responsibility, but assimilated it to the claim of breach of the principle of non-intervention, see *DRC v Uganda*, DRC statement, 11 April 2005, CR 2005/2, 49–50. Yet, in its closing arguments, the DRC requested the Court to find that through its military action Uganda had breached the prohibition of force as well as the principles of territorial sovereignty and non-intervention: DRC statement, 25 April 2005, CR 2005/13, 36–7.
[126] Memorial of the DRC, 198.
[127] Ibid., 232 [5.92].
[128] See, e.g., Ibid., 198, 214, 218, 222, 233.
[129] Ibid., 232–3 [5.93–4].
[130] Counter-memorial of Uganda, 21 April 2001, 180–216; *DRC v Uganda*, 194.

wished to exonerate itself from all of the allegations made by the DRC, so it is safe to assume that Uganda's plea of self-defence was invoked as a general defence applicable to all the breaches claimed by the applicant. Subsequently, during oral arguments before the Court, Uganda, whose legal team included Ian Brownlie as counsel (who had been counsel for Nicaragua in *Nicaragua v US*), expressly cited Article 21 ARS though it did not discuss the scope of this provision in detail.[131]

The Court's judgment did not refer to Article 21 either. Nevertheless, the Court implicitly accepted, at least as a matter of principle, that self-defence lawfully exercised would not constitute an infringement of these other obligations. Thus, after finding that self-defence had not been lawfully exercised, it held that Uganda had breached the prohibition of force and, in addition, the principles of territorial sovereignty and non-intervention.[132] *A contrario*, it may be inferred that had Uganda's plea been successful, these obligations would not have been breached.

### 5.4.3.2 Commercial Obligations

***Nicaragua v US (1986)*** Alongside its claims relating to the rights of territorial sovereignty and non-intervention, Nicaragua also claimed that the mining of, and attack on, the ports of Corinto, Puerto Sandino and El Bluff – the principal Nicaraguan ports which together handled almost all of its trade – constituted a breach of the freedom of commerce and navigation as well as the freedom of transit protected under Articles XIX(1) and XX of the 1956 US–Nicaragua Treaty of Friendship, Commerce and Navigation ('FCN Treaty') respectively.[133] In the preliminary objections phase, the United States made a relevant observation in this regard. Having claimed that it was acting in collective self-defence on behalf of Costa Rica, El Salvador and Honduras,[134] it then argued that the FCN Treaty was subject to the 'usual exceptions relating to … measures for collective or individual self-defense'.[135] Nicaragua, for its part, asserted in

---

[131] Uganda oral statement, 18 April 2005, CR 2005/7, 30 [78].

[132] *DRC v Uganda*, [165], [345.1]. Note that the Court only refers to the principle of non-use of force and the principle of non-intervention in the dispositif, even though the DRC had claimed also a breach of its territorial sovereignty and the Court had addressed it in its reasoning. For the DRC's plea for relief, see Memorial of the DRC, 273.

[133] Memorial of Nicaragua, *Nicaragua*, 110–11. See further: oral statement of Nicaragua, ICJ Pleadings, vol. V, 210–12.

[134] Counter-Memorial of the United States on Preliminary Objections, ICJ Pleadings, vol. II, 60, 219ff.

[135] Ibid., 54. The quote is taken from a report of the Senate Foreign Relations Committee, *Sen Executive Rept. No. 9*, Annex 41, at 4.

the merits phase that the breaches of the FCN Treaty could be justified on the basis of 'exonerating causes traditionally recognized under customary international law and enumerated in Chapter V of the draft articles of the ILC concerning State responsibility',[136] including self-defence. Indeed, Nicaragua continued, '[t]he United States invoked one of these causes in its Counter-Memorial during the first phase of the present case: legitimate self-defense.'[137] According to Nicaragua, however, this plea was not met in fact and, as a result, could not justify the breach of the FCN treaty.[138] The Court, again, accepted this position in principle, though it rejected the plea on the facts: having concluded that the United States' claim of self-defence was unfounded, this plea could not justify the Treaty breaches either.[139]

***Oil Platforms* (2003)** The *Oil Platforms* case concerned the breach of various provisions of the 1955 Iran–US Treaty of Amity through the attacks carried out by the United States on offshore oil complexes, owned for commercial purposes by the National Iranian Oil Corporation.[140] Before the Court, Iran argued that the attacks on the platforms constituted a breach of Article X(1) of the Treaty, pursuant to which '[b]etween the territories of the High Contracting Parties there shall be freedom of commerce and navigation.'[141] In response to this allegation, the United States relied, among others, on the plea of self-defence. In particular, in its Rejoinder of 2001, the United States invoked as defences both the essential security exception under Article XX(1)(d) of the Treaty and, alternatively, self-defence as a circumstance precluding wrongfulness. The United States argued that the destruction of the platforms was a lawful exercise of self-defence and that, for this reason, the alleged breach of the 1955 Treaty was justified. Indeed, expressly citing Article 21, it held that '[a]ny actions of the US deemed incompatible with Article X of the Treaty would not be wrongful by the operation of this principle [of self-defence] of customary international law.'[142]

---

[136] Memorial of Nicaragua, ICJ Pleadings, vol. IV, 112 [427].
[137] Id.
[138] Id.
[139] *Nicaragua*, [282] (noting that the 'justification of self-defence' had already been 'rejected on the legal level').
[140] For the claims, see *Oil Platforms*, [1], [26].
[141] Iran initially pleaded breaches of arts I, IV(1) and X(1) of the 1955 Treaty of Amity, but in its preliminary objection judgment the ICJ limited the claim to breaches of art. X(1), see *Oil Platforms, Preliminary Objections*, 821.
[142] Rejoinder of the United States, 23 March 2001, 141 [5.02].

It must be noted that after having relied explicitly on Article 21 as a defence for the breach of the Treaty of Amity, during the oral proceedings before the Court in early 2003 the United States modified its defensive argument. Its revised forensic strategy was to characterise the Treaty of Amity as a self-contained regime, thus excluding from the Court's jurisdiction any consideration of general international law – probably in an effort to avoid pronouncements on the law on the use of force and self-defence by the UN's main judicial body on the eve of the invasion of Iraq. Thus US counsel explained at length how Article XX(1)(d) constituted a *lex specialis* between the parties, with the consequence that, consistent with Article 55 ARS, this provision excluded the applicability to the dispute under the Treaty of the circumstances precluding wrongfulness of the (general) law of state responsibility. The United States was thus erecting a ring fence between the dispute before the Court and general international law: the self-contained character of the Treaty excluded consideration of the law on the use of force, and the 'special' character of the defence in Article XX(1)(d) excluded consideration of self-defence as a circumstance precluding wrongfulness.[143] This change of argument notwithstanding, not only did the United States not reject in its oral pleadings the principle stated in Article 21, but its insistence that Article XX(1)(d) of the Treaty constituted a *lex specialis* excluding the application of Article 21 can only be evidence of the acceptance by the United States that, absent the *lex specialis*, Article 21 would have been applicable as *lex generalis*.

Iran, for its part, while denying that the plea was met on the facts, agreed in its oral pleading with the statement of principle in the American argument:

> [A]ction otherwise lawfully taken in self-defence could constitute a circumstance precluding wrongfulness in relation to Article X, paragraph 1, of the Treaty. In other words, it accepts the proposition contained in Article 21 of the ILC Articles on the Responsibility of States. There is no express stipulation to that effect in the 1955 Treaty, but there does not need to be. If the US was acting in self-defence in attacking and destroying or attempting to destroy the platforms, then Article X, paragraph 1, of the Treaty is not one of the 'obligations of total restraint' of which [the Court] spoke in the *Nuclear Weapons* Advisory Opinion. Freedom of commerce may suffer when action is taken in self-defence; it is not an 'intransgressible' value.[144]

---

[143] See, generally, Prosper Weil's argument on behalf of the United States at Statement of the United States, 26 February 2003, CR 2003/12.
[144] Statement of Iran, CR 2003/5, 41 [29] (references omitted).

Iran later added that, if made out, self-defence would 'exonerate the United States entirely; it would provide a complete justification for their conduct, in accordance with Article 21 of the ILC's Articles.'[145]

The Court eventually found that the plea of self-defence was not met in fact and that, nevertheless, the United States had not breached the Treaty of Amity either. The Court explained its consideration of the law of self-defence as an application of Article 31(3)(c) VCLT, on the so-called principle of 'systemic integration'.[146] The Treaty of Amity did not exist in a vacuum, so its interpretation required taking into account general international law including the law on the use of force. The law on the use of force was thus 'incorporated' into the Treaty of Amity by way of interpretation – a decision which attracted some criticism.[147] It is unclear why the Court did not follow the parties' argument in this regard: had it understood the role of Article 21, it could have considered the law of self-defence as part of the 'general rules' of the law of responsibility without unduly stretching the limits of the compromissory clause in the Treaty itself.

## 5.5 Justification for the Collateral Impairment of Other Obligations

As reviewed earlier, state practice and international case-law suggest that self-defence acts as a justification for these collateral impairments. Namely, *because* the impairment was caused by a lawful measure of self-defence it is justified. There are also no indications in the practice of states that the defending state be excused for these impairments.[148] Can

---

[145] Statement of Iran, 19 February 2003, CR 2003/7, 51 [3].
[146] *Oil Platforms*, [41].
[147] Some judges disagreed with this aspect of the judgment, see the separate opinions of Higgins, 237 [46]; Buergenthal, 278–83; and Owada, 310 [13–14], 314–19, all in *Oil Platforms*. For scholarly criticism see, e.g., Taft, 'Self-Defense and the *Oil Platforms* Decision' (2004) 29 *Yale JIL* 295; Weil and Richemond-Barak, 'The *Oil Platforms* Case before the International Court of Justice: A Non-Case of International Responsibility' in Ragazzi (ed.), *International Responsibility Today: Essays in Memory of Oscar Schachter* (2005), 329.
[148] For an exception in the literature, see: Tsagourias, 'Self-Defence Against Non-State Actors: The Interaction between Self-Defence as a Primary Rule and Self-Defence as a Secondary Rule' (2016) 29 LJIL 801, at 823–4. Tsagourias's claim that self-defence pursuant to ARS art. 21 is an excuse is, however, premised on the erroneous assumption that *because* it is included in the ARS and *because* the ARS codify secondary rules, *therefore* it must be a secondary rule and, as such, an excuse. The merits of arguments such as this have already been addressed in Chapter 1 of this book. Here it may be sufficient to quote

self-defence's justifying effect be sustained theoretically and, if so, pursuant to what theory? Needless to say, Article 21 remains wholly undertheorised in the scholarship. As this chapter has shown, the very role and scope of the Article are much misunderstood, so it is no surprise that no explanations for the exonerating effect of self-defence in respect of collateral impairments exist in the literature. This section will attempt to fill this void.

A number of theories are from time to time referred to in the scholarship in a bid to explain the exonerating effect of self-defence vis-à-vis the prohibition of force. These theories may serve as a starting point for the analysis of self-defence's interaction with the other obligations owed to the aggressor. Four different theories have been identified in the scholarly literature: (i) interest balancing; (ii) exercise of a right; (iii) exercise of a peremptory right; and (iv) forfeiture of legal protection. These various theories can be classified into two broad categories: consequentialist (i) and deontic (ii, iii, and iv). Regrettably scholars have not engaged in a sustained exposition and analysis of any of these theories. This section will thus try to develop each one as much as it is possible and to provide relevant critiques. The analysis will also draw upon the corresponding debate among (domestic) legal theorists, especially criminal law theorist. In drawing from the debate in domestic law, the attempt is not to transpose domestic law developments and theories into international law. Rather, these works will be used as an aid in the development of the corresponding international law theories and to illuminate the workings and implications of each of these theories.

### 5.5.1 Consequentialist Theories

The legality of the collateral impairment of other obligations may be explained by reference to an act-consequentialist rationale. Pursuant to this theory, there exists, in these circumstances, a conflict between the legally protected interests of the defending state (the interest in protecting its own sovereignty) and the legally protected interests of the aggressor state (whichever interests are protected by the rule impaired). In this conflict, a net benefit results from upholding the superior interest. Although one of the two interests is sacrificed, ultimately that sacrifice avoids a

---

Judge Gaja's remark that such arguments are not 'based on solid ground', at Gaja, 'Primary and Secondary Rules in the International Law of State Responsibility' (2014) 97 *Rivista di diritto internazionale* 990–1.

greater injustice – *summum jus, summa injuria*.[149] Unlike in the case of state of necessity, as will be seen in Chapter 8, the superior interest in circumstances of self-defence has been predetermined by the legal order: the protection of a state's sovereignty is deemed to be superior to the interests of the aggressor state. The application of the right of self-defence thus prevails over the application of the rules protecting the aggressor state's interest(s).

This theory has some appeal. Indeed, it is intuitively plausible that the protection of state sovereignty – especially in the 'extreme circumstance of self-defence, in which the very survival of a state would be at stake'[150] – may take precedence over other obligations. Moreover, the theory can account for the exclusion of 'obligations of total restraint': insofar as they relate to fundamental rules (humanitarian law and human rights) and collective interests (environmental law) they may be considered as superior to the individual interest of the defending state.[151] Lastly, the theory also provides a principled basis to the requirements of necessity and proportionality: these are built into the very terms of the theory, since failure to observe them may cause a greater injury than that avoided.[152]

Nevertheless, there are some significant drawbacks to this theory. To begin with, as will be discussed further in Chapter 8 in connection with state of necessity, other than peremptory rules, international law does not recognise a hierarchy of interests. In absolute terms, then, one state's sovereignty is not superior to another state's right to non-intervention, commercial rights or whatever other interests may be impaired in the circumstances. Moreover, how to explain why the defending state's sovereignty is superior to the aggressor state's sovereignty, such that the latter but not the former can be liable to infringement? Consequently, this

---

[149] Barboza, 'Contramedidas en la reciente codificación de la responsabilidad de los Estados: fronteras con la legítima defensa y el estado de necesidad' (2003) 12 *Anuario Argentino DI* 15, 29–30. Similarly, Spiermann, 'Humanitarian Intervention as a Necessity and the Threat or Use of *Jus Cogens*' (2002) 71 *Nordic JIL* 523, 534 ('Arguably, self-defence is a special case of necessity where the interests protected by Article 2(4) of the Charter are most clearly, or least exceptionally, outweighed by essential interests threatened by a grave and imminent peril, namely the interests of the attacked state and others').
[150] *Nuclear Weapons*, 266 [2.E].
[151] This, of course, requires the assumption that collective interests are deemed superior to individual interests – a not uncontroversial proposition. See, e.g., Crawford's remarks in the context of state of necessity: Crawford, Second Report, [292], discussed further in Chapter 8, Section 8.4.1.
[152] Omichinski, 'Applying the Theories of Justifiable Homicide to Conflicts in the Doctrine of Self-Defense' (1986–7) 33 *Wayne LR* 1447, 1456.

rationale cannot sustain in a principled manner the preeminence given to the right of self-defence over the rights of the aggressor. This obstacle could be overcome by approaching the scale of interests in relative terms. Thus, the balance could be tipped in favour of the defending state by taking into account the aggressor state's wrongdoing (namely, the fact that the aggressor committed a wrongful act). Such reasoning, however, involves a moral judgment about the blameworthiness of the aggressor: it is because what the aggressor has done is wrong that the scales are tipped in the opposite direction.[153] But this manner of proceeding is problematic both in law, since fault is not a requirement of state responsibility,[154] and in practice, due to the character of states as collective entities.[155] Alternatively, the balance could be tipped by taking into account the degree of injury caused to the defending state's interest. Following this approach, it seems clear that, in an extreme case of self-defence threatening the state's survival, the defending state's interest (its very survival) could be superior to the interests of the aggressor (say, its territorial sovereignty or commercial interests). But problems remain. For, outside the case of state survival, what degree of attack is necessary to meet this gravity threshold: would an armed attack, or an aggression or something altogether graver be enough? Also, is this gravity threshold a fixed one or does it vary depending on the interest of the aggressor in question (e.g., one threshold for sovereignty, and a different one for its commercial interests)? If the latter, how to determine the degree of gravity necessary given that there is no scale of interests in international law?

Even if these problems were overcome, which may be possible if gravity is taken as a radically relative threshold to be assessed only on a case-by-case basis,[156] this alternative would nevertheless be under-inclusive, as it might not allow the justification of circumstances falling

---

[153] Proponents of consequentialist rationales for killing in self-defence speak here of the 'moral blame' of an aggressor as diminishing the value of the aggressor's life. For an overview and critique of these views, see Rodin, *War and Self-Defense* (2002), 51–5; Leverick, *Killing in Self-Defence* (2006), 45–50.

[154] See Chapter 1, Section 1.4.2.3.

[155] Indeed, while aggression is (may be) a crime for which the head of state bears international criminal responsibility, the state is not (and cannot be) criminally responsible, so the head of state's fault (more specifically, his or her *dolus*) in connection with the crime may not be attributed to the state as a collective entity.

[156] Note that in the case of state of necessity the relative hierarchy of the interests in question is not determined *a priori*, and is a matter to be assessed by reference to each case. See, Chapter 8, Section 8.4.1. Note, also, that this very open-endedness in the drafting of the provision made it very controversial among ILC members, states and commentators.

## 5.5 JUSTIFICATION FOR COLLATERAL IMPAIRMENTS 209

below the survival threshold (whatever this may be). Perhaps more dangerously, this approach has the potential of rendering all of the restrictions imposed on the exercise of self-defence essentially meaningless. This risk is clearly illustrated by the United Kingdom's argument in *Nuclear Weapons*. According to the United Kingdom: '[t]he needs of a State forced to fight for its survival in the face of massive aggression must weigh heavily in [the] balance'.[157] Indeed almost anything can be subordinated to state survival: Bosnia-Herzegovina, for example, claimed that its right of self-defence could not be limited by a UNSC resolution imposing an arms embargo;[158] and the United Kingdom that nuclear weapons could not be excluded in such a situation.[159] Equally, once survival is preeminent, how can its protection be limited by requirements of necessity and proportionality, or by obligations of total restraint?[160] This approach essentially subordinates the entire legal system to the political fact of existence, it subordinates law to power.[161] It is the ultimate manifestation of law as apology,[162] and it veers, as the language of the ICJ in *Nuclear Weapons* showed, dangerously close to the infamous and now defunct right of self-preservation.[163]

Another version of this theory takes a rule-consequentialist stance.[164] In this version, the benefit is not achieved by upholding the interest of the self-defending state over that of the aggressor; rather, a net benefit is gained from the restoration of legality achieved once the armed attack

---

[157] UK oral statement, *Nuclear Weapons*, 15 November 1995, CR 1995/34, 41.
[158] *Application of the Convention on the Prevention and Punishment of the Crime of Genocide, Order of 8 April 1993, Request for the Indication of Provisional Measures* (1993) ICJ Rep 3, [36].
[159] UK oral statement, *Nuclear Weapons*, CR 95/3, 39–40.
[160] See, on this point, *Nuclear Weapons*, decl Bedjaoui, 273 [22]: 'A State's right to survival is also a fundamental law, similar in many respects to a "natural" law. However, self-defence – if exercised in extreme circumstances in which the very survival of a State is in question – cannot produce a situation in which a State would exonerate itself from compliance with the "intransgressible" norms of international humanitarian law. In certain circumstances, therefore, a relentless opposition can arise, a head-on collision of fundamental principles, neither one of which can be reduced to the other.'
[161] Kohen, 'The Notion of "State Survival" in International Law' in Boisson De Chazournes and Sands (eds), *Nuclear Weapons and the International Court of Justice* (1999), 293, 299–304.
[162] In the sense used by Koskenniemi, *From Apology to Utopia: The Structure of International Legal Argument* (2006).
[163] See, e.g., *Nuclear Weapons*, [96]. For an explanation and critique of the right of self-preservation, see Chapter 8, Section 8.2.2.2.
[164] Rodin, *Self-Defense*, 54.

comes to an end. The risks inherent in this modified theory are all too obvious. If restoration of legality provides, ultimately, a net benefit, then why limit self-defence to necessary and proportionate measures?[165] The rule-consequentialist approach cannot account for, and ultimately undermines, the requirements and conditions of the right of self-defence in international law.

### 5.5.2  Deontic Theories

Rights-based rationales may also provide an account of the legality of the collateral impairments caused by self-defensive force. These theories seek to explain the lawfulness of otherwise wrongful acts by reference to the entitlement (permission) to engage in such behaviour. It is immaterial for these theories whether the entitlement takes the form of, in Hohfeldian terms, a claim-right or a liberty. Of course, whether an entitlement is a claim-right or a liberty would have practical implications in respect of, for example, the existence of an obligation of toleration of, and non-interference with, the relevant conduct. Given these implications, it is fundamental to begin by analysing the internal structure of the right of self-defence through the prism of Hohfeld's fundamental legal conceptions.

#### 5.5.2.1  Preliminary Clarification: The Right of Self-Defence as a Hohfeldian Liberty

Giancarlo Scalese has argued that the entitlement to resort to self-defence constitutes a 'subjective right' or, to put it in Hohfeldian terms, a claim-right of the state victim of an armed attack.[166] Since, he argues, the legal protection of subjective rights is guaranteed by the correlative duty imposed on others not to interfere with the exercise of the right,[167] it follows that the right of self-defence entails both an entitlement to act for the state victim of the armed attack (the right-holder) and the aggressor's duty not to interfere with the exercise of this right. According to Scalese, moreover, the aggressor state's duty of toleration or non-interference is evidenced by Article 30 of the ARS, on the obligation of cessation and guarantees of non-repetition.[168] Indeed, Scalese concludes, any attempt

---

[165] Leverick, *Killing in Self-Defence*, 48–9.
[166] Scalese, *La rilevanza delle scusanti nella teoria dell'illecito internazionale* (2008), 23–7.
[167] Ibid., 25.
[168] Pursuant to ARS art. 30: 'The State responsible for the internationally wrongful act is under an obligation: (a) to cease that act, if it is continuing; (b) to offer appropriate assurances and guarantees of non-repetition, if circumstances so require.'

## 5.5 JUSTIFICATION FOR COLLATERAL IMPAIRMENTS

by the aggressor state to resist or to react against the action in self-defence constitutes a violation of this provision.[169]

The right of self-defence, nevertheless, hardly reflects the internal logical structure of a subjective right, as claimed by Scalese. Fundamentally, the problem is that no correlative obligation can be found to the right of self-defence. To understand this point (and, as will be seen, to identify the character of the entitlement to act in self-defence), Hohfeld's scheme of fundamental legal conceptions and their relations can be useful. The main aspects of his scheme were explained in Chapter 3, but will be summarised here briefly before homing in on the aspects of this scheme that are relevant for the present analysis.

Hohfeld identified what he called fundamental legal conceptions and set out to analyse the relations existing among them.[170] The basic elements of all legal relations, according to Hohfeld, are rights, privileges, powers and immunities. Of interest here are only rights and privileges (the so-called first-order legal relations), subsequently re-labelled by scholars as claim-rights and liberties, respectively.[171] Each of these determine the legal position of a certain subject with respect to a given conduct, and they are paired with correlative positions of others in relation to that same conduct. In Hohfeldian analysis, correlatives are simply two ways of saying the same thing. In the case of claim-rights, to say that A has a claim-right that B do X is *the same as* saying that B owes a duty to A to do X. For example, if State A has the right that State B share a new military technology (under a treaty for the exchange of technology), State B has the duty to share *that* new military technology with State A. Or, to say that A has a privilege or liberty to do X is *the same as* saying that B has a no-right that A not do X.[172] For instance, State A has a freedom to navigate on the high seas and, correlatively, State B has a no-right that A *not* navigate on the high seas. The correlation always exists between two parties, and in respect of the same thing.

Arguments supporting the character of self-defence as a claim-right usually fail precisely on the identification of a correlative duty to the right.

---

[169] Scalese, *Scusanti*, 27.
[170] See Hohfeld, 'Fundamental Legal Conceptions', 16. For the relevance of Hohfeldian analysis to international law, see: Smit Duijzentkunst, *The Concept of Rights in International Law* (unpublished PhD thesis, Cambridge University, 2015), ch. 3.
[171] For the re-naming of rights as claim-rights, see: Mackie, *Ethics: Inventing Right and Wrong* (1977), 173–4. For the re-naming of privileges as liberties, see: Williams, 'The Concept of Legal Liberty' (1956) 56 *Col LR* 1129.
[172] Schlag, 'How to Do Things with Hohfeld' (2015) 78 *Law & Contemp Probs* 185.

Thus, some scholars have argued that self-defence is the correlative right of the obligation not to use force[173] or of the obligation not to engage in aggression.[174] In both cases, however, there is no correspondence between the notions of self-defence and those of use of force (which is broader) and aggression (which is narrower).[175] To be sure, states are under an obligation not to use force (or engage in aggression). But the correlative of this duty is the right to be *free* from force (or aggression) and not the right to resort to self-defence against that force (or aggression). For others, including Scalese, the correlative of self-defence is the duty of the target state not to interfere with (but to tolerate) the use of self-defensive force against it.[176] But here, too, the correlation does not exist, for the right of self-defence and the duty of non-interference do not refer to the same thing. If the victim state uses self-defensive force against the aggressor state, in response to the aggressor's use of force, the victim state's right is about its own acting in self-defence, whereas the aggressor state's obligation is about its own non-interference.[177] On the one hand, the victim has a right to act in self-defence (to do X); on the other, the aggressor has an obligation not to interfere in the self-defensive action (not to do Y). Furthermore, the correlative of the aggressor's obligation not to do Y (not to interfere) is the victim's claim-right that the aggressor not do Y (namely, the right that the aggressor not interfere with its self-defensive action). This latter relation can of course exist, but it does not follow logically from the right of self-defence (nor, for that matter, can it be evidenced in state practice).

Scalese's appeal to ARS Article 30 as evidence of the aggressor state's duty to tolerate the self-defensive force cannot change this conclusion. To be sure, the victim state has a right to the cessation of the armed attack and the aggressor state has a correlative obligation to cease the attack. But this legal relation is a different one from the one concerning self-defence. Indeed, it is simply the relation established under the prohibition of force

---

[173] Randelzhofer, 'Article 51' in Simma (ed.), *The Charter of the United Nations* (2nd edn, 2002), vol. 1, 790.

[174] Giraud, 'La théorie de la légitime défense' (1934) 49 *Recueil* 688, 703; Neff, 'The Dormancy, Rise and Decline of Fundamental Liberties of States' (2015) 4 CJICL 482, 495.

[175] For an analysis of the meaning of the expressions 'use of force', 'armed attack' and 'aggression', see Ruys, *Armed Attack*, ch. 3.

[176] Čepelka, 'Conséquences juridiques', 44–6.

[177] The use of the label 'aggressor state' is not intended to suggest that the reasoning in the text is only applicable in cases of aggression (if this concept is indeed different from that of 'armed attack'). It is simply a convenient label to refer, in few words, to the State author of the armed attack.

## 5.5 JUSTIFICATION FOR COLLATERAL IMPAIRMENTS 213

itself: the victim state retains its right that force not be used against it, so it can claim from the aggressor that it stop its behaviour. Or it can be conceived as a new legal relation (one of the legal relations of responsibility, arising from the wrongful act), pursuant to which the victim state has a right that the aggressor stop its behaviour, and the aggressor has an obligation towards the victim to stop the behaviour. ARS Article 30 simply reflects this latter obligation, which arises as a result of the violation of the prohibition of force, but it is unrelated to the victim state's exercise of self-defence.

In practice, moreover, states do indeed react against self-defensive force either by continuing in their attack or, even, through additional non-forcible measures such as embargoes. For example, in the hypothetical given above, the aggressor can react against the victim's use of self-defence by imposing an embargo on, and breaking off diplomatic relations with, the victim. Moreover, instead of desisting from its initial attack, the aggressor can continue and even intensify its military efforts against the victim. Does the aggressor infringe the victim state's right of self-defence in so doing? Is the aggressor obliged to tolerate the victim's self-defensive force, that is to remain passive in front of it? As seen earlier, nothing in the legal relation of self-defence entitles the victim to demand such behaviour from the aggressor and, correlatively, that relation does not impose on the aggressor an obligation to stop such behaviour. In short, the right of self-defence does not entail an obligation for the aggressor to remain passive in front of the victim's exercise of self-defence.[178] This is not to say that the aggressor's reaction to the self-defensive force would be lawful – at the very least, its prolonged use of force against the victim would constitute a continued infringement of its obligation not to use force against that state[179] and, if obligations of free trade existed, the imposition of an embargo would violate those obligations. The point is, however, that neither of these actions violates the right of self-defence as such.

The right of self-defence is best understood as a Hohfeldian privilege or liberty of the victim state.[180] Privileges or liberties constitute permissions

---

[178] Sicilianos, *Réactions décentralisées*, 46–7.
[179] E.g., Venturini, *Necessità e proporzionalità nell'uso della forza militare in diritto internazionale* (1988), 48; Arroyo Lara, 'Reflexiones en torno a la legítima defensa como causa excluyente la ilicitud (VIII Informe a la CDI)' (1982–3) 1 *Anales de la Universidad de La Laguna* 75, 88–91.
[180] See, e.g., Arroyo Lara, 'Reflexiones', 88–91; Venturini, *Necessità*, 48; Sicilianos, *Réactions décentralisées*, 46–7.

of the legal order to do (or not to do) something. Or, to put it in terms of its Hohfeldian opposite, a situation of liberty is a situation in which a subject *does not* have a duty not to do (or to do) something. To say that A has a liberty to do (or not to do) X is the same as saying that A is under no duty not to do (or to do) X. In terms of correlative jural positions, A's liberty is the equivalent for B of what Hohfeld called a situation of 'no-rights', namely the situation in which B does not have a claim-right against A that it not do (or do) what the liberty permits. So, the correlative of A's liberty is B's no-right. As in the earlier example, State A has a right of free navigation on the high seas and State B has a no-right that State A not navigate on the high seas. What is crucial for present purposes is that liberties do not entail claim-rights for the liberty-holder, which means that they do not imply a correlative duty on the part of others. So to say that A has a liberty to do X does not entail that B has a duty towards A in respect of that liberty. Liberties are thus permissions that the 'law tolerates but does not support by imposing a duty on anyone else.'[181] This means that there is no (correlative) obligation not to interfere with the enjoyment of a liberty. Hohfeld explained this through the following example: when A, the owner of a salad, says to B 'Eat the salad if you can; you have [my] license to do so, but [I] don't agree not to interfere with you', what A derives is the liberty of eating the salad. A would have no claim against B, so that if B manages to hold on to the dish such that A could not actually eat the salad, no right of A would have been violated.[182] Thus B *can* interfere with A's exercise of its liberty and, in so doing, it will not infringe A's liberty.[183] A liberty is not directly protected by the legal system (it can be interfered with), and any 'protection for the action is indirect in deriving from the protective perimeter or ring fence provided by the claim-rights that the agent has, not from the privilege/liberty itself'.[184] That is, the reaction or

---

[181] Stone, *Legal System and Lawyers' Reasoning* (1964), 143.
[182] This is a slightly simplified version of Hohfeld's example, see Hohfeld, 'Fundamental Legal Conceptions', 35–6.
[183] The freedom of navigation was mentioned earlier as an example of a liberty. Now, under UNCLOS, States are forbidden from interfering with the freedom of navigation. This obligation is not derived from the freedom of navigation itself, but is specifically provided for in UNCLOS art. 211. Indeed, the correlative of that duty is not the freedom of navigation, but the freedom from interference. Recall that correlatives represent two different ways of saying the same thing.
[184] Brown, 'Rights, Liberties and Duties: Reformulating Hohfeld's Scheme of Legal Relations?' (2005) 58 *Current Legal Problems* 343, 344.

## 5.5 JUSTIFICATION FOR COLLATERAL IMPAIRMENTS

resistance by B could infringe *other* claim-rights accruing to A, which entail a correlative duty for B.[185]

This analytical explanation more accurately reflects the internal structure of the right of self-defence. In the earlier example, the victim state has a liberty to resort to force in self-defence, but the aggressor is under no duty to tolerate that action. The aggressor's reactions may, of course, infringe the 'protective perimeter' created by the victim's other claim-rights (for example, the right to non-interference in the case of the embargo, or the right to be free from force if the aggression is continuing); but they do not infringe the victim's entitlement to resort to self-defence. Self-defence is therefore a liberty of the victim state.

Now, in the exercise of this liberty, the victim state can encroach upon claim-rights of the aggressor state, in respect of which the victim has a correlative duty. For example, the self-defensive force can encroach upon the aggressor state's (claim-)right to territorial sovereignty (in respect of which the victim state has a correlative duty not to trespass), or the aggressor state's (claim-)right of non-intervention (in respect of which the victim state has a correlative duty of non-intervention), or the aggressor state's (claim-)right to respect the freedom of commerce (in respect of which the victim has a duty to maintain respect), and so on. Why is it the case that the encroachment of these rights of the aggressor by the self-defensive force is lawful? Simply to say that the victim state has a 'right' to self-defence is insufficient in this respect: while the right provides the legal basis for the victim's resort to force, it does not explain why the aggressor state's own rights, in respect of which the victim has a correlative duty and which are impaired by self-defensive force, are not thereby breached. At least three theories have been proposed in this regard,[186] reviewed below.

---

[185] For example, say that there is a free bench in the park with enough space for only one person. Both Amy and Charles see the bench and want to sit on it. They both have a liberty to do so, and neither is obliged to let the other sit. At the same time, both can interfere with the other's sitting on the bench. If Amy sat down, Charles could ask her to move elsewhere or act in an obnoxious manner (say by playing music out loud while Amy is reading) to get Amy to leave. Charles could even push Amy off the bench: her liberty to sit there does not prevent interventions, even of this forceful type. Nevertheless, if Charles did push Amy off the bench, his act would in all likelihood be contrary to his obligation not to interfere with Amy's person (her right to physical integrity, for example). So other (claim-)rights of Amy may protect her against Charles' interference, but her liberty to sit on the bench does not so protect her.

[186] A number of additional theories have been proposed in domestic law in this regard. See, e.g., Miller, 'Killing in Self-Defense' (1993) 7 *Public Affairs Quarterly* 325; Uniacke,

### 5.5.2.2 Unity of the Legal System[187]

First, it has been maintained that, since the determination of wrongfulness requires a holistic assessment of the legal system, 'to be considered unlawful, conduct cannot be in accordance with any legal rule nor, therefore, constitute the performance of an obligation or the exercise of a right'.[188] On this view, so long as there exists a rule in the legal system which permits (or exempts) or commands the conduct, then that conduct may not be classified as unlawful even if it is incompatible with a proscriptive rule in that same system.[189] As a result, since self-defence constitutes a permission of the legal order it follows that conduct adopted in pursuance of that permission will be lawful in relation to the legal order as a whole.

This theory seems to be premised on two assumptions: first, that legal systems require coherence and compatibility between their rules; and, second, that in the event of incompatibility, the rule with which the conduct accords (be it a permission/exemption or a command) takes priority over the rules with which the conduct is incompatible.[190] Whatever its merits in domestic legal orders, this explanation is ill-suited to international law. While it is arguable that the international legal order too contains an assumption of compatibility,[191] the same cannot be said about the second assumption. Indeed, the opposite seems to be true: as the ICJ has remarked, '[t]here can be no doubt that, as a general rule, a particular act may be perfectly lawful under one body of legal rules and unlawful under another'.[192] The existence of incompatible rules is the result of international law's development through a process of 'accretion and cumulation' rather than erosion and reduction, as explained by the *Southern Bluefin Tuna* Tribunal,[193] and by the coexistence of various sources of

---

*Permissible Killing: The Self-Defence Justification of Homicide* (1994), ch. 6; Leverick, *Killing in Self-Defence*.

[187] Scalese, who upholds this theory, simply refers to it as 'exercise of a right', but the label 'unity of the legal system' seems to better capture the essence of this rationale.

[188] Scalese, *Scusanti*, 17 ('per essere ritenuta illecita, una condotta non può risultare conforme ad alcuna norma giuridica né, quindi, rappresentare l'adempimento di un dovere o l'esercizio di un diritto').

[189] The terms permission, exemption, command and proscription are used in the sense explained by Pauwelyn, *Conflict of Norms in Public International Law* (2003), 158–9.

[190] For this critique, see Marinucci and Dolcini, *Manuale di diritto penale* (2nd edn, Giuffrè, 2006), 236–8.

[191] Merkouris, *Article 31(3)(c) VCLT and the Principle of Systemic Integration: Normative Shadows in Plato's Cave* (2015), 169. See further Pauwelyn, *Conflict of Norms*, ch. 5.

[192] *Croatia v Serbia*, [474] (not yet reported).

[193] *Southern Bluefin Tuna Case (Australia v Japan; New Zealand v Japan) (Jurisdiction and Admissibility)* (2000) 23 RIAA 1, [52]. The metaphor was taken from the arguments made

## 5.5 JUSTIFICATION FOR COLLATERAL IMPAIRMENTS 217

law with varying degrees of participation by states. Technical rules exist for the resolution of conflict between rules in the form of presumptions against incompatibility and priority principles.[194] But none of these technical principles establish that in any case of incompatibility, accordance with any one rule of the order is sufficient to establish the conduct's legality in respect of the legal order as a whole.

### 5.5.2.3 Exercise of a Peremptory Right

Another potential explanation is that the right of self-defence is a peremptory rule of international law. Peremptory rules prevail over any other non-peremptory rule of the system, and set aside their application to the extent of inconsistency.[195] In the conflict between the right of self-defence and the (non-peremptory) rights of the aggressor state collaterally impaired, self-defence takes priority thus excluding the violation of those rights.

This theory has a number of benefits. To begin with, it seems to be capable of explaining in a consistent manner the relationship between self-defence and the three sets of legal relations described above. In respect of the first legal relation, the prohibition of force, it was said earlier that self-defence can be construed as a defence to the prohibition (rather than a negative rule-element, as maintained by the ILC). Given the peremptory status of the prohibition, it would be necessary for this relation to be systemically possible that the right of self-defence *also* be peremptory. Moreover, by upholding self-defence as a defence to the prohibition of force, this theory is compatible with the practice of tribunals in allocating

---

on behalf of applicants by James Crawford, see First Round Presentation of Australia and New Zealand, 8 May 2000, *Southern Bluefin Tuna*, 121 (of the unpaginated pdf document), https://icsid.worldbank.org/.

[194] On which see, generally, ILC Fragmentation Report.

[195] A provision to the effect that compliance with a peremptory rule justifies the non-performance of conflicting non-peremptory obligations was proposed by the ILC on second reading; see draft Article 29 *bis*: ILC Report, fifty-first session, ILC Yearbook 1999, vol. II(2), 75–7. According to this provision: 'The wrongfulness of an act of a State is precluded if the act is required in the circumstances by a peremptory norm of general international law'; see Candioti, 2605th meeting, ILC Yearbook 1999, vol. I, 276. States commenting in the Sixth Committee generally agreed with the proposal: Summary of Sixth Committee Debates, 8 February 2000, UN Doc A/CN.4/504, 15 [50]. Note, however, that the text of the draft article concerned situations where the peremptory norm *requires* a certain course of conduct incompatible with a non-peremptory obligation, and not where the peremptory rule authorises or permits such conduct. The draft article as proposed by the ILC relied on a narrow notion of conflict, requiring conflicting *obligations*.

the burden of proof with respect to self-defence on the respondent (instead of allocating the proof of its absence on the claimant).

In respect of the second set of legal relations, insofar as these are not peremptory, the right of self-defence would be able to set them aside, thus excluding their breach by self-defensive force. As a result, the collateral impairment of the aggressor's rights would be lawful.

Finally, in respect of the third set of legal relations, insofar as these are peremptory (and many of these are) and they are intended to impose definitive restraints on the conduct of war, they would constitute the most special (peremptory) rule in the circumstances and, as such, they could set aside the application of the right of self-defence. As a result, the collateral impairment of these rights would remain unlawful.

Nevertheless, there remain significant problems with the theory. In particular, the theory undermines the exclusion of obligations of total restraint from the scope of the defence insofar as these may not have peremptory character. While it is accepted that fundamental human rights and basic rules of humanitarian law belong to *jus cogens*,[196] not all of them do. Thus, they could be set aside by the peremptory right of self-defence if and when they were inconsistent with the exercise of that right. The same could be said of environmental obligations, even though they may have been intended to impose an absolute constraint on states during armed conflict, since these are not currently recognised as part of *jus cogens*. A theory of justification which relies on the notion of peremptory rules thus directly undermines one of the conditions of application of Article 21. At any rate, as already noted earlier, the practice and *opinio juris* of states do not support the peremptory status of the right of self-defence.[197]

#### 5.5.2.4 Forfeiture of Legal Protection

Finally, the legality of the collateral impairment of the rights of the aggressor state may be explained by reference to a rights forfeiture theory. In short, pursuant to this theory, the legality of the collateral impairment of rights belonging to the second set of legal relations by self-defensive force derives from the fact that the aggressor state has, by its conduct, forfeited the protection afforded by the legal system to its interests. As a result, when the victim state resorts to defensive force against the

---

[196] Some human rights and rules of humanitarian law have been identified as belonging to *jus cogens*, see, e.g., ARS art. 40 Commentary, [5] (on 'basic rules of international humanitarian law') and *Barcelona Traction, Light and Power Company, Limited, Judgment* (1970) ICJ Rep 3, [34] (on 'rules concerning the basic rights of the human person').

[197] See van Steenberghe, *Légitime défense*, 118.

## 5.5 JUSTIFICATION FOR COLLATERAL IMPAIRMENTS     219

aggressor, it does not breach the aggressor state's rights since their legal protection has been forfeited. This theory has been proposed by scholars writing in the context of self-defence against non-state actors. In this context, the distinction between the first and second set of legal relations is sharply brought to the surface: while the use of force is targeted against the non-state actor, it takes place in the territory of a third state. The right of self-defence may be lawfully exercised as against the non-state actor, but this says nothing of the encroachment upon the rights of the territorial state. To explain the legality of the encroachment upon the territorial state's rights, scholars have argued that by allowing the operation of the groups from their territory these states forfeit the legal protections afforded by international law.[198] Nevertheless, the theory remains considerably underdeveloped in the scholarship.[199] To test the theory's potential explanatory power, therefore, it will need to be further developed here.

As a first step in this development, the forfeiture theory may need a linguistic and a logical clarification. Critics of the theory of forfeiture in domestic law often point out that the term 'forfeiture' implies the permanent and universal loss of rights.[200] Moreover, they say, the notion has punitive connotations,[201] as evidenced by the fact that historically forfeiture was imposed by courts as a penalty for wrongdoing.[202] Self-defence is neither of these things: it is not punitive and is only temporary. So a theory of self-defence based on the notion of 'forfeiture', if understood in this way, may not work. However, supporters of this theory in domestic law note that there is nothing inherently punitive[203]

---

[198] See, e.g., Reinold, 'State Weakness, Irregular Warfare, and the Right of Self-Defense Post-9/11' (2011) 105 AJIL 244, 285. Similar reasoning underpins the views of these authors (even if they do not use the language of forfeiture): Gazzini, *Changing Rules*, 189; Moir, 'Action Against Host States of Terrorist Groups' in Weller (ed.), *Oxford Handbook of the Use of Force in International Law* (2015), 730.

[199] For an exception (though focusing on the relation between self-defence and the prohibition of force), see Fletcher and Ohlin, *Defending Humanity*.

[200] Kadish, 'Respect for Life and Regard for Rights in the Criminal Law' (1976) 64 *Cal LR* 871, 884; Kaufman, 'Is There a "Right" to Self-Defense?' (2004) 23 *Crim Just Ethics* 20, 25; Wallerstein, 'Justifying the Right to Self-Defense: A Theory of Forced Consequences' (2005) 91 *Virgina LR* 999, 1016.

[201] Noting this connotation: Uniacke, 'In Defense of *Permissible Killing*: A Response to Two Critics' (2000) 19 *Law and Philosophy* 627, 628. For this reason, Uniacke opted not to use the language of 'forfeiture'. Rights forfeiture is, moreover, one of the theories of punishment in domestic legal theory: Wellman, 'The Rights Forfeiture Theory of Punishment' (2012) 122 *Ethics* 371.

[202] See Fletcher, 'The Right to Life' (1980) 63 *Monist* 135, 143.

[203] Uniacke, 'Response', 628.

or permanent[204] about the notion of 'forfeiture'. A temporarily limited and non-punitive sense of the notion of 'forfeiture' can indeed serve as the basis of a theory of Article 21's justifying effect. In what follows, therefore, forfeiture will be understood in this sense.

Turning to the logical clarification, any theory of forfeiture based exclusively on this notion is bound to be only 'half right'.[205] This is because forfeiture occurs in the context of the relations between two parties: the aggressor state and the victim state. The fact of forfeiture must therefore be analysed from both points of view. Under this theory, then, the aggressor state loses the legal protection of its rights temporarily as a result of its armed attack. Correlatively, the victim state is alleviated from its duty of respect and non-interference with those rights; or, what is the same, the victim state now possesses a liberty vis-à-vis the aggressor state in respect of the conduct covered by the forfeited right.[206] These two jural positions, the aggressor's no-right and the victim's liberty (or no-duty), are not separate entities but simply the same fact, the forfeiture, seen from two different angles. David Rodin clearly illustrates the point by reference to self-defence and the right to life:

> The aggressor's loss of the right to life, and the defender's possession of the right to kill are not two independent moral facts that might part company or fail to correspond in a perplexing manner. They are rather simple Hohfeldian correlates of one another; in other words, the same normative fact described from two different perspectives. The aggressor's right to life includes the claim against others that they not kill him. If the aggressor forfeits this right with respect to the defender then he has a no-claim against the defender that he not kill him. But this in turn is just to say that the defender has the right (liberty) to kill him. The absence of the aggressor's right to life and the defender's right to kill are thus internally connected by the logic of normative relations.[207]

Forfeiture, in other words, must be understood in a relational way; as embedded in the normative relations existing between the relevant parties. This means that forfeiture is not, by definition, universal or as against all other members of the legal order: it occurs only in respect of the relations binding the aggressor state and its victim.

---

[204] Thomson, 'Self-Defense' (1991) 20 *Philosophy and Public Affairs* 283, 302; Leverick, *Killing in Self-Defence*, 61.

[205] Lang, 'Why Not Forfeiture?' in Frowe and Lang (eds), *How We Fight: Ethics in War* (2014), 58.

[206] Recall that a liberty is the jural opposite of a duty. If a state has a no-duty not to do X, then it will have a liberty to do X.

[207] Rodin, *Self-Defense*, 75.

## 5.5 JUSTIFICATION FOR COLLATERAL IMPAIRMENTS 221

This theory can successfully explain why the aggressor state's rights in the circumstances are not violated by the exercise of self-defence. By its conduct, the aggressor state forfeits the legal protection of its rights. This means for the victim state that it is no longer under a duty to respect or not to interfere with the aggressor's forfeited rights. In the words used by the ARS, the victim is no longer under an obligation to *perform* its obligations vis-à-vis the aggressor.[208]

Crucially, the theory can also account for the various conditions and limitations of Article 21 in a principled manner. To begin with, the theory can explain the generality of Article 21; namely, its availability in relation to any rights of the aggressor state, regardless of their content or source. Save for a few exclusions considered shortly, the aggressor forfeits the protection that the law affords to its rights – thus opening any of the interests protected by these rights to encroachment by the victim state in the exercise of its right of self-defence. Of course, peremptory rules impose a limit on the aggressor's forfeiture: these rules being non-derogable, the aggressor cannot (unilaterally) forfeit their application.[209] This includes those obligations of total restraint that possess peremptory character. A state acting in self-defence may not, therefore, lawfully impair these obligations as they have not been forfeited by the aggressor. Furthermore, the theory is also capable of explaining the exclusion of those obligations of total restraint not having peremptory character. In this case, the exclusion may be explained by reference to the collective character of the interests that these rights protect. The aggressor state cannot, individually, forfeit the legal protection afforded to a collective interest by the legal order – much in the same way that it cannot consent to their non-performance, as seen in Chapter 4. The theory cannot, however, explain the requirements of necessity and proportionality of the right of self-defence: if the aggressor has forfeited the legal protection of its rights, why should the victim limit its force to what is necessary and proportionate? This obstacle may be overcome by changing the focus of analysis, by moving from the situation of the forfeiting state to that of the state acting in self-defence. It is indeed arguable that necessity and proportionality are conditions intrinsic to the right of self-defence – and, indeed, Rodin has provided an analysis of defensive rights, in general, which shows how these requirements are intrinsic to such rights. This is because defensive rights do not involve absolute liberties but, since defensive rights permit the defence

---

[208] Commentary to Chapter V of Part One, [2].
[209] Thus accounting for the limitation in Article 26 ARS.

of particular goods through harmful or otherwise impermissible measures, they are liberties which 'exist within determinate moral and legal bounds'.[210]

### 5.5.2.5 The Acid Test: Compensation for Material Loss

Each of the theories discussed is able to capture some properties and characteristics of self-defence, while falling short in respect of others. So how to choose between them? One way of doing so is by working out what practical implications may follow from each of these theories. A good acid test in this regard is the duty of compensation in the event of successful invocation of the defence. Given the extant uncertainties as to the circumstances in which compensation may be due, it may be useful to query if any of the theories above has anything to say about the issue of compensation. To this end, consider the following scenario. In the exercise of its right of self-defence, the victim state attacks a commercial port of the aggressor, thereby impairing bilateral conventional obligations to maintain free trade. The victim state's action meets the requirements of the right of self-defence under the *jus ad bellum*, and does not involve an obligation of total restraint. Therefore, the impairment of the conventional right to maintain free commerce may be justified under Article 21. Could the aggressor demand compensation from the victim pursuant to the duty referred to in ARS Article 27(b), since it has suffered a 'material loss' caused by a lawful measure of self-defence? As discussed in Chapter 2, the duty referred to in Article 27(b) remains shrouded in mystery. The provision does not specify the conditions or circumstances in which an obligation to make compensation will arise. Originally, the provision did not include self-defence as one of the defences which, even if successfully invoked, may give rise to an obligation of compensation. Nevertheless, during the second reading of the ARS, this exclusion was deleted and the duty was made potentially available in respect of all of the defences in the ARS. So, can an obligation to make compensation arise in the event of a successful invocation of the justification of self-defence?

There were no suggestions during the ILC work (nor are there suggestions in the scholarship) that compensation should arise in these circumstances (at least, insofar as compensation towards the aggressor state is concerned). Moreover, the case-law involving self-defence also does not evidence that states perceive that compensation is (or should) be due in the circumstances. Nevertheless, it should be noted that of the theories

---

[210] Rodin, *Self-Defense*, ch. 2.

discussed earlier some are more likely than others to (at least) support a potential duty of compensation. As was explained in Chapter 2,[211] the duty of compensation could be grounded on the right of the affected state – in this case, the aggressor state. So it will be crucial to determine whether, in the circumstances, the aggressor state is entitled to the legal protection of its interests. Under a forfeiture theory of self-defence, self-defensive action is lawful because by its own conduct the aggressor state has renounced the protection that the law affords to its interests. When the victim state acts in self-defence it, therefore, neither violates nor infringes – in the sense in which this distinction was made in Chapter 2 – the rights of the aggressor state. No duty of compensation could therefore be grounded on the rights of the aggressor.[212] A consequentialist theory of self-defence, instead (where the action is lawful because it achieves a net benefit), has no effect on the right of the aggressor state: the aggressor state retains the legal protection afforded by the law to its interests. And while its rights are not violated, they are at the very least infringed – and this infringement can be the basis of a duty of compensation.[213] Any choice of a theory to underpin the justifying effect of self-defence should therefore take into account these potential implications.

### 5.5.3 Rights Forfeiture and the Justification of Self-Defence

From the discussion above, it seems that the most persuasive rationale for the justification of the collateral impairments caused by self-defensive force is the forfeiture theory.[214] The theory can explain why there is no breach of these rights and, at the same time, account for the conditions and limitations imposed on Article 21 in a principled manner. Normative and policy reasons may militate in favour of this theory as well. Indeed, the theory responds to the moral and political stigma attached to the use of force and aggression in international relations without, however, presupposing this stigma as the basis of the theory. That the use of force and aggression are stigmatized in international relations can also be seen in the differential treatment of aggressor and victim state in the ILC Articles

---

[211] Chapter 2, Section 2.4.2.
[212] See, e.g., Rodin, *Self-Defense*, 51–2.
[213] Fletcher, 'Right to Life', 149. See further Fletcher, '*Perspectives on Rights*: The Right to Life' (1978–9) 13 *Georgia LR* 1371, 1386; Rodin, *Self-Defense*, 51–2; Rodin, 'Justifying Harm' (2011) 122 *Ethics* 74, 107–8.
[214] For Fletcher and Ohlin, this might be the best theory to explain the legality of self-defence in international law: Fletcher and Ohlin, *Defending Humanity*, 40.

on the Effect of Armed Conflict on Treaties. Article 15 contains a further restriction on the categories of treaties that may be terminated or suspended by an aggressor state.[215] Equally, a forfeiture theory supports the exclusion of any potential right of the aggressor to compensation for material loss caused by self-defence; an exclusion which may also be supported by the principle *ex injuria jus non oritur*. Although the theory cannot account for the requirements of necessity and proportionality, these can, as argued by Rodin, be considered as being built into the right of self-defence itself. As such, a theory of forfeiture need not account for them; rather, the requirements ought to be accounted for by a theory of rights or, more particularly, of defensive rights.

---

[215] Article 15: 'Prohibition of benefit to an aggressor State. A State committing aggression within the meaning of the Charter of the United Nations and resolution 3314 (XXIX) of the General Assembly of the United Nations shall not terminate or withdraw from a treaty or suspend its operation as a consequence of an armed conflict that results from the act of aggression if the effect would be to the benefit of that State'; GA, Effects of Armed Conflicts on Treaties.

# 6

# Countermeasures

## 6.1 Introduction

Pursuant to ARS Article 22:

> The wrongfulness of an act of a State not in conformity with an international obligation towards another State is precluded if and to the extent that the act constitutes a countermeasure taken against the latter State in accordance with chapter II of Part Three.

This provision concerns only one of the functions of countermeasures in the law of state responsibility: its role as a defence, more specifically, as a justification for otherwise wrongful behaviour. This is, as will be explained, only an *incidental* function of the institution of countermeasures. Their primary function is an instrumental one: that of serving the implementation of state responsibility. In this sense, countermeasures are a means of enforcement; perhaps the only means of enforcement equally available to all states, at least from a formal point of view.

The term 'countermeasure' is one of recent adoption, having gained popularity only after it was used in the *Air Service Agreement* award.[1] The expression, nevertheless, had been in use, admittedly without generality or consistency, since the early twentieth century, appearing apparently for the first time in a British diplomatic note of 1915.[2] The ILC did not initially adopt this term when discussing this concept in the framework of the codification of state responsibility, and the question of the proper terminology to use in this regard was uncertain for some time. There was indeed some resistance within the ILC to the use of the term 'countermeasure',[3] in particular because taken literally the term 'meant nothing'.[4] But the term was

---

[1] *Air Service Agreement of 27 March 1946 between the United States of America and France* (1978) 18 RIAA 417, 443–4.
[2] Elagab, *The Legality of Non-Forcible Counter-Measures in International Law* (1988), 2–3.
[3] Alland, 'Countermeasures of General Interest' (2002) 13 EJIL 1221, 1222.
[4] Reuter, 1771st meeting, ILC Yearbook 1983, vol. I, 102 [23].

eventually adopted by the Commission precisely because of its, so-to-speak, neutrality: the term, while still referring to the same practice, was free of the damaging connotations associated with the historical institution of reprisals, of which it was the direct descendant and which evoked memories of abuse, force, repression, punishment and imperialism. The image that best sums up the contemporary perception of the historical practice of reprisals is that of gunboat diplomacy – an image that was recurrent, both explicitly and implicitly, in the comments of both ILC members and States in the Sixth Committee of the UN General Assembly throughout the Commission's work on this topic. As will be seen in this chapter, however, this is only a partial image.

Countermeasures, despite the terminological change, are still regarded with a heavy (and probably healthy) dose of scepticism, and for a number of reasons. To begin with, despite being a means of enforcement formally available to all states, it is a fact that materially some states are better placed to take countermeasures than others and that countermeasures may affect some states more than others. In the words of Julio Barboza, countermeasures are taken by those who can and not by those who may want to.[5] Moreover, due to their unilateral character, countermeasures are especially prone to abuse. Countermeasures have thus been likened to all sorts of wild beasts,[6] mythological beasts even,[7] that need to be 'domesticated' or 'caged'.[8] The metaphor of the wild beast is especially apt, insofar as countermeasures frequently serve as a reminder that international law remains in a 'primitive stage' and that the so-called 'domestic analogy' that some had hoped for – under which international law would develop towards ever more centralisation until it resembled a domestic legal order with centralised enforcement – has not yet materialised.

The ILC faced many difficulties in the codification of the regime of countermeasures. There were innumerable disagreements, both within the Commission and among states in the Sixth Committee, ranging from

---

[5] Barboza, 'Contramedidas en la reciente codificación de la responsabilidad de los Estados: fronteras con la legítima defensa y el estado de necesidad' (2003) 12 *Anuario Argentino DI* 15, 19.
[6] Kabatsi, 2649th meeting, ILC Yearbook 2000, vol. I, 292 [12] ('lions' and 'leopards'); Brownlie, 2649th meeting, ILC Yearbook 2000, vol. I, 301 [19] ('wild animals'). Kateka spoke of countermeasures as belonging to the 'rule of the jungle': 2647th meeting, ILC Yearbook 2000, vol. I, 277 [6].
[7] Bruno Simma is said to have likened countermeasures to an 'elusive dragon' during ILC debates, though the reference could not be found in the summary records of the plenary debates. For the reference, see Kabatsi, 2649th meeting, 292 [12].
[8] Brownlie, 2672nd meeting, ILC Yearbook 2001, vol. I, 34 [1].

## 6.1 INTRODUCTION

the content of the customary law to how to progressively develop the institution. It seems fair to say that most aspects of the Commission's work on countermeasures were fraught with controversy. So much so that the topic of countermeasures was, according to some, one of the most difficult issues that the Commission had tackled in its work on responsibility.[9] In this sea of controversies, however, there was one island of certainty: that countermeasures were *lawful* measures. This much emerged from the practice of states and from the case-law of international tribunals. This being so, countermeasures can *only* be classified as justifications: the countermeasure constitutes at most *prima facie* or apparent breach of the obligation affected, a breach that is precluded by the circumstances in which the measure is adopted. Strictly speaking, of course, it is not the countermeasure itself which precludes wrongfulness. The justification arises from the circumstances which triggered the adoption of the countermeasure, namely the 'previous wrongful act' of the target state.[10]

That countermeasures, if accepted, were lawful was a point simple enough and uncontroversial enough that it gave rise to little debate in both the Commission and in the Sixth Committee. But underneath the apparent simplicity of this statement, there is a hidden complexity. As explained by Omer Elagab:

> The right to resort to countermeasures is built on a paradox: States are permitted as a form of redress to take measures that are in themselves a threat to the order. It is due to this that an aggrieved State is entitled to invoke counter-measures as a justification for retaliatory measures taken against another State which has committed a breach of international law previously.[11]

Indeed, how can a wrong in response to a wrong be right; do two wrongs actually make a right? Can a measure that violates the rights of a state be lawful?[12] Answering this question is the central aim of this chapter.

The argument in this chapter is developed in three steps. Section 6.2 begins with some remarks on the historical institution of reprisals.

---

[9] See, e.g., ILC Report, forty-third session, ILC Yearbook 1991, vol. II(2), 127 [311].
[10] E.g., Venturini, *Necessità e proporzionalità nell'uso della forza militare in diritto internazionale* (1988), 12; Sicilianos, *Les réactions décentralisées à l'illicite* (1990), 27; Pellet, 2672nd meeting, ILC Yearbook 2001, vol. I, 46 [49]; Alland, 'General Interest', 1224 (fn. 13).
[11] Elagab, *Counter-Measures*, 44.
[12] To paraphrase Nicolas Politis, 'Le régime des représailles en temps de paix. Rapport et projets de résolution et de règlement' (1934) 38 *Annuaire IDI* 1, 24.

By focusing equally on the practice and doctrine on forcible and non-forcible reprisals, this section attempts to recalibrate the contemporary representation of reprisals during this period. Section 6.3 considers developments since 1945, focusing primarily on the work of the ILC on countermeasures. As will be explained, the ILC's work on this topic was very comprehensive: most of the views proposed in the literature were discussed, at one point or another, by the Commission and its work elicited the response of a very large number of states in the Sixth Committee. As such, it provides a good repository of the views of states and the scholarship on the topic of countermeasures. The section will explain the dual role of countermeasures in the law of responsibility and it will provide an overview of their current regime as codified in Chapter II of Part Three of the ARS. Section 6.4 then turns to the question whether countermeasures constitute justifications or excuses. Empirically, as noted above, it can be affirmed that countermeasures are lawful measures. Therefore, they must be classified as justifications. But how to explain their legality, given the paradox at their heart? After critically evaluating a number of possible theoretical explanations for the legality of countermeasures, this section argues that the best theory is one based on rights forfeiture: by its own wrongful act, the responsible state forfeits the protection afforded by the law to its interests. In these circumstances, the act of the injured state – even if it impairs one of the interests of the responsible state – is not wrongful since the law's protection of that state's interests has been forfeited.

## 6.2 Reprisals and the Origins of Countermeasures

Reprisals are an old institution of international relations, their origins dating as far back as the Middle Ages. As an institution aimed at the reparation for wrongs to foreign nationals, reprisals have been regarded as the first manifestation of the international responsibility of states.[13]

For many centuries, reprisals were private in character. They were carried out by private citizens, usually the injured citizen, with the authorisation of their sovereign given through letters of reprisal. Reprisals usually involved the seizure of property from the subjects of the wrongdoing sovereign in order to compensate the damage to the injured individual. The institution was based on conceptions of solidarity between the members

---

[13] Anzilotti, *Teoria generale della responsabilità dello stato nel diritto internazionale* (1902), 10–14.

## 6.2 REPRISALS AND THE ORIGINS OF COUNTERMEASURES

of a community, so that each member was personally liable for the wrongs of the community.[14] The consolidation of states as the primary subjects of the emerging law of nations around the seventeenth century had a significant impact on the institution, for states began to centralise and regulate the power to issue letters of reprisal and, in time, became themselves the executors and the target of reprisals.

A fundamental change in the practice of reprisals occurred in the nineteenth century.[15] In addition to centralising the power to order reprisals, states now centralised the power to carry them out too. Reprisals had become public in character,[16] and quickly pervaded interstate relations during this century. Public reprisals are closer to today's countermeasures, so the review of the historical origins of this institution will begin in the nineteenth century. These remarks will be relatively brief, since the history of reprisals has been amply and ably charted in the literature and very little can be added here to this impressive body of work.[17] This overview will also be limited to peace-time reprisals. Even though peace-time

---

[14] Waldock, 'The Regulation of the Use of Force by Individual States in International Law' (1952) 81 *Recueil* 451, 458.

[15] For an overview, see Hindmarsh, 'Self-Help in Time of Peace' (1932) 26 AJIL 315, 319ff.

[16] Noting this development, see Woolsey, *Introduction to the Study of International Law* (1860), 264; Klüber, *Droit des gens moderne de l'Europe* (2nd edn, 1874), 329; Carnazza-Amari, *Trattato sul diritto internazionale pubblico di pace* (2nd edn, 1875), 887; Hall, *International Law* (1880), 312 (fn. 1); Calvo, *Dictionnaire de droit international public et privé* (1885) vol. 2, 162; Calvo, *Le droit international théorique et pratique* (4th edn, 1888) vol. 3, 519; Bry, *Précis élémentaire de droit international public* (1891), 380; Walker, *The Science of International Law* (1893), 156; Despagnet, *Cours de droit international public* (1894), 513; Bonfils, *Manuel de droit international public* (1894), 549; Pradier-Fodéré, *Traité de droit international: Européen et Américain* (1894) vol. 6, 481; Piédelièvre, *Précis de droit international public* (1895) vol. 2, 86; Westlake, *International Law* (1907) vol. 2, 9; Fauchille, *Traité de droit international public* (Paix) (8th edn, 1926) vol. 3, 692.

[17] See, among others, Del Vecchio and Casanova, *Le rappresaglie nei comuni medievali e specialmente in Firenze* (1894); Lafargue, *Les représailles en temps de paix* (1898); Ducrocq, *Représailles en temps de paix: Blocus pacifique suivi d'une étude sur les affaires de Chine (1900–1901)* (1901); Anzilotti, *Teoria*, ch. 1; Guarini, *Le rappresaglie in tempo di pace: storia e dottrina* (1910); Maccoby, 'Reprisals as a Measure of Redress Short of War' (1924–6) 2 CLJ 64; de la Brière, 'Evolution de la doctrine et de la pratique en matière de représailles' (1928) 22 *Recueil* 237; Haumant, *Les représailles* (1934); Colbert, *Retaliation in International Law* (1948); Venezia, 'La notion de représailles en droit international public' (1960) 64 RGDIP 465; de Guttry, *Le rappresaglie non comportanti la coercizione militari nel diritto internazionale* (1985), 5–13; Rinaudo, 'Rappresaglia (storia del diritto)' in Azara and Eula (eds), *Novissimo Digesto Italiano* (1986); Chavarot, 'La pratique des lettres de marque d'après les arrêts du parlement (XIIIe–début XVe siècle)' (1991) 149 *Bibliothèque de l'école des chartes* 51; Elagab, *Counter-Measures*, chaps 1–2; Darcy, 'The Evolution of the Law of Belligerent Reprisals' (2003) 175 *Mil L Rev* 184; Neff, *War and the Law of Nations* (2005), 225–39; Neff, *Justice among Nations* (2014), esp. 88–91, 162–3, 334–6, 345, 400.

and belligerent reprisals shared the same mechanisms, similar concerns and, often, the same requirements and conditions, the institution of belligerent reprisals will not be considered here.[18] Sections 6.2.1 and 6.2.2 outline the regulation of reprisals in the periods 1800–1919 and 1919–45 respectively, and Section 6.2.3 provides some interim conclusions.

### 6.2.1   1800–1919: Classic Age of Reprisals

The entitlement to take reprisals that the law of this period afforded to states was a very broad one: there were no limits in relation to the obligations that could be affected by way of reprisal, and no limits as to the means used which could include (and often actually involved) the use of armed force.[19] Throughout this period, states resorted to reprisals with much frequency. Indeed, reprisals were a prominent feature of the foreign relations of the period, often degenerating into the discredited practice of gunboat diplomacy for which statesmen like the British Prime Minister Lord Palmerston became known. Aptly, Charles de Visscher would later call this period the 'classic age of reprisals ... of all measures of so-called pacific coercion'.[20]

The variety of measures that states took by way of reprisal frequently eluded, if not directly defied, the very meaning of the term 'reprisal'.[21] Etymologically, the term originated in the French word *reprendre* which meant to retake.[22] This term referred to the practice of private reprisals of the previous century, when victims were authorised to seize property from the wrongdoer state or its subjects up to the amount of the damage suffered – they were, in a sense, retaking what was theirs. This practice continued with the public seizing of property, especially of ships

---

[18] On which see, generally, LeFur, *Des représailles en temps de guerre. Représailles et réparation* (1919).

[19] Note that according to some scholars reprisals should not affect the rights of private individuals: Fiore, *Il diritto internazionale codificato* (1890), 295; Bry, *Précis*, 381; Foignet, *Manuel élémentaire de droit international public* (1892), 238; Piédelièvre, *Précis*, 89; Mérignhac, *Traité de droit public international* (1912) vol. 3, 49–50. As the examples reviewed here show, on the whole, states did not respect this requirement.

[20] de Visscher, *Theory and Reality in Public International Law* (3rd edn, 1968), 296.

[21] Lawrence noted that the term 'reprisal' was used in a 'bewildering variety of senses': Lawrence, *The Principles of International Law* (4th edn, 1910), 334. On the terminological imprecision, see Darcy, 'Retaliation and Reprisal' in Weller (ed.), *The Oxford Handbook of the Use of Force in International Law* (2015), 879–83.

[22] Woolsey, *Introduction*, 264; Twiss, *The Law of Nations* (1861), 23; Bry, *Précis*, 380; Rivier, *Principes de droit des gens* (1896) vol. 2, 192–3. Though some noted it might be related to the Latin term 'reprimere' (to repress): Carnazza-Amari, *Trattato*, 880.

## 6.2 REPRISALS AND THE ORIGINS OF COUNTERMEASURES 231

(both public and private), by states in the nineteenth century.[23] But in time, reactions to wrongs were expanded to include a wide range of both actions and omissions, as described later, which did not involve any retaking, literal or figurative, of property.[24]

While frequent and with few limitations, reprisals could nevertheless not be resorted to arbitrarily. The practice of the period suggests that there existed certain minimum requirements and conditions for the taking of these measures. There was, however, no conventional or, in any other way, institutional statement of these conditions, which were instead summarised by scholars in their textbooks. These requirements were not always respected, and the institution, especially in its forcible variety, was the subject of repeated abuse. As many scholars argued at the turn of the twentieth century, reprisals, if they were to survive at all, required stricter and stronger regulation. A growing antipathy towards this institution can be perceived in their writings, an antipathy which was heightened during World War I, during which belligerents engaged in an indiscriminate use of reprisals, which played an important role in the interwar years' debates over, and eventual limitation of, the institution.

### 6.2.1.1 Positive and Negative Reprisals

The scholarly writings of this period tended to classify reprisals into two categories: positive, consisting in some act, and negative, consisting in abstentions.[25] While this was a descriptive classification only, with no practical import,[26] it nevertheless roughly traced the distinction between forcible and non-forcible means of reprisal – a distinction which acquired fundamental importance and normative significance in the interwar years. The distinction will be retained here for explanatory purposes.

---

[23] Note that the seizure was only temporary, until such time as the wrongdoer provided reparation: Davis, *The Elements of International Law* (4th edn, 1916), 264.
[24] As noted later, several scholars denied that omissions could be classified as 'reprisals', since they did not involve, strictly speaking, a retaking of property.
[25] See, e.g., Phillimore, *Commentaries upon International Law* (1857) vol. 3, 67; Halleck, *International Law* (1861), 297, 299; Klüber, *Droit de gens*, 2nd edn, 331 (note (c)); Carnazza-Amari, *Trattato*, 888; Fiore, *Nouveau droit international public* (2nd edn, 1885) vol. 2, 665; de Martens, *Traité de droit international* (1887) vol. 3, 160; Calvo, 3 *Droit international*, 520; Bonfils, *Manuel*, 545–6; Rivier, *Principes*, 192; Ducrocq, *Représailles*, 27–8; Oppenheim, *International Law* (1906) vol. 2, 39; Guarini, *Rappresaglie*, 121. The distinction is attributed to Klüber, see Twiss, *Law*, 29.
[26] On which see de Martens, 3 *Traité*, 160; Politis, 'Le régime des représailles en temps de paix. Rapport préliminaire et questionnaire' (1934) 38 *Annuaire IDI* 23, 25; Sánchez de Bustamante y Sirvén, *Droit international public* (1937) vol. 4, 105.

**Positive Reprisals** Positive reprisals consisted in actions taken by the injured state. Typically, positive reprisals involved the use of force against the target state, with measures ranging from the seizure of property (be it private or public), to pacific blockades,[27] to the temporary occupation of territory of the target state.

A classic example of nineteenth-century armed reprisals is the *Prince of Wales* incident between Britain and Brazil. The *Prince of Wales*, an English merchantman, had foundered off the coast of Rio Grande in Brazil in 1861; its passengers were probably murdered and the cargo plundered by locals. The United Kingdom requested the Brazilian authorities to investigate the incident and later presented a claim for indemnity on behalf of the owner of the ship and cargo.[28] While communications on the *Prince of Wales* were ongoing, in 1862, three British officials from the frigate *Forte* were arrested and questioned on Brazilian soil,[29] an action which the British found offensive and for which they demanded an apology.[30] Brazil refused to provide reparation and apologies for these two incidents,[31] leading the United Kingdom to adopt reprisals to enforce its claims.[32] A few days after the commencement of reprisals, which consisted in the seizure of private merchantmen, Brazil agreed to pay the requested compensation for the

---

[27] Pacific blockades were controversial for much of their existence and were frequently discussed in the literature. Among others, see Gessner, *Le droit des neutres sur mer* (1865), 215–23; Fauchille, *Du blocus maritime: étude de droit international et de droit comparé* (1882), 38–68; Hogan, *Pacific Blockade* (1908); Westlake, 'Pacific Blockade' (1909) 25 LQR 13; Falcke, *Le blocus pacifique* (1919); Washburn, 'The Legality of the Pacific Blockade – I' (1921) 21 *Col LR* 55; Washburn, 'The Legality of the Pacific Blockade – II' (1921) 21 *Col LR* 227; Washburn, 'The Legality of the Pacific Blockade – III' (1922) 21 *Col LR* 442. The IDI also worked on this topic, and adopted a Declaration in 1887, on which see Perels, 'Droit de blocus en temps de paix' (1887–8) 9 *Annuaire IDI* 275.

[28] Mr Christie, British Minister in Rio de Janeiro, to Senhor Taques, Ministry of Foreign Affairs, 17 March 1862, Brazil. *Correspondence respecting the plunder of the wreck of the British barque 'Prince of Wales', on the coast of Brazil, in June 1861; and respecting the ill-treatment of three officers of Her Majesty's ship 'Forte' by the Brazilian police, in June 1862, Command Papers; Accounts and Papers* (1863), at 27–8 (hereinafter '*Correspondence*').

[29] See exchange of letters between Christie and various Brazilian officials in the Ministry for Foreign Affairs: *Correspondence*, 51ff, esp. Nos 45 and 49 (with enclosures).

[30] See the two letters from Christie to the Marquis of Abrantes, Brazilian Minister of Foreign Affairs, 5 December 1862: *Correspondence*, 109–11 (no. 70, enclosures 1 and 2).

[31] The Marquis of Abrantes to Christie, 29 December 1862, *Correspondence*, 118 (no. 72, enclosure 1).

[32] Christie to the Marquis of Abrantes, 30 December 1862, *Correspondence*, 129 (no. 72, enclosure 4), esp. 132.

*Prince of Wales* and agreed to submit the demands in relation to the *Forte* to arbitration.[33]

The *Don Pacifico* incident between the United Kingdom and Greece is another, more controversial example.[34] Pacifico was a Gibraltar-born British national, whose residence in Athens was attacked by a mob during a revolt in 1847. After unsuccessful attempts to obtain compensation from Greece, Pacifico turned to the British government. The United Kingdom made exorbitant demands on his behalf and, when Greece refused to comply, it resorted to reprisals. A British navy squadron blockaded the Bay of Salamis and the Port of Piraeus and seized Greek public and commercial property, until Greece agreed to the British requests. The measures caused consternation within the British Parliament and all over Europe due to their excessive character, even leading France, at one point, to recall its ambassador from London.[35]

Despite their armed nature, forcible reprisals were an institution of the law of peace, often termed, by the English language literature, 'measures short of war'.[36] Conceptually, however, the precise boundary between armed reprisals and war was not clear. Scholars used a range of criteria to distinguish between the two, including whether there was a *justa causa* (necessary for reprisals, but not for war), the effects of hostilities on treaties (suspended or terminated by war, but not by reprisals), and the effects on third parties (who had rights and duties of neutrality in war, but not in situations of reprisal). Towards the end of the century, two different approaches to this question were developed: an objective theory of war, pursuant to which war existed whenever there were sustained armed hostilities between two parties, and a subjective theory, pursuant to which war existed only when there was an *animus belligerandi*.[37] The objective theory tended to collapse reprisals into war, whereas the subjective theory maintained, conceptually at least, the distinction between war and reprisals. In practice, however, the line between war and reprisals was often entirely illusory.[38] This was especially the case when the rights of third

---

[33] See the note from the Brazilian Government of 5 January 1863, BFSP LIV, 790, quoted in de Lapradelle and Politis, *Recueil des arbitrages internationaux* (1905) vol. 2, 237.

[34] On the facts, see Whitten, 'The Don Pacifico Affair' (1986) 48 *Historian* 255. For a legal analysis, see de Lapradelle and Politis, *Recueil des arbitrages internationaux* (1905) vol. 1, 580–9.

[35] On the protests, see Carnazza-Amari, *Trattato*, 891–2; Calvo, 3 *Droit international*, 525–6; Whitten, 'Don Pacifico', 259–67; Grewe, *The Epochs of International Law* (2000), 526–7.

[36] Neff, *War*, 215.

[37] Ibid., 230–6.

[38] de Guttry, *Rappresaglie*, 9; Neff, *War*, 230–6.

states were affected by the measures. The blockade of Venezuelan ports in 1902 by a coalition of European creditor nations, a wide-ranging measure which affected Venezuelan trade with third states, is a fitting illustration of this fuzzy line. Despite insistence by the blockading powers that the measure was peaceful, the United States (an affected third state) asserted that it was an act of war and, in time, even one of the blockading powers (Britain) recognised as much.[39] Scholars indeed regarded it as war;[40] it had been, as T. J. Lawrence said, 'undoubtedly a war, though a little one.'[41]

**Negative Reprisals** In addition to positive measures, states could also employ 'negative reprisals'. The non-payment of debts,[42] withholding of performance of obligations[43] and, on occasion, the unilateral termination of treaties,[44] were often cited as examples of negative reprisals.[45] For several scholars, omissions such as these were difficult to subsume under the term 'reprisal' since they hardly involved the retaking of property.[46] Without refusing to recognise the practice, they simply thought that it was better described by the term 'retaliation'.[47] A review of the practice of the period, including the examples below, shows that the terminology employed in this regard was far from unanimous. The use of the terms 'retaliation' and 'retorsion' to refer to non-forcible measures involving the

---

[39] See Neff, *War*, 233.
[40] Holland, 'War *Sub Modo*' (1903) 19 *LQR* 133; Penfield, 'The Anglo-German Intervention in Venezuela' (1903) 177 *North American Rev* 86; Basdevant, 'L'action coercitive anglo-germano-italienne contre le Venezuela (1902–1903)' (1904) 11 RGDIP 373; Westlake, *International Law* (2nd edn, 1913) vol. 2, 15–16.
[41] Lawrence, *Principles*, 4th edn, 342.
[42] Phillimore, *Commentaries, vol. 3*, 67; Klüber, *Droit de gens*, 2nd edn, 331 (n(c)); Fiore, *Diritto internazionale*, 295; Rivier, *Principes*, 192; Oppenheim, 2 *International Law*, 39.
[43] Wheaton, *Elements of International Law* (Carey, 1836), 210; Phillimore, 3 *Commentaries*, 67; Halleck, *International Law*, 299; Heffter, *Le droit international de l'Europe* (2nd edn, 1866), 210; Bluntschli, *Le droit international codifié* (2nd edn, 1874), 282; Carnazza-Amari, *Trattato*, 888; Hall, *International Law*, 308; Fiore, 2 *Nouveau droit*, 667; de Martens, 3 *Traité*, 160; Calvo, 3 *Droit international*, 520; Foignet, *Manuel*, 238; Despagnet, *Cours*, 513–14; Rivier, *Principes*, 192; Oppenheim, 2 *International Law*, 39; Guarini, *Rappresaglie*, 123; Mérignhac, 3 *Traité*, 51.
[44] Bluntschli, *Droit international*, 282; Calvo, 2 *Dictionnaire*, 161; Bry, *Précis*, 380; Pradier-Fodéré, 6 *Traité*, 462; Piédelièvre, *Précis*, 86–7; Ducrocq, *Représailles*, 28; Guarini, *Rappresaglie*, 123; Mérignhac, 3 *Traité*, 51.
[45] These categories were not conceptually defined, and any given instance of 'negative' reprisal could fall into one or the other category. For example, the non-payment of debts could be, at once, also a failure to perform a conventional obligation whenever the debt was agreed upon by treaty.
[46] Twiss, *Law*, 29–30; Westlake, 2 *International Law*, 6; Pradier-Fodéré, 6 *Traité*, 463.
[47] This suggestion was not strictly accurate, since withholding the payment of debts, for example, was a means of seizing property.

## 6.2 REPRISALS AND THE ORIGINS OF COUNTERMEASURES 235

non-performance of the target state's rights was by no means generalised, and in many instances the term reprisal was used.[48]

A common negative reprisal was the withholding of payments of debts to the wrongdoing state or its nationals. One example of such measures occurred in 1807, during the Napoleonic wars, when the British seized the ships and property of Denmark, a nation with which they were at peace.[49] Denmark considered the seizure to be unlawful and, while still at peace with Britain, issued an ordinance for the sequestration of debts owed by Danish to British subjects and their payment into the Danish treasury.[50] A similar measure was adopted by the United States against China in 1855, when US subjects had suffered damage as a result of ill-treatment by Chinese authorities. Faced with a Chinese refusal to provide reparation for the damage, the United States proceeded to withhold payment of debts to China up to the amount of the damages claimed.[51]

States also withheld (or at least, threatened to do so) the performance of conventional obligations towards the wrongdoer state as a means of reprisal. Thus, during the war of the Fifth Coalition, Napoleon reminded the Swedish Crown (then a neutral state) that if it failed to comply with the Treaty of 24 February 1810,[52] France would consider itself released from fulfilment of the obligations under that treaty. '[S]i vous manquez à vos engagements, je me croirai dégagé des miens', wrote Napoleon.[53] Non-performance of treaty obligations was also intimated by China as a reaction to US legislation prohibiting Chinese immigration,[54] contrary to the 1880 Immigration Treaty.[55] China claimed that the legislation was in breach of the 1880 Treaty,[56] and asserted that as a result it was released

---

[48] Darcy, 'Retaliation', 879–83.
[49] The incident is discussed further in Chapter 8, Section 8.2.2.1.
[50] On which see Wheaton, *Elements of International Law* (8th edn, updated by R. H. Dana, 1866), 391.
[51] Wharton, *A Digest of the International Law of the United States* (2nd edn, 1887) vol. 2, 576, citing Mr Marcy, Secretary of State, to Mr Parker, 5 October 1855, MSS Inst China.
[52] This agreement was a complement to the Treaty of Peace between Russia and Sweden, signed at Friedrichshamn, 17 September 1809, 60 CTS 457, see de Martens, *Nouvelles causes célèbres du droit des gens* (1843) vol. 2, 417.
[53] Letter from Napoleon to the Crown Prince of Sweden, 8 March 1811, in de Martens, 2 *Nouvelles causes*, 418.
[54] Act to execute certain treaty stipulations relating to Chinese immigration of 6 May 1882 (Chinese Exclusion Act), 22 Stat 58; Act of 1 October 1888 (Scott Act), 25 Stat 504; Act of 13 September 1888, 25 Stat 476.
[55] US–China Immigration Treaty (signed in Peking, 17 November 1880), 1 Malloy 237.
[56] See, e.g., Letters from the Tsung-li-yamen to Mr Denby (head of the US legation to China) of 16 June 1890 and 17 June 1890, in (1889) FRUS 188, at 189 and 190 respectively; Letter

236                              COUNTERMEASURES

from 'the observance of all its treaties with the United States'.[57] China's right to resort to 'retaliation' against the United States was recognised by the Chairman of the US Senate Committee on Foreign Relations.[58]

Threats of non-performance of treaty obligations could also seamlessly turn into threats of unilateral termination of the relevant treaty. An example of this is the reaction of Germany towards Switzerland in the Wohlgemuth affair of 1889. The incident concerned the imprisonment and expulsion of a German secret police agent, Mr Wohlgemuth, from Switzerland.[59] Germany complained of the treatment given to its national, which was in contravention to a Swiss–German Treaty of 1876, and demanded an indemnity. It further threatened the adoption of measures of control at the border between the two states,[60] which would 'certainly affect' the rights of Switzerland under the Treaty.[61] Germany further noted that, as a result of the breach, it was entitled to terminate the 1876 Treaty unilaterally[62] and, after the Swiss failed to comply with its demands,[63] proceeded to do so.[64] Finally, Germany also accused Switzerland of allowing anti-German revolutionary activities in its territory in breach of its obligations under a Neutrality Treaty and warned that if Switzerland failed to comply with its neutral duties, then Germany would withhold performance of Switzerland's rights under that same treaty.[65]

---

from Tsui (Chinese ambassador) to Mr Blaine (US Secretary of State), 26 March 1890, in (1889) FRUS 211.

[57] Letter of 8 July 1889 from Chinese Ambassador to American Secretary of State, in FRUS 1889, 132.

[58] (1889) FRUS 135 [3].

[59] The facts of this incident are recounted in (1889) 30 *Archives diplomatiques (2ème sér)* 369–74; 'Chronique: Affaires Wohlgemuth et Lutz' (1889) 16 *Journal de droit international privé*, 418–22; Stowell and Munro, *International cases, arbitrations and incidents illustrative of international law as practiced by independent States* (1916) vol. 1, 137–49.

[60] The measures are referred to in the Interpellation of the Swiss National Council of 21 June 1889, in (1889) 31 *Archives diplomatiques (2ème sér)* 334.

[61] 'Les mesures à prendre à cet effet toucheront certainement aux clauses du traité d'établissement sur l'article 2 duquel le Gouvernement helvétique a une opinion différente de la nôtre', in Letter from the German Chancellor to the German Minister in Berne, 28 June 1889, 31 *Archives diplomatiques (2ème sér)* 336.

[62] Letter of 28 June 1889 (1889) 31 *Archives diplomatiques (2ème sér)* 338.

[63] Interpellation of the Swiss National Council, in (1889) 31 *Archives diplomatiques (2ème sér)* 334 (on the 'unjustified' nature of Germany's retaliatory measures); Letter from Mr Droz, 13 July 1889, ibid., 340 (contesting, on the facts, the German claim of unilateral termination due to breach).

[64] (1889) 31 *Archives diplomatiques (2ème sér)* 341.

[65] Letter from German Chancellor to German Minister in Berne of 5 June 1889, (1889) 31 *Archives diplomatiques (2ème sér)* 335.

### 6.2.1.2 What Limits on the Right to Reprisals?

Despite the longevity and frequency of the practice of reprisals, there were many uncertainties about the institution. First, the law regarding the taking of reprisals was vague. Save for two exceptions, there was no conventional or otherwise institutional statement of the conditions of, or limits on, the recourse to reprisals. The exceptions related to incidental, though no less significant for this reason, aspects of the institution. These were the Declaration on Pacific Blockades of the Institut de Droit International (IDI), adopted in 1887, which had clarified that pacific blockades ought not to affect the rights of third parties,[66] and the Drago-Porter Convention of 1907, set in motion by a letter of protest of the Argentine Minister Luis María Drago after the Venezuelan blockade of 1902,[67] which outlawed the use of force for the collection of debts.[68] In the literature, scholars often included a list of conditions for the lawful taking of reprisals, many of which seem to have had some support in the practice of states.[69] Thus, reprisals could only be taken after the commission of a wrongful act, be it a denial of justice or an infringement of the rights of states; they must be proportionate;[70] and, finally, some element of *sommation* seems to have been necessary.[71] But given the incidence and significance of the practice, the absence of clear regulation was unsatisfactory and it led Lawrence to maintain, in 1915, that there was a clear need for 'international legislation on the subject of reprisals'.[72]

Second, while the institution was often justified due to its aptitude to prevent war – on the basis that it would allow the resolution of the dispute

---

[66] IDI, Déclaration concernant le blocus en dehors de l'état de guerre, (1887–8) 9 *Annuaire IDI* 300.

[67] Letter by Drago, Minister of Foreign Relations of the Argentine Republic, to García Mérou, Minister of the Argentine Republic to the United States (29 December 1902), (1907) 1 AJIL Supp. 1. Drago subsequently developed his argument in: Drago, *Cobro coercitivo de deudas públicas* (1906).

[68] Convention on the Limitation of Employment of Force for Recovery of Contract Debts (The Hague, adopted 18 October 1907, in force 26 January 1910), 205 CTS 250. On this development, see Williams, 'Le droit international et les obligations financières internationales qui naissent d'un contrat' (1923) 1 *Recueil* 289, 326–36.

[69] Generally, Bluntschli, *Droit international*, 284–5; Carnazza-Amari, *Trattato*, 889–90; Calvo, 2 *Dictionnaire*, 161–2; Despagnet, *Cours*, 514; Piédelièvre, *Précis*, 88–9; Oppenheim, 2 *International Law*, 35, 39–41.

[70] This requirement is endorsed by the protests against the British measures in *Don Pacifico*.

[71] In the various instances of practice reviewed here, the states resorting to reprisal first made demands for reparation from wrongdoing states.

[72] Lawrence, *The Principles of International Law* (6th edn, 1915), 344. The call first appeared in 1910, in the 4th edition of the work: Lawrence, *Principles*, 344.

before states felt compelled to turn to war, as the means of last resort[73] – at the turn of the twentieth century scholars began to question its legality, legitimacy and effectiveness. Scholars argued that reprisals were incompatible with the state of peace; that they were nothing more than a tool of oppression of the powerful against the weak; and that reprisals were rarely effective and, even worse, that they frequently escalated disputes thus leading to, rather than away from, war[74] – all concerns that, as will be seen later, continue to be voiced in contemporary international law in relation to the institution of countermeasures. The dangers inherent in the institution came into sight, catastrophically, during World War I, when belligerents time and again invoked reprisals to commit violations of the laws of war against their enemies, leading enemies to adopt counter-reprisals and violate the laws of war in return. These successive and circular invocations of reprisals eventually spiralled into lawlessness.[75] The lesson from the World War was certainly not limited to belligerent reprisals, and in the interwar period many efforts were made to limit, as much as possible, the analogous institution of the law of peace.

### 6.2.2  1919–1945: Period of Transition

As a reaction to the horrors of the war, institutional cooperation among states significantly increased in the interwar period. Among others, the years after World War I witnessed the proliferation of institutional means of dispute settlement.[76] Developments which had begun in 1899 at the Hague Peace Conferences[77] finally crystallised in this period when the ad hoc mechanisms for dispute settlement of the previous century were replaced by permanent institutions, such as the League of Nations and the Permanent Court of International Justice, and mandatory procedures, such as those established in the 1928 General Act of Geneva.[78] Moreover,

---

[73] See, e.g., Carnazza-Amari, *Trattato*, 880; Hall, *International Law*, 311; Mérignhac, 3 *Traité*, 53.

[74] See, e.g., Creasy, *First Platform of International Law* (1876), 401; Funck-Brentano and Sorel, *Précis de droit des gens* (1877), 229; de Martens, 3 *Traité*, 161; Piédelièvre, *Précis*, 90; Ducrocq, *Représailles*, 50; Despagnet, *Cours de droit international public* (3rd edn, 1905), 595–6.

[75] See Hull, A *Scrap of Paper: Breaking and Making International Law during the Great War* (2014), ch. 9.

[76] On this development, see Crawford, 'Continuity and Discontinuity in International Dispute Settlement: An Inaugural Lecture' (2010) 1 JIDS 3 and references therein.

[77] On which see Scott, *The Hague Peace Conferences of 1899 and 1907* (1909), vol. 1.

[78] General Act of Arbitration (Pacific Settlement of International Disputes) (signed 26 September 1928, in force 16 August 1929), 93 LNTS 343. On the historical significance of

for the first time in international law, states established (procedural) limits on war in the Covenant of the League of Nations[79] and, subsequently, prohibited recourse to war as 'an instrument of national policy' through the Kellogg-Briand Pact of 1929.[80] This was a 'new international law',[81] characterised by wider and stronger international cooperation and commitment to peace, and one that represented, according to Arrigo Cavaglieri, a 'period of transition from unilateral means of coercion'.[82]

On the subject of reprisals, two main questions occupied international lawyers during this period: the limitation of reprisals, in particular of armed reprisals, and the elaboration of a regime of reprisals. The next two sections will discuss these developments by reference to forcible and non-forcible reprisals, respectively.

### 6.2.2.1 Outlawing Forcible Reprisals

The strengthening of institutional means of dispute settlement during this period was accompanied by the adoption of rules limiting recourse to war – until then the 'litigation of nations'[83] – in international relations. In the years between 1919 and 1945, war was first limited by the procedural requirements of the Covenant of the League and, subsequently, prohibited in the Kellogg-Briand Pact. The impact of these developments on the legality of armed reprisals was uncertain, and was rendered especially difficult by the terminology employed in these instruments. Both the Covenant and the Pact limited or outlawed 'war', a term which was evocative of the legal institution of war, perfected in the previous century. Reprisals, even in their forcible variety, had traditionally been an institution of the law of peace. So did the limitation or prohibition of 'war' include armed reprisals as well?

The question came sharply to the fore shortly after the establishment of the League, in the Corfu incident between Italy and Greece.[84]

---

the Act, see Borel, 'L'Acte Général de Genève' (1929) 27 *Recueil* 497; Brierly, 'The General Act of Geneva, 1928' (1930) 11 BYIL 119.

[79] Articles 11–15, Covenant of the League of Nations (1919), 13 AJIL Supp. 361.
[80] General Treaty for the Renunciation of War as an Instrument of National Policy (Kellogg-Briand Pact), (1928), 94 LNTS 57.
[81] Kunz, 'The Law of Nations, Static and Dynamic' (1933) 27 AJIL 630, 635.
[82] Cavaglieri, *Corso di diritto internazionale* (1934), 447.
[83] Phillimore, 3 *Commentaries*, 59. Elaborating on the theme of war as the litigation of States, see, generally, Whitman, *The Verdict of Battle: The Law of Victory and the Making of Modern War* (2012).
[84] For a summary of the facts of the incident, see Strupp, 'L'incident de Janina entre la Grèce et l'Italie' (1924) 31 RGDIP 255.

In 1923 the Italian General Tellini and members of his staff, who were part of a delimitation commission between Greece and Albania, were murdered in Janina, Greece. In response, Italy made extensive demands for reparation, which Greece refused to comply with.[85] Its demands unheeded, the Italian government ordered its navy to bomb and occupy Corfu.[86] Greece immediately brought the incident to the attention of the Council of the League. Before the Council, the characterisation of the Italian occupation in Corfu became crucial, for depending on whether it was seen as war or as a 'measure short of war' determined which Articles of the Covenant would be relevant to the incident.[87] The parties' arguments on this issue were representative of the two main theories of war (objective and subjective) mentioned earlier. According to Greece, Italy's conduct constituted an act of war, since the existence of war depended on the nature of the act (objective theory of war).[88] For Italy, instead, its act did not constitute war since its government had clarified that it had no intention of going to war with Greece (subjective theory of war).[89] The implications of these two approaches for the legality of reprisals were clear. The objective view of war engulfed armed reprisals as well, insofar as 'war' depended on the armed nature of an act. Any limitation (or prohibition) on war, then, constituted a limitation (or prohibition) on armed reprisals. The subjective view, instead, maintained a clear division between war and armed reprisals, since the former required the existence of an *animus belligerandi*, at least from one of the parties involved.[90] Absent the intention, armed action including

---

[85] The similarity of Italy's demands to the Habsburg ultimatum to Serbia after the assassination of the Archduke did not go unnoticed: Wright, 'Review: *The Corfu Incident of 1923: Mussolini and the League of Nations* by James Barros' (1966) 60 AJIL 870, 871.

[86] Letter dated 4 September 1923 from M. Salandra to the Secretary-General of the League, submitted to the Council on 5 September 1923, (1923) 4 LNOJ 1414.

[87] Greece brought the issue to the attention of the League under art. 12, as a situation 'likely to lead to a rupture'; though during the discussion, the question was raised whether Italy's actions might not be 'acts of war' between League members, which had been resorted to without following the procedures established in the Covenant and, therefore, subject to sanctions from the Council.

[88] Nicolas Politis (Greece), Council of the League, Sixth Meeting – 1 September 1923, (1923) 4(11) LNOJ 1276, 1277; Ninth Meeting – 5 September 1923, (1923) 4(11) LNOJ 1287, 1289.

[89] Antonio Salandra (Italy), Council of the League, Sixth Meeting – 1 September 1923, (1923) 4(11) LNOJ 1276, 1278.

[90] According to McNair, 'it takes two to make a quarrel, but it is not so the case that it takes two to make a war': 'The Legal Meaning of War, and the Relation of War to Reprisals' (1926) 11 *Transactions Grot Soc* 29, 33.

## 6.2 REPRISALS AND THE ORIGINS OF COUNTERMEASURES 241

armed reprisals would fall under the category of 'measures short of war', which were not prohibited. The dispute was eventually resolved by the Conference of Ambassadors in Paris, which found that Greece was in breach of its obligation to adequately investigate the murder.[91]

The question of the legal characterisation of Italy's measure, which was of wider interest to the League and its members, nevertheless remained open. The Council, mindful of the need to prevent any similar disputes in the future, resolved to ask a Committee of Jurists whether 'measures of coercion … not meant to constitute war' were consistent with the Covenant. The Committee's response was sibylline: these measures, it said, 'may or may not' be consistent with the Covenant.[92] The Committee's reply was the subject of much scrutiny by states[93] and commentators,[94] though no agreement on its meaning could be reached. Indeed, a decade later, the IDI could not provide any further clarity on the point. The Institute's 1934 Regime of Peace-Time Reprisals stated in Article 4 that reprisals were prohibited in the same conditions as recourse to war.[95] But neither the Regime nor its commentary explained whether 'war' was to be understood objectively or subjectively. The IDI, after noting the deep disagreements between proponents of these two theories, simply gave up its effort of resolving the issue.[96] Article 4 was, as a result, no less vague

---

[91] The Conference set up a Commission of inquiry to investigate whether Greece had acted with the required diligence in its investigations of the murder. The Conference eventually held that Greece had acted negligently, and ordered it to provide reparations to Italy. However, it has subsequently emerged that Mussolini arm-wrestled the Conference of Ambassadors to suppress the Commission's report which had in fact found, by three votes to one, that Greece had acted with the required diligence in investigating the murder. See generally Barros, *The Corfu Incident of 1923: Mussolini and the League of Nations* (1965).

[92] Special Committee of Jurists, 'Report: Interpretation of Certain Articles of the Covenant and Other Questions of International Law' (1924) 5 LNOJ 523.

[93] For the reactions of states to the Report, see Société des Nations, Réponses du Comité spécial de juristes visé par la Résolution du Conseil du 28 septembre 1923, Observations des gouvernements des Etats membres de la Société, 22 mars 1926.

[94] E.g., Lowell, 'The Council of the League of Nations and Corfu' (1923) 6 *World Peace Foundation Pamphlet Series* 169; Hudson, 'How the League of Nations Met the Corfu Crisis' (1923) 6 *World Peace Foundation Pamphlet Series* 176; Guani, 'Les mesures de coercition entre membres du Pacte de la Société des Nations envisagées spécialement au point de vue Américain' (1924) 31 RGDIP 285; Hill, 'The Janina-Corfu Affair' (1924) 18 AJIL 98; Politis, 'Les répresailles entre Etats membres de la Société des Nations' (1924) 31 RGDIP 5; Strupp, 'Janina'; Wright, 'Opinion of Jurists on the Janina-Courfou Affair' (1924) 18 AJIL 536.

[95] Article 4, IDI, Résolution du 19 octobre 1934 – Régime des représailles en temps de paix (1934) 38 *Annuaire IDI* 708.

[96] Politis, 'Rapport et avant-projet de résolution et de Règlement suivi des Observations des Membres de la Commission' (1934) 38 *Annuaire IDI* 54, 77.

than the Committee's response had been. Armed reprisals were in a legal limbo, a limbo which the evidence shows was readily exploited by many states.[97]

The question was, at any rate, destined to become moot. By the beginning of World War II, the combination of the treaty-based restrictions on, and prohibition of, war and the growing practice of states, which both asserted a prohibition of force and protested other states' uses of force, eventually crystallised into a general ban on force under customary international law.[98] With the exception of self-defence, all other uses of force permitted until then became prohibited. Insofar as the prohibition related to the use of force itself, it also extended to all other institutions which had, in the past, involved force as their medium. This included, of course, armed reprisals. But note that it was not reprisals themselves that had been prohibited – it was only the use of force as the medium of reprisals. Non-forcible reprisals, as will be seen, remained possible.

#### 6.2.2.2   Regulating Non-Forcible Reprisals

Non-forcible reprisals continued to be permitted throughout the period and were often used (or at least endorsed) in practice. Examples include the French confiscation of the property of German companies in Alsace, in response to Germany's delays in the payment of its war debt in 1922;[99] an opinion of a Swiss minister about the imposition of reciprocal taxes on foreigners whose governments had imposed inequitable taxes on Swiss subjects as a reprisal in 1928;[100] and the responses of states to the Questionnaire of the Preparatory Committee of the 1930 Hague Codification Conference. Australia, Belgium, Czechoslovakia, Finland, Great Britain, Hungary, India, Italy, Japan, New Zealand, Netherlands, Switzerland and South Africa, all confirmed in their responses that reprisals were permissible under international law and that they constituted a situation in which the state 'can disclaim responsibility'.[101] No discussion

---

[97] For examples, see Neff, *War*, 301–3.
[98] On which see Brownlie, *International Law and the Use of Force by States* (1963), ch. 5, esp. 107–11.
[99] *Annual Register*, 1922, 165–6, cited by Elagab, *Counter-Measures*, 29.
[100] *Répertoire suisse de droit international public*, 1914–1939 (1975), vol. 3, 1785–96, cited by Elagab, *Counter-Measures*, 29–30.
[101] League of Nations, Bases of Discussion for the Conference Drawn up by the Preparatory Committee – Responsibility of States for Damage Caused in Their Territory to the Person and Property of Foreigners, 15 May 1929, C.75.M.69.1929.V.3, 128–30.

## 6.2 REPRISALS AND THE ORIGINS OF COUNTERMEASURES 243

on this matter took place at the Hague Codification Conference which, as is well known, failed to complete its work on responsibility.[102]

As to their regulation, it was keenly felt throughout the period that reprisals should have specific and stringent requirements and conditions. The *Naulilaa* award (albeit concerning armed reprisals) was the first institutional articulation of a regime regulating the institution.[103] The Tribunal held that the lawful taking of reprisals must comply with the following requirements: a prior wrongful act, an unsuccessful demand for reparation, proportionality, and be adopted for the purpose of obtaining reparation and a return to legality. Moreover, said the Tribunal, reprisals were limited by the 'experiences of humanity' and the principle of good faith applicable in the relations between states.[104] These requirements were subsequently incorporated into the IDI's Regime of 1934,[105] which contemporary scholars have described as a 'good summation of nineteenth-century practice' on the subject.[106]

The other issue which preoccupied statesmen and scholars throughout this period was that of the relation between reprisals and institutional means of dispute settlement – an issue which has yet to be satisfactorily resolved. This relation was central to the parties' arguments in the PCIJ's case concerning the *Railway Traffic between Lithuania and Poland*,[107] a dispute arising out of the Polish occupation of Vilnius in 1920.[108] During the occupation, the railway sector Landwarów-Kaisiadorys, which connected Vilnius to ports in the Baltic sea, had been destroyed. Poland, who had strong economic interest in the running of the line, contended that Lithuania was under an obligation to reestablish the sectors of the line located within its territory.[109] Lithuania denied that it was obliged to repair

---

[102] On which see, e.g., Borchard, 'Responsibility of States at the Hague Codification Conference' (1930) 24 AJIL 517; Hackworth, 'Responsibility of States for Damage Caused in Their Territory to the Person or Property of Aliens' (1930) 24 AJIL 500.

[103] The incident occurred before Portugal entered the war, so the case was not, strictly speaking, one concerning belligerent reprisals.

[104] *Responsabilité de l'Allemagne à raison des dommages causés dans les colonies portugaises du sud de l'Afrique (sentence sur le principe de la responsabilité) (Portugal c Allemagne)* (1928) 2 RIAA 1011 (*Naulilaa* award), 1026. On the facts leading to the case, and the historical context, see Zollmann, 'L'affaire *Naulilaa* entre le Portugal et l'Allemagne, 1914–1933. Réflexions sur l'histoire politique d'une sentence arbitrale internationale' (2013) 15 *J Hist IL* 201.

[105] Article 6, IDI, Régime des représailles en temps de paix.

[106] Neff, *War*, 229.

[107] *Railway Traffic between Lithuania and Poland* (1931) PCIJ Series A/B No 42, 108.

[108] For a summary of the relevant events, see Brockelbank, 'The Vilna Dispute' (1926) 20 AJIL 583.

[109] *Railway Traffic*, 113–14.

the railway and argued that, in any event, it was justified in withholding the reparation as a 'negative' or 'pacific' reprisal against Poland's continued occupation of its territory.[110] Poland replied that Lithuania's resort to reprisals was unlawful since it had not previously exhausted the dispute settlement procedures of the League's Covenant,[111] a position contradicted by Lithuania.[112] Eventually, the PCIJ did not need to resolve this question since it found that Lithuania had no obligation to repair the railway sector;[113] reprisals were thus unnecessary to ground the legality of Lithuania's conduct.

The relation between reprisals and dispute settlement was also central to the IDI's work on reprisals during the 1930s. Rapporteur Nicolas Politis,[114] who had been the Greek representative in the Council during the Corfu affair, submitted progressive and ambitious proposals to the Institute, including strict conditions for recourse to unilateral measures when dispute settlement institutions were available. But the Resolution adopted by the Institut did not go as far. Article 5 of the Regime set limits on the adoption of reprisals only where there existed specific (treaty-based) obligations of dispute settlement which provided for judicial or arbitral bodies with mandatory jurisdiction, including the power to issue provisional and conservatory measures.[115]

### 6.2.3   Interim Conclusions

The institution of reprisals underwent fundamental changes in the two periods under review. From their private origins, reprisals had become public and, as such, an important feature of interstate relations. Moreover, from their initial narrow scope of retaking of property, the concept had expanded beyond the etymological origins of their label: it encompassed a wide range of measures, consisting in actions and omissions, aimed at obtaining redress for wrongs done. This expansion gave

---

[110] Memorial of Lithuania, *Railway Traffic between Lithuania and Poland* (1931) PCIJ Series C No 54, 130, 208; oral statement of Lithuania, 17th public sitting, 17 September 1931, *Railway Traffic between Lithuania and Poland* (1931) PCIJ Series C No 54, 316 (Annex 2), 342, 348.

[111] Second Memorial of Poland, *Railway Traffic between Lithuania and Poland* (1931) PCIJ Series C No 54, 264, 280–8.

[112] Oral statement of Lithuania, 17 September 1931, *Railway Traffic*, 343–8.

[113] *Railway Traffic*, 122.

[114] Politis urged the IDI to go beyond the letter of the law and to 's'inspirer de leur esprit ainsi que de la tendance générale du droit moderne': Politis, 'Rapport préliminaire', 34.

[115] Article 5, IDI, Régime des représailles en temps de paix.

## 6.2 REPRISALS AND THE ORIGINS OF COUNTERMEASURES 245

rise to doubts as to the meaning and scope of the institution, as evidenced by the fact that in 1923, when discussing the Corfu incident, members of the League's Council could not agree on the meaning of the term 'reprisal' and, in their query to the Committee of Jurists, opted to use instead the vaguer expression 'measures of coercion not meant to constitute war'.[116]

These doubts were in time overcome arguably due, at least in some measure, to the clear and precise definition of the institution given in 1928 by the Tribunal in *Naulilaa*. As explained by the *Naulilaa* award, reprisals consist in:

> an act of self-help on the part of the injured States, responding after an unsatisfied demand to an act contrary to international law on the part of the offending State... [Reprisals] would be illegal if a previous act contrary to international law had not furnished the reason for them. They aim to impose on the offending State reparation for the offense or the return to legality in avoidance of new offenses.[117]

The award, all the while providing for limits and conditions, endorsed a broad conception of reprisals, not restricted to the 'retaking' of property. The definition was subsequently endorsed by the IDI's Resolution of 1934, whose Regime also spelled out in some more detail the legal regulation of the institution. Despite some variation on the details of the regulation between *Naulilaa* and the IDI's Regime, the definitions provided by both these bodies enclosed the three fundamental aspects of the law and practice of reprisals of the time: their consisting in the non-performance of the law (their so-called 'intrinsic illegality', in an expression current today),[118] their role in the enforcement of international law and their exceptional justification, each of which will be considered next.

---

[116] Council of the League, Sixteenth Meeting – 22 September 1923, LNOJ 1320–30. The French representative (Hanotaux) stated, for example, that 'there are several ways of interpreting the expression "right of reprisal" and [he] cannot admit its insertion in a document without knowing precisely what is meant by that expression', at 1323.

[117] *Naulilaa*, 1026. A similar definition can be found in the IDI's 1934 Resolution: art. 1, Régime des représailles, (1934) 38 *Annuaire IDI* 708: 'Les représailles sont des mesures de contrainte, dérogatoires aux règles ordinaires du droit des gens, décidées et prises par un Etat, à la suite des actes illicites commis à son préjudice par un autre Etat, et ayant pour but d'imposer à celui-ci, par pression exercée au moyen d'un dommage, le retour à la légalité.'

[118] Alland, 'The Definition of Countermeasures' in Crawford et al. (eds), *The Law of International Responsibility* (2010), 1131.

### 6.2.3.1 Reprisals as the Non-Performance of the Law

The scholarship and practice of the period overwhelmingly accepted that reprisals entailed the taking of actions involving the non-performance of the rights of the target state.[119] This held true both for forcible and non-forcible reprisals.

In respect of forcible reprisals, the *Forte* incident between the United Kingdom and Brazil noted earlier is illustrative. The incident was submitted by the parties to arbitration and the sole arbitrator, King Leopold of Belgium, held that the conduct of the Brazilian authorities was not an 'offense' against Britain.[120] Following the award, the British government formally expressed 'regrets' for the taking of reprisals against Brazil.[121] This formal expression of regret can be seen as an implicit recognition of the impairment of Brazil's rights by the measures, for there would have been nothing to regret had the United Kingdom acted in accordance with its obligations towards Brazil. Perhaps more clearly, the illegality of the measure of reprisal can be seen in the *Don Pacifico* affair, in which the disproportionate British reprisals against Greece were the subject of reprobation by the House of Lords and of protest by European powers. Finally, in the *Naulilaa* award, the Tribunal held Germany's forcible reprisals against Portugal to be unlawful.[122]

Some contemporary scholarship has nevertheless questioned that in the period prior to 1919 (at least) forcible reprisals consisted in acts that impaired rights of the target state. Since international law at the time did not contain a prohibition of force, it is said, forcible reprisals were of necessity lawful. This is the conclusion that can be derived from Roberto Barsotti's view that: 'at the time when resort to war was unconditionally permitted, the need to define and distinguish between the single measures short of war was not felt, since their lawfulness was never in doubt.'[123] Barsotti is certainly right that there existed, at the time, no prohibition of force. He is

---

[119] In the scholarship, see, e.g., Foignet, *Manuel*, 236; Bonfils, *Manuel*, 545; Despagnet, *Cours*, 513; Oppenheim, 2 *International Law*, 34; Dupuis, 'Règles générales du droit de la paix' (1930) 32 *Recueil* 1, 275; Bourquin, 'Règles générales du droit de la paix' (1931) 35 *Recueil* 1, 220. See also art. 2 of the 1934 Régime de représailles by the IDI.

[120] The award (as well as the parties' memorials) can be found at Ortolan, *Règles internationales et diplomatie de la mer* (4th edn, Plon, 1864) vol. 1, 431–45 (award at 444).

[121] de Lapradelle and Politis, 2 *Recueil*, 242.

[122] *Naulilaa*, 1028.

[123] Barsotti, 'Armed Reprisals' in Cassese (ed.), *The Current Regulation of the Use of Force* (1986), 84. Expressing similar views, see Arangio-Ruiz, Fourth Report on State Responsibility, ILC Yearbook 1992, vol. II(1), 8 [7]; Cassese, *International Law* (2nd edn, 2005), 300.

also probably right that, for this reason, the difference between a reprisal and, say, action in self-defence (also a measure short of war) had only limited legal implications. However, it is an overstatement to say that the lawfulness of the measures 'was never in doubt'. The examples above show how the legality of forcible measures of reprisal was not a given. Indeed, even if the international law of the time did not prohibit force, it did recognise other rights which were potentially impaired by armed reprisals, including the (fundamental) rights to equality and independence. At the very least reprisals entailed the non-performance of these rights of the target state and therefore could, absent justification, constitute violations thereof.[124]

Non-forcible reprisals, too, were acts which entailed the non-performance of rights of the target state. Thus, in the *Wohlgemuth* affair, Germany threatened to adopt measures which 'affected' the rights of Swiss nationals under the 1876 Treaty. In the US–China immigration dispute of the 1880s, China too threatened measures against American nationals contrary to the 1880 Immigration Treaty. Finally, in the *Railway Traffic* case the PCIJ considered that the Lithuanian argument of reprisal would be relevant only if it could be demonstrated that Lithuania was under an obligation to repair the railway.

It was precisely their character as illegal measures that set reprisals apart from all other means of pressure at the disposal of states for the enforcement of international law,[125] such as retorsions and (on some meanings of this term) retaliation.[126]

### 6.2.3.2 Function of Reprisals: Enforcement of International Law

Despite the first attempts at institutionalisation in the interwar years, the international legal order of the period was still highly decentralised. It followed from this decentralisation that its enforcement too was decentralised and, as such, it rested with each member of the community. Therefore, thought some scholars, the institution of reprisals followed from the international legal order as a matter of logical necessity.[127] This

---

[124] See, for example, the observations by Creasy, *First Platform*, 402.
[125] See, e.g., Holtzendorff, *Eléments de droit international public* (1891), 159; Davis, *Elements*, 263–4; De Louter, *Le droit international public positif* (1920) vol. 2, 197, 200.
[126] The leading work on this institution at the time was Rapisardi-Mirabelli, *La ritorsione* (1919).
[127] See, e.g., Carnazza-Amari, *Trattato*, 879; Cavaglieri, 'Règles générales du droit de la paix' (1929) 26 *Recueil* 311, 567; Verdross, 'Règles générales du droit de la paix' (1929) 30 *Recueil* 271, 481; Bourquin, 'Règles générales', 221–2; Hindmarsh, *Force in Peace. Force*

kind of deductive reasoning seemed less aimed at the recognition of the institution – which was amply supported by states – but at its rationalisation. Reprisals were permissible because they provided states with the means to enforce their rights against law-breakers. To be sure, the enforcement of international law could be achieved through a variety of means ranging from 'intangible moral influences to positive measures of coercion.'[128] The Tribunal in *North Atlantic Fisheries* confirmed this much when it said that:

> every State has to execute the obligations incurred by Treaty *bona fide*, and is urged thereto by the ordinary sanctions of International law in regard to observance of Treaty obligations. Such sanctions are, for instance, appeal to public opinion, publication of correspondence, censure by Parliamentary vote, demand for arbitration with the odium attendant on a refusal to arbitrate, rupture of relations, reprisal, etc.[129]

Only reprisals, however, involved a non-performance of obligations as a means of enforcement against another violation of the law. And it was for this reason that their tight regulation was of the utmost importance.

The regulation of reprisals required a clear understanding of what the 'enforcement' of international law meant. As a means to an end, the typology and limits of reprisals were conditioned, if not determined, by the notion of enforcement. Were reprisals backward-looking only, or should they be forward-looking; were they only about compensation, about the restoration of legality, or about punishment and repression? There is evidence that states resorted to reprisals for a variety of different purposes: to obtain redress for injuries suffered,[130] to repress and punish the violator,[131] and, even, for the forward-looking objective of forcing a state to change its behaviour for the future.[132] The literature was equally divided as to the function of reprisals in international law. Thus, for some scholars, reprisals were exclusively punitive in character.[133] For Lassa Oppenheim, reprisals

---

*Short of War in International Relations* (1933, reprinted 1973), 12, 86–8; Cavaglieri, *Corso*, 448; Politis, 'Rapport préliminaire', 26.

[128] Hindmarsh, *Force in Peace*, 5.
[129] *North Atlantic Coast Fisheries Case (Great Britain/US)* (1910) 11 RIAA 167, 186 (emphasis in original).
[130] E.g., some of the examples discussed in Sections 6.2.1 and 6.2.2.
[131] See, e.g., the examples cited by Picchio Forlati, *La sanzione nel diritto internazionale* (1974), 64; Neff, *War*, 229.
[132] Neff, *War*, 226.
[133] E.g., Foignet, *Manuel*, 236; Piédelièvre, *Précis*, 85. The punitive function of reprisals was central to Hans Kelsen's theory of international law, as will be discussed in Sections 6.3

## 6.2 REPRISALS AND THE ORIGINS OF COUNTERMEASURES

were 'exceptionally permitted for the purpose of compelling the [wrongdoing State] to consent to a satisfactory settlement of a difference created by its own international delinquency',[134] a widely shared view among scholars.[135] Others went further, and found the purpose of reprisals was the 're-establishment of the disturbed legal order'.[136] Some still adopted an eclectic understanding of the function of reprisals: for Albert Hindmarsh, for instance, reprisals could serve both remedial and deterrent aims.[137]

No clear picture emerges from the review of both practice and doctrine throughout the period. Doctrinally at least, the answer to this question was often affected by scholars' conception of international law, and of law more generally, and by their understanding of the consequences of the violations of international law. Some of these views, such as those of Hans Kelsen and Roberto Ago, will be discussed in more detail throughout the chapter, since they affected the way in which the ILC began its consideration of the notion of countermeasures during its work on responsibility. It is important to highlight, however, that from very early on the institution of reprisals was closely linked to the institution of responsibility insofar as it was a means to enforce against violations of international law, regardless of what enforcement may have entailed (be it punishment or reparations, or both). And yet, as will be seen shortly, the role of reprisals in the law of responsibility, and therefore their place in the ARS, was questioned by several states during the ILC's codification process.

### 6.2.3.3 Reprisals as Lawful Measures

Because of their role in the enforcement of international law reprisals were lawful acts, despite taking the form of the non-performance of an obligation owed to the target state. States' replies to the questionnaire for the 1930 Hague Codification Conference showed that they deemed reprisals to be lawful and, as such, to constitute a circumstance in which the state could 'disclaim responsibility'. As a matter of positive law, it cannot be doubted that states considered reprisals to be lawful acts. In

---

and 6.4. Roberto Ago endorsed Kelsen's conception of reprisals, see Ago, 'Le délit international' (1939) 68 *Recueil* 415, 428–30, 524–31, 536–7.

[134] Oppenheim, 2 *International Law*, 34.
[135] Wheaton, *Elements*, 209; Phillimore, 3 *Commentaries*, 64; Halleck, *International Law*, 297; Twiss, *Law*, 20, 28; Heffter, *Droit international*, 209; Sandonà, *Trattato di diritto internazionale moderno* (1870), 242; Klüber, *Droit de gens*, 2nd edn, 329; Hall, *International Law*, 309, 311; Holland, *The Elements of Jurisprudence* (3rd edn, 1886), 328; Pradier-Fodéré, 6 *Traité*, 455, 460; Rivier, *Principes*, 191.
[136] Bourquin, 'Règles générales', 223.
[137] Hindmarsh, *Force in Peace*, 58.

the literature, other than Cavaglieri, who raised the possibility (without endorsing it) that reprisals may be 'objectively wrongful' yet their author excused,[138] on the whole scholars viewed reprisals as conduct permitted by international law.

### 6.3 Countermeasures in Contemporary International Law

Non-forcible reprisals, renamed 'countermeasures' during this period,[139] have remained a constant feature of international life. Despite optimistic expectations from the United Nations' collective security and judicial systems[140] – not dissimilar to the hopes expressed in the early 1920s about the League of Nations – the international legal system is still a decentralised one. The 'domestic analogy', which many had hoped for, has not been fulfilled,[141] and international law has remained, in the labels used time and again in this regard, in a 'primitive' or 'archaic' stage.[142] In this state of affairs, countermeasures must remain available to states which would, otherwise, have no generally available means for the enforcement of their rights in international law.

The core development on the subject in the years since 1945 is the codification of a regime of countermeasures and its systematisation within the law of responsibility.[143] The codification process did not alter the three fundamental features of reprisals developed up to 1945: the so-called

---

[138] Cavaglieri, 'Règles', 575.
[139] Commentary to Chapter II of Part Three, [3]. According to Malanczuk, the notion of countermeasures 'covers the traditional area of reprisals as a reaction against an international offence': Malanczuk, 'Countermeasures and Self-Defence as Circumstances Precluding Wrongfulness in the ILC Draft Articles on State Responsibility' (1983) 43 ZaöRV 705, 719.
[140] See, e.g., the pleadings of Albania in the *Corfu Channel* case: Albania, Duplique, 20 September 1948, (1950) ICJ Pleadings, vol. II, 373 [153–4]. See also the oral statement of 12 November 1948, (1950) ICJ Pleadings, vol. III, 295: 'self-redress is only a part of primitive law and has been displaced, at any rate in most cases, by collective action through the United Nations Organization'.
[141] On which see Koskenniemi, 'Solidarity Measures: State Responsibility as a New International Order?' (2002) 72 BYIL 337.
[142] See, e.g., Economides, 2600th meeting, ILC Yearbook 1999, vol. I, 242 [48]; Pellet, 2646th meeting, ILC Yearbook 2000, vol. I, 272 [52]; Dugard, 2648th meeting, ILC Yearbook 2000, vol. I, 283 [1]; Rosenstock, 2667th meeting, ILC Yearbook 2001, vol. I, 17 [53].
[143] Alland, 'International Responsibility and Sanctions: Self-Defence and Countermeasures in the ILC Codification of Rules Governing International Responsibility' in Simma and Spinedi (eds), *United Nations Codification of State Responsibility* (Oceana, 1987), 144 (noting that countermeasures were not traditionally dealt with in the context of responsibility).

'intrinsic illegality' of the countermeasure (that is, their consisting in the non-performance of an obligation owed to the target state), their (legal) justification, and their role in the enforcement of international law. It did, however, finally fulfil Lawrence's wish for more legislation on the subject by providing a detailed articulation of the requirements and conditions for the taking of countermeasures. The codification of this regime was not an easy task. For many, countermeasures were one of the most controversial aspects of the Commission's codification of responsibility,[144] causing serious disagreements both within the Commission and among states in the GA's Sixth Committee. The Commission had to walk a tight line between opposing concerns: the perceived need for (unilateral) self-help remedies in a decentralised system and the limitation of abuses inherent in unilateralism.[145] States disagreed as to the desirability of codifying a regime of countermeasures; according to some, codification would serve to contain the institution, but for others, it would 'counterintuitively'[146] legitimise it. With the support of the majority of states, the Commission chose to include a regime of countermeasures in the ARS, as this was perceived to be the most constructive way of balancing the interests of injured states, by allowing the unilateral enforcement of their rights, and those of weaker states of protection against abuse. The regime eventually adopted in the ARS, a combination of codification and progressive development, contains adequate 'checks and balances'[147] that provide for stringent conditions for the taking of countermeasures while allowing some degree of flexibility.[148]

The Commission's work also clarified the double function that countermeasures play in the law of responsibility. It was generally agreed in the Commission and the Sixth Committee that countermeasures act as a justification. Somewhat more troublesome was, instead, the choice as to countermeasures' primary function in international law. Special Rapporteur Ago's proposals envisaged a punitive (or partly punitive) role for countermeasures, as evidenced in his terminological choices: he referred to countermeasures as (Kelsenian) sanctions. But during the work of the ILC, this view changed fundamentally: countermeasures were not a substantive

---

[144] See, e.g., ILC Report, forty-third session, 127 [311].
[145] See, e.g., the summary of the Commission's debate on Arangio-Ruiz's third and fourth reports: ILC Report, forty-fourth session, ILC Yearbook 1992, vol. II(2), 19–21.
[146] Bederman, 'Counterintuiting Countermeasures' (2002) 96 AJIL 817.
[147] As the Bahraini representative put it: A/C.6/47/SR.26, [18].
[148] Simma and Tams, 'Reacting Against Treaty Breaches' in Hollis (ed.), *The Oxford Guide to Treaties* (2012), 595–604; Crawford, *State Responsibility: The General Part* (2013), 684–6.

consequence of the wrongful act, in the same way as reparations were a consequence of the wrongful act, but only an instrument to induce the wrongdoing state to perform its obligations of cessation and reparation. To reflect this dual function, the ARS deal with countermeasures in two different Parts: in Part One, on the internationally wrongful act, and in Part Three, on the implementation of state responsibility. In the context of Part One, a provision appears in Chapter V among the 'circumstances precluding wrongfulness', Article 22 quoted in the introduction to this chapter, which embodies the principle that measures adopted by way of countermeasure are lawful. In the context of Part Three, the ARS establish a regime of countermeasures including both substantive and procedural conditions.

This section's analysis of countermeasures in contemporary international law will focus on the Commission's work of codification. As already advanced, the choice of focus on the ILC's work is warranted for three interrelated reasons. First, due to its importance in the development and consolidation of this institution; indeed, today, no claim of countermeasures occurs without a reference to the ARS and the Commission's work. Second, because the Commission's work elicited a high volume of responses and comments from states, providing a good sample of, at the very least, their *opinio juris*. Over a period of over twenty years,[149] at least one hundred states expressed their views (individually or collectively) in the Sixth Committee or in written observations to the ILC. Finally, because of its comprehensiveness, since most of the views on countermeasures discussed in the literature were voiced, at some point or another during the decades-long work on the topic, by Commission members and states.

### 6.3.1  The Dual Role of Countermeasures in the Law of Responsibility

Countermeasures have a double role in the law of state responsibility: as a justification *and* as a means for the implementation of state responsibility. The role of countermeasures as a justification was never seriously in doubt during the ILC's codification, despite some occasional appeals for the exclusion of the relevant provision from the project. Somewhat more controversial, however, was the function of countermeasures. Initially conceptualised as one of the legal relations arising from the wrongful act taking the form of a sanction against the wrongdoing state,

---

[149] Between the years 1979, the date of Ago's report on countermeasures, and 2001, the date of Crawford's last report to the Commission.

countermeasures were subsequently recast in instrumental terms, as a means for implementing responsibility. These two functions, and their development in the ILC, are reviewed in this section. Following the order of the ARS, this analysis addresses first the incidental function (Article 22) and then the primary function (Articles 49–54) of countermeasures.

### 6.3.1.1 Incidental Function: A Circumstance Precluding Wrongfulness

In the midst of all the difficulties encountered by the ILC in the codification of countermeasures, one principle was never in doubt: countermeasures entail behaviour not in conformity with what is required by an obligation of the state taking them, but they are nevertheless lawful. As put by Finland:

> Although resort to countermeasures was a matter of extreme delicacy ... [t]here had been no serious disagreement about the principle embodied in article 22 precluding the wrongfulness of an act that would otherwise constitute a breach, if taken as a lawful countermeasure.[150]

This principle has been accepted by states in their practice,[151] and has been endorsed in international case-law both before and after the adoption of the ARS.[152] An overwhelming majority of states also expressly or

---

[150] A/C.6/56/SR.11, [28] (speaking on behalf of Nordic countries).
[151] For a review of practice, see Ago, Eighth Report on State Responsibility, ILC Yearbook 1979, vol. II(1), 41–6. See further the instances of practice examined by de Guttry, *Rappresaglie*, ch. 2, 173; Elagab, *Counter-Measures*, ch. 2; Sicilianos, *Réactions*, 245–90; Focarelli, *Le contromisure nel diritto internazionale* (1994), ch. 1. On the basis of their review of state practice, all these authors conclude that countermeasures justify the non-performance of the rights of the target state.
[152] See *Air Service Agreement*, [80–1]; *United States Diplomatic and Consular Staff in Tehran (USA v Iran)* (1980) ICJ Rep 3, [53]; *Military and Paramilitary Activities in and Against Nicaragua (Nicaragua v USA)* (1986) ICJ Rep 14, [201]; *Gabčíkovo-Nagymaros Project (Hungary/Slovakia)* (1997) ICJ Rep 7, [82]. Investor–state arbitral tribunals too have endorsed it: *Archer Daniels Midland Company and Tate & Lyle Ingredients Americas, Inc v Mexico*, ICSID Case No ARB/(AF)/04/5, Award, 21 November 2007, [121]; *Corn Products International, Inc v Mexico*, ICSID AF Case ARB/(AF)/04/1, Decision on Responsibility, 15 January 2008, [145]; *Cargill, Inc v Mexico*, ICSID Case ARB/(AF)/05/2, Award, 18 September 2009, [381–2]. The NAFTA Tribunals dealt with countermeasures in three disputes between US investors and Mexico. While the approach to the availability of the defence of countermeasures as against investors varied, none of the three tribunals denied, as a matter of principle, that countermeasures were accepted in international law. For an analysis of these cases, see Paparinskis, 'Investment Arbitration and the Law of Countermeasures' (2008) 79 BYIL 264; Parlett, 'The Application of the Rules on Countermeasures in Investment Claims' in Chinkin and Baetens (eds), *Sovereignty, Statehood and State Responsibility: Essays in Honour of James Crawford* (2015), 389.

implicitly supported Article 22 (and its predecessor draft Article 30) in the Sixth Committee.[153] Only Korea,[154] Sri Lanka[155] and Uruguay[156] objected to it in principle; and France argued that countermeasures (like all of the other defences) did not preclude wrongfulness, but were rather excuses.[157] Aside from these few objections, Article 22 rests on solid and historically well-established foundations.

While the principle was unassailable, there were differences of opinion about the analytical explanation of countermeasures' operation as a justification. The various Special Rapporteurs who addressed countermeasures offered at least two different explanations of the manner in which countermeasures precluded the wrongfulness of conduct incompatible with an obligation of the state. Ago had initially espoused the view that countermeasures suspended the 'operation' of the obligation owed to the target state. As a result, since the obligation no longer bound the injured state, the countermeasure could not constitute a breach thereof. As he explained:

> The lawfulness of the act of the State, although conflicting with the terms of an international obligation, lies in the fact that the circumstance found to exist in the particular situation as an exception cancels out that obligation. There is no wrongfulness because in the case in point the obligation is not operative, and consequently there is no breach of the obligation.[158]

---

[153] Expressly endorsing the principle, see Algeria: A/C.6/55/SR.18, [3]; Croatia: A/C.6/55/SR.16: [72]; China: A/C.6/56/SR.11, [62]; Finland (on behalf of the Nordic countries): A/C.6/56/SR.11, [28]; Italy: A/C.6/51/SR.36, [4]; A/C.6/54/SR.24, [25]; Netherlands: A/C.6/54/SR.21, [47]; Slovakia: A/C.6/54/SR.22, [53]; Slovenia: A/C.6/55/SR.18, [21]; Spain: A/C.6/54/SR.21, [20]; United Kingdom: A/C.6/55/SR.14, [33] and A/CN.4/488, 154; United States: A/CN.4/488, 154; Venezuela: A/C.6/56/SR.15, [37]. Brazil had initially objected to the classification of countermeasures as a justification, but subsequently accepted it. Contrast its views in 1979 and then in 2001: A/C.6/34/SR.45, 6–7; A/C.6/56/SR.16, [2]. In turn, Mexico objected to the inclusion of countermeasures in the draft, though it accepted that, if included, they should constitute a justification: A/C.6/51/SR.40, [67].

[154] A/C.6/54/SR.25, [90] ('if an act of an injured State was legitimate under international law the question of its wrongfulness clearly did not arise. There was therefore no justification for retaining': art. 22).

[155] A/C.6/47/SR.27, [2] (art. 30 was 'based on relatively scant jurisprudential material'); A/C.6/49/SR.27, [3].

[156] A/C.6/49/SR.27, [21] (countermeasures 'were wrongful acts in themselves and ... their lawfulness was not obviated by the fact that they were a response to a previous wrongful act'); A/C.6/50/SR.21, [22].

[157] A/C.6/56/SR.11, [70].

[158] Ago, Eighth Report, [84].

On this view, there would have been no difference between countermeasures and the suspension of treaties due to material breach; an elision which would have rendered nugatory the careful procedural guarantees established in the VCLT for the suspension of treaties,[159] thereby eroding the principle *pacta sunt servanda*.

Ago's explanation of the effect of countermeasures was later revised by Special Rapporteurs Riphagen and Arangio-Ruiz, who considered that countermeasures only entitled the state not to comply with the obligation in question: the obligation remained in force, though compliance with it was suspended temporarily.[160] Crawford re-asserted this view in much more explicit terms. He described defences as 'shields' and not 'swords', for defences could prevent a finding of wrongfulness of conduct otherwise contrary to an obligation but they could not strike down the obligation itself.[161] As applied to countermeasures, this meant that countermeasures could only affect the performance of the obligation for as long as the situation lasted,[162] but they could not affect the status of the obligation as such. For this reason, they could not be relied upon to suspend or terminate treaty obligations; non-performance of treaty obligations, on the one hand, and suspension/termination of the treaty itself, both responses to treaty breaches which in the past were covered under the institution of reprisals, had now been separated. This is the view currently upheld by the ARS[163] and endorsed by the ICJ.[164]

#### 6.3.1.2 Primary Function: Implementation of State Responsibility

Countermeasures also have another function in the law of state responsibility: they are a mechanism for the implementation of responsibility, namely the obligations of cessation (if the wrongful act is continuing) and reparation.[165] As Special Rapporteur Crawford remarked in his Second

---

[159] Arts 65–68, Vienna Convention on the Law of Treaties (VCLT) (adopted 23 May 1969, in force 27 January 1980), (1969) 1155 UNTS 331.

[160] See draft art. 9(1) proposed by Riphagen, Sixth Report on the Content, Forms and Degrees of International Responsibility, ILC Yearbook 1985, vol. II(1), 11, pursuant to which 'the injured State is entitled, by way of reprisal, to suspend the performance of its obligations' to the wrongdoing state; and draft art. 11: Arangio-Ruiz, Fourth Report, 22 (the injured state is 'entitled ... not to comply with one or more of its obligations towards' the wrongdoer).

[161] Crawford, Second Report on State Responsibility, ILC Yearbook 1999, vol. II(1), [226].

[162] Crawford, Third Report on State Responsibility, ILC Yearbook 2000, vol. II(1), 86–7.

[163] Commentary to Chapter V of Part I, [2–4]; ARS art. 22 Commentary, [4]; Commentary to Chapter II of Part Three, [4].

[164] *Gabčíkovo-Nagymaros*, 38–9.

[165] ARS art. 49(1).

Report, this instrumental function was the 'main purpose' of countermeasures, their role as a 'circumstance precluding wrongfulness' being solely an 'incidental effect'.[166] Nevertheless, the Commission began its consideration of the topic under a different assumption, that countermeasures constituted a sanction for wrongfulness.

**First Reading: Countermeasures as Sanction**  Special Rapporteur Ago introduced reprisals (as he referred to them) into the project on state responsibility in his Third Report of 1971. Here, in the context of explaining the concepts of the 'internationally wrongful act' and of 'responsibility' in international law, Ago classified reprisals as one of the legal relations arising from the occurrence of a wrongful act. Reprisals, therefore, belonged to the content of responsibility. For Ago 'in any system of law, a wrongful act may give rise, not to a single type of legal relationship, but to a dual form of relationship, each form being characterized by the different legal situations of the subject involved.'[167] These legal relations amounted

> either to giving the subject of international law whose rights have been infringed by the wrongful act the subjective right to claim reparation … from the author of the act or to giving that subject, or possibly a third subject, the faculty to impose a sanction on the subject which has engaged in wrongful conduct.[168]

The wrongful act, in this view, generated two consequences for the injured state: the right to reparation and the faculty to apply a sanction. According to Ago, the sanction, of a repressive or punitive character,[169] was concretised in the notion of reprisals.[170] Reprisals therefore constituted 'responsibility' proper, in the sense that they constituted one of the legal relations arising from the wrongful act. This conceptualisation meant that, aside from a brief mention of the 'incidental effect' of preclusion of wrongfulness in Part One of the ARS, the bulk of the regulation of reprisals would

---

[166] Crawford, Second Report, [393].
[167] Ago, Third Report on State Responsibility, ILC Yearbook 1971, vol. II(1), [36].
[168] Ago, Third Report, [36].
[169] See id.; Ago, Eighth Report, [79]; Ago, Eighth Report on State Responsibility – Add.5–7, ILC Yearbook 1980, vol. II(1), [90]. This view, as noted in Section 6.2, was not uncommon in the literature.
[170] For a discussion of the various meanings of the term 'sanction' and the term as used by Ago and the Commission (in the sense of punishment), see Alland, 'Responsibility and Sanctions', 171–6.

be contained in Part Two, which was concerned with the 'content, forms and degrees of responsibility'.[171]

Ago's conception of reprisals-as-sanctions drew, primarily, from the work of Hans Kelsen.[172] For Kelsen, as is well known, the essential characteristic of law was its being a coercive order.[173] As he explained in the *Pure Theory*:

> the consequence attached in the [hypothetical legal norm] to a certain condition is the coercive act of the state – comprising punishment and the civil or administrative use of coercion – whereby only the conditioning material fact is qualified as an unlawful act, and only the conditioned material fact is qualified as the consequence of the unlawful act.[174]

The 'hypothetical legal norm' thus states that 'under certain conditions (among which the delict plays an important role) a certain consequence (a coercive measure, called the sanction) shall ensue.'[175] Like domestic law – Kelsen's archetypal law – international law responded to these characteristics: it was a coercive order, in which reprisals constituted the sanctions for breach.[176] Indeed, in Kelsen's view, the institution of reprisals provided the proof that international law was 'law properly so called', to use John Austin's expression, insofar as it evidenced its coercive character.[177]

Kelsen's understanding of reprisals-as-sanctions will be discussed again later, as it was accompanied by a theoretical explanation of the legality of the otherwise unlawful act adopted in reaction to a previous wrong. For now, what is significant is the influence that Kelsen's theory had on Ago's own conceptualisation of the place of reprisals in the law of responsibility. Ago accepted Kelsen's view that reprisals are linked to the wrongful act by an 'ought' proposition: namely, that the wrongful act generated, as a consequence, a sanction in the form of a reprisal. But Ago disagreed with Kelsen's characterisation of reparation as a subsidiary (and surrogate) obligation to the obligation breached, and thus as different from

---

[171] Ago, Eighth Report, [83].
[172] Ago, Third Report, [35–6]. See also, in his scholarly work: Ago, 'Délit', 527–31.
[173] See Kelsen, *Introduction to the Problems of Legal Theory: A Translation of the First Edition of the Reine Rechtslehre or Pure Theory of Law* (1997), 26 (sec. 12); Kelsen, 'Théorie du droit international public' (1953) 84 *Recueil* 1, 14.
[174] Kelsen, *Introduction*, 26 (sec. 12).
[175] Kelsen, *Law and Peace in International Relations – The Oliver Wendell Holmes Lectures 1940–1941* (reprinted in 1997), 22.
[176] See, generally, Kelsen, 'Théorie', 32–4; Kelsen, *Law and Peace*, 29–31.
[177] See von Bernstorff, *The Public International Law Theory of Hans Kelsen – Believing in Universal Law* (2010), 87–90.

the sanction.[178] For Ago, both reparation and reprisals constituted legal relations arising from the internationally wrongful act.[179] The difference between reprisals and reparation, as he explained in his Third Report, was the purpose of each of these consequences: reparations had a remedial function as they were aimed at the elimination of the injury caused by the wrongful act, whereas reprisals had a punitive one as they were aimed at 'impos[ing] a penalty' on the wrongdoing state.[180] By his Eighth Report of 1979, however, this categorical view had been softened, as Ago accepted that 'legitimate sanctions' may serve both remedial and punitive purposes.[181] Be that as it may, Ago's conception of reprisals tended to see them as ends in themselves.

The subsequent Special Rapporteurs, Riphagen and Arangio-Ruiz, followed the structure of the responsibility project as it had been envisioned by Ago. They thus continued to deal with countermeasures (as they had by then been renamed) in the context of Part Two of the draft. They, however, moved away from Ago's conception of countermeasures as punitive.[182] These Special Rapporteurs had initially allowed for the possibility that punitive countermeasures be available, if at all, only in respect of state crimes,[183] though this possibility did not materialise and the provisions on countermeasures in response to international crimes were not cast (explicitly, at least) as punitive or repressive in character.[184] In respect of every other breach of international law, countermeasures served to ensure cessation and reparation.[185] Countermeasures were, in Arangio-Ruiz's words, an 'instrumental'[186] consequence of the wrongful act: a means to an end, and not an end in themselves.

---

[178] Kelsen, 'Théorie', 31–2; Kelsen, *Law and Peace*, 32. Kelsen described this as a 'secondary' norm, in that it was a rule directed at the subjects of the legal system and not at its 'organs'. The sanction only was a 'primary' or 'genuine' norm, since it was directed at the organs of the state in charge of enforcing the law. See Kelsen, *General Theory of Law and State* (1945), 61.

[179] Ago, Third Report, [36]. See also Ago, 'Délit', 529.

[180] Ago, Third Report, [36]. This duality of consequences, remedial and punitive, matched Ago's acceptance of both delictual and criminal responsibility of states, a possibility which he introduced in the ARS in the form of the infamous draft art. 19.

[181] Ago, Eighth Report, [79].

[182] Barboza, 'Contramedidas', 22.

[183] E.g., Riphagen, Fourth Report on the Content, Forms and Degrees of International Responsibility, ILC Yearbook 1983, vol. II(1), [58]; Arangio-Ruiz, Fourth Report, 6–7. The proposal was supported by some members of the Commission: ILC Report, forty-fourth session, 24 [155].

[184] Crawford, First Report on State Responsibility, ILC Yearbook 1998, vol. II(1), [51].

[185] Arangio-Ruiz, Fourth Report, [3].

[186] See, Arangio-Ruiz, Third Report on State Responsibility, ILC Yearbook 1991 vol. II(1), [1].

**Second Reading: Instrumental Countermeasures** Many states in the Sixth Committee, commenting during the first reading of the ARS, were critical of the provisions on countermeasures – and for a number of reasons, including the (material) inequality of states which meant that they could be abused by the powerful against the weak,[187] the fact that countermeasures did not belong properly in the law of responsibility,[188] and the inherent risk of abuse.[189] Many were also critical of the conception of countermeasures-as-sanctions, provisionally included in the ARS. An overwhelming majority of states either objected to the punitive aim of countermeasures,[190] or endorsed their role for the purposes of achieving cessation and reparation only.[191] Other states took issue, specifically, with the first-reading Commission's approach to cast countermeasures as a consequence of wrongfulness, as part of the 'content' of international responsibility. For example, Colombia questioned whether countermeasures were a legal consequence of the wrongful act,[192] and Brazil and Mexico both considered that the draft should be limited to the consequences of cessation and reparation and exclude countermeasures.[193] For these three

---

[187] E.g., Brazil: A/C.6/51/SR.34, [64]; Indonesia: A/C.6/47/SR.28, [65]; Mexico: A/C.6/50/SR.21, [61] and A/C.6/51/SR.40, [67]; Morocco: A/C.6/51/SR.36, [38].

[188] Especially France: A/C.6/47/SR.26, [5], A/C.6/48/SR.23, [15] and A/C.6/51/SR.36, [23]; Greece: A/C.6/47/SR.24, [67]; Indonesia: A/C.6/47/SR.28, [65].

[189] E.g., Cameroon: A/C.6/50/SR.24, [2].

[190] Bahrain: A/C.6/47/SR.26, [18]; Belarus: A/C.6/47/SR.27, [81] and A/C.6/56/SR.12, [9]; Brazil: A/C.6/55/SR.18, [65]; Bulgaria: A/C.6/48/SR.26, [41] and A/C.6/49/SR.26, [62]; Chile: A/C.6/47/SR.24, [43]; Cyprus: A/C.6/47/SR.21, [89], A/C.6/54/SR.26, [81], A/C.6/55/SR.18, [32], and A/C.6/56/SR.13, [56]; Egypt: A/C.6/51/SR.39, [70]; France: A/C.6/47/SR.26, [9]; India: A/C.6/47/SR.25, [74] and A/C.6/55/SR.15, [29]; Indonesia: A/C.6/48/SR.22, [81] and A/C.6/51/SR.38, [29]; Iraq: A/C.6/55/SR/16, [36]; Israel: A/C.6/47/SR.27, [21]; Italy: A/C.6/51/SR.36, [5]; Mali: A/C.6/56/SR.13, [26]; Norway (on behalf of Nordic countries): A/C.6/47/SR.25, [34]; Romania: A/C.6/47/SR.29, [24]; Russian Federation: A/C.6/47/SR.28, 23 [105]; Sierra Leone: A/C.6/55/SR.16, [51]; Slovenia: A/C.6/47/SR.26, [36]; Switzerland: A/C.6/47/SR.25, [94]; Thailand: A/C.6/48/SR.28, [86]; Uruguay: A/C.6/47/SR.27, [12]; Venezuela: A/C.6/50/SR.20, [3] and A/C.6/56/SR.15, [37].

[191] Argentina: A/C.6/56/SR.15, [53]; Australia: A/C.6/48/SR.26, [24]; China: A/C.6/47/SR.25, [24]; Costa Rica: A/C.6/55/SR.17, [64]; Croatia: A/C.6/55/SR.16, [72]; Czechoslovakia (as it then was): A/C.6/47/SR.25, [44]; German Democratic Republic (as it then was): A/CN.4/351 and Add.1–3, 18; Iran: A/C.6/47/SR.25, [62]; Japan: A/C.6/47/SR.26, [31]; Kuwait: A/C.6/55/SR.18, [58]; New Zealand: A/C.6/56/SR.11, [54]; Pakistan: A/C.6/47/SR.29, [62]; Poland: A/C.6/47/SR.28, [78]; Slovakia: A/C.6/54/SR.22, [53] and A/C.6/55/SR.16, [66]; South Africa (on behalf of South African Development Community): A/C.6/55/SR.14, [24]; Sri Lanka: A/C.6/49/SR.27, [3]; Turkey: A/C.6/48/SR.28, [99]; United Kingdom: A/C.6/55/SR.14, [33].

[192] A/C.6/56/SR.16, [40] (countermeasures 'were not a logical, automatic consequence of State responsibility and therefore had no place in the law on the responsibility of States').

[193] Brazil: A/C.6/56/SR.16, [2]; Mexico: A/C.6/51/SR.40, [67] and A/C.6/55/SR.20, [37].

states, the Commission ought to leave countermeasures out of the draft. China,[194] the Czech Republic,[195] Russia,[196] Switzerland[197] and Ukraine,[198] also criticised this approach of the Commission's though they remained favourable to the inclusion of countermeasures in the draft. For this latter group of states, countermeasures had no 'logical relation' with Part Two of the draft, as they did not arise automatically from the wrongful act. Instead, they should be seen as a mechanism for the implementation of state responsibility and, for this reason, they suggested that the regime of countermeasures should be relocated to Part Three of the draft.[199]

The definitive conceptual shift on the role of countermeasures from sanction to implementation, from substantive to instrumental, took place during the second reading of the ARS. Very early on in his tenure, Special Rapporteur Crawford emphasised that countermeasures 'should be seen as performing an instrumental function of ensuring compliance, and not as punitive measures or sanctions'.[200] For Crawford, not even in respect of the breach of multilateral obligations and peremptory rules – the notions that replaced, in its essence, the now deleted draft Article 19 on international crimes of states – could countermeasures be punitive. Indeed, in respect of these obligations, Crawford argued that countermeasures could be taken by states other than the injured state, but only with the aim of inducing cessation and reparation,[201] a proposal that both the Commission and states rejected.[202] Nevertheless, albeit without much by way of discussion on the purposes or aims of countermeasures,[203]

---

[194] A/C.6/51/SR.36, [18].
[195] Comments by Governments on All the Draft Articles, Doc A/CN.4/488 and Add.1–3, ILC Yearbook 1998, vol. II(1), 157.
[196] A/C.6/55/SR.18, [51].
[197] A/C.6/55/SR.18, [81].
[198] A/C.6/48/SR.24, [32]. See also A/C.6/51/SR.36, [80].
[199] E.g., China: A/C.6/51/SR.36, [18]; Russia: A/C.6/56/SR.14, [43]; Ukraine: A/C.6/48/SR.24, [32] and A/C.6/51/SR.36, [80].
[200] Crawford, Third Report, [287]. See also Crawford, Second Report, [393]; Crawford, 2645th meeting, ILC Yearbook 2000, vol. I, 264 [65].
[201] Crawford, Third Report, 102–6.
[202] See ARS art. 54 (a non-prejudice clause) and Commentary.
[203] See the comments by Brownlie, 2649th meeting, 301 [90], noting the multitude of purposes of countermeasures: as inducement 'to resort to a dispute settlement procedure; as a reprisal; as a deterrent; as an inducement to abandon a policy; as a form of self-defence (in which case interim measures would apply); or as self-help in order to achieve a settlement'. The Special Rapporteur, he thought, had not 'produced a clear decision as to which of those purposes was to be legitimated ... though the implication of articles 47 and 48 was that it was self-help. In that context the purpose appeared to be to bring

the Commission and states followed Crawford's suggestion to reframe countermeasures as merely instrumental to the implementation of responsibility.[204] To reflect this updated understanding, the Commission moved the topic of countermeasures from Part Two, on the content of responsibility, to Part Three, on the implementation of state responsibility.

Thus, the Commentary currently explains that countermeasures must be taken 'with a view to procuring cessation of and reparation for the internationally wrongful act and not by way of punishment'.[205] As a means of enforcement, therefore, countermeasures were both backward-looking (to induce reparation) and forward-looking (to induce resumed compliance). But they were no longer punitive,[206] at least not formally so.

### 6.3.2 *The Regime of Countermeasures in the Articles on State Responsibility*

Pursuant to the ARS, countermeasures are lawful only if certain conditions and requirements are met. These requirements have been endorsed by states and international courts and tribunals.[207] This section will provide a brief overview of the regime in the ARS, addressing its requirements and conditions in three clusters: (1) (actual) existence of a wrongful act, (2) substantive and (3) procedural requirements.

#### 6.3.2.1  Existence of a Wrongful Act

Countermeasures are a response to a wrongful act committed by the target state,[208] a wrongful act that must actually exist. This is an especially tricky requirement, since injured states will often act on the basis of a unilateral (and therefore subjective) appreciation of the situation. It may occur that, after the event, it is determined that a prior wrongful act

---

about cessation and reparation, but doing so without any procedure of peaceful settlement'. Similarly, Brownlie, 2672nd meeting, 35 [2].

[204] ILC Report, fifty-first session, ILC Yearbook 1999, vol. II(2), 88 [449].
[205] Commentary to Chapter II of Part III, [6].
[206] It could not be otherwise, it may be added, since there exist significant impediments to the conception of countermeasures as punishment in a decentralised legal order, not the least of which is the absence of hierarchy in the relations between States. See Leben, 'Les contre-mesures inter-étatiques et les réactions à l'illicéité dans la société internationale' (1982) 28 AFDI 9.
[207] For recent examples, see *Application of the Interim Accord of 13 September 1995 (FYR Macedonia v Greece)* (2011) ICJ Rep 644, [164]; and the high-fructose corn syrup disputes between Mexico and US investors, cited earlier.
[208] ARS art. 49(1).

did not objectively exist and that the state taking countermeasures has therefore acted wrongfully.[209] Thus, in *Interim Accord*, Greece found that its countermeasures were wrongful acts because Macedonia's conduct, which Greece alleged had triggered its own response, did not constitute a violation of its obligations towards Greece under the Accord.[210] A mere good faith belief that a wrongful act exists is not enough to justify the reactive measures.[211]

### 6.3.2.2 Substantive Requirements

Countermeasures are temporarily constrained in terms of their duration and their effects.[212] First of all, countermeasures must be limited to the temporary non-performance of obligations towards the target state. Countermeasures, providing like all other defences a 'shield' rather than a sword, may not affect the continued existence of the obligation as such.[213] As a result, they may not be relied upon to terminate or suspend treaty obligations towards the wrongdoing state,[214] which can only be achieved by application of the relevant rules in the law of treaties.[215] This temporal element is also ensured by the requirement of reversibility of countermeasures. According to the ARS, countermeasures must be taken 'in such a way as to permit the resumption of performance of the obligations in question.'[216] Note, however, that this is not an absolute standard, since the ARS indicate that this requirement must be fulfilled only 'as far as possible'.[217] Lastly, countermeasures shall be terminated as soon as the target State has ceased the wrongful conduct and provided reparation for the

---

[209] It is thus said that a state adopts countermeasures 'at its own risk': ARS art. 49 Commentary, [3].
[210] *Interim Accord*, [164].
[211] Cf. Damrosch, 'Retaliation or Arbitration – or Both? The 1978 United States–France Aviation Dispute' (1980) 74 AJIL 785, 793–7.
[212] On which see Kamto, 'The Time Factor in the Application of Countermeasures' in Crawford et al. (eds), *The Law of International Responsibility* (2010), 1169.
[213] ARS art. 49(2).
[214] Commentary to Chapter V of Part One, [1].
[215] Article 60 VCLT (on material breach of treaty) and the equivalent customary rule. On the relation between countermeasures and suspension/termination due to material breach of treaty see, generally, Sicilianos, 'The Relationship between Reprisals and Denunciation or Suspension of a Treaty' (1993) 4 EJIL 341, 576; Forlati, *Diritto dei trattati e responsabilità internazionale* (2005); Forlati, 'Reactions to Non Performance of Treaties in International Law' (2012) 25 LJIL 759; Simma and Tams, 'Treaty Breaches'.
[216] ARS art. 49(3).
[217] ARS art. 49(3).

injury; namely, as soon as the aims pursued by the countermeasures have been achieved.[218]

According to ARS Article 51,[219] countermeasures must be proportionate.[220] This is a well-established requirement in general international law. Under this requirement, countermeasures must be 'commensurate to the injury suffered'.[221] As the Commentary explains, the proportionality calculus is both quantitative and qualitative,[222] and must take into account the injury suffered, the gravity of the wrongful act and the rights in question (both those affected by the prior wrong and those affected by the countermeasure),[223] the type of measure adopted by the injured state and its degree of intensity.[224] Finally, proportionality may be linked to the purpose of the measure.[225] In practice, proportionality may be difficult to determine due, especially, to the non-reciprocal character of countermeasures.[226] Indeed, since an injured state can take countermeasures through *any* obligation owed to the target state, the proportionality analysis involves a comparison between 'different integers'.[227] Ultimately, as the Commentary acknowledges, the assessment of proportionality 'is not an easy task and can at best be accomplished by approximation'.[228]

Finally, certain obligations are excluded from the scope of countermeasures. These are established in Article 50(1), an exclusionary clause listing obligations that cannot be affected by the measures.[229] These

[218] ARS art. 53.
[219] In the 1850s, the British reprisals against Greece in the *Don Pacifico* affair elicited protest from other European powers due to their disproportion to the damage caused to the British national; see Section 6.2.1.1. See also *Naulilaa*, 1028; IDI, Régime des représailles en temps de paix, Article 6(2); *Air Service Agreement*, [83]; *Gabčíkovo-Nagymaros*, [85].
[220] ARS art. 51. See, generally, Cannizzaro, 'The Role of Proportionality in the Law of International Countermeasures' (2001) 12 EJIL 889; Franck, 'On Proportionality of Countermeasures in International Law' (2008) 102 AJIL 715; O'Keefe, 'Proportionality' in Crawford et al. (eds), *The Law of International Responsibility* (2010), 1158.
[221] ARS art. 51.
[222] ARS art. 51 Commentary, [6].
[223] Id.
[224] Ibid., [1].
[225] See, e.g., Cannizzaro, 'Proportionality'.
[226] The Commentary notes in this regard that countermeasures affecting the same or closely related obligations are more likely to be proportionate: ARS art. 49 Commentary, [5].
[227] Franck, 'Proportionality', 729.
[228] *Air Service Agreement*, [83].
[229] On which see, generally, Borelli and Olleson, 'Obligations Relating to Human Rights and Humanitarian Law' in Crawford et al. (eds), *The Law of International Responsibility* (2010), 1177; Leben, 'Obligations Relating to the Use of Force and Arising from Peremptory Norms of International Law', ibid., 1197; Boisson de Chazournes, 'Other Non-derogable Obligations', ibid., 1205.

include: (a) the prohibition of force, (b) obligations for the protection of fundamental human rights, (c) obligations of a 'humanitarian character prohibiting reprisals', and (d) 'other obligations under peremptory rules of international law'. The latter paragraph reaffirms, in the context of countermeasures, the general exclusion of defences in the case of breach of peremptory rules contained in Article 26 ARS. Furthermore, Article 50(2) indicates that a state which has taken countermeasures must continue to fulfil any obligations of dispute settlement binding it to the target state and to respect the inviolability of diplomats, their premises, archives and documents.

These exclusions are largely accepted in practice;[230] nevertheless, on a conceptual level, there were disagreements in the ILC as to their rationale.[231] Special Rapporteur Crawford acknowledged that the exclusions 'embod[ied] no clear principle',[232] and he has recently stated in his scholarly work that the absence of a single underlying rationale was due to the fact that it had not been 'possible in the ILC and among States to find agreement on a more rigorous basis'.[233] Disagreements as to the rationale of these exclusions persist to this day and, as noted in the literature, these uncertainties have a significant impact on certain aspects of the application of countermeasures.[234] Section 6.4 will consider the question of the rationale of these exclusions, in the context of examining the theoretical explanations for countermeasures' justifying effect: the choice of theory in this regard may affect the rationale for the exclusions.

### 6.3.2.3 Procedural Conditions

A state adopting countermeasures must also fulfil certain procedural conditions. First of all, the injured state must call on the target state to provide cessation or reparation (*sommation*).[235] This is a well-established requirement,[236] and some scholars consider that countermeasures are justified, strictly speaking, by the wrongdoing state's failure to perform its

---

[230] Crawford, *General Part*, 690.
[231] See, e.g., Simma, 2646th meeting, ILC Yearbook 2000, vol. I, 270 [31] (on human rights exclusion); Pellet, 2682nd meeting, ILC Yearbook 2001, vol. I, 113 [70].
[232] Crawford, Fourth Report on State Responsibility, ILC Yearbook 2001, vol. II(1), [64].
[233] Crawford, *General Part*, 690.
[234] See Paparinskis, 'Investment Treaty Arbitration and the (New) Law of State Responsibility' (2013) 24 EJIL 617.
[235] ARS art. 52(1)(a).
[236] *Naulilaa*, 1026; IDI, Régime des représailles en temps de paix, art. 6(1). More recently, see *Gabčíkovo-Nagymaros*, [84].

obligations of cessation and reparation and not by the initial wrongful act.[237] The purpose of *sommation* is to give the target state an opportunity to review its conduct, offer justifications or excuses if any exist (in which case countermeasures are excluded as explained in Chapter 2),[238] and to comply with its obligations of cessation or reparation. Additionally, the injured state must notify the target state of its decision to take countermeasures and make an offer to negotiate with that state.[239] This is not a strict requirement, as the ARS make provision for urgent countermeasures when this is necessary for the preservation of the injured state's rights.[240]

The entitlement to take countermeasures may be affected by the existence of obligations of dispute settlement between the parties. This was one of the most controversial aspects of the Commission's work,[241] just as it had been in the interwar period both within the League of Nations (in the Corfu incident) and the IDI during its work on the 1934 Regime. Article 52(3) of the ARS establishes that a state may not take countermeasures if the wrongful act has ceased and the dispute is pending before a tribunal competent to make binding decisions for the parties,[242] or, if already taken, countermeasures must cease without delay.[243] Nevertheless, countermeasures may be taken if the target state fails to implement its obligations of dispute settlement in good faith.[244] Moreover, this limitation is applicable only where there exists, as between the parties, a mandatory mechanism for the settlement of disputes capable of issuing binding decisions on the parties. On this point, international law has not changed much since the interwar period, as this solution is substantially similar to that of the IDI's 1934 Regime.

As to standing, the ARS entitle any state injured by a wrongful act to resort to countermeasures. In accordance with the definition of 'injured

---

[237] E.g., Čepelka, 'Les conséquences juridiques du délit en droit international contemporain', *Acta Universitatis Carolinae, Iuridica, Monographia* (1965) vol. 3, 49–50; Zemanek, 'The Unilateral Enforcement of International Obligations' (1987) 47 ZaöRV 32, 35.
[238] See Chapter 2. That countermeasures cannot be taken against justified conduct has also been asserted by: Zoller, *Peacetime Unilateral Remedies: An Analysis of Countermeasures* (1984), 94; Elagab, *Counter-Measures*, 51.
[239] ARS art. 52(1)(b).
[240] ARS art. 52(2).
[241] See, e.g., the symposium on 'Countermeasures and Dispute Settlement' in (1994) 5 EJIL 20–115. See also Schachter, 'Dispute Settlement and Countermeasures in the International Law Commission' (1994) 88 AJIL 471.
[242] ARS art. 52(3).
[243] Id.
[244] ARS art. 52(4).

state' in the ARS, a state is injured in the case of a breach of a bilateral obligation owed to it or, in the case of a multilateral obligation, if the breach 'especially affects' it.[245] The ARS leave unresolved the question whether, in the case of multilateral obligations, states not especially affected by the breach ('States other than an injured State')[246] may adopt countermeasures for the protection of the collective interest.[247] Special Rapporteur Crawford's proposal to include a provision entitling these states to take countermeasures in the collective interest was rejected since, as the Commentary indicates, state practice in this regard was too 'limited and rather embryonic' for codification.[248] Nevertheless, since the adoption of the ARS, practice seems to be moving towards their recognition.[249]

### 6.4 Countermeasures as Justifications

Countermeasures, when they comply with the requirements and conditions specified above, are lawful measures. Positive law is clear in this respect. But how can this legality be explained theoretically? This is an important question that scholars have frequently undervalued on the basis that any effort in this regard would have no practical import; it would be, in other words, theory for theory's sake.[250] Nevertheless, as was argued in the introduction, it is through these theoretical explanations that a mass of otherwise unrelated practices can be collated into an institution of the legal order[251] and that difficult aspects of these institutions can be resolved or at least illuminated. For example, a theoretical articulation of the institution may provide a principled account of the obligations excluded from

---

[245] See ARS art. 42(a) and (b)(1), defining 'injured state' for the purposes of the ARS.
[246] ARS art. 48.
[247] ARS art. 54.
[248] ARS art. 54 Commentary, [3].
[249] See, e.g., Tams, *Enforcing Obligations Erga Omnes in International Law* (2005); Proukaki, *The Problem of Enforcement in International Law* (2011); Dawidowicz, 'Third-party Countermeasures: Observations on a Controversial Concept' in Chinkin and Baetens (eds), *Sovereignty, Statehood and State Responsibility: Essays in Honour of James Crawford* (2015), 340.
[250] Venezia, 'Répresailles', 468–9; de Guttry, *Rappresaglie*, 21–2 (fn. 29). Kalshoven apparently denies any relevance to theoretical explanations in this regard, only to then concede that the 'debate cannot … be denied a certain fundamental significance', in view of potential practical and normative implications, see Kalshoven, *Belligerent Reprisals* (2nd edn, 2005), 21.
[251] On the relevance of theory in this regard, see Morgenthau, 'Théorie des sanctions internationales' (1935) 16 RDILC (3rd ser.) 474.

the scope of countermeasures. This final section, therefore, will consider several plausible theoretical accounts of the legality of countermeasures.

### 6.4.1 Theorising the Legality of Countermeasures

How can it be the case that, in Nicolas Politis' words, 'an act contrary to law can nevertheless be recognised by it as lawful?'[252] At least four theoretical explanations have been put forward to answer this question: (1) states act as 'organs' of the international community when they adopt countermeasures, (2) countermeasures involve the suspension of obligations towards the wrongdoing state, (3) consequentialist and (4) deontic rationales. Of these, the second explanation, upheld by Ago during his tenure as Special Rapporteur, has already been dismissed and so will not be considered again here.[253] Aside from the first of these theories, supported by Kelsen and the Vienna School, the other rationales have been referred to in international legal scholarship only in a rather superficial way. The following discussion will, therefore, try to develop each theory as much as it is possible and to provide relevant critiques of each one of them. Given the absence of writings in contemporary international law on the matter, and with the caveat made in the introduction to this book, the analysis in this Section will, when necessary, draw upon the work of theorists working within domestic law to develop these theories.

#### 6.4.1.1 States as Organs of the International Community

Pursuant to this theory, countermeasures are lawful because they constitute the execution of a sanction by the injured state acting on behalf of the international community. The theory was elaborated by Kelsen[254] and the Vienna School,[255] and was subsequently endorsed by other

---

[252] Politis, 'Régime des représailles', 24.
[253] Ago, Eighth Report, [84]. Endorsing Ago's rationale, see Alland, *Justice privée et ordre juridique international* (1994), 140–2. Historically, a similar rationale was supported by Strupp, 'Règles générales du droit de la paix' (1934) 47 *Recueil* 259, 568. Similarly, see Westlake, 2 *International Law*, 6; Strupp, 'Janina', 283 ('les règles juridiques doivent disparaître devant le droit de représailles, naturellement lorsque ce droit est exercé par l'Etat lésé par un délit international vis-à-vis de l'Etat lésant').
[254] This thesis is developed in a number of works; see Kelsen, *Unrecht und unrechtsfolge im volkerrecht* (1932); Kelsen, 'Théorie générale du droit international public. Problèmes choisis' (1932) 42 *Recueil* 117; Kelsen, *Law and Peace*. Situating this aspect of Kelsen's work in his overall theory, see Zolo, 'Hans Kelsen: International Peace through International Law' (1998) 9 EJIL 306.
[255] See, e.g., Kunz, 'Static and Dynamic'; Kunz, 'The Theory of International Law' (1938) 32 *ASIL Proc* 23. For an overview of the Vienna School's approach, see von Bernstorff, *Hans*

scholars,[256] including a young Roberto Ago.[257] Kelsen's represents the most sophisticated version of this theory, so this brief exposition will refer to his work.

According to Kelsen, a legal community exists whenever there is a sphere of interests protected by law and force is permitted only as a sanction, imposed by the legal community, for the infringement of the community's rules.[258] In modern domestic legal orders, the state monopolises force and reserves its use only as a sanction against delicts. The sanction (Kelsen's hypothetical norm) is applied by an organ of the state which thereby acts on behalf of the legal community.[259] Thus, an executioner does not commit murder when he carries out a death penalty even though his actions bring about the death of an individual.[260] Primitive legal communities respond to these characteristics as well: a sphere of interests is protected by law, force is monopolised by the community and is used to sanction infringements of the law in the form of impairment of those interests. But there is a crucial difference, in that primitive legal communities do not possess 'special' organs in charge of applying sanctions. Rather, the sanctions are applied by the members of the community itself:

> In primitive law the individual whose legally protected interests have been violated is himself authorized by the legal order to proceed against the wrongdoer with all the coercive measures provided by the legal order. This is called self-help. Every individual takes the law into his own hands.[261]

Force is monopolised by the community, but its execution is decentralised to its members through a norm which authorises them, in certain circumstances, to apply force.[262] When executing an (authorised) sanction, in the form of a vendetta or blood-revenge, the victim therefore acts as an organ of the legal community and his action is lawful.

For Kelsen international law constitutes a primitive legal community. Like modern domestic legal orders, international law possesses sanctions against wrongdoing, as evidenced by the practice of reprisals

---

*Kelsen*, 84–90. von Bernstorff finds the origins of this theory in the writings of Kaltenborn in the mid-nineteenth century, ibid., at 85–6.

[256] See also Guggenheim, *Traité de droit international public* (1954) vol. 2, 84–5; D'Amato, 'The Coerciveness of International Law' (2009) 52 GYIL 437.
[257] Ago, 'Délit', 424–31.
[258] Kelsen, *General Theory*, 20–2.
[259] Kelsen, *Law and Peace*, 12.
[260] The analogy is taken from Ago, 'Délit', 536.
[261] Kelsen, *Law and Peace*, 49.
[262] Ibid., 49–50.

## 6.4 COUNTERMEASURES AS JUSTIFICATIONS

(and – though this was a more controversial claim – by the just war theory). But unlike domestic legal orders, international law has no 'central government, no courts, no administrative organs' and 'no special organs exist to execute' sanctions for the breach of its rules.[263] This does not mean that international law is not law properly so called. There is between domestic and international law merely a difference of degree: domestic law is centralised whereas international law is decentralised – indeed it has the highest degree of decentralisation occurring in positive legal systems.[264] This means that in the absence of a 'special organ', the execution of the sanction is entrusted to each member of the legal community: 'General international law is in this respect, too, a primitive law. It has the technique of self-help. It is the State violated in its rights that is authorized to react against the violator by resorting to war or reprisals.'[265] A state thus authorised acts like an organ of the international community; or, put differently, 'it is the international legal community itself that reacts against the violator of the law through the medium of the State resorting to reprisal' (or to just war).[266] When an injured state takes reprisals against its wrongdoer it acts no more unlawfully than an executioner who carries out a death sentence.

This is certainly a neat and intrinsically consistent theory, though it suffers from some fundamental drawbacks. Leaving aside the possible accuracy of the theory at the time it was formulated (in the interwar years), the central premise of the theory, that countermeasures constitute the sanction of international law, is an inaccurate representation of contemporary international practice. As noted earlier, the conception of countermeasures-as-sanctions was rejected by both states and the ILC in favour of an instrumental understanding of this institution. Furthermore, there are difficulties with the notions of the 'international legal community' and of the state as an 'organ' of that community. In particular,

---

[263] Kelsen, 'Sanctions in International Law under the Charter of the United Nations' (1945–6) 31 *Iowa LR* 499, 500.
[264] Kelsen, *General Theory*, 325–6.
[265] Ibid., 327.
[266] Kelsen, *Law and Peace*, 57. See also Kelsen, 'Collective Security and Collective Self-Defence under the Charter of the United Nations' (1948) 42 AJIL 783, 783: 'Since the state, in exercising self-help by taking enforcement action against another state under definite conditions determined by international law, acts on authorization of general international law, it may be considered to act as an organ of the international community constituted by this law, so that its action may be interpreted as reaction of the international community against violations of law. It is through the individual state that the international community acts, although this reaction is completely decentralized.'

as Leo Gross has shown, the metaphor of the state as an 'organ' of the community is both empirically inaccurate and normatively difficult to maintain.[267] While historically interesting and also important – it provided a powerful response to the Austinian ontological challenge to international law when it was first formulated – the theory cannot provide a satisfactory explanation for the legality of countermeasures in contemporary international law.

### 6.4.1.2 Consequentialist Theories

Consequentialist theories can provide a plausible theoretical explanation of the legality of countermeasures. As already explained in Chapter 5 in relation to self-defence, consequentialism comes in two variants: act- and rule-consequentialism, both of which can explain the legality of this institution.

Pursuant to act-consequentialism, as explained by Julio Barboza, countermeasures are legal because they protect a superior interest or, otherwise put, they constitute a lesser evil.[268] Barboza explains that countermeasures generate a conflict between the legally protected interests of the injured state and those of the target state, and in these circumstances a net benefit is gained from allowing the impairment of the interests of the wrongdoer rather than those of the injured state. The interests of the wrongdoer thus give way to those of the injured state, with the result that the latter's countermeasure is lawful. The theory is simple and explanatory, and it has the benefit of being able to account, in a principled manner, for (most of) the conditions and requirements of countermeasures. Necessity and proportionality, for example, are implicit in the very terms of the theory, since failure to observe them may cause a greater injury than that initially inflicted.[269] Similarly, the theory can also account for the exclusion of peremptory rules and other collective interests from the scope of countermeasures, since these would be, by definition, superior to the individual interest of the injured state.

But the theory is not unproblematic. To begin with, there is some circularity in the argument. Indeed, Barboza does not actually explain why

---

[267] Gross, 'States as Organs of International Law and the Problem of Autointerpretation' in *Essays on International Law and Organization* (1998) vol. 1, 167–97.

[268] Barboza, 'Contramedidas', 30. Historically, Hall had maintained a similar view: *International Law*, 311 (reprisals are justified because 'they are means of avoiding the graver alternative of war').

[269] Omichinski, 'Applying the Theories of Justifiable Homicide to Conflicts in the Doctrine of Self-Defense' (1986–7) 33 *Wayne LR* 1447, 1456.

## 6.4 COUNTERMEASURES AS JUSTIFICATIONS

the wrongdoer's interests should give way to those of the injured state: he merely asserts that they do. And yet, this is an essential aspect of the theory since, aside from peremptory rules, international law establishes no hierarchy among interests: the interests of the wrongdoer are on the same plane as those of the injured state. So why should the interests of the former bend to those of the latter? As in the case of self-defence, it could be argued that the balance is tipped in favour of the injured state by taking into account the responsibility of the wrongdoing state in the calculus.[270] But, again, this entails importing concepts of moral blameworthiness into the analysis, which are difficult to assess in international law. In addition, the theory is potentially underinclusive. Consider the following scenario. State A and State B have a treaty for the transfer of technology necessary for the maintenance of railway lines. State A fails to meet its payments to State B for the technology and, as a countermeasure, State B withholds the transfer of the agreed technology. Assume that the countermeasure is temporary, reversible, necessary and complies with all the procedural conditions. It is also a proportionate countermeasure, since it affects the 'same or [a] closely related obligation'.[271] After the adoption of the countermeasures, as a result of an earthquake, State A's railway line between its major cities is damaged thus preventing important communications between the two, an interruption which has labour, economic and other effects on both the government and, most importantly, the population of State A. The damage can only be restored with the technology that B has withheld as a countermeasure. Can it still be said that the interest of State A in the performance of the treaty obligation (the transfer of technology) is somehow inferior to State B's interest in the performance of the same treaty obligation (the payment of the price)? State A's interests may well be of higher moral value and, nevertheless, State B's countermeasure would be lawful in the circumstances.[272] Act-consequentialism cannot explain

---

[270] Proponents of consequentialist rationales for killing in self-defence speak here of the 'moral blame' of an aggressor as diminishing the value of the aggressor's life. For an overview and critique of these views, see Rodin, *War and Self-Defense* (2002), 51–5; Leverick, *Killing in Self-Defence* (2006), 45–50.

[271] ARS art. 49 Commentary, [5]. Of course, it is not always the case that equivalent countermeasures are proportionate: Focarelli, *International Law as a Social Construct* (2012), 351–2.

[272] It could be argued that this effect would render the countermeasure disproportionate. Case-law has specified that, among others, 'effects' must also be taken into account in assessing a countermeasure's proportionality. In *Gabčíkovo-Nagymaros*, the Court referred to the 'effects of the countermeasure' (at [85, 87]), and in *Air Service* the Tribunal took into account the effect of the measures on aircraft operators (at [83]). The question is which effects must be taken into account. This is a difficult issue, and it cannot

why, in these circumstances, a net benefit is gained from upholding the interests of State B (the injured state) over those of State A (the wrongdoing state), so that the theory must fail as a description of the current practice of countermeasures. (The theory is nevertheless useful, in that it may point out situations in which countermeasures may not be desirable, such as the hypothetical scenario just discussed.)

Pursuant to the rule-consequentialist account,[273] the legality of countermeasures is explained by the net benefit gained from the enforcement of international law, rather than the superiority of the interest of the injured state. The net benefit would derive from restoring respect in international legality and by the (potential) deterrent effect of enforcement. Aside from the difficult empirical claim regarding deterrence, the risks inherent in this modified theory are patent. If enforcement provides, ultimately, a net benefit to the legal order as a whole, then why limit countermeasures to necessary and proportionate measures?[274] Pushed to the extreme, this theory could bring back the understanding of countermeasures-as-sanctions.[275] But as already explained earlier, punitive countermeasures are both systemically untenable and empirically ruled out.

### 6.4.1.3  Deontic Theories

Countermeasures' legality may finally be explained through rights-based theories. It was said in Chapter 5, in the context of self-defence, that these theories explain the lawfulness of otherwise wrongful acts by reference to the entitlement (permission) to engage in such behaviour and that it is immaterial whether the entitlement is a claim-right or a liberty.[276] Nevertheless, since different practical implications may follow from the characterisation of the right to take countermeasures as one or the other type of entitlement, this section begins by analysing the internal structure of this entitlement.

---

be expanded upon here. It seems reasonable, however, that the effects to be taken into account must have a direct causal link with the measure in question. Such a direct link is evident in the *Air Service* case, in which the suspension of flight routes protected under the agreement directly affected the air carriers. In the hypothetical, the damage to the train lines was not the direct consequence of the countermeasure, but rather of a natural disaster.

[273] On which see: Rodin, *Self-Defense*, 54.
[274] Leverick, *Killing in Self-Defence*, 48–9.
[275] Making an analogous argument, in the context of the domestic law of self-defence, see: Kadish, 'Respect for Life and Regard for Rights in the Criminal Law' (1976) 64 *Cal LR* 871, 883.
[276] Chapter 5, Section 5.5.2.1.

## 6.4 COUNTERMEASURES AS JUSTIFICATIONS

**Preliminary Clarification: Countermeasures as Hohfeldian Liberties**
As in the case of self-defence, the Italian scholar Giancarlo Scalese has argued that the entitlement to take countermeasures constitutes a 'subjective right' of the injured state.[277] For Scalese, it is only 'natural' that countermeasures constitute a subjective right: subjective rights, generally, are composed by a bundle of 'powers', including the power to defend the legal situation protected by the right itself.[278] Since the entitlement to take countermeasures derives from a subjective right (as a 'power' to defend the legal situation protected by the right) it, too, must be a subjective right.[279] Scalese then explains that subjective rights are protected by the legal order through the imposition of a correlative duty on others not to interfere with the exercise of the right.[280] To characterise countermeasures as claim-rights entails both an entitlement to act for the injured state (the right-holder), as well as a correlative duty not to interfere with the exercise of that right for the target state. According to Scalese, the target state's duty of toleration or non-interference with the exercise of countermeasures is evidenced by ARS Article 30, on the obligation of cessation and guarantees of non-repetition. Indeed, Scalese concludes, any attempt by the target state to resist or to react against the countermeasure is a violation of the obligation in Article 30.[281]

The classification of countermeasures as a subjective right may, however, be challenged – on the same grounds as his classification of self-defence as a subjective right was challenged in Chapter 5. The Hohfeldian scheme of fundamental legal conceptions is again helpful for this purpose. Since the analysis undertaken here mirrors that in Chapter 5, this section will not include an exposition of Hohfeld's scheme; the remarks made in that chapter are applicable *mutatis mutandis* to the present explanation.[282]

To begin with, contrary to Scalese's suggestion, the character of subjective legal positions is not determined by their normative derivation (whatever this might mean) but rather by the internal logical structure of the entitlement itself. In the case of countermeasures, this internal

---

[277] Scalese, *La rilevanza delle scusanti nella teoria dell'illecito internazionale* (2008), 23–7.
[278] Ibid., 25.
[279] This conclusion does not necessarily follow and, indeed, scholars discussing the relationship between the 'right' of self-defence and the right to life usually hold that self-defence is a liberty attached to the (claim-) right to life. See, e.g., Ashworth, 'Self-Defence and the Right to Life' (1975) 34 CLJ 282, 283.
[280] Scalese, *Scusanti*, 25.
[281] Ibid., 27.
[282] For an explanation of the scheme as it is relevant for this analysis, see Chapter 5, Section 5.5.2.1. For a general exposition of Hohfeld's scheme, see Chapter 3, Section 3.2.1.2.

logical structure does not respond to the characteristics of a subjective or claim-right. Indeed, it is not possible to identify the existence of a correlative obligation of the target State not to interfere with the countermeasure adopted by the injured state.[283] This is best illustrated with an example. Consider the right to inviolability of diplomatic premises. This is a claim-right, in that State A has a right to the inviolability of its diplomatic premises in the territory of State B and, as a correlative, State B has an obligation not to interfere with the diplomatic premises of State A. If B interferes with A's diplomatic premises, say through surveillance of the premises by its secret services, A will be entitled to request B to cease the breach (and thus cease the interference) and provide reparation. Is the same true of the entitlement to take countermeasures? Taking the same example, if State B does not satisfy the request for cessation and reparation, A could take countermeasures to induce B to cease the conduct and make reparation.[284] To this end, State A may choose to freeze accounts belonging to State B in A's banks. Now, say that State B, having received notice that A intends to freeze the assets, immediately transfers them to banks in its own territory or in the territory of a third state. Or, say that after A freezes B's assets, State B adopts unfriendly acts such as recalling its ambassador and breaking diplomatic relations with A. If there were a duty not to interfere with the taking of the countermeasures, then these acts would be unlawful.[285] And yet, B's transfer of its funds from A's banks and its decision to break diplomatic relations are not considered to be unlawful. State B could also adopt unlawful acts against State A, in reaction to A's countermeasures. For example, State B could prevent the transit of A's commercial aircraft through its airspace, in contravention of bilateral or multilateral agreements. Even in this scenario, B's conduct would not infringe A's right to resort to countermeasures: at most, it would infringe *other* rights binding it to A (part of the so-called 'protective perimeter'), such as the bilateral or multilateral agreements on civil aviation.

Countermeasures, like self-defence,[286] are thus better understood as liberties.[287] Liberties constitute a permission to do (or not do) something

---

[283] Venturini, *Necessità*, 17; Sicilianos, *Réactions*, 47.
[284] This discussion assumes that all the procedural and substantive conditions for the taking of countermeasures are met.
[285] See Ago, 'Délit', 429–30; Sicilianos, *Réactions*, 47.
[286] See Chapter 5, Section 5.5.2.1.
[287] There was indeed criticism at the ILC 'for any language which implied that countermeasures were a positive or "subjective" right of the injured State': ILC Report, fifty-second session, ILC Yearbook 2000, vol. II(2), 56 [318].

## 6.4 COUNTERMEASURES AS JUSTIFICATIONS

and, since they do not entail claim-rights, they correlatively do not imply a duty on the part of others. A liberty is not, therefore, directly protected by the legal system, and any 'protection for the action is indirect in deriving from the protective perimeter or ring fence provided by the claim-rights that the agent has, not from the privilege/liberty itself.'[288] This analytical explanation more accurately reflects the internal structure of the right to take countermeasures. Relying again on the example used earlier, State A has a liberty to take countermeasures against State B, but State B is under no duty not to interfere with the countermeasure. Consequently, State B may resist and even react against A's countermeasure, without thereby infringing that entitlement. If at all, the resistance or reaction will infringe other claim-rights of State A's 'protective perimeter', such as, in the example, the conventional right of commercial overflight.

As with self-defence, Scalese's appeal to ARS Article 30 as evidence of the target State's duty to tolerate the countermeasure is unavailing. The obligation to cease the wrongful conduct is a different legal relation from the right to take countermeasures: it is one of the legal relations generated by the wrongful act, which entails a claim-right of the injured state to demand certain behaviour from the wrongdoing state. Failure by the wrongdoing state to perform this obligation is a breach of Article 30 and, in addition, it could be a continuing breach of the initial obligation. In the diplomatic premises example above, if despite State A's demands and its countermeasures, State B maintains its surveillance of the diplomatic premises of State A, it does not thereby violate A's countermeasures. B's conduct will be a continuing violation of its obligation to respect A's diplomatic inviolability and, in addition, a breach of its obligation of cessation under Article 30. Any claim by State A in this regard will be about the performance of the substantive obligation breached and of Article 30, and not about interferences with its taking of countermeasures. Indeed, Article 30 could be breached by the responsible State's failure to comply with the injured State's request whether or not countermeasures had been adopted.

Having ascertained that countermeasures constitute a liberty of the injured State, the next step is to explain why the infringement of the target state's rights is not unlawful.[289] After all, the right to take countermeasures

---

[288] Brown, 'Rights, Liberties and Duties: Reformulating Hohfeld's Scheme of Legal Relations?' (2005) 58 *Current Legal Problems* 343, 344.

[289] For an explanation of this difficulty, see Rodin, *Self-Defense*, 49–50; Kaufman, 'Is There a "Right" to Self-Defense?' (2004) 23 *Crim Just Ethics* 20, 23; Leverick, 'Defending Self-Defence' (2007) 27 OJLS 563, 571.

consists in the liberty *not to* perform an obligation owed to the target state. Or, what is the same, to deny the target state's corresponding claim-right. In the diplomatic premises hypothetical, State B has a claim-right that State A not seize its assets (generically, that it not do X); correlatively, State A has an obligation not to seize the assets of State B (generically, it has an obligation not to do X). By virtue of the countermeasure, State A has the liberty *to do* the very X contemplated by its duty towards State B; in this case, seize the assets. So State A's doing X (seizing the assets) in the exercise of the liberty infringes State B's claim-right that it not do X. So why is State B's claim-right not infringed by A's countermeasure? At least two rationales have been proposed in this regard,[290] reviewed below.

**Unity of the Legal System**  The first of these rationales maintains that, since the determination of wrongfulness requires a holistic assessment of the legal system, 'to be considered unlawful, conduct cannot be in accordance with any legal rule nor, therefore, constitute the performance of an obligation or the exercise of a right'.[291] This theory was already dismissed in Chapter 5 and the objections made there are equally applicable to countermeasures.[292]

**Forfeiture Theory**  A more successful explanation of the legality of countermeasures can be found in the theory of rights forfeiture, already developed in Chapter 5. In short, the legality of countermeasures derives from the fact that the wrongdoing state has, by its conduct, forfeited the legal protection of its rights. As a result, when the injured state adopts countermeasures against it, it does not breach the target state's rights since the target state has forfeited the law's protection of those rights. This explanation of countermeasures' legality was explicitly supported, if with brief and superficial remarks, by Charles Dupuis[293] and by ILC member Laurel Francis.[294]

---

[290] A number of additional theories have been proposed in domestic law in this regard. See, e.g., Miller, 'Killing in Self-Defense' (1993) 7 *Public Affairs Quarterly* 325; Uniacke, *Permissible Killing: The Self-Defence Justification of Homicide* (1994), ch. 6; Leverick, *Killing in Self-Defence*.

[291] Scalese, *Scusanti*, 17 ('per essere ritenuta illecita, una condotta non può risultare conforme ad alcuna norma giuridica né, quindi, rappresentare l'adempimento di un dovere o l'esercizio di un diritto').

[292] Chapter 5, Section 5.5.2.2.

[293] Dupuis, 'Règles générales', 275 (reprisals constitute 'moyens licites à l'encontre d'une souveraineté qui a perdu droit au respect et s'est dépouillée de la protection du droit international par les infractions qu'elle y a commises').

[294] Francis, 1545th meeting, ILC Yearbook 1979, vol. I, 59 [3].

## 6.4 COUNTERMEASURES AS JUSTIFICATIONS

A forfeiture theory of countermeasures, like for self-defence, must be premised on a non-punitive and temporarily limited notion of forfeiture of legal protection. Equally, it must be built and examined in a relational way; as embedded in the legal relations between the relevant parties.[295] Forfeiture occurs in the context of the relations between two parties: the wrongdoing state and the injured state. The fact of forfeiture must therefore be analysed from both points of view. From the wrongdoing state's side, this state loses the legal protection of its rights temporarily. The situation of the wrongdoing state can therefore be described, in Hohfeldian terms, as one of no-rights. Correlatively, from the injured state's side, this state is alleviated from its duty of non-interference with the rights of the wrongdoing state the protection of which it has forfeited.[296] The situation of no-duty is the jural opposite of a liberty – that is, to have a liberty to do X is the same as not being under a duty not to do X. This liberty is *precisely* the liberty afforded to the injured state by the countermeasure. Thus, when it acts in pursuance of that liberty the state taking countermeasures does not impair the rights of the wrongdoing state – the wrongdoer being in a position of no-rights, the injured state does not have a duty to respect those rights.

The situations of no-right of the wrongdoing state and the liberty of the injured state (or its no-duty, to put it in opposite terms) represent the same fact, the forfeiture, seen from the two different angles. Forfeiture therefore is not universal or as against all other members of the legal order. Of course, the intersubjective extent of the forfeiture depends on the underlying legal relations. In the case of bilateral obligations, it is limited to the relations between the two parties. So, the wrongdoing state's forfeiture is limited to the non-performance *by* the injured state of obligations binding it *to* the injured state. Crucially, though, if the obligations are multilateral the wrongdoing state's forfeiture may involve more parties, plausibly as many states as are bound by the collective obligation.

The forfeiture theory struggles to accommodate all of the conditions and requirements of countermeasures. It is, nevertheless, able to rationalise these various elements systematically. As to the substance of countermeasures, the theory can account for their non-reciprocal character.

---

[295] Rodin, *Self-Defense*, 75.
[296] As was said in Chapter 5, claim-rights are protected by the legal system through the imposition of correlative duties of respect and non-interference. By contrast, liberties are 'tolerated' but not protected by the system, since there is no duty on the part of others not to interfere with their enjoyment.

If the wrongdoing state has forfeited the legal protection of its rights, then the injured state may target any of them by way of countermeasure. The theory can also explain the exclusion of peremptory rules, fundamental human rights and humanitarian law. As to peremptory rules, these are, by definition, non-derogable rules with the result that states may not forfeit them. In turn, fundamental human rights and humanitarian law (if they do not belong to *jus cogens*) may not be forfeited by a wrongdoing state because the forfeiture would affect beneficiaries of the right other than the state itself, that is individuals.[297] The rationale for the exclusion of fundamental human rights and humanitarian law, as was advanced earlier, was controversial during the ILC debates. Riphagen had grounded the exclusion on the notion of objective regimes and the collective interests that these protect.[298] Arangio-Ruiz, in turn, relied on principles of humanity.[299] Crawford returned to the same rationale as Riphagen, justifying the exclusion on the basis that these constitute rights vested in beneficiaries other than the state target of the countermeasure.[300] This rationale was not generally acceptable to the ILC, but it nevertheless seems to be the most persuasive way of explaining why fundamental human rights and humanitarian law are excluded from the scope of countermeasures. This explanation could be challenged on the basis that to rationalise these two exclusions under the same principle may come at the cost of nuance, for this rationalisation overlooks the difference between human rights, the direct beneficiary of which is the individual, and humanitarian law, in which the prohibition of reprisals benefits individuals only indirectly, since individuals are, as it were, the object rather than subject of the rule. It can be countered, nevertheless, that this distinction may not be sustainable or desirable *de lege ferenda*, given the increased recognition of individual personality under international law. From a policy point of view, moreover, a rationale based on the non-forfeiture of rights benefitting third parties[301] can ground other

---

[297] This rationale could extend to protect individuals from being the target of countermeasures generally, so long as they are beneficiaries of the rights affected. Thus, investor rights (if classified as substantive rights) could be excluded from the scope of countermeasures. Of course, whether additional exclusions are recognised on the basis of this rationale needs to be verified in state practice.

[298] Riphagen, Fourth Report, [88–9].

[299] Arangio-Ruiz, Third Report, 32–4; Fourth Report, [78]. Article 14 and commentary, ILC Report, forty-seventh session, ILC Yearbook 1995, vol. II(2) 71–4 [17–24].

[300] Crawford, Third Report, [340], [349]. For Crawford *all* human rights (and not just 'fundamental' ones) were excluded from the scope of countermeasures.

[301] Note that the use of the expression 'third parties' in this context was contested by several ILC members, see, e.g., Simma, 2646th meeting, ILC Yearbook 2000, 270 [31]; Pellet,

## 6.4 COUNTERMEASURES AS JUSTIFICATIONS

potential and possibly desirable exclusions such as integral obligations (e.g. environmental law)[302] and also other rights vested (in some way) on individuals (e.g. investment law).[303] Of course, any further exclusions would need to be corroborated in the practice and *opinio juris* of states.

Matters are more complex in respect of the exclusion of dispute settlement obligations and diplomatic law, for it is difficult to explain why a state may not forfeit these rights. A principled explanation may be achieved, however, by changing the focus of the analysis, by moving, as it were, from the wrongdoing state's legal position to the injured state's. These limitations could potentially be construed as limitations on the right to take countermeasures. From this standpoint, these are not arbitrary limitations. As to dispute settlement obligations, these partake in the same rationale as the right to countermeasures: they are both instrumental to the implementation of responsibility. It seems logical, then, to prevent these obligations from being targeted by countermeasures. The same rationale may be applied to diplomatic law, in that the diplomatic channel is essential to the resolution of the dispute and, ultimately, the implementation of responsibility.[304] Alternatively, diplomatic law may be

---

2646th meeting, ILC Yearbook 2000, 273 [57]. The criticism relied on the notion of 'third-parties' as applicable to the law of treaties, in the sense of an entity not a party to a given treaty. Individuals are certainly not third parties in human rights law in this sense. Nevertheless, it is undoubted that the obligations arising under human rights law are both owed inter-state and state–individual. To target a countermeasure at the state–state level necessarily has effects on the rights of individuals, who conceptually are third parties to that relation. See also Paparinskis, 'Law of Countermeasues', 331–2.

[302] Human rights exclusions could come under this category as well. After all, as argued by Simma during the second reading of the ARS, human rights obligations are integral and cannot be 'bilateralized', see Simma, 2646th meeting, 270 [31].

[303] Whether countermeasures can affect investor rights is an uncertain issue. Arbitral tribunals have taken widely different views, on the basis of the character of the rights granted to investors (substantive or procedural) under investment treaties: cf. *ADM v Mexico*, *CPI v Mexico* and *Cargill v Mexico*. There are reasonable policy grounds to uphold either view. On the one hand, it seems reasonable to exclude individuals from being targeted by countermeasures against their home state on fairness grounds. On the other, however, it is often the case that there is no other better way to pressure the home state into complying with its obligations, see Parlett, 'Rules on Countermeasures', 403–4. Moreover, to allow countermeasures against investors of the responsible state could go some way towards redressing the material imbalance inherent in the institution of countermeasures insofar as investment and capital usually flow from developed towards developing states, see Tomuschat, 'Are Counter-measures Subject to Prior Recourse to Dispute Settlement Procedures?' (1994) 5 EJIL 77, 78.

[304] Article 50 Commentary, [2, 12]. As stated by Arangio-Ruiz, this exclusion was important for 'securing of the normal channels of communication among States. Certainly, the possibility of effective uninterrupted communication is an essential requirement of

seen as an external limitation on the injured state's right. Insofar as diplomatic law constitutes a *lex specialis*,[305] it is excluded from the scope of countermeasures by virtue of ARS Article 55.[306]

The requirements of necessity and proportionality may also be grounded on this theory – though admittedly this requires some ingenuity. Both domestic[307] and international law[308] scholars have argued that these two requirements are undercut by the very basis of the theory, the wrongdoer's forfeiture of legal protection. For if the wrongdoing state is not protected by law, then what binds the injured state to take countermeasures only as a last resort and in a proportionate manner? After all, it is not bound to perform its obligations towards the wrongdoing state, so whether it performs proportionately or disproportionately is not legally relevant. This critique may be overcome by – again – shifting the focus from the wrongdoing state's forfeiture to the injured state's right, and relating these limitations to the latter's right. As Judith Jarvis Thomson has written, 'a proportionality requirement flows very naturally out of the fact that some rights are more stringent than others, a fact that any plausible theory of rights must accommodate.'[309] The right to take countermeasures is a stringent entitlement, as only with such stringent conditions is it possible to minimise abuse. Thus it is reasonable that conditions of necessity and proportionality be built into the injured state's entitlement to take countermeasures.[310]

The theory may also accommodate the temporal aspect of countermeasures. In domestic law, as seen in Chapter 5,[311] one of the main criticisms against the theory of forfeiture is its permanence. Furthermore, even if forfeiture were only temporary, it has been argued that the theory has difficulty

---

international relations both in times of crisis and under normal conditions': Arangio-Ruiz, Fourth Report, [87].

[305] On diplomatic law as *lex specialis*, see *Tehran Hostages*, 40.
[306] See, e.g., Elagab, *Counter-Measures*, 116–22; Barboza, 'Contramedidas', 40.
[307] Fletcher, 'The Right to Life' (1980) 63 *Monist* 135, 143; Omichinski, 'Theories', 1456; Kasachkoff, 'Killing in Self-Defense: An Unquestionable or Problematic Defense?' (1998) 17 *Law and Philosophy* 509, 517.
[308] Making this criticism in the context of self-defence, see Farhang, 'Self-Defence as a Circumstance Precluding Wrongfulness' (2015) *Utrecht LR* 1, 11–12.
[309] Thomson, 'Self-Defense' (1991) 20 *Philosophy and Public Affairs* 283, 302 (fn. 13). For a similar view, see McMahan, *Killing in War* (2009), 9–10.
[310] For a theoretical explanation of the limitations of necessity and proportionality as 'intrinsic elements' of defensive rights, see Rodin, *Self-Defense*, ch. 2. On the rationale of requirement of proportionality in respect of the entitlement to take countermeasures in international law, see O'Keefe, 'Proportionality', 1159–60.
[311] Chapter 5, Section 5.4.2.4.

## 6.4 COUNTERMEASURES AS JUSTIFICATIONS

explaining why (and when) rights are regained.[312] Again, this critique may be overcome by reference to the rights-forfeiture matrix. The right to take countermeasures is triggered by the existence of a wrongful act on the part of the wrongdoing state. So the right is a conditional one, limited by the continued existence of its triggering condition. This solution has been criticised on the basis that 'the triggering conditions should not be part of the limitations on the defense.'[313] But there is no logical reason why this should be so, and it is perfectly plausible that a conditional right exists only for so long as the triggering condition lasts. In this sense, the condition limits the temporal scope of the right. If the right to countermeasures (and, therefore, the forfeiture of legal protection) is only temporary then, when the wrongdoer complies with its obligations of cessation and reparation, the injured state's entitlement to take countermeasures ceases.

Lastly, the procedural requirements of countermeasures, *sommation* and, where available, dispute settlement obligations, present some difficulties for this theory. If the trigger of countermeasures is the wrongful act,[314] then the wrongdoing state forfeits the legal protection of its rights at the moment it commits that act. The injured state would be, therefore, entitled to take countermeasures immediately since the wrongdoer would have, from the moment of its wrongful act, forfeited the legal protection of its interests. How then to explain these procedural requirements? A possibility is to consider that the triggering condition consists in the combination of the wrongful act *and* unsuccessful *sommation*.[315] The right would thus not emerge until after the injured state had complied with this requirement. Alternatively, these requirements may be seen as a corollary of the condition of necessity. If countermeasures are a mechanism of last resort,[316] then other avenues must be exhausted before taking

---

[312] For an interesting thought experiment exploring precisely this difficulty, see Thomson, *Self-Defense and Rights (Lindley Lecture)* (1976).

[313] Grabczynska and Ferzan, 'Justifying *Killing in Self-Defence*' (2007) 99 *J Crim L & Criminology* 235, 246.

[314] See, e.g., Malanczuk, 'Countermeasures', 714 ('it is reasonable to assume that the illegality of the initial act of the delinquent State constitutes the legality of the response by precluding the wrongfulness of the act taken against the offender').

[315] On which see Dominicé, 'Observations sur les droits de l'Etat victime d'un fait internationalement illicite' in Dominicé et al. (eds), *L'ordre juridique international entre tradition et innovation* (1997), [177, 224–8, 296] (paragraph cited is the online version, available at http://books.openedition.org/iheid/1351); Lukashuk, 2646th meeting, ILC Yearbook 2000, vol. I, 268 [7].

[316] Commentary to draft art. 47, [1]. According to Crawford, they are measures of 'later (if not final) resort': Crawford, 'Overview of Part Three of the Articles on State Responsibility' in Crawford et al. (eds), *The Law of International Responsibility* (2010), 932.

this route: this includes the invocation of the responsibility of the wrongdoing state (through a notice of claim),[317] and the exhaustion of mandatory dispute settlement mechanisms (where available). As long as these options remain available, the countermeasure will be unnecessary. Urgent countermeasures for the preservation of the injured state's rights can also be grounded on their being necessary in the circumstances.

The theory is certainly not free from criticism. To begin with, it is not able to account, on a single underlying rationale, for all of the requirements and conditions of the institution. As Crawford remarked, countermeasures are a complex institution, so it is difficult to accommodate all of its conditions and requirements under a single principle. At the very least, however, the theory is able to provide a matrix along which these various requirements can be systematised. Second, it may be objected that the theory is built on a specific notion of forfeiture and, for this reason, it may be accused of ad-hocism. A certain degree of ad-hocism is inevitable, in that the theory is developed by reference to the institution as it is currently recognised (it is developed applying a bottom-up approach, in the sense discussed in Chapter 3),[318] rather than starting from first principles. Third, the dividing line between suspension of rights and suspension of performance (the forfeiture of legal protection) is very fine indeed, to the point where it may be queried whether reference to 'forfeiture' instead of suspension is not just a semantic artifice. As to the difference between suspension of rights and suspension of performance, while the line may be fine it is an important conceptual and practical distinction.[319] This is best seen by reference to treaty law: while the suspension of a treaty-right would entail the suspension of provisions of the treaty, the suspension of performance of a treaty-right would not affect the continued status of the relevant treaty provision. To achieve the former, the procedures in the VCLT would need to be followed; to achieve the latter, no such procedures exist or are necessary.

### 6.4.1.4  The Acid Test: Compensation for Material Loss

Each of the theories discussed is able to capture some properties and characteristics of countermeasures, while falling short in respect of others. As with self-defence in the previous chapter, these theories will be tested by

---

[317] ARS arts 42 and 43, respectively.
[318] See Section 3.4.
[319] Crawford, *General Part*, 682–4.

## 6.4 COUNTERMEASURES AS JUSTIFICATIONS 283

reference to the duty of compensation referred to in ARS Article 27(b). Given the uncertainties relating to the circumstances in which the duty will arise, it may be useful to consider whether any of the theories above have any implications on the existence of this duty.

Take the diplomatic premises scenario described above. It may be recalled that State A froze, by way of countermeasure, assets belonging to State B located within its territory to induce it to provide reparation for the violation of State A's diplomatic premises in State B. State A is successful in its action, and State B withdraws from the premises (cessation), provides indemnities for damages caused and an apology to State A (reparation). State A immediately cancels the freezing order, and State B is able to access its funds again. However, during the period that the countermeasures were in place, State B missed a repayment deadline for lack of sufficient funds (which were frozen by State A). As a result, B must now pay moratory interest to its creditors. Can B demand compensation from A, since this is a 'material loss' caused by the countermeasures?

As with self-defence, there were no suggestions during the ILC work (nor in the scholarship) that compensation should arise in these circumstances (at least, vis-à-vis the target state). Likewise, the case-law does not evidence that states perceive that compensation is (or should be) due in the circumstances. Nevertheless, as was said in Chapter 2, some theories are more likely than others to (at least) support a potential duty of compensation. In that chapter, it was said that the duty of compensation could be grounded on the right of the affected state.[320] The different theories underlying countermeasures take different views on whether the target state, as a result of its wrongful act, retains the protection of its interests by the legal order. Under a forfeiture theory, countermeasures are lawful *because* by its own conduct the responsible state has renounced the protection that the law affords to its interests. When the injured state takes countermeasures, therefore, it neither violates nor infringes the rights of the responsible state. No duty of compensation could therefore be grounded on the rights of the responsible state.[321] In contrast, under a consequentialist theory (where the action is lawful because it achieves a net benefit) there is no effect on the rights of the responsible state: this state retains the legal protection afforded by the law to its interests. And while its rights are not violated, they are

---
[320] Section 2.4.
[321] See, e.g., Rodin, *Self-Defense*, 51–2.

at the very least infringed – and this infringement can be the basis of a duty of compensation.[322]

### 6.4.2 Grounding the Justification of Countermeasures on Rights Forfeiture

Forfeiture theory possesses the strongest explanatory power for the justification of countermeasures. This theory can accommodate the character of countermeasures as a right of states and it can account in a systematic way for the various requirements and limitations of countermeasures currently recognised. Equally, as in relation to self-defence, the theory excludes that a duty of compensation may arise in the circumstances – an exclusion which is also supported by the maxim *ex injuria jus non oritur*.

Of course, difficulties remain with this theory as evidenced both here and in Chapter 5. More development may be necessary for this (or other theories) to explain the 'paradox' at the heart of countermeasures. This is all the more important since there are lingering doubts as to the precise boundaries of this institution. Even though countermeasures may be less noxious in contemporary conditions, they are nevertheless an established institution in international law, unlikely to disappear from interstate relations. Sovereignty and decentralisation are not contingent phenomena in international law, they are rather immanent features. While talk of international law as a 'primitive legal order' implies that this is merely a temporary state of affairs and that, perhaps unavoidably, in time international law too will respond to the features of modern legal systems,[323] the domestic analogy has not materialised and, as Martti Koskenniemi has argued,[324] it is also implausible that it will ever materialise. Countermeasures will thus continue to play a prominent role in the international legal order. For this reason, certainty and clarity about the institution of countermeasures, including on a more conceptual and theoretical level, is of fundamental importance.

---

[322] Fletcher, 'Right to Life', 149. See further Fletcher, '*Perspectives on Rights*: The Right to Life' (1978–9) 13 *Georgia LR* 1371, 1386; Rodin, *Self-Defense*, 51–2; Rodin, 'Justifying Harm' (2011) 122 *Ethics* 74, 107–8.
[323] Campbell, 'International Law and Primitive Law' (1988) 8 OJLS 169, 193.
[324] Koskenniemi, 'Solidarity Measures'. Cf. Dinstein, 'International Law as a Primitive Legal System' (1986–7) 19 *NYU J Int'l L & Pol* 1.

# 7

# Force Majeure

## 7.1 Introduction

*Force majeure* is a defence recognised in most legal systems of the world – indeed, variations of this plea have been recognised in legal systems for millennia.[1] With different terms, and occasionally different conditions, legal systems accept the total or partial exoneration for torts, delicts, and other offences, occurring in connection with supervening events that are irresistible, either because of their power or because of their unforeseeability.[2] These various rules are the legal manifestations of the adage that no one should be bound to perform the impossible (*ad impossibilia nemo tenetur*).[3] The plea of *force majeure* as a defence to legal wrongs is often considered to constitute a general principle of law.[4] Moreover, studies have been undertaken to demonstrate its metajuridical character: the idea at the heart of *force majeure* pleas has deep roots in human thinking about morality and responsibility.[5]

[1] The notion of *force majeure* is said to have originated in Roman law, though there is evidence that analogous concepts existed in early Babylonian law, see Hoppe and Wright, 'Force Majeure Clauses in Leases' (2007) 21 *Probate and Property* 8, 9. In Roman law, see, e.g. Volterra, *Istituzioni di Diritto Privato Romano* (1961), 622 (fn. 2); Guarino, *Diritto Privato Romano* (9th edn, 1992), 1012; de Robertis, *La responsabilità contrattuale nel Diritto Romano dalle origini a tutta l'età postclassica* (1996), 136ff.

[2] Generally, Jones and Schlechtriem, 'Breach of Contract (Deficiencies in a Party's Performance)' in Von Mehren (ed.), *International Encyclopedia of Comparative Law* (1976) vol. 7 (Contracts in General), ch. 15.

[3] Sibert, *Traité de droit international public* (1951) vol. 1, 333.

[4] Wolff, 'Les principes généraux du droit applicables dans les rapports internationaux' (1931) 36 *Recueil* 479, 523; Ripert, 'Les règles de droit civil applicables aux rapports internationaux' (1933) 44 *Recueil* 569, 619–20; Grapin, *Valeur internationale des Principes généraux du droit* (1934), 118; Verdross, 'Les principes généraux du droit dans la jurisprudence internationale' (1935) 52 *Recueil* 191, 215; Scheuner, 'L'influence du droit interne sur la formation du droit international' (1939) 68 *Recueil* 95, 163.

[5] The commentary to a survey conducted in France in 1984 concerning the 'sentiment of responsibility' identified that even persons not familiar with the legal concept of *force majeure* sensed that when damage is caused by 'meteorological elements of a certain violence' nobody should answer for it. The study posed the following question to citizens: 'You

Article 23 of the ARS articulates this idea in the international legal order.[6] Pursuant to this provision:

1. The wrongfulness of an act of a State not in conformity with an international obligation of that State is precluded if the act is due to *force majeure*, that is the occurrence of an irresistible force or of an unforeseen event, beyond the control of the State, making it materially impossible in the circumstances to perform the obligation.
2. Paragraph 1 does not apply if:
   (a) the situation of *force majeure* is due, either alone or in combination with other factors, to the conduct of the State invoking it; or
   (b) the State has assumed the risk of that situation occurring.

As the Commentary explains, the plea concerns a situation in which a state is 'in effect compelled to act in a manner' incompatible with its obligations.[7] The 'compulsion' so to act is the result of the occurrence of an irresistible force or of an unforeseen event, which is beyond the control of the state.[8] In short, this external event, which can be either natural or anthropogenic,[9] must be the cause of the material impossibility to perform the obligation.[10] The Commentary adds that the state must have 'no real possibility' of escaping the effects of this external event, and that an increased difficulty of performing its obligations will not be enough.[11]

---

have placed a pot of flowers on the windowsill of the dwelling of which you are a tenant. It falls and injures a passer-by. A tornado made the pot fall. Who is responsible?' According to the survey, 62 per cent of the participants felt they were responsible for the injuries, but 30 per cent considered that nobody should be responsible. This result evidenced both a strong sense of responsibility for damages (in the sense that the injured person must obtain reparation), and the extent to which certain external events are accepted as exonerating one from responsibility, see Antonmattei, *Contribution à l'étude de la force majeure* (1992), 7 (fn. 3).

[6] On *force majeure* in international law see generally: UN Secretariat, '"*Force Majeure*" and "Fortuitous Event" as Circumstances Precluding Wrongfulness: Survey of State Practice, International Judicial Decisions and Doctrine', ILC Yearbook 1978, vol. II(1); Szurek, *La force majeure en droit international* (doctoral thesis, Université Paris II Panthéon-Assas, 1996), vol. 1; Gutiérrez-Espada, *El hecho ilícito internacional* (2005), 142–4; Bjorklund, 'Emergency Exceptions: State of Necessity and *Force Majeure*' in Muchlinski and Ortino (eds), *Oxford Handbook of International Investment Law* (2007), 459; Szurek, 'Force Majeure' in Crawford et al. (eds), *The Law of International Responsibility* (2010), 475; Paddeu, 'A Genealogy of *Force Majeure* in International Law' (2011) 82 BYIL 381; Crawford, *State Responsibility: The General Part* (2013), 295–301.
[7] ARS art. 23 Commentary, [1].
[8] Ibid., [2].
[9] Ibid., [3].
[10] Ibid., [2].
[11] Ibid., [3].

When the state is 'compelled' to act in a manner incompatible with its obligations in these circumstances, its conduct is actually 'involuntary or [it] involves no element of free choice'.[12] It is this aspect of the plea that distinguishes it from the state of necessity, a cognate of the plea of *force majeure*, which, according to the Commentary, 'does not involve conduct which is involuntary or coerced'.[13] It is particularly important to demarcate these two defences since they can both arise from the same supervening event.[14] The plea is excluded if the state has unequivocally assumed the risk of the situation occurring or if it has contributed to the situation of *force majeure*.[15] The customary character of this defence is well established, and there was no real controversy in the ILC and the Sixth Committee as to whether it should be included in a codification of the law of state responsibility.

An historical analysis of the plea shows that the conception of the plea was not always unanimous. Does *force majeure* exonerate because it excludes the causal link between the non-performance of obligation and the state; because it excludes the state's fault; or because the state is coerced to act in a certain way by the circumstances? These competing conceptions of the plea can be gleaned from the practice and scholarship on *force majeure* throughout many centuries. Each of these conceptions corresponds to a different analytical explanation of the operation of the plea as affecting causation, the constitution of the wrongful act (by exclusion of one of its elements, fault) or, as will be seen, responsibility for a wrongful act. Agreement on the conception of *force majeure* was only reached during the second reading of the ARS, when the ILC settled on the idea of 'involuntariness' or exclusion of 'free choice'.[16] That is, on the idea that *force majeure* exonerates because the situation compels the state to act in a manner inconsistent with its obligations and, therefore, the state's action in the circumstances is involuntary. Similarly – and perhaps correlatively – persisting doubts remain as to the plea's classification as a justification or an excuse. In the case of consent, self-defence

---

[12] Ibid., [1].
[13] ARS art. 25 Commentary, [2].
[14] Thus, a fire can destroy the object of an obligation (for example, destroy one's grain fields so that it is not possible to deliver the goods to a buyer) or it can imperil one's interests (for example, by threatening to destroy one's grain field *unless* one burns the neighbour's house first to prevent the fire from spreading). The same fact (the fire) can thus generate a situation of *force majeure* (the former) and one of necessity (the latter).
[15] ARS art. 23 Commentary, [9–10].
[16] Ibid., [1].

and countermeasures, as the previous chapters showed, the practice very clearly conveys that these acts are lawful. As such, these defences must be classed as justifications. But in respect of *force majeure*, the practice is not clear. This is partly because invocations of *force majeure* are themselves rare and are even more rarely successful, thus making it difficult to assess whether in any given case the plea has acted to preclude wrongfulness or responsibility. In addition, scholars have often disagreed on the point,[17] and states have not been forthcoming in expressing their views.

This chapter will commence with some historical notes on the development of *force majeure* in the law of state responsibility. Section 7.2 will provide an overview of the main developments on this notion until 1945. The developments in the nineteenth century and early twentieth century are of special importance in this regard, as it is in this period that the current conception of *force majeure* consolidated. Section 7.3 will consider the contemporary formulation of the defence, tracing the ILC's work as well as the practice of states from 1945 onwards. Finally, Section 7.4 will address the question of the classification of *force majeure* as a justification or an excuse. As will be shown, the rationale of the plea relies on the compulsion of the state to act in a manner incompatible with its obligations. This rationale – together with other aspects of the plea – suggests that the defence is 'individualised',[18] in the sense that the rule focuses on the situation of the invoking state rather than on the act itself. Individualisation is a characteristic feature of excuse defences. Moreover, the absence of choice or, in other words, the constriction of a subject's free will, is construed by (domestic) legal theorists as a theory of excuse. On these bases, the chapter will conclude by proposing to classify *force majeure* as an excuse.

## 7.2 Historical Notes on the Development of the Plea of *Force Majeure*

References to *force majeure* can be found in the early works on the law of nations. These are, however, rather scattered and do not present a coherent understanding of *force majeure* or of its role as a defence to responsibility;

---

[17] Cf. Christakis, 'Les "circonstances excluant l'illicéité": une illusion optique?' in Corten et al. (eds), *Droit du pouvoir, pouvoir du droit: Mélanges offerts à Jean Salmon* (2007), 244 (justification); Crawford, *General Part*, 319 (excuse).

[18] In the sense used by George Fletcher, and explained in Chapter 1, Sections 1.2 and Chapter 3, Section 3.3.1.1. See, e.g., Fletcher, 'The Individualization of Excusing Conditions' (1973–4) 47 *S Cal LR* 1269.

for this reason, they will not be considered here.[19] In practice the plea took centre stage in the nineteenth century, in the context of claims relating to damages caused to foreigners during internal struggles. This practice was central in developing the defence as it is currently understood: while initially 'force majeure' was used as a descriptive term to refer to certain external events (the 'insurrections' or 'civil wars' themselves), by the beginning of the twentieth century *force majeure* had become a legal term of art, denoting situations of impossibility of performance caused by supervening events (including by insurrections and civil wars). In the judicial and arbitral practice of the first half of the twentieth century a defence of *force majeure* slowly consolidated, in which states could disclaim responsibility whenever circumstances beyond their control produced an impossibility of performance.

For ease of exposition, the nineteenth and twentieth century developments will be considered separately in the next two sections, though it should be noted that there is no clear break between these two periods in respect of the development of the plea. As a result, the sources (especially those around the turn of the century) will not be dogmatically separated into pre- or post-1900; rather, they will be treated in one or the other section on the basis of substantive considerations. These developments will then be drawn together in the concluding remarks of this section.

### 7.2.1 The Force Majeure *of Revolutions in the Nineteenth Century*

Historically, the nineteenth century witnessed numerous wars of independence, primarily in Latin America, nationalist revolutions in Europe and imperialist expansions in Asia and Africa.[20] Foreigners residing in these territories often suffered damage in connection with these various conflicts. Their national states often took up their causes, and espoused their claims against the host states – initially through diplomatic means and, as the century progressed, ever more through third-party dispute settlement mechanisms such as mixed-claims commissions.[21] Very often, the claims were presented mostly by what Arnulf Becker Lorca refers to as states in

---

[19] On which see Paddeu, 'Force Majeure', 398–403. See also Berlia, 'La guerre civile et la responsabilité internationale de l'Etat' (1937) 11 RGDIP 51.

[20] See, generally, Rodríguez, *The Independence of Spanish South-America* (1998); Blanning, *The Nineteenth Century: Europe 1798–1914* (2000); Chamberlain, *The Scramble for Africa* (2013).

[21] On this development, see Parlett, *The Individual in the International Legal System* (2011), 47–65.

the 'centre' as against those in the 'peripheries' and 'semi-peripheries',[22] and their arguments usually turned on the extent of host state obligations towards foreigners. It was in this setting that the rather entrenched positions on the standard of treatment of aliens (international minimum standard or national treatment), which would later stall every effort at codification of the responsibility of states for damages to aliens, first emerged. Host states wishing to deny wrongdoing in these circumstances usually relied on a combination of arguments, ranging from the standard of treatment of nationals to the exercise of the state's right of self-preservation.[23] Often, too, these states turned to the notion of *force majeure*. These disputes proved to be a fertile ground for the development and finessing of the law of responsibility generally, but also for the consolidation and configuration of the concept of *force majeure* in interstate relations.

In its widest formulation, *force majeure* was invoked by host states to exclude all responsibility for damage caused in connection with an external, unforeseen or irresistible, event. Domestic struggles (including revolts, insurrections and civil wars) were characterised as *forces majeures*, as superior forces, and all injuries occurring in connection with the struggle were attributed to the event itself. In this way, the state avoided *any* responsibility for injuries caused to foreigners: these injuries were not the state's doing, but the result of a superior force.[24] The state was as much an innocent victim of this superior force as the injured foreigners themselves. An example of this position can be seen in the Belgian response to claims by the United Kingdom and United States in relation to damage caused to their nationals during the bombardment of Antwerp, as part of the 1830 Belgian insurrection.[25] According to the Belgian authorities, 'the consequences of open war are events of chance or of superior force

---

[22] See, generally, Becker Lorca, *Mestizo International Law* (2015).

[23] See, e.g., the diplomatic note of Prince Schwartzenberg addressed to the British Crown on behalf of the Kingdom of Two Sicilies and the Grand Duke of Tuscany of 1850, cited by Arias, 'The Non-Liability of States for Damages Suffered by Foreigners in the Course of a Riot, an Insurrection or a Civil War' (1913) 7 AJIL 724, 742.

[24] Among writers, this view was maintained by Despagnet, *Cours de droit international public* (Larose, 1894), 344. Despagnet later reiterated this view noting that it corresponded with the practice of states. He acknowledged that compensation was sometimes offered (on a gratuitous basis) and that legal scholarship and the IDI tended to accept limited instances of responsibility in these circumstances: Despagnet, *Cours de droit international public* (3rd edn, 1905), 378ff.

[25] For a summary of the facts of this incident, see Laurent, 'State Responsibility: A Possible Historic Precedent to the Calvo Clause' (1966) 15 ICLQ 395; Laurent, 'Anglo-American Diplomacy and the Belgian Indemnities Controversy 1836–42' (1967) 10 *Historical Journal* 197.

['*force majeure*' in the French version], for which no one is responsible'.[26] In this extreme position, insurrections, revolts, wars, and so on, were said to 'constitute' *forces majeures* and all claims for damages arising therefrom were denied, regardless of any direct causation between the damage and the state organs' own actions.[27]

This extreme position was opposed by many other states and was widely criticised in the literature.[28] These criticisms usually denied that there was a necessary causal link between the superior force and the damage, and focused instead on the direct causation of the damage by the state organs' conduct. Thus, the United Kingdom's response to the Belgian statement above emphasised that, although in war 'unavoidable necessity excuses many acts which lead to the destruction of private property',[29] the damage caused to its nationals had resulted from acts of the Belgian volunteers. These acts, it added, were 'not unavoidable, nor were they necessary'.[30] The distinction between damage caused by the event and damage caused by the state's officials was better articulated some years later by British Law Officer Dodson in an opinion concerning the effects of the Neapolitan Insurrection of 1848 on British property in Messina. According to Dodson, 'redress cannot be demanded for the suffering parties' in the case of accidental occurrences in the 'ordinary operations of war', namely cases where property was 'destroyed by the ordinary operations of war, or in the case of towns bombarded, or taken by storm, or of a country laid waste for the purpose of securing a frontier or stopping the

---

[26] UN Secretariat, '"*Force Majeure*" and "Fortuitous Event"', 106 [162], citing (1841–2) 30 BFSP 224.

[27] For another example, see the French response to Spanish claims for indemnities in respect of the Saida Incident of 1881, reported in Kiss, *Répertoire de la pratique française en matière de droit international public* (1962) vol. 3, 618–19.

[28] See, e.g., Brusa, 'Responsabilité des Etats à raison des dommages soufferts par des étrangers en cas d'émeute ou de guerre civile' (1898) 17 *Annuaire IDI* 96. In the early twentieth century, see Rougier, *Les guerres civiles et le droit des gens* (1903), 473; Nys, *Le droit international: les principes, les théories, les faits* (1905) vol. 2, 227; Wiesse, *Reglas de derecho internacional aplicables a las guerras civiles* (2nd edn, 1905), 78–9, 87; Podestá-Costa, 'La responsabilidad del Estado por daños irrogados a la persona o a los bienes de extranjeros en luchas civiles' (1939) 34 *Revista de derecho internacional* (La Habana) 5, 50. Edwin Borchard did not address *force majeure* in relation to these types of damages. He did, however, note Brusa's report to the IDI and the position he took there on *force majeure* in a footnote. Further, he considered damages consequent upon legitimate acts of war during an international war to be due to 'necessity or *force majeure*', see Borchard, *The Diplomatic Protection of Citizens Abroad* (1915), 256.

[29] UN Secretariat, '"*Force Majeure*" and "Fortuitous Event"', 106, citing (1841–2) 30 BFSP 232.

[30] Ibid., citing (1841–2) 30 BFSP 232.

progress of the enemy or of making approaches to a town intended to be attacked.[31] Nevertheless, he added, there was an exception to this general principle: where the destruction 'was intentional and wanton, without provocation and without necessity'.[32] In these cases, the state owed a duty of reparation to the injured foreigners. A similar approach was later followed by Max Huber in *British Claims in the Spanish Zones of Morocco*. In his report, Huber accepted that the fact of the revolt itself, and the injuries caused by it, were a case of *force majeure*. The state was, therefore, not responsible for their occurrence as such. However, the state retained the obligation to exercise vigilance in the circumstances, so the mere existence of a 'certain connection' between the damage and the revolt was insufficient to exclude the state's responsibility. Thus, it was necessary to examine, individually, what the state organs had done or failed to do in relation to each claim.[33] In sum, on this view, there was a difference between, on the one hand, damage caused as an incident of the fighting – as collateral damage, we would say today – and, on the other, damage directly caused by the state organs' conduct in fighting the insurrection.[34] The former was the result of the *force majeure*, the latter resulted from the 'free volition'[35] of the state and, therefore, engaged its responsibility.[36]

Among commentators the view was increasingly upheld that states were responsible for their own acts even during internal revolts, but that under certain circumstances in which the state's will had been 'coerced' and its conduct, therefore, 'compelled', it could disclaim its responsibility. In these arguments, *force majeure* became a notion concerned with state will. Scholars presented a range of views in this regard, in which *force majeure* played a wider or narrower role. At the wider end of the spectrum, there were those like the Argentine jurist Carlos Calvo for whom all acts adopted by the state in a domestic struggle were 'coerced' by the circumstances. The state should not be responsible for these acts since it was

---

[31] *Insurrection in Sicily* (1848) 2 McNair Intl L Op 251, 252.
[32] Ibid., 251.
[33] Huber, Rapport sur les responsabilités de l'Etat dans les situations visées par les réclamations britanniques, *British Claims in the Spanish Zone of Morocco* (1924) 2 RIAA 639, 642.
[34] The same could be said of natural events: the state is not responsible for the occurrence of an earthquake and the damages caused by it. It is, however, responsible for the acts of its own organs in connection with the event, say if the state could have taken precautions to minimise damage and failed to do so.
[35] Rougier, *Guerres civiles*, 474 (speaking of 'volonté libre').
[36] Among the writers, the following maintained (versions) of this position: Fiore, *Nouveau droit international public* (2nd edn, 1885) vol. 1, 572, 583–8; Wiesse, *Le droit international appliqué aux guerres civiles* (1898), 47.

## 7.2 HISTORICAL NOTES ON THE DEVELOPMENT OF THE PLEA 293

not a guarantor of the safety of foreigners from cases of *force majeure*.[37] At the other end of the spectrum was Emilio Brusa, writing as rapporteur on responsibility to the IDI.[38] Brusa was critical of the reliance on the concept of *force majeure* to exclude the responsibility of the state for damages caused to foreigners during domestic struggles. In his view, *force majeure* excluded the voluntariness of conduct, whereas voluntariness played a fundamental role in war and insurrection. It was thus wrong to describe the state's acts in those circumstances as 'coerced'; on the contrary, the state's acts in quashing the insurrection were willed and, as such, engaged the state's responsibility.[39] Julius Goebel's views seemed to chart a middle ground. He too disapproved of the notion of *force majeure* as used in this context, which he dismissed as a 'doctrine of municipal law which [had] been transferred to international jurisprudence to enable a State to escape liability where it otherwise would be responsible'.[40] Goebel thought that it was 'obviously impossible to absolutely eliminate the element of will' in relation to the state's conduct during domestic revolts. He conceded, however, that the state's will could be eliminated in certain circumstances, and that this depended on the gravity and intensity of the situation.[41] An internal revolt amounting to the degree of the American Civil War, for example, constituted *force majeure* in which the will of the state was eliminated.[42] In such circumstances, the state was not responsible for damage caused by its compelled actions.

In their wider or narrower forms, all these views led to sweeping conclusions: the state's will was either eliminated or undisturbed, its acts were either all coerced or all voluntary. The sweeping nature of these positions may have been the result of the manner in which the relevant claims were handled – usually by diplomatic means. Claimant states presented a collection of claims, often requesting lump sums, rather than discrete claims relating to the injury suffered by each one of their nationals. Host states responded with equally general arguments. As third-party dispute

---

[37] Calvo, *Le droit international théorique et pratique* (3rd edn, 1880) vol. 1, 429.
[38] Brusa's report, in particular its premises and framework, was so divisive that the IDI could not examine the resolution that he proposed therein. A subsequent report was later presented by Louis de Bar and Brusa in 1900, which eventually led to the adoption of the Réglement sur la responsabilité des Etats à raison des dommages soufferts par des étrangers en cas d'émeute, d'insurrection ou de guerre civile (1900) 18 *Annuaire IDI* 254.
[39] Brusa, 'Responsabilité', 97. Similarly: Wiesse, *Reglas*, 87.
[40] Goebel, 'The International Responsibility of States for Injuries Sustained by Aliens on Account of Mob Violence, Insurrections and Civil War' (1914) 8 AJIL 802, 813.
[41] Ibid., 815.
[42] Id.

settlement became an increasingly used mechanism, claims began to be presented individually in relation to each national (or at least in groups of similar claims arising from the same set of facts). This forced the parties to argue about specific injuries and, in turn, required tribunals to assess each discrete claim on its own merits – as had been suggested by Arbitrator Huber in the *Spanish Zones of Morocco* case. By the early twentieth century, tribunals dealing with *force majeure* pleas proceeded to individualised assessments of the respondent state's ability to perform the specific obligation under scrutiny in the circumstances.

### 7.2.2 Force Majeure *in Judicial and Arbitral Practice of the Early Twentieth Century*

*Force majeure* was invoked in several arbitral and judicial proceedings in the early twentieth century. In all cases, the dispute arose against a background that included internal revolts or international wars (and sometimes both), and the non-performance of the obligation had occurred in that setting. The cases and the (relevant) holdings by the tribunals will be briefly summarised in this subsection, and their findings will be assessed in Section 7.2.3.

#### 7.2.2.1 *French Company of Venezuelan Railroads* (1904)

The French Company of Venezuelan Railroads was engaged for the construction, maintenance and operation of railway lines in the western part of Venezuela. The company's operations had been disturbed and interrupted multiple times by a series of external events. In order to avoid bankruptcy, the company had suspended its operations altogether.[43] The company claimed damages from the Venezuelan government before the Franco-Venezuelan mixed-claims commission. In their arguments before the commission both parties referred to the notion of *force majeure*.[44] The company claimed that its suspension of operations had resulted from *force majeure*, caused by the revolution and by the government's failure to service its debts to the company.[45] The Venezuelan Commissioner

---

[43] *French Company of Venezuelan Railroads* (1904) 10 RIAA 285, 291–2, 304, 338. These included a combination of events, among others the failure of Venezuela to pay its contractual debt to the company, damages caused to the company's assets by natural events (floods) and by the actions of officials and insurgents during the Crespo revolution.
[44] As presented by the French and Venezuelan Commissioners.
[45] *French Company*, 317–18, 343.

## 7.2 HISTORICAL NOTES ON THE DEVELOPMENT OF THE PLEA 295

responded that the same *force majeure* that had compelled the company to suspend operations (the revolution), had made it impossible for the state to service its debt to the company.[46] Indeed, all of the government's resources were 'consumed by the imperative necessities of war'.[47] In these circumstances, the government could not be responsible for the injury caused to the company.

The umpire upheld the Venezuelan plea, explaining that the situation in the country was part of those 'misfortunes' which were incidental to government, business, and human life alike. Moreover,

> The claimant company was compelled by *force majeure* to desist from its exploitation in October, 1899; the respondent Government, from the same cause, had been prevented from paying its indebtedness to the claimant company. The umpire finds no purpose or intent on the part of the respondent Government to harm or injure the claimant company in any way or in any degree. Its acts and its neglects were caused and incited by entirely different reasons and motives.[48]

### 7.2.2.2 *Russian Indemnity* (1912)

The 1879 Peace Treaty of Constantinople, adopted after the 1877–8 Turco-Russian War, established the sum of the indemnity owed by the Ottoman Empire to the Russian Empire in consequence of the war.[49] After the adoption of the Treaty, the Ottoman Empire endured a number of insurrections and participated in international wars, all of which had adverse effects on its finances and prevented the timely service of its debt.[50] A dispute arose in respect of the payment of debt and of the obligation to pay interest-damages,[51] which the parties submitted to arbitration by special agreement. *Force majeure* was relevant to the claim of interest-damages. In this connection, the Ottoman Empire's response was two-pronged: in the first instance, it denied the existence of an obligation

---

[46] Ibid., 327.
[47] Ibid., 314.
[48] Ibid., 353.
[49] *Russian Indemnity Case (Russia/Turkey)* (1912) Scott Hague Court Rep 297, 304. For a historical background, see Milgrim, 'An Overlooked Problem in Turkish–Russian Relations: The 1878 War Indemnity' (1978) 9 *International Journal of Middle East Studies* 519.
[50] Waibel, *Sovereign Defaults before International Courts and Tribunals* (2011), 89.
[51] Note that the award uses the expression 'interest-damages' in view of a controversy between the parties in respect of the character of the damages sought and in respect of the obligation to pay those damages, see *Russian Indemnity*, 312–13.

to pay interest-damages as a matter of customary law, and, in the alternative, it invoked the defence of *force majeure*.[52]

In respect of the first defensive argument, Turkey maintained that interest-damages did 'not exist' in international law 'unless expressly stipulated'. The argument was complex, and rested on the assumption that states are not debtors like private entities. Indeed, to find a state bound to an obligation it had not accepted, like the obligation to pay interest-damages, posed the 'risk of compromising the political life of the State, injuring its vital interests, upsetting its budget, preventing it from defending itself against an insurrection of [sic] foreign attack'.[53] For this reason, defaulting states could simply not be treated like private debtors. It is important to point out that this was an argument about the existence of an obligation in international law, and not a defence for the claimed breach of the (existing) obligation to pay the debt to Russia. Turkey cared to clarify this much in its written rejoinder, stating that its argument did not involve the invocation of the notion of 'self-preservation' as a defence for the failure to service its debt, as the Russians had (mis)understood in their own written arguments.[54] The Tribunal rejected Turkey's argument and held that interest-damages were due under international law.[55]

The Ottoman Empire's second (alternative) defensive argument concerned exoneration for failure to pay the principal on time. In this context, Turkey invoked *force majeure*. A series of unforeseen events, said Turkey, had caused for it an 'impossibility to service' its debts to the Russian Empire;[56] for Turkey this was, as Russia too had recognised in diplomatic correspondence, an 'absolute impossibility'.[57] Interest-damages could therefore not arise since Turkey had a valid defence for the non-performance of the obligation to pay. In response, Russia denied that *force majeure* could afford Turkey a defence. It did not reject the plea as a matter of law, but it was sceptical that *force majeure* could last for the period of twenty years during which the Ottoman Empire had failed to pay its debt. At most, Russia argued, the Ottoman Empire could invoke the state of necessity to protect its vital interests but, even in this case, it was farfetched to think that the payment of a relatively modest sum

---

[52] Ibid., 310–11.
[53] Ibid., 310.
[54] *Contre-Réplique présentée au nom du Gouvernement de l'Empire Ottoman* (1912), 28 [280].
[55] *Russian Indemnity*, 310.
[56] *Contre-Mémoire présenté au nom du Gouvernement de l'Empire Ottoman* (1911), 44 [123].
[57] *Empire Ottoman, Contre-Mémoire*, 64 [183].

could be a 'sort of suicide for the Sublime Porte'.[58] In its rejoinder, Turkey maintained that its argument had been misrepresented by Russia: the Ottoman Empire's defence was based on *force majeure*, and not on the self-preservation of the state or of its interests. Sure *force majeure* had some relation with the 'right of self-preservation' but they were not 'la même chose'.[59]

In the award, the Tribunal went on to cite Russia's remarks about the 'case of necessity' in addressing the Ottoman Empire's plea of *force majeure*, thus mixing two things which, as the parties were aware, were not 'la même chose'.[60] The Tribunal accepted that *force majeure* was recognised in international law, since 'international law must adapt itself to political necessities'.[61] However, having reformulated the defence as one requiring a threat to the state's existence (rather than impossibility, as it had been argued by Turkey), it rejected it on the facts as it found that it was an 'exaggeration' to admit that the payment of the sum owed 'would imperil the existence of [Turkey] or seriously compromise its internal or external situation'.[62]

### 7.2.2.3  *The SS Wimbledon* (1923)

The case concerned the right of free passage through the Kiel Canal as established by Article 380 of the Treaty of Versailles.[63] Germany, a party to the Treaty, had refused passage to the English steamship *Wimbledon*, time-chartered to carry military materiel to the Polish base at Danzig during the Russo-Polish War, a war in respect of which Germany had declared its neutrality. Anticipating possible defences of the respondent, the applicant states argued that Germany could not free itself 'from the duty of carrying out [that] obligation' since there was no material or legal impossibility of performance. Indeed, it was not possible to speak of *force majeure* or state of necessity in the circumstances.[64] Yet Germany needed a 'juridical reason' to justify the 'voluntary non-performance' of its obligation.[65] Germany, however, dismissed the applicants' arguments. Its conduct was not in breach of the Treaty, so it was unnecessary to rely

---

[58] *Réplique présentée au nom du Gouvernement Impérial de Russie* (1912), 32–3.
[59] *Empire Ottoman, Contre-Réplique*, 28 [280].
[60] *Russian Indemnity*, 317.
[61] Id.
[62] Ibid., 317–18.
[63] Treaty of Versailles (28 June 1919) 225 CTS 188, (1919) 13 AJIL Supp 151.
[64] Applicants' oral statement, PCIJ Series C No 03/4, 284 (Annex 27, English translation).
[65] Ibid., 288.

on defences. Germany agreed that there had been no 'factual impossibility' or a situation which would have 'unavoidably forced' it not to fulfil its obligation.[66] The PCIJ eventually found Germany in breach of its obligation under the Treaty.[67]

### 7.2.2.4  *Serbian* and *Brazilian Loans* (1929)

The disputes concerned the monetary basis for payment of loans to French bondholders.[68] The loans had been issued in gold-francs and until 1914 they had been serviced in French-francs, equal in value to the gold-franc. In 1914 France established a forced currency regime, and in 1924 it passed legislation to stabilise the value of its currency on the basis of the gold-franc at the value of one fifth of a gold-franc. Serbia and Brazil continued to pay their loans at the current value of the French franc throughout.[69] In 1924, the French bondholders contested the debt service in French-francs at the current value, demanding payment in gold-francs for the remaining debt and of the difference in arrears for the payments that had been made in French-francs.[70]

Before the PCIJ both Serbia and Brazil invoked *force majeure* against the French claim.[71] Serbia argued, first, that the economic dislocation caused by the war, the circumstance which 'most dominated the will of individuals', had forced it to issue the bonds.[72] Further, it invoked *force majeure* in respect of the failure to pay the bonds in gold-francs insofar as the law of 5 August 1914 had made it 'materially' impossible for Serbia to pay in the stipulated currency.[73] Brazil, in turn, invoked *force majeure*

---

[66]  German oral statement, PCIJ Series C No 03/4, 306 (Annexes 29–31). The quotations are a literal translation of the French language transcript. The PCIJ's English translation states that '[t]here was no impossibility whatever for Germany to carry out the Treaty; nor has Germany contravened the Treaty'; see ibid. at 314.

[67]  *The SS 'Wimbledon'* (1923) PCIJ, Series A No 01, 15, 30.

[68]  *Case Concerning the Payment of Various Serbian Loans Issued in France (France v Kingdom of the Serbs, Croats and Slovenes)* (1929) PCIJ, Series A No 20, 5; *Case Concerning the Payment of Various Brazilian Loans Issued in France (France v Brazil)* (1929) PCIJ, Series A No 20, 93.

[69]  *Serbian Loans*, 37–8.

[70]  For a summary of facts, see Sander, '*Brazilian Loans Case* and *Serbian Loans Case*' in Wolfrum (ed.), *Max Planck Encyclopedia of Public International Law* (2008–, available at www.mpepil.com).

[71]  The precise legal basis of *force majeure* was unclear in the defence of both respondents. Indeed, the law applicable to the dispute raised difficult issues, see Waibel, *Sovereign Defaults*, 63ff.

[72]  Serbia, oral statement, PCIJ Series C No 16-III(2), 211.

[73]  Memorial of Serbia, PCIJ Series C No 16-III(3), 459.

in respect of the obligation to service the loans in gold-francs, which it said had become impossible in view of French municipal law: this was the case of *force majeure* also known as '*fait du prince*'.[74] Having found that the gold-franc was a standard of value, the PCIJ rejected the *force majeure* pleas of both respondent states since the French Law of 1914 had not made it impossible for either Serbia or Brazil to service their debts in the equivalent amount in French-francs.[75]

### 7.2.2.5 *Société Commerciale de Belgique* (1939)

A dispute between Greece and Belgium arose out of the failure of Greece to perform an arbitral award entitling the Société Commerciale de Belgique (Socobelge) to damages.[76] Greece and Socobelge had entered into a contract in 1925 for the construction of a railway line. Following a number of events, including the world financial crisis of the early 1930s, Greece defaulted on its debt including its payments to Socobelge. In 1932, in a process led by the League of Nations, Greece agreed to amended schedules for repayments to its bondholders. The following year, Socobelge initiated arbitral proceedings against Greece under the concession contract. The Tribunal found that Greece was in breach of its contractual obligations, permitted the rescission of the contract, and awarded damages to Socobelge.[77] Greece duly implemented the award, but failed to comply with the provisions concerning damages. In this connection, it argued that its service of foreign debt was tightly regulated by other international arrangements, including under the League of Nations, and these arrangements had obliged it to defer payment to Socobelge. Considering such a deferral to be a repudiation of the debt, Belgium, acting on behalf of Socobelge, submitted the dispute to the PCIJ. Belgium claimed that by failing to execute the award, Greece had rejected the award's status as *res judicata* and breached the acquired rights of a foreign national, which, in turn, constituted a breach of Greece's international obligations.[78]

---

[74] Memorial of Brazil, PCIJ Series C No 16, 153. See also Counter-Memorial of Brazil, PCIJ Series C No 16, 235, 241, 243.
[75] *Serbian Loans*, 39–40; *Brazilian Loans*, 120.
[76] For a detailed account of the facts leading to this case, see Reisman, 'The Supervisory Jurisdiction of the International Court of Justice: International Arbitration and International Adjudication' (1996) 258 *Recueil* 9, 233ff.
[77] Memorial of Belgium, PCIJ Series C No 87 (1939), Annexes 7 and 8, containing the arbitral awards.
[78] *Société Commerciale de Belgique* (1939) PCIJ Series A/B No 78, 160, 161–2.

Greece invoked *force majeure*, a 'pressing necessity' as it described it, as a defence against the Belgian claim. Greece adduced its participation in World War I, its absorption of over one million refugees, and the global financial crisis, all events that were external to Greece and that had occurred against its will. In these circumstances it was 'totally'[79] impossible for it to pay in full and immediately the sum owed to Socobelge pursuant to the award.[80] Greece added that it had been 'constrained by the case of *force majeure*' to forgo its obligations under the award.[81] In response, Belgium agreed in law with the Greek defence,[82] though it considered that only a 'factual impediment' could give rise to *force majeure* and no such impediment existed in the case.[83] Ultimately, the PCIJ did not pronounce on the question of *force majeure*, since Greece had acknowledged on record that it in no way wished to repudiate the awards.[84] The PCIJ noted, however, that though the financial circumstance of Greece could not affect its obligation to service its debts, the debtor's capacity to pay could be taken into account in subsequent payment arrangements.[85]

### 7.2.3 An Assessment

Two interrelated trends can be identified in the development of the plea of *force majeure* throughout this period. The first one concerns the conception of *force majeure*: initially a descriptive term, used to designate a certain typology of event, *force majeure* eventually became a rule of the legal order which concerned a situation of impossibility of performance. Second, as the understanding of *force majeure* changed, so did the rationale of its exonerating effect. These two developments are addressed in turn.

#### 7.2.3.1 Changing Conceptions of *Force Majeure*

The first significant development was a conceptual one. In the early cases and literature, the expression '*force majeure*' was used in a descriptive sense. It represented a typology of external event possessing certain characteristics of irresistibility or unforeseeability.[86] Thus, an internal revolt, an

---

[79] Counter-Memorial of Greece, PCIJ Rep Series C No 87, 99–100.
[80] Ibid., 91.
[81] Rejoinder of Greece, PCIJ Rep Series C No 87, 142.
[82] Belgium, oral statement, PCIJ Series C No 87(3), 236.
[83] Ibid., 260.
[84] *Socobelge*, 174–5.
[85] Ibid., 176–7.
[86] *Force majeure* was also understood in this way in France, see Radouant, *Du cas fortuit et de la force majeure* (1920), 4.

## 7.2 HISTORICAL NOTES ON THE DEVELOPMENT OF THE PLEA

international war, or an earthquake, were said to 'constitute' *force majeure*.[87] The language is telling: once the event 'constitutes' *force majeure*, no more scrutiny is required. The injuries resulting from the event cannot be attributed to the state and, consequently, cannot engage the state's responsibility. Thus, Belgium's assertion in 1830 that 'the consequences of open war are events of chance or of superior force' for which no one was responsible.

As the century wore on, however, *force majeure* became a legal term of art, referring to a particular set of circumstances in which the will of the state was constrained and the state was, therefore, compelled to act in a manner incompatible with its obligations.[88] *Force majeure* still involved unforeseen or irresistible events, but it was now a concept concerned with state will. In short, *force majeure* was a defence afforded to a state because, as a result of the occurrence of an external event, it had failed to perform an obligation involuntarily. Note that the notion of involuntariness used in this context was not necessarily equivalent to a physical involuntariness – it was not the situation of the ship that, dragged into a foreign port by strong currents, causes damage to a pier.[89] In these situations the state is the instrument, rather than the agent, of the damage, as will be explained in more detail later. Involuntariness in this context was a normative concept, in that it denoted a situation in which the will of the state had been coerced or compelled.

The difficulty was, of course, that of determining the circumstances in which it was possible to say that the state had acted involuntarily. Practice and doctrine slowly settled on a standard of impossibility of performance in this regard. Only where, as a result of the external event, performance of the obligation had become impossible could it be said that the state had been compelled or coerced to act in a manner contrary to that obligation. That is, only where there was an impossibility to perform the obligation could the non-performance of that obligation be involuntary. This development can be seen very clearly, for example, in the Turkish pleading in

---

[87] For statements to this effect see, e.g., *Petrocelli Case* (1903) 10 RIAA 591; *American Electric and Manufacturing Company Case (Damages to Property)* (1903–5) 9 RIAA 145, 146; *Bembelista Case* (1903) 10 RIAA 717, 718; *The Dunn Case (Chile/UK)* (1895), *Reclamaciones presentadas al Tribunal Anglo-Chileno 1894–1896* (1896) vol. 1, 538; Klüber, *Droit des gens moderne de l'Europe* (2nd edn, 1874), 369; Rolin, 'Consultation' in de la Pradelle (ed.), *Causes célèbres du droit des gens: les Suisses et les dommages de guerre* (1931), 261, 266–7; Sánchez de Bustamante y Sirvén, *Droit international public* (1936) vol. 3, 526.

[88] As a 'situation-based' defence: Szurek, 2 *Force Majeure*, 409–16; or a 'global' defence: Radouant, *Du cas fortuit*, 10–13; Antonmattei, *Contribution*, 10. This change is discussed in Paddeu, 'Force Majeure', 436–46.

[89] See further Section 7.4.1.

*Russian Indemnity*, the Serbian and Brazilian defences in the *Loans* cases, and the Belgian response in *Socobelge*, all of which assessed the plea of *force majeure* against a standard of impossibility.[90]

What kind and degree of impossibility was required? A number of different typologies of impossibility were recognised in the international law of the time. The law of treaties, for example, envisaged a diverse range of 'impossibilities' as grounds for termination or suspension of treaties including physical,[91] legal[92] and moral.[93] In the context of *force majeure*, the practice does not reveal a wholly consistent standard. Various adjectives were used to describe the impossibility required, which referred to both qualitative and quantitative criteria. As to the type, references were made to a 'material'[94] or even 'factual'[95] impossibility of performance. This suggested that, contrary to the law of treaties, legal and moral impossibility would not be enough.[96] As to degree, there were references to 'absolute'[97] and 'total'[98] impossibility. A few sources opted for a lower degree of impossibility, related to situations of threats to the state's survival. In these latter situations, the state retained the possibility to perform its obligation, it *can* perform the obligation, but only at the cost of an extreme sacrifice (its existence). This is the situation that Special Rapporteur Roberto Ago

---

[90] In addition to the cases reviewed, see *William Yeaton Case* (1885) 3 *Moore Arbitrations* 2944, 2948; *Kummerow et al v Venezuela* (1903) 9 RIAA 369, 400; *Michel Macri v Turkey*, Turco-Romanian Arbitral Tribunal, 19 January 1928, 7 TAM 981, 982. In the literature, see Garner, 'Responsibility of States for Injuries Suffered by Foreigners within Their Territories on Account of Mob Violence, Riots and Insurrections' (1927) 21 *ASIL Proc* 49, 63; Cavaglieri, 'Règles générales du droit de la paix' (1929) 26 *Recueil* 311, 553–4; Ripert, 'Les règles', 619; Grapin, *Principes*, 118; Basdevant, 'Règles générales du droit de la paix' (1936) 58 *Recueil* 471, 555; Podestá-Costa, 'Responsabilidad', 50.

[91] E.g., von Martens, *Traité de droit international* (1883) vol. 1, 531–2; Macri, *Teorica del diritto internazionale* (1884) vol. 2, 2; Rivier, *Principes de droit des gens* (1896) vol. 2, 134–5.

[92] E.g., Rivier, *Principes*, 134–5; Bonfils, *Manuel de droit international public* (Fauchille ed., 4th edn, 1905), 477.

[93] E.g., Phillimore, *Commentaries upon International Law* (1855) vol. 2, 61; Klüber, *Droit de gens*, 2nd edn, 234; von Martens, 1 *Traité*, 532.

[94] Applicants' oral statement, *Wimbledon*, PCIJ Series C No 03/4, 284 (Annex 27, English translation); Memorial of Serbia, *Serbian Loans*, PCIJ Series C No 16-III(3), 459.

[95] German oral statement, *Wimbledon*, PCIJ Series C No 03/4, 306 (Annexes 29–31); Belgium oral statement, *Socobelge*, PCIJ Series C No 87, 260.

[96] The Brazilian plea of *fait du prince* in *Brazilian Loans* came close to an argument of legal impossibility, in that the availability of gold had been made impossible by a Decree of the French State. Though the pleadings suggest that the claim related to the unavailability, in the markets, of gold-francs – thus a physical impossibility.

[97] *Empire Ottoman, Contre-Mémoire*, 64 [183].

[98] Counter-Memorial of Greece, *Socobelge*, PCIJ Rep Series C No 87, 99–100.

would later call 'relative impossibility'.[99] Examples of this approach can be seen in the Greek argument in *Socobelge* and the Tribunal's award in *Russian Indemnity*. Nevertheless, this lower degree of impossibility was by no means the norm. Moreover, in at least one of the cases in which it was asserted, *Russian Indemnity*, this approach was the result of a conflation of arguments (state of necessity and *force majeure*) that the parties had presented and clearly understood to be different (recall that they were not 'la même chose'). Rather, the context in which these claims were made (and usually dismissed) suggests that the impossibility referred to had indeed to be absolute and, moreover, physical: an actual inability to perform the obligation. By way of illustration, only if Serbia's (or Brazil's) obligation was to repay the loans in gold-francs and gold-francs had become unavailable as a result of an unforeseen or irresistible event would the plea have been met.

### 7.2.3.2  What Rationale for the Plea?

There were also different explanations as to why the plea of *force majeure* exonerated the state for conduct in contravention of its obligations. Two main trends can be identified in the practice and literature of the period; both roughly coinciding with the different conceptions of *force majeure* mentioned earlier.[100]

First, the rationale of the defence was often found in its exclusion of the causal link between the state's conduct and the damage in question. This is evident, for instance, in Robert Phillimore's explanation of *force majeure* (an instance of 'physical necessity' as he called it): 'a ship may be compelled by a storm, which is *vis major*, to put into an interdicted port; the master may *protest*, as the nautical phrase is, against the wind and the waves but he cannot bring his action – there is no person against whom he can have his remedy'.[101] In the context of internal struggles, Calvo also explained the exonerating effect of *force majeure* (if only partly) on the 'accidental' occurrence of the damages.[102] In this same context, France and Spain agreed in relation to the Saida incident

---

[99] See Section 7.3.1.1.
[100] Szurek arrives at the same conclusion: Szurek, 1 *Force Majeure*, 289–99. For an analogous conclusion, in respect of Roman law, see Gerkens, '*Vis maior* and *vis cui resisti non potest*' in Van Den Bergh and Van Niekerk (eds), *Ex iusta traditum: Essays in Honour of Eric H Pool* (2005), 111.
[101] Phillimore, *Commentaries upon International Law* (1857) vol. 3, 191.
[102] Calvo, 1 *Droit international*, 429.

of 1881 that in the 'ordinary case of *force majeure*' damages arose out of 'the hazards of war'.[103] The damage was, as such, due to an external event and not causally attributable to the state. This rationale coincided with the descriptive conception of *force majeure* mentioned earlier: if the event was a *force majeure*, damages occurring in connection with it were causally attributed to the event itself thus excluding the state's responsibility.

In the second rationale, *force majeure* exonerated the state from responsibility because its conduct, in the circumstances, was involuntary. This rationale, as was observed earlier, was paired with *force majeure* as a legal concept requiring impossibility of performance resulting from the external event. In several of the sources, discussions about *force majeure* centred on the notion of state will and on whether the relevant act, in the circumstances, could be considered as involuntary as a result of external coercion or compulsion.[104] This view accepted that the non-performance of the obligation was causally attributable to the state's own conduct (and not to the external event as such), but it objected that the state had voluntarily engaged in that conduct. Involuntariness in this context involved not just physical involuntariness (where the state is the instrument, rather than the agent of the damage) but also normative involuntariness (where the state's conduct had been coerced or compelled). Thus, in *French Company*, Venezuela claimed that the Crespo revolution had 'compelled' it to breach its obligations towards the company;[105] in *Russian Indemnity* the Tribunal recognised that the 'situation' had 'forced' Turkey to 'make special application of a large part of its revenues', preventing it from fulfilling its debt;[106] and, in *Serbian Loans*, the Serbian argument of *force majeure* referred (among others) to its having been forced to issue the bonds by external events happening 'against its will'.[107] An additional example can be seen in the statement by Brazil, in respect of claims concerning damages caused during the 1893–4 civil war, arguing that it had been 'compelled by *force majeure*' to ensure its safety by adopting measures injurious to foreigners.[108] The assumption

---

[103] Kiss, *Répertoire*, 618–19.
[104] See, e.g., Brusa, 'Responsabilité', 97; Rougier, *Guerres civiles*, 474; Wiesse, *Reglas*, 87. Goebel's critique also implies a notion of *force majeure* premised on involuntariness, see 'International Responsibility', 815.
[105] *French Company*, 314.
[106] *Russian Indemnity*, 317–18.
[107] Oral statement of Serbia, PCIJ Series C No 16-III(2), 211.
[108] Reproduced in (1894) 1 RGDIP 164.

## 7.2 HISTORICAL NOTES ON THE DEVELOPMENT OF THE PLEA

underlying these discussions was, of course, that the state's responsibility could only be engaged when its acts were free and voluntary.[109]

Involuntariness in this context was also often explained as an absence of fault. *Force majeure* exonerated, therefore, because the conduct adopted by the state did not involve elements of intention or negligence. The umpire in *French Company* noted that the Venezuelan conduct which had harmed the claimant had not been committed with 'purpose' or 'intent'.[110] Similarly, in *Prats*, the Mexican Commissioner explained that:

> There is no responsibility without fault (*culpa*) and it is too well known that there is no fault (*culpa*) in having failed to do what was impossible. The fault is essentially dependent upon the will, but as the will completely disappears before the force, whose action cannot be resisted, it is a self-evident result that all the acts done by such force, without the possibility of being resisted by another equal or more powerful force, can neither involve a fault nor an injury nor a responsibility.[111]

This view assumed that responsibility was premised on fault – or at least, that in respect of some obligations, especially obligations of diligence towards foreigners, responsibility required proof of fault.

Reviewing *Prats* and other cases, Ago concluded in an article published in the late 1930s that subjective fault was the generally agreed upon rationale of *force majeure*.[112] But Ago's assertion may be too categorical. While it is certainly true, as the *Prats* case shows, that the language of fault was often used in connection with *force majeure*, it cannot definitively be concluded that references to 'fault' in this context always involved *culpa* in a subjective (or psychological) sense.[113] To begin with, the term 'fault' was used throughout this period to mean two quite different things: alongside *culpa* in the subjective sense, 'fault' was also often understood in an objective sense, meaning simply a breach of international law.[114] When

---

[109] See, e.g., *Sambiaggio Case* (1903) 10 RIAA 499, 513 ('it cannot reasonably be said that [the State] should be responsible for a condition of affairs created without its volition').

[110] *French Company*, 353.

[111] *Salvador Prats v United States* (1874) 3 Moore Arbitrations 2886, 2895. Similarly, see *Piola Case (Italy/Peru)*, Case No 63 (1901) 15 RIAA 444, 445, and *French Company*, 353.

[112] E.g., Ago, 'La colpa nell'illecito internazionale', *Scritti sulla responsabilità internazionale degli Stati* (1979, first published 1939) vol. 1, 286, 299ff.

[113] Indeed, as already noted in Chapter 3, Section 3.3.3, it is doubtful whether Ago's concept of fault was psychological. Palmisano has convincingly argued that in Ago's work, the term 'fault' referred to will (in the sense of voluntariness, not intention). See Palmisano, 'Colpa dell'organo e colpa dello Stato nella responsabilità internazionale: Spunti critici di teoria e di prassi' (1992) 19–20 *Comunicazioni e studi* 623, 657–8.

[114] E.g., Fauchille, *Traité de droit international public (Paix)* (8th edn, 1922) vol. 1, 515; Salvioli, 'Les règles générales de la paix' (1933) 46 *Recueil* 1, 96.

used in this latter meaning, *force majeure*'s exclusion of 'fault' was simply an exclusion of the breach. Second, the majority of the practice then existing involved damages caused to foreigners, in respect of whom the state only had due diligence obligations.[115] These obligations are breached through negligent conduct, so invocations of *force majeure* in relation to these breaches would, of course, require some inquiry into the state's (subjective) fault. It is interesting to note that references to *force majeure* eventually disappeared from tribunals' consideration of claims of injury to foreign nationals in this context: if the state had merely to show a degree of diligence, then 'accidental' occurrences caused by an external event simply did not constitute a dereliction of duty by the state.[116] The factual situation of impossibility (which gives rise to *force majeure*) had been 'swallowed'[117] by the due diligence obligation itself.[118]

### 7.3 *Force Majeure* in Contemporary International Law

Despite the significant amount of practice in the period until 1945, some doubts remained as to the customary status of the plea of *force majeure* in the second half of the twentieth century. Thus, during the Vienna Conference, a number of states were doubtful that this 'domestic law concept' had been recognised in international law.[119] Doubts concerning the customary status of the defence were assuaged by the UN Secretariat's impressive compilation of practice in relation to this defence published

---

[115] The content of due diligence obligations was first articulated by the *Alabama Claims* Tribunal, on which see Lozano Contreras, *La noción de debida diligencia en derecho internacional público* (2007), ch. 1.

[116] Addressing the damage as 'accidental' and, therefore, not a breach of the state's obligation of diligence towards foreigners, see *Martini Case* (1903) 10 RIAA 644, 668 (damage due to the existence of war not attributable to Venezuela); *Cresceri Case (Italy/Peru), Case No 71* (1901) 15 RIAA 449, 451; *Brissot et al v Venezuela* (1898) 3 Moore Arbitrations 2949, 2967 (Commissioner Little), 2969 (Commissioner Findlay).

[117] To use Claire Finkelstein's expression: 'When the Rule Swallows the Exception' in Meyer (ed.), *Rules and Reasoning: Essays in Honour of Frederick Schauer* (1999), 147.

[118] In respect of due diligence obligations, moreover, *force majeure* does not operate as a defence. Rather, insofar as these obligations are limited by possibility, proof of an external event leading to impossibility to perform is tantamount to a denial of the claim. See Zegveld, *Accountability of Armed Opposition Groups in International Law* (2002), 217; Lozano Contreras, *Debida diligencia*, 220–8. On this point see Chapter 4, Section 4.3.2.

[119] See, e.g., *Official Records of the United Nations Conference on the Law of Treaties, First Session (Summary Records of the Plenary Meetings and of the Meetings of the Committee of the Whole)*, 16 March–24 May 1968, Sixty-second Meeting of the Committee of the Whole, remarks by the United States, at 363; France, Poland and USSR, at 364.

## 7.3 CONTEMPORARY INTERNATIONAL LAW

in 1978.[120] Attesting to this is the fact that neither states nor Commission member contested the inclusion of *force majeure* in the ARS: the principle it represented was acceptable to all (though its formulation required some tweaking). The Commission's work on the defence helped the crystallisation of the defence at customary law, in that it elicited positive reactions from states. Moreover, as will be seen later, in none of the instances of practice in which the defence was invoked since 1945 did states contest its customary recognition.

There also remained some lingering disagreements over the precise requirements and the rationale of the plea from the previous period. First, in relation to the requirements of the plea, the Commission – and alongside it, states – endorsed a conception of *force majeure* involving an impossibility to perform obligations due to the occurrence of a supervening event. Nevertheless, some uncertainties persist as to the kind and degree of impossibility required. In respect of kind, the ARS require a material impossibility of performance. As to degree, however, matters are less clear. On first reading, the Commission endorsed a standard of absolute impossibility; but the adjective 'absolute' was eventually removed on second reading. This change has led some scholars to query whether something less than 'absolute' impossibility may be enough to enliven the plea.[121] Second, in respect of the rationale, the Commission endorsed a will-based rationale for the plea.[122] *Force majeure* exonerates because the conduct adopted in the circumstances is 'involuntary' and not, as stated by the Secretariat's Memorandum, because it implied 'the total absence of ... subjective fault'.[123]

This section reviews both state practice as well as the Commission's work on *force majeure*. It begins with a review of the ILC's codification since, as will be seen, much of the contemporary practice, including primarily states' reactions to the Commission's work, has been significantly influenced by the developments in the ILC. It then reviews the relevant practice of states, both in the form of states' views expressed during ILC codification and in arbitral and judicial proceedings. The section concludes with a consideration on the standard of impossibility of performance, given some recent statements in the literature which have tended to water-down this concept into one of increased difficulty of performance.

---

[120] UN Secretariat, '"*Force majeure*" and "Fortuitous event"'.
[121] See Section 7.3.3.
[122] ARS art. 23 Commentary, [1].
[123] UN Secretariat, '"*Force Majeure*" and "Fortuitous Event"', 67 [7], 69 [15].

### 7.3.1 *The ILC's Codification of Article 23*

#### 7.3.1.1 First Reading: A Fault-Based Rationale for *Force Majeure*?

In his Eighth Report presented to the Commission in 1979, Special Rapporteur Ago described the plea of *force majeure* as one concerned with the impossibility to perform an obligation due to the occurrence of an external event, be it natural or anthropogenic,[124] which was unforeseen or irresistible.[125] The report noted that there were many concepts dealing with the consequences of the occurrence of these types of events, including *force majeure*,[126] state of necessity[127] and fortuitous event.[128] Indeed, all these concepts, in one way or another, concerned the situation of an obligor following the occurrence of such events. Nevertheless, there were some important conceptual differences among these various notions. These differences related to two aspects: the position of the state vis-à-vis

---

[124] Ago, Eighth Report on State Responsibility, ILC Yearbook 1979, vol. II(1), [107]. This view was supported by some ILC members, e.g., Sucharitkul, 1572nd meeting, ILC Yearbook 1979, vol. I, 202 [6]. But others thought that *force majeure* was limited to natural events: Vallat, 1570th meeting, ILC Yearbook 1979, vol. I, 195 [64]; Ushakov, 1571st meeting, ILC Yearbook 1979, vol. I, 198 [16–17]; and again Ushakov, 1572nd meeting, ILC Yearbook 1979, vol. I, 204 [15]; Verosta, 1571st meeting, ILC Yearbook 1979, vol. I, 199–200 [24].

[125] Ago, Eighth Report, [103].

[126] Ago's draft art. 31 stated that:
1. The international wrongfulness of an act of a State not in conformity with what is required of it by an international obligation is precluded if it is absolutely impossible for the author of the conduct attributable to the State to act otherwise.
2. The international wrongfulness of an act of a State not in conformity with what is required of it by an international obligation is likewise precluded if the author of the conduct attributable to the State has no other means of saving himself, or those accompanying him, from a situation of distress, and in so far as the conduct in question does not place others in a situation of comparable or greater peril.
3. The preceding paragraphs shall not apply if the impossibility of complying with the obligation, or the situation of distress, are due to the State to which the conduct not in conformity with the obligation is attributable.

See Ago, Eighth Report, 66.

[127] For Ago's draft art. 33, submitted to the Commission in the following year, see Ago, Eighth Report on State Responsibility – Add.5–7, ILC Yearbook 1980, vol. II(1), 51.

[128] Draft art. 32, proposed by Ago, stated that: 'The international wrongfulness of an act of a State not in conformity with what is required of it by an international obligation is precluded if, owing to a supervening external and unforeseeable factor, it is impossible for the author of the conduct attributable to the State to realize that its conduct is not in conformity with the international obligation': Ago, Eighth Report, 66.

its obligation following the occurrence of the event (the type and degree of impossibility of performance) and the (corresponding) extent to which the external event had constrained the will of the state, compelling it to adopt the conduct in question.

The defence of *force majeure* proposed by Ago covered two different situations, which Ago called 'absolute' and 'relative' impossibility of performance.[129] An absolute impossibility involved a situation in which the state faced a 'material'[130] inability to comply. A relative impossibility involved a situation in which the state could 'theoretically comply with the obligation but at the cost of a sacrifice that could not reasonably be required of it'.[131] The situation of relative impossibility envisaged by Ago, moreover, concerned exclusively the state organ himself (as opposed to the state) and the situation in which his life (or that of individuals entrusted to his care) was in danger. In the case of absolute impossibility the conduct was 'entirely *involuntary*', in the case of relative impossibility the 'will of the organ exist[ed] in *theory* but in practice [was] nullified' by the situation.[132] These characteristics separated *force majeure* from the other supervening-event concepts. With respect to fortuitous event, this defence required an epistemological (rather than material) impossibility: it was an impossibility 'to realize' that the conduct adopted was incompatible with an obligation of the state.[133] For example, where as a result of the malfunction of radar a military aircraft enters the airspace of a foreign state. Similarly, *force majeure* differed from the state of necessity since in this case the conduct of the state, which must protect one of its vital interests from an imminent peril, was 'undeniably intentional'.[134]

The three situations of impossibility identified in Ago's report (absolute, relative and epistemological) are certainly distinct conceptually. Nevertheless, Ago's articulation of these different factual situations into rules was not wholly principled or consistent. As Francis Vallat observed, the principles proposed by the Special Rapporteur were acceptable, but 'it was the manner in which those principles were to be expressed that gave rise to difficulty'.[135] For example, why treat absolute and relative impossibility in one article called '*force majeure*' when relative impossibility was

---

[129] Ago, Eighth Report, [106].
[130] Ibid., [106–7].
[131] Ibid., [106].
[132] Id.
[133] Ibid., [104].
[134] Ibid., [102].
[135] Vallat, 1571st meeting, ILC Yearbook 1979, vol. I, 201 [30].

in fact closer to the situation of necessity?[136] Indeed, in the case of relative impossibility it is possible for the organ to comply with the state's obligation, but that organ chooses not to comply with the obligation in order to protect himself from danger. Similarly, in the case of necessity, the state has the possibility to comply with its obligations but it chooses not to do so in order to protect one of its essential interests. Moreover, even though *force majeure* and fortuitous event differed in terms of the kind of impossibility (one was material and the other epistemological), they both required an absolute inability to comply with the obligation; so why treat them separately? The difficulty lay in the fact that it was not clear whether Ago was basing the distinction among the various articles on the kind of impossibility, on the degree of impossibility, or both. And yet, the ground of distinction chosen would affect the articulation of the corresponding provisions.

These issues were discussed at some length in the Commission. Although unaided by differences of opinion regarding the adequate terminology to use to refer to these notions, the Commission eventually managed to agree on most of the substantive points. The Commission decided to separate the scenarios of absolute and relative impossibility and address the latter in an autonomous provision – eventually known as 'distress'.[137] Equally, the Commission struggled to distinguish between *force majeure* and fortuitous event: in practice the use of the terms was rather inconsistent and, moreover, in both cases the impossibility was absolute. The Commission thus decided to merge them in a single provision and leave to 'legal science' the task of studying and determining the identity or difference between the two notions.[138]

The debates in the Commission (and the solutions eventually adopted) clearly show that the provision on *force majeure* was the articulation of a defence relating to absolute impossibility of performance. Indeed, it was because of the different degree of impossibility required by distress that this notion had been removed from the provision concerning *force majeure* and placed on its own in what became draft Article 32. By the

---

[136] A similarity which was noted by the ILC in the commentary to draft art. 31, see ILC Report, thirty-first session, ILC Yearbook 1979, vol. II(2), 122–3 [3].

[137] Riphagen, 1579th meeting, ILC Yearbook 1979, vol. I, 234 [2]. During the debates, this suggestion had also been made by, e.g., Vallat, 1571st meeting, 201 [31]; Vallat, 1572nd meeting, ILC Yearbook 1979, vol. I, 202 [1]; Tsuruoka, 1572nd meeting, ILC Yearbook 1979, vol. I, 205 [21]. On this development, see Chapter 9, Section 9.3.

[138] ILC Report, thirty-first session, 123 [5–6].

## 7.3 CONTEMPORARY INTERNATIONAL LAW

same token, the previously separate provision on fortuitous event (Ago's proposed Article 32), which concerned a different kind of impossibility (epistemological), was included in the provision on *force majeure* on the basis that they shared the same degree of impossibility: absolute.[139]

Nevertheless, when the Commission redrafted the provision proposed by Ago, it changed the wording relating to the impossibility of performance. Ago's proposed draft Article had required an 'absolute impossibility of performance' and in his report Ago had remarked that in international practice, *force majeure* required a 'material and absolute impossibility'.[140] The ILC opted not to use the adjective 'absolute' in the text of draft Article 31 and replaced it with the term 'material'. In relevant part, the article adopted on first reading stated:

> The wrongfulness of an act of a State not in conformity with an international obligation of that State is precluded if the act was due to an irresistible force or to an unforeseen external event beyond its control which made it materially impossible for the State to act in conformity with that obligation or to know that its conduct was not in conformity with that obligation.[141]

It is difficult to infer from this change that the Commission considered that *force majeure* required less than an absolute impossibility of performance. Indeed, the Drafting Committee explained that the use of the word 'material' instead of 'absolute' was intended to 'convey the idea of an objective rather than a subjective criterion for determining the situation of impossibility'.[142] This change was arguably prompted by the concerns expressed by many Commission members about the subjectivity of certain aspects of the provision – for example, was the requirement of unforeseeability a subjective one (unforeseen for the invoking state) or an objective one (unforeseen by any state or, plausibly, an equivalent of the concept of *bon père de famille*: the well-governed state)?[143] The change to 'material' was intended to address some of these concerns. If the impossibility was a 'material' one, even though it ought to be assessed by reference to a specific state and a specific obligation, then it could be

---

[139] Tabibi, 1571st meeting, ILC Yearbook 1979, vol. I, 198 [11]; Sucharitkul, 1572nd meeting, 202 [6]. Note, however, that some queried whether it was necessary to qualify impossibility with an adjective: Vallat, 1570th meeting, 195 [64].

[140] Ago, Eighth Report, [124]. See also Ago, 1573rd meeting, ILC Yearbook 1979, vol. I, 205 [1–2].

[141] ILC Report, thirty-first session, 122.

[142] But it did not elaborate further on this point: Riphagen, 1579th meeting, 234 [3].

[143] On which see Szurek, 2 *Force Majeure*, 500ff.

ascertained objectively. Crucially, this linguistic change was not, as has subsequently been argued, a way of watering down the requirement of absolute impossibility towards one of difficulty of performance, as high as that difficulty might be.[144] The examples given in the commentary to draft Article 31 corroborate this. The draft commentary states, for example, that a 'temporary impossibility' existed where 'the unforeseen destruction of the means of transport to be used made it temporarily impossible to transfer particular food-stuffs to another State.'[145] It is here not a matter of increased difficulty in the transport, say through a longer route or more onerous means – but of temporary inability to do so. Equally, a material impossibility to perform an 'obligation to act' would exist where 'an earthquake destroyed property to be handed over to another State, or if an insurrection removed part of a State's territory from its control and thus prevented it, in that part of its territory, from adopting the necessary measures to protect foreign agents or other aliens.'[146] In all cases, the obligations are actually impossible, and not simply more onerous, to perform.

As to the rationale of the defence, the Commission did not settle the question whether it related to the state's fault or its free will. The Commission, in other words, did not answer the question about the relevance of the involuntary nature of the conduct adopted in a situation of *force majeure*: was it relevant because it represented the coercion of the state's will or because it excluded that the state had acted with fault? Ago – who had previously held that *force majeure*'s rationale was grounded on exclusion of fault – used the terms 'involuntary' and 'unintentional' in his report almost as if they were synonyms. There seems to have been a slight preference for describing conduct adopted as a result of a fortuitous event as 'unintentional' (for the state organ does not know)[147] and conduct adopted as a result of *force majeure* as 'involuntary' (for the state has no alternative option).[148] But this preference (if it is one) is not consistent throughout the report, so not much can be inferred from it. The Commission's discussion does not shed any further light on the point; there are only sparse observations relating to fault in this context.[149] Unhelpfully, the commentary

---

[144] As to which see Section 7.3.3.
[145] ILC Report, thirty-first session, 123 (fn. 620).
[146] Ibid., 124 (fn. 621).
[147] Ago, Eighth Report, [104].
[148] Ibid., [106].
[149] For an exception, see Sucharitkul, 1572nd meeting, 203 [8] ('account had to be taken of a subjective element that found expression in the degree of diligence displayed by the author of the conduct attributable to the State').

to draft Article 31 indicated that *force majeure* concerned '*involuntary*, or at least unintentional, conduct'.[150] The use of the disjunctive 'or' here suggests that the Commission perceived that there was a difference between the two scenarios. There is no doubt that fortuitous event (the impossibility to know) concerned subjective fault insofar as it concerned a mental state, so the reference to the 'unintentional' character of the conduct most certainly relates to conduct adopted as a result of this type of event.[151] But did it extend also to situations of material impossibility? No express answer can be gleaned from Ago's report, the Commission's debate, or the commentary to draft Article 31.

#### 7.3.1.2 Second Reading: Excluding Fault

Special Rapporteur Crawford's report on *force majeure* was supportive of retaining draft Article 31. Nevertheless, he proposed a number of changes to the provision – some more controversial than others – including on the two points of interest to this chapter: the standard of impossibility and the issue of fault.

On the standard of impossibility, the Special Rapporteur endorsed the requirement of 'material impossibility' contained in the first-reading Article. The report does not expressly articulate what Crawford understood 'material impossibility' to mean. However, a brief remark in the report suggests that his understanding of this standard was not as strict as that endorsed on first reading. In distinguishing *force majeure* from impossibility of performance in the law of treaties, Crawford noted that 'the "degree of difficulty" associated with force majeure ... though considerable, is less than that required' by VCLT Article 61.[152] Later, during the debates within the Commission, he dismissed a suggestion to use the expression 'absolute and material impossibility of performance' in the provision, with a view to aligning the draft Article with the language used by the *Rainbow Warrior* Tribunal (discussed later).[153] Crawford's rejection of this suggestion was not a principled one. Rather

---

[150] ILC Report, thirty-first session, 123 [4] (emphasis in original).
[151] ILC Report, thirty-first session, 132 [37].
[152] Crawford, Second Report on State Responsibility, ILC Yearbook 1999, vol. II(1), [259]. Note, however, that the differences between impossibility as per ARS art. 23 and VCLT art. 61 are more complex than the latter simply being more stringent than the former. See Paddeu, 'Force Majeure', 467–76.
[153] Kateka, 2591st meeting, ILC Yearbook 1999, vol. I, 171 [22]; He, 2591st meeting, ILC Yearbook 1999, vol. I, 172 [25]; Kamto, 2592nd meeting, ILC Yearbook 1999, vol. I, 179 [29].

than object to it on the grounds that the impossibility required was not absolute (was it relative?), the Special Rapporteur simply said that it was 'unnecessary' to use the adjective 'absolute' to qualify the type of impossibility required by *force majeure*.[154] Furthermore, a request from a member of the Commission for clarification as to what 'actual' or 'material' impossibility meant, and what the difference was between 'absolute' impossibility and 'increased difficulty' of performance, was left unanswered.[155]

Crawford also proposed to eliminate all references to 'subjective' elements from draft Article 31. This meant, first of all, dealing with the question that the first-reading Commission had left to 'legal science' to resolve: the fortuitous event and the situation of epistemological impossibility. Crawford argued that no distinction could be discerned from international practice between *force majeure* and fortuitous event, and that the notion of *force majeure* was sufficiently broad to cover both situations.[156] Moreover, the language of 'impossibility to know' of the breach should be deleted from the text of the Article for it suggested that 'responsibility depends on the State "knowing" that its conduct is wrongful, yet in general such knowledge is not required.'[157] Of course, an innocent mistake of fact could provide a defence in certain circumstances, where the ignorance of a fact was 'essential' to a state's 'responsibility *in the circumstances*, and without which the conduct in question could not have been wrongful.'[158] This was the case, for instance, of a mistake as 'to the location of an aircraft, owing to an undetected fault in navigational equipment'.[159] But Crawford thought that draft Article 31 should be formulated without the 'introduction of overtly subjective elements.'[160] Aside from two vigorous critics of this proposed change,[161] Commission members agreed to remove these subjective elements and limit the provision to *force majeure* for the occurrence of a material impossibility.

Eliminating all subjective elements required also dealing with the fault-laden language present throughout the commentary to draft Article 31: thus, the use of the term 'unintentional' in the commentary to draft

---

[154] Crawford, 2592nd meeting, ILC Yearbook 1999, vol. I, 179 [35].
[155] He, 2591st meeting, 172 [25].
[156] Crawford, Second Report, [265].
[157] Ibid., [262].
[158] Id.
[159] Id.
[160] Id.
[161] Simma and Hafner, 2592nd meeting, ILC Yearbook 1999, vol. I, 176–7.

Article 31 was not repeated in the Commentary to Article 23. The Commentary now states that in the case of *force majeure* 'the conduct of the State which would otherwise be internationally wrongful is involuntary or at least involves no element of free choice.'[162]

### 7.3.2 Force Majeure *in the Practice of States since 1945*

Aside from the few states that were sceptical of the recognition of *force majeure* in international law during the 1968 session of the Vienna Conference on the law of treaties, noted earlier, on the whole, the practice since 1945 has confirmed the customary status of this plea. These instances of practice are reviewed here, before turning to the classification of *force majeure* as a justification or an excuse in the final part of this chapter.

#### 7.3.2.1  States' Views in the Sixth Committee

States in the Sixth Committee were generally favourable to the provision on *force majeure*.[163] A few states objected to the 'subjective' elements of draft Article 31 as adopted on first reading. For Austria, the provision mixed subjective and objective elements in 'a manner likely to blur rather than determine' the scope of the provision;[164] for France, *force majeure* should be limited to an assessment of 'objective facts';[165] and for Italy 'the drafting of article 31(1) was perhaps not altogether appropriate in that it' referred to knowledge of the breach.[166] As was just seen, these subjective elements were removed by the Commission on second reading, a decision which met the express approval of states in the Sixth Committee. The Czech Republic thus welcomed the deletion of references to fault since

---

[162] ARS art. 23 Commentary, [1].
[163] On first reading: Algeria: A/C.6/34/SR.49, [35]; Austria: A/C.6/34/SR.47, [61]; India: A/C.6/34/SR.51, [63]; Italy: A/C.6/34/SR.47, [25]; Jordan: A/C.6/34/SR.51, [56]; Kenya: A/C.6/34/SR.43, [4]; Mexico: A/C.6/34/SR.41, [47]; Mongolia: A/C.6/34/SR.50, [38]; Netherlands: A/C.6/34/SR.39, [6]; Spain: A/C.6/34/SR.44, [5]; Syria: A/C.6/34/SR.51, [13]; Trinidad and Tobago: A/C.6/34/SR.49, [23]; Venezuela (on behalf of the parties to the Pact of Cartagena): A/C.6/34/SR.44, [16]. On second reading: Algeria: A/C.6/55/SR.18, [6]; Russia: A/C.6/55/SR.18, [53]. In writing, see German Democratic Republic: Comments and Observations of Governments on Part 1 of the Draft Articles on State Responsibility for Internationally Wrongful Acts, A/CN.4/414, ILC Yearbook 1988, vol. II(1), 5 [47]; United Kingdom: Comments and Observations Received from Governments, A/CN.4/488 and Add.1–3, ILC Yearbook 1998, vol. II(1), 133.
[164] A/CN.4/488, 133.
[165] Id.
[166] A/C.6/34/SR.47, [25].

they were 'misleading and were contrary to the notion of general elements required for the establishment of a State's responsibility'.[167] Specifically on the question of knowledge, Germany maintained that '[t]here was no general requirement in international law that a State must know that its conduct was not in conformity with an obligation'.[168] For Venezuela, the 'proposal to eliminate the subjective element implied in the phrase "to know that its conduct was not in conformity with that obligation", was also a sound one'.[169]

For the most part states did not comment on the standard of impossibility or on the rationale of the plea. As to the latter, Morocco accepted that 'the wrongfulness of an act could be precluded by the involuntary conduct of a state'.[170] Similarly, the United Kingdom accepted that in situations of *force majeure* the state's conduct was involuntary.[171] As to the standard of impossibility, only Slovakia, during the second reading of the Articles, requested that a clear distinction be made between 'material or actual inability to comply and circumstances making such compliance more difficult'.[172] Aside from these few, and not especially critical remarks, on the whole, states were satisfied with the Commission's choices on these matters.

### 7.3.2.2   Arbitral and Judicial Practice

**Events of *Force Majeure*: *de Wytenhove* (1950) and *Ottoman Lighthouses* (1956)**   These two cases are dealt with together insofar as both tribunals employed, somewhat anachronistically, the term *force majeure* in a descriptive sense. In both cases, the tribunal considered that the external event had excluded the existence of a causal link between the state's conduct and the damage. The state could not, consequently, be held responsible.

In *de Wytenhove*, claimants had lost their furs due to a fire while the items were being relocated by a merchant to protect them from bombings during World War II. The Conciliation Commission exonerated Italy from responsibility since the loss of the furs was a 'fortuitous event' which had not resulted from Italy's acts of war.[173]

---

[167] A/C.6/54/SR.22, [38].
[168] A/C.6/54/SR.22, [6].
[169] A/C.6/54/SR.23, [53].
[170] A/C.6/34/SR.48, [31].
[171] A/CN.4/488, 130.
[172] A/C.6/54/SR.22, [54].
[173] *De Wytenhove Case (France/Italy)* (1950) 13 RIAA 228.

A similar approach is discernible in *Ottoman Lighthouses*. Greece invoked *force majeure* in respect of Claim 15, concerning damage caused to a lighthouse in Paspargos during World War I. The lighthouse had been taken over by Greece from the claimants in 1915 and, having been destroyed by Turkish bombings in 1916, Greece had repaired the lighthouse with materials of inferior quality. The lighthouse was restored to the owner in 1919, who subsequently claimed damages for its diminished value. The Tribunal excluded Greece's responsibility, holding that:

> there must ... be a causal relationship between the act and the damage; however, the prejudice caused by the impossibility for Greece of returning the lighthouse to the Company in its original state was caused not by Greece's seizure but by the bombardment, which damaged it severely; that bombardment constituted a case of *force majeure* that would have affected it even if it had remained in the hands of the company.[174]

***Rights of US Nationals in Morocco* (1952)**   In *Rights of US Nationals in Morocco*, concerning the application to US nationals of a decree of the French Republic of Morocco regulating imports into the French Zone of Morocco, France invoked *force majeure* against the claim of the United States that the decree breached conventional obligations of free trade between the United States and Morocco. France argued that measures of non-convertibility of currency adopted after World War II, a fact 'external' to Morocco, entailed that it was no longer 'physically possible' for Morocco 'to choose the countries with which it wishes to trade'.[175] *Force majeure* was a limitation on Morocco's freedom of choice: the events were a 'constraint that prevented the State from performing its obligation'.[176] The United States did not contest this statement of the rule, solely objecting to the argument on the facts.[177]

***Rainbow Warrior* (1990)**   The facts of the *Rainbow Warrior* were summarised in the Introduction to this study and will be considered again in great detail in Chapter 9.[178] Of interest, here, is to note that the Tribunal considered the plea of *force majeure* in respect of France's unilateral removal of its agents from Hao. France had mentioned the notion of *force majeure* in a diplomatic note to New Zealand explaining the reasons for

---

[174] *Ottoman Empire Lighthouses Concession (France v Greece)* (1956) 12 RIAA 155, 219–20.
[175] France oral statement, *Rights of US Nationals in Morocco (France v USA)* (1952) ICJ Pleadings, vol. II 140, 182–3.
[176] Ibid., 183.
[177] US oral statement, *Rights of US Nationals in Morocco*, ICJ Pleadings, vol. II, 241, 248–9.
[178] Section 9.3.2.2.

the removal of the agents, but later, before the Tribunal, argued that it had not actually intended to rely on this defence.[179] Nevertheless, the Tribunal considered that 'the invocation of "*force majeure*" has not been totally excluded' and thus proceeded to examine it.[180] In so doing, the Tribunal endorsed the Commission's formulation of draft Article 31 and its commentary. In particular, the Tribunal explained that *force majeure* involved a situation of 'absolute and material impossibility of performance' and that in these circumstances the conduct adopted by the state is 'involuntary or at least unintentional'.[181] The plea, however, failed on the facts.

*LAFICO v Burundi* (1991)   The Libyan Arab Republic Burundi Holding Company ('HALB'), a joint corporation owned by LAFICO (on behalf of Libya) and Burundi, operated in Burundi and was managed by LAFICO. Burundi, claiming threats to the peace and to the external and internal security of the state, broke off diplomatic relations with Libya and expelled all Libyan nationals from its territory, including the director general of LAFICO. Subsequently, Burundi requested the liquidation of HALB.[182] Part of the dispute turned on the role of LAFICO, through two Libyan nationals, in the operation of HALB. In particular, on whether it was necessary to liquidate HALB in view of its inoperative status consequent on the inability of the Libyan representatives to participate in the operation of the company as they could not be present in Burundi. Burundi contended that HALB's functioning had been impaired by the absence of LAFICO managers, due to the lawful interruption of diplomatic relations. This had caused a situation in which it was 'objectively impossible' for the managers to participate in the work of HALB. But Burundi was not responsible for this 'objective impossibility'. In addressing Burundi's argument of 'objective impossibility', the Tribunal turned, among others, to draft Article 31 adopted by the Commission in 1979. It endorsed the provision as adopted, and dismissed the plea as 'the alleged impossibility is not the result of an irresistible force or an unforeseen external event beyond the control of Burundi'.[183]

*Gabčíkovo-Nagymaros* (1994)   The plea of *force majeure* was not relevant to the dispute in *Gabčíkovo-Nagymaros*. Nevertheless, it was referred

[179] *Rainbow Warrior (New Zealand v France)* (1990) 20 RIAA 215, [76].
[180] Id.
[181] Ibid., [77].
[182] *Libyan Arab Foreign Investment Company (LAFICO) v Burundi* (1991) 96 ILR 279, 300–1.
[183] *LAFICO v Burundi*, 317–18.

to by Hungary in one of its pleadings in an effort to distinguish this plea from the state of necessity (which had been invoked by Hungary). According to Hungarian counsel, *force majeure* concerned situations in which the will of the author of the conduct was 'practically absent'.[184]

*Aucoven v Venezuela (2003)* Venezuela raised a defence of *force majeure* in respect of its failure to comply with a 1993 concession agreement with Aucoven, for the undertaking of works and the subsequent management of the Caracas–La Guaira highway system. The project's economic viability was heavily reliant on the increase of tolls for the use of the highway. A first, and insufficient, increase of the tolls by the government in 1997 caused violent protests in Caracas and the state of Vargas, leading the government to eliminate tolls altogether. Shortly thereafter, Aucoven terminated the concession agreement and filed arbitral claims against Venezuela. Venezuela invoked *force majeure* in respect of its failures to increase tolls arguing that, in view of the previous violent reactions by the local population, it had been impossible for it to further raise the tolls as required by the agreement. The defence of *force majeure* was invoked under clause 41(2) of the agreement itself (and not under international law).[185] The dispute was governed by Venezuelan law and international law, which 'prevail[ed] over conflicting national rules'.[186]

Venezuela argued that the standard of impossibility required by the Venezuelan law on administrative contracts did not require 'that the force majeure event be irresistible; it suffice[d] that by all reasonable judgment the event impede[d] the normal performance of the contract'.[187] Aucoven, instead, argued that the applicable standard was the international law requirement of 'absolute' impossibility.[188] The Tribunal held that it was 'not satisfied that international law impose[d] a different standard which would be called to displace the application of national law'.[189] Without deciding whether the requirement of impossibility was met – since it had already dismissed the plea of *force majeure* on the basis that the protests had been foreseeable – the Tribunal nevertheless remarked that it was

---

[184] Hungary oral statement, *Gabčíkovo-Nagymaros*, 4 March 1997, CR 1997/3, 70.
[185] *Autopista Concesionada de Venezuela v Bolivarian Republic of Venezuela* ICSID Case ARB/00/5, Award, 23 September 2003, [107].
[186] Ibid., [105].
[187] Ibid., [121].
[188] Id.
[189] Ibid., [123].

'rather inclined to find that, in consideration of [previous] events and of the risk of [their] repetition, the impossibility requirement' appeared to be fulfilled.[190]

### 7.3.3 A Postscript on the Standard of Material Impossibility

The development of the plea described so far shows the existence of variation in respect of the standard of impossibility required by the plea of *force majeure*. Different adjectives are used in this connection, and it is often unclear whether these adjectives are intended to qualify the *kind* of impossibility or the *degree* of that impossibility (whatever its kind may be). The Commission's choice to use the expression 'material impossibility of performance' in Article 23 without an explanation as to its meaning in the Commentary has further deepened the uncertainties around this standard. All that the Commentary indicates in this connection is that material impossibility refers to an 'actual impossibility'[191] and that it is more than an increased difficulty of performance.[192]

Scholarly literature has recently argued that material impossibility must not be 'absolute'. The argument is based on the distinction between the requirement of impossibility under Article 23 and that under VCLT Article 61. Pursuant to Article 61, the impossibility that may ground the suspension or termination of a treaty must involve the permanent or temporary 'disappearance or destruction of an object indispensable for the execution of the treaty'.[193] During the Vienna Conference, Mexico had suggested to expand Article 61 to include all the cases covered by the notion of *force majeure*, such as cases of 'impossibility to deliver an article by a given date owing to a strike, the closing of a port or a war, or of the possibility that a rich and powerful State, faced with temporary

---

[190] Ibid., [124].
[191] ARS art. 23 Commentary, [5].
[192] Ibid., [2].
[193] Pursuant to VCLT art. 61: '1. A party may invoke the impossibility of performing a treaty as a ground for terminating or withdrawing from it if the impossibility results from the permanent disappearance or destruction of an object indispensable for the execution of the treaty. If the impossibility is temporary, it may be invoked only as a ground for suspending the operation of the treaty. 2. Impossibility of performance may not be invoked by a party as a ground for terminating, withdrawing from or suspending the operation of a treaty if the impossibility is the result of a breach by that party either of an obligation under the treaty or of any other international obligation owed to any other party to the treaty.'

difficulties, might be obliged to suspend its payments.'[194] Some states had been sceptical of this proposal, since in their view the concept of *force majeure* remained ill-defined in international law.[195] Mexico eventually withdrew the proposal which was, consequently, not put to a vote.[196] This, as the ICJ later interpreted it, meant that the requirement of impossibility in Article 61 is stricter than that in Article 23.[197] Therefore, scholars have concluded, Article 23 must not involve an absolute impossibility.[198]

There are a number of practical and conceptual difficulties with this view. To begin with, the practice reviewed earlier generally points in the direction of an absolute degree of impossibility. The only case in which a lower standard was explicitly endorsed, *Aucoven*, was not decided on this point and, at any rate, Venezuela relied on the notion of *force majeure* as contemplated in its administrative law and the relevant investment contract.

Second, the argument is not compatible with the ILC's own explanation for the choice of the adjective 'material' as a replacement for 'absolute' in the text of draft Article 31, as shown earlier. Indeed, the ILC removed distress from the provision on *force majeure* because it concerned a relative as opposed to an absolute impossibility of performance, which was the subject of the provision on *force majeure*. Similarly, the ILC incorporated fortuitous event into the provision on *force majeure* because it involved a situation in which it is absolutely impossible for the state organ to know that it is acting contrary to international law (note: it is not more difficult to know, but impossible). Moreover, Special Rapporteur Crawford's remark that *force majeure* requires a

---

[194] *Official Records of the United Nations Conference on the Law of Treaties, First Session (Summary Records of the Plenary Meetings and of the Meetings of the Committee of the Whole)*, Sixty-second Meeting of the Committee of the Whole, 361.
[195] See, ibid., remarks by the United States, at 363; France, Poland and USSR, at 364.
[196] Ibid., 365.
[197] *Gabčíkovo-Nagymaros Project (Hungary/Slovakia)* (1997) ICJ Rep 7, [102], noting that: 'During the conference, a proposal was made to extend the scope of the article by including in it cases such as the impossibility to make certain payments because of serious financial difficulties ... Although it was recognized that such situations could lead to a preclusion of the wrongfulness of non-performance by a party of its treaty obligations, the participating States were not prepared to consider such situations to be a ground for terminating or suspending a treaty, and preferred to limit themselves to a narrower concept.' See also Szurek, 'Force Majeure', 475.
[198] Crawford, *General Part*, 299; Tzanakopoulos and Lekkas, '*Pacta Sunt Servanda* versus Flexibility in the Suspension and Termination of Treaties' in Tams et al. (eds), *Research Handbook on the Law of Treaties* (2014), 329–30.

lower 'degree of difficulty'[199] than that in VCLT Article 61 was, at best, oblique. The Commission did not discuss this observation, and from the few comments made during the debates, it appears that the Commission worked under the assumption that *force majeure* concerned an absolute impossibility.[200]

Third, those who argue that the provision does not require absolute impossibility do not actually specify what might be enough to enliven the plea. Clarity on the standard of impossibility contemplated in Article 23 requires that two things be kept separate: the kind of impossibility and the degree of impossibility. The adjective 'material' refers to the kind of impossibility. This adjective was chosen to indicate that the standard was an objective one, but it also suggests that the impossibility be a physical one. Admittedly the meanings of the term 'material' include both physical senses as well as senses related to significance or relevance.[201] Nevertheless, the Commission's work on *force majeure* supports a meaning of 'material' related to physical possibility. This is borne out by the examples given in the commentary to the old draft Article 31, as well as the commentary to Article 23 in which the Commission describes material impossibility as an '*actual* impossibility'.[202] The adjective absolute, in turn, refers to the degree of impossibility. If the material impossibility required by Article 23 is not absolute then it must be a relative one. To recall, relative impossibility concerns the situation in which the state *can* comply with its obligations, but compliance comes at a high cost so it cannot be expected of it to comply. In essence, compliance is made more onerous, or more difficult, in the circumstances. However, a mere increased difficulty does not amount to material impossibility, as the Commentary affirms. So what degree of difficulty will be required? Would threats to an essential interest of the state be a sufficiently high difficulty to meet the standard? If this were the case, then the situation would be one where the state had a choice between complying with its obligation even at the cost of harm to one of its interests (it is this potential harm that makes compliance more difficult), or failing to comply so as to protect its interest – it would be, in short, a situation of necessity. Conceptually at least, the defence of *force majeure* must be formulated as requiring an absolute impossibility of performance if it is not to slide into the concept of state of necessity

---

[199] Crawford, Second Report, [259].
[200] See also Szurek, 'Force Majeure', 479–80.
[201] See meanings I and III in the *Oxford English Dictionary*.
[202] ARS art. 23 Commentary, [5].

(but without the rigid conditions imposed on the necessity plea in international law which, as will be seen in the next chapter, are intended to guard against its abuse).

Finally, the argument relies on a *non sequitur*. That the type and degree of impossibility envisaged in Article 61 are stricter than that in Article 23 does not entail that only the former is absolute. To be sure, the VCLT requirement of impossibility is certainly stricter: the impossibility must result from the 'destruction' of an object and that object must be 'essential' to the performance of the treaty as a whole. Article 23, in contrast, contains no such limitations. So the factual scenario envisaged is certainly a narrower one. The difference concerns the *facts* from which the impossibility results and the properties of that object in relation to the treaty in question; but it does not concern the degree of impossibility itself.[203]

Of course, it may be queried whether it is desirable to formulate the defence in Article 23 as one requiring an absolute impossibility to perform, and whether there may be good reasons to lower the degree of impossibility required. After all, in its current stringent formulation the plea is almost never made out and one may wonder whether, in these circumstances, the defence has any useful function at all. But this is a separate question – one about *lex ferenda*, rather than *lex lata* – and its consideration must take careful notice of the fine, yet significant, differences between kinds and degrees of impossibility, and between the legal articulation of these various situations. Most importantly, one ought to be very careful not to unknowingly transform the substance of the plea of *force majeure* into that of the plea of necessity, given that the requirements of the former do not offer similar protections to the state whose rights are affected by the invocation of the plea as the requirements of the latter.

## 7.4 *Force Majeure* as an Excuse

Few states and commentators have considered the classification of *force majeure* as a justification or an excuse. Among states, only France,[204] India[205] and Japan[206] have expressed the view that *force majeure* constitutes

---

[203] For a similar conclusion, see Forlati, *Diritto dei trattati e responsabilità internazionale* (2005), 159–63, esp. 162.

[204] Comments and Observations Received from Governments, A/CN.4/492, ILC Yearbook 1999, vol. II(1), 133.

[205] A/C.6/54/SR.23, [33].

[206] A/CN.4/492, 107.

an excuse. Commentators' opinions are also divided, while for some *force majeure* operates as a justification,[207] for others it constitutes an excuse.[208] In practice, moreover, the plea is rarely successful, rendering it difficult to test its effects, and whether it operates by excluding wrongfulness or responsibility. In contrast with the defences considered in the previous three chapters, in respect of which it was clear from the practice of states that their application entails the legality of the relevant conduct, positive law provides no clear answer in the case of *force majeure*.

Thus, unlike in the previous three chapters where the classification of the plea followed a (mostly) bottom-up approach, the absence of a clear indication in the positive law as to the effects of *force majeure* requires that its classification take a top-down approach. The analysis will, therefore, work from the concept and the rationale of the plea, the concept of justification and excuse, and the way in which arguments about *force majeure* have been presented, to propose a classification for the plea. As will be seen, the plea of *force majeure* is individualised, in that it focuses on the state rather than the act and on whether the state acted voluntarily when it failed to perform its obligation. On this basis, the plea can be classified as an excuse, a classification that, as will be seen, is also supported by policy reasons. This chapter will conclude with some remarks on the theory of excuse that underlies the plea of *force majeure*. Given the plea's rationale (that the state acts involuntarily), the defence may be explained by reference to a theory of free will which will, therefore, be construed as a theory of excuse. This same rationale, as will be seen in the next two chapters, also underlies the plea of distress and could, potentially, underpin an excuse of necessity.

### 7.4.1   Explaining the Rationale

In contemporary international law, *force majeure* is accepted as a defence to responsibility because the conduct adopted in the circumstances is, as stated in the Commentary to Article 23, 'involuntary or involves no element of free choice'.[209] This rationale, based on the (in)existence of state will in relation to the impugned conduct, was central to the conceptual shift on the defence of *force majeure* at the turn of the century. *Force majeure*

---

[207] E.g., Szurek, 1 *Force Majeure*, 307–14; Christakis, 'Illusion', 244.
[208] E.g., Scalese, *La rilevanza delle scusanti nella teoria dell'illecito internazionale* (2008), 63; Crawford, *General Part*, 319.
[209] ARS art. 23 Commentary, [1].

moved from a descriptive term referring to a superior force, to a normative one referring to the position of the state vis-à-vis its obligation(s) subsequent to, and as a result of, the occurrence of one such 'superior force'. In these circumstances, had the state voluntarily omitted to comply with its obligations or had it been coerced or compelled to act in that way? In many of the disputes reviewed in this chapter, the parties and the tribunal explained the situation of *force majeure* by reference to the will of the state, or more properly by reference to the constraints placed on it. In *French Company*, the Tribunal spoke of the Venezuelan government's conduct as 'compelled' by the circumstances;[210] in *Wimbledon* the applicants opposed the (potential) plea of *force majeure* with Germany's 'voluntary' closure of the canal;[211] in *Serbian Loans* the applicant argued that the circumstances (in particular, the French Law of 1924) had 'forced' it to pay the debt in French-francs;[212] in *Socobelge* too, Greece's non-performance of the award had been 'constrained by a case of *force majeure*';[213] in *Rights of US Nationals* Morocco had been left with 'no choice' following external events;[214] and for Hungary, in *Gabčíkovo-Nagymaros*, in a case of *force majeure* the will of the state was 'practically absent'.[215] The Commentary, following the language of these various cases, indicates that *force majeure* involves 'involuntary' conduct or conduct 'involving no element of free choice'. What does it mean, however, for conduct to be involuntary?

Involuntariness can be understood, as mentioned earlier, in a physical sense, related to the power to act.[216] The state has no power to act in cases where, for instance, as a result of strong currents a public vessel is dragged into foreign prohibited waters – an example included in the Commentary to Article 23.[217] The act of entering into the foreign waters is certainly attributable to the flag state of the vessel;[218] but it cannot be said that the captain directed the vessel into foreign waters. Even if he acted to avoid his vessel being dragged – say by steering it in the opposite direction – the vessel would have been dragged by the overpowering currents. This would be an involuntary entry. It is the result of an irresistible force, beyond the

---

[210] *French Company*, 353.
[211] Applicants' oral statement, PCIJ Series C No 03/4, 288 (Annex 27, English translation).
[212] Serbia, oral statement, PCIJ Series C No 16-III(2), 211
[213] Rejoinder of Greece, PCIJ Rep Series C No 87, 142.
[214] France, oral statement, *Rights of US Nationals in Morocco*, ICJ Pleadings, vol. II, 182–3.
[215] *Gabčíkovo-Nagymaros*, Hungary, oral statement, CR 1997/3, 70.
[216] Pink, 'The Will' in Craig (ed.), *Routledge Encyclopedia of Philosophy* (1998).
[217] ARS art. 23 Commentary, [6].
[218] Christakis, 'Illusion', 253–4.

control of the shipmaster; the state organ simply had no power to prevent it or to overcome it. The situation is no different from that where an individual, pushed by a mob or by strong winds, treads and injures a toddler. In these circumstances the state is acted through, rather than acting itself; it is an instrument rather than an agent. In the Latin maxim, the state *non agit sed agitur*.[219] Of course, these will be only rare occurrences in international law which are, especially in what concerns the right of refuge from the perils of navigation (and of aviation), already recognised as part of the law of the sea and the law of aviation.[220]

But involuntariness can also be a normative concept, related not so much to the power to act but to the capacity to choose.[221] This capacity to choose may be constrained by the circumstances, and this is precisely the most common scenario described in the practice reviewed earlier. In most of these cases, states invoking *force majeure* referred to their acts as having been coerced or compelled by the circumstances.

That the state's capacity to choose can be constrained or coerced is accepted in international law. To be sure, there is no general concept of coercion applicable across international law – but it is a factual circumstance that is taken into account by different rules, to different degrees, and to different effects. For example, coercion can constitute an unlawful act if it amounts to an interference in the internal affairs of a state. In this context, according to *Nicaragua*, a state acts unlawfully if 'it uses methods of coercion in regard to such choices which must remain free ones'.[222] Equally, coercion amounting to a threat of the use of force is a ground for the invalidation of treaties.[223] In *Aminoil*, for instance, the Tribunal recognised that the freedom to consent to an agreement may be limited by 'constraint'.[224] Duress was also pleaded by Mauritius in the *Chagos Islands* arbitration in an effort to invalidate its acceptance of independence in the terms 'imposed' by the United Kingdom, namely, the acceptance of detachment of the Chagos Archipelago as a condition of

---

[219] E.g., Scalese, *La rilevanza delle scusanti nella teoria dell'illecito internazionale* (2008), 64.
[220] On which see Chapter 9, Section 9.2.
[221] Strawson, 'Free Will' in Craig (ed.), *Routledge Encyclopedia of Philosophy* (2011).
[222] *Military and Paramilitary Activities in and Against Nicaragua (Nicaragua v USA)* (1986) ICJ Rep 14, [206].
[223] VCLT art. 52: 'A treaty is void if its conclusion has been procured by the threat or use of force in violation of the principles of international law embodied in the Charter of the United Nations.' On which see Corten, 'Article 52 (1969)' in Corten and Klein (eds), *The Vienna Conventions on the Law of Treaties: A Commentary* (2011) vol. 2, 1201.
[224] *Kuwait v American Independent Oil Company (Aminoil)* (1984) 66 ILR 518, [44].

the independence of Mauritius.²²⁵ The ARS also recognise a situation of coercion in Article 18: thus, a state that coerces another into committing a wrongful act is itself responsible.

As far as *force majeure* is concerned, the state's will is coerced by the situation of impossibility deriving from the supervening event. Unlike in the case of physical involuntariness described earlier, in this case the supervening event does not act through the state, as it were, but rather creates a material impossibility to comply with the obligation and, thereby, constrains the state's capacity to choose whether to comply with that obligation. Moreover, since the material impossibility required by the plea is absolute, the state must have *no* other choice but to fail to comply in the circumstances – thus, its conduct involves 'no element of free choice'. In Paul Reuter's words, *force majeure* involves a situation of 'irresistible coercion' for the state.²²⁶ By way of example, if the Serbian debt had to be serviced in gold-francs, and gold-francs had become unavailable as a result of the French Law, then it would have had no available means to comply with the obligation. Similarly, if the state were obliged to return a work of art to another state, as a form of reparation for instance,²²⁷ and as a result of an earthquake or a fire the works of art were destroyed, the state would have no available means to comply with its obligation. The state may *want* to comply, but it is actually impossible for it to do so. The state has simply no choice in the matter.

The complete absence of choice, which determines the involuntariness of the conduct, is a crucial element in the differentiation between *force majeure* and the other supervening-event defences, state of necessity and distress. In the case of the plea of necessity the state has a binary choice: either it complies with its obligation, to the detriment of one of its essential interests; or it fails to comply, to the detriment of the (non-essential) interests of the state affected by its conduct.²²⁸ The choice is even wider in the case of distress: for the distressed agent there must be no other *reasonable* way of acting, as he judged the situation at the time. So there may be multiple options, but only one of them is reasonable.²²⁹ In these cases the state *can* comply, but it does not want to.

---

[225] Application of Mauritius, 1 August 2012, *Mauritius v UK*, PCA, vol. 1, 109–12; Mauritius, oral statement, Hearing Transcript, Day 3, *Mauritius v UK*, PCA, vol. 3, 248–50.
[226] Reuter, 1571st meeting, ILC Yearbook 1979, vol. I, 200 [25].
[227] E.g., *Case Concerning the Temple of Preah Vihear (Cambodia v Thailand)* (1962) ICJ Rep 6, 36–7.
[228] See Chapter 8, esp. Section 8.4.4.
[229] See Chapter 9, esp. Section 9.4.

### 7.4.2 Force Majeure *as an Excuse*

In the absence of practice that might permit a, so to speak, bottom-up answer to this question, a tentative classification can be made by approaching the question from the top-down. Namely, by proceeding from the concepts of justification and excuse and determining whether *force majeure*, as formulated in Article 23 and taking account of its rationale, responds to the characteristics of either of the two categories of defence. This is, of course, only a tentative classification which will need confirmation in the practice of states.

It may be recalled from the analysis in Part I of this study, that justifications are defences that focus on the conduct whereas excuses focus on the actor; indeed, it is conduct that is either lawful or wrongful, and the actor that is either responsible or excused. Of course, the focus of any given defence on act or on actor is not exclusive. Nevertheless, each defence will *preponderantly* focus on either the actor or its conduct. To take an uncontroversial example of a justification, in the case of countermeasures the analysis focuses on whether the countermeasure was a response to a previous illegality and whether it meets certain requirements and conditions (is it proportionate, and does it affect permitted or prohibited obligations?). Of course, the analysis takes into account certain properties of the state invoking countermeasures: which of its rights were breached by the responsible state, what effects did the breaches have, or what is the purpose of its adoption of the measure? But these are relevant to the analysis of proportionality or necessity of the measure; they are, in a sense, ancillary to the central analysis of the plea which is the countermeasure itself. In the case of *force majeure* the focus of analysis is not on the act, but rather on the situation of the invoking state itself. Could the state have foreseen the external event, or could the state have controlled it; and what effect did the external event have on the state; did it compel it to act contrary to its obligations? The analysis is, in a sense, individualised in that it looks to the state, to the specific circumstances in which it finds itself, and whether, in these circumstances, it retains the capacity to comply with the relevant obligation. Note, however, that the individual character of the analysis does not entail its subjectivity. As noted earlier, the 'material' character of the impossibility entails an objective standard: it is not just that *this* state finds it impossible to comply, but rather that any state in the same circumstances and in relation to the same obligation would have found it impossible to comply.[230] As an individualised defence, *force majeure* responds more closely to the concept of excuse than to that of justification. It is thus plausible to classify it as an excuse.

The classification of *force majeure* as an excuse may further be endorsed on policy grounds. In particular, on the consequences that this characterisation would have for the application of ARS Article 18, which envisages the situation where a state coerces another state into committing a wrongful act.[231] Pursuant to this provision, a coercing state is responsible only insofar as the coerced state's act is wrongful.[232] Coercion of a state is, indeed, a form of derived responsibility – it depends on the illegality of the principal actor's conduct. The derivative character of this responsibility is systemically necessary, given that coercion can involve a state's responsibility for the wrongful act of another even if the coercion is itself lawful.[233] Now, if the coerced state has a justification, which renders its conduct lawful, then the coercing state will have participated in the commission of a lawful act. Consequently, the coercing state (so long as its own act of coercion is not itself prohibited by international law) cannot be responsible for the act of the coerced state: its responsibility would have no legal basis.[234] Thus, if State A coerces State B to engage in conduct contrary to a right of State C, and State C had at any rate consented to that act by State B, then there can be no responsibility for State A since State B's act is lawful.

A particular difficulty arises here in respect of *force majeure*. According to the Commentary to Article 18:

> The equation of coercion with *force majeure* means that in most cases where article 18 is applicable, the responsibility of the coerced State will be precluded *vis-à-vis* the injured third State ... Coercion amounting to *force majeure* may be the reason why the wrongfulness of an act is precluded *vis-à-vis* the coerced State.[235]

---

[230] Here, there are certain difficulties, in that the standard of comparison is unsettled. Szurek argues that the standard for these purposes is that of the 'well-governed state', see Szurek, 2 *Force Majeure*, 500ff.
[231] These same remarks are applicable, *mutatis mutandis*, to a state directing another state to commit a wrongful act, which is the subject of ARS art. 17. On this point see also Chapter 1, Section 1.3.3.2.
[232] ARS art. 23 Commentary, [1].
[233] Ibid., [3].
[234] Recall that 'responsibility' is defined as the legal consequences arising from a wrongful act.
[235] ARS art. 23 Commentary, [4].

In short, if the coercion reaches the level of *force majeure*, then the coerced state's act will be lawful and, consequently, it will not be responsible for it. Indeed, it would be unfair to hold it responsible since 'the coercing State is the prime mover in respect of the conduct and the coerced State is merely its instrument.'[236] Nevertheless:

> there is no reason why the wrongfulness of that act should be precluded *vis-à-vis* the coercing State. On the contrary, if the coercing State cannot be held responsible for the act in question, the injured State may have no redress at all.[237]

But this conclusion does not stand. If the coercing state's responsibility *derives from* the wrongfulness of the act of the coerced state, then the legality of the latter's conduct on the basis of *force majeure* necessarily affects the coercing state's responsibility. Just as in the hypothesis of consent mentioned earlier, the coercing state's responsibility would have no legal basis. The injured state would thus remain without redress. The policy aim of avoiding unfair treatment to the coerced state, ultimately undermines the policy aim of ensuring fair treatment to the injured state. To ensure that the injured state retains an avenue for redress in these circumstances, while at the same time making a concession for the situation of the coerced state, the best solution is to classify *force majeure* as an excuse. This way, the coerced state's act remains wrongful, but the coerced state will not be responsible for it (it will be excused). Since the excuse is individualised, the coercing state cannot benefit from it and its responsibility towards the injured state can rest on the wrongfulness of the coerced state's conduct.

### 7.4.3 Theorising the Excuse of Force Majeure: A Free Will Theory

*Force majeure* can therefore be classified as an excuse and there are good policy reasons to do so as well. The final question to consider is how to sustain this classification theoretically. In domestic legal orders, defences concerned with involuntariness are usually grounded on theories of free will, as explained in Chapter 3. Pursuant to these theories, since the basis of responsibility is rational and free choice-making, then whenever will or choice is lacking there is no basis to ascribe responsibility to the agent

---

[236] Commentary to Chapter IV of Part One, [6].
[237] ARS art. 23 Commentary, [4].

## 7.4 FORCE MAJEURE AS AN EXCUSE

even though his act is a violation of a proscription in the legal order.[238] Is it possible to construe a similar theory in international law?

The roles of will and free will in the concept of state responsibility have not been discussed to a great extent in the literature and, unavoidably, have received even less attention in state practice. Still, occasional references can be found in the scholarship, though these are articulated more in the form of axiomatic assertions than analytic explanations. According to Ian Brownlie, for example, the theory of 'objective responsibility rests on the notion of the voluntary act',[239] a view repeated by Crawford in the most recent edition of *Brownlie's Principles*.[240] Analogous views were expressed by Georg Schwarzenberger (on more than one occasion)[241] and by Marcel Sibert.[242] Others, instead, have focused on the notion of free will. For example, Paul Fauchille asserted in 1922 that 'sans liberté pas de responsabilité',[243] and for Paul Widenbaum, writing in 1938, '[i]nternational law as well as municipal accepts as basic principle the doctrine that each individual – person or state – is free to decide his actions and is therefore responsible for them'.[244] More recently, Ago maintained that the 'objective element' of the internationally wrongful act, namely the conduct in breach of the state's international obligations, requires the state to 'freely exercise or refrain from exercising its subjective right, its faculty or power, and [to] freely fulfil or violate the obligation'.[245] Moreover, François Rigaux has expressly indicated that responsibility is premised on the existence of free will,[246] and Crawford notes that state responsibility can only be engaged

---

[238] See Chapter 3, Section 3.4.2.2. See, generally, Horder, *Excusing Crime* (2007), 35. It is not excluded that such theory may be applicable to corporate subjects, at least under so-called 'doctrines of identification'. As explained by Andrew Simester, pursuant to theories of identification 'the corporation is imputed with a package comprising some designated (senior) individual's conduct and culpability. At least at international law, analogous doctrines of identification are required to recognise the state as an agent, and in principle such doctrines could also impute excuses', see Simester, 'Necessity, Torture and the Rule of Law' in Ramraj (ed.), *Emergencies and the Limits of Legality* (2008), 302.

[239] Brownlie, *State Responsibility* (1983), 38; restated in Brownlie, *Principles of Public International Law* (7th edn, 2008), 437.

[240] Crawford, *Brownlie's Principles of Public International Law* (2012), 556.

[241] Schwarzenberger, 'The Fundamental Principles of International Law' (1955) 87 *Recueil* 191, 351; Schwarzenberger and Brown, *Manual of International Law* (6th edn, 1976), 146.

[242] Sibert, *Traité*, 311.

[243] Fauchille, 1 *Traité*, 427.

[244] Weidenbaum, 'Necessity in International Law' (1938) 14 *Transactions Grot Soc* 105, 117.

[245] Ago, Third Report on State Responsibility, ILC Yearbook 1971, vol. II(1), [51].

[246] Rigaux, 'International Responsibility and the Principle of Causality' in Ragazzi (ed.), *International Responsibility Today: Essays in Memory of Oscar Schachter* (2005), 81.

where the state has a normal capacity to act.[247] As far as states are concerned, the following statement by Germany in the *Wimbledon* case is especially relevant:

> Any diminution of Germany's right to declare herself neutral in future conflicts is not only incompatible with sovereignty, it is also a diminution of her liberty of action from a moral point of view. Liberty of conscience, which should exist for a State no less than an individual, and the possibility of responsibility would be done away with.[248]

It can be inferred from these statements that the responsibility of a state is premised on its free will: its ability to choose its own conduct. As such the consequences of a wrongful act can only arise if the act was itself voluntarily adopted in circumstances in which the state had a normal capacity to act.[249]

It follows from the above that, where this capacity is disturbed, then the state may be excused from the legal consequences of its wrongful acts. This conclusion represents the extension, to the law of responsibility, of the effects of coercion in other branches of international law. This is not to say there is a general concept of duress or coercion in international law; nevertheless, it seems clear that under certain circumstances, the legal order recognises that acts adopted under some form of constraint on the state's will do not produce legal effects. For instance, in the law of treaties the coercion of the state (or of its organs) determines the invalidity of treaties.[250] In the law of responsibility, coercion of the state's will – within the conditions and requirements established by the formulation of the defences – can exclude the legal consequences of the wrongful act. An excuse of *force majeure* can, therefore, be supported by a free will theory.

Now, a free will theory of excuse nevertheless falls short of explaining, or grounding, the plea in its current formulation. In particular, it is incapable of accommodating in a principled manner the exclusion of the plea where the state has contributed to the occurrence of the situation of *force majeure*. Indeed, if the plea is afforded because the state acted under

---

[247] Crawford, *Brownlie's Principles*, 552.
[248] Germany, oral statement, PCIJ Series C No 03/1, 342 (Annexes 29–31).
[249] The first reading of the ARS included a provision on the 'capacity' to act of the state, though this was understood to relate to the personhood of the entity – namely, whether it was recognised as a subject of the legal order. See Ago, First Report on State Responsibility, ILC Yearbook 1969, vol. II, 195–7; ILC Report, twenty-fifth session, ILC Yearbook 1973, vol. II, 176–9.
[250] On which see VCLT art. 52, and Corten, 'Article 52 (1969)', vol. 2, 1201.

circumstances in which its will was coerced – why does it matter whether that coercion resulted from endogenous or exogenous causes, or a combination of the two? Of course, the requirement of non-contribution is a well-established restriction of the plea, recognised at customary law, and it is unlikely to be rejected because it cannot be sustained by the theory underlying the defence.

As was said in Chapter 2, moreover, this theory is capable of sustaining a difference between the various excuses on the basis of the extent of compulsion it creates. It would thus allow for a distinction between total and partial excuses: where the act is entirely involuntary then excuse can be total, whereas where the act is partially involuntary then excuse can be partial. This may have an impact on the potential duty to compensate for material damage.

These considerations are, of course, only embryonic. A free-will theory of excuse in international law still requires further development, as does the possibility of distinguishing between total and partial excuse. Nevertheless, the practice available so far allows to make a reasonable argument in favour of the classification of the plea, as well as the identification of its underlying theory, as an excuse. Only the practice of states can, however, confirm this tentative classification.

# 8

# State of Necessity

## 8.1 Introduction

Pursuant to ARS Article 25:

1. Necessity may not be invoked by a State as a ground for precluding the wrongfulness of an act not in conformity with an international obligation of that State unless the act:
    (a) is the only way for the State to safeguard an essential interest against a grave and imminent peril; and
    (b) does not seriously impair an essential interest of the State or States towards which the obligation exists, or of the international community as a whole.
2. In any case, necessity may not be invoked by a State as a ground for precluding wrongfulness if:
    (a) the international obligation in question excludes the possibility of invoking necessity; or
    (b) the State has contributed to the situation of necessity.

The development of this general defence in international law and within the ILC's codification of state responsibility has been fraught with difficulties and filled with controversy, as this chapter will highlight.

These difficulties result from a combination of linguistic and substantive imprecisions concerning the concept of necessity. Linguistically, the term 'necessity' has various different meanings,[1] as noted by the Tribunal in *Indus Waters Kishengaga*.[2] At least two main meanings of this term can be found: 'necessity' may express unavoidability in the laws of physical causation, or it may express a situation or predicament. Necessity as

---

[1] See, e.g., McKean, 'The Law of Necessity' (1932) 36 *Dick LR* 237, 244; Christakis, ' "Nécessité n'a pas de Loi?" Rapport général sur la nécessité en droit international' in Christakis (ed.), *La nécessité en droit international* (2007), 9.

[2] *Indus Waters Kishengaga Arbitration (Pakistan v India)* PCA, Partial Award, 18 February 2013, [219–27] (parties' arguments); [397–9] (Tribunal's decision).

## 8.1 INTRODUCTION

unavoidability of events is legally translated in the notion of *force majeure*, that superior, uncontrollable, and unavoidable, force that causes a material impossibility to perform. Indeed, it was not unusual, historically, to address such natural events as 'unavoidable necessity'.[3] In contrast to the apparent certainty of necessity as unavoidability, necessity as predicament concerns the uncertain.[4] In law, necessity as predicament refers to circumstances of an extraordinary character, which exceed the bounds of the law's regular framework, and are addressed through rules of necessity.

Just as it has many meanings, the concept of necessity also plays multiple functions in the law.[5] These functions are oftentimes described with two Latin maxims originating in medieval canon law: *necessitas non habet legem* and *necessitas facit legem*.[6] Neither of these maxims expresses legal rules. It is not the case that necessity generates the right to engage in certain conduct, or that necessity, literally, opens the door to non-legality. In the words of the umpire in the *Faber* case: '[t]he rights of an individual are not created or determined by his wants or even his necessities'.[7] The same holds true for states. The maxims refer, rather, to the ordinary notion of necessity and describe the manners in which this notion relates to the legal order: necessity may highlight areas of absent or insufficient legal regulation (it has no law), and it may inspire the creation or modification of rules of law (it makes law).[8] This is the *opinio necessitatis* which often accompanies the *opinio iuris* in customary law.[9]

---

[3] Paddeu, 'A Genealogy of *Force Majeure* in International Law' (2011) 82 BYIL 381, 386.
[4] For the intellectual history of necessity-of-predicament as a notion concerned with the unknown, see Heathcote, *State of Necessity and International Law*, unpublished thesis, Graduate Institute of International and Development Studies, 2005, 35–78.
[5] Generally, Sperduti, 'Introduzione allo studio delle funzioni della necessitá nel diritto internazionale' (1943) 22 *Rivista di diritto internazionale* 19.
[6] On the origin of these maxims, see Roumy, 'L'origine et la diffusion de l'adage canonique *Necessitas non habet legem* (VIIIe–XIIIe s.)' in Mueller and Sommar (eds), *Medieval Church Law and the Origins of the Western Legal Tradition: A Tribute to Kenneth Pennington* (2006), 457. On these maxims see, generally, Agamben, *State of Exception* (2005), 24–30.
[7] *Faber* case (1903) 10 RIAA 438, 466.
[8] Borsi, 'Ragione di guerra e stato di necessità nel diritto internazionale' (1916) 5 *Rivista di diritto internazionale* 157, 182, 184; Perassi, 'Necessità e stato di necessità nella teoria dommatica della produzione giuridica' (1917) *Rivista di diritto pubblico* 271; Rapisardi-Mirabelli, *I limiti d'obbligatorietà delle norme giuridiche internazionali* (1922), 121–3; Heathcote, *Necessity*, ch. 4; Montini, 'La necessità ambientale e le sue diverse funzioni nel diritto internazionale contemporaneo' in Spinedi et al. (eds), *La codificazione della responsabilità internazionale degli Stati alla prova dei fatti* (2006), 159; Tsagourias, 'Necessity and the Use of Force: A Special Regime' (2010) 41 NYIL 11, 12; Cassella, *La nécessité en droit international* (2011), 461–505 (to avoid ambiguities, she rejects the use of sources language: 461–2).
[9] Thirlway, *The Sources of International Law* (2014), 78–9.

To emphasise again, new rules are not created by the fact of necessity alone. To put it another way, necessity is not a formal source of law.[10] Necessity may, however, prompt the setting in motion of the regular (and formal) processes of law creation and modification, resulting in the adoption or recognition of new necessity-based rules or rules in 'necessity's image', to use Sarah Heathcote's evocative expression.[11] As stated by Thailand in the Sixth Committee of the UN General-Assembly: 'As international law continue[s] to evolve, what had formerly been allowed might be prohibited, as a consequence of a necessity recognised by the international community.'[12] Such necessity-based rules include, for example, the right of self-defence,[13] angary,[14] refuge in distress,[15] expropriation, and security exceptions in bilateral investment treaties. These rules (may) also include 'state of necessity', a general and abstract rule recognised as a defence to breaches of international law. It is because of the existence of specific necessity-inspired rules that Article 25(2)(a) excludes the application of the general defence when the necessity situation has already been catered to by the substantive (or primary) rule in question. Necessity, in short, relates to the law in different ways: it may highlight absent or deficient regulation, it may prompt the adoption of new rules and it may be a rule in itself.

Failure to perceive these essential distinctions is at the core of rather unsophisticated argumentation about the plea of necessity in customary international law. The language of necessity is present in all necessity-inspired provisions: e.g., the necessity of self-defence, the necessity of emergency measures to address threats to the state's 'essential security interests', and so on. Not all references to 'necessity' in the practice of states constitute references to the general rule 'state of necessity'. A state's appeal to necessity in the context of self-defence, for example, says nothing about that state's views on the recognition of a general plea of necessity. This is an important reminder, since much of the nineteenth-century practice invoked in support of the recognition of a general defence of 'state of necessity' concerned necessity-inspired rules, in particular the

---

[10] On the notion of formal sources, see ibid., ch. 1.
[11] Heathcote, *Necessity*, 131–2.
[12] A/C.6/35/SR.56, [50] (observation made while discussing the topic of injurious consequences of acts not prohibited by international law).
[13] Tsagourias, 'Necessity', 13–15.
[14] Scalese, *La rilevanza delle scusanti nella teoria dell'illecito internazionale* (2008), 141.
[15] Rapisardi-Mirabelli, *Limiti d'obbligatorietà*, 124–5.

## 8.1 INTRODUCTION

rights of self-preservation and of self-defence.[16] To consider that this practice is in any way relevant state practice for the purposes of ascertaining the recognition of a general defence of state of necessity, as some do,[17] presents notable legal difficulties. Legally, the practice is relevant to the special rule *only*, and the state's *opinio juris* is, therefore, limited to that rule.

To avoid these (and other) difficulties, this chapter will use the term 'necessity' in its ordinary sense (clarifying, where necessary, which of the two senses mentioned earlier is relevant), and 'state of necessity', 'defence of necessity' or 'plea of necessity' to refer to the general rule. In so doing, this chapter will not follow the terminology employed by the English version of the ARS.[18] It will also refer to 'situation of necessity' as the set of factual circumstances that the 'state of necessity' is concerned with. As will be shown in Sections 8.2 and 8.3, this situation of necessity is currently understood to concern a predicament resulting from a clash of interests: the essential interests of the invoking state, on the one hand, and the interests of the injured state or of the international community as a whole, on the other. This preferred terminology is not, however, imposed on the materials discussed, and the language employed by the relevant practice and authors will be maintained. So reference will be made to the 'right of necessity', the 'justification of necessity' and the 'excuse of necessity' depending on the expressions used in the sources.

There are many meanings of necessity and many rules of necessity. It is no wonder that the notion and its legal accommodation have been so controversial. Against this cacophony of necessities, this chapter seeks to elucidate the conceptualisation, and to identify the rationale, of state of necessity in international law. Focused on the general and abstract rule of necessity, the chapter addresses other (specific) necessity-based rules

---

[16] That specific necessity-based rules cannot support the recognition of a general rule was emphasised as well by Ago in respect of military necessity and necessity-based rules in the law of war: Ago, Eighth Report on State Responsibility – Add.5–7, ILC Yearbook 1980, vol. II(1), [49].

[17] E.g., Barboza, 'Necessity (Revisited) in International Law' in Makarczyk (ed.), *Essays in International Law in Honour of Judge Manfred Lachs* (1984), 28; Boed, 'State of Necessity as a Justification for Internationally Wrongful Conduct' (2000) 3 *Yale HR & Development LJ* 1, 4–7; Sloane, 'On the Use and Abuse of Necessity in the Law of State Responsibility' (2012) 106 AJIL 447, 455.

[18] Note that the French version of the ARS refers to *état de nécessité* and the Spanish version to *estado de necesidad*.

only incidentally, and then only when required for a better understanding of the development of the general defence. Equally, the chapter's main focus is not the customary status of the defence at international law although the identification of the defence's conceptualisation and rationale will require an assessment of relevant state practice and *opinio juris*. Incidentally, then, the chapter will assess the status of the plea in international law as well.

Section 8.2 begins with an historical analysis of the plea of necessity in international law. The section argues against the received opinion, to show that the contemporary defence of necessity's roots cannot be found far back in international law's history. The section shows that the conceptualisation and rationale of the international rule has changed throughout its history, as a reflection of the contemporaneous stage of development of international law, generally, and the law of state responsibility, in particular. The contemporary (general and abstract) defence of necessity, it will be concluded, was a novel rule doctrinally elaborated only in the first half of the twentieth century. This novel rule was not immediately accepted in practice, not least because of its infamous invocation by Germany in justification of the 'rape of Belgium'.[19] This historical analysis is both longer and more in depth than that in other chapters in this study; this is required by the critical stance taken in this chapter against the mainstream narrative about the plea: that it has a rich history in international law and, for this reason, its recognition in contemporary international law is (virtually) a given. Section 8.3 addresses the codification (and corresponding 'rehabilitation') of state of necessity by the ILC and discusses the practice concerning the defence from 1945 to the present day. Section 8.4 then argues that the rationale of the plea of necessity in contemporary international law concerns the protection of superior interests. This rationale, premised on consequentialist reasoning, is compatible with justification-type defences based on a theory of lesser evils. As a result, state of necessity – as currently codified in the ARS – must be classified as a justification. This is, as will be shown, a counterintuitive classification since the trend in international law is to portray state of necessity as an excuse. The chapter will therefore conclude with a proposal for the reconceptualisation of the defence as an excuse by recasting the plea as one concerned with a coerced act, that is with a situation in which the state's freedom of choice is constrained by the circumstances.

---

[19] On which see Zuckerman, *The Rape of Belgium: The Untold Story of World War I* (2004).

## 8.2 State of Necessity in International Law: Historical Notes

The historical development of the general rule of necessity (as opposed to particular rules in necessity's image) is here addressed in three stages: (i) seventeenth and eighteenth centuries, during which the early-modern international lawyers discussed a so-called 'right of necessity'; (ii) the nineteenth century, during which no general rule of necessity (as a right or a defence) was recognised; and (iii) 1900–45, during which doctrine formulated and, later, states occasionally relied upon, the defence of necessity as a general and abstract rule.

### 8.2.1 Seventeenth and Eighteenth Centuries: The Natural Right of Necessity

#### 8.2.1.1 The Early-Modern International Lawyers

The early-modern international lawyers recognised in their systems of natural law and the law of nations a so-called 'right of necessity'.[20]

The 'right of necessity' was addressed in the context of the rights of property and dominion, and was a 'tacit exception',[21] as Grotius put it, to the institutions of property and dominion which had been established at the time of the original compact.[22] As examples of these situations, Grotius referred to the destruction of a neighbour's house in order to preserve one's own, and to the cutting of another ship's ropes to disentangle one's own.[23] Vattel, in turn, discussed a right to the exceeding foodstuffs of other nations, which could be requested or taken by force,[24] the right to

---

[20] On which see, generally, Moriaud, *De la justification du délit par l'état de nécessité* (1889), 128–39; Rodick, *The Doctrine of Necessity in International Law* (1928), ch. 1; Weidenbaum, 'Necessity in International Law' (1938) 14 *Transactions Grot Soc* 105, 113–16; Foriers, *De l'état de nécessité en droit pénal* (1951), 108–10; Pillitu, *Lo stato di necessità nel diritto internazionale* (1981), 20–9; Salter, 'Hugo Grotius: Property and Consent' (2001) 29 *Political Theory* 537; Salter, 'Grotius and Pufendorf on the Right of Necessity' (2005) 26 *Hist Pol Thought* 285; Cassella, *Nécessité*, 29–35.

[21] 'For some of the Laws of GOD [sic], however general they be, seem to admit of *tacit* Exceptions in Cases of extreme Necessity', the same was true of human laws. See Grotius, *De jure belli ac pacis [1625]* (2005), I.4.§vii.

[22] Grotius, *Jure belli*, I.4.§7; Wolff, *Jus gentium methodo scientifica pertractatum [1764]* (1934) vol. 2, §338; Vattel, *Droit des gens ou principes de la loi naturelle* (1916), II.§120.

[23] Grotius, *Jure belli*, II.2.§vi.4.

[24] Vattel, *Droit*, II.§120.

use the things of another nation, like its vessels, wagons, horses, and 'even the personal labour of foreigners'.[25] Equally, for Vattel the right of necessity included the case of a vessel 'obliged to enter a road which belongs to you, in order to shelter herself from a tempest'.[26] According to these authors, the right over the things of others in situations of necessity was grounded on the fiction of the revival of the 'original community of goods', pursuant to which the situation of extreme necessity revived the natural law right to the use of things, things which had been held in common before the introduction of private property.[27] The necessitous could thus make use of the things necessary to his survival as a matter of right and without infringement of the rights of others.[28]

This right of necessity was not absolute: these authors recognised some restrictions to it. For example, the necessitous was under an obligation of restitution and, in case of equal necessities, the right of the owner prevailed. Identifying the legal basis for, and the rationale of, these restrictions, which are broadly analogous to the ones still recognised today in ARS Article 25, was as problematic then as it is now. Grotius, for instance, was aware of the logical contradiction between these restrictions and the theoretical explanation of the right: if the necessitous exercised a right over the needed things which were held in common and not individually by the owner, then there was no legal basis for restitution or for the owner's preferential right over those things. He nevertheless maintained that:

> Truth of it is, this Right is not absolute, but limited to this, that Restitution shall be made when that Necessity's over. For it is sufficient that it go so far and not further, to maintain the Laws of natural Equity against the Rigour of the Rights of a Proprietor.[29]

It was, in short, equitable to provide restitution.

Pufendorf criticised the obligation of restitution as a contradiction in Grotius' work: if the necessitous had taken things held in common to which it had a natural right, why would he have to make restitution? For Pufendorf the inconsistency could be overcome by grounding the right of

---

[25] Vattel, *Droit*, II.§121.
[26] Vattel, *The Law of Nations* (2008), I.23.§288; II.9.§128.
[27] Grotius, *Jure belli*, II.2.§ii.1; Wolff, *Jus gentium*, §342. The 'original community' rationale for the taking of other's property when in situations of necessity had been developed by the canon lawyers and legists of the late Middle Ages. Noting the Medieval roots of Grotius' arguments on this point see Pillitu, *Necessità*, 21; Tierney, *The Idea of Natural Rights* (1997), 333; Salter, 'Grotius and Pufendorf'.
[28] Wolff, *Jus gentium*, §338; Vattel, *Droit*, II.§117.
[29] Grotius, *Jure belli*, II.2.§vii–ix.

## 8.2 STATE OF NECESSITY: HISTORICAL NOTES

necessity on a different theory – which Grotius had expressly rejected[30] – the duty of charity of the owner under the laws of humanity. Pursuant to this duty, Pufendorf explained, owners must come to the aid of those in need.[31] Since the situation of necessity did not exclude the property rights of the owner, the necessitous would be using or taking the property of others (and not his own). The obligation of restitution (which subsisted only where it was possible)[32] could thus be founded on the (continuing) right of property of the owner.[33]

Vattel, who returned to the Grotian theory of original community, sidestepped the theoretical difficulty, acknowledged by Grotius and highlighted further by Pufendorf, by simply appealing to the practice of European states – he marked the turn towards positivism, after all – all the while failing to point to any specific examples of this practice.[34]

In addition to the rights of property and dominion, these authors recognised a broader and general 'right' of necessity. Grotius, for example, indicated that all laws contained a tacit exception of necessity: all divine laws, because God could not have imposed absolutely strict laws, and all human laws, because legislators could not have intended to ignore man's frailty.[35] Throughout *De jure belli*, Grotius identified necessity-based exceptions to the laws of war, including the right of self-defence,[36] and established exceptions to the rights of those not participating in war (*'his qui in bello medii sunt'*).[37] An example of the latter was the passage

---

[30] Grotius, *Jure belli*, II.2.§vi.4.
[31] Pufendorf, *De jure naturae et gentium [1688]* (Clarendon, 1934), II.6.§v.
[32] Where restitution was not possible, Pufendorf recognised that the necessitous would have a duty to show gratitude to the owner: Pufendorf, *Jure naturae*, II.6.§vi. Indeed, his construction of the right of necessity as one based on the duty of charity had implications beyond the mere situation of necessity. The owner's possibility to exercise the duty of charity and show kindness to others had an important societal function: the owner's kindness was met by the deserving poor's gratitude, and the bond thereby formed was essential to life in society, see Salter, 'Grotius and Pufendorf', 297–8.
[33] Pufendorf, *Jure naturae*, II.6.§vi. Pufendorf's theory was not, however, wholly consistent. While no incompatibilities existed between the *ratio* and these restrictions to the right of necessity where the owner voluntarily complied with the duty of charity, the same is not apparent in case of owners failing to comply with this duty. These owners, according to Pufendorf, 'lost their property and their merit', and the needy person could, in consequence, take his things 'on the same grounds' as a perfect (e.g., enforceable) right: Pufendorf, *Jure naturae*, II.6.§vi. In these cases, if the owner had lost its property, what was the basis of restitution? Pufendorf does not say.
[34] Vattel, *Droit*, II.§121.
[35] Grotius, *Jure belli*, I.4.§7.
[36] Grotius, *Jure belli*, III.1.§ii.1 (italics in original).
[37] Grotius, *Jure belli*, III.17.§i.

through, and occupation of, neutral territory by belligerent forces,[38] an instance of the application of the 'right of necessity' which was widespread in the practice of states before the rise of the contemporary law of neutrality,[39] and which would later be invoked by Germany in 1914 as justification of the invasion of Belgium and Luxembourg. Vattel's right of necessity was equally broad. He defined it as:

> The right which mere necessity gives to certain acts, otherwise unlawful, when without the doing of those acts it is impossible to fulfil an indispensable obligation. We must be perfectly sure that in the given instance the obligation is really indispensable and that the act in question is the only means of fulfilling it. If one or the other of these two conditions is wanting, the right of necessity does not exist.[40]

Thus, necessity allowed a state to 'dispense' from fulfilling its treaty obligations without violation of the treaty.[41] In cases of 'very urgent' necessity,[42] treaties may become 'hurtful' to the state and, in consequence, lose their obligatory force.[43] Like Grotius, Vattel maintained that, during war, in a case of 'urgent necessity' a belligerent may forcefully pass through neutral territory and may temporarily seize a neutral town.[44] Finally, the duty of self-preservation, generally limited to just and lawful means,[45] entitled the state to encroach upon the liberty and freedom of others in cases of extreme necessity.[46] It was this instance of 'necessity' that states resorted to in the nineteenth century, and which forms the basis of the practice frequently discussed, today, as relevant to the plea of necessity.

Pufendorf's right of necessity was, perhaps, broader than that of Grotius and Vattel. In contrast to these authors, Pufendorf's right of necessity extended, beyond circumstances of self-preservation, to the protection of property.[47] Moreover, the right of necessity endowed man

---

[38] Grotius, *Jure belli*, II.2.§x, also III.17.§i.
[39] Neff, *The Rights and Duties of Neutrals* (2000), 16.
[40] Vattel, *Droit*, II.§119.
[41] Vattel, *Droit*, II.§170.
[42] Vattel, *Droit*, III.§107. In respect of treaties of alliance, Vattel said that if the state could not give assistance 'without putting itself in evident danger' this circumstance 'dispenses' the state from its fulfilment, see III.§92. This was due to the fact that the state could not enter into treaties contrary to its indispensable duties of self-preservation and self-protection, see II.§160.
[43] Vattel, *Droit*, III.§92.
[44] Vattel, *Droit*, III.§122.
[45] 'A laudable end cannot justify any means', Vattel at I.§184.
[46] Vattel, *Droit*, II.§§18–19, III.§122.
[47] Pufendorf, *Jure naturae*, II.6.§viii.

with three different entitlements. Alongside the right over the things of others grounded, as noted, on duties of charity, Pufendorf maintained that necessity entitled man with rights over his own person and rights over the person of others.[48] These two entitlements found their *ratio* in human frailty.[49]

The 'right of necessity' of the early-modern lawyers appeared to be a general one: it had ramifications in different areas of the law of peace and the law of war. It frequently operated as an autonomous and discrete legal rule (as the exception to the right of property and dominion). Yet, in other circumstances it appeared to be the source of legal entitlements: Pufendorf thus referred to rights over things, over one's own body, and over other persons arising from necessity. Equally, the right of necessity was at the basis of the rights of belligerents during war,[50] of the right of passage over neutral territory,[51] of the dispensation of treaty obligations,[52] and of the duty of self-preservation.[53] As the source of legal entitlements, the right of necessity came closer to what was defined in Section 8.1 as the ordinary notion of necessity which operates as the inspiration for law creation and change. It can indeed be queried whether this general right of necessity was properly understood as an entitlement of states. It rather seems that the 'right of necessity' that these authors discussed is better understood as the 'law of necessity', providing the *material* rather than the *formal* source of legal entitlements; after all, the term *jus* in *jus necessitatis* may be interpreted as meaning both 'right' and 'law'. In any case, their approaches and rationales to the right of necessity would not survive in the nineteenth century, though at the end of the eighteenth century they were central to the arguments of the United Kingdom in the matter of *The Neptune*.

### 8.2.1.2 'Necessity' as Original Community in *The Neptune*

'Necessity' as a revival of original communism was invoked and discussed in *The Neptune* case of 1797,[54] one of the early arbitrations decided

---

[48] Pufendorf, *Jure naturae*, II.6.§iii.
[49] Pufendorf, *Jure naturae*, II.6.§i.
[50] E.g., Grotius, *Jure belli*, III.1.§ii.1; Wolff, *Jus gentium*, §782 ('no greater force can be used against an enemy than necessity demands, which alone excuses one using force and transfers all the blame to the one against whom it is used').
[51] Pufendorf, *Jure naturae*, II.6.§viii; Vattel, *Droit*, II.§123.
[52] Vattel, *Droit*, III.§92.
[53] Vattel, *Droit*, II.§§18–19, III.§122.
[54] For a historico-legal background to this dispute, see Neff, *Neutrality*, 63ff. Note that the value of this incident as relevant practice in respect of state of necessity has been

under the Jay Treaty.[55] *The Neptune*, an American vessel on voyage from Charleston to Bordeaux, carrying rice among other things, was stopped and seized by the British navy in April 1795. The Admiralty Court of London ordered the sale of *The Neptune*'s cargo to the British government at the invoice price plus 10 per cent profit.[56] The owner claimed that it was owed the commercial price at which the articles would have sold in Bordeaux.[57] Before the Claims Commission, the British government rejected the claim arguing that the seizure was lawful as the merchandise constituted contraband and, in the alternative, that the seizure was a lawful preemptive purchase to provide for a threatened famine.[58] On this latter claim, agents for the British Crown asserted that the 'capture was made under such circumstances of distress as rendered the act lawful against the neutral'.[59]

Deciding by majority, the Commissioners rejected the British argument.[60] The majority opinions interpreted the British argument of preemptive purchase as one of necessity: the Commissioners noted that the Orders in Council, pursuant to which the seizure had been performed, had been issued to provide for a threatened famine.[61] The opinions closely followed the formulation of necessity in Grotius' *De jure belli*. Commissioner Pinkney, in particular, emphasised that necessity ought to be 'extreme', it must be real and pressing, and no other means of overcoming it must be available to the state.[62] This necessity by 'the law of nature suspends … *sub modo* the rights of others'.[63] That is, when made with a view 'to our own preservation or defence under the pressure of that imperious and unequivocal necessity which breaks down the distinctions of property, and, upon certain conditions, revives the original right of using things as if they were common'.[64] But these extremes were not met in fact, so the British plea was rejected.[65]

---

questioned: Verdross, 'Les principes généraux du droit dans la jurisprudence internationale' (1935) 52 *Recueil* 191, 209–10; Heathcote, *Necessity*, 137.

[55] Treaty of Amity, Commerce and Navigation between his Britannick Majesty and the United States (Jay Treaty), London 19 November 1794, 52 CTS 249.
[56] *The Neptune* (1797) 4 Moore Arbitrations 3843.
[57] Ibid., 3844.
[58] Id.
[59] Cited by Commissioner Gore, ibid., 3846.
[60] Ibid., 3853 (Gore); 3874–5 (Pinkney); 3885 (Trumbull).
[61] Ibid., 3873.
[62] Id.
[63] Ibid., 3859.
[64] Ibid., 3860.
[65] Ibid., 3853 (Gore); 3874–5 (Pinkney).

## 8.2.2 The Long Nineteenth Century (1800–1914): Twilight of the General 'Right of Necessity'

The general right of necessity of the early-moderns, if such a right was recognised, did not survive the nineteenth century. Few authors asserted the right and, in practice, even fewer states invoked a general right (or rule) of necessity. Rather, the nineteenth-century practice frequently cited as relevant to the contemporary defence of necessity concerned a specific legal entitlement, the fundamental right of self-preservation, and a specific typology of conduct, the use of force short of war. The stereotypical example of this practice was the *Caroline* incident, in which the British minister in Washington justified the sinking of the *Caroline* as a 'necessity of self-defence and self-preservation'.[66]

Alongside this practice on the use of force, today's *jus ad bellum*, the notion of 'necessity' was frequently invoked in the regulation of the conduct of hostilities, today's *jus in bello*. In this context, it took the form of 'military necessity'. Given the specialised content of the notion of 'military necessity', it will not be addressed in this book any further.[67] The notion of necessity was also frequently invoked, this time as a defence, in prize courts by vessels captured while entering prohibited waters or while blockade-running. In this context 'necessity' provided a specific defence for ships in distress; for this reason, it will be addressed in Chapter 9 in relation to the defence of distress.

### 8.2.2.1 A Difficult Start: The Seizure of the Danish Fleet (1807)

Already in the early nineteenth century, the 'right of necessity' was the subject of much controversy. In 1807, in the midst of the Napoleonic wars, the United Kingdom captured Copenhagen and seized and destroyed part of the fleet of Denmark, a neutral state.[68] In Parliament, Secretary of State Canning stated his views in respect of the seizure of the fleet:

> Was it to be contended that in a moment of imminent danger and impending necessity we should have abstained from the course which prudence and policy dictated in order to meet these calamities that threatened our

---

[66] Fox to Forsyth (6 February 1838), in Manning, *Diplomatic Correspondence of the United States–Canadian Relations* (1943) vol. 3, 422. (Hereafter, Manning, 3 *Correspondence*.)
[67] For an overview of this doctrine and references see Turns, 'Military Necessity', in *Oxford Online Bibliographies* (www.oxfordbibliographies.com).
[68] For an account, see Creasy, *First Platform of International Law* (1876), 350ff.

security and existence because if we fell under the pressure we should have the consolation of having the authority of Pufendorf to plead?[69]

The Opposition did not dispute the legal basis of Canning's argument:

> [I]t may be said that … a threat from a third power existed … If our conduct could be at all justified on this ground, it must be on the necessity of anticipating the views of the enemy with regard to the Danish fleet. No writer on International Law, or on any other law, or on common justice, had ever maintained that one power could be justified in taking from another power what belonged to it, unless a third power meant, and was able to take the same thing. The justification of this step must, therefore, rest on the necessity of it which would depend on the circumstances…[70]

The measure was, however, contested by Napoleon and 'the other foreign enemies of England.'[71] It was significant that, though only a few years had passed since *The Neptune*, the argument of necessity no longer relied on the revival of the original community of goods, but emphasised the reason of state.

Such an unambiguous invocation of necessity was not, however, characteristic of the practice of the period 1800–1914. In later instances of practice concerning the use of force to avoid (allegedly) imminent dangers, states appealed to different legal notions, including self-preservation and self-defence. This new terminology was the consequence of an important doctrinal development, which would be prevalent in legal scholarship for over a century and would provide a legal basis to numerous abuses in practice, the theory of fundamental rights of states.[72]

### 8.2.2.2 Necessity and the Fundamental Right of Self-Preservation

**The Fundamental Rights of States and the Right of Self-Preservation**
The idea of fundamental rights of states had been present in the law of nations since the work of Wolff and of Vattel.[73] But the legal articulation of a doctrine or theory of fundamental rights occurred only after the French Revolution. In 1793 the National Convention was presented with a draft Declaration on the Rights and Duties of Nations,

---

[69] Hansard, Parliamentary Reports, vol. X, 283.
[70] Ibid., 253–4.
[71] Creasy, *First Platform*, 353.
[72] Generally, see Pillet, *Recherches sur les droits fondamentaux des Etats* (1899); Cavaglieri, *I diritti fondamentali degli Stati nella Società Internazionale* (1906); Gidel, 'Droits et devoirs des nations, théorie classique des droits fondamentaux des États' (1925) 10 *Recueil* 537.
[73] Jouannet, *The Liberal-Welfarist Law of Nations* (2012), 124.

## 8.2 STATE OF NECESSITY: HISTORICAL NOTES

modelled after the 1789 Declaration on Rights and Duties of Man and Citizen, prepared by the Abbé Grégoire.[74] The declaration on the rights of states was not adopted, but its core idea that states, like individuals, had inherent or natural rights was subsequently developed by international lawyers from different legal traditions.[75] With varying terminology, this doctrine was upheld by scholars in both Europe and America, from both Continental and Common law traditions, including: Henri Bonfils,[76] Pasquale Fiore,[77] William Hall,[78] Henry Halleck,[79] August Wilhelm Heffter,[80] Alphonse Rivier,[81] Georg von Martens[82] and Henry Wheaton.[83]

In broad terms, the fundamental rights of states were those rights 'inherent' in statehood: states were entitled to them by the mere fact of their existence.[84] These included, usually, the rights of self-preservation, independence, equality, respect and commerce.[85] The doctrine initially derived from natural law, but its theoretical underpinnings varied throughout the century to accommodate different jurisprudential theories developed, throughout the century, to explain the foundation of international law. Thus, as the nineteenth century advanced, fundamental rights were successively said to derive from history, sociology and, even, positive law.[86] The theory of fundamental rights would be abandoned in the first half of the twentieth century in connection with the growing prevalence of positivism, partly due to the difficulties of positivism in providing a consistent and convincing basis to the idea of fundamental rights.[87] But for the time being, it affected international affairs in important ways.

---

[74] Ibid., 37.
[75] Cavaglieri, *Diritti*, 33–5.
[76] Bonfils, *Manuel de droit international public* (1894), 121–2.
[77] Fiore, *Nouveau droit international public* (2nd edn, 1885) vol. 1, 323–4; Fiore, *Il diritto internazionale codificato* (1890), 103. Also Carnazza-Amari, *Traité de droit international public en temps de paix* (1880) vol. 1, 372–3.
[78] Hall, *International Law* (1880), 36.
[79] Halleck, *International Law* (1861), 82.
[80] Heffter, *Le droit international de l'Europe* (3rd edn, 1873), 59ff.
[81] Rivier, *Principes de droit des gens* (1896) vol. 1, 255.
[82] de Martens, *Traité de droit international* (1883) vol. 1, 387.
[83] Wheaton, *Elements of International Law* (1836), 81ff.
[84] E.g., Klüber, *Droit des gens moderne de l'Europe* (1831), 65; Ortolan, *Règles internationales et diplomatie de la mer* (4th edn, 1864) vol. 1, 49; de Martens, 1 *Traité*, 388; Rivier, *Principes*, 255; Despagnet, *Cours de droit international public* (2nd edn, 1899), 163; Nys, *Le droit international* (1905) vol. 2, 176; Bonfils, *Manuel de droit international public* (Fauchille ed., 4th edn, 1905), 124.
[85] Cavaglieri, *Diritti*, 24.
[86] Yet, none of these subsequent theories could explain the fundamental character of these rights and they were eventually abandoned: Jouannet, *Liberal-Welfarist*, 125.
[87] Generally Cavaglieri, *Diritti* (1906).

Fundamental rights were not only inherent in statehood, for some scholars they also *constituted* statehood. Their suppression entailed for the state in question the loss of its status as a subject of international law. Their maintenance thus became paramount, and it is easy to see why, as a result, the right of self-preservation took a preeminent role.[88] The right of self-preservation was indeed said to be 'primary' or 'cardinal', and it was said to be the source of all other fundamental rights.[89] Moreover, it also often constituted a state's duty towards its people.[90] For all the apparent defensive character of this right, it was not infrequently noted that self-preservation was not limited to the protection of the existence of the state but also included the state's right to self-perfection.[91] It is arguably for this reason that commerce was included in the list of fundamental rights.

The right of self-preservation endowed the state with all the rights necessary to its successful attainment, both internally and externally.[92] Internally, self-preservation entitled the state to organise its army, levy taxes, erect fortifications, and regulate the entry and stay of foreigners.[93] It also provided it with the right to fight insurrections,[94] a right appealed to in disputes concerning damages caused to foreigners during internal strife.[95] Externally, the rights attendant on self-preservation included the rights to security,[96] self-defence,[97] and intervention.[98]

---

[88] See further Jouannet, *Liberal-Welfarist*, 105–6.

[89] Twiss, *The Law of Nations* (1861), 144; Calvo, *Dictionnaire de droit international public et privé* (1885) vol. 1, 180; Piédelièvre, *Précis de droit international public* (1894) vol. 1, 172; Rivier, *Principes*, 255.

[90] Halleck, *International Law*, 92; de Martens, 1 *Traité*, 388; Rivier, *Principes*, 278; Nys, 2 *Droit international*, 180.

[91] Carnazza-Amari, *Trattato sul diritto internazionale pubblico di pace* (2nd edn, 1875), 299; Fiore, *Trattato di diritto internazionale* (3rd edn, 1887) vol. 1, 308; Rivier, *Principes*, 265; Nys, 2 *Droit international*, 178; Mérignhac, *Traité de droit public international* (1905) vol. 1, 246.

[92] Halleck, *Elements of International Law and Laws of War* (1866), 57; Calvo, *Dictionnaire*, 180.

[93] Klüber, *Droit des gens*, 68; Phillimore, *Commentaries upon International Law* (1854) vol. 1, [225–6]; Halleck, *International Law*, 92; de Martens, 1 *Traité*, 389; Fiore, *Trattato*, 301; Foignet, *Manuel élémentaire de droit international public* (1892), 66; Nys, 2 *Droit international*, 180; Mérignhac, 1 *Traité*, 240.

[94] Foignet, *Manuel*, 66.

[95] E.g., by the Austrian Prince Schwartzenberg in respect of a British claim for damages caused during the 1849 and 1850 insurrections in Tuscany and Sicily. Cited in Arias, 'The Non-Liability of States for Damages Suffered by Foreigners in the Course of a Riot, an Insurrection or a Civil War' (1913) 7 AJIL 724, 742.

[96] Twiss, *Law*, 12–13; Creasy, *First Platform*, 149–50.

[97] Wheaton, *Elements*, 81; Twiss, *Law*, 11, 144; Carnazza-Amari, *Trattato*, 301; Bonfils, *Manuel*, 125.

[98] Wheaton, *Elements*, 82; Hall, *International Law*, 242.

Self-preservation also granted the state the right to conclude treaties of alliance,[99] and to request information from neighbouring states in relation to their measures and plans of military self-aggrandisement.[100] These corollary rights varied in name and scope, and were frequently somewhat overlapping. Moreover, they could be exercised both as precautionary measures to avert impending danger, and as reactive measures to repel attacks, both external (from other states) and internal (against insurgents).[101] One such corollary right, according to some, was the 'right of necessity'.

**A Discrete Right: The Right of Necessity as a Corollary of the Right of Self-Preservation** Some part of the doctrine, including Carlos Calvo,[102] Guillaume de Garden,[103] Joachim Klüber[104] and Giacomo Macri,[105] recognised a discrete right of necessity, deriving from the right of self-preservation. Rivier could potentially be included in this list insofar as he contemplated an 'excuse of necessity' which, despite employing different terminology, was substantially similar to the 'right of necessity' of these scholars.[106] According to these authors, the right of necessity was characterised by a situation of conflicting rights, namely a situation in which the state's right to existence, for instance, clashed with another state's right to territorial integrity (when, e.g., an attack was being prepared from a neighbouring state). In this situation, the right of necessity entitled the state whose existence was at issue to set aside the rights of other states. In the words of Garden: 'it cannot be doubted that in an extreme case, when something directly threatens the self-preservation of the state, all must give way, every engagement, every obligation must cede'.[107] The state's self-preservation, at the basis of the right of necessity, trumped every other obligation of the state so that its measures of protection, even if contrary to the rights of other states, were lawful. These authors warned that the right of necessity ought not be confused with reason of state, a political

---

[99] Phillimore, 1 *Commentaries*, [225]; Carnazza-Amari, *Trattato*, 304.
[100] Halleck, *International Law*, 93.
[101] Calvo, *Le droit international théorique et pratique* (3rd edn, 1880) vol. 1, 309.
[102] Calvo, *Dictionnaire*, 180. However, he did not include it in *Le droit international public*.
[103] de Garden, *Traité complet de diplomatie* (1833) vol. 1, 266.
[104] Klüber, *Droit des gens*, 75–6; views restated in Ott's updated edition of the book: Klüber, *Droit des gens moderne de l'Europe* (2nd edn, 1874), 75–7.
[105] Macri, *Teorica del diritto internazionale* (1883) vol. 1, 90.
[106] Rivier, *Principes*, 277–8.
[107] de Garden, *Traité*, 266. Also Klüber, *Droit des gens*, 76, and 75 of 2nd edn.

doctrine, or the *droit de convenance*, since it was limited by the previous exhaustion of other means and by an obligation to make reparation.[108]

The right of necessity advocated by these authors retained the name and, roughly, the definition and limitations of the right of necessity of the early-moderns. Yet it differed from the early-modern lawyers' right in one fundamental respect: it moved away from the theory of the revival of original communism, and was grounded on the primacy of the right of self-preservation. If self-preservation was the primary right, it took priority over all other rights such that any action in its furtherance, including in breach of another state's right, was lawful. Indeed, it was of the essence of this doctrine that action in self-preservation was lawful. As these authors' exposition of the doctrine clearly shows, the right of self-preservation, as a result of its preeminence, trumped other rights, rendering action adopted in pursuance with it – even if incompatible with other states' rights – lawful.

Despite the nominal *éloignement* from the *droit de convenance* and the political doctrine of reason of state, the right of necessity recognised by these authors was seemingly limitless and, ultimately, was able to provide a legal basis to politically motivated uses of force. The right of necessity cloaked with legality displays of pure power-politics – it was a right to commit a wrong when this wrong was necessary for the attainment of political ends. For this reason, it was harshly criticised. It found vocal critics in Bonfils,[109] Paul Pradier-Fodéré[110] and John Westlake.[111] It was not, moreover, upheld by the majority of commentators nor appealed to, autonomously, by states in their practice. Rather, states invoked the right of self-preservation, in the name of which they engaged in the abuses and violations that critics of the right of necessity had warned against.

**Inspiring Rights: The 'Necessity of Self-Defence and Self-Preservation'**
The material scope of the right of necessity upheld by the authors mentioned earlier was frequently addressed under the banner of the fundamental right of self-preservation. The practice concerning self-preservation has been extensively analysed in doctrinal commentary,[112] so this section will discuss in depth only two instances: the *Caroline* incident and the *Fur*

---
[108] de Garden, *Traité*, 267. Also Klüber, *Droit des gens*, 76, and 75 of 2nd edn.
[109] Bonfils, *Manuel*, 124.
[110] Pradier-Fodéré, *Traité de droit international: Européen et Américain* (1885) vol. 1, 373.
[111] Westlake, *International Law* (2nd edn, 1910) vol. 1, 307–8.
[112] Cavaglieri, *Lo stato di necessità nel diritto internazionale* (1917), 73–86; Heathcote, *Necessity*, 200–31.

*Seals* arbitration. These two cases stand out from the practice of the rest of the century in view of the parties' comprehensive arguments on self-preservation, self-defence and necessity. While certainly a limited sample, these instances can nevertheless provide a better grasp of the understanding that states had of these notions at the time.

*The Caroline Incident (1837)* On 29 December 1837, British forces entered the territory of the United States and apprehended and destroyed the *Caroline*, a steamer used by Canadian insurgents, moored off Fort Schlosser in the American bank of the Niagara River.[113] The incident caused outrage in the United States and gave rise to a protracted diplomatic correspondence between the two states, in which the notions of self-preservation, self-defence and necessity were invoked. The parties largely agreed on the legal principles applicable to the incident: the state's territory was inviolable save for specific exceptions. But the parties remained, even after the resolution of the dispute, in disagreement on whether the facts of the case supported the plea of exception invoked by the United Kingdom.

Following the events, the United States' Secretary of State Forsyth complained of the acts to the British minister in Washington, Fox, and demanded an explanation.[114] In his response, Fox invoked the 'necessity of self-defence and self-preservation' to justify the British measure.[115] A formal request for redress was presented to the British government in March 1838 by Stevenson, the US minister in London. Stevenson rejected the justification invoked by Fox in his earlier correspondence: while he recognised that the inviolability of sovereign territory was subject to limited exceptional circumstances, he held that none of these were present in the *Caroline* case. Stevenson indicated that in times of war, the territory of neutrals could exceptionally be invaded in cases 'arising out of necessity, and self-preservation, which suspend in favor of a belligerent *sub modo* the right of a neutral nation'.[116] In times of peace it was agreed that there could be 'no entry into the territory of an independent state, but where consent is first given; or where entry is innocent and unjustly refused; or in cases of extreme state necessity'.[117] Moreover, this necessity

---

[113] For an exposition of the facts, see Jones, 'The *Caroline* Affair' (1976) 28 *Historian* 485.
[114] Forsyth to Fox (5 and 19 January 1838), in Manning, 3 *Correspondence*, 32, 33.
[115] Fox to Forsyth (6 February 1838), in Manning, 3 *Correspondence*, 422.
[116] Stevenson to Palmerston (22 May 1838), in Manning, 3 *Correspondence*, 454.
[117] Id.

'must be imminent, and extreme, and involving impending destruction'.[118] Stevenson's letter went unanswered for nearly two years. In the meantime, the British law officers Dodson, Campbell and Rolfe had opined that the British measure was justified by self-preservation.[119]

The matter of the *Caroline* was, during these two years, addressed in the context of a separate, but related, incident – the arrest in 1840 of Alexander McLeod, a British citizen, and his trial in New York for alleged involvement in the sinking of the *Caroline*. His arrest and trial angered Britain and forced the British government to acknowledge the 'publick [sic] character' of the attack on the *Caroline*: in a note of protest on McLeod's arrest and trial, Fox held that McLeod could not be made personally responsible for the sinking since the measure was a public act.[120] He further justified the British measure by emphasising that it had been adopted 'in the strictest ... self-defence, rendered absolutely necessary by the circumstances of the occasion for the safety and protection of Her Majesty's subjects'.[121] McLeod was eventually found not guilty on the evidence before the New York Court.[122]

In April 1841 the new American Secretary of State, Webster, addressed a note to Fox in which he recognised that 'a just right of self-defence attaches always to nations, as well as to individuals, and is equally necessary for the preservation of both'.[123] To exercise this right, it was indispensable to show a 'necessity of self-defence, instant, overwhelming, leaving no choice of means, and no moment for deliberation'.[124] Moreover, the measures 'justified by the necessity of self-defence, must be limited by that necessity, and kept clearly within it'. Such a necessity, Webster argued, was not present in the British case.[125] In his reply, sent to Stevenson, the American minister in London, Lord Palmerston, held that the destruction of the *Caroline* had been 'a justifiable act of self-defence ... for the protection of British Subjects and their Property, and for the Security

---

[118] Ibid., 454–5.
[119] Opinion of 21 February 1838, 2 *McNair Intl L Op* 226; Opinion of 25 March 1839, 2 *McNair Intl L Op* 228.
[120] Fox to Forsyth (13 December 1840), in Manning, 3 *Correspondence*, 604.
[121] Fox to Forsyth (29 December 1840), in Manning, 3 *Correspondence*, 606.
[122] See Green, 'Docking the *Caroline*: Understanding the Relevance of the Formula in Contemporary Customary International Law Concerning Self-Defense' (2006) 14 *Cardozo JICL* 429, 435.
[123] Webster to Fox (24 April 1841), in Manning, 3 *Correspondence*, 140.
[124] Ibid., 145.
[125] Id.

## 8.2 STATE OF NECESSITY: HISTORICAL NOTES

of' British territories.[126] Lord Ashburton, British Special Minister to the United States, later replied to Webster's note in 1842. Having been instructed by Lord Aberdeen, the British Foreign Secretary, to invoke the plea of self-defence,[127] Ashburton said that he agreed with the statement of the law made by Webster:

> A strong overpowering necessity may arise, when this great principle [of territorial integrity] may and must be suspended. It must be so for the shortest possible period, during the continuance of an admitted overruling necessity, and strictly confined within the narrowest limits imposed by that necessity. Self-defence is the first law of our nature and it must be recognised by every code which professes to regulate the conditions and relations of man. Upon this modification, if I may call it, of the great general principle, we seem also agreed...[128]

The dispute was eventually settled with an apology on the part of the British government.[129]

This incident is frequently invoked by contemporary legal scholarship as a precedent for the defence of state of necessity.[130] Indeed, James Crawford has even found in the last statement quoted the 'answer' to the 'criticism that the early cases are inapposite insofar as they do not embody an *opinio juris* that necessity precludes wrongfulness.'[131] Two related arguments

---

[126] Palmerston to Stevenson (27 August 1841), in Manning, 3 *Correspondence*, 644–5.

[127] Aberdeen to Ashburton (8 February and 25 April 1842), in Manning, 3 *Correspondence*, 693, 704, respectively. Not, as suggested by the British law officers, 'self-preservation'.

[128] Ashburton to Webster (28 July 1842), in Manning, 3 *Correspondence*, 767.

[129] Ashburton to Webster (28 July 1842), and Webster to Ashburton (6 August 1842) in Manning, 3 *Correspondence*, 770–1 and 187, respectively.

[130] Article 25 Commentary, [5]. See also Ago, Eighth Report – Add.5–7, [57]. In doctrine see, e.g., Malanczuk, 'Countermeasures and Self-Defence as Circumstances Precluding Wrongfulness in the International Law Commission's Draft Articles on State Responsibility' in Spinedi and Simma (eds), *United Nations Codification of State Responsibility* (1987), 241–3; Johnstone, 'The Plea of "Necessity" in International Legal Discourse: Humanitarian Intervention and Counter-terrorism' (2005) 43 *Columbia J Trans'l L* 337, 344.

[131] Crawford, *General Part*, 310. Crawford bases his argument on the following quote from Lord Ashburton of the United Kingdom (in Manning, 3 Correspondence, 767):

> [I]t is admitted by all writers, by all Jurists, by the occasional practice of all nations, including your own, that a strong overpowering necessity may arise, when this great principle [the obligation of respect for the independent territory of another state] may and must be suspended. It must be so for the shortest possible period, during the continuance of an admitted over-ruling necessity, and strictly confined within the narrowest limits imposed by that necessity... Agreeing therefore on the general principle and on the possible exception to

are offered in support of this assessment of the incident. First is a linguistic argument pursuant to which at the time of the *Caroline* incident the term 'self-preservation' was a synonym of, or a substitute label for, the defence of necessity. Accordingly, the reference to self-preservation in the diplomatic exchanges of these states must be understood as an invocation of the plea of necessity. The second is a substantive argument, grounded on the distinction between precautionary and reactive forcible measures. This argument relies on the recognition, in nineteenth-century international law, of distinct legal bases for the adoption of precautionary and reactive forcible measures in times of peace: necessity for the former and self-defence for the latter. According to this view, it is significant that in the incident the responsibility of the United States was never at issue;[132] the British measure thus ought to have been a precautionary one. Since the British seizure of the *Caroline* was a precautionary measure, therefore the appropriate legal ground of defence at issue in this case was that of necessity and not that of self-defence.[133]

Neither of these two arguments is convincing, and for a number of reasons. As a matter of law, the legal texts of the period (and of the period before) do not evidence identity between the notion of self-preservation and the defence of necessity. As was noted earlier, a general right of necessity was not generally recognised in the literature of the period and, for those who did recognise it, the right of necessity was a corollary of the fundamental right of self-preservation. While certainly associated, these two notions, let alone these two entitlements, were not identical. These two points of law are developed in more detail later,[134] but this brief observation is sufficient at this stage to reject the first argument.

> which it is liable, the only question between us is whether this occurrence came within the limits fairly to be assigned to such exception ...
>
> But this quote omits, after the sentence ending in 'limits imposed by that necessity', the following sentence: 'Self-defence is the first law of our nature and it must be recognised by every code which professes to regulate the conditions and relations of man.' Once this sentence is added to the text, the meaning radically changes for it contextualises the references to 'necessity' as conditions of the 'first law of our nature', that is, self-defence.

[132] E.g., Bowett, *Self-Defence in International Law* (1958), 59–60 (though note that at 270, Bowett relied on the *Caroline* as a precedent for anticipatory self-defence); Sicilianos, *Les réactions décentralisées à l'illicite* (1990), 29; Gazzini, *The Changing Rules on the Use of Force in International Law* (2005), 130.

[133] Note that to reach this conclusion, this argument too assumes the identity between the notions of 'self-preservation' and 'necessity'.

[134] See also, e.g., Alland, 'International Responsibility and Sanctions: Self-Defence and Countermeasures in the ILC Codification of Rules Governing International

## 8.2 STATE OF NECESSITY: HISTORICAL NOTES

Further, there is no merit in the identification of separate legal bases for precautionary and reactive measures. For those upholding it, the right of necessity concerned precautionary measures. But the right of self-preservation and the right of self-defence were not so limited: both these rights allowed the taking of precautionary *and* reactive forcible measures.[135] It thus cannot follow from the alleged precautionary character of the British measure that the correct legal basis for its action was necessity and not, for instance, self-defence. On the facts of the case, moreover, these arguments misread the correspondence between the parties to the dispute. To begin with, despite initial hesitations, the exchanges between the parties, taken as a whole, point to the notion of self-defence as the agreed legal ground for the action of the British: the parties' disagreement did not concern the legal ground for the measure, but whether that legal ground was met in fact.[136] To be sure, the early communications between the parties contain the language of self-preservation; for example, Fox's initial reaction was to invoke 'the necessity of self-defence and self-preservation'. But this should not be surprising: the rights of self-preservation and self-defence were related to one another. Indeed, as the brief survey of the doctrine of fundamental rights of states explained, the right of self-defence was a corollary of the fundamental right of self-preservation. That is to say, the right of self-defence found its source as a legal rule in the fundamental right of self-preservation. In this light, it can be understood why, for instance, the British minister Fox spoke of 'self-defence and self-preservation'. But as the diplomatic exchanges continued, and the parties offered more detailed legal arguments, it became evident that the legal rule appealed to was that of self-defence. Thus Webster's notes refer to the right of self-defence and Lord Aberdeen unambiguously instructed Lord Ashburton to plead self-defence in his communications with the American government – and this, even after the British law officers recommended that the Crown invoke self-preservation and emphasise

---

Responsibility' in Simma and Spinedi (eds), *United Nations Codification of State Responsibility* (1987), 152–3.

[135] Jennings, 'The *Caroline* and McLeod Cases' (1938) 32 *AJIL* 82, 91. Even further, Neff argues that in the nineteenth century self-defence was always precautionary: Neff, *War and the Law of Nations* (2005), 241–2. Indeed, many contemporary scholars who maintain a right of anticipatory self-defence cite the *Caroline* incident as authority for this right, e.g., Bowett, *Self-Defence*, 270; Deeks, '"Unwilling or Unable": Toward a Normative Framework for Extraterritorial Self-Defense' (2012) 52 *Va J Int'l L* 483, 502.

[136] See Waldock, 'The Regulation of the Use of Force by Individual States in International Law' (1952) 81 *Recueil* 451, 463.

the precautionary character of the measure. Further, it is not clear that the parties characterised the sinking of the *Caroline* as a precautionary measure. To the contrary, the parties discussed at length the legality of the American toleration of rebels in its territory and the consequent loss of neutral status of the United States.[137] Indeed, textbooks of the period subsequently discussed the *Caroline* incident in the context of a state's right to use force against irregulars operating from the territory of neighbouring states.[138]

Finally, it does not appear from the correspondence that the notion of 'necessity', mentioned by the parties in their arguments, provided a discrete legal ground of justification for the British measure. The term 'necessity', in the context in which it was used by the parties, described one of the factual preconditions for the use of force by the British: hence, Webster's 'necessity of self-defence', and Fox's 'necessity of self-defence and self-preservation'.[139] In this sense, the 'necessity' referred to was no different from the requirement of necessity in the modern right of self-defence.[140]

The *Caroline* incident is, consequently, better characterised as an example of self-defence; and it is, indeed, in relation to this notion that the literature of the nineteenth century discussed this incident.[141] Yet, even in this context, the incident has more historical than legal relevance to the

---

[137] E.g., Fox to Forsyth (19 December 1840), 606 ('The place where the vessel was destroyed was nominally it is true within the Territory of a friendly Power: but the friendly power had been deprived through overbearing piratical violence, of the use of its proper authority over that portion of Territory. The Authorities of New York had both even been able to prevent the Artillery of the State from being carried off publickly at midday to be used as instruments of war against Her Majesty's subject'); Fox to Webster (12 March 1841), 616 (referring to the US 'permission' to the rebels to organise themselves in its territory); Webster to Fox (24 April 1941), 141 (objecting to the UK claim that the United States 'permitted' the presence of rebels in its territory); Palmerston to Stevenson (27 August 1841), 659–60 (arguing that it was possible that 'the Government of New York knowingly and intentionally permitted the Band of Invaders to organize and equip themselves within the State, and to arm themselves for War against British Territory out of the Military Stores of the State ... In [this] case the British Authorities in Canada had a right to retaliate War for War'), all in Manning, *Correspondence*, vol. 3.

[138] E.g., Phillimore, 1 *Commentaries*, [228–30].

[139] Similarly Tsagourias, 'Necessity', 13.

[140] Green, 'Docking', 450–1. A requirement emphasised by the ICJ in *Military and Paramilitary Activities in and Against Nicaragua (Nicaragua v United States of America)* (1986) ICJ Rep 14, [194–5]; *Oil Platforms (Islamic Republic of Iran v United States of America)* (2003) ICJ Rep 161, [43]; *Case Concerning Armed Activities on the Territory of the Congo (DRC v Uganda)* (2005) ICJ Rep 168, [147]. On which see, generally, Gardam, *Necessity, Proportionality and the Use of Force by States* (2010).

[141] See references in Brownlie, *International Law and the Use of Force by States* (1963), 43 (fn. 5).

current right of self-defence.[142] The invocation of the right of self-defence was made in a legal framework which distinguished, formally, between the states of war and peace. While there existed no prohibition on resort to war at the time, international law nevertheless (and, perhaps, paradoxically) regulated the resort to force during peace.[143] By appealing to self-defence, the United Kingdom (and the United States) were attempting to contain the dispute within the bounds of the state of peace – namely, they were trying to avoid the creation of a new state of war. So it was highly significant, not just politically but also legally, that they be able to classify the incident as one concerning the exercise of self-defence. The memory of the 1812 war between Britain and the United States was still fresh, and diplomats on either side of the Atlantic did their best to avoid, in the circumstances, the renewal of hostilities. Indeed, the possibility of war was a constant worry in the parties' correspondence,[144] even leading the Czar of Russia to offer to mediate between the parties in the interests of peace.[145] It was with this in mind that the parties approached their legal arguments in respect of the sinking of the *Caroline*: the right of self-preservation and its attendant entitlement, applicable in times of peace, provided a legal ground for the 'peaceful' use of force in international relations,[146] which could contain their dispute and avoid the renewal of (formal) war between them.

*Fur Seals (1893)* Following the acquisition of Alaska, in the years 1868–73, the United States adopted legislation regulating sealing off the Pribilof Islands in the Bering Sea.[147] Enforcing these statutes, American navy vessels had visited and searched, and subsequently confiscated, fourteen

---

[142] See Sicilianos, *Réactions*, 29; Kolb, 'La légitime défense des Etats au XIXème siècle et pendant l'époque de la Société de Nations' in Kherad (ed.), *Légitimes défenses* (2007), 43. But see Kearly, 'Raising the *Caroline*' (1999) 17 *Wisconsin ILJ* 325.
[143] O'Connell, *The Power and Purpose of International Law* (2011), 156.
[144] E.g., Stevenson to Forsyth (9 Feb 1841), at 612; Stevenson to Webster (9 March 1841), at 614; Stevenson to Webster (18 March 1841), at 619, all in Manning, *Correspondence*, vol. 3.
[145] Stevenson to Webster (19 April 1841), in Manning, 3 *Correspondence*, 627.
[146] As evidenced by the fact that these rights were addressed under the 'law of peace', and not the 'law of war'. Some writers, however, disagreed with this characterisation opting, instead, for a half-way between peace and war, see Halleck, *International Law*, 96, for whom these were 'belligerent' measures; Calvo, 1 *Droit international*, 311, for whom the measures constituted an 'imperfect war'. See generally Lamberti-Zanardi, *La legittima difesa nel diritto internazionale* (1972), 7–8; Neff, *War*, 215–50.
[147] *Fur Seals Arbitration* (1893) 1 Moore Arbitrations 755, 763. On which see Blodgett, 'The Fur Seal Arbitration' (1894) 3 *Northwestern LR* 73; Brown, 'Fur Seals and the Bering Sea Arbitration' (1895) 26 *Journal of the American Geographical Society of New York* 326.

Canadian sealing schooners in the period 1886–9 while on the high seas. The British protested the actions taken by the US navy and the ensuing dispute was submitted to arbitration, where the parties presented extensive arguments in respect of the US visitation of British vessels at sea.

Before the Tribunal, the United States defended its action by invoking self-defence. According to the United States:

> the right of self-defense on the part of a nation is a perfect and paramount right to which all others are subordinate, and which upon no admitted theory of international law has ever been surrendered; that it extends to all the material interests of a nation important to be defended; that in the time, the place, the manner, and the extent of its execution it is limited only by the actual necessity of the particular case … and that whenever an important and just national interest of any description is put in peril for the sake of individual profit by an act upon the high sea, even though such act would be otherwise justifiable, the right of the individual must give way, and the nation will be entitled to protect itself against the injury by whatever force may be reasonably necessary, according to the usages established in analogous cases.[148]

The United States argued that the protection of the seals from extinction was a 'common interest of all nations',[149] and that their extinction would involve a 'serious and permanent injury to the rights of the Government and people of the US'.[150] The right of self-defence, recognised in international law, gave the United States a right to protect these interests. It was with a view to such protection that the United States had passed the disputed legislation. Moreover, since the right of self-defence was not territorially limited, the United States could enforce this protective legislation extraterritorially, namely, on the high seas.[151] Specifically in respect of visitation on the British-flagged ships, the United States added that the right of self-defence granted states the right to stop and search foreign vessels both in times of peace and in times of war. So long as the necessity to perform such a search was present, it was immaterial whether there existed a state of war: 'Whenever the necessity arises, the right arises'.[152]

For the United Kingdom, the American claim was unprecedented.[153] As to the right of visitation in times of peace, the British agent maintained

---

[148] *Fur Seals*, 839–40.
[149] Ibid., 776, 779.
[150] Ibid., 785.
[151] Ibid., 783, 840.
[152] Ibid., 868; also 842.
[153] Ibid., 819.

## 8.2 STATE OF NECESSITY: HISTORICAL NOTES

that the 'greatest number of instances recognised by International Law of rights of self-defence and self-preservation' were belligerent rights, resting 'on the true basis of all exceptional acts of self-defence or self-preservation – the genuine emergency of danger'.[154] The right of visitation was a belligerent right, excluded in times of peace.[155] At any rate, the United Kingdom concluded that no necessity existed in the case justifying the American measure: so it was 'idle to try to treat this case as a case of necessary self-defence or self-preservation'.[156]

Both parties referred to the *Caroline* incident in their explanations of the 'right of self-defence'.[157] More so than in that incident, the arguments of the parties in this case clearly show the role of 'necessity' as a factual condition for the exercise of self-defence and self-preservation. In the words of the US agent, already quoted, 'Whenever the necessity arises, the right [of self-defence] arises'.[158] Again, as in the *Caroline*, 'necessity' was not invoked as an autonomous legal rule.

The Tribunal eventually decided that the United States had no right to protect the seals outside its territorial seas.[159] While it did not address the arguments of self-defence and self-preservation, there is evidence that the majority of the Tribunal rejected a proposal to include a reference in the *dispositif* of the award endorsing the recognition of these rights.[160]

### 8.2.2.3 Whither the Right of Necessity in International Law?

The practice and scholarly literature of this period do not support the recognition of an autonomous rule of necessity in international law. States did not invoke a right of necessity, or any general rule of necessity for that matter. To be sure, states did use the language of necessity. Though in these invocations, necessity described one of the factual conditions for the exercise of other legal entitlements. So it was that states referred to the 'necessity of' self-preservation and self-defence, in respect of the seizure of the Danish fleet, the *Caroline* incident and in the *Fur Seals* arbitration. Only a minority of scholars endorsed an autonomous rule of necessity, in the form of a right of necessity, during the century. In contrast, the majority of commentators addressed the factual situations that this

---

[154] Ibid., 892.
[155] Ibid., 902.
[156] Ibid., 894.
[157] Ibid., 867 (United States); 893–4 (United Kingdom).
[158] Ibid., 868; also 842.
[159] Ibid., 938–9.
[160] Ibid., 920.

minority discussed under the right of necessity within the context of the right of self-preservation and its attendant rights, especially those of self-defence (and intervention). The right of necessity, if one had ever existed, had been subsumed in the fundamental right of self-preservation.

It is this subsumption of the right of necessity in the right of self-preservation that has led contemporary scholars to maintain that throughout the nineteenth century 'necessity was equated with "self-preservation".'[161] This assertion, however, overstates the point. To begin with, the right of self-preservation was a much broader category than the purported right of necessity upheld by certain scholars. The purported rule of necessity, even taken in the widest form recognised at the time by the likes of Garden and Klüber, concerned solely inter-state, forcible, and precautionary measures. In turn, the right of self-preservation had both internal (domestic) and external (inter-state) manifestations, it encompassed both forcible and non-forcible measures, and it entitled the state to adopt both precautionary as well as reactive measures. Of course differences of opinion existed on this question, but the overall impression from the writings and practice of the period was that the right of self-preservation encompassed, but was not limited to, the purported rule of necessity. In other words, scholarship and practice of the nineteenth century did not simply replace the term 'right of necessity' for that of 'right of self-preservation' in their work and their mutual dealings respectively – which is what the contemporary equation argument entails.

As a consequence of this, an invocation of self-preservation need not entail an invocation of the purported rule of necessity. This holds true even where the action sought to be justified by self-preservation was forcible, extraterritorial and of a precautionary character.[162] Indeed, other entitlements corollary to the right of self-preservation allowed the adoption of extraterritorial, precautionary and forcible measures. This was certainly the case of the rights of self-defence[163] and intervention.[164] Accordingly,

---

[161] E.g., Barboza, 'Necessity', 28. More recently Boed, 'Necessity', 4–7; Sloane, 'Necessity', 455.

[162] Similarly, Bin Cheng identifies territorial and external applications for the 'principle of self-preservation' and includes 'necessity' as one such external application, see Bin Cheng, *General Principles of Law as Applied by International Courts and Tribunals* (1953), 69.

[163] Neff, *War*, 241–2.

[164] E.g., Lawrence, *Handbook of Public International Law* (2nd edn, 1885), 32–4; Woolsey, *Introduction to the Study of International Law* (5th edn, 1886), 43–4; Bry, *Précis elémentaire de droit international public* (1891), 122. See, early in the twentieth century, Ellery Stowell's discussion of intervention for self-preservation as a necessity-based concept: Stowell, *Intervention in International Law* (1921), 392–3. (Note that the author is

an invocation of self-preservation in respect of an extraterritorial, forcible and precautionary measure need not entail an appeal to the presumed right of necessity for in the absence of more specific statements in each instance, such an invocation could equally be seen as an appeal to the rights of self-defence or intervention.[165] The best that can be said is that invocations of self-preservation were appeals to the fundamental right of self-preservation itself – and not to any other legal entitlements actually or purportedly existing at the time and which were not specifically mentioned by states.

At the same time, the right of self-preservation and its corollary right of self-defence were entitlements inspired by the notion of necessity in its ordinary meaning. It may be recalled that one of the accepted meanings of necessity is as a situation of predicament, and what greater predicament than threats to one's existence? The right of self-defence was, perhaps, the utmost rule in 'necessity's image'. The connection between these rules and (ordinary) necessity is made explicit in the references to necessity in the context of self-preservation, self-defence and intervention. Yet this necessity is not a reference to a discrete legal rule – but to the set of factual conditions required for the exercise of these rights.[166] Thus, Fox's 'necessity of self-defence and self-preservation', but also Webster's 'necessity of self-defence', and the US agent's statement in *Fur Seals* that '[w]henever the necessity arises, the right arises'.[167] Equally, in the statement of Lord Ashburton (to which Crawford attributed *opinio juris* in respect of the plea of necessity), the concept of necessity was used in connection with that of 'self-defence', which Ashburton declares to be 'the first law of our nature [which] must be recognised by every code which professes to regulate the conditions and relations of man.'[168] That is, necessity also imposed the limits of this 'first law of our nature', that of self-defence.

As noted in the introduction to this chapter, the notion of necessity plays an important role in legal development and change by highlighting insufficiencies in legal regulation. A situation of necessity may inspire law creation and change. In this connection, Emmanuelle Jouannet has described how historico-legal developments of the period, including

addressing the existence of a legal entitlement to intervention, with the necessity of self-preservation as the inspiration of this entitlement.)

[165] O'Connell, *Power and Purpose*, 156.
[166] Tsagourias, 'Necessity', 13.
[167] *Fur Seals*, 868.
[168] Ashburton to Webster (28 July 1842), in Manning, 3 *Correspondence*, 767.

the consolidation of states as sovereign entities and exclusive subjects of the law of nations, resulted in an increased emphasis on the protection of the state's independence and continued existence. The need to maintain the continued existence of the state inspired the creation of a legal right: the right of self-preservation.[169] In respect of this right, then, necessity operated as a material source of law.[170] It is probably this relation, between ordinary necessity and the notion of self-preservation, that Brownlie was alluding to when he maintained that necessity was, at the time, a broader category than self-preservation.[171]

Though a necessity-inspired rule, the recognition and invocation of a right of self-preservation by states no more supports an autonomous rule of necessity in international law than do other necessity-inspired rules, like the right of self-defence,[172] the right of angary[173] or the right of distress.[174] Indeed, nobody claims that invocations of self-defence are precedents for the purported rule of necessity. The practice concerning the right of self-preservation cannot consequently be invoked in support of the recognition, during the nineteenth century, of an autonomous legal rule of necessity – and as such, as relevant state practice for today's defence of state of necessity. Furthermore, insofar as this practice concerned exclusively the use of extraterritorial force it is inadequate to support a *general* rule of necessity applicable in respect of all obligations.

By way of conclusion, a linguistic observation can be made. Much is made about the terminological confusion which prevailed in this field throughout the period, which has led some to conclude that these various terms were used interchangeably.[175] While the clarity and precision of the contours of these notions cannot be pushed too far and acknowledging that the language used was not entirely consistent and uniform,[176] neither

---

[169] Explaining the emphasis on self-preservation in nineteenth-century international law (the 'liberal' international law) see Jouannet, *Liberal-Welfarist*, 105–6.
[170] This argument was put forward by Heathcote, *Necessity*, 208, though in respect of the adoption of the 1871 London Protocol. The argument is, however, valid more broadly.
[171] Brownlie, *Use of Force*, 42.
[172] Tsagourias, 'Necessity', 13–15.
[173] Stowell, *Intervention*, 401–2; Scalese, *Scusanti*, 141.
[174] That specific necessity-based rules cannot support the recognition of a general rule was emphasised as well by Ago in respect of military necessity and necessity-based rules in the law of war: Ago, Eighth Report – Add.5-7, [49].
[175] The observation as to the interchangeable use of these notions has been a constant feature of the literature in this field. See, e.g., Winfield, 'Grounds of Intervention in International Law' (1924) 5 BYIL 149, 151–2; Gross and Ní Aoláin, *Law in Times of Crisis* (2006), 330; Agius, 'The Invocation of Necessity in International Law' (2009) 56 NILR 95, 98.
[176] On which see Brownlie's propositions and their qualifications about the meaning and use of these notions in the relevant period: Brownlie, *Use of Force*, 46–9.

can it be maintained that these terms were used as if they had no distinct meanings at all. There seem to have been, at the very least, some basic distinctions between these notions:

- *Necessity*: When used in connection with the rights of self-preservation and self-defence, the term 'necessity' referred to the factual condition for the exercise of those rights. 'Whenever the necessity arises, the right arises', would claim the United States before the Tribunal in *Fur Seals*.
- *Right of self-preservation*: It was a very broad right concerning the protection of the continued existence of the state as a political entity as well as its self-protection having internal and external manifestations, entitling the state to precautionary and reactive measures, which could be both forcible and non-forcible.
- *Right of self-defence*: It is a corollary of the right of self-preservation, usually concerned solely with external and forcible aspects of self-preservation, though sufficiently broad to include both precautionary and reactive measures.[177]

Ultimately, these were proto-notions still in a state of flux, which were slowly refined through the practice and by the legal scholarship of the century. Indeed, the practice and doctrine of this period, rather than clearly supporting one or other rule existing in contemporary international law, are perhaps better likened to the *nebula* from which the rules existing now would originate and develop[178] – the right of self-defence and state of necessity among them.

### 8.2.3  1914–1945: Towards State of Necessity in International Law

#### 8.2.3.1  A Doctrinal Development: State of Necessity in the Law of State Responsibility

Towards the end of the nineteenth century and, particularly, at the beginning of the twentieth, scholars of international law began to discuss a defence of necessity. At least two parallel developments in international and domestic law underpin the doctrinal elaboration of this defence. In international law, these were, first, the maturation of the law of responsibility as a distinct topic from the second half of the nineteenth century;[179] and, second, the demise of the theory of fundamental rights of states, following the affirmation of positivism as the mainstream jurisprudential

---

[177] Similarly, Jennings, 'Caroline', [91].
[178] Kolb, 'Légitime', 25.
[179] Brownlie, *State Responsibility* (1983), 6–7.

theory.[180] At the domestic level, this was the inclusion in codes and legislation of the late nineteenth century of defences of necessity,[181] which had given rise to a flourishing literature on the topic,[182] and which provided a model on the basis of which the international law rule of necessity could be formulated.

**New Frameworks: The Rule of Necessity and the Law of State Responsibility**  Throughout the first part of the twentieth century some part of the scholarship, primarily Anglo-American, continued to refer to the right of self-preservation. Often this occurred in the context of revised and updated editions of nineteenth-century texts,[183] while on other occasions self-preservation was accepted as an excuse.[184] These few invocations notwithstanding, the right (or excuse, as some now referred to it) of self-preservation would eventually succumb. The growing influence of positivism as the jurisprudential foundation of international law eclipsed the doctrine of fundamental rights and, with it, the right of self-preservation. Moreover, the right of self-preservation had grown unpopular throughout the nineteenth century in view of the abuses perpetrated through invocations of this right, so that alongside the demise of the natural right came the abandonment of the language of self-preservation as well.

The disappearance of this right (and its language) left a vacuum in international law: what rule of this system would now provide for the protection and preservation of states?[185] As Arrigo Cavaglieri noted,[186]

---

[180] Generally, Cavaglieri, *Diritti*, 1906.
[181] For an overview, discussing the legislations of Brazil, Germany, Austria-Hungary, Portugal, Italy, Japan and China, see Foriers, *Nécessité*, 157–66. For an overview of the common law, see Stephen, *History of the Criminal Law of England* (1883) vol. 2, 108.
[182] E.g., Moriaud, *Justification*; Civoli, 'In torno alla legittima difesa e allo stato di necessità. Studio storico' (1893) 37 *Rivista penale* 21; Fabisch, *Essai sur l'état de nécessité* (1903); Brasiello Teucro, *Lo stato di necessità nel diritto romano e nel sistema legislativo vigente* (1903).
[183] E.g., Davis, *The Elements of International Law* (4th edn, 1916), 92; Phillipson, *Wheaton's Elements of International Law* (5th edn, 1916), 87. The Dutch jurist De Louter also continued to refer to the 'fundamental right of self-preservation': De Louter, *Le droit international public positif* (1920) vol. 1, 240. Wilson continued to accept a right of self-preservation, but limited only to the performance of acts that did not infringe the rights of other states. If in its exercise, the rights of others were infringed, the invoking state would have committed a wrongful act and its responsibility would be engaged: Wilson, *International Law* (8th edn, 1922), 77.
[184] Strisower, cited in Cavaglieri, *Diritti*, 91; Oppenheim, *International Law* (2nd edn, 1912) vol. 1, 184.
[185] Cavaglieri, *Necessità*, 14.
[186] Id.

## 8.2 STATE OF NECESSITY: HISTORICAL NOTES

legal writers filled the void with an abstract and general rule of necessity, the characterisation of which varied. A material necessity (the need for a rule about state preservation) gave rise to a general rule of necessity. Several authors, including Giuseppe Cavarretta,[187] Jean Pierre Adiren François,[188] Karl Strupp[189] and Karl Wolff,[190] argued for the existence of a right of necessity. Others, instead, recognised defences of necessity, sometimes as a justification and others as an excuse. Fiore[191] and Rivier,[192] both in the nineteenth century, Emanuel Ullmann,[193] and, at least initially, Cavaglieri,[194] maintained that state of necessity operated as an excuse. In turn, Roberto Ago,[195] Dionisio Anzilotti,[196] Scipione Gemma,[197] Franz von Holtzendorff,[198] Paul Heilborn[199] and Franz von Liszt,[200] all characterised state of necessity as a justification.

These differing characterisations were not rigorously maintained by the authors supporting them. In particular, the boundary between right and justification of necessity was often unclear and unexplained. For instance, both von Liszt, who classified state of necessity as a justification,[201] and

---

[187] Cavarretta, *Lo stato di necessità nel diritto internazionale: parte generale* (1910).
[188] François, 'Règles générales du droit de la paix' (1936) 66 *Recueil* 1, 182.
[189] Strupp, 'Règles générales du droit de la paix' (1934) 47 *Recueil* 259, 567.
[190] Wolff, 'Les principes généraux du droit applicables dans les rapports internationaux' (1931) 36 *Recueil* 479, 520.
[191] For Fiore, 'necessity' provided a defence for the non-performance of obligations: Fiore, 1 *Nouveau droit*, 192–3 and 585. Subsequently, he recognised that state responsibility was excluded in case of measures necessary to attend to the security of the state: Fiore, *Trattato*, 133.
[192] Rivier referred to an 'excuse of necessity' which, he noted, some part of the doctrine called 'droit de nécessité'. For Rivier, this language was misleading as it disguised the 'true nature' of necessity, namely, an exceptional notion of restrictive application: Rivier, *Principes*, 278. Rivier's point was more semantic than conceptual: the word 'excuse' intended to emphasise the restrictive and exceptional character of this legal entitlement. In its legal effects, however, the 'excuse of necessity' was no different from the 'right of necessity': the conduct in question remained lawful.
[193] Cited in Cavaglieri, *Necessità*, 18.
[194] Cavaglieri, *Diritti*, 149.
[195] Ago, 'Le délit international' (1939) 68 *Recueil* 415, 540.
[196] Anzilotti, 'La responsabilité internationale des Etats à raison des dommages soufferts par des étrangers' (1906) 13 RGDIP 285, 303–4; Anzilotti, 'Corso di diritto internazionale', *Opere di Dionisio Anzilotti* (reprint of 3rd edn originally published in 1927, 1955), 414–9.
[197] Gemma, *Appunti di diritto internazionale* (1923), 240.
[198] Cavaglieri, *Necessità*, 19.
[199] Cited in Cavaglieri, *Diritti*, 92.
[200] von Liszt, *Le droit international: Exposé systématique* (translation of 1913 9th edn, 1927), 201–2.
[201] Id.

Ago, who classified it as a 'circumstance precluding wrongfulness',[202] indicated that necessity granted the state a 'right' to act in the protection of its interests. It was perhaps for this reason that Strupp contended that it did not matter whether necessity was characterised as a 'right' or a 'circumstance precluding wrongfulness' – so long as it was accepted by positive law.[203] This may have been simply a semantic distinction (after all, some justifications may be explained as Hohfeldian liberty-rights as was seen in previous chapters),[204] perhaps one intended to highlight that the plea of necessity was a concept of the law of responsibility. Or it may also have been a result of unarticulated theoretical assumptions about the defence: as seen in previous chapters, justifications based on consequentialist theories cannot be reduced to rights – be they claim- or liberty-rights.[205] While such an argument is unlikely to have been made in these terms – Hohfeld only elaborated his scheme of fundamental legal conceptions in 1913 – it is not impossible that these authors were working from the intuition that a difference existed between a justification of this type and a right. Finally, to speak of a defence, or even justification, of necessity could have avoided the primarily negative and critical baggage of the 'right of necessity', of which these authors were certainly aware.

Whatever the case, the language of justification which was increasingly used in this regard represented a shift in the framework for the development of the rule of necessity: from the state's substantive (and fundamental) rights to the law of responsibility.

**New Conceptions: The Rule of Necessity as a Conflict of Interests**
While disagreeing on the character of the rule of necessity as a right, a justification or an excuse, the doctrinal writings of this period show a trend which transcended these differences: the situation contemplated by the rule of necessity. The rule of necessity, or 'state of necessity' as it was frequently referred to, concerned situations in which the state faced an irreconcilable clash of interests. In Strupp's definition:

> la situation, à constater objectivement, dans laquelle un état est menacé d'un grand danger, actuel ou imminent, susceptible de mettre en question son existence, son statut territorial ou personnel, son gouvernement ou sa forme même, de limiter, voire d'anéantir son indépendance ou sa capacité

---

[202] Ago, 'Délit', 533, 540.
[203] Strupp, 'Recueil', 567.
[204] See, e.g., Chapter 5, Section 5.5.2.1, and Chapter 6, Section 6.4.1.3.
[205] Rodin, *War and Self-Defence* (2002), 28.

d'agir, situation à laquelle il ne peut échapper qu'en violant certains intérêts d'autres états protégés par le droit de gens.[206]

It was no longer a clash of two rights; between, on the one hand, the state's right of self-preservation and, on the other, the right of the other state.[207] Building on jurisprudential developments, including Rudolf Jhering's work on the notion of interest and the explanation of rights as legally protected interests, these authors recast the rule of necessity as a notion concerned with conflicting interests: the interest of the invoking state and the interest of the injured state.[208]

This understanding of the rule of necessity as a clash of interests presented a new, fundamental difficulty: which of the clashing interests ought to prevail? Nineteenth-century doctrine had solved the clash of rights through the (given) superiority of the right of self-preservation. But positivists of the early twentieth century could not rely on this jusnaturalist solution, so they appealed to the notion of 'vital' or 'essential' interests. Authors like Ago,[209] Anzilotti,[210] François[211] and Gemma[212] thus maintained that the state's existence was an essential or vital interest; a solution which seemed to be, in essence, simply a rebranding of the former right of self-preservation as an 'essential interest'. Other authors simply pointed to interests which appeared to be vital for the state's existence and preservation. Thus Strupp referred to the state's territory, government and population. Whether the interest in a state's own preservation (or territory, government, population and so on) was recognised in positive law or not, there was still a tinge of naturalism to these arguments insofar as they relied on what seemed to be an absolute hierarchy of values among interests which was determined by the reason of the thing – thus preservation, or territory, or government, and so on, prevailed over all other interests. So, in accordance with positivist methodology, these authors sought to ground the state's interest in its own existence on positive law. Anzilotti, for instance, explained that by submitting to law, states had pledged to

---

[206] Strupp, 'Recueil', 568.
[207] Wolff, 'Principes', 521. Cf. Ellery Stowell, who continued to consider the question as one of clash of rights and as a matter of the 'relativity of rights': Stowell, *The Diplomacy of the War of 1914* (1915), 452–3; and Stowell, *Intervention*, 399.
[208] Verdross, 'Règles générales du droit de la paix' (1929) 30 *Recueil* 271, 488. See also Basdevant, 'Règles générales du droit de la paix' (1936) 58 *Recueil* 471, 552; Cavaglieri, 'Règles générales du droit de la paix' (1929) 26 *Recueil* 311, 557.
[209] Ago, 'Délit', 544.
[210] Anzilotti, 'Responsabilité (II)', 304; Anzilotti, 'Corso', 416–17.
[211] François, 'Règles générales', 183.
[212] Gemma, *Appunti*, 240.

sacrifice their particular interests insofar as necessary to achieve the collective interests guaranteed by law. This pledge could not be swayed, in Anzilotti's view, other than when the state's existence was at stake.[213] In other words, the state's self-preservation was an essential interest because states agreed it was so. But if states agreed that their existence ought to be protected, even at the cost of the rights of other states, why not recognise a right to such protection? The appeal to positive law on this point distorted the new conceptualisation of the rule: if the state's existence was protected by positive law, the clash in the situation of necessity became, again, a clash of rights.

Even more abstractly, Wolff argued that the interest relevant for the rule of necessity was the superior interest in the circumstances. The state's self-preservation, at any rate, was the 'greatest' interest of all.[214] Even without listing the 'essential interests', for Wolff there was no difficulty in determining which interest was superior in the event of a particular conflict: it seemed clear that the interest in sovereignty was superior to the interest over territory which, in turn, was superior to the interest over a portion of territory.[215] The balance to be struck was both qualitative (for example, sovereignty was a superior interest to territory) and quantitative (for example, the whole territory was a superior interest to a portion thereof). Wolff's theory relativised the rule of necessity,[216] foreshadowing the approach later adopted by the ILC.

The identification of the essential, vital or superior interests relevant to the rule of necessity gave rise to one of the most controversial aspects of this new defence: none of the arguments put forward by supporters of the defence was satisfactory, and the notion remained vague and subjective. It epitomised, as its detractors would point out, the rule's susceptibility to abuse. Before turning to these critiques, the theoretical explanations proposed by doctrine for the new rule will be outlined.

**New Theories for the Rule of Necessity**  Contemporaneous developments on the rule of necessity in domestic law highlighted a variety of theoretical groundings for this rule: ranging from the idea of moral constraint, to the (in)utility of punishing individuals acting out of necessity.[217]

---

[213] Anzilotti, 'Responsabilité (II)', 304.
[214] Wolff, 'Principes', 517.
[215] Ibid., 518.
[216] Wolff, 'Principes', 518, 521.
[217] For an account of other rationales discussed in domestic law throughout this period see Foriers, *Nécessité*, 120–55; Pergola, 'Fondamento giustificativo dello stato di necessità' (1909) 70 *Rivista penale* 405.

## 8.2 STATE OF NECESSITY: HISTORICAL NOTES

International lawyers too discussed the theories underlying the rule of necessity. These different approaches affected the operation of the rule and, in turn, its characterisation as a justification or excuse, though these consequences were not always fully worked out by the various scholars writing on the topic. The theories proposed by international law doctrine can be roughly classified into subjective (focusing on the state) and objective (focusing on the act) theories.

Subjective rationales relied on the notion of state will. For instance, Cavaglieri maintained that state of necessity's exonerating effect was grounded on its exclusion of the state's culpable will: the conflict between its interests and its obligations limited and constrained the state's will.[218] The exclusion of state affected the imputation of the act to the state,[219] and since imputation was an element of the wrongful act, its exclusion entailed that no wrongful act had been committed.[220] Cavaglieri would later become one of the foremost critics of the rule of necessity, and in his later work he seemed to accept that, if such rule were recognised at all, it could at most exclude the responsibility of the actor without affecting the wrongfulness of the conduct. Moreover, true to his orthodox voluntaristic-positivism, he would also reject absence of fault as the rationale of the excuse.[221] The German author Emanuel Ullmann, instead, considered that state of necessity provided a defence in view of the situation in which the state was placed by the conflict of interests. This required a subjective assessment of the position of the state relative to the circumstances and, consequently, excluded the legal consequences of the wrongful act (responsibility), but not its attribution or wrongful character.[222]

At least four different objective theories can be found among scholars: first, the neutrality of international law in relation to the necessitated act; second, the suspension of international law by the situation of necessity; third, necessity as a limitation intrinsic to all international obligations; and, fourth, the superiority of the interest safeguarded through the necessitated act. Each of these will be briefly reviewed.

The first rationale was supported by the German author Paul Heilborn. In his view, international law was simply 'neutral' to the act adopted in a situation of necessity. Where two interests clashed irreconcilably,

---

[218] Cavaglieri, *Diritti*, 147.
[219] Id.
[220] Ibid., 147, 151.
[221] Cavaglieri, *Corso di diritto internazionale* (1934), 442.
[222] Ullmann, *Völkerrecht* (Siebeck, 1908), 145, cited by Cavaglieri, *Necessità*, 18.

international law had no interest either to impose the fulfilment of the law or to grant a right to infringe the law in a situation of necessity.[223] The necessitated act was *hors la loi*: neither lawful, nor wrongful.[224] This was a dangerous rationale, particularly in the context of a legal system which had not – yet – regulated the use of force. If the necessitated act was *hors la loi* then there was no way to limit the means employed or the degree of injury to the other state's interests that was acceptable. It is not difficult to see why it was criticised even by commentators sympathetic to the recognition of a rule of necessity in international law.[225]

Second, it was argued that the situation of necessity temporarily suspended international law, such that the necessitated act was not in contravention of an international obligation of the state. For Holtzendorff the law could simply not solve the clash between irreconcilable interests, so international law was temporarily suspended while the conflict was resolved.[226] This rationale eventually led to extralegality as well, though through a different route from the previous one. Its difficulties were, again, patent: as with Heilborn, the suspension rationale seemingly legitimated the use of force to solve the conflict of interests. Ago presented what appeared as a narrower version of the rationale: the situation of necessity temporarily suspended the specific obligation conflicting with the state's essential interest, and not the law as a whole. In his view, this approach was backed by positive law – though not much by way of practice was adduced in support of this contention.[227] Ago's theory was not limited to state of necessity, but reflected what he considered to be the rationale of all defences in international law. It has already been discussed in previous chapters, and will be returned to – for what respects the plea of necessity – later on in this chapter.

The third objective rationale, proposed by Anzilotti, maintained that necessity established a limitation upon the binding force of all international

---

[223] Cited in Cavaglieri, *Necessità*, 19.
[224] On 'extra-legality' models in respect of emergency situations, see, generally, Gross and Ní Aoláin, 'Emergency, War and International Law' (2001) 70 *Nordic JIL* 29; Gross and Ní Aoláin, *Law in Times of Crisis*, ch. 3.
[225] See, e.g., LeFur, 'La théorie du droit naturel depuis le XVII siècle et la doctrine moderne' (1927) 18 *Recueil* 259, 430.
[226] Holtzendorff, cited in Cavaglieri, *Necessità*, 18–19.
[227] Ago, 'Délit', 544. As discussed in Chapter 1, Ago maintained at the ILC that all circumstances precluding wrongfulness operated by suspending the obligation with which they conflict. See Ago, Eighth Report on State Responsibility, ILC Yearbook 1979, vol. II(1), [55]. See also ILC Report, thirty-first session, ILC Yearbook 1979, vol. II(2), 109 [10].

obligations. Anzilotti's theory, premised on his voluntarist conception of international law, suggested that states could not have consented to be bound by international obligations as far as self-destruction: the state's will was not suicidal. Conversely, it was only logical that states had bound themselves to perform obligations only so long as that performance did not pose a risk of self-destruction. When self-destruction was at stake, the obligations reached their logical end and did not, therefore, constrain the state's ability to attend to its survival. State of necessity was, then, a justification: the conduct adopted in the circumstances was not prohibited.[228] In his later work, Anzilotti updated this theory to render it compatible with his revised jurisprudential position on the foundation of international law: the law's limitation in situations of necessity was now derived from the collective will of states (they all agreed that self-destruction was the limit of obligation), and no longer from the presumed prudence of individual states.[229]

Finally, the fourth objective rationale relied on the superiority of the interest of the invoking state. Thus, Franz von Liszt explained that interests *prépondérants* prevailed over the 'legitimate interests of a third State'.[230] Similarly, for Karl Wolff the rule of necessity excluded the wrongfulness of conduct because international law demanded the protection of the superior interest. Indeed, the protection of the superior interest was not only lawful, but commendable since it was socially desirable.[231] This rationale was not free from logical and practical difficulties, as its critics noted. But it is the rationale that garnered the most support in international law throughout the twentieth century.

### 8.2.3.2 Fearing Anarchy and Chaos: Rejecting the Rule of Necessity

During the years 1900–45, doctrinal opinions on the rule of necessity were profoundly divided. The chasm between supporters and deniers intensified after the invocation of necessity by the German Chancellor to justify the invasion of Luxembourg and Belgium in 1914 in breach of the permanent neutrality of these two states. The invasion of Belgium and Luxembourg epitomised the risks inherent in the rule of

---

[228] Anzilotti, 'Responsabilité (II)', 303–4. For a critique of his view, see Rapisardi-Mirabelli, *Limiti*, 119–21.
[229] Anzilotti, 'Corso', 418.
[230] von Liszt, *Droit*, 201–2.
[231] Wolff, 'Principes', 517–18.

necessity: unjustified uses of force in international relations, leading to anarchy and chaos. Doctrinal writings against the rule of necessity proliferated, such that Strupp (a supporter) acknowledged in 1934 that the majority of scholars rejected the rule.[232] Scholarly critiques were comprehensive: commentators denied the positive law character of the rule, disputed the notion of essential interests, warned against the subjectivity of the rule, and pointed to the institutional deficiencies of international law as a bar to the rule's recognition.

**The 'Rape' of Belgium and Luxembourg**   On 4 August 1914, Germany invaded Belgium, a permanently neutral state, in what became the first campaign of World War I.[233] The day before, it had invaded Luxembourg, also a permanently neutral state. Germany, which maintained that it had been informed of an imminent French attack through Belgium,[234] explained that its 'imperious duty of preservation' required it to prevent this attack by occupying Belgium first.[235] In these circumstances, the neutrality treaties were no more than 'scraps of paper'.[236] On the day of the invasion, the German Chancellor von Bethmann-Hollweg invoked necessity to 'excuse' the invasion:

> Necessity knows no law. Our troops have occupied Luxembourg, and perhaps have already entered Belgian territory. Gentlemen, that is a breach of international law … We have been obliged to refuse to pay attention to the justifiable protests of Belgium and Luxembourg. The wrong – I speak openly – the wrong we are thereby committing we will try to make good as soon as our military aims have been attained. He who is menaced, as we are, and is fighting for his all can only consider how he is to hack his way through.[237]

---

[232] Strupp, 'Recueil', 567.
[233] Belgium had been neutralised by the Treaty for the Definitive Separation of Belgium from Holland between Austria, France, Great Britain, Prussia, Russia and Belgium (signed at London 15 November 1831), 82 CTS 255; and later the Treaty between Belgium and the Netherlands relating to the Separation of Their Respective Territories (signed at London 18 April 1839), 88 CTS 427.
[234] See Commission on the Responsibility of the Authors of the War and on Enforcement of Penalties, 'Report Presented to the Preliminary Peace Conference – 29 March 1919' (1920) 14 AJIL 95, 109–10.
[235] Text in Zuckerman, *Rape of Belgium*, 11.
[236] See, generally, Hull, *A Scrap of Paper: Breaking and Making International Law during the Great War* (2014).
[237] Cited in the Report of the Commission on the Responsibility of the Authors of the War and on Enforcement of Penalties, Presented to the Preliminary Peace Conference – 29 March 1919, (1920) 14 AJIL 95, 111.

## 8.2 STATE OF NECESSITY: HISTORICAL NOTES 373

This action was the 'single most famous infringement of neutral rights in history'.[238] It met with the objections of, among others, Great Britain,[239] France,[240] Italy,[241] Japan[242] and Russia,[243] and would eventually provide the basis for the attribution of blame to Germany for the beginning of the War. This attribution of blame was later formalised in the Versailles Treaty which provided in Article 232(3) that Germany had violated the Treaty of 1839 and imposed on this state an obligation of reparation,[244] thus implicitly rejecting the German justification for the invasion. The attribution of guilt to Germany for the origins of the War may be questioned both in terms of its accuracy as well as its historiographic value;[245] nevertheless, the prevailing sense at the time that Germany was the culprit for the horrors of 1914–18 pervaded through and shaped the debate about the notion of necessity in international law.

The Chancellor's address to the Reichstag on the invasion of Belgium and Luxembourg was generally perceived as political in nature;[246] and so it led German scholars to attempt to provide it with legal foundations.[247] To this end, they invoked self-defence,[248] state of necessity[249] and

---

[238] Neff, *Neutrality*, 159. By no means the only one during the war: the Allies too invoked military necessity to invade Greece and Shantung, see Rodick, *Doctrine*, 113ff.

[239] *La Guerre de 1914: recueil de documents intéressant le droit international* (Pedone, 1916) vol. 1: 47 (doc 41); vol. 2: 106 (doc 444), 363 (doc 659).

[240] *Recueil de documents*, vol. 1: 49 (doc 43); vol. 2: 106 (doc 444), 363 (doc 659).

[241] *La Guerre de 1914: recueil de documents intéressant le droit international* (Pedone, 1916) vol. 2, 106 (doc 444), 363 (doc 659).

[242] 2 *Recueil de documents*, 106 (doc 444).

[243] Ibid., 106 (doc 444), 363 (doc 659).

[244] Treaty of Versailles (28 June 1919) 225 CTS 188, (1919) 13 AJIL Supp 151. See also the Report of the Commission on the Responsibility of the Authors of the War and on Enforcement of Penalties, Presented to the Preliminary Peace Conference – 29 March 1919, 107–12.

[245] See, e.g., Clark, *The Sleepwalkers: How Europe Went to War in 1914* (2013).

[246] Mueller, cited in de Visscher, *Belgium's Case: A Juridical Enquiry* (1916), 19–20; see also Renault, *First Violations of International Law by Germany: Luxembourg and Belgium* (1917), 40.

[247] For a summary, and refutation, of these arguments, see generally de Visscher, *Belgium*; Phillipson, *International Law and the Great War* (1915), chaps 2 and 8; Garner, *International Law and the World War* (1920) vol. 2, chaps 28 and 29.

[248] Self-defence was addressed by Strupp, von Liszt and Kohler, cited in de Visscher, 'Les lois de la guerre et la théorie de la nécessité' (1917) 24 RGDIP 74, at 77, 81, 82, respectively. This argument relied on knowledge of an imminent attack from France. Critics accepted the invocation of self-defence as a matter of law, but disputed it on the facts: Phillipson, *Great War*, 30–1; de Lapradelle, 'The Neutrality of Belgium' (1914) *North American Rev* 847, 851; de Visscher, *Belgium*, 27–8; de Visscher, 'Les lois', 76–7.

[249] Most notably by Kohler in his brochure *Not kennt kein Gebot* published in 1915, whose argument is summarised by Hazan, *L'état de nécessité en droit pénal interétatique et international* (1949), 68–70.

the doctrine of *Kriegsraison geht vor Kriegsmanier*.[250] Their arguments were challenged by other academics, in particular by the Belgian scholar Charles de Visscher in his 1916 work *Belgium's Case: A Juridical Inquiry*.[251] The German occupation became the paradigmatic embodiment of the abuses that the recognition of a general rule of necessity might lead to. It was argued that the doctrines of necessity and *Kriegsraison* had the potential to annihilate international law.[252] The memories of World War I still fresh, scholars launched on a campaign against the recognition of a rule of necessity in international law.

**A Different Battlefield: The Intellectual Dispute over the Recognition of a Rule of Necessity** The impact that the invocation of necessity (and its proxy *Kriegsraison*)[253] as a justification for the German occupation had on academic opinion on this defence is best exemplified in Cavaglieri's post-war turn against the rule of necessity. Whereas in 1906 he had been favourable to a defence of necessity,[254] in 1917 his views had radically changed. His *Lo stato di necessità nel diritto internazionale* is a thorough and critical examination of the theory and practice of this defence in international law, concluding against its recognition by positive law and against the desirability of such recognition.

---

[250] E.g., Niemeyer, 'International Law in War' (1915) 13 *Mich LR* 175. See the reply by Reeves to Niemeyer published in the same volume: Reeves, 'The Neutralization of Belgium and the Doctrine of *Kriegsraison*' (1915) 13 *Mich LR* 179. The doctrine of *Kriegsraison* was said to have been first articulated by the German jurist Lüder, whose work was translated and quoted *in extenso* in Westlake, *Chapters on the Principles of International Law* (1894), 239. The reception of the doctrine was mixed: contrast Rivier, *Principes de droit des gens* (1896) vol. 2, 242; Anzilotti, cited in Borsi, 'Ragione di guerra', 159; and Westlake, *Chapters*, 238ff; Oppenheim, *International Law* (1906) vol. 2, 78–9.

[251] de Visscher, *Belgium's Case: A Juridical Enquiry* (1916).

[252] E.g., Root, 'The "Great War" and International Law' (1921) 83 *Advocate of Peace Through Justice* 225, 225.

[253] The precise relation between *Kriegsraison* and state of necessity is unclear. For Cavaglieri, the concepts were distinct insofar as state of necessity was aimed at the protection of legally relevant interests, whereas *Kriegsraison*'s purpose was the attainment of military or political (not legal) goals: Cavaglieri, *Necessità*, 48–9. Borsi and de Visscher, instead, thought that the distinction between the two notions was artificial: technological developments in the means of warfare entailed that every war posed a potential threat to the state's existence (a legally protected interest). *Kriegsraison* was thus a specific manifestation of state of necessity applicable in times of war: Borsi, 'Ragione di guerra', 161–2; de Visscher, 'Les lois', 95. Whether or not a manifestation of the discrete rule of necessity in international law, it appears clear that the doctrine of *Kriegsraison*, like the doctrine of military necessity, was inspired by necessity in its ordinary sense.

[254] Cavaglieri, *Diritti*, 145ff.

## 8.2 STATE OF NECESSITY: HISTORICAL NOTES 375

Three main objections were raised by legal scholars against the rule of necessity: (i) that it was not recognised by positive international law; (ii) that the structure of international law could not support its recognition; and (iii) that this defence could only lead to anarchy, chaos, and the demise of international law, by legitimising might over right.

First, on the status of the defence in international law, alongside Cavaglieri,[255] authors like Alfred Verdross and Charles Basdevant too maintained that state practice did not show that states had recognised this rule as part of positive law.[256] Similarly, critics maintained that state of necessity was not a general principle.[257]

Second, critics argued that the structure of international law rendered it ill-suited to recognise a rule of necessity. The analogical application of public, criminal and private law necessity rules and their rationales was inadequate. Public and criminal law rules of necessity failed because the rationales of both were premised on the hierarchical relation between state and individual.[258] Private law necessity was more appealing insofar as the relations between individuals in domestic legal systems were, like the relation between states in international law, horizontal or on a footing of equality.[259] Yet, the analogy with a private law rule of necessity grounded on the exclusion of fault was inadequate since it was not settled that fault was a necessary requirement of international responsibility.[260] Equally, analogies with necessity-defences grounded on interest balancing or the superiority of one of the interests were also inadequate: it was not possible to identify in international law the 'general social advantage' the preponderance of which authorised the 'sacrifice of the lesser interest'.[261] Detractors of the rule of necessity would adduce time and again the complexity of the process of interest balancing and the difficulties in the identification of protection-worthy interests (indeed, they

---

[255] Cavaglieri, *Necessità*, 22–5; Cavaglieri, 'Règles', 559.
[256] Verdross, 'Règles', 489.
[257] de Visscher, *Belgium*, 39; Verdross, 'Règles', 490; Cavaglieri, 'Règles', 558; Basdevant, 'Règles', 553.
[258] Cavaglieri, *Necessità*, 26–7. Similar arguments in respect of criminal law necessity were made by de Visscher, *Belgium*, 39; Verdross, 'Règles', 490.
[259] Cavaglieri, *Necessità*, 27.
[260] Ibid., 30. Note that this was the argument he had maintained in 1906: Cavaglieri, *Diritti*, 147. For a review of the relevant debates on the requirement of fault at the time, see Palmisano, 'Colpa dell'organo e colpa dello Stato nella responsabilità internazionale: Spunti critici di teoria e di prassi' (1992) 19–20 *Comunicazioni e Studi* 623.
[261] de Visscher, *Belgium*, 42, 45. See also Cavaglieri, *Necessità*, 28.

still do today).[262] Critics noted the vagueness of the notion of essential interest,[263] and maintained that international law lacked a scale of values or interests and that this rendered the identification of essential interests and the assessment of their superiority inherently subjective.[264] The matter was entirely left to the unilateral assessment of the invoking state.[265] For example, it seemed clear that on the occasion of Germany's occupation of Belgium, the Belgian right of independence was superior to Germany's 'right to development', and yet Germany had held its own right to be superior.[266] In view of its unilateral and subjective character, the rule of necessity required independent third-party adjudication.[267] Yet no binding procedures of dispute settlement existed in international law.[268] It could further be added that, at any rate, states would have been unwilling to submit their disputes concerning 'vital interests' to third-party adjudication, as noted by James Brierly in another context.[269]

Rules of necessity, ran the critics' third main objection, led to the 'most arbitrary subjectivism, [and] real anarchy'.[270] For Coleman Phillipson '[n]o law [could] tolerate the plea of necessity, when the conduct involved is directly contrary to the behests of that law'.[271] He continued, '[o]nce the factitious and spurious kinds of "necessity" are admitted or even tolerated by the society of nations, all international law and comity become nugatory, all conventions and established institutions for regulating international dealings will prove futile'.[272] For Fauchille too '[t]he purported right of necessity must be rejected. It would excuse the worst injustices, the most heinous violations of the independence and equality of states'.[273] This notion legitimised might over right, force over law,[274] and it was

---

[262] See, e.g., Sloane, 'Necessity'.
[263] de Visscher, *Belgium*, 45; Cavaglieri, *Necessità*, 34; LeFur, 'Théorie', 432–3.
[264] Fauchille, *Traité de droit international public (Paix)* (8th edn, 1922) vol. 1, 419.
[265] Cavaglieri, 'Règles', 560.
[266] LeFur, 'Théorie', 432–3. This assessment was made even by scholars sympathetic to a rule of necessity: Stowell, *The Diplomacy of the War of 1914*, 452–3.
[267] Rapisardi-Mirabelli, *Limiti*, 122.
[268] LeFur, 'Théorie', 434; Basdevant, 'Règles', 553.
[269] Brierly, 'Vital Interests and the Law' (1944) 21 BYIL 51.
[270] Cavaglieri, 'Règles', 560.
[271] Phillipson, *Great War*, 28–9.
[272] Ibid., 32. A similar view was held by Wehberg, co-editor of the *Zeitschrift fur Volkerrecht* with Kohler, who withdrew from the publication of Kohler's brochure. Wehberg maintained that Kohler's views 'ultimately end in the negation of international law', cited in Renault, *First Violations*, 58–9 (fn. 1).
[273] Fauchille, 1 *Traité*, 420.
[274] LeFur, 'Théorie', 430.

inherently absurd, much like 'a constitution recognising the right to revolution'.[275] It had to be rejected 'impitoyablement'.[276]

### 8.2.3.3 Lagging Behind: Protection of Essential Interests in the Practice of States

During this period states were ambiguous and ambivalent about the rule of necessity. Outright statements of support or critique were rare, though it was clear that states asserted the legality of the protection of their essential interests – even at the cost of breaching their international obligations. They did so, however, not by invoking a rule of necessity, but by invoking the defence of *force majeure*. Assessing these invocations by states is no easy task: no irrefutable conclusions can be drawn from them. They suggest, however, that at the time states had not generally accepted a discrete rule of necessity in international law, though the necessity (in the ordinary sense) of such a rule may have started to manifest itself.

**The Defence of Necessity at the 1930 Hague Codification Conference**
Only a few states addressed necessity during the work of the Preparatory Committee and during the 1930 Codification Conference. Romania stated that '[i]n principle, a sovereign state may enact any measures it thinks necessary to ensure its existence',[277] a statement redolent of the superseded right of self-preservation. Closer to a defence of necessity was Portugal's proposal during the Conference to include 'state of emergency' as a 'circumstance in which the state could decline responsibility'.[278] Speaking against the recognition of a discrete rule of necessity, Switzerland suggested that a clear distinction be drawn between self-defence, an acceptable defence to responsibility, and 'the law of necessity, which can be used as a cloak to cover every form of injustice and arbitrariness'.[279] Denmark's objection was even more forceful, though the argument was one of *lex ferenda* (which implied the recognition of a rule of the necessity at the time): it was desirable, it said, if in the future an attempt was made 'to limit as far as possible, if not to abolish completely, the far-reaching right

---

[275] Rapisardi-Mirabelli, *Limiti*, 123.
[276] Bourquin, 'Règles générales du droit de la paix' (1931) 35 *Recueil* 1, 220.
[277] League of Nations, Bases of Discussion for the Conference Drawn up by the Preparatory Committee – Responsibility of States for Damage Caused in Their Territory to the Person and Property of Foreigners, Official No C.75.M.69.1929.V, vol. 3, 23.
[278] Acts of the Conference for the Codification of International Law, vol. 4, Official No C.351(c).M.145(c).1930.V, Minutes of the Third Committee, Annex I, 227.
[279] C.75.M.69.1929.V, vol. 3, 58, 61–2, 65, 69.

of necessity recognised by former international law, and particularly the former right of war'.[280]

Sparse references are also found to so-called 'financial necessity', namely, situations of necessity affecting the fulfilment of financial obligations. In reply to the Preparatory Committee's questionnaire South Africa stated that:

> If through adverse circumstances beyond its control, a state is actually placed in such a position that it cannot meet all its liabilities and obligations, it is virtually in a position of distress. It will then have to rank its obligations and make provision for those which are of a more vital interest first. A state cannot, for example, be expected to close its schools and universities and its courts, to disband its police force and to neglect its public services to such an extent as to expose its community to chaos and anarchy merely to provide the money wherewith to meet its moneylenders, foreign or national ...[281]

Portugal held a similar view: if the state was unable to pay its debt due to 'external conditions and circumstances independent of its control, the risks should be borne equally by foreign creditors and nationals of the state'.[282]

The Preparatory Committee did not include a defence of necessity as a case in which the state could decline responsibility. Nevertheless, it added an exception of 'financial necessity' in Bases 4 and 9 in respect of the state's responsibility for the suspension or modification of the service of debts.[283] Neither the rule of necessity nor financial necessity was addressed during the Conference.

### Essential Interests and *Force Majeure* in International Disputes

*French Company of Venezuelan Railroads* (1904)  The case, already reviewed in Chapter 7,[284] concerned claims for compensation presented by *French Company* to the Venezuelan government in connection with the company's bankruptcy. Venezuela invoked the plea of *force majeure*,[285] arguing that it had been impossible for it to service its debt

---

[280] Ibid., 126.
[281] Ibid., 37.
[282] Ibid., 39.
[283] Basis of Discussion 4 (repudiation of debts by legislative organs), and Basis of Discussion 9 (repudiation of debts by the executive), C.75.M.69.1929.V, 40, 48, respectively.
[284] Section 7.2.2.1.
[285] *French Company of Venezuelan Railroads* (1904) 10 RIAA 285, 329.

## 8.2 STATE OF NECESSITY: HISTORICAL NOTES

to the company in view of 'those circumstances, under which every resource was consumed by the imperative necessities of war'.[286]

The Umpire upheld the Venezuelan plea of *force majeure*, reasoning that performance would pose a danger to the state's existence:

> [The Government's] first duty was to itself. Its own preservation was paramount. Its revenues were properly devoted to that end. The appeal of the company for funds came to an empty treasury, or to one only adequate to the demands of the war budget.[287]

*Russian Indemnity* (1912) The dispute concerned interest-damages owed by the Ottoman Empire to Russian nationals, in view of delays in the service of the principal. The defence of the Ottoman Empire, as explained in Chapter 7, was two-pronged: first it denied the existence of interest-damages in international law, and, in the alternative, it invoked the defence of *force majeure* (among others).[288] Only in the context of the latter was the plea of necessity raised. While rebutting the Ottoman Empire's plea of *force majeure*, Russia argued that at most Turkey could invoke the 'case of necessity' to protect its vital interests. But even then, Russia argued that it was farfetched to think that the payment of a relatively modest sum could be a 'sort of suicide for the Sublime Porte'.[289] In its rejoinder, Turkey clarified that its argument had been misrepresented by Russia: it was a claim about *force majeure*, and not one about the 'right of self-preservation' of the state, that it had raised in defence. Turkey conceded that *force majeure* had some relation with the 'right of self-preservation', but it emphasised that they were not 'la même chose'.[290]

The Tribunal, as was noted, conflated the arguments about state of necessity and *force majeure*. It quoted Russia's remarks on the 'case of necessity' as an approval – in principle – of Turkey's invocation of *force majeure*.[291] The Tribunal upheld the Turkish plea as a matter of international law, observing that 'international law must adapt itself to political necessities'.[292] But it denied that it was met in fact: it was an 'exaggeration' to admit that the payment of the sum owed 'would

---

[286] Ibid., 314.
[287] Id.
[288] *Russian Indemnity Case (Russia/Turkey)* (1912) Scott Hague Court Rep 297, 310–11. See Chapter 7, Section 7.2.2.2.
[289] *Réplique présentée au nom du Gouvernement Impérial de Russie* (1912), 32–3.
[290] *Contre-Réplique présentée au nom du Gouvernement de l'Empire Ottoman* (1912), 28 [280].
[291] *Russian Indemnity*, 317.
[292] Id.

imperil the existence of [Turkey] or seriously compromise its internal or external situation'.[293]

*The SS Wimbledon* (1923)   The defence of necessity did not play a substantial role in the dispute concerning the closure of the Kiel Canal contrary to the Versailles Treaty.[294] Nevertheless, the parties to the case made relevant statements on this defence in their oral pleadings. Applicants argued that Germany was precluded from invoking the defence of necessity to justify the closure of the Canal. The French agent acknowledged that 'the plea of necessity' was a principle of international law which would furnish grounds for 'frustrating the rule of free passage'.[295] Subsequently, the Italian agent cast doubt on the recognition of this plea in international law. For the Italian agent, it was not possible 'to speak of ... that concept which had been expressly sanctioned in the first book of the German Civil Code relating to the exercise of rights in general (sect 227), and which, besides, lends itself to controversy; I mean the *status necessitatis*'.[296] Germany later confirmed that it had not invoked the *jus necessitatis*, or any other defences for that matter, since its position was that its conduct was permitted by the Treaty of Versailles.[297]

*Serbian Loans* (1929)   The dispute concerned the mode of payment of Serbian loans to French bondholders, which had been issued in gold-francs.[298] The respondent argued, among others, that the service of the debt in gold-francs would jeopardise its financial stability in view of the economic dislocation caused by World War I.[299] Serbia's interest in its own financial stability took precedence over its creditors' rights.[300] The Court rejected the argument, holding that 'the economic dislocations caused by the war did not release the debtor state', though such dislocations 'may present equities which will doubtless receive appropriate consideration' in subsequent negotiations.[301]

---

[293] Ibid., 317–18.
[294] *The SS 'Wimbledon'* (1923) PCIJ, Series A No 01, 15.
[295] PCIJ Series C No 03/4, vol. 2, 178–9.
[296] Ibid., 284.
[297] Ibid., 306.
[298] *Case Concerning the Payment of Various Serbian Loans Issued in France (France v Kingdom of the Serbs, Croats and Slovenes)* (1929) PCIJ Series A No 20, 5.
[299] PCIJ Series C No 16/3, 458–9.
[300] Ibid., 458.
[301] Phillipson, *Great War*, 32; Basdevant, 'Règles', 551; Weidenbaum, 'Necessity', 105.

*Société Commerciale de Belgique* (1939)   The safeguarding of the state's vital interests was more clearly articulated in the Greek plea in this case. The case concerned the payment of compensation to the Société Commerciale de Belgique (Socobelge) by Greece as established in arbitral awards. Following the financial crisis of the early 1930s, Greece's foreign debt repayment had been tightly regulated by international instruments, including by the League of Nations.[302] In Greece's view, its debt to the Socobelge was not a foreign debt but a private one and, consequently, it should be deferred. Greece argued that the deferral was not wrongful having been due to a situation of *force majeure*, which it characterised as one of 'nécessité impérieuse'.[303] Greece buttressed this argument by reference to its national interests (including the stability of its national currency, economic existence of the state and the normal functioning of its public services), which took precedence over the rights of foreign creditors.[304] Greece stated that:

> The Government ... anxious for the vital interests of the Hellenic people and for the administration, economic life, health situation and security, both internal and external, of the country, could not take any other course of action; any Government in its place would do the same.[305]

During the oral phase, Greek counsel explained that:

> there occur from time to time external circumstances beyond all human control which make it impossible for Government to discharge their duty to creditors and their duty to the people; the country's resources are insufficient to perform both duties at once. It is impossible to pay the debt in full and at the same time to provide the people with a fitting administration and to guarantee the conditions essential for its moral, social and economic development. The painful problem arises of making a choice between the two duties; one must give way to the other in some measure: which?[306]

To answer this question, Greek counsel cited the works of Gaston Jèze, Albert de Lapradelle, Nicolas Politis and Verdross and concluded that:

---

[302] *Société Commerciale de Belgique* (1939) PCIJ Series A/B No 78, 160.
[303] Greece Counter-Memorial, PCIJ Rep Series C No 87, 91, 100.
[304] Greece Counter-Memorial, 101; Greece Rejoinder, PCIJ Rep Series C No 87, 141.
[305] Greece Counter-Memorial, 101 (English translation from UN Secretariat, '"Force Majeure" and "Fortuitous Event" as Circumstances Precluding Wrongfulness: Survey of State Practice, International Judicial Decisions and Doctrine', ILC Yearbook 1978, vol. II(1), [276]).
[306] Greece, PCIJ Rep Series C No 87(3), 204–5 (English translation from UN Secretariat, '"Force Majeure" and "Fortuitous Event"', [281]).

Doctrine recognizes in this matter that the duty of a Government to ensure the proper functioning of its essential public services outweighs that of paying its debts. No state is required to execute, or to execute in full, its pecuniary obligation if this jeopardizes the functioning of its public services and has the effect of disorganizing the administration of the country. In the cases in which payment of its debt endangers economic life or jeopardizes the administration, the Government is, in the opinion of authors, authorized to suspend or even reduce the service of debt.[307]

In addition, Greece invoked the award in *Russian Indemnity*, South Africa's response to the questionnaire of the Preparatory Committee to the Codification Conference, and Bases of Discussion 4 and 9 submitted to the Conference.[308] While it referred to this defence as *force majeure*, Greece noted that it was sometimes referred to by others as 'state of necessity'.[309]

In its response, Belgium agreed that 'a State is not obliged to pay its debts' if payment would 'jeopardize its essential public interests'.[310] Eventually, the Court did not address the argument of *force majeure*, since Greece had stated on record that it did not wish to repudiate its debt,[311] though it noted that Greece's financial difficulties could be taken into account in subsequent payment arrangements.[312]

### 8.2.4 An Assessment: State of Necessity between Substance and Form

The defence of necessity, which was slowly coming to be known as 'state of necessity', originated in a doctrinal development of the late nineteenth and early twentieth century. As noted by Cavaglieri, this doctrinal elaboration was intended to cover the field left open by the demise, at the hands of legal positivism, of that infamous jusnaturalist notion, the right of self-preservation. The rule of necessity was formulated in abstract and general terms and concerned situations of conflict of interests. Some authors continued to characterise it as a clash of rights – a matter with which Ago

---

[307] Greece: PCIJ Rep Series C No 87(3), 205 (English translation from UN Secretariat, '"*Force Majeure*" and "Fortuitous Event"', [281]).
[308] Greece: PCIJ Series C No 87(3), 207–9.
[309] Ibid., 209.
[310] Belgium: PCIJ Series C No 87(3), 236.
[311] *Socobelge*, 174–5.
[312] Ibid., 176.

would later take issue in his report to the ILC in 1980[313] – but such an articulation of the rule was slowly waning.

Throughout the period, commentators disagreed on the rationale of the rule. These rationales frequently relied on domestic analogies to public, criminal, and private law rules of necessity. The analogy was often problematic, and critics pointed to these deficiencies to show the inadequacy of the transposition and thereby show the non-recognition of a rule of necessity in international law. Of all the proposed rationales, the theory relying on the superiority of the interest safeguarded in the circumstances seemed the more amenable to the characteristics of the international legal system. To be sure, the rationale was not free from criticism. It was noted that the lack of a scale of values or interests in international law resulted in subjectivism, particularly dangerous in a system which also lacked binding dispute settlement.

Aside from scholarly and theoretical arguments, commentators fundamentally disagreed on the positive law recognition of the rule of necessity and the extent of the divergence on this point suggests, at the very least, that an assessment of the practice of states of the period would yield no unambiguous answer. A contextual analysis of the practice of this period must take into account two important factors. First, that the rule had only recently been formulated by legal scholars. To recall, the rule as formulated addressed conflicts of interests in a general and abstract manner and was usually characterised as a defence in the context of the law of responsibility. This means, second, that the practice of the previous century could not completely and fully support this new rule, since the old practice concerned, primarily, the use of force (a narrow field) pursuant to the right of self-preservation (a substantive and specific rule). Indeed, the circumscribed field of the previous practice creates a problem for the identification of the general and abstract customary rule: would those instances of practice not have pointed to the existence of a specific rule allowing the use of force for the protection of the state's existence at the cost of any rights of any third state, rather than a general rule allowing the state to breach any engagement for the protection of unspecified 'essential interests'?

Bearing these considerations in mind, what does the practice of the period 1900–45 reveal about the status of the rule of necessity in international law? The first thing to note is that, in substance, states agreed that, when their essential interests faced threats, they could address that

---

[313] See Section 8.3.1.1 below.

threat even at the cost of the rights of other states. States also agreed that 'essential interests' included the existence of the state, the state's economic stability and the maintenance of the state's public services. Notably, however, in international judicial proceedings, states articulated their claims through a rule of *force majeure* and not through the rule of 'state of necessity' (or through a 'right of necessity'). As discussed in Chapter 7, during this period *force majeure* was crystallising as a defence concerned with material and absolute impossibility of performance. The case-law of this period, and in particular the tribunals' rejection of the substance of the invoking states' arguments, was instrumental in shaping the contours of the defence of *force majeure* as one concerned with impossibility of performance due to unforeseen and irresistible forces – and not one concerned with increased difficulty of performance. When seen from the standpoint of the plea of necessity, this case-law highlights the fracture existing between, on the one hand, the substance of states' claims (difficulty of performance in view of threats to its interests) and, on the other, the formal articulation of those claims as *force majeure* (concerned with absolute and material impossibility). This is often written off as the (inaccurate) use of the expressions *force majeure* and state of necessity as synonymous.[314] Yet, these two notions had been distinguished for centuries and had separate lineages, as both this chapter and Chapter 7 have shown. The fracture between substance and form rather produces the impression that 'state of necessity' was not a recognised rule in international law at the time: if it had been, why did states not invoke this notion expressly?

Failure expressly to invoke the plea of necessity is even more troubling if one considers that, in parallel to these disputes, states had referred to state of necessity and, specifically, to 'financial necessity' in the context of the Hague Codification Conference. Significantly, Greece, which had relied on the Bases of Discussion and states' observations to the Preparatory Committee on 'financial necessity' in the oral pleadings of *Socobelge*, called its defence '*force majeure*'. And it noted, in passing, that 'some' called this defence 'state of necessity' – without itself subscribing to this nomenclature.

In view of this evidence, it may at least be queried whether, in the interwar years, the invocation of *force majeure* instead of the defence of necessity was not a choice dictated by forensic strategy. The defence of *force majeure* had been broadly recognised as part of international law, whereas the relatively recent defence of necessity had earned a bad reputation after its infamous invocation to justify one of the most confronting

---

[314] As argued by, among others, Ago, Eighth Report, [100].

acts of World War I, indeed the act that precipitated the war itself, the German invasion of Belgium and Luxembourg. Disdainfully, scholars of the period had referred to state of necessity as a 'German notion' and had attempted to demonstrate how, by invoking it, Germany had improperly transposed its domestic law to the international field.[315] States too noted the German origins of this defence; Italy, for example, referred to *status necessitatis* as a German doctrine in the *Wimbledon* case. But whether or not the formal invocation of *force majeure* in respect of claims which substantively fell within the notion of state of necessity was a choice dictated by forensic strategy, the fact remains that the substance of states' claims was at variance with their form; that the states' practice in this respect, purporting to protect their essential interests, was at variance with their expressed and implied opinions with respect to the defence of necessity.

Lastly it may be noted that the practice of this period, save for the *Wimbledon* case, related to disputes concerning the fulfilment of financial obligations against a background of considerable economic upheaval. It can thus be asked whether this practice does not reflect agreement on a specific rule in respect of situations of necessity affecting financial obligations: the 'financial necessity' included in the Bases of Discussion. This point is persuasively made by Heathcote who argues that this practice crystallised into a rule of 'financial necessity' granting the debtor state the possibility to renegotiate the payment of its debt taking into account its financial position. Indeed, the PCIJ, in both *Serbian Loans* and *Socobelge*, ultimately suggested a negotiated solution taking into account the new economic position of the debtor state. A similar solution was reached in the dispute arising out of Bulgaria's failure to pay Greece the debt arising out of the *Forests of Central Rhodope* award.[316] Before the League of Nations' Council, to which the dispute had been submitted, Bulgaria pleaded its financial position to request the performance of its obligation through means other than payment in cash. Greece accepted the Bulgarian proposal and stated its readiness to reach a negotiated agreement.[317] If the argument is correct, and a specific necessity-based rule crystallised in respect of financial difficulties, then this practice does not lend any more support to a general rule of necessity in

---

[315] E.g., de Visscher, *Belgium*, 39; Kaeckenbeck, 'Divergences between British and Other Views on International Law' (1919) 4 *Transactions Grot Soc* 213, 229. Also noting its German 'origins': Higgins, *The Law of Nations and the War* (1914), 28–9; Renault, *First Violations*, 78; Ripert, 'Les règles de droit civil applicables aux rapports internationaux' (1933) 44 *Recueil* 569, 619.

[316] *Socobelge*, 176.

[317] LONJ, 15th year, no 11 (part 1), November 1934, 1432.

international law than the practice on the right of self-preservation of the previous century.

The picture painted by the practice of this period does not, in consequence, lend itself to definite and definitive conclusions. The most that can be said is that, while there was a perceived need for a defence that states could invoke to justify breaches committed for the safeguarding of their essential interests, no such rule had yet crystallised. In any event, these instances of practice were certainly short of the 'general practice' required by the then newly adopted Article 38(1)(b) of the Statute of the PCIJ.

## 8.3 New Beginnings: Rehabilitating State of Necessity at the International Law Commission

It fell to the ILC to rehabilitate the defence of necessity in international law. The credit goes, especially, to Special Rapporteur Ago, whose extensive report on state of necessity was comprehensive, analytical, critical and 'courageous'.[318] He convinced the Commission to include this defence, thus rescuing it from the damning judgments it had been subjected to in the interwar and early post-war years. The ILC's tentative inclusion of the defence set in motion the feedback loop between the Commission and the ICJ which, mostly ignoring state practice, would culminate in the ICJ's statement that 'substantial authority' supported the recognition of this rule in international law.[319] This dialogue between the ILC and the ICJ also catalysed scholarly opinions on the recognition of this defence: the number of sceptical voices has since dwindled dramatically.[320] Today, only few remain who contest the positive recognition of this rule.[321]

*Pace* the ILC and the ICJ, doubts remain on the defence's status at customary law. While the practice of recent years (particularly practice

---

[318] Schwebel, 1616th meeting, ILC Yearbook 1980, vol. I, 171 [9].
[319] A 'normative Ponzi' scheme, in Villalpando's words: Villalpando, 'On the International Court of Justice and the Determination of Rules of Law' (2013) 26 LJIL 243, 248.
[320] Among the sceptics: Guggenheim, *Traité de droit international public* (1954) vol. 2, 62; Sørensen, 'Principes de droit international public' (1960) 101 *Recueil* 1, 219–20; Sereni, *Diritto internazionale* (1962) vol. 3, 1528–9 (stating that 'it appears' that this plea is recognised in international law, all the while remaining sceptical); Jiménez de Aréchaga, 'International Responsibility' in Sørensen (ed.), *Manual of Public International Law* (1968), 542–4; Rousseau, *Droit international public* (1983) vol. 5, 91–2.
[321] Most forcefully, see Yamada, 'State of Necessity in International Law: A Study of International Judicial Cases' (2005) 34 *Kobe Gakuin LJ* 107; Heathcote, 'Est-ce que l'état

parallel and subsequent to the ILC work on responsibility) upholds this defence, it is not clear that the practice before this period supported its recognition as a customary law rule. And while recent practice is favourable, it would appear to fall short of the generality, uniformity, and consistency required as evidence of a customary rule.[322] This notwithstanding, contemporary practice and doctrine on this defence concur on the conceptualisation of the defence as one concerning situations of clashing interests. Equally, agreement that the interest protected must be of an 'essential' character, and that the interest impaired must be inferior, suggest, as will be discussed in Section 8.4, that the defence is premised on a theory of lesser evils, pursuant to which the protection of superior interests takes priority over the fulfilment of international law obligations protecting lesser interests.

### 8.3.1 Codifying State of Necessity at the International Law Commission

The reputation of the rule of necessity had been seriously damaged after World War I. In the interwar period, states refrained from invoking the defence, opting to invoke *force majeure* to justify their alleged breaches of international law while protecting their essential interests, and doctrinal opinion was heavily polarised. It fell on the ILC and, particularly, on its very forceful Special Rapporteur Ago to reinstate this defence in international law, ultimately leading to its inclusion as a circumstance precluding wrongfulness in the ARS.

Ago's exposition on state of necessity in his last report was praised by its peers at the ILC.[323] Writing outside the Commission, two members noted how Ago had 'masterfully'[324] and 'brilliantly'[325] managed to convince the ILC to include this general defence. This, Ago had achieved by surgically detaching state of necessity from its troubled past: the right of self-preservation and the right of necessity. He noted that 'the concepts of self-preservation and state of necessity are in no way identical, nor are they indissolubly linked in the sense that one is merely the basis and

---

de nécessité est un principe de droit international coutumier?' (2007) 1 RBDI 53; Sloane, 'Necessity'.

[322] In the words of the ICJ: *North Sea Continental Shelf Cases (FR Germany/Denmark; FR Germany/Netherlands)* (1969) ICJ Rep 3, [74].

[323] Barboza, 1617th meeting, ILC Yearbook 1980, vol. I, 175 [20].

[324] Schwebel, 'The Thirty-Second Session of the International Law Commission' (1980) 74 AJIL 961, 963.

[325] Barboza, 'Necessity', 27.

justification of the other'.³²⁶ Avoiding all reference to self-preservation and relying on the practice of states, Ago proposed a neutralised and abstract formulation for the defence as a conflict of interests, grounded on the superiority of the interest in the circumstances. Skilfully, Ago managed to have it both ways: to distance state of necessity from the notion of self-preservation, all while relying on the practice concerning self-preservation to support the customary status of the defence.

Special Rapporteur Crawford's task during the second reading of the ARS was considerably smoother: though some disagreements persisted, he did not face strong opposition to his proposal to retain state of necessity in the ARS. Each of these stages of the drafting will be analysed in turn.

### 8.3.1.1 First Reading: The Inclusion of State of Necessity in the Draft Articles

**Breaking Through: Ago's State of Necessity**   Ago defined state of necessity as a 'situation' in which the essential interests of one state were gravely threatened by an unforeseen event or by the 'foreseeable but unavoidable consequence of factors which had long been present'.³²⁷ Ago opposed this formulation to the 'right of necessity': the defence did not concern a clash of rights (the right of self-preservation or the right of necessity, on the one hand, and another state's subjective right, on the other), but a clash of an essential interest against the (lesser) right of another state.³²⁸ Crucially, the essential interest, while legally relevant, was not legally protected; if it were, it would qualify as a right, and the clash of rights formulation of the defence would reemerge.

---

[326] Ago, Eighth Report – Add.5–7, [8].
[327] Ibid., [2].
[328] Ibid., [2]. Ago's proposed draft article stated that:
  1. The international wrongfulness of an act of a State not in conformity with what is required of it by an international obligation is precluded if the state had no other means of safeguarding an essential interest threatened by a grave and imminent peril. This applies only in so far as failure to comply with the obligation towards another State does not entail the sacrifice of an interest of that other State comparable or superior to the interest which it was intended to safeguard. 2. Paragraph 1 does not apply if the occurrence of the situation of "necessity" was caused by the State claiming to invoke it as a ground for its conduct. 3. Similarly, paragraph 1 does not apply: (a) if the international obligation with which the act of the State is not in conformity arises out of a peremptory norm of general international law, and in particular if that act involves non-compliance with the prohibition of aggression; (b) if the international obligation with which the act of the State is not in conformity is laid down by a conventional interest which, explicitly or implicitly, precludes the applicability of any plea of "necessity" in respect of non-compliance of said obligation', ibid., [81].

## 8.3 STATE OF NECESSITY IN THE ILC

Ago provided a list of examples of essential interests, including 'the existence of the state itself', the state's 'political or economic survival, [the] continued functioning of essential services, [the] maintenance of internal peace, [the] survival of a sector of the population, [the] preservation of the environment of its territory or part thereof'.[329] However, no definition of the notion of essential interest could (or needed to) be provided, since:

> how essential a given interest may be naturally depends on the totality of the conditions in which a state finds itself in a variety of specific situations; it should therefore be appraised in relation to the particular case in which such an interest is involved, and not predetermined in the abstract.[330]

The character of the interest as essential was a matter of 'relation of proportion, rather than [of] absolute value'.[331]

Without calling it a *ratio* (Ago appeared suspicious of 'theories' or 'foundations' of the plea),[332] Ago pointed to the superiority, in the circumstances, of the interest of the invoking state as the foundation of the defence. Arguably, this was the function of the adjective 'essential' qualifying the safeguarded 'interest'. Indeed, Ago clarified that state of necessity was excluded where the interest of the invoking state and those of the injured state were 'comparable and equally essential'.[333] This was all the more relevant since the conflict arose between qualitatively distinct entities: an interest, on the one hand, and a right on the other.[334] The superior interest took precedence since to admit the contrary would produce a greater injustice: *summum jus, summa injuria*.[335] This was a consequentialist take on the defence: the maximisation of justice demanded that, in the circumstances, the inferior right give way. This rationale excluded, *a priori*, the invocation of the defence in respect of breaches of peremptory rules,[336] a point that was 'self-evident', for if states could not, through agreement, derogate from peremptory rules, surely they could not unilaterally derogate from them – even in a state of necessity.[337]

---

[329] Ibid., [2, 12].
[330] Ibid., [12].
[331] Ibid., [15].
[332] Ago gives the impression that it was because of these theories or foundations that the defence was abused in the past: ibid., [76].
[333] Ago, 1613th meeting, ILC Yearbook 1980, vol. I, 156 [7].
[334] Id.
[335] Ago, Eighth Report – Add.5-7, [80].
[336] Ibid., [16, 54, 79].
[337] Ago, 1612th meeting, ILC Yearbook 1980, vol. I, 154 [45]. Cf. Spiermann, 'Humanitarian Intervention as a Necessity and the Threat or Use of *Jus Cogens*' 71 *Nordic JIL* 523, 536–8.

Ago expressly rejected will-based rationales which some part of the doctrine had proposed in the past. In his view, the situation of necessity did not constrain the will of the state. On the contrary, in adopting one or the other course of conduct the state acted 'voluntarily' and 'deliberately'; the state organ deciding to breach an obligation with a view to the protection of an essential interest was 'definitely not in a situation likely to nullify the element of volition'.[338] This distinguished state of necessity from *force majeure*, which, as discussed in Chapter 7, annihilates the state's volition or leaves it 'no element of free choice'[339] and further distinguished it from distress in which the state organ had 'virtually' no choice.[340]

**The Commission's Views and the Adoption of Draft Article 33** The Commission included state of necessity as a defence in the project in what became draft Article 33.[341] This it did, however, only after lengthy discussions in which ILC members voiced doubts and concerns about the plea.[342] In an effort to minimise these concerns,[343] the Commission agreed to draft the article in the negative form, on the model of VCLT Article 62 on the *clausula rebus sic stantibus*.[344] In this way the exceptional defence became 'even more of an exception',[345] to use Tsuruoka's words. While the Commission agreed to include state of necessity in the draft, it is unclear whether members agreed on the positive law status of the defence.[346]

The debates in the Commission addressed three points relevant to this monograph: (i) the meaning of essential interest; (ii) the method and parameters of interest balancing; and (iii) whether state of necessity should be characterised as a justification or as an excuse.[347]

On the first point, Commission members were unsure about what essential interests were, and how to determine their essential character.[348]

---

[338] Ago, Eighth Report – Add.5–7, [2].
[339] Article 23 Commentary, [1].
[340] Ago, Eighth Report – Add.5–7, [2].
[341] ILC Report, thirty-second session, ILC Yearbook 1980, vol. II(2), 33.
[342] Noted by the Commission in ILC Report, thirty-second session, 49 [31].
[343] Mostly concerned about the subjective character of the defence, and the risk of abuse that such subjectivity could entail. See Schwebel, 1616th meeting, 171 [10]; Yankov, 1617th meeting, ILC Yearbook 1980, vol. I, 173 [7]; Pinto, 1618th meeting, ILC Yearbook 1980, vol. I, 178 [3].
[344] ILC Report, thirty-second session, 51 [40].
[345] Tsuruoka, 1617th meeting, ILC Yearbook 1980, vol. I, 177 [33].
[346] Cf. the views of Barboza, 1617th meeting, 176 [23]; Reuter, 1614th meeting, ILC Yearbook 1980, vol. I, 164 [26]; Ushakov, 1614th meeting, ILC Yearbook 1980, vol. I, 165 [38].
[347] For a more detailed discussion of the Commission's debates, see Heathcote, *Necessity*, 80–93.
[348] E.g., Díaz-González, 1615th meeting, ILC Yearbook 1980, vol. I, 166 [2].

Christopher Pinto drew attention to the many meanings of the term 'interest',[349] and Alexander Yankov noted that without a 'legal yardstick' it was difficult to determine which interests were essential.[350] Nikolai Ushakov, a staunch critic of the defence, observed that every state would consider its own interests to be essential.[351] Some members of the Commission suggested that these problems could be avoided by defining essential interests in the commentary.[352] For others definitions were unnecessary: Julio Barboza explained that even though no definition could be given of essential interests, any difficulties could be dispelled by mentioning examples of essential interests in the commentary.[353] At the very minimum, it was agreed that essential interests were not limited to the state's existence.[354] Ago did not address these points in his concluding remarks to the Commission, and the position stated in his report that the essential character of an interest is relative and fact-specific made its way into the commentary to draft Article 33.[355]

The second problem presented by Ago's proposed article was the balancing exercise: how was the comparison between an essential interest (whatever it may be) and the injured state's right to be performed? After all, these were two qualitatively different entities. Ushakov noted that the comparison of two interests (or two rights) was difficult,[356] and for Yankov the point remained that a yardstick was needed and Ago's report did not indicate what this yardstick was.[357] Moreover, as others noted, no 'universally accepted scale of values' existed in international law.[358] Countering these criticisms, Barboza, backing the Special Rapporteur, said that it was 'obvious' that 'it would not be possible for the Commission to establish some kind of scale of interests'.[359] Yet, in his view, no great difficulties would arise in practice.[360] Yankov replied that even if the scale of values need not establish an absolute hierarchy of interests, the 'basic problem of

---

[349] Pinto, 1618th meeting, 178 [2].
[350] Yankov, 1617th meeting, 173 [2].
[351] Ushakov, 1635th meeting, ILC Yearbook 1980, vol. I, 271 [48].
[352] Šahović, 1615th meeting, ILC Yearbook 1980, vol. I, 167 [9].
[353] Barboza, 1617th meeting, 175–6 [22].
[354] ILC Report, thirty-second session, 49 [32].
[355] Id.
[356] Ushakov, 1614th meeting, 165 [37].
[357] Yankov, 1617th meeting, 173 [2].
[358] Pinto, 1618th meeting, 178 [2].
[359] Barboza, 1617th meeting, 175–6 [22].
[360] Id.

measuring that relativity remained'.[361] In the absence of such a yardstick, Pinto added, the balancing operation could 'pose problems which would seriously impair the utility of the concept of necessity'.[362] Willem Riphagen attempted to solve the conundrum by raising the discussion to a higher level of abstraction: the clash was between rules of international law, a rule protecting the state's essential interest (the defence of necessity) and a rule protecting another state's interest (the subjective right in question)[363] – but this was just a different way of restating the same problem without actually solving it. Ultimately, members agreed that the Commission 'did not feel that it had to take a stand' on this point: 'acceptance of one or the other explanations was of no relevance in determining the content of the rule which it had to formulate'.[364] The Commission's Report to the General Assembly thus reasserted Ago's position on the matter: while the interest sacrificed had to be less important than the interest protected, the assessment of the relative hierarchy depended on the circumstances.[365] One hierarchy was nevertheless clear: state of necessity was excluded in the case of breach of peremptory rules.[366]

Third, and last, the Commission discussed the character of the defence of necessity: should the plea act as a circumstance precluding wrongfulness, as Ago suggested, or rather as a circumstance precluding responsibility? Members of the Commission, including Stephen Schwebel and Paul Reuter, suggested that the wrongfulness of the necessitated conduct was not precluded, the defence only affecting the extent of the invoking state's responsibility. In their view, this characterisation appeared more compatible (and coherent) with the requirement that compensation for damages be made to the victim state,[367] a requirement which was contained in Ago's proposal. But in his reply Ago rejected this view in a question-begging statement: it was 'wrong', he said, 'to attribute to state of necessity the value of a cause attenuating rather than precluding wrongfulness. The essential value of a plea of necessity was that it would take the blame of wrongfulness away from the act of the state'.[368] Namely, state of

---

[361] Yankov, 1617th meeting, 173 [2].
[362] Pinto, 1618th meeting, 178 [2].
[363] Riphagen, 1614th meeting, ILC Yearbook 1980, vol. I, 160–1 [1–4].
[364] ILC Report, thirty-second session, 35 [4].
[365] Ibid., 49 [32], in conjunction with 50 [35].
[366] ILC Report, thirty-second session, 50 [37].
[367] Schwebel, 1614th meeting, ILC Yearbook 1980, vol. I, 163 [20]; Reuter, 1614th meeting, 163–4 [22].
[368] Ago, 1614th meeting, ILC Yearbook 1980, vol. I, 165 [33].

necessity was a justification because it was of the essence of state of necessity to be a justification.

After these debates, the Commission agreed to adopt draft article 33 in the following terms:

1. A state of necessity may not be invoked by a State as a ground for precluding the wrongfulness of an act of that State not in conformity with an international obligation of the State unless:
   (a) the act was the only means of safeguarding an essential interest of the State against a grave and imminent peril;
   (b) the act did not seriously impair an essential interest of the State towards which the obligation existed.
2. In any case, a state of necessity may not be invoked by a State as a ground for precluding wrongfulness:
   (a) if the international obligation with which the act of the State is not in conformity arises out of a peremptory norm of general international law;
   (b) if the international obligation with which the act of the State is not in conformity is laid down by a treaty which, explicitly or implicitly, excludes the possibility of invoking the state of necessity with respect to that obligation;
   (c) if the State in question has contributed to the occurrence of the state of necessity.[369]

The Commission's commentary endorsed Ago's report in its relevant parts: the defence was conceptualised as a conflict between an (essential) interest and a right (protecting an inferior interest).[370] Even though the language proposed by Ago had changed in this regard (the reference to the victim state's 'comparable or superior interest' had been replaced with a requirement of a 'serious impairment' of an 'essential interest' of the victim state), this change did not affect the basic assumption that the interest protected had to be superior to the interest affected. Indeed, as explained by the Chairman of the Drafting Committee, Verosta, the change was intended to bring clarity to the provision and the new wording was intended to 'imply a comparison between the two interests involved'.[371] Moreover, the 'essential' character of the interest protected and the comparison with the interest impaired was relative, and required an assessment of the circumstances of

---

[369] ILC Report, thirty-second session, 34.
[370] ILC Report, thirty-second session, 49 [31].
[371] Verosta, 1635th meeting, ILC Yearbook 1980, vol. I, 271 [46].

the case.[372] State of necessity, the commentary continued, provided a defence for wrongful conduct since the 'essential' interest prevailed over the 'inferior' right in the situation of conflict.[373] Indeed, to allow essential interests to perish through the strict application of the law, namely the upholding of the 'inferior' right, was unacceptable: *summum jus, summa injuria*.[374] Finally, the commentary indicated that state of necessity operated as a justification.[375]

### 8.3.1.2  Second Reading and the Adoption of Article 25

The second reading of the provision benefitted from the seal of approval given to it by the ICJ. In *Gabčíkovo-Nagymaros* the Court, notably without any analysis of state practice and *opinio juris*, recognised the customary character of the defence.[376] This judgment gave a 'powerful boost' to the defence,[377] which had the effect of overshadowing the not insignificant contrary opinion expressed by the *Rainbow Warrior* Tribunal a few years before.[378] Crawford's task as Special Rapporteur was thus less herculean than Ago's had been, as Commission members did not, on the whole, oppose the inclusion of this defence in the draft.[379]

**Two Not So 'Minor' Changes: Taking Account of Community Interests** Crawford introduced what he characterised as a 'minor' change to draft Article 33 but which led to a significant modification of the defence.[380] To reflect developments in contemporary international law, Crawford maintained that the plea could not be invoked if the act in necessity injured an interest of the international community. This addition was important since not all *erga omnes* obligations – protecting community interests – involved peremptory rules which, as noted earlier, had already been excluded from the scope of the plea. Thus (individual) essential interests of the acting state could not, in general, be

---

[372] Id.
[373] Id.
[374] Id.
[375] Id.
[376] *Gabčíkovo-Nagymaros Project (Hungary/Slovakia)* (1997) ICJ Rep 7, [51]. Contrast this case with, e.g., the Court's extensive analysis of state practice and *opinio juris* in other cases, such as *Nicaragua* and *Jurisdictional Immunities of the State (Germany v Italy: Greece intervening)* (2012) ICJ Rep 99.
[377] Bodansky and Crook, 'Symposium: The ILC's State Responsibility Articles: Introduction and Overview' (2002) 96 AJIL 773, 788.
[378] *Rainbow Warrior (New Zealand v France)* (1990) 20 RIAA 215, 254 [78].
[379] Concern was expressed by Kateka, 2591st meeting, ILC Yearbook 1999, vol. I, 171 [23]; Lukashuk, 2591st meeting, ILC Yearbook 1999, vol. I, 173 [41].
[380] Crawford, Second Report on State Responsibility, ILC Yearbook 1999, vol. II(1), [292].

invoked to justify the breach of (community) interests protected by *erga omnes* obligations.[381] Yet community interests did not, like peremptory rules, absolutely exclude the plea. Special Rapporteur Crawford noted that there could be 'a single unforeseen case' (though he did not clarify which this case was) in which community interests ought not to prevail over the necessity claim for the protection of a state's essential interests. In such cases:

> the balance to be struck by paragraph 1(b) is not a balance between the interests of the respondent State and the individual interests of the State or States complaining of a breach. What matters is the extent of the injury to the interests protected by the obligation [...].[382]

Although this suggestion can be problematic, in essence it merely restated the view that for the purposes of the defence the character of the interests was a relative matter, and that the assessment of the essential character must take into account both the quality of interest protected and the interest impaired, and the extent of injury caused to each.

Commission members had mixed opinions on the inclusion of community interests in the provision. For Maurice Kamto the change introduced uncertainty.[383] Alain Pellet saw no reason to 'create a balance between essential interests of States and of the international community. States had particular interests, and he did not follow the logic for drawing such a parallel, which would be purely artificial'.[384] Further, Constantin Economides 'failed to see why the interest of a State towards which the obligation existed had to be essential, whereas the interest of the international community did not. The interest of the international community also had to be essential'.[385] But other members were favourable to this change,[386] and the Commission eventually accepted it.[387] No member commented on the 'single unforeseen case' in which, according to the Special Rapporteur, the plea could be invoked to protect a state's essential interests against community interests.

The Drafting Committee added a further, if implicit, reference to community interests, the second major change to draft Article 33. In the

---

[381] Id.
[382] Id.
[383] Kamto, 2592nd meeting, ILC Yearbook 1999, vol. I, [32].
[384] Pellet, 2591st meeting, ILC Yearbook 1999, vol. I, 173 [40].
[385] Economides, 2591st meeting, ILC Yearbook 1999, vol. I, 173 [39].
[386] Gaja, 2591st meeting, ILC Yearbook 1999, vol. I, 171 [21].
[387] Candioti, 2605th meeting, ILC Yearbook 1999, vol. I, 283 [64].

Committee's view, Crawford's change brought the provision into line with contemporary developments, but it had fallen short of full compatibility with contemporary international law. Many Commission members had thus suggested that 'it ought to be possible to invoke necessity in order to protect the essential interest not only of the State but also of the international community'. To reflect this suggestion, the Committee modified the Article's text to apply to the protection of *'an* essential interest'.[388] The protection of community interests is now expressly noted in the Commentary to Article 25, which states that the 'essential interest' may refer to 'particular interests of the State and its people, as well as of the international community as a whole'.[389] Community interests had thus trickled down at both ends of the state of necessity equation. Yet this late (almost as an afterthought) inclusion prevented any meaningful discussion on a crucial question: the standing, so to speak, required to invoke the defence for the protection of community interests. As it stands, the rule implies that *any* state may invoke state of necessity to protect a community interest, allowing a *violatio popularis*, as it were, in the name of community interests. The point is complex, and remains largely unaddressed in doctrinal commentary.[390]

**A Justification or an Excuse?** Special Rapporteur Crawford briefly discussed the characterisation of state of necessity as an excuse or a justification. As noted in Chapter 1, Crawford had addressed the distinction between justification and excuse in broad terms, effectively reopening a debate that appeared to have been definitively closed by Ago. In his, admittedly brief, observations he maintained that 'necessity' was better viewed as an excuse. The characterisation was based on the previous behaviour of the victim state: unlike in cases of self-defence and countermeasures, in which the conduct sought to be justified was a reaction to a previous wrong, in the case of necessity the victim state was innocent.[391] However, following Crawford's recommendation, discussed in Chapter 1, the ILC did not take a position on the classification of the plea as a justification or an excuse.

---

[388] Id. (emphasis added).
[389] Article 25 Commentary, [15].
[390] With the exception of Heathcote, who addresses (and refutes) this possibility as a form of *actio popularis*: Heathcote, *Necessity*, 121–6.
[391] Crawford, Second Report, [231].

### 8.3.1.3  Article 25 and the Commission's Commentary

The Commission adopted the defence of necessity in what became ARS Article 25, cited in the introduction to this chapter. The Commentary explains that 'necessity', as the defence is called, denotes an exceptional situation in which to protect an essential interest from a 'grave and imminent peril' a state fails to perform, for the time being, 'some other international obligation of lesser weight or urgency'.[392] This exceptional situation arises where 'there is an irreconcilable conflict between an essential interest on the one hand and an obligation of the State invoking necessity on the other'.[393] Following the line set by the Commission on first reading, the Commentary indicates that 'the extent to which an interest is "essential" depends on all the circumstances, and cannot be prejudged'.[394] What matters is whether 'the interest relied on ... outweigh[s] all other considerations, not merely from the point of view of the acting State but on a reasonable assessment of the competing interests, whether these are individual or collective'.[395]

While not defining 'essential interests', the Commentary notes that the defence 'extends to particular interests of the State and its people, as well as of the international community as a whole'.[396] It also notes that in practice the plea had been invoked to protect 'a variety of interests, including safeguarding the environment, preserving the very existence of the State and its people in time of public emergency, or ensuring the safety of a civilian population',[397] all examples that, as will be seen, states have appealed to in practice when invoking the plea of necessity.

Finally, in keeping with Crawford's suggestion, the Commentary does not indicate the character of state of necessity as a justification or excuse. Indeed, the Commentary refers to this defence both as a 'circumstance precluding wrongfulness' and as an 'excuse for non-performance'.[398] At any rate, the Commentary suggests that the effect of state of necessity derives from the superiority of the interest protected by the invoking state,[399] the same *ratio* that Ago had proposed and that, as will be seen, typically underpins justifications of necessity in domestic systems.

---

[392] ARS art. 25 Commentary, [1].
[393] Ibid., [2].
[394] Ibid., [15].
[395] Ibid., [17].
[396] Ibid., [15].
[397] Ibid., [14].
[398] Ibid., [2–3].
[399] Ibid., [1].

### 8.3.2 State of Necessity in the Practice of States since 1945

Article 25, and the ILC's work on state of necessity, represented the culmination of doctrinal developments which had begun early in the twentieth century, and slowly been reflected in subsequent practice: a general and abstract defence of necessity, not limited to self-preservation, concerned with a situation of conflicting interests in which the superior interest is given priority. It remains to investigate whether, since 1945, state practice contemporaneous and posterior to the ILC work supports the defence's formulation.

#### 8.3.2.1 Reactions to the Work of the International Law Commission on State of Necessity

Over fifty states commented on the provision on state of necessity throughout its drafting stages. Of these, roughly half, including Argentina,[400] Australia,[401] Bulgaria,[402] Canada,[403] Chile,[404] Egypt,[405] Ethiopia,[406] Finland,[407] Greece,[408] India,[409] Iraq,[410] Italy,[411] Jamaica,[412] Japan,[413] Kenya,[414] Portugal,[415] Slovakia,[416] Spain,[417] Sri Lanka,[418] Tunisia,[419] the United States[420] and Zaire,[421] who all commented during the first reading of the ARS, and Cuba,[422] Mexico[423] and the Netherlands,[424] during the

---

[400] A/C.6/35/SR.50, [25].
[401] A/C.6/55/SR.16, [43].
[402] A/C.6/35/SR.59, [11].
[403] A/C.6/35/SR.48, [7].
[404] A/C.6/35/SR.47, [7].
[405] A/C.6/35/SR.52, [52].
[406] A/C.6/35/SR.51, [44].
[407] A/C.6/35/SR.48, [50].
[408] A/C.6/35/SR.52, [35].
[409] A/C.6/35/SR.54, [31].
[410] A/C.6/35/SR.51, [56].
[411] A/C.6/35/SR.49, [32].
[412] A/C.6/35/SR.53, [50].
[413] A/C.6/35/SR.48, [32].
[414] A/C.6/35/SR.56, [60].
[415] A/C.6/35/SR.58, [16].
[416] A/C.6/55/SR.22, [55].
[417] A/C.6/35/SR.55, [10].
[418] A/C.6/35/SR.49, [8].
[419] A/C.6/35/SR.52, [45].
[420] A/C.6/35/SR.51, [3].
[421] A/C.6/35/SR.54, [63].
[422] A/C.6/54/SR.28, [93].
[423] A/C.6/54/SR.23, [20].
[424] A/C.6/55/SR.21, [51].

second reading, found the inclusion of the provision to be acceptable. The rest either objected to it or expressed serious doubts about its inclusion in the ARS.[425] Byelorussia (as it then was),[426] the then Czechoslovakia,[427] Libya,[428] Mongolia,[429] Romania,[430] Russia[431] and Ukraine,[432] on first reading, and then Indonesia[433] and the United Kingdom[434] on second reading, expressly objected to it. Nevertheless, serious doubts and concerns about potential abuses were expressed by many states, including those in favour of its codification in the ARS. Critics of the plea noted that it was contrary to international peace and security, and impaired the sovereign equality of states.[435] To avoid the risk of abuse, some states requested that mandatory dispute settlement should follow an invocation of the plea.[436] Others, noting the similarities between the plea and the VCLT provision on *rebus sic stantibus*, suggested that just like for Article 62 VCLT procedures be put in place for the invocation of state of necessity.[437]

Concerning the formulation of the defence, numerous states noted the vagueness of the expression 'essential interest' and requested further clarification.[438] While some agreed with the Commission's view that the

---

[425] Expressing doubts: on first reading: Sweden: Comments of Governments on Part One of the Draft Articles on State Responsibility for Internationally Wrongful Acts, A/CN.4/342 and Add.1-4, ILC Yearbook 1981, vol. II(1), 71, at 77; United Kingdom: A/C.6/35/SR.51, [9]; Comments by Governments on all the Draft Articles, A/CN.4/488 and Add.1-3, ILC Yearbook 1998, vol. II(1), 81, at 134-5; and later on during the second reading as well: Comments and Observations Received from Governments, A/CN.4/515 and Add.1-3, ILC Yearbook 2001, vol. II(1), 41, at 56; and A/C.6/56/SR.11, [22]. Russia also objected during the second reading: A/C.6/56/SR.14, [50].

[426] A/C.6/35/SR.57, [41] and Comments and Observations of Governments on Part One of the Draft Articles on State Responsibility for Internationally Wrongful Acts, A/CN.4/351 and Add.1-3, ILC Yearbook 1982, vol. II(1), 15, at 17-18.

[427] A/C.6/35/SR.54, [15-16] and Comments and Observations of Governments on Part One of the Draft Articles on State Responsibility for Internationally Wrongful Acts, A/CN.4/362, ILC Yearbook 1983, vol. II(1), 1, at 2 [4].

[428] A/C.6/35/SR.57, [34].

[429] A/C.6/35/SR.53, [28] and A/CN.4/342 and Add.1-4, 76 [7].

[430] A/C.6/35/SR.50, [1].

[431] A/CN.4/351 and Add.1-3, 19 [3] (as USSR).

[432] A/C.6/35/SR.56, [34].

[433] A/C.6/55/SR.18, [39].

[434] A/CN.4/515, 56.

[435] Romania: A/C.6/35/SR.50, 1.

[436] Iraq: A/C.6/35/SR.51, [57]; Libya: A/C.6/35/SR.57, [34]; Mexico: A/C.6/35/SR.48, [22] and A/C.6/56/SR.14, [11]; Netherlands: A/C.6/35/SR.44, [29] and A/C.6/35/SR.51, [3].

[437] Netherlands: A/C.6/35/SR.44, [29].

[438] Byelorussia: A/C.6/35/SR.57, [41], and A/CN.4/351 and Add.1-3, 17-18; France: A/C.6/35/SR.50, [40]; Hungary: A/C.6/35/SR.55, [44]; Israel: A/C.6/35/SR.50, [14]; Italy: A/C.6/35/SR.49, [34]; Libya: A/C.6/35/SR.57, [34]; Mexico: A/C.6/54/SR.23, [20]; Mongolia:

value of the interests was a relative question,[439] others thought this was an insufficient explanation.[440] In particular, states feared the potentially broad interpretation of essential interests. Italy sought to limit the notion by indicating that it should not include political interests: state of necessity ought not to concern the state as a political entity, but the state as an aggregate of human beings.[441] Iraq disagreed: 'The state was a political institution, and political interest often connoted matters vital to the existence and well-being of the state itself'.[442] In general, states seemed to accept the defence in respect of interests such as the environment,[443] the well-being of the population,[444] and financial interests.[445]

Very few states discussed the foundation of this plea. Some seemed to agree that the superiority of the interest safeguarded must take priority over the particular obligation infringed.[446] Others also pointed to the need to weigh all the circumstances of the case to make this assessment.[447] However, some noted the difficulties in balancing or weighing the interests of two states: according to Mongolia '[i]t is virtually impossible to establish whose interests are essential when the interests of two States clash'.[448] Further, corroborating the Commission's views, some states emphasised the voluntary and free character of the necessitated conduct.[449]

Equally, few states addressed the character of the defence as a justification or an excuse. For Britain,[450] France,[451] India,[452] Japan[453] and

---

A/C.6/35/SR.53, [28] and A/CN.4/342 and Add.1–4, 76 [7]; Philippines: A/C.6/35/SR.53, [15]; Portugal: A/C.6/35/SR.58, [16]; Russia: A/C.6/56/SR.14, [50].

[439] Ethiopia: A/C.6/35/SR.51, [45]; Iraq: A/C.6/35/SR.51, [57].
[440] United Kingdom: A/CN.4/515, 56 [3].
[441] A/C.6/35/SR.49, [33].
[442] A/C.6/35/SR.51, [58].
[443] Finland: A/C.6/35/SR.48, [50]; United Kingdom: A/CN.4/515, 56 [2].
[444] Id.
[445] Bulgaria: A/C.6/35/SR.59, [11]; Finland: A/C.6/35/SR.48, [50]; United Kingdom: A/CN.4/515, 56 [2]; Sri Lanka: A/C.6/35/SR.49, [8]; Trinidad: A/C.6/35/SR.56, [25].
[446] Ethiopia: A/C.6/35/SR.51, [45]; Finland: A/C.6/35/SR.48, [50]; Mexico: A/C.6/35/SR.45, [14]; A/C.6/54/SR.21, [51].
[447] Iraq: A/C.6/35/SR.51, [57]; Mongolia: A/C.6/35/SR.53, [28].
[448] Mongolia: A/CN.4/342 and Add.1–4, 76 [7], also at A/C.6/35/SR.53, [28]. Further: Hungary: A/C.6/35/SR.55, [44].
[449] Argentina: A/C.6/35/SR.50, [25]; Kuwait: A/C.6/35/SR.49, [27].
[450] A/CN.4/488, 130.
[451] A/CN.4/488, 130, 133.
[452] A/C.6/54/SR.23, [33].
[453] Comments and Observations Received from Governments, A/CN.4/492, ILC Yearbook 1999, vol. II(1), 101, at 107.

## 8.3 STATE OF NECESSITY IN THE ILC

Russia,[454] state of necessity was an excuse. Brazil and Thailand, in turn, agreed that the defence was a justification.[455]

### 8.3.2.2 Invoking State of Necessity in Dispute Settlement

**Protecting Environmental Interests: 'Ecological Necessity'** 'Ecological necessity' is not – or not yet – a discrete legal category. This expression is, instead, frequently used to describe cases in which state of necessity has been invoked to protect environmental interests.[456] The most relevant dispute concerning 'ecological necessity' is the *Gabčíkovo-Nagymaros Project* case before the ICJ, between Hungary and Slovakia.

In 1977, Hungary and the then Czechoslovakia agreed to the construction of a barrage system in the Danube, between Gabčíkovo (in Slovakia) and Nagymaros (in Hungary). The system, as stipulated in the 1977 Treaty, constituted a 'joint operation' the financing, contracting and operation of which would be shared in equal measure by the parties. Work started in

---

[454] A/C.6/55/SR.18, [53].
[455] Brazil: A/C.6/35/SR.47, [23]; Thailand: A/C.6/35/SR.56, [48].
[456] On which see Montini, 'Necessità ambientale'; Fitzmaurice, 'Necessity in International Environmental Law' (2010) 41 NYIL 159. The *Torrey Canyon* incident is not discussed here since the United Kingdom did not invoke state of necessity to justify its conduct with respect to the vessel: ARS art. 25 Commentary, [9]. The United Kingdom did not invoke any legal grounds as explanation for its conduct, which did not, at any rate, give rise to protests from other states. The United Kingdom seemed to rely on the vessel's status as a wreck, after its abandonment by the owner; on which see Spinedi, 'Problemi di diritto internazionale sollevati dal naufragio della *Torrey Canyon*' (1967) *Rivista di diritto internazionale* 655, 670; Cahier, 'Changements et continuité du droit international' (1985) 195 *Recueil* 9, 291. These factual circumstances severely undermine this case as an instance of state of necessity. Detracting further from the precedential relevance of this instance is the fact that the United Kingdom, commenting on draft art. 33 adopted on first reading and noting references to *Torrey Canyon* in the commentary to this provision, maintained that 'further consideration is required as to whether there is a need for a provision concerning action taken by a State to cope with environmental emergencies which pose an immediate threat to its territory (as envisaged in the commentary at [16]). If so, this would be akin to *force majeure* or distress, and might be considered in that context. It would not, however, in the British Government's view, provide in itself a sufficient basis for any wider provision concerning necessity': A/CN.4/488, 134–5. This position of the United Kingdom seems coherent with its attitude to the sinking of the *Amoco Cadiz* in 1978, which caused the largest oil pollution to that date. Unlike in *Torrey Canyon*, the United Kingdom did not destroy the wreck, see Rousseau, 'Chronique des faits internationaux' (1978) RGDIP 1125. Despite it being irrelevant practice in respect of the defence of necessity, the *Torrey Canyon* incident clearly evidences the function of necessity (in its ordinary sense): having highlighted factual circumstances not adequately regulated by international law, the incident led to the adoption of the Convention Relating to Intervention on the High Seas in Cases of Oil Pollution Casualties, (1969) 970 UNTS 211, as noted by Heathcote, *Necessity*, 172.

1978, in accordance with the agreed Schedule of Work. At Hungary's initiative, the works were slowed down in 1983 and subsequently accelerated in 1989. But following internal controversies about the project, Hungary suspended the work at Nagymaros on 13 May 1989, pending the conclusion of ecological studies undertaken by competent authorities. In July 1989, Hungary suspended work at Dunakiliti (in the Gabčíkovo sector) and, in October 1989, abandoned the work at Nagymaros. Throughout this time, negotiations between the parties continued with a view to investigating alternative solutions for the alleged environmental problems caused by the project. Eventually, Czechoslovakia decided to begin work on the so-called Variant C, a unilateral modification of the project as originally envisioned, which would be implemented from October 1992.[457] On 19 May 1992, Hungary transmitted to Czechoslovakia a *note verbale* terminating the 1977 Treaty. In 1993, the parties agreed to submit their dispute to the ICJ.

Before the Court, Hungary invoked state of necessity to justify its suspension of works under the 1977 Treaty.[458] On the substance and status of this defence, the parties agreed that state of necessity was recognised by international law and that it was reflected in the then draft article 33 adopted on first reading by the ILC.[459] During the oral phase of the case, Slovakia, who had succeeded to the treaty after the dissolution of Czechoslovakia, raised some doubts about the recognition of necessity by positive international law and noted several doctrinal opinions against it.[460] It did not, however, push this argument any further.

The parties also debated the essential character of the interests at stake in the case, thus supporting the formulation and *ratio* of the first-reading defence. Hungary maintained that through the suspension and later abandonment of the works it sought to protect the 'ecological balance' of the region[461] and the guarantee of fresh water supply for the local population and future generations on either side of the border.[462] It also added that state of necessity was not limited to threats to the state's existence, but included the protection of the environment.[463] Further, although it

---

[457] *Gabčíkovo-Nagymaros*, [20–3].
[458] Memorial of the Republic of Hungary, 2 May 1994, vol. 1, 281ff.
[459] *Gabčíkovo-Nagymaros*, [50].
[460] Slovakia, oral statement, 25 March 1997, CR 1997/9, 58; 14 April 1997, CR 1997/14, 25.
[461] Hungary Memorial, 285 [10.10], 288 [10.22], 289 [10.25], 293 [10.40].
[462] Hungary Memorial, 289 [10.24], 291 [10.37–38]; Hungary, oral statement, 4 March 1997, CR 1997/3, 73; 5 March 1997, CR 1997/4, 23–4.
[463] Hungary: CR 1997/3, 72.

## 8.3 STATE OF NECESSITY IN THE ILC

recognised that economic interests could be essential for a state, Hungary stated that economic interests would rarely be essential for the purposes of the plea of necessity since they were 'capable of adjustment and compensation'.[464] The suspension of the works would only affect an economic interest of Slovakia. Indeed, counsel for Hungary pointed out that Czechoslovakia had described the 1977 Treaty as merely a 'building contract'.[465] It followed from this characterisation of the Slovak interest at stake, that Hungary's ecological interests were superior.

Slovakia's response was two-pronged: first, it argued that the interest protected by Hungary was non-essential, and second, that the Slovak interests infringed were essential. On the first point, Slovakia initially denied that state of necessity applied to any interest other than the state's existence.[466] It later changed this position, and during the hearings, it conceded that the preservation of the 'ecological balance' of the region was an essential interest for the purposes of the plea.[467] At any rate, according to Slovakia, the real concern of Hungary was not the environment: this was just a (convenient) cloak for Hungary's real goal, the protection of its finances.[468] Second, as to its own 'essential' interests, noting that the ILC had not provided guidance on their identification,[469] Slovakia listed the prevention of repeated flooding affecting Slovakia's population, its pursuit of sustainable development, and the production of clean energy, all of which were incorporated in the 1977 Treaty.[470] For Slovakia, contrary to Hungary's assertion, the Treaty was not a mere 'building contract'.[471] With this, Slovakia had turned Hungary's argument on its head: it was not Slovakia's, but Hungary's interests that were financial in character and, therefore, inferior in the circumstances. Slovakia went further, and denied that financial interests could ever be safeguarded under the plea of necessity.[472]

In its judgment, the Court noted that state of necessity, as reflected in draft article 33, was recognised in customary law.[473] The Court underscored

---

[464] Hungary: CR 1997/4, 24.
[465] Hungary, oral statement, 10 April 1997, CR 1997/12, 71.
[466] Counter-Memorial Submitted by the Slovak Republic, 5 December 1994, vol. 1, 298 [10.41].
[467] Slovakia: CR 1997/9, 63; CR 1997/14, 70.
[468] Slovakia: Memorial, 325 [8.31–33]; Reply, 105 [5.12].
[469] Slovakia, CR 1997/9, 63.
[470] Slovakia: Counter-Memorial, 298–9 [10.42]; CR 1997/9, 61; 26 March 1997, CR 1997/10, 17–18; CR 1997/14, 72.
[471] Slovakia: CR 1997/14, 72.
[472] Slovakia, Counter-Memorial, 298 [10.41].
[473] *Gabčíkovo-Nagymaros*, [51].

the exceptional character of the defence,[474] and explained that the successful invocation of the plea did not mean that the state had acted 'in accordance with its obligations', at most, it meant that the state would 'not incur international responsibility by acting as it did.'[475] As to the invocation of the plea, the Court held that the determination of whether the conditions of state of necessity were met was not a matter for the 'sole judgment' of the state concerned.[476] In respect of the character of the interests protected, the Court noted that according to the ILC their essential character should be assessed on a case-by-case basis. Like the ILC, the Court had no difficulty to accept the essential character of environmental interests.[477] It did not discuss, however, whether the interests invoked by Hungary were superior to those of Slovakia or whether, if considered to be essential, Slovakia's interests had been seriously impaired. There was no need to: the Court found that Hungary had been unable to prove, with the evidence available at the time, that its interests were threatened by a 'grave and imminent' peril and, on this basis, dismissed the plea.[478]

'Financial Necessity': State of Necessity in Investment Arbitration   State of necessity has also been invoked in numerous investment treaty arbitrations instituted following the Argentine financial crisis of the early 2000s. In response to claims by investors that Argentina's measures to address the crisis infringed their conventionally protected rights, Argentina has invoked the plea of necessity. In all cases, Argentina has invoked the plea as a justification. The tribunals seized of these disputes have adopted widely different decisions, even though the factual matrix of the disputes was virtually identical in all claims.[479] Moreover, the tribunals have adopted

---

[474] Id.
[475] *Gabčíkovo-Nagymaros*, [48].
[476] Id.
[477] Ibid., [53].
[478] Ibid., [54].
[479] The literature on this point is vast. See, among others, Leben, 'L'etat de nécessité dans le droit international de l'investissement' (2005) 349 *Cahiers de l'arbitrage* 19; Bjorklund, 'Emergency Exceptions: State of Necessity and *Force Majeure*' in Muchlinski and Ortino (eds), *Oxford Handbook of International Investment Law* (2007), 459; Martinez, 'Is Invoking State Defences in Investment Arbitration a Waste of Time and Money?' (2008) 15 *Croat Arb YB* 89; Viñuales, 'State of Necessity and Peremptory Norms in International Investment Law' (2008) 14 *Law & Bus Rev Am* 79; Valenti, 'Lo stato di necessità nei procedimenti arbitrali ICSID contro l'Argentina' (2008) 91 *Rivista di diritto internazionale* 114; Binder, 'Changed Circumstances in International Investment Law: Interfaces between the Law of Treaties and the Law of State Responsibility with a Special Focus on the Argentine Crisis' in Binder et al. (eds), *International Investment Law in the 21st Century: Essays in Honour of Christoph Schreuer* (2009), 608; Cortés Martín, 'El estado de

## 8.3 STATE OF NECESSITY IN THE ILC

differing (and often incorrect) assessments of the relation between the so-called 'non-precluded-measures' clauses in the treaties and the general defence of necessity.[480] While these differences render any general appraisal of the case-law rather difficult, it at least appears that the parties and the tribunals upheld the customary status of the defence and accepted ARS Article 25 as an accurate statement of the customary defence.[481]

In general, the approach of the parties and the tribunals to Article 25 corroborated the conceptualisation of the defence as a clash of interests and, albeit implicitly, the plea's superior interest rationale. In its argument – at least as recounted in the various awards – Argentina first identified its essential interests, and then maintained that its conduct had not impaired an essential interest of the co-contracting states. Among its essential interests, Argentina appealed to the protection of its 'existence and independence'[482] (even referring to 'self-preservation'[483]), and the well-being of its population guaranteed through access to public services, the maintenance of public order, and the functioning of public institutions.[484]

---

necesidad en materia económica y financiera' (2009) 25 AEDI 119; Reinisch, 'Necessity in Investment Arbitration' (2010) 41 NYIL 137; Martinez, 'Invoking State Defenses in Investment Treaty Arbitration' in Waibel et al. (eds), *The Backlash Against Investment Arbitration: Perceptions and Reality* (2010), 315; Alvarez-Jiménez, 'Foreign Investment Protection and Regulatory Failures as States' Contribution to the State of Necessity under Customary International Law – A New Approach' (2010) 27 *J Int'l Arb* 144; Gazzini, 'Foreign Investment and Measures Adopted on Grounds of Necessity: Toward a Common Understanding' (2010) 7(1) TDM; Cristani, 'The Sempra Annulment Decision of 29 June 2010 and Subsequent Developments in Investment Arbitration Dealing with the Necessity Defence' (2011) 15 *Int'l Comm LR* 237; Waibel, *Sovereign Defaults before International Courts and Tribunals* (2011), ch. 5; Subramanian, 'Too Similar or Too Different: State of Necessity as a Defence under Customary International Law and the Bilateral Investment Treaty and Their Relationship' (2012) 9 *Manchester J Int'l Economic L* 68; Lozano Contreras, 'El estado de necesidad y las cláusulas de emergencia contempladas en los APPRI: los casos argentinos ante el CIADI' (2013) 65 REDI 101.

[480] On which see Kurtz, 'Adjudging the Exceptional at International Law: Security, Public Order and Financial Crisis' (2008) 59 ICLQ 325.

[481] Only in one case, under the Argentina–UK BIT, claimants contested the customary status of the defence, relying on the United Kingdom's objection. In their view, the defence was either not part of customary law or, at any rate, not applicable under the BIT since the United Kingdom had been a 'persistent objector': *BG Group Plc v Argentina*, UNCITRAL Award, 24 December 2007, [400].

[482] E.g., *Enron Corporation and Ponderosa Assets LP v Argentine Republic*, ICSID Case ARB/01/3, Award, 22 May 2007, [289].

[483] *EDF International SA, SAUR International SA and Leon Participaciones Argentinas SA v Argentine Republic*, ICSID Case ARB/03/23, Award, 11 June 2012, [507].

[484] E.g., *Sempra Energy International v Argentine Republic*, ICSID Case ARB/02/16, Award, 29 September 2007, [326]; *BG Group*, [393]; *National Grid Plc v Argentine Republic*, UNCITRAL Award, 3 November 2008, [245].

It may be noted that Argentina did not invoke its economic interests in this context. Indeed, other than in *CMS* (the first award dealing with the necessity plea) where Argentina asserted 'that economic interest qualifies as an essential interest of the State when threatened by grave and imminent peril',[485] in subsequent cases the state's economic interests became merely instrumental to its existence and independence, and to the wellbeing of its population – the essential interests the measures sought to protect. In general, claimants and tribunals have accepted the essential character of these interests.[486]

As to the interests impaired, there are two relevant considerations: that of the beneficiary of the interests, and that of the essential character of those interests. As to the first point, as related in the awards, Argentina's arguments have addressed solely the interests of its co-contracting state (and the international community as a whole). On the whole, Argentina has disregarded the interests of investors, although it has frequently noted that the measures were not discriminatory against them.[487] The views of tribunals in this regard have ranged from complete disregard of investor's interests[488] to the characterisation of investors as the direct beneficiaries of BITs.[489] For the former tribunals, the clash of interests exists between the two co-contracting parties and for the latter between the host state and the investor. In between these two poles, other tribunals have accounted for investors' interests in an indirect manner, by conceptualising the protection of investors as an interest of the co-contracting state.[490] These contrasting views are, in part, a practical consequence of the unsettled debate on

---

[485] *CMS Gas Transmission Company v Argentine Republic*, ICSID Case ARB/01/8, Award, 12 May 2005.

[486] *LG&E Energy Corp, LG&E Capital Corp, LG&E International Inc v Argentine Republic*, ICSID Case ARB/02/1, Liability, 3 October 2006, 46 ILM 40, [257]; *Metalpar SA and Buen Aire SA v Argentine Republic*, ICSID Case ARB/03/5, Award, 6 June 2008, [208]; *Suez Sociedad General de Aguas de Barcelona SA and InterAgua Servicios Integrales del Agua SA v Argentine Republic [Suez-InterAgua]*, ICSID Case ARB/03/17, Liability, 30 July 2010, [238]; *Suez Sociedad General de Aguas de Barcelona SA and Vivendi Universal SA v Argentine Republic [Suez-Vivendi]*, ICSID Case ARB/03/19, Liability, 30 July 2010, [260]; *Enron Corporation and Ponderosa Assets LP v Argentine Republic*, ICSID Case ARB/01/3, Annulment, 30 July 2010, [358–60]; *Total SA v Argentine Republic*, ICSID Case ARB/04/1, Liability, 27 December 2010, [222 (fn. 267)]; *Impregilo Spa v Argentine Republic*, ICSID Case ARB/07/17, Award, 21 June 2011, [346]. Cf. *EDF*, [518] (claimant contesting the Argentine characterisation of its interest).

[487] *Enron*, [295]; *Sempra*, [334]; *BG Group*, [395]; *Metalpar SA and Buen Aire SA v Argentine Republic*, [134]; *National Grid*, [208–9]; *EDF*, [558].

[488] *Impregilo*, [354].

[489] *Enron*, [342]; *Sempra*, [392].

[490] *CMS*, [357–8]. See also *Suez-InterAgua*, [239]; *Suez-Vivendi*, [261].

## 8.3 STATE OF NECESSITY IN THE ILC

the status of investors under bilateral investment treaties.[491] But they may also betray a difficulty intrinsic in the plea of necessity: although its drafters clearly had interstate relations in mind, like all of Part One of the ARS, the plea of necessity is applicable to *all* obligations of international law, including obligations owed to non-state actors, such as investors. For, indeed, and this is the second point mentioned above, whether the interest impaired is essential or not is necessarily affected by who the beneficiary of the relevant interest is. The case-law identifies the interest of the co-contracting states as being either financial or as relating to the fulfilment of the rights of their investors under the BIT. When addressing investor interests, moreover, these tend to be classified as financial. Where tribunals have focused on the co-contracting party's interest, these have been deemed to be non-essential.[492] At any rate, as explained by the Tribunal in *Impregilo*, '[t]he interests of a small number of Contracting State's nationals or legal entities are not consistent with or qualify as an "essential interest" of that State'[493] – an assertion which raises the question whether a larger number might. In turn, where investor interests were taken into account, at least one tribunal (*Enron*) thought that these were essential (to the investor itself).[494] In at least one instance, Argentina pointed to the 'purely patrimonial' character of the interests impaired to dismiss their status as essential.[495]

Ultimately, in all but two cases the tribunal rejected Argentina's necessity plea.[496] These rejections were not based on the difficulties in assessing the relative essential character of the interests at stake. Rather, it usually turned on one of two (if not both) issues: first, the requirement of non-contribution to the situation of necessity, namely the degree of contribution of Argentina to the crisis itself;[497] and, second, the fact that the

---

[491] For a summary of the different approaches, and their consequences for general defences see Paparinskis, 'Investment Treaty Arbitration and the (New) Law of State Responsibility' (2013) 24 EJIL 617. See also Orrego-Vicuña, 'Softening Necessity' in Arsanjani (ed.), *Looking to the Future: Essays on International Law in Honour of W Michael Reisman* (2010), 747. On the position of investors under BITs, see Roberts, 'Power and Persuasion in Investment Treaty Interpretation: The Dual Role of States' (2010) 104 AJIL 180, 184–5 (and literature cited therein).
[492] *CMS*, [357–8]. See also *Suez-InterAgua*, [239]; *Suez-Vivendi*, [261].
[493] *Impregilo*, [354].
[494] *Enron*, [342]; *Sempra*, [392].
[495] *National Grid*, [208].
[496] The plea was upheld in *LG&E* and *Continental Casualty Company v Argentine Republic*, ICSID Case ARB/03/9, Award, 5 September 2008. Annulment proceedings in *LG&E* are currently suspended by agreement of the parties.
[497] See, e.g., *CMS*, [329]; *Enron*, [312]; *Sempra*, [354]; *National Grid*, [262]; *Suez-InterAgua*, [242–3]; *Suez-Vivendi*, [264–5]; *Impregilo*, [358]; *EDF*, [1173].

impleaded measures were not the 'only way' to deal with the crisis.[498] Be that as it may, this case-law lends support to the current formulation of the defence and its superior-interest *ratio*.

The dispute in *von Pezold v Zimbabwe*, the only case in which the plea of necessity has been raised so far outside of the Argentina cases, also corroborated the formulation of Article 25 as well as the conflict of interests understanding of the plea. Zimbabwe raised the plea of necessity to justify the expropriation without compensation of land to satisfy the demands of the Settlers/War Veterans.[499] The parties and the Tribunal agreed that ARS Article 25 reflected the 'legal test' for the plea of necessity under international law (but did not specifically refer to its customary recognition).[500] The Tribunal found that none of the requirements of Article 25 had been met in fact and, for this reason, rejected Zimbabwe's plea. Of relevance, here, are only the considerations which pertain to the interest-balancing exercise. As to the essential interests protected, Zimbabwe claimed to be acting to safeguard its existence, political and economic survival (the 'ongoingness' of the state, as the respondent put it).[501] The claimants did not contest that these interests were essential.[502] The Tribunal also agreed in principle,[503] though it found that in fact the measures were intended to ensure the survival not of the state, but of the government and its president at a political level – and these could not be protected under Article 25.[504] In relation to the interests impaired, the Tribunal found in favour of the claimants, who argued that the Zimbabwean measures were discriminatory insofar as they targeted white farmers and that, for this reason, they impaired an essential interest of the international community as a whole protected by the prohibition of discrimination.[505] Claimants also argued that since the measures constituted a breach of the prohibition on racial discrimination, and this prohibition was recognised as a peremptory rule of international law, the plea of necessity was excluded by application of

---

[498] See, e.g., *Enron*, [309]; *Sempra*, [351]; *Suez-InterAgua*, [238, 243]; *Suez-Vivendi*, [260, 265]; *Total*, [223]; *EDF*, [1172].
[499] *von Pezold et al v Republic of Zimbabwe*, ICSID Case ARB/10/15, Award, 28 July 2015, [613].
[500] Ibid., [613] (Zimbabwe); [617] (claimants); [624] (Tribunal).
[501] Ibid., [614].
[502] Ibid., [627].
[503] Ibid., [628].
[504] Ibid., [631].
[505] See ibid., claimants' argument [619–22, 649]; Tribunal's decision [657].

ARS Article 26.[506] The Tribunal agreed with claimants that the measures impaired an essential interest of the international community and that it was, at any rate, excluded by ARS Article 26.[507]

It may be wondered whether the Tribunal would have rejected the plea *even if* it had found that Zimbabwe's measures actually safeguarded an essential interest in the sense of Article 25, for example the state's survival. In such a case there would have been a clash between an individual interest (state survival) and a collective one (non-discrimination) – the exceptional situation that Crawford had referred to in his report. It is not clear from the Tribunal's reasoning how it would have approached the balancing or weighing of these two interests. It may have taken the dogmatic (and absolute) view that collective interests are superior to individual interests or, if following the lead of the Special Rapporteur, it could have considered which of the two interests, *in the circumstances*, ought to take precedence. It must be noted that conceptually, this is a distinct question from that of the peremptory status of the obligation breached: Article 25 requires the determination of a relative priority, namely, priority in the specific context taking into account not only the nature of the interests in question but also the extent of the harm threatened. In this contextual and relativised analysis it would be possible to find that the individual interest was superior in the circumstances. Nevertheless, even if this were the case, the plea could still be excluded if the collective interest in question was protected by a rule of *jus cogens*.[508]

Finally, it may be noted that for Zimbabwe, state of necessity acted as a justification since 'a State that successfully invokes necessity is excluded from any wrongfulness caused by the act of the State.'[509]

---

[506] Ibid., [621–2].

[507] Ibid., [657]. The Tribunal explained, improperly, that 'Zimbabwe's violation of its obligation *erga omnes* means that it has breached ILC Article 26', id. Of course, ARS Article 26 cannot be breached, as it does not itself impose an obligation on states. It is simply a (substantive) condition of application of the defences.

[508] Article 26 and its Commentary do not specify if the provision is applicable only where there is a 'serious breach' of a peremptory rule, as required by ARS art. 41. It must be inferred from this that even a trivial breach will be enough to exclude the availability of defences. This inference is supported by the Commentary's clarification that 'the circumstances precluding wrongfulness in Chapter V of Part One do not authorize or excuse *any* derogation from a peremptory norm of general international law', at [4] (emphasis added).

[509] *von Pezold*, [616].

### Miscellaneous Cases: The Generality of the Defence of Necessity[510]

*M/V Saiga (No 2)* (1999) This dispute arose out of the wrongful arrest and detention by Guinea of the *M/V Saiga*, a bunkering vessel flagged in St Vincent and the Grenadines engaged in the sale of gas-oil off the coast of Guinea, including in Guinea's EEZ. St Vincent and the Grenadines instituted proceedings against Guinea under UNCLOS Annex VII before ITLOS. The main aspect of the dispute concerned the compatibility with UNCLOS of the extension of Guinea's jurisdiction to prescribe and enforce its customs laws against foreign-flagged vessels beyond the territorial sea.[511] The plea of necessity arose in connection with this point.

Guinea argued that the prescription and enforcement of its customs laws beyond the territorial sea was grounded on the variously termed principle of self-protection, self-help or necessity.[512] In Guinea's view, customary law recognised a 'principle of self-protection in case of grave and imminent perils which endanger essential aspects of [the state's] public interests'.[513] In application of this principle, Guinea had adopted and enforced laws forbidding bunkering in its EEZ to protect its financial interests.[514] Guinea's argument straddled (conceptually) the plea of necessity and necessity in its ordinary meaning. In essence, and in a similar way to the US argument in *Fur Seals*, the reference to necessity was as a material source (or source of inspiration) for the state's right to regulate its EEZ – thus, necessity in its ordinary meaning. St Vincent and the Grenadines denied that there was a principle of international law allowing Guinea to protect itself against 'unjustified economic activities' in its EEZ affecting its public interests.[515] If anything, it could invoke state

---

[510] The *Corfu Channel* case is not discussed here because, as demonstrated by Corten, the UK argumentation in the case did not rely on an autonomous defence of necessity. Rather, the references to necessity in the pleadings concerned a condition for the exercise of other legal entitlements, e.g. right of intervention or right of self-help: Corten, *Le droit contre la guerre* (2nd edn, 2014), 390–4. In other words, as in the *Caroline* incident and the *Fur Seals* arbitration, the United Kingdom referred to necessity in its ordinary meaning, and not as a distinct defence in the international legal order.

[511] On the distinction between jurisdiction to prescribe and jurisdiction to enforce, see O'Keefe, 'Universal Jurisdiction: Clarifying the Basic Concept' (2004) 3 JICJ 735, 736–44.

[512] See, e.g., Counter-Memorial Submitted by Guinea, 16 October 1998, [112]. Also noted by the applicant in Reply, 19 November 1998, [137], and the Tribunal in *M/V Saiga (No 2) (St Vincent and the Grenadines v Guinea)* ITLOS, Judgment 1 July 1999, [128].

[513] Rejoinder submitted by Guinea, 28 December 1998, [97].

[514] ITLOS/PV.99/15, 16 March 1999, 6–7.

[515] St Vincent and the Grenadines oral statement: ITLOS/PV.99/7/Rev.1, 11 March 1999, 13.

## 8.3 STATE OF NECESSITY IN THE ILC    411

of necessity but, in any event, the plea was not met. Citing draft Article 33 adopted by the ILC on first reading and *Gabčíkovo-Nagymaros*, the applicant held that state of necessity could not be invoked unless the conduct in question was the 'only means' to safeguard an essential interest from a grave and imminent peril. While it was ready to accept that Guinea's financial interests might be essential, the detention of the *Saiga* was not the only means to protect Guinea's interests and no 'grave and imminent threat' existed.[516]

The Tribunal rejected Guinea's claims. The Tribunal distinguished the 'broad notion of public interest or self-protection' from the plea of necessity.[517] As to the plea, the Tribunal noted that it was recognised in customary law, citing the ICJ's *Gabčíkovo-Nagymaros* judgment,[518] and held that two cumulative conditions were required for the successful invocation of the plea: the conduct had to be the 'only means' to protect an essential interest from a grave and imminent peril, and it must not seriously impair an essential interest of another state.[519] In the case of the *Saiga*, the first condition was not met: there was no evidence of a grave and imminent peril to the state's financial interests (though there was no discussion as to the essential character of financial interests), nor was the conduct adopted the only means to protect that interest.[520]

While not expressly identifying the rationale of the plea invoked, the structure of the parties' arguments and the Tribunal's judgment reveal acceptance of the superior interest rationale.

*Legality of Use of Force (Serbia v Belgium) (1999)*    In April 1999 Serbia instituted proceedings before the ICJ and requested provisional measures against ten NATO member states in relation to the air-strike campaign launched against it. During the provisional measures hearing, Belgium, one of the respondents, invoked state of necessity as a justification for the alleged breach of the prohibition on the use of force.[521] For Belgium, state of necessity was 'enshrined in all branches of the law' and 'unquestionably

---

[516] Reply, [138]; ITLOS/PV.99/7/Rev.1, 12.
[517] *M/V Saiga*, [129].
[518] Ibid., [133–4].
[519] Ibid., [133].
[520] Ibid., [135].
[521] Belgium also rehashed old arguments favouring the narrow reading of the prohibition: so long as force was not used against the 'territorial integrity or political independence' of another state, there was no breach of the prohibition, *Legality of Use of Force (Serbia v Belgium)*, CR 1999/15, Wednesday 10 May 1999, 17.

acknowledged in international law' as reflected in draft Article 33. Belgium defined the defence as 'the cause which justifies the violation of a binding rule in order to safeguard, in face of grave and imminent peril, values which are higher than those protected by the rule which has been breached'.[522]

The interests protected by the intervention, according to Belgium, were 'rights of *jus cogens*',[523] which were 'essential values' threatened by an impending humanitarian catastrophe.[524] These were the 'right to life and physical integrity, the prohibition of torture',[525] and 'the collective security of an entire region'.[526] The obligation allegedly breached was the rule prohibiting the use of force. Belgium did not characterise this obligation as *jus cogens*, thus placing it in the rank of 'inferior' value as compared with the interests it sought to safeguard.

Serbia did not comment on the Belgian argument,[527] and the Court did not address the plea in its Order.[528]

*Palestinian Wall (2004)* In 2003, the General Assembly requested the ICJ to render an advisory opinion on the legality of the construction of a wall by Israel in Occupied Palestinian Territory. Some of the states which took part in the proceedings discussed the possible invocation of state of necessity as a defence by Israel in their submissions to the Court.

France noted that Israel was confronted with 'grave threats to its security'[529] and that it could invoke the defence of necessity in respect of measures to address those 'grave threats'.[530] It noted, moreover, that in assessing the defence the Court would need to address 'the gravity of the threats to Israel's security; the set of steps taken by the Government of Israel to deal with them, the construction of the wall being only one of those steps; and the violations of Palestinian rights caused by the

---

[522] CR 1999/15, 18. The text quoted is the 'uncorrected' translation of the pleadings available on the Court's website (not paginated). Page references are to the original statement in French.
[523] Id.
[524] Ibid., 15–16.
[525] Id.
[526] Ibid., 18.
[527] CR 1999/25, Wednesday 12 May 1999.
[528] *Legality of the Use of Force (Federal Republic of Yugoslavia v Belgium), Provisional Measures, Order of 2 June 1999* (1999) ICJ Rep 124.
[529] Written statement of the French Republic, 30 January 2004, *Palestinian Wall*, [47].
[530] Ibid., [47, 50].

## 8.3 STATE OF NECESSITY IN THE ILC

construction of the wall'.[531] Malaysia and Saudi Arabia's remarks focused on the peremptory character of the rights impaired by the wall. Malaysia contended that the wall 'constitutes a violation of peremptory norms of international law, such as the right to self-determination of peoples and the respect of the territorial integrity of other countries'.[532] Saudi Arabia, in turn, stated that Israel could not rely on ARS Article 25 since 'the separation wall clearly impairs the rights of the Palestinian people' including self-determination,[533] a right arising under peremptory rules.[534] Finally, Syria stated that 'necessity, in general, is a contradiction between two legal interests; one is sacrificed for the sake of upholding the other'.[535] Syria was opposed to the recognition of this defence in international law since (in language reminiscent of the early-twentieth-century sceptics) its acceptance would pose a 'great danger to the stability of ... international relations', and ultimately lead to 'international chaos'.[536] Moreover, Syria noted that the balancing of interests could not be performed in international law in the absence of an accepted scale of interests.[537] At any rate (quoting the scrapped draft Article 33), Syria noted that the defence could not succeed in respect of the construction of the wall since the wall affected 'the sovereignty and independence of the targeted state', one of the 'most important interests' of states.[538]

The Court discussed the defence of necessity only briefly, reasserting its customary status. On the facts, the Court rejected that state of necessity was applicable since the construction of the wall along the chosen route was not the only means to safeguard Israeli interests from peril.[539]

Once again the references to the conflict of interests, and the opposition between superior and inferior interests, in the submissions of states suggest that the underlying explanation of the defence lay in the superiority of the interest protected.

---

[531] Ibid., [57].
[532] Malaysia, oral statement, CR 2004/4, 24 February 2004, 28–9
[533] Written statement of the Kingdom of Saudi Arabia, 30 January 2004, [30].
[534] Ibid., [39].
[535] Memorandum Presented by the Syrian Arab Republic in Implementation of Section (2) of Article (66) of the ICJ Statute and the Court Decision of 19 December 2003, [18].
[536] Ibid., [19].
[537] Ibid., [20–1].
[538] Ibid., [22].
[539] *Legal Consequences of the Construction of a Wall in the Occupied Palestinian Territory* (2004) ICJ Rep 136, [140].

### 8.3.3 A Customary Defence?

Since 1945, the plea of necessity has been invoked by only a handful of states. In the order in which they were addressed in this section: Hungary, Argentina, Zimbabwe and Belgium. A broader number of states have endorsed the defence, be it in the Sixth Committee of the General Assembly or before the ICJ in advisory proceedings. Nevertheless, many remain that question it. *Pace* the ICJ and other tribunals, it is still debatable whether this practice is sufficiently general and consistent to support the customary status of the defence. Be that as it may, the existing practice is at least uniform in respect of the conceptualisation and requirements of the defence, as codified in Article 25 ARS.

## 8.4 State of Necessity between Justification and Excuse

Leaving aside the persisting doubts as to the defence's customary status, the practice which exists supports the formulation of the defence as a clash of interests in which the superior interest in the circumstances prevails. The primacy of superior interests, lesser evils or balancing of interests as it is also known, is traditionally seen as a theory of justification – already considered in Chapters 5 and 6. Indeed, the superior interests rationale is the stereotypical theory underpinning justification defences in domestic law. If grounded on this rationale – as the practice suggests it is – then state of necessity in international law must also be classified as a justification. This is a counterintuitive conclusion, since states and tribunals are increasingly partial towards an excuse of necessity and the prevailing sentiment among commentators is to classify it as such. It seems certainly desirable to classify the plea as an excuse – to retain the wrongfulness of the necessitated act may discourage states from breaching the law even in difficult circumstances. Yet, to classify state of necessity as an excuse is incompatible with its current formulation. Indeed, only with difficulty can a superior interests *ratio* ground an excuse defence. The superior interests rationale is act-focused (rather than actor-focused) and, moreover, its consequentialist logic is at odds with the wrongfulness of the act in question.

This section further examines the superior interests rationale, a consequentialist theory of justification already considered in previous chapters, and what this implies for the defence, in particular in respect of the potential duty of compensation. Finally, given the wish for, and the desirability of, classifying the plea of necessity as an excuse, and by way of conclusion

## 8.4 BETWEEN JUSTIFICATION AND EXCUSE

of this chapter, this section will make a proposal for the reconceptualisation of the plea, through a recalibration of the focus of the plea on the invoking state, that may support its classification as an excuse.

### 8.4.1 Identifying the Rationale: Superiority of the Interest Safeguarded

The ARS Commentary states that the defence refers to 'exceptional cases where the only way a State can safeguard an essential interest threatened by a grave and imminent peril is, for the time being, not to perform some other international obligation of lesser weight or urgency'.[540] With few exceptions, states commenting on the ILC work and states invoking the plea of necessity in international disputes accepted the conceptualisation of the defence as a conflict between an essential and a non-essential or inferior interest.[541] Equally, the practice reviewed suggests that states, if only implicitly, accepted that the exonerating effect of the defence for the breach of an obligation lies in the superiority of the interest of the invoking state as against the interest protected by the obligation impaired.

As already mentioned earlier, the determination as to the superior or inferior character of the interests is not made in the abstract.[542] Indeed, other than in the case of interests protected by peremptory rules, international law recognises no hierarchy of values or interests. The analysis is therefore a relative and contextual one, which takes into account both qualitative and quantitative criteria. These include the subject matter of the interests in question, as well as the potential harm to them. For example, in *Gabčíkovo-Nagymaros*, Hungary referred to the 'irreversibility' of the damage to the ecological balance of the region in assessing the essential character of its interests.[543] As the Commentary explains:

> The extent to which a given interest is 'essential' depends on all the circumstances, and cannot be prejudged. It extends to particular interests of the

---

[540] ARS art. 25 Commentary, [1].

[541] For a survey of the development of the superior interest rationale in domestic law (criminal and private), see Viganò, *Stato di necessità e conflitti di doveri: Contributo alla teoria delle cause di giustificazione e delle scusanti* (2000), 66ff.

[542] Cf. Song, 'Between Scylla and Charybdis: Can a Plea of Necessity Offer Safe Passage to States in Responding to an Economic Crisis without Incurring Liability to Foreign Investors?' (2008) 19 *Am Rev Int'l Arb* 235, 250–1.

[543] For further examples, see *CMS*, [319]: 'A first question the Tribunal must address is whether an essential interest of the state was involved in the matter. Again here the issue is to determine the gravity of the crisis. The need to prevent a major breakdown, with all its social and political implications, might have entailed an essential interest of the State in which case the operation of the state of necessity might have been triggered'; *Enron*,

State and its people, as well as of the international community as a whole. Whatever the interest may be, however, it is only when it is threatened by a grave and imminent peril that this condition is satisfied.[544]

In other words, interests may or may not be essential, in relation to one another, depending on the circumstances.[545] Thus, in *Gabčíkovo-Nagymaros* Hungary noted that financial interest *could* be essential,[546] and in *M/V Saiga* St Vincent and the Grenadines that they 'might' be essential.[547]

When introduced in the ARS by Ago, the plea of necessity sought to safeguard essential but not legally protected interests of the invoking state against the legally protected interests (the rights) of the injured state. But this formulation is difficult to maintain in contemporary international law.[548] With the ever-growing density of the international legal order, most essential interests are (or may eventually be) protected or regulated under some international legal principle or rule. A state invoking the plea of necessity is thus likely to be able to point to some rule or principle of the legal order which protects the essential interest(s) it attempts to safeguard with its actions. By way of illustration, Belgium asserted in *Legality of Use of Force* that the essential character of the interests safeguarded through its conduct, including the right to life and the right to be free from torture, was supported by the recognition of those interests in peremptory rules of the legal order. Though the interests safeguarded were recognised rules of the legal order (and were, therefore, legally protected), these rules did not entitle Belgium to act against Serbia's territorial sovereignty or to act against Serbia at all. The legal basis of Belgium's action had to be found elsewhere – in the plea of necessity. So the plea can be invoked to safeguard legally protected essential interests, so long as the relevant rule or principle does not provide the state with an entitlement to act against the injured state. If it did, then the situation would turn into

---

[306]: 'Yet, the argument that such a situation compromised the very existence of the State and its independence so as to qualify as involving an essential interest of the State is not convincing.'

[544] ARS art. 25 Commentary, [15].
[545] Similarly, Boed, 'Necessity', 27–8; Spiermann, 'Intervention', 531; Laursen, 'The Use of Force and (the State of) Necessity' (2004) 37 *Vanderbilt J Transnat'l L* 485, 503; Benvenuti, 'Lo stato di necessità alla prova dei fatti' in Spinedi et al. (eds), *La codificazione della responsabilità internazionale degli Stati alla prova dei fatti* (2006), 126.
[546] Hungary: CR 97/4, 24.
[547] Reply, [138]; ITLOS/PV.99/7/Rev.1, 12.
[548] I am grateful to my reviewers for highlighting this issue.

## 8.4 BETWEEN JUSTIFICATION AND EXCUSE

a normative conflict, as the state in question would be both permitted to act, and prohibited from acting, in a certain way.

Once the superior (or inferior) character of the relevant interests has been established, then the two must be balanced. As the ARS Commentary indicates, if the plea is to be successful, then 'the interest relied on must outweigh all other considerations, not merely from the point of view of the acting State but on a reasonable assessment of the competing interests, whether these are individual or collective'.[549] This is an attempt to render the analysis of the plea more objective: it is not just the perspective of the invoking state that is relevant; rather, a tribunal or other decision-maker must look at the situation as a whole and determine, on a 'reasonable assessment of the competing interests', what interest ought to prevail or, what is the same, what is the lesser of two evils. This way of proceeding can be gleaned from the practice as well. Thus, as stated by France in *Palestinian Wall*, the plea of necessity required the consideration of a multiplicity of circumstances, including 'the gravity of the threats to Israel's security; the set of steps taken by the Government of Israel to deal with them, the construction of the wall being only one of those steps; and the violations of Palestinian rights caused by the construction of the wall'.[550] In *Gabčíkovo-Nagymaros* too, the Court affirmed that the assessment of the plea required taking into account not only the interests of the invoking state, but also any countervailing interest of the injured state.[551]

The assessment of the (relative) superiority of the interests involved in these situations is not an easy one.[552] Where the interests in question involve the same subject matter, a quantitative criterion could be relied upon: as noted by Wolff, cited earlier, it seems reasonable that the loss of a small portion of territory is a lesser evil than the loss of a larger portion. But what about interests related to different subject matters? How to assess the relative value of the interests in human life and the maintenance of peace in international relations, at issue in the Belgian pleading in *Legality of Use of Force*; or the relative value of respect of treaty commitments (the principle *pacta sunt servanda*) and the protection and well-being of a state's population, at issue in the Argentine crisis disputes? Additionally, since state of necessity operates so long as the harm to those interests remains

---

[549] Ibid., [17].
[550] Written statement of the French Republic, 30 January 2004, *Palestinian Wall*, [57].
[551] *Gabčíkovo-Nagymaros*, [58].
[552] On which see Sloane, 'Necessity'.

only a potentiality:[553] how can the harm caused be estimated with any certainty? To be sure, these difficulties are not exclusive to international law. Even in domestic law, where the scale of values tends to be clearer and is often codified, the lesser evils rationale has generated much debate and controversy.[554] But the risks involved in these assessments, made unilaterally by the invoking party, often in haste and in difficult circumstances, are heightened in the international legal order given the absence of a mandatory judiciary that can oversee every invocation of the plea.

Lastly, it must be noted that the superior interests rationale supports some of the requirements and conditions of the plea. To begin with, it follows from this rationale that the plea is excluded if the interests impaired by the necessitated act are themselves superior to the interest safeguarded (Article 25(1)(b)). Further, the requirement of proportionality is implicit in the logic of the rationale. Nevertheless, the two exclusions in Article 25(2) are not easily reconcilable with the theory. After all, if what matters is the protection of superior interests, then it should be irrelevant whether a rule protecting an inferior interest excludes the plea. Equally, it should be irrelevant where the peril originated, be it in causes endogenous or exogenous to the invoking state.

### 8.4.2 State of Necessity as a (Counterintuitive) Justification

The superior interests rationale rests on act-consequentialist premises,[555] that is, the necessitated act is judged in accordance with the result it achieves. While the act may be incompatible with the strict letter of the law, it ultimately achieves the protection of a superior interest or, at the very least, it prevents a greater evil. This result is desirable and socially more beneficial than adherence to the letter of the law. In Ago's words, 'the fundamental requirement of respect for the law' must not 'ultimately lead to the kind of situation that is perfectly described by the adage *summum*

---

[553] State of necessity is a prophylactic defence, applicable only so long as the damage to the interests is imminent and has not yet materialised, that is so long as it remains a 'threat' to those interests: Paddeu, '*Force Majeure*', 463–6.

[554] See, e.g., Alexander, 'Lesser Evils: A Closer Look at the Paradigmatic Justification' (2005) 24 *Law & Philosophy* 611; Simons, 'Exploring the Intricacies of the Lesser Evils Defense' (2005) 24 *Law & Philosophy* 645; Berman, 'Lesser Evils and Justification: A Less Close Look' (2005) 24 *Law & Philosophy* 681.

[555] On which see Frey, 'Act-Utilitarianism' in Lafollette (ed.), *The Blackwell Guide to Ethical Theory* (2000), 165; Sinnott-Armstrong, 'Consequentialism' in Zalta (ed.), *Stanford Encyclopedia of Philosophy* (2012), http://plato.stanford.edu/entries/consequentialism/.

*jus, summa injuria*.[556] For Heathcote this means that 'the purpose or spirit of the law should take priority over its explicit provisions'.[557]

Thus superior interest (or lesser evils) constitutes a theory of justification.[558] Domestic legal systems that recognise a justification of necessity, ground the plea on this theory.[559] This is because it is perceived that the net benefit achieved by the necessitated act should be permitted, if not praised, by the legal order. Indeed, in international law, states invoking the plea of necessity maintain that their conduct was *lawful* and not that they are excused despite their conduct being unlawful. Whether an act produces an overall net benefit is an objective question – and objectivity is, indeed, the hallmark of justification defences. To be sure, there remains some element of subjectivity,[560] in that the initial assessment is made, unilaterally, by the invoking state. But then, this subjectivity is a feature of the international legal order in which, more often than not, states must 'auto-interpret' situations and act at their own risk.[561] Ultimately, the success

---

[556] Ago, Eighth Report – Add.5–7, [80].

[557] Heathcote, *Necessity*, 361. While considering that state of necessity is not, cannot, and should not be a rule of international law, Heathcote agrees that, if premised on this rationale, the purported rule of necessity operates as a justification.

[558] Upholding this characterisation, see Pillitu, *Necessità*, 325; Kohen, 'The Notion of "State Survival" in International Law' in De Chazournes and Sands (eds), *Nuclear Weapons and the International Court of Justice* (1999), 309–10; Bücheler, *Proportionality in Investor-State Arbitration* (2015), 293. On different grounds, Dupuy too maintains that state of necessity operates as a justification: Dupuy, 'Le fait générateur de la responsabilité des Etats' (1984) 188 *Recueil* 8, 39–40.

[559] Among civil law jurisdictions, see, e.g., Argentina: Art. 34(3) Código Penal, see Sierra and Cantaro, *Lecciones de derecho penal* (2005), 247; Chile: sec. 10(7) Criminal Code, see Politoff et al., 'Chile' in *International Encyclopaedia of Laws (Criminal Law: Suppl. 24)* (2003), 88; Italy: Art. 54 Codice Penale, on which see Viganò, *Stato di necessità*, 114–32; Germany: see secs 228 and 904 of the BGB (civil law), and sec. 34 of the STGB (criminal law) a translation of which can be found at Bernsmann, 'Private Self-Defence and Necessity in German Penal Law and in the Penal Law Proposal – Some Remarks' (1996) 30 *Israel LR* 171, 180; Morocco: Art. 124(2) Criminal Code, see Amzazi, 'Morocco' in *International Encyclopaedia of Laws (Criminal Law: Suppl. 11)* (1997), 65; Portugal: Art. 34 Criminal Code, see Faria, 'Portugal' in *International Encyclopaedia of Laws (Criminal Law: Suppl. 48)* (2013), 66; Spain: Art. 20 Criminal Code, see Bachmaier Winter and del Moral García, 'Spain' in *International Encyclopaedia of Laws (Criminal Law: Suppl. 46)* (2012), 99. In the common law, see sec. 3.02 of the US Model Penal Code which, according to Viganò, *Stato di necessità*, 113, has been adopted by roughly half of the US states. The matter is more complicated in the United Kingdom, where there remain doubts as to the recognition of a general justification of necessity.

[560] On which Cassella, *Nécessité*, 195–211.

[561] See Gross, 'States as Organs of International Law and the Problem of Autointerpretation' in *Essays on International Law and Organization* (1998) vol. 1. In this sense, state of necessity is indeed no different from countermeasures or self-defence. In each of these cases, it

of the plea requires that its factual and legal requirements be verifiable 'not only from the point of view of the invoking state, but on a reasonable assessment of the competing interests, whether these are individual or collective',[562] as noted earlier.

Superior interests is a different principle of justification from the one underpinning consent, self-defence and countermeasures. This difference has important implications in practice. Consent, self-defence and countermeasures are grounded on the absence of legal protection of the interest impaired, be it as a result of the affected state's voluntary renunciation (consent) or of forfeiture through conduct (self-defence and countermeasures). The state against which the defence is invoked does not possess a right that the invoking state not act in that manner. In Hohfeldian terms, that state is in a position of no-right with respect to the invoking state (it does not have a right that the invoking state not act in a certain way). Or, what is the same, the invoking state possesses a liberty so to act: this state is entitled to adopt that course of conduct. In contrast, under a superior interests rationale, the affected state retains its right against the invoking state that it not act in a certain way and, by the same token, the invoking state possesses a permission of the legal order to act against the injured state.[563] This situation is difficult to represent by means of Hohfeldian analysis: insofar as the affected state retains its rights as against the invoking state, its position cannot be assimilated to one of no-rights. By the same token, then, the invoking state's permission cannot be reduced to a Hohfeldian liberty, for the correlation (the no-right of the other party) would be missing.[564] This situation was explained in Chapter 3 by means of an example from David Rodin's work. It may be worth quoting the example here again, as the point is not a simple one. Consider the situation of a farmer who burns his neighbour's field to prevent a wild fire from engulfing a town (or his own house). In this situation:

> The neighbour has a right not to have his field destroyed, but the farmer's action is justified in the circumstances because it is overwhelmingly the lesser evil. What is distinctive about this case, however, is that the

---

is the state taking the measure that must unilaterally assess that the triggering condition (a wrongful act or an armed attack) has occurred. This it does, at its own risk, as it may subsequently turn out to be the case that the target state's conduct was not a wrongful act or an armed attack.

[562] ARS art. 25 Commentary, [17].
[563] Rodin, *Self-Defense*, 29.
[564] Recall that in the Hohfeldian scheme, correlative legal conceptions are simply two ways to describe the same thing – albeit from different angles.

farmer does not have a simple Hohfeldian liberty to burn the field, since the neighbour's claim-right against having his property destroyed does not disappear in the face of the justification ... What this implies is that justifications arising from consequentialist considerations (in particular 'lesser evil' justifications) are not reducible to a simple Hohfeldian relation.[565]

To use an international law example, consider the situation in the *Legality of Use of Force* case. Assume, for the sake of the argument, that state of necessity was a plea available as against the use of force. In this case, Serbia would have a right that Belgium not use force against it and that it respect its territorial sovereignty. And yet, if Belgium's use of force was limited to the protection of the civilian population from an impending genocide, it would not be difficult to agree that the interests protected by Belgium are superior. Nevertheless, Belgium would not have a liberty to impair Serbia's territorial sovereignty or its right to be free from the use of force. Indeed, Serbia's rights (claim-rights) entail correlative duties for Belgium. And these rights (and their correlative obligations) do not disappear in the situation of necessity. Thus, on the one hand, Serbia retains its claim-right that Belgium not use force or trespass into its territory, correlatively Belgium retains its duty not to use force and not to trespass; and, on the other hand, Belgium is nevertheless justified in using force and in trespassing. It was precisely because of this difficulty that it was said in Chapter 3 that lesser evils justifications, like state of necessity, provide, in Suzanne Uniacke's words, a 'weak' justification.[566] Likewise, as will be seen in the next section, it is precisely because of this particular characteristic of the plea of necessity – that the affected state retains its rights, and yet the invoking state is permitted to act against those rights – that the question of the duty to compensate the affected state has been controversial.

### 8.4.3 *A Duty of Compensation?*

A consequence of classifying state of necessity as a justification is that it raises considerable difficulty in determining whether a duty of compensation may arise: after all, the state has acted pursuant to a permission granted by the legal order, such that its conduct is lawful. Nevertheless, it has often been argued that a duty of compensation for the material loss caused to the state affected by the necessity measure should arise regardless. As already advanced in Chapter 2, this is a difficult question which

---

[565] Ibid., 28.
[566] Uniacke, *Permissible Killing*, 27.

both legal theorists and moral philosophers have considered at length. Already Grotius and Pufendorf adopted widely different views on the point: indeed, Grotius' assertion that a duty of compensation arose for the party invoking necessity was one of the aims of Pufendorf's critique of his remarks on the 'right of necessity'. Pufendorf was, it can be added, equally unsuccessful in his theoretical justification of compensation in the circumstances. The most that either of these scholars could say is that compensation would have been equitable, or fair.[567] Indeed, the affected state, whose rights are sacrificed, is in a different position to the state target of self-defence or countermeasures: while in the latter the target state has itself committed a wrongful act against the invoking state, the former is innocent. It seems only fair that it be compensated for its sacrifice. And yet, if the state who invokes necessity commits no wrongful act, if it acts lawfully, why should it provide compensation? Is it not the point of the defence to exclude any consequences (including pecuniary repercussions) for the invoking state?

As was said in Chapter 2, compensation is not incompatible with the legality of the necessitated act. Moreover, there is at least a convincing reason to impose this duty, namely to prevent states from shifting the burden of protecting their own interests on to other states.[568] Indeed, international law scholars seem to be generally in favour of such a duty.[569] Nevertheless, it is doubtful whether positive law at present recognises the existence of this duty.[570] A number of cases are often invoked as precedent, including *Neptune*,[571] the *General Company of the Orinoco*,[572] the League of Nations' report in relation to the property of Bulgarian Minorities in Greece,[573] *Gabčíkovo-Nagymaros*,[574] and the awards in *CMS*,[575] *Enron*,[576] *Sempra*[577]

---

[567] See Section 8.2.1.2.
[568] ARS art. 27 Commentary, [5]. See also Crawford, *General Part*, 318.
[569] See Reinisch and Binder, 'Debts and State of Necessity' in Boholavsky and Cernic (eds), *Making Sovereign Financing and Human Rights Work* (2014), 125 and references cited therein.
[570] Arguing in favour of compensation in these cases, see Bücheler, *Proportionality*, 243, 290–6.
[571] Esp. *Neptune*, 3874–5 (per Pinkney).
[572] *Company General of the Orinoco* (1905) 10 RIAA 184.
[573] League of Nations, 'Report of the Commission of Enquiry on the Incidents on the Frontier between Bulgaria and Greece, Doc No C.727.M.270.1925.VII' (1926) 7 LNOJ 196.
[574] *Gabčíkovo-Nagymaros*, [48].
[575] *CMS*, [392–4].
[576] *Enron*, [345].
[577] *Sempra*, [394].

and *EDF*.[578] But this case-law is far from consistent. As for *The Neptune* case, aside from the fact that this precedent predates the contemporary defence of necessity by over a century, it should be noted that the applicable law by the Commission included 'justice, equity and the law of nations', as per Article VII of the Jay Treaty. As a result, very little can be inferred from this case 'as to the positive law between States at the time'.[579] In *General Company of the Orinoco*, compensation was not due as a result of the facts presumptively justified by necessity (namely the unilateral termination of the concession contract), rather, it was due for the breach of the concession contract before its termination;[580] it was, in other words, reparation for wrongful conduct. The compensation suggested by the League of Nations' Commission of Enquiry for the taking of Bulgarian property in Greece – taken over by the Greek government to house refugees of Greek origins arriving from Turkey – is also better understood as a reparation for wrongful conduct.[581] The statements in *CMS*, *Enron*, *Sempra* and *EDF* were made in *obiter dicta*, insofar as the tribunals had already rejected the plea. At any rate, other arbitral tribunals dealing with disputes arising out of the Argentine crisis have taken the opposite view in respect of virtually identical facts.[582] In *Gabčíkovo-Nagymaros*, too, the Court's statement is merely *obiter* and falls short of a confirmation of the customary status of this duty.[583] The arbitral and judicial practice, certainly important both as a subsidiary means for the determination of rules of law and for its role in the development of the law, is far too scarce and inconsistent to allow drawing any hard conclusions on the existence of a duty of compensation.

Moreover, as far as state practice and *opinio juris* are concerned, there are significant discrepancies. Hungary,[584] Russia[585] and Slovakia[586]

---

[578] *EDF*, [1171], [1177]. Later restated by the Annulment Committee in *EDF International SA, SAUR International SA and Leon Participaciones Argentinas SA v Argentine Republic*, ICSID Case ARB/03/23, Annulment, 5 February 2016, [330].

[579] Heathcote, *Necessity*, 137.

[580] See Forteau, 'Reparation in the Event of a Circumstance Precluding Wrongfulness' in Crawford et al. (eds), *The Law of International Responsibility* (2010), 889.

[581] Heathcote, *Necessity*, 223–4.

[582] See, e.g., *LG&E*, [264].

[583] *Gabčíkovo-Nagymaros*, [48].

[584] See, e.g., CR 1997/3, 4 March 1997, 87 (Court's translation); CR 1997/4, 5 March 1997, 24–5 [36]; CR 1997/5, 6 March 1997, 64; CR 1997/6, 7 March 1997, 60, 66 (Court's translation).

[585] A/C.6/55/SR.18, 10 [53].

[586] See, e.g., CR 1997/11, 27 March 1997, 56–7.

have acknowledged the existence of the duty; Argentina,[587] Chile[588] and Zimbabwe[589] have rejected it. Commenting on the ILC's work, Denmark (on behalf of the Nordic countries),[590] the Netherlands[591] and Poland[592] generally supported Article 27 (and its predecessor draft Article 35), though it is not clear that they specifically supported the duty of compensation referred to in the second paragraph of the Article since (i) their remarks often emphasised the duty to resume compliance with the underlying obligation (paragraph (a) of the Article); and (ii) in any event, paragraph (b) does not itself provide for this duty but is drafted only as a without-prejudice clause (so, at most, they accepted that this was a possibility). But for France,[593] Japan[594] and Slovakia[595] further analysis of the duty referred to in Article 27(b) was necessary. Moreover, during both the first and second readings of the ARS, the majority of states were silent on the matter. As this review shows, the practice and case-law are both very limited and inconsistent. Any argument for the customary recognition of a duty of compensation is, therefore, far from convincing. Equally unpersuasive is any argument based on general principles:[596] as already indicated in Chapter 2, there is significant variation in the manner in which domestic legal orders address this issue.[597]

There is thus a persuasive reason to impose a duty of compensation, and yet there is no evidence in positive law of a discrete rule attaching a duty of compensation to the invocation of the plea of necessity.[598] A duty of

---

[587] See *CMS*, [389]; *CMS (Annulment)*, [139]; *Enron*, [344–5]; *Sempra*, [393–4]; *BG Group*, [398].

[588] A/C.6/35/SR.47, [8–9].

[589] *von Pezold v Zimbabwe*, [615]. The tribunal did not address the question.

[590] A/C.6/54/SR.22, 2 [3].

[591] A/C.6/54/SR.21, 7–8 [52]. For the Netherlands, paragraph (b), the provision should be limited to *force majeure*, state of necessity and distress: UN Doc A/CN.4/515 and Add.1–3, 57.

[592] A/C.6/54/SR.21, 8 [57].

[593] France wished to delete the Article because, in its view, it was unacceptable to assert that compensation followed even if conduct was justified 'in such a general and imprecise way': UN Doc A/CN.4/515 and Add.1–3, 56. It seemed that the underlying principle was acceptable to it, but that further refinement was necessary.

[594] A/C.6/54/SR.22, 3 [9].

[595] A/C.6/54/SR.22, 10 [57].

[596] E.g., *CMS*, [390].

[597] For references see Christie, 'The Unwarranted Conclusions Drawn from *Vincent v Lake Erie Transportation Co* Concerning the Defence of Necessity' (2005) 5 *Issues in Legal Scholarship* 7 (fns 72 and 73, contrasting the laws of the United Kingdom and the United States – in the text of the article – and France and Germany).

[598] See also Akehurst, 'International Liability for Injurious Consequences Arising Out of Acts Not Prohibited by International Law' (1985) 16 NYIL 3, 12 ('whether compensation is

compensation could potentially be based on certain other legal doctrines, already mentioned in Chapter 2. First, the duty of compensation could be based on the *right* of the affected state. As was said in Chapter 2, legal theorists have drawn a distinction between the violation and infringement of rights, where a violation is the combination of infringement and wrongfulness. In the case of necessity, while the right of the affected state may not be violated (the act is justified and, as such, lawful) it is still infringed and it may be necessary to make good this infringement. Indeed, it could be argued that absent compensation, the infringement becomes a violation. Second is the doctrine of unjust enrichment. The state invoking necessity derives a benefit to the detriment of the affected state – a state which, it may be worth recalling, has no obligation to bear the burden of the protection of the invoking state's interests. As explained by Michael Akehurst, '[a] State which commits an act of necessity expropriates the right of another State in order to safeguard its own essential interest. Such expropriation constitutes unjust enrichment unless it is accompanied by compensation'.[599] As noted in Chapter 2, the choice between these two approaches may affect the calculation of compensation: in the former approach, compensation is determined by the extent of the infringement on the affected state's right; in the latter, it is determined by the extent of the enrichment of the invoking state.

If no legal basis can be found to attach compensation to the plea of necessity, because there is no specific customary obligation in this regard or because neither of the two legal doctrines just mentioned are accepted as potential bases for this duty, then one last option to ensure that compensation is due all the while allowing some leeway for the invoking state which finds itself in difficult circumstances could be to reframe the plea of necessity as an excuse.[600] This approach could resolve the question of the legal basis of compensation: compensation would be based on the wrongfulness of the conduct in question and, in this sense, it would be a form of reparation *not excluded* by the defence. However, the approach still falls short of specifying the circumstances in which the plea would afford only a partial excuse, excluding all other forms of reparation save for compensation for material loss – an issue which will require further doctrinal development and the endorsement of state practice.

---

payable *de lege lata* is open to doubt. *De lege ferenda*, however, acts of necessity ought always to be accompanied by compensation').
[599] Akehurst, 'International Liability', 12–13.
[600] On which see Section 8.4.4.

### 8.4.4 A Proposal for Excusing Necessity

The characterisation of state of necessity as a justification is far from unanimous, as was just noted. Some states, in submitting observations to the ILC, maintained that it was an excuse;[601] the point was made in no uncertain terms by the ad hoc Committee in *CMS*;[602] and legal scholarship increasingly leans towards classifying the plea as an excuse.[603] But the current formulation of the plea in the ARS is inadequate to sustain this classification. Indeed, to say that an act which achieves greater justice (or avoids a greater harm) is wrongful is incompatible with the logic of the consequentialist formulation of the plea. It would thus be mistaken to insist on characterising the defence as currently formulated as an excuse. Nevertheless, the ARS's formulation of the defence should not be an impediment to its development at customary law or, rather, to its crystallisation as a customary rule in different form from that contemplated in the ARS. The question that arises, then, is how to reformulate the plea to support its classification as an excuse.

It may be recalled from Chapter 3 that excuses possess subjective elements. 'Subjective' is not here a reference to fault or intention – indeed, the plea would certainly fail on the basis of a fault-based rationale since, as noted by the ARS Commentary, the invoking state acts *voluntarily*.[604] To say that excuses possess subjective elements means simply that these are defences that focus on the actor, in this case on the state and, in particular, on the specific circumstances of the actor at the time of the impugned conduct. Thus, as was said there, these are 'individualised' defences. So the first thing to do in recasting the plea of necessity as an excuse is to move away from the act (and whether it achieves greater justice, or a lesser evil), and concentrate on the actor (in particular, on the circumstances in which the actor found itself). The interest potentially harmed and the extent of the impending harm can remain central questions, but

---

[601] See Section 8.3.2.1.
[602] *CMS Gas Transmission Company v Argentine Republic*, ICSID Case ARB/01/8, Annulment, 25 September 2007, [129].
[603] E.g., Higgins, *Problems and Process: International Law and How We Use It* (1994), 40; Johnstone, 'Necessity', 352–6; Orrego-Vicuña, 'Softening Necessity', 742; Ryngaert, 'State Responsibility, Necessity and Human Rights' (2010) 41 NYIL 79, 96–7; Tsagourias, 'Necessity'.
[604] As described by the ARS art. 25 Commentary, [2]. On this point, see Chapter 3, Section 3.3.3, explaining why a fault-based conception of excuses in international law is not necessary and why it is not desirable, since it would preclude the characterisation of state of necessity as an excuse.

the crucial issue should be whether the law could expect the state, in those circumstances, to behave differently. If the law is made for 'normal' circumstances, is it possible to expect that its subjects behave accordingly even in abnormal circumstances? Or do the abnormal circumstances affect the way in which the state acts?

Domestic legal orders that recognise an excuse of necessity often rely on notions of coercion or duress to explain the situation in which the individual finds him- or herself. The circumstances of necessity are, in other words, circumstances that limit the individual's free will, in the sense that they coerce the individual's choice as to his actions. As was seen in Chapter 7, this same theory underpins the plea of *force majeure* in international law and, as will be seen in Chapter 9, it can also ground the defence of distress. Coercion, or restrictions on a state's freedom of choice, could also ground the excuse of necessity.[605] In normal circumstances, the state would have had a range of options open to it to protect its essential interest. But in the situation of necessity, where there is a grave and imminent harm to one of the state's essential interests, the state's choice is restricted: it may need to act quickly, or choose means providing immediate or short-term relief, or be limited in terms of the typology of measures to adopt in view of the interest at issue and the kind (and degree) of harm foreseen. Thus, its choice to act, while a voluntary one, is not an entirely free one. In keeping with the desire to restrict the plea as much as possible, the degree of coercion required should be a high one. Only where the state's available means for the protection of its interests have been limited to one – the one that requires the breach of the rights of a third state – will the plea be available. To use the language of Article 25(1)(a), the impairment of another state's rights must be 'the only way' to protect that interest. In essence, the state's freedom has been reduced to two options: to let its interest be harmed or, even worse, perish *or* protect it at the expense of another state's rights.[606]

The other requirements and conditions of the plea are difficult to accommodate in a coercion-based theory. If the point of the plea is to make a concession for the predicament in which the invoking state finds itself, then it is immaterial what rights of the injured state are thereby

---

[605] See also Scalese, *Scusanti*, 102–3.
[606] Note that the degree of coercion required here is weaker than that required for *force majeure*. In the case of *force majeure* the state has only one option: not to perform its obligations. In the case of excusing necessity, the state has two options: to let its interests be harmed, or to infringe an obligation to protect its interests. Despite the different degrees, in both cases the state's will is coerced.

impaired (whether they protect essential interests of the injured state, or they exclude the possibility of invoking the plea) or where the peril originates from (be it causes endogenous or exogenous to the invoking state). So long as there is a situation of necessity and the conduct adopted by the state is the 'only' way to protect its interests – essential interest, of course – then the invoking state's will has been coerced. This is not to say that no limitations can be recognised. But it must nevertheless be acknowledged that these requirements and conditions are ad hoc and external to the theoretical explanation of the plea.[607]

With the caveats made earlier, an excuse of necessity could be restated as follows:

1. State of necessity may not be invoked by a State as a ground for precluding its responsibility for the commission of a wrongful act unless:
   (a) there exists a grave and imminent peril to an essential interest of the State; and
   (b) the State's act is the only way to safeguard its essential interest in the circumstances.
2. In any case, state of necessity may not be invoked by a State as a ground for precluding responsibility if:
   (a) the State's act seriously impairs an essential interest of the State or States towards which the obligation exists, or of the international community as a whole;
   (b) the international obligation in question excludes the possibility of invoking necessity; or
   (c) the State has contributed to the situation of necessity.

This formulation retains all the requirements and conditions in ARS Article 25, but it emphasises the illegality of the conduct adopted in the circumstances and makes the lack of choice (the act is the 'only way') a more central aspect of the plea by including it as part of the definition of the plea and not, as in the current version of Article 25, as a situation excluding the invocation of the plea. Without straying much from the text that was found acceptable by states, this formulation can help recalibrate

---

[607] This is not problematic, given that the current requirements and conditions are largely accepted. However, it could be more problematic for new restrictions to the plea: the possibility of grounding restrictions or expansions of any rule on its own rationale may go some way to legitimating them and render them more acceptable to states. There may be some more reticence where the restrictions may not be brought back to the underlying rationale of the defence, as exemplified by the suspicion with which some of the restrictions imposed on countermeasures were received, on which see Chapter 6.

the focus of the plea from whether the act achieves the greater good (by protecting the superior interest) to the situation of the state invoking the plea, in particular the impending threat to its interests and the limited choice available to it in respect of the means through which to protect that interest.

To argue for state of necessity as an excuse, ultimately, reflects the unease and concern surrounding the recognition and application of this plea in international law. The sacrifice of a state's rights for the protection of another state's interests, however essential the latter may be, is at odds with the equality of states. Even if justice or equity, allegedly pursued through the protection of the superior interest or through concessions to states in situations of predicament, may be tolerable or desirable, it remains that the means to achieve those ends are contrary to the mandate of the law. While there exist limits and restrictions on the means used, state of necessity ultimately legitimises the Machiavellian 'ends justify means' and brings this notion closer to its political cognate, the *raison d'état*. State of necessity involves a 'unilateral derogation from otherwise binding obligations' on the basis of uncontrolled subjective judgment, and in this it seems to be 'even more audacious than the concept of *jus cogens*: it permits the non-legal to trump the legal',[608] even if only temporarily. Any invocation of this plea, whether as a justification or an excuse, must be treated with utmost scepticism.

---

[608] Heathcote, *Necessity*, 2–3.

# 9

# Distress

## 9.1 Introduction

Pursuant to ARS Article 24:

1. The wrongfulness of an act of a State not in conformity with an international obligation of that State is precluded if the author of the act in question has no other reasonable way, in a situation of distress, of saving the author's life or the lives of other persons entrusted to the author's care.
2. Paragraph 1 does not apply if:
    (a) the situation of distress is due, either alone or in combination with other factors, to the conduct of the State invoking it; or
    (b) the act in question is likely to create a comparable or greater peril.

The ILC's Commentary explains that the defence is limited to situations where there exist threats to life and that circumstances of threats to physical integrity are excluded.[1] The threats to life must relate either to the state organ's own life, or that of individuals entrusted to his care; in the latter case, there must be a 'special relationship' between the state agent and the individuals in danger (regardless of the individuals' nationality).[2] In these circumstances, the state organ who acts in a manner incompatible with his state's international obligations does so voluntarily, though his conduct is not the product of free choice. In the Commission's words, in these circumstances, 'choice is effectively nullified by the situation of peril'.[3] Unlike in the state of necessity, the conduct adopted by the distressed state organ need not be 'the only way' to save life, but the only 'reasonable way'. The criterion of reasonableness accounts for the fact that the state organ will not always have the time or means to evaluate different courses of

---

[1] ARS art. 24 Commentary, [1].
[2] Ibid., [7]. On the irrelevance of nationality, see [1].
[3] Ibid., [1].

conduct. Thus, Article 24 attempts to 'strike a balance between the desire to provide some flexibility regarding the choices of action by the agent in saving lives and the need to confine the scope of the plea having regard to its exceptional character'.[4] Nevertheless, the defence will be unavailable if the act in question is likely to create a comparable or greater peril, which must be determined by reference to the context of saving lives;[5] the plea is, in this sense, limited by a requirement of proportionality. Finally, there is a requirement of non-contribution: the plea will fail if the invoking state contributed to bringing about the situation of distress.[6]

The defence of distress, a necessity-based rule as will be seen,[7] was elaborated by the Commission on the basis of a specific and longstanding body of practice in international law: the right of refuge of vessels in distress, later extended to aircraft in distress.[8] Surely, the Commission thought, the underlying rationale of the right of refuge – humanitarian considerations – applied beyond the strict circumstances of the law of the sea? These considerations had already led to the recognition of an analogous right for aircraft in distress, and it was perhaps arbitrary to protect human life in certain circumstances but not others. After all, situations of distress were not limited to the perils of navigation and aviation. So it seemed reasonable to make it generally available. Article 24 was, without a doubt, an instance of progressive development by the Commission and its customary status remains to be confirmed.[9]

This chapter will begin by considering the historical antecedents of Article 24. Section 9.2 will offer brief remarks on the historical evolution of the right of refuge and will focus, more extensively, on a forgotten, yet very interesting, body of practice in the nineteenth century: that of distress, a defence in prize law for the violation of lawfully established blockades. To be sure, this practice does not constitute relevant state practice to support the customary status of Article 24 – and indeed, it is not assessed here for the purposes of making a customary law determination. Both the

---

[4] Ibid., [6].
[5] Ibid., [10].
[6] Ibid., [9].
[7] As noted by, inter alia, Pillitu, *Lo stato di necessità nel diritto internazionale* (1981), 284–91; Salmon, 'Les circonstances excluant l'illicéité' in Zemanek and Salmon (eds), *La responsabilité internationale* (1987), 126; Scalese, *La rilevanza delle scusanti nella teoria dell'illecito internazionale* (2008), 148–9; Cassella, *La nécessité en droit international* (2011), 65–6.
[8] Tracing these developments: Lissitzyn, 'The Treatment of Aerial Intruders in Recent Practice and International Law' (1953) 47 AJIL 559.
[9] See Daillier et al., *Droit international public* (8th edn, 2009), 877–8. But see Szurek, 'Distress' in Crawford et al. (eds), *The Law of International Responsibility* (2010), 481.

right of refuge and the plea of distress in prize law were underpinned by humanitarian considerations, and it was by extension of this humanitarian aim that the plea of distress was first imagined at the ILC. It may thus be useful to understand the reasons for their recognition, as well as their practical application, as this may shed some light on the potential application and operation of Article 24. Section 9.3 then reviews the work of the ILC on the development of this defence. As will be seen, the adoption of draft Article 32 in 1979 met with tepid support among states in the Sixth Committee. The *Rainbow Warrior* Tribunal's reliance on this provision in 1990 had an important legitimising effect,[10] ultimately cementing the plea in the ARS, though practice in relation to it remains scarce.[11] Finally, Section 9.4 will consider the characterisation of distress as a justification or an excuse.

## 9.2 Historical Antecedents of the Defence of Distress

The defence of distress was only formulated by the ILC in the late 1970s; historical materials surveyed show that no such general defence was recognised in the past. Nevertheless, there existed in the past specific rules to cater to situations of distress – or, what is the same, situations of necessity involving threats to an individual's life. These took the form of a right of refuge of vessels, widely recognised in the law of the sea, and a defence for the unlawful entry of vessels into lawfully established blockades. This section will only give a brief outline of the right of refuge through the centuries; this material has been amply covered in the specialised literature and it is not necessary to address it here in any detail.[12] More time will be spent on the defences to blockade violations, in view of the fact that they have not been studied thus far and that their interpretation and application

---

[10] In the case of *Rainbow Warrior (New Zealand v France)* (1990) 20 RIAA 217.

[11] In his work as ILC Special Rapporteur on the responsibility of international organisations, Gaja noted that '[i]nstances in which distress was invoked in order to preclude wrongfulness of an act of a State are rare': Fourth Report on Responsibility of International Organisations, ILC Yearbook 2006, vol. II(1), [33].

[12] See, e.g., Chircop, 'Ships in Distress, Environmental Threats to Coastal States, and Places of Refuge: New Directions for an *Ancien Regime*?' (2002) 33 *ODIL* 207; Chircop, 'The Customary Law of Refuge for Ships in Distress' in Chircop and Linden (eds), *Places of Refuge for Ships: Emerging Environmental Concerns of a Maritime Custom* (2006), 163; Chircop et al., 'Characterising the Problem of Places of Refuge for Ships' in Chircop and Linden (eds), *Places of Refuge for Ships: Emerging Environmental Concerns of a Maritime Custom* (2006), 1; Noyes, 'Places of Refuge for Ships' (2008) 37 *Denv J Int'l L & Pol'y* 135; Morrison, *Places of Refuge for Ships in Distress* (2012).

by prize courts may aid in the elucidation of the concept, conditions and rationale of the contemporary plea of distress.

### 9.2.1 *The Law of the Sea and the Right of Entry in Distress*

The idea that vessels in danger due to the perils of navigation were allowed to take refuge in foreign coasts and ports is of ancient, yet unknown, origins. The right, which as will be seen is an expression of humanitarian considerations, can be traced back as far as the Egyptian kingdom,[13] and was included in the so-called Consolato del Mare and the Rolls of Oleron during the Middle Ages.[14] Most importantly the right has been recognised by states for many centuries.[15] A right of refuge has been included in bilateral treaties of Friendship and Navigation since at least the seventeenth century. A notable example from the eighteenth century is the Jay Treaty of 1794, in which the British 'consented' to allowing American vessels to take shelter in their ports in cases of 'stress of weather, danger from enemies, or other misfortune'.[16] The right of refuge became an established feature of the international law of the sea during the nineteenth century.[17] The precise content of this entitlement varied, though it was usually extended to all ships (merchant, fishing and military) in times of peace, with some modification during war.[18] Additionally, the distressed ships were entitled to a number of privileges while in the coastal state's waters, such as exemption from customs charges and immunity from the coastal

---

[13] See, e.g., Azuni, *The Maritime Law of Europe* (1806) vol. 1, 189.
[14] Chircop, 'Customary Law of Refuge', 171-3.
[15] A thorough review of the customary law in this area, in historical perspective, is provided by Chircop, 'Customary Law of Refuge', 171-3; and Morrison, *Refuge*, ch. 4.
[16] Article 23, Treaty of Amity, Commerce and Navigation between His Britannick Majesty and the United States of America (Jay Treaty), London 19 November 1794, 52 CTS 249.
[17] On which see, e.g., Ortolan, *Règles internationales et diplomatie de la mer* (1845) vol. 1, 160; Hautefeuille, *Des droits et des devoirs des nations neutres en temps de guerre maritime* (2nd edn, 1858) vol. 1, 345; Halleck, *International Law* (1861), 171-2; Heffter, *Le droit international de l'Europe* (3rd edn, 1873), 160-1; Sandonà, *Trattato di diritto internazionale moderno* (1870), 447; Twiss, *The Law of Nations* (2nd edn, 1875), 446; Bluntschli, *Le droit international codifié* (3rd edn, 1881), 207; Calvo, *Dictionnaire de droit international public et privé* (1885) vol. 1, 243; Bonfils, *Manuel de droit international public* (Fauchille ed., 4th edn, 1905), 357-8, see also 5th edn, 375-6; Mérignhac, *Traité de droit public international* (1907) vol. 2, 388; Wheaton, *Elements of International Law* (5th edn, 1916), 156; Laun, 'Le régime international des ports' (1926) 15 *Recueil* 1, 63.
[18] Noyes, 'Ships in Distress' in Wolfrum (ed.), *Max Planck Encyclopedia of Public International Law* (2009–, available at www.mpepil.com), sec. D. The only exclusion concerned belligerent ships entering enemy ports in distress, id.

state's jurisdiction.[19] This right continues to be recognised in contemporary international law, and it is codified in Article 18(2) of UNCLOS.[20] Moreover, the customary right has been extended to aircraft in distress as well.[21]

Recent developments – in particular related to environmental or other security concerns of the coastal state – have called into question the continued recognition of the right (at least as it extends to ships). Thus, in a few now-infamous instances, coastal states refused refuge to distressed vessels, such as the *Erika*, the *Prestige* and the *Castor*, with devastating environmental consequences when these ships sank and caused significant amounts of oil to spill into the sea.[22] On at least one occasion, access was also controversially denied, without explanation, by Chinese port authorities in Hong Kong to two American warships in search of refuge from a storm in 2007.[23] Coastal states have thus reasserted their right of sovereignty over their duties of humanity towards distressed vessels. Such refusals might not, as of yet, have challenged the right of refuge as such though they are tending to limit it. It is not impossible that the ground lost by the right of refuge vis-à-vis coastal state sovereignty may be regained by way of the plea of distress in Article 24. Indeed, if the state organs'

---

[19] See, e.g., *Kate A Hoff (The Rebecca) (USA v United Mexican States)* (1929) 4 RIAA 444, 447. In some circumstances the distressed vessel could lose its immunity; for example, when it was engaged in the slave trade, see *The Enterprise (United Kingdom/United States of America)* (1853) 4 *Moore Arbitrations* 4349; *The Hermosa (United Kingdom/United States of America)* (1853) 4 *Moore Arbitrations* 4374; *The Creole (United Kingdom/United States of America)* (1853) 4 *Moore Arbitrations* 4375.

[20] Article 18(2), United Nations Convention on the Law of the Sea (UNCLOS) (adopted 10 December 1982, entered into force 16 November 1994), (1982) 1833 UNTS 397. For a thorough analysis of the right of refuge in contemporary international law, see Morrison, *Refuge*. Further references can also be found at: US Department of State, Collection of Sources on Entry into Port under *Force Majeure*, at http://2001-2009.state.gov/s/l/2007/112701.htm.

[21] On which see, generally, Dugard, 'Jurisdiction over Persons on Board an Aircraft Landing in Distress' (1981) 30 ICLQ 902.

[22] On which see, generally, Murray, 'Any Port in a Storm? The Right of Entry for Reasons of *Force Majeure* or Distress in the Wake of the *Erika* and the *Castor*' (2002) 63 *Ohio St LJ* 1465; Foley and Nolan, 'The *Erika* Judgment – Environmental Liability and Places of Refuge: A Sea Change in Civil and Criminal Responsibility That the Maritime Community Must Heed' (2008) 33 *Tulane Maritime LJ* 41; Donner, 'Offering Refuge Is Better Than Refusing' (2008) 7 *JoMA* 281; Noyes, 'Distress', [17–20]; Whitehead, 'No Port in a Storm: A Review of Recent History and Legal Concepts Resulting in the Extinction of Ports of Refuge' (2009) 58 *Naval LR* 65.

[23] Julian Barnes, 'US Takes Issue with China Snub', *LA Times*, 28 November 2007, at http://articles.latimes.com/2007/nov/28/world/fg-uschina28; CNN, 'China Tells More US Vessels to Keep Out', 30 November 2007, at http://edition.cnn.com/2007/US/11/30/china.us/.

lives were at stake, it may be possible for public ships to ignore the coastal state's refusal and invoke, in order to justify or excuse entry, Article 24.

## 9.2.2 Blockade Violations in Distress in the Long Nineteenth Century

The other historical instance in which the notion of distress played a significant part concerned the violation of blockades by distressed ships.

A 'clear and incontrovertible right of belligerents',[24] the main purpose of blockade as a measure of war was to cut off all trade and intercourse of the enemy. The right of blockade crystallised as a right of belligerents in the late eighteenth century,[25] and during the nineteenth century, some claimed (and practised) a right of 'pacific' blockade.[26] A blockade involved the stationing of vessels off an enemy's coasts creating a cordon beyond which enemy and neutral vessels could not navigate. One of the fundamental requirements of a lawfully established blockade was effectiveness: an ineffective blockade was considered to be lifted.[27] Effectiveness was measured by the existence of a 'real and apparent danger' of capture for ships attempting to enter the blockaded area.[28] Ships entering and leaving the blockaded area would reveal the blockade's ineffectiveness and, ultimately, lead to its demise.[29] Blockading squadrons thus endeavoured to prevent ships from entering the area, and belligerent states discouraged the practice of blockade-running – which had become a lucrative business[30] – by

---

[24] Phillimore, *Commentaries upon International Law* (1857) vol. 3, 291.
[25] For a concise but comprehensive summary of the history of the institution of blockade, see Bargrave Deane, *The Law of Blockade* (1870), 16; Fauchille, *Du blocus maritime: étude de droit international et de droit comparé* (1882).
[26] See Chapter 6, Section 6.2.
[27] Article 4, Declaration of Paris Respecting Maritime Law, 16 April 1856, 115 CTS 1. And later Article 2 of the 'Final Protocol and Declaration of the London Naval Conference' (1909) 3 AJIL Supp 179.
[28] *The Olinde Rodrigues* (1899) 174 US 510, 515. Also IDI, Règlement international des prises maritimes, sec. 35. In the literature, see Kleen, *Lois et usages de la neutralité d'après le droit international conventionnel et coutumier des états civilisés* (1898) vol. 1, 569; Holtzoff, 'Some Phases of the Law of Blockade' (1916) 10 AJIL 53, 55. This was the compromise solution between the so-called 'Continental' and 'Anglo-American' approaches to prize law. As to the Continental approach, see Despagnet, *Cours de droit international public* (1894), 624; Kleen, *Lois*, 571. On the Anglo-American approach, see Halleck, *International Law*, 539; Oppenheim, *International Law* (1906) vol. 2, 407–8.
[29] Halleck, *International Law*, 545; Kleen, *Lois*, 570.
[30] In reality, it appears that blockade-running may have been less lucrative than the mythology suggests, see Lebergott, 'Through the Blockade: The Profitability and Extent of Cotton Smuggling, 1861–1865' (1981) 41 *Journal of Economic History* 867.

subjecting the breaching vessels to confiscation and, after prize proceedings in prize courts, to forfeit.[31]

Throughout the nineteenth century, the interpretation and application of the right of blockade, like much of the practice and scholarship of this period on the rights and duties of neutrals, was subject to contrasting Continental European and Anglo-American approaches.[32] What constituted a blockade violation therefore differed depending on the approach. Under the Continental approach, a material act of breach was necessary for the ship to be liable to capture.[33] The ship had to be caught *in flagrante delicto* while attempting to cross the line of the blockading squadron.[34] Such an approach was consonant with the Continental understanding that notification of the blockade should be made individually to each ship arriving at the blockaded area.[35] On this view, a breach occurred only when, after notification, the vessel attempted nonetheless to enter the area.[36] Pursuant to the Anglo-American approach, instead, a breach of blockade required the presence of three elements: an effective blockade, intention to breach the blockade and some 'act of violation'.[37] It was unnecessary that the vessel be caught *in flagrante*: the breach of the blockade commenced from the moment when the ship set sail to a blockaded port with the intention to enter.[38] Indeed, the mere fact of approaching the blockading squadron to solicit information on the blockade was held

---

[31] The effect of the capture on the cargo depended on other circumstances, including whether it belonged to the ship owner, or whether, if belonging to a third party, the commander of the ship knew its intended destination: *The Mercurius* (1798) 1 C Rob 83, 84–5. Note that unlawful capture rendered the capturing state liable to compensation; see, e.g., IDI, Règlement international des prises maritimes, sec. 9.

[32] On the contrasting approaches, see, generally, Kaeckenbeck, 'Divergences between British and Other Views on International Law' (1919) 4 *Transactions Grot Soc* 213. That these contrasting approaches existed was later denied by Lauterpacht, 'The So-called Anglo-American and Continental Schools of Thought in International Law' (1931) 12 BYIL 31.

[33] Fauchille, *Blocus*, 322; Rivier, *Principes de droit des gens* (1896) vol. 2, 431.

[34] *La Marthe-Magdeleine* (year IX), in de Pistoye and Duverdy, *Traité de prises maritimes* (1859), 378–80. Bluntschli, *Droit international*, 486.

[35] See, e.g., *La Louisa* (1847), in de Pistoye and Duverdy, *Traité*, 382. See also Article 7 of the 1870 Instructions addressées par S. Exc. l'Amiral Ministre Secrétaire d'Etat au Département de la Marine et des Colonies, in Barboux, *Jurisprudence du Conseil des prises pendant la guerre de 1870–1871* (1872), 135 (Annex I). In doctrinal commentary, see Ortolan, *Règles internationales et diplomatie de la mer* (1845) vol. 3, 314; Fiore, *Il diritto internazionale codificato* (1890), 387.

[36] E.g., *La Caroline* (1830), de Pistoye and Duverdy, *Traité*, 381.

[37] E.g., *The Betsey* (1798) 1 C Rob 93, 93; Wheaton, *Elements of International Law* (1836), 344.

[38] E.g., *The Columbia* (1798) 1 C Rob 154; *The Circassian* (1864) 69 US (2 Wall) 135.

to constitute a violation thereof.[39] This approach was consistent with the Anglo-American view that notification of the blockade made to neutral governments was presumed to have been made to all its citizens,[40] which allowed US and British vessels to apprehend neutral ships on the high seas so far as it could be proved that it was their intention to enter a blockaded port.[41]

Once apprehended and brought before prize courts, the ship masters often invoked 'distress', 'stress of weather', 'urgent necessity' and so on, to justify their entry into the blockaded area and thus prevent forfeiture. The different approaches to blockade violations mentioned above affected the relevance of these defences in prize proceedings. Practice shows that the plea was much more commonly raised in Anglo-American prize courts than in European ones. This was because, under the Anglo-American approach, the mere approaching of the vessel (whether it had in fact been notified of the blockade or not) to the cordon was enough to warrant its capture. Any defences, if relevant, would be considered not by the blockading squadron but by prize courts. In contrast, the Continental practice of individual notification meant that a vessel approaching the blockading squadron in distress would be able to explain its condition to the blockading squadron, without violating the blockade.[42] Notwithstanding these differences in the practice of states, a defence of distress was generally recognised for the entry into or exit from a blockaded area. Indeed, the 1882 Resolution on Maritime Prizes of the Institut de Droit International (IDI) accepted that merchant vessels had permission to enter the blockaded port due to 'bad weather', but only after confirmation by the commander of the blockade that the 'situation of *force majeure*' persisted.[43] More importantly, the defence was included in the London Declaration,[44] an instrument widely praised as having brought consensus to the two

---

[39] *The James Cook* (1810) Edwards 261, 263–4 ('it has been determined over and over again that a ship is not at liberty to go up to the mouth of a blockaded port even to make inquiry; that in itself is a consummation of the offence, and amounts to an actual breach of the blockade').

[40] E.g., *The Ringende Jacob* (1799) 1 C Rob 89, 91.

[41] For a statement and critique of this approach, see Twiss, 'The Doctrine of Continuous Voyages, as Applied to Contraband of War and Blockade' (1877–8) 3 *Law Mag & Rev* 1; Fauchille, *Blocus*, 337ff.

[42] Fauchille, *Blocus*, 350; Despagnet, *Cours*, 636.

[43] IDI, Règlement international des prises maritimes, sec. 40.

[44] Article 7, Declaration of London, 1909: 'in circumstances of distress ... a neutral vessel may enter a place under blockade'. See also the report of the conference in 'General Report on the Declaration Concerning the Laws of Naval Warfare Presented to the London Naval Conference on Behalf of Its Drafting Committee' (1914) 8 AJIL Supp 88, 96.

approaches,[45] and for having codified the 'general principles of international law' on maritime warfare.[46]

The case-law on these defences shows that prize courts tended to scrutinise defences very closely, in view of the possible consequences that violations may have had on the continued existence of the blockade.[47] A successful defence, as explained by the British judge Sir William Scott (later Lord Stowell) in *The Eleanor*, must fulfil the following requirements:

> it must be an urgent distress; it must be something of grave necessity: such as is spoken of in our books, where a ship is said to be driven in by stress of weather. It is not sufficient to say it was done to avoid a little bad weather, or in consequence of foul winds; the danger must be such as to cause apprehension to the mind of an honest and firm man. I do not mean to say that there must be an actual physical necessity existing at the moment; moral necessity would justify the act; where, for instance, the ship had sustained previous damage, so as to render it dangerous to the lives of the persons on board to prosecute the voyage: Such a case, though there might be no existing storm, would be viewed with tenderness; but there must be at least a moral necessity.[48]

This holding was frequently relied upon by both US and British courts sitting in prize and provided the standard by which to determine the validity of the plea. For example, in *The Diana*, the US Supreme Court directly quoted *The Eleanor* and held that, although a vessel could be 'in such distress as to justify her in attempting to enter a blockaded port', 'nothing less than an uncontrollable necessity, which admits of no compromise, and cannot be resisted' will be upheld in justification of the offence.[49] Moreover, the situation of distress must not have been created by the master himself for, otherwise, the defence would only be 'a part of the mechanism of the fraud'.[50] For example, distress caused by the ship master's intoxication was not an acceptable defence: in *The Shepherdess* the court held that 'a master cannot, on any principle of law, be allowed to stultify

---

[45] A '*media sententia*' in the words of the Drafting Committee: 'Report', 90. See also Macdonell, 'The Declaration of London' (1910) 11 *J Soc Comp L* 68, 68; Scott, 'The Declaration of London of February 26, 1909' (1914) 8 AJIL 274, 302. Note, nevertheless, that the United Kingdom was unsatisfied with this compromise solution and refused to ratify the Declaration. For a discussion and critique of the British position, see Root, 'The Real Significance of the Declaration of London' (1912) 6 AJIL 583.

[46] Preliminary Provision, 'Declaration of London, 1909', 190.

[47] Upton, *The Law of Nations Affecting Commerce during War* (1863), 285; Walker, *The Science of International Law* (1893), 523; Gregory, 'The Law of Blockades' (1903) 12 *Yale LJ* 339, 347.

[48] *The Eleanor* (1809) Edwards 135, 161.

[49] *The Diana* (1868) 74 US 354, at 360–1. See also *The New York* (1818) 16 US (3 Wheat) 59.

[50] *The Eleanor*, 161.

himself by the pretended or real use of spirituous liquors'.[51] Equally, loss of the compass of the ship was not an acceptable defence.[52]

Even though the plea was widely recognised, the terminology used to refer to it was rather inconsistent, in particular between Continental and Anglo-American sources. Continental scholars tended to use the language of *force majeure* to refer to the situation of the ship, where the expression '*force majeure*' was used in different senses. For Paul Fauchille, for example, '*force majeure*' referred to the defence available to a ship which was dragged into the blockaded area by strong winds or currents.[53] For Frantz Despagnet, instead, the '*force majeure*' compelled or forced the captain to enter into the blockaded area.[54] The IDI's resolution on maritime prize similarly stated that 'merchant vessels are allowed to enter, due to bad weather, in the blockaded port, but only after the commander of the blockade has certified the persistence of the *force majeure*'.[55] Fauchille's *force majeure* dragged the ship into the blockaded area (it acted on the ship), Despagnet's and the IDI's did not: it acted on the captain, and compelled him to seek refuge. In this second scenario, the defence was analogous to the notion of *détresse* of Johann Bluntschli,[56] Carlos Calvo[57] and Richard Kleen.[58] According to these scholars, *détresse* concerned the situation in which the master of a ship was compelled or forced to enter the blockaded area by the perils of navigation (including by 'superior forces').[59] The Anglo-American practice and doctrine on defences for blockade violations predominantly used, instead, the terms 'necessity' and 'distress'. For example, J. B. Scott held in *The Charlotta* that the breach of the blockade would be 'justified' by 'the alleged distress' of needing repairs, but that if there was 'no such necessity' the defence would not be accepted.[60] In *The Major Barbour*, the District Court for the Southern District of New York noted that the captain claimed to be 'excused for seeking a blockaded port for necessary repairs, supplies or shelter' and

---

[51] *The Shepherdess* (1804) 5 C Rob 262, 266. Alcohol intoxication of a ship's commander and sailors was a common phenomenon at the time: Simpson, *Cannibalism and the Common Law* (1986), 104.
[52] *The Elizabeth* (1810) 1 Edwards 198.
[53] Fauchille, *Blocus*, 350.
[54] E.g., Despagnet, *Cours*, 636.
[55] IDI, Règlement international des prises maritimes, sec. 40.
[56] Bluntschli, *Droit international*, 488.
[57] Calvo, *Dictionnaire*, 243.
[58] Kleen, *Lois*, 606–7.
[59] See, e.g., Calvo's definition of distress as 'Dénûment extrême, danger pressant, la situation même qui cause ce danger': Calvo, *Dictionnaire*, 243.
[60] *The Charlotta* (1810) Edwards 252, 252.

agreed that 'an act done clearly from necessity, and fairly and with good faith, in entering a blockaded port, will be excused'.[61] In *The Diana*, the US Supreme Court held that 'attempted evasions of the blockade would be excused upon pretenses of distress and danger'.[62] 'Necessity' and 'distress' thus denoted a situation in which the perils of navigation, such as 'stress of weather',[63] the 'state of the wind',[64] the want of provisions or the need of repairs,[65] posed a threat to the vessel, its crew and cargo. In such circumstances, the ship's master was compelled to enter the blockaded area to seek refuge. Indeed, only a compelled entry would afford a defence in these circumstances.[66] The entry into the blockaded area must be, in the words of Henry and Bargrave Deane,[67] William Hall[68] and Godfrey Lushington,[69] the consequence of 'an absolute necessity'.

Despite the use of different terminology, judges and scholars across the Channel and across the Atlantic were articulating the same concern: that there existed exceptional and extraordinary circumstances (a situation of distress) in which a ship's master was compelled or forced to put into a blockaded port. In these circumstances of peril, frequently caused by superior forces of nature (the *forces majeures*), the vessel entering the blockaded port should not be subjected to the penalties imposed for blockade violation. The defence of distress thus performed, in the context of blockades, the same function that the right of refuge performed in the law of the sea generally: to exempt from responsibility those vessels entering into prohibited waters when necessary to protect the vessels, life on board, and even the ship's cargo.

### 9.2.3 Distress and Humanitarian Considerations

The right of refuge of ships in distress, as well as the defence to the violation of blockades, were expressions of humanitarian considerations. It

---

[61] *The Major Barbour* (1862) Blatchford 167, 171. Further, *The Courier* (1810), Edwards 249, 250–1 (a 'case of necessity'); *The Rising Dawn* (1863), Blatchford 368, 369.
[62] *The Diana* at 360–1.
[63] *The Eleanor*, 161.
[64] *The Charlotta*, 253.
[65] Also the *The Hurtige Hane* (1799) 2 C Rob 124 (want of water); and *The Fortuna* (1803) 5 C Rob 27 (want of provisions, strong winds).
[66] E.g., *The Panaghia Rhomba* (1858) 2 Roscoe 635, 637 ('the attempt to enter Odessa was the result of imperative and overruling compulsion').
[67] Bargrave Deane, *Blockade*, 39.
[68] Hall, *International Law* (1880), 628.
[69] Similarly, Lushington, *A Manual of Naval Prize Law* (1866), 51.

was for this reason that the exception was granted to *any* ship in distress, regardless of its character, whether in peace or in war.[70] Indeed, precisely because of the humanitarian aims of these institutions, refuge was sometimes offered even to privateers.[71] These humanitarian aims were explicitly referred to both in practice and by scholars. In the literature, the reference to these considerations can be found across many centuries. Among the early-modern natural lawyers, Grotius grounded the right of refuge of ships in distress on 'maxims of natural equity';[72] for Pufendorf it would have been a 'barbarous inhumanity, to deny the liberty of harmless access to shore' in these cases;[73] and for Burlamaqui this was a right arising 'purely from humanity'.[74] Vattel too recognised humanitarian treatment for distressed vessels.[75] The emphasis placed on humanitarian considerations by these authors is not in the least surprising in view of their – very frequently – religious background and the natural law tradition within which they were writing. These pious responses were nevertheless not affected by the materialisation of Grotius' impious hypothesis. Though the inexistence of God had not (and has not) been proved, his existence had become irrelevant to the positive international lawyers of the nineteenth century. Even so, humanitarian considerations did not disappear from the understanding of these situations. Indeed, similar remarks could be found in the writings of nineteenth-century scholars. Thus, Bluntschli,[76] Georges Bry,[77] Carlos Calvo,[78] Pasquale Fiore,[79] Henry Halleck,[80] Laurent Hautefeuille,[81] Ernest Nys[82] and Travers Twiss,[83] all emphasised this humanitarian rationale.

---

[70] Morrison, *Refuge*, 10. Note that today, still, the right of refuge is based on humanitarian considerations.
[71] E.g., Twiss, *Law of Nations*, 2nd edn, 451.
[72] Grotius, *De jure belli ac pacis libri tres, 1625* (2005), II.2.§vi.3.
[73] Pufendorf, *Of the Law of Nature and Nations* (Kennet trans., 4th edn, 1729), III.3.§viii.
[74] Burlamaqui, *The Principles of Natural and Politic Law* (2006), IV.2.§xlvi.
[75] Vattel, *The Law of Nations* (2008), II.7.§94.
[76] Bluntschli, *Droit international*, 208.
[77] Bry, *Précis elémentaire de droit international public* (4th edn, 1901), 95, 188–9.
[78] Calvo, *Le droit international théorique et pratique* (3rd edn, 1880) vol. 3, 489.
[79] Fiore, *Nouveau droit international public* (2nd edn, 1885) vol. 1, 541.
[80] Halleck, *International Law*, 171–2. See also Halleck, *Elements of International Law and Laws of War* (1866), 94–5.
[81] Hautefeuille, 1 *Des droits*, 345ff. See also Hautefeuille, *Histoire des origines, des progrès et des variations du droit maritime international* (1858), esp. at 65ff, 239ff, 417ff and 516ff.
[82] Nys, *Le droit international* (1905) vol. 2, 160.
[83] Twiss, *Law of Nations*, 2nd edn, 446.

Prize courts, too, often remarked on the humanitarian aims of these two institutions. J. B. Scott held in *The Eleanor* that a '[r]eal and irresistible distress must be at all times a sufficient passport for human beings under any such application of human laws',[84] a statement endorsed by the US Supreme Court in *The New York*.[85] In *The Nabby*, the Court of Vice Admiralty at Halifax, Nova Scotia, held that '[r]eal distress is a passport even through the savage land, it appeals at once to sentiments universally felt, at its approach, the rigour of law is softened, and the violence of war becomes composed by the sacred influence of humanity.'[86] And early in the twentieth century, the Tribunal in *North Atlantic Fisheries* described the right of refuge as the 'exercise in large measure of those duties of hospitality and humanity which all civilized nations impose upon themselves and expect the performance of from others.'[87]

These references to humanity were, in essence, a showing of compassion for the predicament of the captain and his crew. As Scott put it in *The Eleanor*, any action taken in such difficult circumstances should be viewed 'with tenderness'.[88] Could it have been expected of the ship's master to face the predicament at the cost of his life and that of his crew; and would anyone have behaved differently in the circumstances? As prize courts remarked, the master was forced, coerced, or compelled, to enter into that port – even when the port was closed to him. Sure, the captain chose to enter that port, but the point was that this was not a free choice.[89] Indeed, 'the fact that [the vessel] may be able to come into port under its own power can obviously not be cited as conclusive evidence that the plea is unjustifiable', for if the captain waited until his ship was wrecked then he would 'obviously ... not be using his best judgment'.[90] The best judgment was to seek refuge.

As will be seen in the next section, it was precisely the humanitarian aims of the plea that Ago appealed to, to explain the development and inclusion in the ARS of what became Article 24.

---

[84] *The Eleanor*, 159–60.
[85] *The New York*.
[86] Decided in August 1818, Reported in the *Quebec Mercury* no 43, Tuesday, 27 October 1818, at 356, quoted by Morrison, *Refuge*, 118.
[87] *North Atlantic Coast Fisheries Case (Great Britain/US)* (1910) 11 RIAA 167, 194.
[88] *The Eleanor*, 161.
[89] Thus, where choice was available, courts rejected the plea. A British Court denied the plea as it was not proven that the master of the ship 'could not have gone to another port not blockaded' to seek refuge: *The Panaghia Rhomba*, 638.
[90] *Kate A Hoff (The Rebecca)*, 447.

## 9.3 The Defence of Distress in Contemporary International Law

By the time the ILC commenced its work on state responsibility, international law did not recognise a general defence of distress, applicable in respect of every rule of international law. Accordingly, with few exceptions, scholars did not include a defence of distress in their treatment of state responsibility.[91] One of the few exceptions was Eduardo Jiménez de Aréchaga.[92] In the context of remarks on the plea of necessity, Jiménez de Aréchaga noted that no general defence of necessity was recognised by international law. Rather, international law recognised 'particular rules... making allowance for varying degrees of necessity';[93] that is, international law recognised necessity-inspired rules or, in Heathcote's words, rules in 'necessity's image'. These rules, such as the right of refuge, were adopted in recognition of 'humanitarian considerations', and they concerned the human dimension of the state's organs and not 'the state as a body politic'.[94] While exceptional at the time, Jiménez de Aréchaga's views eventually found a loud outlet: the *Rainbow Warrior* Tribunal, which he had presided.

### 9.3.1 First Reading: Formulating the Defence of Distress in the International Law Commission

#### 9.3.1.1 Ago's 'Relative Impossibility of Performance'

The defence of distress was first formulated by the ILC in 1979, taking inspiration from a proposal in Ago's report on *force majeure*. Ago's report on this defence noted that the same type of supervening events (unforeseen

---

[91] See, e.g., Gemma, *Appunti di diritto internazionale* (1923); de Visscher, 'La responsabilité internationale des Etats', *Bibliotheca Visseriana* (1924) vol. 2, 107; Anzilotti, *Corso di diritto internazionale* (3rd edn, 1928), 413; Cavaglieri, 'Règles générales du droit de la paix' (1929) 26 *Recueil* 311, 554; Strupp, *Eléments du droit international public universel, Européen et Américain* (2nd edn, 1930) vol. 1, 342; and later Strupp, 'Règles générales du droit de la paix' (1934) 47 *Recueil* 259, 557; Bourquin, 'Règles générales du droit de la paix' (1931) 35 *Recueil* 1, 220; Basdevant, 'Règles générales du droit de la paix' (1936) 58 *Recueil* 471; Sánchez de Bustamante y Sirvén, *Droit international public* (1936) vol. 3, 526; Ago, 'Le délit international' (1939) 68 *Recueil* 415, 532; Rousseau, *Principes généraux du droit international public* (1944) vol. 1, 365ff.

[92] The other exception was Rolando Quadri, *Diritto internazionale pubblico* (5th edn, 1968), 226.

[93] Jiménez de Aréchaga, 'International Responsibility' in Sørensen (ed.), *Manual of Public International Law* (1968), 543.

[94] Jiménez de Aréchaga, 'Responsibility', 543. Also Quadri, *Diritto*, 226.

or irresistible) could result in two conceptually distinct situations. First, a supervening event could give rise to an absolute impossibility of performance. This was 'a real and insurmountable situation of being materially unable to act in conformity with the obligation'.[95] As explained in Chapter 7, this was a situation in which the state had in fact no choice but to fail to perform its obligations. For Ago, the failure to perform in these circumstances was 'involuntary'.[96] Second, these supervening events could create a 'relative impossibility' of performance: 'a situation in which the State organ could theoretically comply with the obligation but at the cost of a sacrifice that could not reasonably be required of it'.[97] In the situation of relative impossibility of performance the 'will of the organ exist[ed] *in theory* but in practice [was] nullified by a perilous situation.'[98] In other words, the state organ's freedom to choose to comply with the state's international obligations was constrained by the situation of relative impossibility, and as a result the conduct adopted in the circumstances was, albeit voluntary, not free.[99] This type of situation, Ago noted, was 'more often than not' referred to as *force majeure*, though these situations were also called 'emergency' or '*détresse*'.[100]

As examples of relative impossibility of performance, Ago mentioned the right of refuge of vessels and aircraft in distress.[101] These examples belonged to a narrow and specific context only, so Ago inquired whether there existed 'a rule of general application, valid for conduct not in conformity with an international obligation regardless of the content of the obligation'.[102] Ago reported doctrinal disagreements on the matter,[103] but he noted that in practice the right of refuge had been extended by analogy and included in other international conventions. For example, it had been included as an exception to the prohibition on the discharge of oil into the sea if discharge was necessary 'for the purpose of securing the safety of the ship, preventing damage to the ship or cargo, or saving life

---

[95] Ago, Eighth Report on State Responsibility, ILC Yearbook 1979, vol. II(1), [111].
[96] Ibid., [106].
[97] Id.
[98] Id. (emphasis in original).
[99] Ibid., [135].
[100] Ibid., [129].
[101] Ibid., [130–2].
[102] Ibid., [133].
[103] Ibid., [134] referring to the opposing views of Quadri (noted earlier) and Lamberti-Zanardi (for whom distress applies 'in regard to specific obligations only').

at sea'.[104] While these were particular conventional rules, their 'rationale' could be extended 'if only by analogy' to comparable cases.[105] Ago thus asked: '[w]ould a governmental organ pursued by insurgents or rioters who are determined to destroy it be committing an internationally wrongful act if it sought safety by entering a foreign embassy without permission?'[106] Certainly not, he thought. At any rate, Ago noted that the circumstances in which the defence applied were limited and that the state organ would have 'little material opportunity of breaching many international obligations of its State ... simply in order to save its life in a situation of distress.'[107]

As to the conditions of this circumstance, Ago stated that it was applicable whenever there was a threat to the life or personal integrity of the organ in question: the protection of 'something other than life ... may also represent an interest that is capable of severely restricting an individual's freedom of decision and compel him to act in a manner which is justifiable but not in conformity with an international obligation of the State of which it is an organ.'[108] Ago also added a requirement of proportionality: the defence applied only if the 'interest protected' by the conduct adopted to safeguard the distressed state organ was 'to some extent proportionate to the interest ostensibly protected by the [breached] obligation.'[109] Indeed, the interest pursued by the obligation breached must be 'markedly less important than that of protecting the life of the organ' in question. For example, if the conduct seeking to protect the life of 'one person or of a small group of persons, endangered the life of a greater number of human beings', the defence would be unacceptable.[110]

Ago included this defence in paragraph 2 of Article 31, pursuant to which:

> The international wrongfulness of an act of a State not in conformity with what is required by it by an international obligation is ... precluded if the

---

[104] Ago, Eighth Report, [132]. Quoting, at fn 282, the following: Article IV(1)(a) of the International Convention for the Prevention of Pollution of the Sea by Oil, (1954) 327 UNTS 8, and Article V of the Convention on the Prevention of Marine Pollution by Dumping of Wastes and Other Matter, (1972) 1046 UNTS 120.
[105] Ago, Eighth Report, [134].
[106] Id.
[107] Id.
[108] Ibid., [135].
[109] Ibid., [138] (note that the numbering of the paragraph is out of sequence: it should be numbered '136').
[110] Id.

author of the conduct attributable to the State has no other means of saving himself, or those accompanying him from a situation of distress, and insofar as the conduct in question does not place others in a situation of comparable or greater peril.[111]

### 9.3.1.2  Distress as a Discrete Defence: The Adoption of Draft Article 32 at the International Law Commission

The discussion of Ago's report at the Commission highlighted some disagreement in respect of a defence based on relative impossibility of performance. For the critics, there were two main issues with Ago's proposal. First, they disputed that the general defence could be formulated on the basis of practice in a special field of international law. For example, for Francis Vallat, this generalisation would entail important challenges, 'not the least of which was the meaning of distress itself; what amounted to distress and to whom and in what circumstances it applied'.[112] The problem would be better handled within the specific context in which it had been frequently raised,[113] namely the law of the sea. Second, Commission members questioned the 'human dimension' of the defence: they took issue with the defence's aim to protect the life of state organs '*qua* human beings'.[114] Nikolai Ushakov urged the Commission to confine its work to situations involving the state only.[115] Vallat, in turn, pointed to a difficulty in the provision: if the defence concerned individuals and the decision to breach the international obligation of the state was left to the individual alone, then the link between that individual as a state organ and the state would be severed.[116] Supporters did not think these difficulties were insurmountable.[117] In particular, in respect of the human dimension of the plea, Paul Reuter pointed out that it was not unusual to refer to the state organ separately from the state: the Vienna Convention on the Law of Treaties, for example, contained provisions on coercion of the state and coercion of a state organ.[118] Besides, as Ago reminded

---

[111] Ibid., [153].
[112] Vallat, 1572nd meeting, ILC Yearbook 1979, vol. I, 202 [2].
[113] Id.
[114] Ago, 1573rd meeting, ILC Yearbook 1979, vol. I, 207 [9].
[115] Ushakov, 1572nd meeting, ILC Yearbook 1979, vol. I, 204 [14].
[116] Vallat, 1572nd meeting, 202 [3].
[117] Some members thought it enshrined a 'general principle': Reuter, 1571st meeting, ILC Yearbook 1979, vol. I, 200 [27]; Sucharitkul, 1572nd meeting, ILC Yearbook 1979, vol. I, 202 [5].
[118] Reuter, 1571st meeting, 200 [26].

the Commission, the provision could not exclude the so-called 'human dimension': 'it was not the State itself but its agent that was in such a situation. The fact that a human being was at the centre of the situation could not be disregarded'.[119]

On the whole the ILC was satisfied with the provision and decided to retain it. However, the Commission considered that, partly due to the 'human dimension' of distress, 'relative impossibility' was sufficiently different from *force majeure* (the situation of 'absolute impossibility') to warrant its treatment in an autonomous provision.[120] The Commission thus adopted draft Article 32, pursuant to which:

> The wrongfulness of an act of a State not in conformity with an international obligation of that State is precluded if the author of the conduct which constitutes the act of that State had no other means, in a situation of extreme distress, of saving his life or that of persons entrusted to his care.[121]

The Commission's draft commentary broadly traced Ago's report. It explained that in cases of distress the conduct in question was not 'entirely involuntary' since the state organ has, if only theoretically, a choice between complying with the international obligation and saving himself. Further, it characterised this choice as not 'a real choice' or 'free choice' since the state organ was aware that by adopting 'the conduct required by the international obligation he, and the persons entrusted to his care, will almost inevitably perish'. In these circumstances, the possibility of acting in accordance with the international obligation is 'only apparent' since it is 'nullified' by the extreme peril.[122]

### 9.3.2  State Reactions and the Rainbow Warrior *Affair (1979–1999)*

#### 9.3.2.1  State Reactions to Draft Article 32

States expressed conflicting views on draft Article 32 in the Sixth Committee and in observations submitted to the ILC. A number of states,

---

[119] Ago, 1573rd meeting, 206-7 [8]. A view shared by Quentin-Baxter, 1572nd meeting, ILC Yearbook 1979, vol. I, 204 [17].
[120] See, e.g., Reuter, 1571st meeting, 200 [28]; Vallat, 1571st meeting, ILC Yearbook 1979, vol. I, 201 [31]; Vallat, 1572nd meeting, 202 [1]; Tsuruoka, 1572nd meeting, ILC Yearbook 1979, vol. I, 205 [21].
[121] Riphagen, 1579th meeting, ILC Yearbook 1979, vol. I, 234 [5].
[122] ILC Report, thirty-first session, ILC Yearbook 1979, vol. II(2), 133 [2].

including Austria,[123] India,[124] Jordan,[125] Kenya,[126] Mongolia[127] and the United States,[128] found the provision to be acceptable. For Italy it was a 'classical [case] for precluding wrongfulness',[129] and for Chile the defence was acceptable since 'requirements of elementary justice called for certain exceptions to the normal rule'.[130] Other states, however, found the provision to be problematic. In particular, the Netherlands,[131] Sweden[132] and Ukraine[133] questioned the Commission's formulation of a general defence on the back of practice existing within a specialised field. For Byelorussia (as it then was) the draft article 'provided for separate, private cases of distress'.[134] For France, the provision needed further study.[135]

Few states addressed this defence in written observations submitted to the ILC in the following years: Mongolia objected to its inclusion;[136] Japan wished to expand the plea to cover other 'vital interests' of individuals, including economic interests;[137] and the United Kingdom wished to expand it to the protection of individuals *not* entrusted to the care of a state organ, so as to make allowances for 'emergency humanitarian action'.[138] France – not without some irony, as will be seen in the next section – wished to word it more narrowly to avoid its invocation 'for injurious ends'.[139]

---

[123] A/C.6/34/SR.47, [61].
[124] A/C.6/34/SR.51, [63].
[125] A/C.6/34/SR.51, [56].
[126] A/C.6/34/SR.43, [4].
[127] A/C.6/34/SR.50, [38]. In written comments to the ILC, Mongolia later requested that defence be formulated more precisely: Comments of Governments on Part I of the Draft Articles on State Responsibility for Internationally Wrongful Acts, A/CN.4/342 and Add.1–4, ILC Yearbook 1981, vol. II(1), [7].
[128] A/C.6/34/SR.45, [4].
[129] A/C.6/34/SR.47, [25].
[130] A/C.6/35/SR.47, [7].
[131] Comments and Observations of Governments on Part One of the Draft Articles on State Responsibility for Internationally Wrongful Acts, A/CN.4/351 and Add.1–3, ILC Yearbook 1982, vol. II(1), 19.
[132] A/CN.4/342 and Add.1–4, 77.
[133] A/C.6/34/SR.47, [46].
[134] A/C.6/34/SR.44, [22].
[135] A/C.6/34/SR.48, [13].
[136] Comments by Governments on All the Draft Articles, UN Doc A/CN.4/488 and Add.1–3, ILC Yearbook 1998, vol. II(1), 134.
[137] Comments and Observations Received from Governments, A/CN.4/492, ILC Yearbook 1999, vol. II(1), 107.
[138] A/CN.4/488, 134.
[139] Id.

### 9.3.2.2 Boosting the Defence: The *Rainbow Warrior* Arbitration

More than anything else, however, it was the award in *Rainbow Warrior* that cemented distress as a defence in the law of responsibility. The *Rainbow Warrior* Tribunal was deaf to the mixed reception of draft Article 32 in the Sixth Committee just reviewed: it endorsed the defence in no uncertain terms, relying only on the work of the ILC and the scholarly views of the Tribunal's own president.[140]

The sinking of the Greenpeace ship and its context were explained at some length in the Introduction to this study. Of relevance here are only the facts relating to the repatriation of the two French agents. To recall, Major Mafart and Captain Prieur were bound to spend three years in isolation in a French Military facility in Hao, as decided by the UN Secretary-General. Pursuant to the Secretary-General's Ruling, the agents could not be removed before the expiry of the three years without the 'mutual consent' of the parties.[141] Mafart and Prieur were duly transferred by New Zealand to French authorities, and they arrived in Hao on 22 July 1986. In 1987, France requested New Zealand's consent to repatriate Mafart alleging a medical emergency.[142] The following year, France requested the consent of New Zealand to repatriate Prieur, initially alleging pregnancy-related complications[143] and subsequently invoking 'humanitarian considerations' in view of her father's terminal illness.[144] In both instances, New Zealand asked that France allow its appointed physician to examine the agents and verify the severity of their medical conditions. France thwarted New Zealand's efforts on both occasions, invoking time constraints and (domestic) legal impediments to the access of foreign aircraft to its military facility in Hao.[145] France eventually repatriated the agents unilaterally. Mafart left on a military aircraft,[146] and Prieur on a

---

[140] For a critique of this endorsement, see Davidson, 'The *Rainbow Warrior* Arbitration Concerning the Treatment of the French Agents Mafart and Prieur' (1991) 40 ICLQ 446, 456; Weil, 'Le droit international en quête de son identité: cours général de droit international public' (1992) 237 *Recueil* 11, 175–7.

[141] *UN Secretary-General: Ruling on the Rainbow Warrior Affair between France and New Zealand* (1987) 26 ILM 1346, 1370.

[142] For the facts concerning Mafart's case, see *Rainbow Warrior (New Zealand v France)* (1990) 20 RIAA 215, 226–40.

[143] Ibid., [47–8]. The facts concerning Prieur's case are summarised at *Rainbow Warrior*, 240–4.

[144] Ibid., [52].

[145] Ibid., [22, 24, 30] (Mafart); [51–4] (Prieur).

[146] Ibid., [25].

special flight that had been arranged from Paris.[147] Only Mafart's medical condition was later confirmed to have required treatment not available in Hao by a New Zealand appointed physician, who examined Mafart in Paris.[148] Neither agent returned to Hao to complete the three-year period of isolation after the stabilisation of the medical reasons that required their repatriation. New Zealand claimed that France had thus breached its obligations under the Secretary-General's Ruling and, after fruitless attempts to reach a diplomatic solution, the dispute was submitted to arbitration.

Before the Tribunal, France attempted to explain its conduct by invoking 'the whole theory of special circumstances that exclude or "attenuate" illegality'.[149] According to France, its actions had responded to what it variously described as 'circumstances of extreme urgency',[150] 'obvious humanitarian considerations'[151] and the 'very special circumstances' of the case.[152] There is no evidence in the award of a French invocation of draft Article 32 or of any direct reliance on a defence of distress; but it may be worth recalling that only a few years earlier, France had been very sceptical of this draft provision.[153] New Zealand interpreted France's argument as based on 'factors beyond France's control, such as humanitarian reasons of extreme urgency making the action necessary'[154] to which, it thought, the defences of *force majeure* and distress may be relevant. In any event, New Zealand argued, these defences were not applicable to treaty breaches.[155]

In addressing these arguments, the Tribunal relied heavily on the ILC work on state responsibility.[156] Among the 'circumstances precluding

---

[147] Ibid., [56].
[148] Ibid., [28].
[149] Ibid., [76].
[150] Ibid., [71].
[151] Ibid., [70].
[152] Ibid., [66].
[153] A/C.6/34/SR.48, [13].
[154] *Rainbow Warrior*, [73].
[155] New Zealand's main argument in this regard was that the defences from the law of responsibility were not applicable to treaty breaches, since the VCLT already contained (specific) provisions on suspension and termination. As is well-known, the Tribunal rejected the argument affirming, in no uncertain terms, that the law of responsibility was applicable generally, regardless of the conventional origin of the obligation at issue: *Rainbow Warrior*, [73].
[156] Relying perhaps too heavily on the ILC's work: Charpentier, 'L'affaire du *Rainbow Warrior*: la sentence arbitrale du 30 avril 1990 (Nouvelle Zélande c. France)' (1990) 36 AFDI 395, 397.

wrongfulness' adopted by the Commission, the Tribunal found that the defence relevant to the case was that of distress, a defence which involved 'elementary humanitarian considerations'.[157] The Tribunal's exposition of this defence closely traced the ILC's commentary adopted on first reading and stated that the defence concerned cases of extreme urgency in which the life or physical integrity of a state organ was under threat. It recalled that in the situation of distress, the state organ's free will was curtailed such that its decision whether to comply with the state's obligation was therefore not a 'real' or 'free' one. Equally, the Tribunal noted that state practice on distress usually concerned boundary violations by vessels or aircraft, but, citing the Commission's work, it maintained that it was 'applicable, if only by analogy, to other comparable cases'.[158] The Tribunal then stated that draft Article 32 had been 'generally accepted'[159] and backed this affirmation with only two sources: the ILC work and one scholarly opinion. As to the former, the reception of draft Article 32 by states in the Sixth Committee had been rather ambivalent, as was just seen. As to the latter, this was the Tribunal president's own scholarly work. The award quoted a passage from Max Sørensen's edited *Manual of Public International Law*, in which Jiménez de Aréchaga denied that state of necessity was a general rule in international law and that, instead, there existed specific rules allowing for varying degrees of necessity. These specific rules reflected, moreover, not the principle of necessity, but humanitarian considerations. Remarkably, the author's name was missing from the source provided in the citation.[160]

Having found that this defence was relevant to the case, the Tribunal proceeded to reformulate the question that it had to address. For the Tribunal, a successful invocation of distress required that France prove the following three requirements:

1. The existence of very exceptional circumstances of extreme urgency involving medical or other considerations of an elementary nature, provided always that a prompt recognition of the existence of those exceptional circumstances is subsequently obtained from the other interested party or is clearly demonstrated.

---

[157] *Rainbow Warrior*, [78].
[158] Id.
[159] Id.
[160] Id. Indeed, the quotation is often attributed to Sørensen; see, e.g., Chatterjee, 'The *Rainbow Warrior* Arbitration between New Zealand and France' (1992) 9 *J Int'l Arb* 17, 27.

2. The reestablishment of the original situation of compliance with the assignment in Hao as soon as the reasons of emergency invoked to justify the repatriation disappeared.
3. The existence of a good faith effort to try to obtain the consent of New Zealand in terms of the 1986 Agreement.[161]

In this reformulation, the Tribunal had transformed the obligation not to remove the agents without the 'mutual consent' of the parties into an obligation of best efforts: France did not need to obtain consent, it only needed to show that it had attempted to do so in good faith. This manoeuvre had a fundamental impact on the role played by distress in the application of the relevant law to the facts. Indeed, the transformation of the obligation of result (to obtain consent) into an obligation of conduct (to attempt to obtain consent in good faith) had the effect of collapsing the defence into the obligation itself: the factual situation of distress (the medical emergency) thus became relevant evidence of the good faith of France such that if it could be proved that the fact existed, then France would not have been in breach of its obligations. This is precisely what the Tribunal went on to find in respect of Mafart: France had notified New Zealand of Mafart's condition; an examination by a New Zealand physician in Hao would have been impossible; and, eventually, his condition was confirmed by a New Zealand-appointed physician in Paris. These facts evidenced that France's attempt to obtain New Zealand's consent had been done in good faith. Consequently, France had not breached its obligation (as the Tribunal had reformulated it).[162] As to the 'extreme urgency and the humanitarian considerations invoked by France', these, said the Tribunal, '*may* have been circumstances excluding responsibility for the unilateral removal ... of Mafart'.[163] But they were not necessary: France's conduct did not contravene its obligation. Contrary to arbitrator Keith's views in dissent,[164] the conduct of France was lawful because it *fulfilled* its obligations and not as a result of the application of distress as a circumstance precluding wrongfulness. In the case of Prieur the Tribunal found that France had breached its obligation to request in good faith New Zealand's consent. Her pregnancy did not show the need for medical attention unavailable in Hao,[165] and her removal had been presented

---

[161] *Rainbow Warrior*, [79].
[162] Ibid., [80–8].
[163] Ibid., [99] (emphasis added).
[164] Ibid., diss op Keith, 276 [4].
[165] Ibid., [99].

by France as a *fait accompli*.¹⁶⁶ Moreover, since there was no situation of 'extreme urgency' or 'humanitarian considerations' the 'responsibility' of France could not be excluded on these grounds.¹⁶⁷

The Tribunal thus endorsed the plea of distress as formulated by the ILC, but did not actually apply it to justify (or excuse) the conduct of France. For even in the case of Mafart, often cited as an instance of the successful application of the plea, the Tribunal's reasoning was such that the formulation of the obligation of France had 'swallowed' the defence: the situation of distress was, therefore, merely a fact that could prove France's good faith efforts to obtain the consent of New Zealand. Nevertheless, the award was certainly significant in one respect: it alerted to a situation, beyond the traditional ones involving trespass into foreign territory to seek refuge, in which the plea developed by the Commission would have been relevant. Even though doubts may have lingered as to the customary character of the plea, it had become clear that a general defence of distress was (potentially) necessary in international law.

### 9.3.3 *Progressive Development and the Adoption of Article 24*

The final Special Rapporteur, James Crawford, took notice of these (and other)¹⁶⁸ developments in his report of 1999,¹⁶⁹ and argued in favour of retaining the defence in the draft. It was clear to the Commission that the defence did not have customary status and that the generality of the defence was 'a novel feature of draft article 32'; the draft Article was, in short, a 'case of progressive development'.¹⁷⁰ Nevertheless, Crawford gave at least three reasons in support of retaining it. First, the defence had received a 'generally favourable response' from states.¹⁷¹ Second, the defence of distress was relevant also 'outside the context of ships or aircraft', as the *Rainbow Warrior* award had demonstrated.¹⁷² Finally, and in response to critics within the ILC, Crawford argued that a defence of distress was necessary to address the inter-state consequences of the exercise of the right of refuge by public ships. On this last point, the Special Rapporteur disagreed with those members of the Commission who

---

¹⁶⁶ Ibid., [94–5].
¹⁶⁷ Ibid., [99].
¹⁶⁸ Including the codification of the right of refuge in Article 18(2) of UNCLOS.
¹⁶⁹ Crawford, Second Report on State Responsibility, ILC Yearbook 1999, vol. II(1), [270].
¹⁷⁰ ILC Report, fifty-first session, ILC Yearbook 1999, vol. II(2), 81 [365].
¹⁷¹ Crawford, Second Report, [272].
¹⁷² Ibid., [271].

thought that the defence of distress was irrelevant since the circumstances in which it could arise were covered by the right of refuge. In his view, even in the case of the right of refuge, the defence was necessary. Indeed, the right of refuge extended only to the captain of the vessel in his private capacity, but it said nothing about the encroachment of his national state on the territory of the coastal state. According to Crawford:

> In practice, although the primary rules might provide a defence for the individual captain of a ship ... they were not applicable to the issue of State responsibility. Where the captain was a State official, his or her conduct was attributable to the State and raised the question of the responsibility of that State [for the violation of the coastal State's territorial integrity]. Hence the need for a draft article on distress.[173]

Crawford's point was based on what may be called the *dédoublement* of the ship's master as an individual and as a state organ. The right of refuge covered him as an individual: it exempted him, personally, from the legal consequences of his entry into a prohibited port arising under the domestic law of the coastal state. But it did not cover him as a state organ – thus, the state's responsibility could still be engaged insofar as the organ's conduct was attributable to it and that conduct involved a trespass into another state's territory. Thus, a defence of distress was necessary to explain why the entry was not a breach of the flag state's international obligations.

Crawford also proposed some modifications to the scope of the plea and to the text of the draft Article. First, the plea had to be limited to situations in which human life was at stake. To extend the defence to threats to the agent's personal integrity raised the question of where to draw the lower limit. Second, the defence should be available where the state organ 'reasonably believed' that the situation was life-threatening. The threat to life must 'be apparent and have some basis in fact', but it was the case that 'in situations of genuine distress' there may not be time to conduct the necessary perusal to determine the actuality of the danger.[174] For this reason, it was better to frame the defence in terms of the state organ's 'reasonable belief in a life-threatening situation'.[175] Finally, Crawford also rejected the proposal to extend the defence to individuals not related to the state, as had been argued by the United Kingdom as seen earlier. Crawford's rejection of this proposal was grounded on the rationale of the defence:

---

[173] ILC Report, fifty-first session, 81 [364].
[174] Crawford, Second Report, [273].
[175] Id.

the compulsion induced in the state organ by the situation of distress. When the situation threatened the lives of individuals not linked to the state, then the state organ may have a moral duty to act to save lives, but the circumstances could not be said to provoke a compulsion to act. As such they fell outside the scope of the defence.[176]

The plea of distress did not give rise to many disagreements in the Commission. On the whole, its members supported the Special Rapporteur's proposal to limit the defence to cases involving a threat to the lives of the state organ or individuals entrusted to his care.[177] Crawford's most controversial proposal, the inclusion of the criterion of 'reasonable belief', was eventually accepted albeit in modified form.[178] While Commission members feared that the inclusion of that expression might render the defence too subjective,[179] they accepted the gist of the proposal. Namely, the recognition that in situations of distress the state organ in question might not have the time (or means) at his disposal to carefully assess the reality of the risk to his life or that of persons entrusted to his care. The point was that '[s]ituations of that kind called for a certain latitude within the limits of which immediate measures had to be taken'.[180]

Few states commented on what became Article 24 in the Sixth Committee. States were generally supportive of the defence, though they criticised certain aspects of its formulation.[181] Only Poland objected to the inclusion of a discrete provision of distress,[182] and India was the only state to characterise the defence as a circumstance precluding responsibility: it was a circumstance which 'exonerate[d] the state from the consequences of wrongful conduct'.[183] With the overall backing of the General Assembly, the Commission adopted Article 24, in the terms quoted in the introduction to this chapter.

---

[176] Crawford, 2592nd meeting, ILC Yearbook 1999, vol. I, 180 [40].
[177] E.g., Rosenstock, 2591st meeting, ILC Yearbook 1999, vol. I, 171 [24]; Kateka, 2591st meeting, ILC Yearbook 1999, vol. I, 171 [22]; Kamto, 2592nd meeting, ILC Yearbook 1999, vol. I, 179 [30]. Cf. Pellet, 2591st meeting, ILC Yearbook 1999, vol. I, 172 [30].
[178] Candioti, 2605th meeting, ILC Yearbook 1999, vol. I, 282–3 [60–1].
[179] It was criticised by Economides, 2591st meeting, ILC Yearbook 1999, vol. I, 173 [36]; Kamto, 2592nd meeting, 179 [31].
[180] Crawford, 2592nd meeting, 180 [39].
[181] The Netherlands and Slovakia objected to the criterion of 'reasonable belief' as it added an element of subjectivity to the defence which could lead to its abuse: A/C.6/54/SR.21, [49], and A/C.6/54/SR.22, [55], respectively. The Czech Republic, in turn, approved of the limitation of the defence to situations in which there existed a threat to life: A/C.6/54/SR.22, [38].
[182] A/C.6/56/SR.13, [32–3].
[183] A/C.6/54/SR.23, [33].

### 9.3.4 Customary Status Pending

Since the adoption of the ARS in 2001, there have been no invocations of distress as a defence to state responsibility. The question as to its customary status, therefore, remains pending. On second reading, states showed an overall favourable disposition towards it; but on the whole, only very few states actually expressed any views – thus falling well short of the requirement of generality of state practice and *opinio juris* necessary to identify a customary rule. To be sure, the defence is certainly an important one, given its express humanitarian purpose of protecting the lives of state organs (or others entrusted to their care). Moreover, as Crawford pointed out, it seems that the defence is analytically necessary to exclude any state responsibility issues in the exercise of the right of refuge by public vessels. It may also be that the defence becomes a practically relevant one in the future. Given the trend among coastal states to limit the exercise right of refuge, highlighted in Section 9.2.1, often denying altogether this right, it may be queried whether (public) vessels in distress may choose nevertheless to defy these orders and put into port to seek refuge.

## 9.4 Classifying Distress as Justification or Excuse

The final question that remains to be considered is whether the defence of distress should be classified as a justification or an excuse. The materials reviewed thus far present an equivocal picture. On the one hand, much emphasis is placed on the humanitarian aims of the plea, on how it cannot be expected of a state organ to comply with the state's obligations when in distress, and on the compulsion or coercion exerted by the situation of distress on the state organ's free will. As will be seen, all of these indications point in the direction of the classification of the plea as an excuse. On the other hand, however, there is some emphasis on the balancing of interests at the core of the plea: the interest in life (that of the organ or others entrusted to his care) and the interest protected by the obligation impaired in the circumstances. This emphasis, instead, points in the direction of the classification of the plea as a justification. Both possibilities will be reviewed in turn, before providing some concluding remarks.

### 9.4.1 Distress as an Excuse

The defence of distress in Article 24 has a humanitarian aim; in this, it shares the same rationale as the right of refuge and the defence to blockade

## 9.4 DISTRESS AS JUSTIFICATION OR EXCUSE

violations. These humanitarian aims of the plea are uncontroversial. In *Rainbow Warrior* the Tribunal specifically referred to the 'elementary humanitarian considerations' involved in the plea: must a human being perish, to ensure international law is respected? For Ago, this much could not be expected of anyone; when the state organ faces threats to his life, or to the life of those entrusted to his care, it can simply not be required of that state organ, as an individual, to act in accordance with the state's obligations.

The prize case-law on blockade violations, as well as the work of the ILC on the defence of distress indicate that the conduct adopted by the distressed state organ is a coerced one.[184] In the circumstances of distress, the state organ is compelled to act in a manner inconsistent with the state's international obligations. As the Commentary clarifies, this conduct is not a free one. Sure, the state organ voluntarily performs the conduct; but his freedom to choose how to act 'is effectively nullified by the situation of peril'.[185] The state organ can perform the obligation in the sense that it is materially possible for him to do so; but this is not a feasible option. Distress, in this sense, shares the same explanation as *force majeure* and as the (potential) excuse of necessity: in all cases, the state is compelled by the circumstances to adopt a course of conduct which is incompatible with its obligations; this is a course of conduct which impairs the rights of a third (innocent) state. However, as explained in Chapter 7, these defences differ in respect of the degree of impossibility caused by the circumstances and this has an impact on the degree of coercion (or, from the opposite angle, the extent of the choice available to the state). *Force majeure* requires an impossibility that is absolute: the state has no option but to fail to perform the obligation. Absent any choice in the matter, the state's conduct must be considered involuntary. In the case of distress, instead, the impossibility is only relative: the state organ has a number of options for it can choose to perish, or it can choose to save its life and, in this case, a number of more or less onerous options may be open to it. Nevertheless, it cannot be expected of the state organ to sacrifice its life (or that of individuals entrusted to his care), so even if this is an option it is not a feasible one. The state organ is therefore coerced to choose the option which while protecting its life, entails non-performance of the

---

[184] See, e.g., Ago, Eighth Report, [106, 135]; Crawford, 2592nd meeting, [40].
[185] ARS art. 24 Commentary, [1]. In the literature, see Capotorti, 'Cours général de droit international public' (1994) 248 *Recueil* 9, 259; Scalese, *Scusanti*, 102–3; Szurek, 'Distress', 483; Crawford, *State Responsibility: The General Part* (2013), 301.

obligation of the state of which it is an organ. The conduct is voluntary, but it is not an entirely free one.

That the coercion envisaged by the plea relates to the state organ rather than to the state itself (as in *force majeure* or the potential excuse of necessity)[186] is not problematic. It is, rather, an expression of the so-called 'human dimension' of distress, a dimension which was criticised by several members of the Commission. Yet, this 'human dimension' is certainly not an anomaly in international law. As pointed out by Reuter during the first reading of the provision, the law of treaties, for instance, takes into account situations in which a treaty has been entered into through coercion of the state's representative. Thus, VCLT Article 51 establishes that '[t]he expression of a State's consent to be bound by a treaty which has been procured by the coercion of its representative through acts or threats directed against him shall be without legal effect.' The threats are not against the state, but against the state organ itself: VCLT Article 51, like Article 24, regards the state organ *as an individual*.[187] This human dimension means that the plea contains an element of subjectivity (precisely what certain ILC members disliked about it). Thus, the situation of distress and the state organ's response must be analysed from the point of view of the state organ at the time. Of course, there are some limits: the situation of distress must have some basis in fact. But some flexibility must be allowed to the state organ, as he may be required to act at once without being able to ascertain the gravity of the threat, or to consider multiple possible ways of averting the danger. Subjectivity, in this context, does not mean arbitrariness. Subjectivity, however, is a significant factor for the classification of the plea as a justification or an excuse. As discussed in Chapter 1 and Chapter 3, excuses are primarily subjective defences in the sense that the focus of analysis in an excuse defence is the agent itself, rather than the act.

Coercion-based theories, as was seen in Chapters 7 and 8, on *force majeure* and state of necessity respectively, are traditionally seen in domestic law as grounding excuse-defences. An agent can be responsible insofar as its acts are freely adopted; by the same token, responsibility

---

[186] As noted by Enrique Candioti, it is 'the author of the act, and not the State, that [is] in distress': Candioti, 2605th meeting, [61]. See also Nollkaemper, 'Concurrence between Individual Responsibility and State Responsibility in International Law' (2003) 52 ICLQ 615, 635 ('the distress of the individual author of the act, not of an abstract state').

[187] On which see Tenekides, 'Les effets de la contrainte sur les traités à la lumière de la Convention de Vienne du 23 mai 1969' (1974) 20 AFDI 79; Distefano, 'Article 51 (1969)' in Corten and Klein (eds), *The Vienna Conventions on the Law of Treaties: A Commentary* (2011) vol. 2, 1179.

may be diminished or even excluded if the act is not the product of free choice. This being the case, the defence of distress could be classified as an excuse – a classification which, as seen, is in keeping with its subjective character.

Nevertheless, a coercion theory and, therefore, a classification of the plea as an excuse, cannot account for the limitations imposed on the defence. Thus, if the point is that the state is excused because its agent's freedom to choose was diminished – why is it relevant that the choice causes an equal or greater peril? The rationale concerns the actor, not the consequences of its act. For similar reasons, it seems irrelevant what the origins of the peril are: be they exogenous or endogenous, or a combination thereof. So long as there is a situation of distress and the conduct adopted by the state is the only reasonable way to protect its interests – then the invoking state will have been coerced. This is not to say that no limitations can be recognised. But it must nevertheless be acknowledged that these requirements and conditions are ad hoc and external to the plea's underlying theory.[188]

### 9.4.2 Distress as a Justification

The other alternative is to classify the plea as a justification. Indeed, as formulated in the ARS and explained in the Commentary, distress could also be characterised as a justification on the basis of a lesser evils theory: as was just seen, there is some element of balancing between interests in the plea. The humanitarian aims of the plea can indeed be accommodated in an interest-balancing framework: states may agree that the interest in the protection of life is superior to other interests protected by international law. As a result, this interest ought to prevail whenever it comes into conflict with any of the other interests safeguarded by international legal norms.[189] As the Commentary explains:

> Distress can only preclude wrongfulness where the interests sought to be protected (e.g. the lives of passengers or crew) clearly outweigh the other interests at stake in the circumstances. If the conduct sought to be excused

---

[188] This is not problematic, given that the current requirements and conditions are largely accepted. However, it could be more problematic for new restrictions to the plea: the possibility of grounding restrictions or expansions of any rule on its own rationale may go some way to legitimating it and render it more acceptable to states. There may be some more reticence where the restrictions may not be brought back to the underlying rationale of the defence, as exemplified by the suspicion with which some of the restrictions imposed on countermeasures were received in the ILC, on which see Chapter 6.
[189] ARS art. 24(2).

endangers more lives than it may save or is otherwise likely to create a greater peril it will not be covered by the plea of distress.[190]

In contrast with the state of necessity, where the interest sought to be protected is undetermined (it simply has to be 'essential'), in the case of distress the rule itself stipulates the specific interest for which it is available: the protection of life. Nevertheless, this interest is not superior in all circumstances: its superiority is relative and the plea is excluded when the act is 'likely to create a comparable or greater peril' than the one avoided. The determination of the relative weight of these interests is contextual and will depend on qualitative and quantitative elements, that is the substance of the obligations at issue as well as the degree of the potential harm caused. In addition, as the Commentary explains, the words 'comparable or greater peril' in Article 24(2) 'must be assessed in the context of the overall purpose of saving lives.'[191] In this way, the Commentary gives this balancing exercise an explicit teleological flavour: it is not just an assessment of the competing weights of two interests, but of their competing weight in relation to the protection of life.

The lesser evils explanation for this defence is capable of grounding the requirement of proportionality: as noted in previous chapters, proportionality is inherent in the theory of lesser evils. It is also capable of accommodating limits as to the means employed (the 'no other reasonable way' requirement) as an unreasonable way may result in comparable or greater peril. Nevertheless, this theoretical explanation is incapable of accounting for the requirement of non-contribution to the situation of distress. After all, if what matters is the protection of the superior interest in the circumstances, then it should be irrelevant where the peril originated, be it in endogenous or exogenous causes to the invoking state. Moreover, while the humanitarian aims of the plea can be reconciled with the theory, this explanation falls short of accommodating its human dimension, namely 'the fact that a human being was at the centre of the situation'.[192] The defence is a recognition of human frailty, of the fact that human beings are not required to act like heroes, to sacrifice themselves on the altar of the law when doing so comes at the cost of their own existence – and a superior interests rationale fails to capture this by obscuring the actor in order to focus on the act and the net-benefit achieved by the act.

---

[190] ARS art. 24 Commentary, [10].
[191] Id.
[192] Ago, 1573rd meeting, 206–7 [8]. A view shared by Quentin-Baxter, 1572nd meeting, ILC Yearbook 1979, vol. I, 204 [17].

### 9.4.3 *Justification or Excuse?*

Positive law, by way of the practice and *opinio juris* of states, is silent on this question – indeed, it is still debatable whether the defence of distress is recognised as part of customary law at all. In addition, the little practice that exists in this regard is insufficient to determine whether, in the views of states, the defence should be classified as a justification or an excuse. As was seen, only one state, India, expressly stated in its observations on past drafts of Article 24 that this defence should be classified as an excuse. Arguably, one could attribute to France the view that the plea acts as a justification given the way in which it presented its defence in *Rainbow Warrior*. But then this could be contradicted by the view expressed in the Sixth Committee that all defences in the ARS must constitute excuses since they are secondary rules.[193] In the absence of any practice from which to glean the views of states on this question, the classification of distress as a justification or an excuse cannot be performed following a bottom-up approach, an approach which is most in keeping with the consensual basis of international law. A top-down approach will therefore be necessary, one that takes into account a variety of factors starting from the concepts of justification and excuse, the formulation of the defence, and potential implications of each classification.

In the case of distress, the centre of gravity of the plea seems to be the state organ and not its act: the focus is on the situation of the state organ, whether its life or that of individuals entrusted to his care were in danger, and how he decided to act to avert that danger. The requirement that the act not cause an equal or greater peril is of course a relevant one, but it seems to operate more as a limitation of the plea (that is, the plea will fail in these circumstances) than as its main consideration. This fact would militate in favour of its classification as an excuse. Likewise, as already mentioned, the classification of the plea as an excuse is more likely to capture the human dimension of the plea: the fact that its recognition is an acknowledgment of human frailty and that there exist circumstances capable of bending the will of individuals. If the plea were a justification, by contrast, it would focus on the act and whether the act in question achieved the purpose of saving life.

In terms of the implications of classifying distress as a justification or an excuse, the classification of the plea as an excuse is likely to undercut

---

[193] A/C.6/56/SR.11, [70].

the very humanitarian aim of the plea by maintaining the wrongfulness of the conduct in question. Indeed, this consideration might discourage state organs from acting to protect lives in these circumstances – perhaps not when their own life is at stake, but possibly when it is the lives of those entrusted to the state organ's care that are in danger.[194] In contrast, the value of human life is highlighted by classifying the plea as a justification insofar as this classification upholds the superior value of human life over other legally protected interests, by maintaining that the conduct adopted in the circumstances is lawful, and it makes the saving of life the central point of the analysis. Indeed, as the Commentary notes, the very balancing between the interests at stake, those of the invoking and the affected state, must be assessed 'in the context of the overall purpose of saving lives'.[195] Given these different implications, it may be necessary to consider which of the two classifications is preferable from a policy perspective: is it better to discourage or encourage the protection of life at the cost of the non-performance of international law obligations?

The duty of compensation, which as seen in Chapters 5 and 6, provided an acid test for the competing theories of justification underlying the pleas of self-defence and countermeasures, is not of much help in assessing the comparative benefits of classifying distress as a justification or an excuse. In the case of self-defence and countermeasures, it is generally accepted that neither of the two defences should give rise to a duty of compensation for material loss – at least as between the invoking state and the aggressor or wrongdoing state, as the case may be. Thus, the theory which was most likely to exclude any duty of compensation was thought to have the best explanatory power in each case. But in the case of distress, the sentiment in respect of compensation for material loss is quite unclear. Indeed, it may be said that this is the case *par excellence* which shows the difficulties implicit in the duty of compensation for material loss, and domestic law literature has discussed it as such. Much of the domestic legal literature that has considered the existence of a duty of compensation has done so precisely in relation to a case that, under international law, would be classified as one of distress: that of a ship master entering a port to shield himself from danger

---

[194] For an argument along these lines, see Christie, 'The Unwarranted Conclusions Drawn from *Vincent v Lake Erie Transportation Co* Concerning the Defence of Necessity' (2005) 5 *Issues in Legal Scholarship*.

[195] Id.

## 9.4 DISTRESS AS JUSTIFICATION OR EXCUSE 463

and causing damage to the port in the process. It is the case of *Vincent v Lake Erie*[196] which, more than others, has stimulated the debate. In that case, the steamship *Reynolds* was moored on the claimant's dock when a storm developed. The captain kept fast to the dock, while the wind and waves, continually hitting the ship, pushed it against the dock resulting in its damage. The owner of the dock sued the owners of the vessel for the damage. In a brief judgment, the Supreme Court of Minnesota decided that the *Reynolds* had been justified in not leaving the dock during the storm, but nevertheless awarded compensation to the owner of the dock.[197] Subsequent doctrinal commentary has discussed at length both whether compensation should have been awarded at all and, if so, its potential legal basis – but none of the explanations or theories proposed to support or reject the court's decision has received general assent.[198] It is not clear what the inclination of states is in this regard but, in any event, it would seem that this factor would not be determinative in respect of the classification of the plea as a justification or an excuse: in both cases, the theory underpinning the defence is capable of accommodating a duty of compensation. If classified as a justification, this is because the plea would be grounded on a consequentialist rationale which, as was seen in previous chapters, is capable of sustaining a duty of compensation. If classified as an excuse, this is because the plea could only offer partial exoneration and, as such, exclude all consequences of wrongfulness except for compensation for material loss. Thus the duty of compensation, which was helpful in the assessment of competing theories in respect of other defences, is unlikely to be of much help in the case of distress.

The factors militating in one or other direction are more or less equally stacked. There are benefits and draw-backs in each case. It seems most in keeping with the overall aim to protect human life that the defence be classified as a justification, thus ensuring that the fear of acting

---

[196] *Vincent v Lake Erie Transportation Co* Supreme Court of Minnesota (1910) 109 Minn 456, 124 NW 221.
[197] Ibid., 460 (per O'Brien J.; Lewis J. and Jaggard J. dissenting, at 460–1).
[198] See, e.g., the symposium on this case in (2005) 5(2) *Issues in Legal Scholarship*, available at www.degruyter.com/view/j/ils.2005.5.issue-2/issue-files/ils.2005.5.issue-2.xml. Further references can be found in the various contributions to the symposium. A comprehensive and illustrative overview of the various legal and moral arguments on the point can be found in Sugarman, 'The "Necessity" Defense and the Failure of Tort Theory: The Case against Strict Liability for Damages Caused while Exercising Self-Help in an Emergency' (2005) *Issues in Legal Scholarship*, Article 1.

wrongfully (which would follow from its classification as an excuse) is not a consideration clouding state agents who find themselves in such circumstances. But there is no evidence in the practice of states that they value human life more than other interests protected by international law. Thus, by way of example, the right to life as enshrined in human rights instruments is not absolute.[199] By contrast, it is most in keeping with the human dimension of the plea to classify it as an excuse. This classification seems supported by the historical practice in prize courts, which tended to focus on the situation of the vessel and on whether the circumstance were such as to compel the captain to put into an interdicted port. This study thus (tentatively) classifies distress as an excuse. Nevertheless, this classification needs to be confirmed in the practice of states. Any state invoking distress in the future will need to consider both possibilities, and take into account the practical, policy and normative implications of each classification.

---

[199] Human rights instruments thus protect individuals from the 'arbitrary deprivation of life'. See, e.g., art 4(1) of the International Covenant on Civil and Political Rights, GA Res 2200A (XXI) (in force 23 March 1976) 999 UNTS 171.

# Conclusion

There is conduct that is unlawful, there is conduct that is justified, and there is conduct for which, despite being unlawful, the actor is excused – thus began Chapter 1 of this book, paraphrasing Vaughan Lowe's words.[1] The distinctions referred to in this phrase are often intuitively made – they are, one could say, the result of pre-theoretical intuitions. As Lowe reminded us, no dramatist, no novelist would confuse them, and no philosopher or theologian would conflate them. It seems that, in no small part, it was this intuition that underpinned the observation, made by several scholars, that Chapter V of Part One of the ARS is nothing more than a 'grab-bag of rules',[2] or that the provisions in this chapter do not self-evidently belong to the same category.[3] This study homed in on this intuition and attempted to elaborate it conceptually and analytically so as to provide the legal tools necessary to reflect it in the legal order. The study thus explored the notions of justification and excuse – the notions that domestic legal orders use to translate the above intuition. These concepts were developed in the domestic (criminal) law of Continental European jurisdictions at the turn of the twentieth century, precisely for the purpose of classifying the defences recognised in the legal order. They remain fundamental notions in this regard, though additional categories have since been developed in an effort further to refine the classification of defences.[4] International law has flirted with these notions, time and again, since the early twentieth century; but to date, they remained largely in need of study. This book, by focusing exclusively on these notions in the context of international law, has attempted to fill this gap.

---

[1] To paraphrase Lowe, 'Precluding Wrongfulness or Responsibility: A Plea for Excuses?' (1999) 10 EJIL 405, 406. In turn, borrowing from J. L. Austin's famous 'Plea for Excuses' (1956–7) 57 *Proc Arist Soc* 1.
[2] Rosenstock, 'The ILC and State Responsibility' (2002) 96 AJIL 792, 794.
[3] Crawford, *State Responsibility: The General Part* (2013), 274.
[4] On which see Husak, 'Beyond the Justification/Excuse Dichotomy' in Cruft et al. (eds), *Crime, Punishment, and Responsibility: The Jurisprudence of Antony Duff* (2011), 141.

International law scholarship has been shy to engage with this question and, to date, only few works exist that tackle the issue head on.[5] As a result, this study navigated through relatively uncharted waters. Uncharted international waters at least. Indeed, the topic is much more advanced in domestic law, where the question of the classification of defences has been discussed in Continental Europe since the early twentieth century and in the common law since, at least, the second half of the twentieth century when J. L. Austin's famous 'Plea for Excuses' put it squarely on the map.[6] The advances made by domestic theorists (including their critiques), primarily within the field of criminal law, were a useful source of inspiration and provided important insights for this work. To restate a disclaimer made in the Introduction to this study, these insights were not transposed as such to international law but were nevertheless relied upon insofar as they provided a greater conceptual and theoretical awareness to illuminate the enquiry in this book. At any rate, even though it is often (tautologically) said that state responsibility is 'neither civil nor criminal,'[7] it cannot be denied that international responsibility shares some of the concepts and the language of *both* the domestic law systems of civil and criminal responsibility. The most evident example in this regard is the notions of complicity in the wrongful act of another state and that of the complex, continuous or instantaneous act.[8] And indeed, as borne out by the research carried out for this book, the notions of justification and excuse, as well as the understanding of defences in the international law of responsibility, have borrowed much from domestic criminal law debates.[9]

Starting from the developments in domestic law, and building on the (relatively scant) available state practice and the work of the ILC, and by reference to other characteristics of the legal order and the system of responsibility (for example, the exclusion of fault as a general requirement of responsibility), Chapter 3 defined justification and excuse as follows: justifications constitute defences that relate to properties or characteristics

---

[5] For exceptions, see Christakis, 'Les "circonstances excluant l'illicéité": une illusion optique?' in Corten et al. (eds), *Droit du pouvoir, pouvoir du droit: Mélanges offerts à Jean Salmon* (2007), 223; Scalese, *La rilevanza delle scusanti nella teoria dell'illecito internazionale* (2008).

[6] Austin, 'A Plea for Excuses' (1956–7) 57 *Proc Arist Soc* 1.

[7] Pellet, 'The Definition of Responsibility in International Law' in Crawford et al. (eds), *The Law of International Responsibility* (2010), 12.

[8] See Distefano, 'Fait continu, fait composé et fait complexe dans le droit de la responsabilité' (2006) 52 AFDI 1.

[9] Note, for example, that Ago's own 'Le délit international' relied heavily on criminal law doctrine in its chapter on the 'circumstances precluding wrongfulness': Ago, 'Le délit international' (1939) 68 *Recueil* 415, ch. 5.

of acts – they go to the question of whether any given conduct is wrongful or lawful; excuses, in turn, constitute defences that relate to properties or characteristics of actors – they go to the question of whether any given actor is responsible for its wrongful conduct.

Chapter 1 of this book argued that the law of state responsibility in international law is systemically capable of accommodating a distinction between justification and excuse, as these were defined. The system of responsibility in international law is built upon a distinction between the internationally wrongful act (an act which constitutes a breach of an international obligation of a state) and the responsibility following from that act (namely the legal consequences of cessation and reparation which flow from the wrongful act). The structure of the ARS itself reflects this distinction: Part One relates to the internationally wrongful act, and Part Two to the content of the international responsibility of a state. This distinction is crucial to upholding the unity of the system of responsibility. International law, unlike domestic law, does not recognise a distinction between criminal, tortious and contractual responsibility. This means that the law of responsibility codified in the ARS is applicable to *all* and *every* breach of international law, so long as there is no special regime,[10] regardless of the source (conventional or customary) or substance of the obligation breached. And yet, there are significant substantial differences between the 'infinite variety', to use again Richard Baxter's words, of states' obligations. Some require fault; some require damage; some require states to obtain a given result; others to engage in certain conduct, and so on.[11] This variety is accounted for in the law of responsibility precisely through the distinction between the single, unitary, conception of the internationally wrongful act (a breach of international law), and a modular conception of responsibility involving a set of distinct possible legal relations arising from the wrongful act: cessation and reparation, including restitution, compensation and satisfaction. To a fixed notion of wrongful act are attached modular consequences of responsibility, which depend on the content of the obligation breached. This conceptual distinction (between the wrongful act and its consequences, or 'responsibility' proper) is one that can also support the distinction between justifications and excuses:

---

[10] See ARS art. 55 and Commentary.
[11] For a classification of obligations in international law, see Combacau and Alland, '"Primary" and "Secondary" Rules in the Law of State Responsibility: Categorizing International Obligations' (1985) 16 NYIL 81; Marchesi, *Obblighi di condotta e obblighi di risultato* (2003).

justifications deny that there is a wrongful act, whereas excuses exclude the consequences of that wrongful act.

That international law can theoretically accommodate the distinction was never really disputed in international legal scholarship and practice. Indeed, not even Ago, who was one of the most fervent objectors of the notion of excuses in international law as seen in Chapter 1, denied that the distinction was possible. He simply queried whether there would be any use, given his understanding of international law, to actually draw the distinction as a matter of positive law. But Ago's position, as shown in Chapter 1, is far from definitive or determinative. Indeed, the ILC never unqualifiedly went along with Ago's position – adopting it provisionally on first reading, and reopening, and ultimately leaving open, the debate on second reading.

Indeed, contrary to Ago's views on the matter, and as amply shown in Chapter 2, there exist practical problems of international law the solution to which may be dictated, affected or, at the very least, highlighted, by the distinction between justification and excuse. Most crucially, the distinction has clear implications in respect of the responsibility of accessory states to the wrongful act of another state and in relation to the entitlement to suspend or terminate treaties following a material breach pursuant to VCLT Article 60. As for accessorial responsibility, a clear example is that of complicity, codified in ARS Article 16. The accomplice state's responsibility is derivative since its conduct is only wrongful insofar as it aids or assists in the commission of a wrongful act by another state. Absent the wrongful act of the other state, the accomplice's own conduct is not wrongful[12] and, therefore, the accomplice state will not be responsible. It thus becomes apparent how whether the principal actor possesses a justification for its conduct (its conduct not being wrongful) or whether the state is excused (its conduct remains wrongful) has an impact on the responsibility of the accomplice. In turn, in respect of the entitlement to suspend or terminate a treaty following a material breach, as per VCLT Article 60, this entitlement only follows to the extent that the material breach is wrongful. So if the author of the material breach possesses a justification, rendering its conduct lawful, other treaty parties cannot invoke the entitlement in Article 60. The opposite answer applies in the

---

[12] Unless, of course, it is in and of itself conduct contrary to an international obligation of the accomplice state. An example would be the provision of weapons and other military equipment to the principal state, which may constitute an indirect use of force by the accomplice state in breach of Article 2(4) of the UN Charter.

case where the author of the material breach possesses an excuse, for in this case the conduct would remain wrongful and could therefore trigger the right in Article 60. Generalising from this example, it could be said that the distinction between justification and excuse determines the availability of *all* consequences of wrongfulness not included in the concept of responsibility: since excuses only preclude responsibility (namely, cessation or reparation), they may not preclude other consequences of wrongfulness which will, therefore, remain available even if the invoking state is excused. Of course, none of these consequences will be available in the case of justifications for, in this case, the precondition of these consequences (namely, a wrongful act) would be missing.

The problem of compensation for material loss caused by a state that benefits from a defence, which is often pointed to as an example of the implications of drawing the distinction (if not as the reason for drawing it), is, instead, one that cannot be resolved by the distinction between justification and excuse. The simplistic solution afforded by this distinction (that justifications do not generate compensation, but excuses do), is much too lacking in nuance. On the one hand, there may be certain excuses which do not warrant a duty of compensation (e.g., *force majeure*). On the other, there may be certain justifications which may warrant such a duty. This is most clearly the case of state of necessity, as these are situations in which an 'innocent' state will be made to bear the burden of the protection of the interests of the invoking state and, precisely for this reason, it is often asserted (unfortunately, without much by way of analytical argument) that it should entail a duty of compensation. The situations in which the potential duty of compensation is due are, therefore, not clearly mapped out by drawing the boundary between justification and excuse: the duty, indeed, cuts across the distinction. Nevertheless, it should not be concluded from this that the distinction between justification and excuse has no relevance to this question. For one, the distinction is useful in isolating the issues which require resolution. In respect of justifications, since conduct is lawful, any duty of compensation will require the identification of a specific and persuasive rationale, much in the same way that regimes of strict liability (or liability for lawful conduct) are grounded on specific rationales. In this connection, the theories underpinning the various justification defences may be helpful. Thus, justifications based on rights forfeiture theories (self-defence and countermeasures) can be treated differently from consequentialist justifications (like state of necessity). In the former case, it can be said that the lawful conduct did not affect any rights of the target state, since the legal protection of these rights was forfeited, so there is no basis for a duty of compensation. In the latter case, instead, while the conduct is lawful it is still possible to say that the conduct affected a right of the target state, and this can be the basis of a duty of compensation. In the case of excuses, in turn, it is possible to ground a duty of compensation on the wrongfulness of the act and say, for example, that excuses provide only partial exoneration. The question then becomes one about the circumstances in which excuses afford total or only partial exoneration. To be sure, these are all questions for which there are currently no answers. But these various factors can prove relevant in respect of the existence of a duty of compensation. Thus, in negotiations between the parties or, potentially, in the decision of an international tribunal factors including whether the conduct is lawful (justification) or wrongful (excuse) and the underlying rationale of the justification (is it a rights forfeiture theory or a consequentialist one) or of the excuse (is it a free will theory and if so, what was the degree of restriction of the state's freedom), may be relevant to the weighing of the equities of the case and, thereby, to the determination of whether compensation is due.

There are thus practical problems of international law the solution to which may hinge on, be affected, or be highlighted by, the classification of defences as either justifications or excuses. Of course, international law may opt to resolve these questions by means other than the distinction between justification and excuse or to adopt solutions different from those reached by means of this distinction. For example, states may decide that Article 60 may be triggered even when the breach is justified or that it may not be triggered when a treaty-party has an excuse for its material breach. That the solutions outlined above follow, by logical implication, from the distinction between justification and excuse does not make them binding as such. Nevertheless, the solution dictated by the distinction may be acceptable to states and subsequently harden into positive law. Where these solutions were not ultimately accepted by positive law, the distinction would nevertheless have had the merit of illuminating the problem, potential options and consequences. It seems safe to conclude that, even if not itself providing the solution to these practical problems, the distinction between justification and excuse possesses practical importance.

Chapters 1 and 2 thus argued that the distinction is possible in international law (it can be accommodated by the system of responsibility) and that it is useful (it has practical consequences). Chapter 3 then set out to develop the concepts of justification and excuse *for* international law and to clarify some of their properties and characteristics. It was thus clarified that justifications constitute permissions of the legal order and that, as a result, justified conduct is lawful conduct and not, as some have argued, that it is 'non-wrongful'. Likewise, in respect of excuses, it was clarified that they do not (and need not) relate to the concept of fault understood in a subjective sense. Chapter 3 also identified potential theories of justification and excuse and explained the relevance of both concept and theory of defences in the classification of defences as justifications or excuses.

The classification of defences into these two categories is no simple task. It is possible to argue that the classification is a matter for the legislator (or for the practice of states, as the case may be), but this would simply beg the question – ultimately, there must have been some basis even for the legislator to perform this classification. Domestic law theory has identified two different approaches to the classification: a top-down and a bottom-up approach. In the former, one starts from the theory of justification or excuse, and formulates a defence which responds to the logic of that theory. Thus, one could start from a consequentialist theory and thereby design a defence of necessity to follow that logic: this is necessity as a lesser evil. Or one could start from a theory of free will and design a defence of necessity to follow that logic: this is necessity as the constrainer of free will which compels the agent to act. On the bottom-up approach, instead, one starts from the formulation of the defence and working up through its practice, its rationale, and the concept of justification and excuse, arrives at a potential theory which may explain its effect and, on that basis, performs the classification. Thus, one could start from the formulation of the plea of countermeasures, attest that in practice states accept that countermeasures are permissible, and as such lawful, that the rationale of the plea is the enforcement of international law, and one arrives at a potential deontic theory: the target state, by its conduct, forfeits the protection of its rights. This is a theory of justification and, therefore, countermeasures are a justification. As far as international law is concerned, the second approach seems more in tune with its voluntaristic premises as it starts from the practice of states. Theorists admit, however, that more often than not the classification of defences will require a combination of the two approaches above and may involve also other factors, such as policy or normative considerations. The classification of defences is, in some measure, more an art than a science. Part II of this book bears this out: it relies on elements of both top-down and bottom-up reasoning in reaching the classification of each of the defences.

The book argued that consent, self-defence, countermeasures and (as currently formulated) state of necessity can all be classified as justifications.

In respect of the first three, the state practice available largely supports this conclusion. As for state of necessity, there exist some dissenting voices both among states as well as international tribunals. On the whole, however, the available state practice seems to side with its classification as a justification. This study then attempted to determine the theoretical grounds upon which the effect of these defences as justifications could be based. Different theories were essayed to explain the effect of justifications, ranging from the renunciation of legal protection, to rights forfeiture and to lesser evil (or consequentialist) rationales. Chapter 4 argued that consent can be explained on the basis of a renunciation theory and Chapters 5–6 argued that both self-defence and countermeasures can be explained by a rights forfeiture theory. These are both deontic theories that can, at a very high level of abstraction, be assimilated since in both cases the premise of justification is that the invoking state acts with a permission of the legal order (taking the form of a Hohfeldian liberty or privilege) and that the interest affected in the circumstances is not protected by the legal order (be it as a result of voluntary renunciation in the case of consent, or as a result of forfeiture by conduct in the case of self-defence or countermeasures). State of necessity, as explained in Chapter 8, is instead better supported by a superior interest theory or lesser evil – a rather different type of theory from the previous one, since it relies on consequentialist premises. The necessitated act is deemed lawful because, in the circumstances, it achieves a net benefit: as between two interests, it has achieved the protection of the superior one. State of necessity does grant a permission to act, but this permission cannot be explained in terms of rights (*rectius*, liberties) in the Hohfeldian scheme; indeed, the permission afforded by state of necessity cannot be reduced to one of the Hohfeldian (first order) fundamental legal concepts. This is why theorists often distinguish between strong justifications (the former) and weak justifications (the latter). Likewise (one may say, correlatively), the plea of necessity cannot be explained by the absence of protection of the interests impaired: the state whose interests are impaired possesses a right that the invoking state not act as it did.

*Force majeure* (Chapter 7) and distress (Chapter 9) were, instead, classified as excuses. Here the practice is much less clear – to the extent that there has been any practice at all in the past few decades. From a theoretical standpoint, these excuses were explained by reference to a free will theory. This theory possesses rather different premises from the theories of justification, as it concerns the concept of state will and the circumstances in which that will is manifested: it focuses, that is, on the extent to which the circumstances of *force majeure* or of distress coerced the will of the state, thereby compelling the state to act in breach of its international obligations. The theory may be criticised as involving an element of anthropomorphisation of the state.[13] But then, insofar as the notion of state will constitutes the premise of the contemporary legal order (at least in its positivist variant), a certain degree of anthropomorphisation is built into the system as a whole. Of course, there are not insignificant difficulties in determining the will of corporate entities, especially as complex an entity as the state: whose will counts as the will of the state for these purposes, is it the state as a whole or only the implicated state organ?[14] This is especially important in respect of the defences.[15] In *Rainbow Warrior*, for instance, was it the circumstances of Major Mafart and Captain Prieur that were relevant to the defence of distress or was it the circumstances of the state officials, in France, who ultimately took the decision (and therefore acted in breach of an international obligation) to repatriate the two?[16] These are certainly complex practical difficulties, but they do not affect the conceptual premise. And if the conceptual premise is accepted, then it must also be accepted that the expression of that will can be affected, and that in some circumstances the manifestation of that will may be coerced or compelled by the circumstances. In short, it must be accepted that the will may not be free. This much seems obvious as a question of fact. It is, moreover, already recognised by certain rules of the legal order. For instance, in the field of treaty-law, the consequence of coercion in the expression of will in relation to the treaty itself is the invalidity of the act in question.[17] It could be possible to add that in the field of responsibility, the consequence of coercion of the will is that of excluding the consequences of the coerced act. Thus, when the circumstances of *force majeure*

---

[13] On the risks of which, see Dickinson, 'The Analogy between Natural Persons and International Persons in the Law of Nations' (1917) 26 *Yale LJ* 564.

[14] This difficulty is not exclusive to the notion of excuse. Take the example of customary law: whose acts and *opinio juris* should count in case of contradiction or disagreement as between state organs? For an example of this, see *Case Concerning the Temple of Preah Vihear (Cambodia v Thailand)* (1962) ICJ Rep 6.

[15] The answer may vary. For example, in the case of *force majeure* it is the circumstances relating to the state as a whole which matter; in the case of distress, the focus is on the circumstances of the specific state organ implicated.

[16] On which see Charpentier, 'L'affaire du *Rainbow Warrior*: la sentence arbitrale du 30 avril 1990 (Nouvelle Zélande c. France)' (1990) 36 AFDI 395, 399–400.

[17] See VCLT art. 51 (on coercion of the state's representative, which invalidates the act of consent); art. 52 (on coercion of the state through the use of force, which renders the treaty void).

or distress (or, potentially, of necessity if this plea were to be recast as an excuse) compel a state or one of its organs to act in a manner incompatible with international law, that act will not bear the legal consequences of responsibility for the state that so acted.

As already mentioned, to elaborate the classification explained above, this book relied on state practice, as far as this was available, but it also engaged in the investigation and elaboration of theories of justification and excuse. The identification and development of theories of justification and excuse can be helpful both in assessing the defences currently recognised in the legal order (do they actually reflect the logic of justification or excuse?) as well as in the potential development of new defences. As explained by the domestic criminal lawyer Michael Corrado, in remarks that are applicable to both justification and excuse:

> if we can find the underlying theory, then not only can we regularize the scheme of existing excuses, we can also decide about *proposed* excuses ... we can at least *consider* each proposed excuse in the light of the most plausible theory.[18]

As was mentioned in the Introduction to this book, individual defences are not inherently justifications or excuses. Rather, they can be formulated to reflect the logic of either one. The choice as to the classification of any individual defence as a justification or excuse responds to a variety of factors, including normative, moral and other policy considerations. Understanding the theories of justification and excuse is thus instrumental in the formulation (or reformulation) of defences. For instance, given recent calls in the literature and some part of the practice of states and international tribunals to cast state of necessity as an excuse, one may begin reformulating this defence (which at present reflects a rationale of justification) along the lines of the preferable theory of excuse. Thus, Chapter 8 proposed that the defence of state of necessity be reframed so as to emphasise the element of compulsion or coercion of the state's will created by the situation of grave and imminent threats to an essential interest – to reflect, in short, the logic of the free will theory of excuse.

The theory of defences has until now been mostly overlooked in the international law literature. Therefore, this study, to develop its argument, had to identify the relevant theories and elaborate them *for* the

---

[18] Corrado, 'Notes on the Structure of a Theory of Excuses' (1991–2) 82 *J Crim L & Criminology* 465, 466. A similar view is expressed by Mantovani, *Principi di diritto Penale* (2nd edn, 2007), 177–8.

international legal order as much as it was possible and as much as it was necessary for the purposes of the argument in this work. Against this background, this book may be seen as an initial exploration into this field. But much remains to be done: there are uncertainties and difficulties that will need to be ironed out by doctrinal engagement with the topic as well as in light of subsequent developments in the law. For example, as discussed in Chapters 5 and 6 respectively, a forfeiture theory of self-defence or countermeasures is unable to explain the limitation of these justifications by requirements of necessity and proportionality. After all, if the state is exercising a liberty and the target state has renounced its rights (it possesses, in Hohfeldian terms, a no-right), how then to limit the invoking state to only what is necessary and proportionate? Moreover, one of the hardest obstacles for this theory is the leap that it makes from the no-right of the target party to the positive entitlement of the other. To use an example from domestic law, to say that an individual loses its right to life by its own aggression does not of itself entail a positive right on the part of the victim to kill him. The wrongdoer's no-right is the correlative of the invoking state's liberty. But, as has been noted by domestic law theorists, to have a *liberty* to do something is not the same as being justified in doing it.[19] While a state may be entitled to take countermeasures, is it ever justified for it to take the measure or is it, perhaps, better for it to use other, ideally multilateral, means to obtain the enforcement of its rights? Is it ever justified (in a normative, rather than positive law sense) for the state to breach international law? Theoretically, this is something that may need further exploration in the context of international law, just as it remains in need of explanation in domestic law. Likewise, free-will-based theories of excuse have difficulty explaining the limitation of *force majeure* and distress (as well as the potential excuse of necessity) by requirements of non-contribution: if what matters are the circumstances in which the entity's will was expressed, then is it relevant whether the factors contributing to the situation are exogenous or endogenous to the state invoking the defence? More generally, can any of these theories (of both justification and excuse) actually provide a complete account of all the conditions and requirements of each defence; and is this necessary?[20]

---

[19] Steinhoff, 'Self-Defense as Claim Right, Liberty, and Act-Specific Agent-Relative Prerogative' (2016) 35 *Law and Philosophy* 193, 196.

[20] Recall the discussions within the ILC in relation to the substantive limitations on countermeasures, and the dissatisfaction caused to some by the fact that these limitations were not all reducible to the same underlying principle, see Chapter 6, Section 6.3.2.2.

And should we strive to provide a monistic theory for all justifications and, likewise, for all excuses; or can a plurality of theories (e.g., renunciation, forfeiture, lesser evil) be accommodated by the legal order? And would this make any difference in theory or in practice? The study, as can be seen, raises numerous questions – many more than it can itself hope to answer.

The notions of justification and excuse proposed in this work were developed with a view to reflecting the thinking of the ILC, as well as the views and practice of states and international tribunals. But these concepts too require further investigation. As was seen in Chapter 3, there remain many doubts about the very notions of justification and excuse and, more importantly, about their boundaries. Do justifications involve morally right conduct, or is this consideration irrelevant; must a state invoking a justification have done it for the right reasons, or is it enough that – even though it may have acted for different reasons – the conditions for the justification objectively exist? Do excuses exclude any considerations of fault, or can this notion be – somehow – incorporated into the analysis? And if so, would excuses be available *only* in respect of obligations which contain an element of fault? Are justifications exclusively objective defences (since they relate to conduct) and excuses exclusively subjective (since they relate to the actor), or do they, to some degree, combine both aspects?[21] Answers to these questions will require testing the concepts of justification and excuse in the practice of states and in the literature, through the elaboration and analysis of their limits, possibly by way of hypothetical scenarios and other thought experiments.[22]

---

[21] Certain justifications possess subjective elements. Take the example of state of necessity. While the *quid* of the analysis is whether the state conduct in question protects an interest deemed to be superior, by reference to certain quantitative and qualitative criteria, it is undeniable that the analysis involves a consideration of the situation of the state invoking the defence. And this imports elements of subjectivity: in the absence of an absolute hierarchy of interests or values in international law, the analysis is necessarily relative and what may be essential for a given state in a given circumstance may not be the essential for another state in another, different, situation. Subjectivity forms part of this very analysis. By the same token, excuses retain some objective elements: for example, the standard of material impossibility in *force majeure* is an objective standard. It is not relevant whether the state thinks it is in a position of impossibility, what matters is whether that situation of impossibility exists in fact. To what extent, then, are justifications objective and excuses subjective?

[22] These have proved extremely useful in the analogous domestic law debate. Think, for example, of the following famous thought experiments: Carneades' plank (discussed among others by Cicero and Kant), on which see: Finkelstein, 'Two Men on a Plank' (2001) 7 *Legal Theory* 279; Ghanayim, 'Excused Necessity in Western Legal Philosophy' (2006) 19 *Canadian J of L & Juris* 31; Cohan, 'Two Men and a Plank: The Argument from

## CONCLUSION

Even if the boundaries between the two categories of defences are never fully determined, their respective areas never hermetically sealed, these concepts will remain important to legal practice and doctrine. As Riccardo Pisillo Mazzeschi has said:

> les distinctions juridiques sont caractérisées par un certain relativisme, c'est-à-dire par le fait que ces distinctions sont rarement capables de créer des lignes de démarcations ou des dichotomies nettes et absolues, mais que le plus souvent elles laissent à l'interprète une certaine marge d'appréciation. Toutefois nous sommes fermement convainçu que les distinctions juridiques, même avec ces limites, servent à l'interprète comme outils indispensables pour situer et systématiser de la meilleure manière possible, et selon un standard de rationalité convainçant, les données du phénomène juridique.[23]

Systematisation, as noted by Pisillo Mazzeschi, goes beyond the mere organisation of rules and concepts – to distinguish between justification and excuse involves more than simply arranging the defences in accordance with their likeness. The systematisation of defences is of relevance to the law of responsibility as a whole, for it upholds the structured framework of the law of responsibility in international law. It may be recalled from Chapter 1 that the German criminal lawyer Albin Eser drew a distinction between structured and flat systems of responsibility, the former represented through the metaphor of a house with several levels and the latter as a one-storey bungalow. The distinction between justification and excuse[24] clearly points in the direction of the system of international

---

a State of Nature' (2007–8) 29 *Whittier LR* 333; the 'trolley problem': initially developed by Thomson, 'Killing, Letting Die, and the Trolley Problem' (1976) 59 *Monist* 204; see also Hallborg, 'Comparing Harms: The Lesser Evil Defense and the Trolley Problem' (1997) 3 *Legal Theory* 291; the lone hiker scenario, on which see: Feinberg, 'Voluntary Euthanasia and the Inalienable Right to Life (Tanner Lecture)' (1978) 7 *Philosophy and Public Affairs* 93; and finally the 'ticking bomb scenario', see, e.g., Moore, 'Torture and the Balance of Evils' (1989) 23 *Israel LR* 284; Ambos, 'May a State Torture Suspects to Save the Life of Innocents' (2008) 6 *JICJ* 261.

[23] Pisillo Mazzeschi, 'Responsabilité de l'état pour violation des obligations positives relatives aux droits de l'homme' (2008) 333 *Recueil* 175, 223.

[24] Note that the distinction between obligations and defences asserted in the Commentary to Chapter V of Part One, at [8], which is at the basis of the further distinction between justification and excuse (as categories of defences), is crucial to this structured system as well. As was mentioned in the Introduction to this book, the distinction between obligations and defences is a theoretically complex one and it exceeds the scope of this work. However, as a matter of positive law, it can be observed that states (and tribunals) reason about obligations and defences as distinct categories and this observation, reflected in the ARS, was accepted as an assumption upon which this work is based. For legal theoretical works on the distinction between obligations and defences see the papers referred to at fn. 25.

responsibility as a structured one. This structured system, which had been discussed by the Commission during the codification of the ARS, involves (at least) three separate stages:

> The first level involved focusing on the existence of a rule. The second level involved determining if there was a reason precluding the unlawfulness. The third level involved looking to 'subjective' circumstances connected with the mental state of the person or State entity that had committed the act.[25]

To elaborate further, this structure would require, first, a determination whether any given conduct is compatible with an obligation of the state (whether it meets the requirements of the definition of the obligation); second, whether the conduct, despite meeting the requirements of the definition of the obligation, is wrongful; and, third, whether the state, despite having engaged in conduct which is in breach of one of its obligations, bears responsibility for that breach. For each of these elements, a respondent state will have corresponding grounds of exoneration: denials that the conduct is incompatible with the obligation (including denials of attribution), defences which exclude that the conduct is a breach of the obligation (justifications), and defences which relate to the responsibility of the actor (excuses).[26]

This structured analysis, which involves the partitioning of the reasoning into sequential steps, is crucial to the better understanding of 'the function and operation of legal rules'[27] and to the more rational application of those rules to the facts of a dispute. This is a function which

---

[25] ILC Report, fifty-first session, ILC Yearbook 1999, vol. II(2), 54 [98] (summarising debate on draft art. 16). Similarly, see Simma, 2568th meeting, ILC Yearbook 1999 vol. I, 13–14 [9] (who proposes a similar structure to the German tripartite theory of crime, composed of '*prima facie* breach', wrongfulness and responsibility). For a different 'tripartite' structure, see Condorelli and Kress, 'The Rules of Attribution: General Considerations' in Crawford et al. (eds), *The Law of International Responsibility* (2010), 224 (speaking of a 'tripartite' structure of attribution, breach and 'absence of circumstances precluding wrongfulness').

[26] This should not be read to mean that there is a logical order of priority between these steps. International tribunals usually do follow a sequential order where defences are invoked: they begin by assessing the conduct in light of the obligation and then consider the defence. Tribunals usually follow a sequential order where defences are invoked: they begin by assessing the conduct in light of the obligation and then consider the defence. See, e.g., *Military and Paramilitary Activities in and Against Nicaragua (Nicaragua v United States of America)* (1986) ICJ Rep 14, [226]. But the order of analysis can be reversed in the interest of judicial economy: *Continental Casualty Company v Argentine Republic*, ICSID Case ARB/03/9, Award, 5 September 2008, [161].

[27] Talmon, '*Jus Cogens* after *Germany v Italy*: Substantive and Procedural Rules Distinguished' (2012) 25 LJIL 979, 984.

should not be underestimated since, as noted by Paul Reuter, international responsibility constitutes the 'laboratory'[28] in which the continuing process of refinement, adjustment and clarification of international obligations takes place. Most importantly, however, the partitioning of the reasoning into sequential steps as described ultimately contributes to the clarity, certainty, and predictability of the legal order, and these are values which are 'not to be discarded lightly'.[29]

---

[28] Reuter, *Droit international public* (6th edn, 1983), 213.
[29] Talmon, '*Germany v Italy*', 1002.

# BIBLIOGRAPHY

Abass, A. 'Consent Precluding State Responsibility: A Critical Analysis' (2004) 53 *International and Comparative Law Quarterly* 211.
Agamben, G. *State of Exception* (Chicago: University of Chicago Press, 2005).
Agius, M. 'The Invocation of Necessity in International Law' (2009) 56 *Netherlands International Law Review* 95.
Ago, R. 'Le délit international' (1939) 68 *Recueil des cours de l'Académie de droit international* 415.
  'La colpa nell'illecito internazionale' in *Scritti sulla responsabilità internazionale degli Stati* (first published 1939, Napoli: Jovene, 1979) vol. 1, 273.
Akande, D. and Liefländer, T. 'Clarifying Necessity, Imminence, and Proportionality in the Law of Self-Defence' (2013) 107 *American Journal of International Law* 563.
Akehurst, M. 'International Liability for Injurious Consequences Arising Out of Acts Not Prohibited by International Law' (1985) 16 *Netherlands Yearbook of International Law* 3.
Alaimo, M. L. 'La natura del consenso nell'illecito internazionale' (1982) *Rivista di diritto internazionale* 257.
Alexander, L. 'A Unified Excuse of Preemptive Self-Protection' (1999) 74 *Notre Dame Law Review* 1475.
  'Lesser Evils: A Closer Look at the Paradigmatic Justification' (2005) 24 *Law & Philosophy* 611.
Alexandrov, S. A. *Self-Defense Against the Use of Force in International Law* (The Hague: Martinus Nijhoff, 1996).
Alland, D. 'International Responsibility and Sanctions: Self-Defence and Countermeasures in the ILC Codification of Rules Governing International Responsibility' in Simma, B. and Spinedi, M. (eds), *United Nations Codification of State Responsibility* (New York: Oceana, 1987), 152.
  *Justice privée et ordre juridique international* (Paris: Pedone, 1994).
  'Countermeasures of General Interest' (2002) 13 *European Journal of International Law* 1221.
  'The Definition of Countermeasures' in Crawford, J. et al. (eds), *The Law of International Responsibility* (Oxford: Oxford University Press, 2010), 1127.

Alldridge, P. 'Rules for Courts and Rules for Citizens' (1990) 10 *Oxford Journal of Legal Studies* 487.
Alvarez-Jiménez, A. 'New Approaches to the State of Necessity in Customary International Law: Insights from WTO Law and Foreign Investment Law' (2008) 19 *American Review of International Arbitration* 463.
Alvarez-Jiménez, A. 'Foreign Investment Protection and Regulatory Failures as States' Contribution to the State of Necessity under Customary International Law – A New Approach' (2010) 27 *Journal of International Arbitration* 144.
Ambos, K. 'Toward a Universal System of Crime: Comments on George Fletcher's *Grammar of Criminal Law*' (2006–7) 28 *Cardozo Law Review* 2647.
  'May a State Torture Suspects to Save the Life of Innocents' (2008) 6 *Journal of International Criminal Justice* 261.
Amerasinghe, C. *Evidence in International Litigation* (Leiden: Martinus Nijhoff, 2005).
Amzazi, M. 'Morocco' in *International Encyclopaedia of Laws (Criminal Law: Suppl. 11)* (The Hague: Kluwer, 1997).
Antonmattei, P.-H. *Contribution à l'étude de la force majeure* (Paris: LGDJ, 1992).
Antonopoulos, C. *Counterclaims before the International Court of Justice* (The Hague: TMC Asser, 2001).
Anzilotti, D. *Teoria generale della responsabilità dello stato nel diritto internazionale* (Florence: Lumachi, 1902).
  'La responsabilité internationale des Etats à raison des dommages soufferts par des étrangers' (1906) 13 *Revue générale de droit international public* 5, 285.
  'Corso di diritto internazionale' in *Opere di Dionisio Anzilotti* (reprint of 3rd edn originally published in 1927, Padova: CEDAM, 1955).
Appolis, G. 'Le règlement de l'affaire du *Rainbow Warrior*' (1987) 91 *Revue générale de droit international public* 9.
Arangio-Ruiz, G. 'Counter-Measures and Amicable Dispute Settlement Means in the Implementation of State Responsibility: A Crucial Issue before the International Law Commission' (1994) 5 *European Journal of International Law* 20.
Arias, H. 'The Non-Liability of States for Damages Suffered by Foreigners in the Course of a Riot, an Insurrection or a Civil War' (1913) 7 *American Journal of International Law* 724.
Arnolds, E. and Garland, N. F. 'The Defence of Necessity in Criminal Law: The Right to Choose a Lesser Evil' (1974) 65 *Journal of Criminal Law & Criminology* 289.
Arroyo Lara, E. 'Reflexiones en torno a la legítima defensa como causa excluyente la ilicitud (VIII Informe a la CDI)' (1982–3) 1 *Anales de la Universidad de La Laguna* 75.
Ashworth, A. 'Self-Defence and the Right to Life' (1975) 34 *Cambridge Law Journal* 282.
Auerbach, C. 'On Professor Hart's Definition and Theory in Jurisprudence' (1956–7) 9 *Journal of Legal Education* 39.

Aust, H. P. *Complicity and the Law of State Responsibility* (Cambridge: Cambridge University Press, 2011).
'Circumstances Precluding Wrongfulness and Shared Responsibility' in Nollkaemper, A. and Plakokefalos, I. (eds), *Principles of Shared Responsibility* (Cambridge: Cambridge University Press, 2014), 169.
Austin, J. L. 'A Plea for Excuses' (1956–7) 57 *Proceedings of the Aristotelian Society* 1.
Azuni, D. A. *The Maritime Law of Europe* (New York: Riley, 1806) vol. 1.
Bachmaier Winter, L. and del Moral García, A. 'Spain' in *International Encyclopaedia of Laws (Criminal Law: Suppl. 46)* (The Hague: Kluwer, 2012).
Bacigalupo, E. *Manual de derecho penal (Parte general)* (Bogotá: Temis, 1996).
Balladore-Pallieri, G. *Diritto internazionale pubblico*, 7th edn (Milano: Giuffrè, 1956).
Bannelier, K. and Christakis, T. '*Volenti non fit injuria*? Les effets du consentement à l'intervention militaire' (2004) 50 *Annuaire Français de droit international* 102.
Barbier, S. 'Assurances and Guarantees of Non-Repetition' in Crawford, J. et al. (eds), *The Law of International Responsibility* (Oxford: Oxford University Press, 2010), 551.
Barboux, H. M. *Jurisprudence du Conseil des prises pendant la guerre de 1870–1871* (Paris: Sotheran, Baer & cie, 1872).
Barboza, J. 'Necessity (Revisited) in International Law' in Makarczyk, J. (ed.), *Essays in International Law in Honour of Judge Manfred Lachs* (The Hague: Martinus Nijhoff, 1984), 27.
   'Contramedidas en la reciente codificación de la responsabilidad de los Estados: fronteras con la legítima defensa y el estado de necesidad' (2003) 12 *Anuario Argentino de derecho internacional* 15.
Bargrave Deane, H. *The Law of Blockade* (London: Longmans, 1870).
Baron, M. 'Justifications and Excuses' (2005) 2 *Ohio State Journal of Criminal Law* 387.
   'Is Justification (Somehow) Prior to Excuse? A Reply to Douglas Husak' (2005) 24 *Law & Philosophy* 595.
Barros, J. *The Corfu Incident of 1923: Mussolini and the League of Nations* (Princeton: Princeton University Press, 1965).
Barsotti, R. 'Armed Reprisals' in Cassese, A. (ed.), *The Current Regulation of the Use of Force* (Dordrecht: Martinus Nijhoff, 1986), 79.
Bartels, L. 'The Relationship Between the WTO Agriculture Agreement and the SCM Agreement: An Analysis of Hierarchy Rules in the WTO Legal System' (2016) 50 *Journal of World Trade* 7.
Basdevant, J. 'L'action coercitive anglo-germano-italienne contre le Venezuela (1902–1903)' (1904) 11 *Revue générale de droit international public* 373.
   'Règles générales du droit de la paix' (1936) 58 *Recueil des cours de l'Académie de droit international* 471.
Baxter, R. R. 'International Law in "Her Infinite Variety"' (1980) 29 *International and Comparative Law Quarterly* 549.

Bederman, D. J. 'Counterintuiting Countermeasures' (2002) 96 *American Journal of International Law* 817.
Beknazar, T. B. 'Russian Indemnity Arbitration' in Wolfrum, R. (ed.), *Max Planck Encyclopaedia of Public International Law* (www.mpepil.com, Oxford: Oxford University Press, 2009–).
Ben Mansour, A. 'Consent' in Crawford, J. et al. (eds), *The Law of International Responsibility* (Oxford: Oxford University Press, 2010), 439.
Bennouna, M. 'Le règlement des differends peut-il limiter le 'droit' de se faire justice a soi-même?' (1994) 5 *European Journal of International Law* 61.
Bentham, J. *An Introduction to the Principles of Morals and Legislation* (first published in 1823, J. H. Burns and H. L. A. Hart, eds, Oxford: Clarendon Press, 1996).
Benvenuti, P. 'Lo stato di necessità alla prova dei fatti' in Spinedi, M. et al. (eds), *La codificazione della responsabilità internazionale degli Stati alla prova dei fatti* (Milano: Giuffrè, 2006), 107.
Berlia, G. 'La guerre civile et la responsabilité internationale de l'Etat' (1937) 11 *Revue générale de droit international public* 51.
Berman, M. N. 'Justification and Excuse, Law and Morality' (2003) 53 *Duke Law Journal* 1.
  'Lesser Evils and Justification: A Less Close Look' (2005) 24 *Law & Philosophy* 681.
Bernsmann, K. 'Private Self-Defence and Necessity in German Penal Law and in the Penal Law Proposal – Some Remarks' (1996) 30 *Israel Law Review* 171.
Bettiol, G. and Pettoello-Mantovani, L. *Diritto penale parte generale*, 12th edn (Padova: CEDAM, 1988).
Bin Cheng. *General Principles of Law as Applied by International Courts and Tribunals* (London: Stevens, 1953).
Binder, C. 'Changed Circumstances in International Investment Law: Interfaces Between the Law of Treaties and the Law of State Responsibility with a Special Focus on the Argentine Crisis' in Binder, C. et al. (eds), *International Investment Law in the 21st Century: Essays in Honour of Christoph Schreuer* (Oxford: Oxford University Press, 2009), 608.
Bjorklund, A. 'Emergency Exceptions: State of Necessity and *Force Majeure*' in Muchlinski, P. and Ortino, F. (eds), *Oxford Handbook of International Investment Law* (Oxford: Oxford University Press, 2007), 459.
Blanning, T. *The Nineteenth Century: Europe 1798–1914* (Oxford: Oxford University Press, 2000).
Blodgett, H. 'The Fur Seal Arbitration' (1894) 3 *Northwestern Law Review* 73.
Bluntschli, J. C. *Le droit international codifié*, 2nd edn (Lardy trans, Paris: Guillaumin, 1874).
  *Le droit international codifié*, 3rd edn (Lardy trans, Paris: Guillaumin, 1881).
Bodansky, D. and Crook, J. R. 'Symposium: The ILC's State Responsibility Articles: Introduction and Overview' (2002) 96 *American Journal of International Law* 773.

Boed, R. 'State of Necessity as a Justification for Internationally Wrongful Conduct' (2000) 3 *Yale Human Rights & Development Law Journal* 1.
Bohlander, M. *The German Criminal Code: A Modern English Translation* (Oxford: Hart, 2008).
  *Principles of German Criminal Law* (Oxford: Hart, 2009).
Bohlen. 'Incomplete Privilege to Inflict Intentional Invasions of Interests of Property and Personality' (1926) 39 *Harvard Law Review* 307.
Boisson de Chazournes, L. 'Other Non-derogable Obligations' in Crawford, J. et al. (eds), *The Law of International Responsibility* (Oxford: Oxford University Press, 2010), 1205.
Bonfils, H. *Manuel de droit international public* (Paris: Rousseau, 1894).
  *Manuel de droit international public*, 4th edn (Fauchille ed., Paris: Rousseau, 1905).
  *Manuel de droit international public*, 7th edn (Fauchille ed., Paris: Rousseau, 1914).
Borchard, E. M. 'Harvard Draft on the Law of Responsibility of States for Damage Done in their Territory to the Person or Property of Foreigners' (1929) 23 *American Journal of International Law Special Supplement* 131.
  *The Diplomatic Protection of Citizens Abroad* (New York: Banks Law, 1915).
  'Responsibility of States at the Hague Codification Conference' (1930) 24 *American Journal of International Law* 517.
Borel, E. 'L'Acte Général de Genève' (1929) 27 *Recueil des cours de l'Académie de droit international* 497.
Borelli, S. and Olleson, S. 'Obligations Relating to Human Rights and Humanitarian Law' in Crawford, J. et al. (eds), *The Law of International Responsibility* (Oxford: Oxford University Press, 2010), 1177.
Borsi, U. 'Ragione di guerra e stato di necessità nel diritto internazionale' (1916) 5 *Rivista di diritto internazionale* 157.
Botterell, A. 'In Defence of Infringement' (2008) 27 *Law & Philosophy* 269.
Bourquin, M. 'Règles générales du droit de la paix' (1931) 35 *Recueil des cours de l'Académie de droit international* 1.
Bowett, D. *Self-Defence in International Law* (Manchester: Manchester University Press, 1958).
  'The Impact of Security Council Decisions on Dispute Settlement Procedures' (1994) 5 *European Journal of International Law* 89.
Brecher, B. *Torture and the Ticking Bomb* (Oxford: Blackwell, 2007).
Brierly, J. L. 'The General Act of Geneva, 1928' (1930) 11 *British Yearbook of International Law* 119.
  'Vital Interests and the Law' (1944) 21 *British Yearbook of International Law* 51.
Brockelbank, W. 'The Vilna Dispute' (1926) 20 *American Journal of International Law* 583.
Bronaugh, R. 'Freedom as the Absence of an Excuse' (1964) 74 *Ethics* 161.
Brown, J. S. 'Fur Seals and the Bering Sea Arbitration' (1895) 26 *Journal of the American Geographical Society of New York* 326.

Brown, V. 'Rights, Liberties and Duties: Reformulating Hohfeld's Scheme of Legal Relations?' (2005) 58 *Current Legal Problems* 343.
Brownlie, I. *International Law and the Use of Force by States* (Oxford: Clarendon Press, 1963).
  *State Responsibility* (Oxford: Oxford University Press, 1983).
  *Principles of Public International Law*, 7th edn (Oxford: Oxford University Press, 2008).
Brusa, E. 'Responsabilité des Etats à raison des dommages soufferts par des étrangers en cas d'émeute ou de guerre civile' (1898) 17 *Annuaire de l'Institut de droit international* 96.
Bry, G. *Précis elémentaire de droit international public* (Paris: Larose, 1891).
  *Précis elémentaire de droit international public*, 4th edn (Paris: Larose, 1901).
Bücheler, G. *Proportionality in Investor-State Arbitration* (Oxford: Oxford University Press, 2015).
Burlamaqui, J. J. *The Principles of Natural and Politic Law* (1747, Nugent trans., Indianapolis: Liberty Fund, 2006).
Byrd, S. 'Wrongdoing and Attribution: Implications Beyond the Justification-Excuse Distinction' (1986–7) 33 *Wayne Law Review* 1289.
Cahier, P. 'Changements et continuité du droit international' (1985) 195 *Recueil des cours de l'Académie de droit international* 9.
Calvo, C. *Le droit international théorique et pratique*, 3rd edn (Paris: Pedone-Lauriel, 1880) vols 1–3.
  *Dictionnaire de droit international public et privé* (Paris: Rousseau, 1885) vols 1 and 2.
  *Le droit international théorique et pratique*, 4th edn (Paris: Pedone-Lauriel, 1888) vol. 3.
Campbell, A. 'International Law and Primitive Law' (1988) 8 *Oxford Journal of Legal Studies* 169.
Campbell, K. 'Offence and Defence' in Dennis, I. H. (ed.), *Criminal Law and Justice* (London: Sweet & Maxwell, 1987).
Cannizzaro, E. 'The Role of Proportionality in the Law of International Countermeasures' (2001) 12 *European Journal of International Law* 889.
  (ed.), *The Law of Treaties Beyond the Vienna Convention* (Oxford: Oxford University Press, 2011).
Capotorti, F. 'L'extinction et la suspension des traités' (1971) 134 *Recueil des cours de l'Académie de droit international* 417.
  'Cours général de droit international public' (1994) 248 *Recueil des cours de l'Académie de droit international* 9.
Carnazza-Amari, G. *Trattato sul diritto internazionale pubblico di pace*, 2nd edn (Milano: Maisner, 1875).
  *Traité de droit international public en temps de paix* (Montanari-Revest trans., Paris: Larose, 1880) vol. 1.

Caron, D. 'The ILC Articles on State Responsibility: The Paradoxical Relationship Between Form and Authority' (2002) 96 *American Journal of International Law* 857.

Cassella, S. *La nécessité en droit international* (The Hague: Martinus Nijhoff, 2011).

Cassese, A. *International Law*, 2nd edn (Oxford: Oxford University Press, 2005).

'On the Use of Criminal Law Notions in Determining State Responsibility for Genocide' (2007) 5 *Journal of International Criminal Justice* 875.

Cavaglieri, A. *I diritti fondamentali degli Stati nella Societá Internazionale* (Padova: Librai-Editori, 1906).

*Lo stato di necessità nel diritto internazionale* (Roma: Athenaeum, 1917).

'Règles générales du droit de la paix' (1929) 26 *Recueil des cours de l'Académie de droit international* 311.

*Corso di diritto internazionale* (Napoli: Rondinella, 1934).

Cavarretta, G. *Lo stato di necessità nel diritto internazionale: parte generale* (Palermo: Reber, 1910).

Čepelka, Č. 'Les conséquences juridiques du délit en droit international contemporain' in *Acta Universitatis Carolinae, Iuridica, Monographia* (Prague: Universita Karlova, 1965) vol. 3.

Chamberlain, M. E. *The Scramble for Africa* (London: Routledge, 2013).

Charpentier, J. 'L'affaire du *Rainbow Warrior*' (1985) 31 *Annuaire Français de droit international* 210.

'L'affaire du *Rainbow Warrior*: le règlement interétatique' (1986) 32 *Annuaire Français de droit international* 873.

'L'affaire du *Rainbow Warrior*: la sentence arbitrale du 30 avril 1990 (Nouvelle Zélande c. France)' (1990) 36 *Annuaire Français de droit international* 395.

*L'affaire Rainbow Warrior et la responsabilité internationale des États* (Saarbrücken: Europa-Institut, 1991).

Chatterjee, C. 'The *Rainbow Warrior* Arbitration Between New Zealand and France' (1992) 9 *Journal of International Arbitration* 17.

Chavarot, M.-C. 'La pratique des lettres de marque d'après les arrêts du parlement (XIIIe–début XVe siècle)' (1991) 149 *Bibliothèque de l'école des chartes* 51.

Chin, G. J. 'Unjustified: The Practical Irrelevance of the Justification/Excuse Distinction' (2009) 43 *Michigan Journal of Law Reform* 79.

Chircop, A. 'Ships in Distress, Environmental Threats to Coastal States, and Places of Refuge: New Directions for an Ancien Regime?' (2002) 33 *Ocean Development & International Law* 207.

'The Customary Law of Refuge for Ships in Distress' in Chircop, A. and Linden, O. (eds), *Places of Refuge for Ships: Emerging Environmental Concerns of a Maritime Custom* (Leiden: Nijhoff, 2006), 163.

et al. 'Characterising the Problem of Places of Refuge for Ships' in Chircop, A. and Linden, O. (eds), *Places of Refuge for Ships: Emerging Environmental Concerns of a Maritime Custom* (Leiden: Nijhoff, 2006), 1.

Christakis, T. 'Les "circonstances excluant l'illicéité": une illusion optique?' in Corten, O. et al. (eds), *Droit du pouvoir, pouvoir du droit: Mélanges offerts à Jean Salmon* (Bruxelles: Bruylant, 2007), 223.

'"Nécessité n'a pas de Loi"? Rapport général sur la nécessité en droit international' in Christakis, T. (ed.), *La nécessité en droit international* (Paris: Pedone, 2007), 9.

'Quel remède à l'éclatement de la jurisprudence CIRDI sur les investissement en Argentine? La décision du comité ad hoc dans l'affaire *CMS c. Argentine*' (*2007*) 111 *Revue générale de droit international public* 879.

Christakis, T. and Bannelier, K. 'La légitime défense en tant que "circonstance excluant l'illicéité"' in Kherad, R. (ed.), *Légitimes défenses* (Paris: LGDJ, 2007), 233.

'La légitime défense a-t-elle sa place dans un code sur la responsabilité internationale?' in Constantinides, A. and Zaikos, N. (eds), *The Diversity of International Law: Essays in Honour of Professor Kalliopi K Koufa* (Leiden: Martinus Nijhoff, 2009), 519.

Christie, G. 'The Unwarranted Conclusions Drawn from *Vincent v Lake Erie Transportation Co* Concerning the Defence of Necessity' (2005) 5 *Issues in Legal Scholarship*, article no 7.

Civoli, C. 'In torno alla legittima difesa e allo stato di necessità. Studio storico' (1893) 37 *Rivista Penale* 21.

Clark, C. *The Sleepwalkers: How Europe Went to War in 1914* (London: Penguin, 2013).

Clark, R. 'State Terrorism: Some Lessons from the Sinking of the *Rainbow Warrior*' (1988) 20 *Rutgers Law Journal* 393.

Cohan, J. A. 'Two Men and a Plank: The Argument from a State of Nature' (2007–8) 29 *Whittier Law Review* 333.

Cohen, F. S. 'Transcendental Nonsense and the Functional Approach' (1935) 35 *Columbia Law Review* 809.

Cohen, J. and Hart, H. 'Theory and Definition in Jurisprudence' (1955) 29 *Proceedings of the Aristotelian Society (Supplemental Volume)* 213.

Colbert, E. S. *Retaliation in International Law* (New York: King's Crown Press, 1948).

Coleman, J. L. *Risks and Wrongs* (Oxford: Oxford University Press, 1992).

Colvin, E. 'Exculpatory Defences in Criminal Law' (1990) 10 *Oxford Journal of Legal Studies* 381.

Combacau, J. and Alland, D. '"Primary" and "Secondary" Rules in the Law of State Responsibility: Categorizing International Obligations' (1985) 16 *Netherlands Yearbook of International Law* 81.

Condorelli, L. 'Le règlement des différends en matière de responsabilité internationale des Etats: quelques remarques candides sur le débat à la CDI' (1994) 5 *European Journal of International Law* 106.

Condorelli, L. and Kress, C. 'The Rules of Attribution: General Considerations' in Crawford, J. et al. (eds), *The Law of International Responsibility* (Oxford: Oxford University Press, 2010), 221.

Conforti, B. 'Cours général de droit international public' (1988) 212 *Recueil des cours de l'Académie de droit international* 9.
Corrado, M. 'Notes on the Structure of a Theory of Excuses' (1991–2) 82 *Journal of Criminal Law & Criminology* 465.
Corten, O. 'The Controversies Over the Customary Prohibition on the Use of Force: A Methodological Debate' (2005) 5 *European Journal of International Law* 803.
  'Breach and Evolution of the International Customary Law on the Use of Force' in Cannizzaro, E. and Palchetti, P. (eds), *Customary International Law on the Use of Force: A Methodological Approach* (Leiden: Martinus Nijhoff, 2005), 119.
  'Article 52 (1969)' in Corten, O. and Klein, P. (eds), *The Vienna Conventions on the Law of Treaties: A Commentary* (Oxford: Oxford University Press, 2011) vol. 2, 1201.
  *Le droit contre la guerre*, 2nd edn (Paris: Pedone, 2014).
Cortés Martín, J. M. 'El estado de necesidad en materia económica y financiera' (2009) 25 *Anuario Español de derecho internacional* 119.
Crawford, J. 'International Law and Foreign Sovereigns: Distinguishing Immune Transactions' (1983) 54 *British Yearbook of International Law* 75.
  'Counter-Measures as Interim Measures' (1994) 5 *European Journal of International Law* 66.
  'Revising the Draft Articles on State Responsibility' (1999) 10 *European Journal of International Law* 435.
  *The International Law Commission's Articles on State Responsibility* (Cambridge: Cambridge University Press, 2002).
  'Continuity and Discontinuity in International Dispute Settlement: An Inaugural Lecture' (2010) 1 *Journal of International Dispute Settlement* 3.
  'Overview of Part Three of the Articles on State Responsibility' in Crawford, J. et al. (eds), *The Law of International Responsibility* (Oxford: Oxford University Press, 2010), 931.
  *Brownlie's Principles of Public International Law*, 8th edn (Oxford: Oxford University Press, 2012).
  *State Responsibility: The General Part* (Cambridge: Cambridge University Press, 2013).
  'Sovereignty as a Legal Value' in Crawford, J. and Koskenniemi, M. (eds), *Cambridge Companion to International Law* (Cambridge: Cambridge University Press, 2013).
  'Chance, Order, Change: The Course of International Law' (2013) 365 *Recueil des cours de l'Académie de droit international* 9.
  'The International Court of Justice and the Law of State Responsibility' in Tams, C. and Sloane, J. (eds), *The Development of International Law by the International Court of Justice* (Oxford: Oxford University Press, 2013), 75.

et al. 'Towards an International Law of Responsibility: Early Doctrine' in Boisson de Chazournes, L. and Kohen, M. (eds), *International Law and the Quest for Its Implementation: Liber Amicorum Vera Gowlland-Debbas* (Leiden: Martinus Nijhoff, 2010), 377.

Crawford, J. and Olleson, S. 'The Exception of Non-Performance: Links Between the Law of Treaties and the Law of State Responsibility' (2001) 21 *Australian Yearbook of Internatioanl Law* 55.

'The Character and Forms of International Responsibility' in Evans, M. D. (ed.), *International Law*, 4th edn (Oxford: Oxford University Press, 2014), 443.

Crawford, J. et al. (eds), *The Law of International Responsibility* (Oxford: Oxford University Press, 2010).

Creasy, E. *First Platform of International Law* (London: John van Voorst, 1876).

Cristani, F. 'The Sempra Annulment Decision of 29 June 2010 and Subsequent Developments in Investment Arbitration Dealing with the Necessity Defence' (2011) 15 *International Community Law Review* 237.

Czapliński, W. and Danilenko, G. M. 'Conflict of Norms in International Law' (1990) 21 *Netherlands International Law Review* 3.

D'Amato, A. 'The Coerciveness of International Law' (2009) 52 *German Yearbook of International Law* 437.

d'Argent, P. 'Du commerce à l'emploi de la force: l'affaire des plates-formes pétrolières (arrêt sur le fond)' (2003) 49 *Annuaire Français de droit international* 266.

Daillier, P. 'The Development of the Law of Responsibility through the Case Law' in Crawford, J. et al. (eds), *The Law of International Responsibility* (Oxford: Oxford University Press, 2010), 37.

et al. *Droit international public*, 8th edn (Paris: LGDJ, 2009).

Daman, M. 'Cross-Border Hot Pursuit in the EU' (2008) 16 *European Journal of Crime, Criminal Law & Criminal Justice* 171.

Damrosch, L. F. 'Retaliation or Arbitration – or Both? The 1978 United States-France Aviation Dispute' (1980) 74 *American Journal of International Law* 785.

Dan-Cohen, M. 'Decision Rules and Conduct Rules: On Acoustic Separation in Law' (1985) 97 *Harvard Law Review* 625.

Darcy, S. 'The Evolution of the Law of Belligerent Reprisals' (2003) 175 *Military Law Review* 184.

'Retaliation and Reprisal' in Weller, M. (ed.), *The Oxford Handbook of the Use of Force in International Law* (Oxford: Oxford University Press, 2015), 879.

David, E. 'Primary and Secondary Rules' in Crawford, J. et al. (eds), *The Law of International Responsibility* (Oxford: Oxford University Press, 2010), 27.

Davidson, J. 'The *Rainbow Warrior* Arbitration Concerning the Treatment of the French Agents Mafart and Prieur' (1991) 40 *International & Comparative Law Quarterly* 446.

Davies, P. 'Defences and Third Parties: Justifying Participation' in Dyson, A., Goudkamp, J. et al. (eds), *Defences in Tort* (Oxford: Hart, 2015), 107.

Davis, G. B. *The Elements of International Law*, 4th edn (New York: Harper & Brothers, 1916).
Davis, N. 'Rights, Permission, and Compensation' (1985) 14 *Philosophy & Public Affairs* 374.
Dawidowicz, M. 'Third-Party Countermeasures: Observations on a Controversial Concept' in Chinkin, C. M. and Baetens, F. (eds), *Sovereignty, Statehood and State Responsibility: Essays in Honour of James Crawford* (Cambridge: Cambridge University Press, 2015), 340.
de Francesco, G. *Diritto penale. I fondamenti* (Torino: Giappichelli, 2008).
de Garden, G. C. *Traité complet de diplomatie* (Paris: Treuttel et Wurtz, 1833) vol. 1.
de Guttry, A. *Le rappresaglie non comportanti la coercizione militare nel diritto internazionale* (Milano: Giuffrè, 1985).
de Hoogh, A. '*Jus Cogens* and the Use of Armed Force' in Weller, M. (ed.), *Oxford Handbook of the Use of Force in International Law* (Oxford: Oxford University Press, 2015), 1161.
 'Restrictivist Reasoning on the *Ratione Personae* Dimension of Armed Attacks in the Post 9/11 World' (2016) 29 *Leiden Journal of International Law* 19.
de la Brière, Y. 'Evolution de la doctrine et de la pratique en matière de représailles' (1928) 22 *Recueil des cours de l'Académie de droit international* 237.
de Lapradelle, A. 'The Neutrality of Belgium' (1914) *North American Review* 847.
de Lapradelle, A. and Politis, N. *Recueil des arbitrages internationaux* (Paris: Pedone, 1905) vols 1 and 2.
de Louter, J. *Le droit international public positif* (Oxford: Oxford University Press, 1920) vols 1 and 2.
de Martens, C. *Nouvelles causes célèbres du droit des gens* (Leipzig: Brockhaus, 1843) vol. 2.
de Martens, F. F. *Traité de droit international* (Paris: Marescq Ainé, 1883) vol. 1.
 *Traité de droit international* (Paris: Marescq Ainé, 1887) vol. 3.
de Oliveira Mazzuoli, V. *Curso de direito international public*, 6th edn (São Paulo: Revista dos Tribunais, 2012).
de Pistoye, A. and Duverdy, D. C. *Traité de prises maritimes* (Paris: Durand, 1859).
de Robertis, F. *La responsabilità contrattuale nel Diritto Romano dalle origini a tutta l'età postclassica* (Bari: Caducci, 1996).
de Visscher, C. *Belgium's Case: A Juridical Enquiry* (London: Hodder and Stoughton, 1916).
 'Les lois de la guerre et la théorie de la nécessité' (1917) 24 *Revue générale de droit international public* 74.
 'La responsabilité internationale des Etats' in *Bibliotheca Visseriana* (Brill, 1924) vol. 2.
 *Theory and Reality in Public International Law*, 3rd edn (Princeton: Princeton University Press, 1968).

Deeks, A. '"Unwilling or Unable": Toward a Normative Framework for Extraterritorial Self-Defense' (2012) 52 *Virginia Journal of International Law* 483.

Del Mar, K. 'The Effects of Framing International Legal Norms as Rules or Exceptions: State Immunity from Civil Jurisdiction' (2013) 15 *International Community Law Review* 143.

Del Vecchio, A. and Casanova, E. *Le rappresaglie nei comuni medievali e specialmente in Firenze* (Bologna: Zanichelli, 1894).

Dempsey, M. M. and Herring, J. 'Why Sexual Penetration Requires Justification' (2007) 27 *Oxford Journal of Legal Studies* 467.

Despagnet, F. *Cours de droit international public* (Paris: Larose, 1894).

  *Cours de droit international public*, 2nd edn (Paris: Larose, 1899).

  *Cours de droit international public*, 3rd edn (Paris: Larose, 1905).

di Amato, A. *Criminal Law in Italy* (The Hague: Kluwer, 2011).

Díaz Barrado, C. M. *El consentimiento, causa de exclusión de la ilicitud del uso de la fuerza en Derecho Internacional* (Zaragoza: Universidad de Zaragoza, 1989).

Dickinson, E. D. 'The Analogy Between Natural Persons and International Persons in the Law of Nations' (1917) 26 *Yale Law Journal* 564.

Dickson, D. 'Bomb Scandal Highlights French Testing' (1985) 229 *Science* 948.

Dietrich, J., 'Accessorial Liability in the Law of Tort' (2011) 31 *Legal Studies* 231.

Dinstein, Y. 'International Law as a Primitive Legal System' (1986–7) 19 *New York University Journal of International Law & Politics* 1.

  *War, Aggression and Self-Defence*, 5th edn (Cambridge: Cambridge University Press, 2012).

Distefano, G. 'Fait continu, fait composé et fait complexe dans le droit de la responsabilité' (2006) 52 *Annuaire Français de droit international* 1.

  'Article 51 (1969)' in Corten, O. and Klein, P. (eds), *The Vienna Conventions on the Law of Treaties: A Commentary* (Oxford: Oxford University Press, 2011) vol. 2, 1179.

Dominicé, C. 'Observations sur les droits de l'Etat victime d'un fait internationalement illicite' in Dominicé, C. et al. (eds), *L'ordre juridique international entre tradition et innovation* (Paris: PUF, 1997), 261.

Dominicé, C. 'The International Responsibility of States for Breach of Multilateral Obligations' (1999) 10 *European Journal of International Law* 353.

Dominicé, C. 'Attribution of Conduct to Multiple States and the Implication of a State in the Conduct of Another State' in Crawford, J. et al. (eds), *The Law of International Responsibility* (Oxford: Oxford University Press, 2010), 281.

Donner, P. 'Offering Refuge Is Better Than Refusing' (2008) 7 *Journal of Maritime Affairs* 281.

Dörr, O. and Randelzhofer, A. 'Article 2(4)' in Simma, B. et al. (eds), *The Charter of the United Nations: A Commentary* (Oxford: Oxford University Press, 2012) vol. 1, 200.

Doswald-Beck, L. 'The Legal Validity of Military Intervention by Invitation of the Government' (1985) 56 *British Yearbook of International Law* 189.
Drago, L. M. *Cobro coercitivo de deudas públicas* (Buenos Aires: Coni Hermanos, 1906).
Dressler, J. 'New Thoughts about the Concept of Justification on the Criminal Law: A Critique of Fletcher's Thinking and Rethinking' (1984–5) 32 *University of California in Los Angeles Law Review* 61.
  'Justifications and Excuses: A Brief Review of the Concepts and the Literature' (1986–7) 33 *Wayne Law Review* 1155.
  *Understanding Criminal Law* (New York: Matthew Bender, 1987).
Duarte d'Almeida, L. 'Defining "Defences"' in Dyson, A. et al. (eds), *Defences in Tort* (Oxford: Hart, 2015), 35.
  *Allowing for Exceptions: A Theory of Defences and Defeasibility in Law* (Oxford: Oxford University Press, 2015).
Ducrocq, L. *Représailles en temps de paix: Blocus pacifique suivi d'une étude sur les affaires de Chine (1900–1901)* (Paris, 1901).
Dugard, J. 'Jurisdiction over Persons on Board an Aircraft Landing in Distress' (1981) 30 *International & Comparative Law Quarterly* 902.
Dupuis, C. 'Règles générales du droit de la paix' (1930) 32 *Recueil des cours de l'Académie de droit international* 1.
Dupuy, P.-M. 'Le fait générateur de la responsabilité des Etats' (1984) 188 *Recueil des cours de l'Académie de droit international* 8.
  'The International Law of State Responsibility: Revolution or Evolution' (1989–90) 11 *Michigan Journal of International Law* 105.
Elagab, O. Y. *The Legality of Non-Forcible Counter-Measures in International Law* (Oxford: Oxford University Press, 1988).
Eser, A. 'Justification and Excuse' (1976) 24 *American Journal of Comparative Law* 621.
  'Justification and Excuse: A Key Issue in the Concept of Crime' in Eser, A. (ed.), *Justification and Excuse: Comparative Perspectives* (Freiburg, 1987), 18.
Fabisch, J. *Essai sur l'état de nécessité* (Lyon: Legendre, 1903).
Falcke, H. P. *Le blocus pacifique* (Leipzig: Arthur Rosserberg, 1919).
Falkof, G. '"State of Necessity" Defence Accepted in *LG&E v Argentina* ICSID Tribunal' (2006) 3(5) *Transnational Dispute Management*.
Farhang, C. 'Mapping the Approaches to the Question of Exemption from International Responsibility' (2013) 60 *Netherlands International Law Review* 93.
  'The Notion of Consent in Part One of the Draft Articles on State Responsibility' (2014) 27 *Leiden Journal of International Law* 55.
  'Self-Defence as a Circumstance Precluding the Wrongfulness of the Use of Force' (2015) 11 *Utrecht Law Review* 1.

Faria, M. P. B. R. 'Portugal' in *International Encyclopaedia of Laws (Criminal Law: Suppl. 48)* (The Hague: Kluwer, 2013).
Fauchille, P. *Du blocus maritime: étude de droit international et de droit comparé* (Paris: Rousseau, 1882).
  *Traité de droit international public (Paix)*, 8th edn (Paris: Rousseau, 1922) vol. 1.
  *Traité de droit international public (Paix)*, 8th edn (Paris: Rousseau, 1926) vol. 3.
Favre, A. 'Fault as an Element of the Illicit Act' (1964) 52 *Georgetown Law Journal* 566.
Feinberg, J. 'Voluntary Euthanasia and the Inalienable Right to Life (Tanner Lecture)' (1978) 7 *Philosophy & Public Affairs* 93.
Ferrer Beltrán, J. and Ratti, G. B. 'Defeasibility and Legality: A Survey' in Ferrer Beltrán, J. and Ratti, G. B. (eds), *The Logic of Legal Requirements: Essays on Defeasibility* (Oxford: Oxford University Press, 2012), 11.
Ferzan, K. K. 'Clarifying Consent: Peter Westen's The Logic of Consent' (2006) 25 *Law & Philosophy* 193.
  'Justification and Excuse' in Deigh, J. and Dolinko, D. (eds), *The Oxford Handbook of Philosophy of Criminal Law* (Oxford: Oxford University Press, 2011), 239.
Finkelstein, C. O. 'When the Rule Swallows the Exception' in Meyer, L. (ed.), *Rules and Reasoning: Essays in Honour of Frederick Schauer* (London: Hart, 1999), 147.
  'Two Men on a Plank' (2001) 7 *Legal Theory* 279.
Fiore, P. *Nouveau droit international public*, 2nd edn (Antoine trans., Paris: Pedone-Lauriel, 1885) vols 1 and 2.
  *Trattato di diritto internazionale*, 3rd edn (Torino: Unione Tipografico-Editrice, 1887) vol. 1.
  *Il diritto internazionale codificato* (Roma: Unione Tipografico-Editrice, 1890).
Firth, S. 'The Nuclear Issue in the Pacific Islands' (1986) 21 *Journal of Pacific History* 202.
Fitzmaurice, G. 'The General Principles of International Law Considered from the Standpoint of the Rule of Law' (1957) 92 *Recueil des cours de l'Académie de droit international* 1.
Fitzmaurice, M. 'Necessity in International Environmental Law' (2010) 41 *Netherlands Yearbook of International Law* 159.
Fitzmaurice, M. and Olufemi, E. *Contemporary Issues in the Law of Treaties* (Utrecht: Eleven, 2005).
Fletcher, G. P. 'Fairness and Utility in Tort Theory' (1972) 85 *Harvard Law Review* 537.
  'Proportionality and the Psychotic Aggressor: A Vignette in Comparative Criminal Theory' (1973) 8 *Israel Law Review* 367.
  'The Individualization of Excusing Conditions' (1973–4) 47 *Southern California Law Review* 1269.
  'The Right Deed for the Wrong Reason: A Reply to Mr. Robinson' (1975–6) 23 *University of California in Los Angeles Law Review* 293.

*Rethinking Criminal Law* (Oxford: Oxford University Press, 1978).
'Should Intolerable Prison Conditions Generate a Justification or an Excuse for Escape' (1978-9) 26 *University of California in Los Angeles Law Review* 1355.
'Perspectives on Rights: The Right to Life' (1978-9) 13 *Georgia Law Review* 1371.
'The Right to Life' (1980) 63 *Monist* 135.
'Rights and Excuses' (1984) 3 *Criminal Justice Ethics* 17.
*Rethinking Criminal Law* (Oxford: Oxford University Press, 2000).
*The Grammar of Criminal Law* (Oxford: Oxford University Press, 2007).
Fletcher, G. P. and Ohlin, J. *Defending Humanity: When Is Force Justified and Why* (Oxford: Oxford University Press, 2013).
Flöckher, A. *De l'intervention en droit international* (Paris: Pedone, 1896).
Focarelli, C. *Le contromisure nel diritto internazionale* (Milano: Giuffrè, 1994).
*International Law as a Social Construct* (Oxford: Oxford University Press, 2012).
Foignet, R. *Manuel élémentaire de droit international public* (Paris: Rousseau, 1892).
Foley, V. and Nolan, C. 'The *Erika* Judgment – Environmental Liability and Places of Refuge: A Sea Change in Civil and Criminal Responsibility That the Maritime Community Must Heed' (2008) 33 *Tulane Maritime Law Journal* 41.
Fontanelli, F. and Bjorge, E. '*Application of the Interim Accord of 13 September 1995 (The Former Yugoslav Republic of Macedonia v Greece)* Judgment of 5 December 2011' (2012) 61 *International & Comparative Law Quarterly* 775.
Foriers, P. *De l'état de nécessité en droit pénal* (Brussels: Bruylant, 1951).
Forlati, S. *Diritto dei trattati e responsabilità internazionale* (Milano: Giuffrè, 2005).
'Reactions to Non Performance of Treaties in International Law' (2012) 25 *Leiden Journal of International Law* 759.
Forteau, M. 'Reparation in the Event of a Circumstance Precluding Wrongfulness' in Crawford, J. et al. (eds), *The Law of International Responsibility* (Oxford: Oxford University Press, 2010), 887.
Foster, C. *Science and the Precautionary Principle in International Courts and Tribunals* (Cambridge: Cambridge University Press, 2011).
Foster, D. 'Necessity Knows No Law! *LG&E v Argentina*' (2006) 9 *International Arbitration Law Review* 149.
Fouret, J. '"*CMS c/LG&E*" ou l'état de nécessité en question' (2007) 2 *Revue de l'arbitrage* 249.
Fox, G. H. 'Intervention by Invitation' in Weller, M. (ed.), *Oxford Handbook on the Use of Force* (Oxford: Oxford University Press, 2015), 816.
Franck, T. M. *Recourse to Force* (Cambridge: Cambridge University Press, 2002).
'On Proportionality of Countermeasures in International Law' (2008) 102 *American Journal of International Law* 715.
François, J. 'Règles générales du droit de la paix' (1936) 66 *Recueil des cours de l'Académie de droit international* 1.
Frey, R. 'Act-Utilitarianism' in LaFollette, H. (ed.), *The Blackwell Guide to Ethical Theory* (Oxford: Blackwell, 2000), 165.

Frowein, J. A. '*Kosovo* and *Lotus*' in Fastenrath, U. et al. (eds), *From Bilateralism to Community Interest: Essays in Honour of Bruno Simma* (Oxford: Oxford University Press, 2011), 923.
Fry, J. D. 'Coercion, Causation, and the Fictional Elements of Indirect Responsibility' (2007) 40 *Vanderbilt Journal of Transnational Law* 611.
Funck-Brentano, T. and Sorel, A. *Précis de droit des gens* (Paris: Plon, 1877).
Gaja, G. '*Jus Cogens* Beyond the Vienna Convention' (1981) 172 *Recueil des cours de l'Académie de droit international* 271.
  'Primary and Secondary Rules in the International Law of State Responsibility' (2014) 97 *Rivista di diritto internazionale* 981.
  'Interpreting Articles Adopted by the International Law Commission' (2014) 85 *British Yearbook of International Law*.
Galiani, F. *De' doveri de' principi neutrali verso i principi guerreggianti, e di questi verso i neutrali* (1782).
Gardam, J. G. *Necessity, Proportionality and the Use of Force by States* (Cambridge: Cambridge University Press, 2010).
Gardner, J. 'Fletcher on Offences and Defences' (2003-4) 39 *Tulsa Law Review* 817.
  'The Gist of Excuses' in Gardner, D. (ed.), *Offences and Defences: Selected Essays in the Philosophy of Criminal Law* (Oxford: Oxford University Press, 2007), 121.
  'In Defence of Defences' in Gardner, J. (ed.), *Offences and Defences: Selected Essays in the Philosophy of Criminal Law* (Oxford: Oxford University Press, 2007), 77.
Garner, J. W. *International Law and the World War* (London: Longmans, 1920) vol. 2.
  'Responsibility of States for Injuries Suffered by Foreigners Within Their Territories on Account of Mob Violence, Riots and Insurrections' (1927) 21 *American Society of International Law Proceedings* 49.
Gattini, A. 'La notion de la faute à la lumière du projet de convention de la Commission du droit international sur la responsabilité internationale' (1992) 3 *European Journal of International Law* 253.
  'Smoking/No Smoking: Some Remarks on the Current Place of Fault in the ILC Draft Articles on State Responsibility' (1999) 10 *European Journal of International Law* 397.
Gazzini, T. *The Changing Rules on the Use of Force in International Law* (Manchester: Manchester University Press, 2005).
  'Foreign Investment and Measures Adopted on Grounds of Necessity: Toward a Common Understanding' (2010) 7(1) *Transnational Dispute Management*.
Gemma, S. *Appunti di diritto internazionale* (Bologna: Zanichelli, 1923).
Gerkens, J.-F. '*Vis maior* and *vis cui resisti non potest*' in van den Bergh, R. and van Niekerk, G. (eds), *Ex iusta traditum: Essays in Honour of Eric H Pool* (Pretoria: University of South Africa, 2005), 109.
Gessner, L. *Le droit des neutres sur mer* (Berlin: Stilke et van Muyden, 1865).

Ghanayim, K. 'Excused Necessity in Western Legal Philosophy' (2006) 19 *Canadian Journal of Law & Jurisprudence* 31.

Gidel, G. 'Droits et devoirs des nations, théorie classique des droits fondamentaux des États' (1925) 10 *Recueil des cours de l'Académie de droit international* 537.

Giraud, E. 'La théorie de la légitime défense' (1934) 49 *Recueil des cours de l'Académie de droit international* 688.

Goebel, J. 'The International Responsibility of States for Injuries Sustained by Aliens on Account of Mob Violence, Insurrections and Civil War' (1914) 8 *American Journal of International Law* 802.

Gomaa, M. M. *Suspension or Termination of Treaties on Grounds of Breach* (The Hague: Martinus Nijhoff, 1996).

Gordley, J. 'Damages under the Necessity Doctrine' (2005) 5 *Issues in Legal Scholarship*, article no 2.

Goudkamp, J. *Tort Law Defences* (Oxford: Hart, 2013).

Gourgourinis, A. 'The Distinction between Interpretation and Application of Norms in International Adjudication' (2011) 2 *Journal of International Dispute Settlement* 31.

Grabczynska, A. and Ferzan, K. K. 'Justifying *Killing in Self-Defence*' (2007) 99 *Journal of Criminal Law & Criminology* 235.

Graefrath, B. 'Complicity in the Law of International Responsibility' (1996) 29 *Revue Belge de droit international* 370.

Grando, M. *Evidence, Proof, and Fact-Finding in WTO Dispute Settlement* (Oxford: Oxford University Press, 2009).

Grapin, P. *Valeur internationale des Principes généraux du droit* (Paris: Domat-Montchrestien, 1934).

Gray, C. *Judicial Remedies in International Law* (Oxford: Clarendon, 1987).

*International Law and the Use of Force*, 3rd edn (Oxford: Oxford University Press, 2008).

*International Law and the Use of Force*, 4th edn (Oxford: Oxford University Press, 2012).

Green, J. A. 'The *Oil Platforms* Case: An Error in Judgment?' (2004) 9 *Journal of Conflict & Security Law* 357.

'Docking the *Caroline*: Understanding the Relevance of the Formula in Contemporary Customary International Law Concerning Self-Defense' (2006) 14 *Cardozo Journal of International & Comparative Law* 429.

'Questioning the Peremptory Status of the Prohibition of the Use of Force' (2011) 32 *Michigan Journal of International Law* 215.

Greenawalt, K. 'The Perplexing Borders of Justification and Excuse' (1984) 84 *Columbia Law Review* 1897.

'Distinguishing between Justification and Excuse' (1986) 49 *Law & Contemporary Problems* 89.

Greenwood, C. 'The Concept of War in Modern International Law' (1987) 36 *International & Comparative Law Quarterly* 283.

Gregory, C. N. 'The Law of Blockades' (1903) 12 *Yale Law Journal* 339.
Grewe, W. G. *The Epochs of International Law* (Michael Byers ed., Berlin: de Gruyter, 2000).
Gross, L. 'States as Organs of International Law and the Problem of Autointerpretation' in *Essays on International Law and Organization* (The Hague: Martinus Nijhoff, 1998) vol. 1, 167.
Gross, O. and Ni Aolain, F. 'Emergency, War and International Law' (2001) 70 *Nordic Journal of International Law* 29.
  *Law in Times of Crisis* (Cambridge: Cambridge University Press, 2006).
Grotius, H. *De jure belli ac pacis* (1625, Tuck ed., Indianapolis: Liberty Fund, 2005).
Grzebyk, P. *Criminal Responsibility for the Crime of Aggression* (London: Routledge, 2013).
Guani, A. 'Les mesures de coercition entre membres du Pacte de la Société des Nations envisagées spécialement au point de vue Américain' (1924) 31 *Revue générale de droit international public* 285.
Guarini, G. B. *Le rappresaglie in tempo di pace: storia e dottrina* (Roma: Società Cartiere Centrali, 1910).
Guarino, A. *Diritto Privato Romano*, 9th edn (Napoli: Jovene, 1992).
Guastini, R. *Le fonti del diritto. Fondamenti teorici* (Milano: Giuffrè, 2010).
Guggenheim, P. *Traité de droit international public* (Genève: Georg & Cie, 1954) vol. 2.
Guillaume, G. 'L'affaire du Rainbow Warrior et son règlement' in Guillaume, G. (ed.), *Les grandes crises internationales et le droit* (Paris: Seuil, 1994), 219.
Gur-Aye, M. 'Should a Criminal Code Distinguish between Justification and Excuse?' (1992) 5 *Canadian Journal of Law & Jurisprudence* 215.
  'Justifying the Distinction between Justifications and Power (Justification vs Power)' (2011) 5 *Criminal Law & Philosophy* 293.
Gutiérrez-Espada, C. *El hecho ilícito internacional* (Madrid: Dykinson, 2005).
Hackworth, G. H. 'Responsibility of States for Damage Caused in Their Territory to the Person or Property of Aliens' (1930) 24 *American Journal of International Law* 500.
Hage, J. *Studies in Legal Logic* (Heidelberg: Springer, 2005).
Hall, J. 'Comment on Justification and Excuse' (1976) 24 *American Journal of Comparative Law* 638.
Hall, W. E. *International Law* (Oxford: Clarendon Press, 1880).
Hallborg, R. 'Comparing Harms: The Lesser Evil Defense and the Trolley Problem' (1997) 3 *Legal Theory* 291.
Halleck, H. *International Law* (San Francisco: Bancroft, 1861).
  *Elements of International Law and Laws of War* (Philadelphia: Lippincott, 1866).
Hameed, A. 'Legislation and Law on the International Plane' (2015), University of Cambridge Faculty of Law Research Paper No 35/2015, available at http://papers.ssrn.com/sol3/papers.cfm?abstract_id=2614614.

Hannikainen, L. *Peremptory Norms (Jus Cogens) in International Law* (Helsinki: Lakimesliiton Kustannus, 1988).

Hart, H. 'Definition and Theory in Jurisprudence' in *Essays in Jurisprudence and Philosophy* (reprint, first published in 1953, Oxford: Oxford University Press, 1985), 1.

Hart, H. L. A. 'Legal Responsibility and Excuses', in Hart, H. L. A. (ed.), *Punishment and Responsibility: Essays in the Philosophy of Law*, 2nd edn (Oxford: Oxford University Press, 2008), 29.

Hassemer, W. 'Justification and Excuse in Criminal Law: Theses and Comments' (1986) *Brigham Young University Law Review* 573.

Haumant, A. *Les représailles* (Paris: Girard, 1934).

Hautefeuille, L. B. *Des droits et des devoirs des nations neutres en temps de guerre maritime*, 2nd edn (Paris: Guillaumin, 1858) vol. 1.

*Histoire des origines, des progres et des variations du droit maritime international* (Paris: Guillaumin, 1858).

Hazan, E. T. *L'état de nécessité en droit pénal interétatique et international* (Paris: Pedone, 1949).

Heathcote, S. 'State of Necessity and International Law', unpublished thesis, Graduate Institute of International and Development Studies, 2005.

'Est-ce que l'état de nécessité est un principe de droit international coutumier?' (2007) 1 *Revue Belge de droit international* 53.

Heffter, A. W. *Le droit international de l'Europe*, 2nd edn (Bergson trans., Paris: Cotillon, 1866).

*Le droit international de l'Europe*, 3rd edn (Bergson trans., Paris: Cotillon, 1873).

Herring, J. *Criminal Law: Texts, Cases, and Materials*, 6th edn (Oxford: Oxford University Press, 2014).

Higgins, A. P. *The Law of Nations and the War* (Oxford: Oxford University Press, 1914).

Higgins, R. *Problems and Process: International Law and How We Use It* (Oxford: Clarendon, 1994).

Hill, D. J. 'The Janina-Corfu Affair' (1924) 18 *American Journal of International Law* 98.

Hindmarsh, A. 'Self-Help in Time of Peace' (1932) 26 *American Journal of International Law* 315.

*Force in Peace. Force Short of War in International Relations* (1933, reprinted in London: Kennikat Press, 1973).

Hodges, H. G. *Doctrine of Intervention* (Princeton: Banner Press, 1915).

Hoffheimer, M. H. 'Codifying Necessity: Legislative Resistance to Enacting Choice-of-Evils Defenses to Criminal Liability' (2007) 82 *Tulane Law Review* 191.

Hogan, A. E. *Pacific Blockade* (Oxford: Clarendon, 1908).

Hohfeld, W. N. 'Some Fundamental Legal Conceptions as Applied in Judicial Reasoning' (1913) 23 *Yale Law Journal* 16.

*The Elements of Jurisprudence*, 3rd edn (Oxford: Clarendon Press, 1886).
Holland, T. 'War *Sub Modo*' (1903) 19 *Law Quarterly Review* 133.
Holtzendorff, F. V. *Eléments de droit international public* (Paris: Rousseau, 1891).
Holtzoff, A. 'Some Phases of the Law of Blockade' (1916) 10 *American Journal of International Law* 53.
Hoppe, J. and Wright, W. '*Force Majeure* Clauses in Leases' (2007) 21 *Probate & Property* 8.
Horder, J. *Excusing Crime* (Oxford: Oxford University Press, 2007).
Horowitz, D. L. 'Justification and Excuse in the Program of the Criminal Law' (1986) 49 *Law & Contemporary Problems* 109.
Hruschka, J. 'On the History of Justification and Excuse in Cases of Necessity' in Byrd, S. and Hruschka, J. (eds), *Kant and Law* (Aldershot: Ashgate, 2006), 323.
Hudson, M. O. 'How the League of Nations Met the Corfu Crisis' (1923) 6 *World Peace Foundation Pamphlet Series* 176.
Hull, I. V. *A Scrap of Paper: Breaking and Making International Law during the Great War* (Ithaca: Cornell University Press, 2014).
Hurd, H. M. 'Justification and Excuse, Wrongdoing and Culpability' (1998–9) 74 *Notre Dame Law Review* 1551.
  'Blaming the Victim: A Response to the Proposal that Criminal Law Recognize a General Defense of Contributory Responsibility' (2005) 8 *Buffalo Criminal Law Review* 503.
Hurst, C. B. 'The Effect of War on Treaties' (1921) 2 *British Yearbook of International Law* 37.
Husak, D. N. *Philosophy of Criminal Law* (New Jersey: Rowman & Littlefield, 1987).
  'Justifications and the Criminal Liability of Accessories' (1989–90) 80 *Journal of Criminal Law & Criminology* 491.
  'The Serial View of Criminal Law Defences' (1992) 3 *Criminal Law Forum* 369.
  'Partial Defenses' (1998) *Canadian Journal of Law and Jurisprudence* 167.
  'On the Supposed Priority of Justification to Excuse' (2005) 24 *Law & Philosophy* 557.
  'Beyond the Justification/Excuse Dichotomy' in Cruft, R. et al. (eds), *Crime, Punishment, and Responsibility: The Jurisprudence of Antony Duff* (Oxford: Oxford University Press, 2011), 141.
Jackson, M. *Complicity in International Law* (Oxford: Oxford University Press, 2015).
Jagota, S. P. 'State Responsibility: Circumstances Precluding Wrongfulness' (1985) 16 *Netherlands Yearbook of International Law* 249.
Jeffries, J. C. and Stephan, P. B. 'Defenses, Presumption, and Burden of Proof in the Criminal Law' (1979) 88 *Yale Law Journal* 1325.
Jenks, W. 'The Conflict of Law-Making Treaties' (1953) 30 *British Yearbook of International Law* 401.
Jennings, R. Y. 'The *Caroline* and McLeod Cases' (1938) 32 *American Journal of International Law* 82.

Jescheck, H.-H. 'Evolución del concepto jurídico de la culpabilidad en Alemania y Austria' (2003) 5(1) *Revista Electrónica de Ciencia Penal y Criminología*.

Jiménez de Aréchaga, E. 'International Responsibility' in Sørensen, M. (ed.), *Manual of Public International Law* (London: MacMillan, 1968), 541.

Johnstone, I. 'The Plea of "Necessity" in International Legal Discourse: Humanitarian Intervention and Counter-terrorism' (2005) 43 *Columbia Journal of Transnational Law* 337.

Jones, G. H. and Schlechtriem, P. 'Breach of Contract (Deficiencies in a Party's Performance)' in Von Mehren, A. T. (ed.), *International Encyclopedia of Comparative Law* (Leiden: Martinus Nijhoff, 1976) vol. 7 (Contracts in General).

Jones, H. 'The *Caroline* Affair' (1976) 28 *Historian* 485.

Jouannet, E. *The Liberal-Welfarist Law of Nations* (Cambridge: Cambridge University Press, 2012).

Kadish, S. 'Respect for Life and Regard for Rights in the Criminal Law' (1976) 64 *California Law Review* 871.

'Excusing Crime' (1987) 75 *California Law Review* 257.

Kaeckenbeck, G. 'Divergences between British and Other Views on International Law' (1919) 4 *Transactions of the Grotian Society* 213.

Kalshoven, F. *Belligerent Reprisals*, 2nd edn (The Hague: Martinus Nijhoff, 2005).

Kammerhofer, J. 'Oil's Well That Ends Well? Critical Comments on the Merits Judgment in the *Oil Platforms* Case' (2004) 17 *Leiden Journal of International Law* 695.

'Gaps, the Nuclear Weapons Advisory Opinion and the Structure of International Legal Argument between Theory and Practice' (2010) 80 *British Yearbook of International Law* 333.

*Uncertainty in International Law: A Kelsenian Perspective* (London: Routledge, 2011).

'The Resilience of the Restrictive Rules on Self-Defence' in Weller, M. (ed.), *Oxford Handbook of the Use of Force in International Law* (Oxford: Oxford University Press, 2015), 627.

Kamto, M. 'La volonté de l'Etat en droit international' (2004) 310 *Recueil des cours de l'Académie de droit international* 9.

'The Time Factor in the Application of Countermeasures' in Crawford, J. et al. (eds), *The Law of International Responsibility* (Oxford: Oxford University Press, 2010), 1169.

Kasachkoff, T. 'Killing in Self-Defense: An Unquestionable or Problematic Defense?' (1998) 17 *Law & Philosophy* 509.

Kasenetz, E. D. 'Desperate Times Call for Desperate Measures' (2010) 41 *George Washington Law Review* 709.

Kaufman, W. 'Is There a "Right" to Self-Defense?' (2004) 23 *Criminal Justice Ethics* 20.

Kazazi, M. *Burden of Proof and Related Issues: A Study on Evidence before International Tribunals* (The Hague: Kluwer Law International, 1996).

Kearly, T. 'Raising the *Caroline*' (1999) 17 *Wisconsin International Law Journal* 325.
Kelsen, H. 'Théorie générale du droit international public. Problèmes choisis' (1932) 42 *Recueil des cours de l'Académie de droit international* 117.
  *Unrecht und unrechtsfolge im volkerrecht* (Wien: Springer, 1932).
  *General Theory of Law and State* (Wedberg trans., Cambridge, MA: Harvard University Press, 1945).
  'Sanctions in International Law under the Charter of the United Nations' (1945–6) 31 *Iowa Law Review* 499.
  'Collective Security and Collective Self-Defence under the Charter of the United Nations' (1948) 42 *American Journal of International Law* 783.
  'Théorie du droit international public' (1953) 84 *Recueil des cours de l'Académie de droit international* 1.
  *Law and Peace in International Relations – The Oliver Wendell Holmes Lectures, 1940–1941* (Buffalo, NY: William S Hein & Co, 1997).
  *Introduction to the Problems of Legal Theory: A Translation of the First Edition of the Reine Rechtslehre or Pure Theory of Law* (B. Litschewski Paulson and S. L. Paulson trans, Oxford: Oxford University Press, 1997).
Kentin, E. 'Economic Crisis and Investment Arbitration: The Argentine Cases' in Kahn, P. and Wälde, T. (eds), *New Aspects of International Investment Law* (The Hague: Nijhoff, 2007), 629.
Kerbrat, Y. 'Interaction between the Forms of Reparation' in Crawford, J. et al. (eds), *The Law of International Responsibility* (Oxford: Oxford University Press, 2010), 574.
Kirgis, F. L. 'Some Lingering Questions about Article 60 of the Vienna Convention on the Law of Treaties' (1989) 22 *Cornell International Law Journal* 549.
Kiss, A. *Répertoire de la pratique française en matière de droit international public* (Paris: CNRS, 1962).
Klabbers, J. *International Law* (Cambridge: Cambridge University Press, 2013).
Kleen, R. *Lois et usages de la neutralité d'après le droit international conventionnel et coutumier des états civilisés* (Paris: Marescq Ainé, 1898) vol. 1.
Klepper, H. 'Torts of Necessity: A Moral Theory of Compensation' (1990) 9 *Law & Philosophy* 223.
Klüber, J.-L. *Droit des gens moderne de l'Europe* (Paris: Aillaud, 1831).
Klüber, J.-L. *Droit des gens moderne de l'Europe*, 2nd edn (Ott ed., Paris: Pedone-Lauriel, 1874).
Knoops, G.-J. A. *Defenses in Contemporary International Criminal Law* (The Hague: Martinus Nijhoff, 2008).
Koh, K. and Tan, Y. 'Singapore' in *International Encyclopaedia of Laws (Criminal Law: Suppl. 5)* (The Hague: Kluwer, 1995).
Kohen, M. 'The Notion of "State Survival" in International Law' in Boisson de Chazournes, L. and Sands, P. (eds), *Nuclear Weapons and the International Court of Justice* (Cambridge: Cambridge University Press, 1999), 293.

Kolb, R. 'La légitime défense des Etats au XIXème siècle et pendant l'époque de la Société de Nations' in Kherad, R. (ed.), *Légitimes défenses* (Paris: LGDJ, 2007), 67.
'Conflits entre normes de *jus cogens*' in Corten, O. et al. (eds), *Droit du pouvoir, pouvoir du droit: Mélanges offerts à Jean Salmon* (Brussels: Bruylant, 2007), 481.
*The International Court of Justice* (Oxford: Hart, 2013).
*Peremptory International Law – Jus Cogens: A General Inventory* (Oxford: Hart, 2015).
Koskenniemi, M. 'Solidarity Measures: State Responsibility as a New International Order?' (2002) 72 *British Yearbook of International Law* 337.
*From Apology to Utopia: The Structure of International Legal Argument* (reissued with new epilogue, Cambridge: Cambridge University Press, 2006).
Kramer, M. *Objectivity and the Rule of Law* (Cambridge: Cambridge University Press, 2007).
Kunz, J. 'The Law of Nations, Static and Dynamic' (1933) 27 *American Journal of International Law* 630.
'The Theory of International Law' (1938) 32 *American Society of International Law Proceedings* 23.
'Adjudging the Exceptional at International Law: Security, Public Order and Financial Crisis' (2008) 59 *International & Comparative Law Quarterly* 325.
*La Guerre de 1914: recueil de documents intéressant le droit international* (Paris: Pedone, 1916) vols 1–2. https://archive.org/details/laguerrede1914re01pari
Lafargue, P. *Les représailles en temps de paix* (Paris: Rousseau, 1898).
Lamberti-Zanardi, P. *La legittima difesa nel diritto internazionale* (Milano: Giuffrè, 1972).
Lang, G. 'Why Not Forfeiture?' in Frowe, H. and Lang, G. (eds), *How We Fight: Ethics in War* (Oxford: Oxford University Press, 2014), 38.
Lanovoy, V. 'Complicity in an Internationally Wrongful Act' in Nollkaemper, A. and Plakokefalos, I. (eds), *Principles of Shared Responsibility* (Cambridge: Cambridge University Press, 2014), 134.
Laun, R. 'Le régime international des ports' (1926) 15 *Recueil des cours de l'Académie de droit international* 1.
Laurent, P. H. 'State Responsibility: A Possible Historic Precedent to the Calvo Clause' (1966) 15 *International & Comparative Law Quarterly* 395.
'Anglo-American Diplomacy and the Belgian Indemnities Controversy 1836–42' (1967) 10 *Historical Journal* 197.
Laursen, A. 'The Use of Force and (the State of) Necessity' (2004) 37 *Vanderbilt Journal of International Law* 485.
'The Judgment of the International Court of Justice in the *Oil Platforms* Case' (2004) 73 *Nordic Journal of International Law* 135.
Lauterpacht, H. 'The So-Called Anglo-American and Continental Schools of Thought in International Law' (1931) 12 *British Yearbook of International Law* 31.

Lawrence, T. J. *Handbook of Public International Law*, 2nd edn (Cambridge: Deighton, Beel & Co, 1885).
*The Principles of International Law*, 4th edn (Boston: DC Heath & Co, 1910).
*The Principles of International Law*, 6th edn (Boston: DC Heath & Co, 1915).
Leben, C. 'Les contre-mesures inter-étatiques et les réactions à l'illicite dans la société internationale' (1982) 28 *Annuaire Français de droit international* 9.
'L'etat de nécessité dans le droit international de l'investissement' (2005) 349 *Cahiers de l'arbitrage* 19.
'Obligations Relating to the Use of Force and Arising from Peremptory Norms of International Law' in Crawford, J. et al. (eds), *The Law of International Responsibility* (Oxford: Oxford University Press, 2010), 1197.
Lebergott, S. 'Through the Blockade: The Profitability and Extent of Cotton Smuggling, 1861–1865' (1981) 41 *Journal of Economic History* 867.
Lefeber, R. 'Case Analysis: The *Gabčíkovo-Nagymaros Project* and the Law of State Responsibility' (1998) 11 *Leiden Journal of International Law* 609.
LeFur, L. *Des représailles en temps de guerre. Représailles et réparation* (Paris: Sirey, 1919).
'La théorie du droit naturel depuis le XVII siècle et la doctrine moderne' (1927) 18 *Recueil des cours de l'Académie de droit international* 259.
Lenckner, T. 'The Principle of Interest Balancing as a General Basis of Justification' (1986) *Brigham Young University Law Review* 645.
Lepard, B. D. *Customary International Law: A New Theory with Practical Applications* (Cambridge: Cambridge University Press, 2010).
Lesaffer, R. 'Too Much History: From War as Sanction to the Sanctioning of War' in Weller, M. (ed.), *Oxford Handbook of the Use of Force in International Law* (Oxford: Oxford University Press, 2015), 35.
Leverick, F. *Killing in Self-Defence* (Oxford: Oxford University Press, 2006).
'Defending Self-Defence' (2007) 27 *Oxford Journal of Legal Studies* 563.
Linderfalk, U. 'The Effect of *Jus Cogens* Norms: Whoever Opened Pandora's Box, Did You Ever Think about the Consequences?' (2007) 18 *European Journal of International Law* 853.
Lissitzyn, O. J. 'The Treatment of Aerial Intruders in Recent Practice and International Law' (1953) 47 *American Journal of International Law* 559.
Londoño Lázaro, M. C. *Las garantías de no repetición en la jurisprudencia Interamericana. Derecho Internacional y cambios estructurales del Estado* (México DF: Tirant lo Blanch, 2014).
Lowe, V. 'Precluding Wrongfulness or Responsibility: A Plea for Excuses?' (1999) 10 *European Journal of International Law* 405.
Lowell, A. L. 'The Council of the League of Nations and Corfu' (1923) 6 *World Peace Foundation Pamphlet Series* 169.
Lozano Contreras, F. *La noción de debida diligencia en derecho internacional público* (Barcelona: Atelier, 2007).

'El estado de necesidad y las cláusulas de emergencia contempladas en los APPRI: los casos argentinos ante el CIADI' (2013) 65 *Revista Española de derecho internacional* 101.

Lubell, N. *Extraterritorial Use of Force against Non-State Actors* (Oxford: Oxford University Press, 2010).

Lushington, S. G. *A Manual of Naval Prize Law* (London: Butterworths, 1866).

Maccoby, S. 'Reprisals as a Measure of Redress Short of War' (1924–6) 2 *Cambridge Law Journal* 64.

MacCormick, N. *Rhetoric and the Rule of Law: A Theory of Legal Reasoning* (Oxford: Oxford University Press, 2005).

Macdonell, J. 'The Declaration of London' (1910) 11 *Journal of the Society of Comparative Legislation* 68.

Mackie, J. L. *Ethics: Inventing Right and Wrong* (London: Penguin, 1977).

Macri, G. *Teorica del diritto internazionale* (Messina: Fratelli d'Angelo, 1883) vol. 1.

  *Teorica del diritto internazionale* (Messina: Fratelli d'Angelo, 1884) vol. 2.

Malanczuk, P. 'Countermeasures and Self-Defence as Circumstances Precluding Wrongfulness in the ILC Draft Articles on State Responsibility' (1983) 43 *Zeitschrift für ausländisches öffentliches Recht und Völkerrecht* 705.

  'Countermeasures and Self-Defence as Circumstances Precluding Wrongfulness in the International Law Commission's Draft Articles on State Responsibility' in Spinedi, M. and Simma, B. (eds), *United Nations Codification of State Responsibility* (New York: Oceana, 1987), 197.

Mancini, M. *Stato di guerra e conflitto armato nel diritto internazionale* (Torino: Giappichelli, 2009).

  'The Effects of a State of War or Armed Conflict' in Weller, M. (ed.), *Oxford Handbook of the Use of Force in International Law* (Oxford: Oxford University Press, 2015), 988.

Manning, W. R. *Diplomatic Correspondence of the United States–Canadian Relations* (Washington: Carnegie Endowment, 1943) vol. 3.

Mantovani, F. *Principi di diritto penale*, 2nd edn (Padova: CEDAM, 2007).

Marchesi, A. *Obblighi di condotta e obblighi di risultato* (Milano: Giuffrè, 2003).

Marinucci, G. and Dolcini, E. *Manuale di diritto penale*, 2nd edn (Milano: Giuffrè, 2006).

Marks, S. 'Treaties, State Responsibility and Remedies' (1990) 49 *Cambridge Law Journal* 387.

Martin, A. 'Investment Disputes after Argentina's Economic Crisis: Interpreting BIT Non-Precluded Measures and the Doctrine of Necessity under Customary International Law' (2012) 29 *Journal of International Arbitration* 49.

Martinez, A. 'Is Invoking State Defences in Investment Arbitration a Waste of Time and Money?' (2008) 15 *Croatian Arbitration Yearbook* 89.

  'Invoking State Defenses in Investment Treaty Arbitration' in Waibel, M. et al. (eds), *The Backlash against Investment Arbitration: Perceptions and Reality* (The Hague: Kluwer, 2010), 315.

McAuley, F. 'Theory of Justification and Excuse: Some Italian Lessons' (1987) 35 *American Journal of Comparative Law* 359.

McDougall, C. *The Crime of Aggression under the Rome Statute of the International Criminal Court* (Cambridge: Cambridge University Press, 2013).

McGregor, L. 'Torture and State Immunity: Deflecting Impunity, Distorting Sovereignty' (2007) 18 *European Journal of International Law* 903.

McKean, F. G. J. 'The Law of Necessity' (1932) 36 *Dickinson Law Review* 237.

McMahan, J. *Killing in War* (Oxford: Clarendon Press, 2009).

McNair, A. D. 'The Legal Meaning of War, and the Relation of War to Reprisals' (1926) 11 *Transactions of the Grotian Society* 29.

Mérignhac, A. *Traité de droit public international* (Paris: LGDJ, 1905) vol. 1.

Mérignhac, A. *Traité de droit public international* (Paris: LGDJ, 1907) vol. 2.

Mérignhac, A. *Traité de droit public international* (Paris: LGDJ, 1912) vol. 3.

Merkouris, P. *Article 31(3)(c) VCLT and the Principle of Systemic Integration: Normative Shadows in Plato's Cave* (Leiden: Brill, 2015).

Merle, R. and Vitu, A. *Traité de droit criminel: Droit pénal général*, 6th edn (Paris: Cujas, 1988).

Messineo, F. 'Maps of Ephemeral Empires: The ICJ and the Macedonian Name Dispute' (2012) 1 *Cambridge Journal of International & Comparative Law* 169.

  'Multiple Attribution of Conduct' in Nollkaemper, A. and Plakokefalos, I. (eds), *Principles of Shared Responsibility* (Cambridge: Cambridge University Press, 2014), 60.

Migliorino, L. 'Sur la déclaration d'illicéité comme forme de satisfaction: à propos de la sentence arbitrale du 30 avril 1990 dans l'affaire du *Rainbow Warrior*' (1992) 96 *Revue générale de droit international public* 61.

Milanović, M. 'The Lost Origins of Lex Specialis: Rethinking the Relationship between Human Rights and International Humanitarian Law' in Ohlin, J. (ed.), *Theoretical Boundaries of Armed Conflict and Human Rights* (Cambridge: Cambridge University Press, 2016).

Milgrim, M. R. 'An Overlooked Problem in Turkish–Russian Relations: The 1878 War Indemnity' (1978) 9 *International Journal of Middle East Studies* 519.

Milhizer, E. R. 'Justification and Excuse: What They Were, What They Are and What They Ought to Be' (2004) 78 *St John's Law Review* 725.

Miller, S. 'Killing in Self-Defense' (1993) 7 *Public Affairs Quarterly* 325.

Mills, A. 'Rethinking Jurisdiction in International Law' (2013) 84 *British Yearbook of International Law* 187.

Moir, L. 'Action against Host States of Terrorist Groups' in Weller, M. (ed.), *Oxford Handbook of the Use of Force in International Law* (Oxford: Oxford University Press, 2015), 720.

Monaco, R. *Manuale di diritto internazionale pubblico* (Torino: UTET, 1960).

Montague, P. 'Rights and Duties of Compensation' (1984) 13 *Philosophy & Public Affairs* 79.

'Davis and Westen on Rights and Compensation' (1985) 14 *Philosophy & Public Affairs* 390.

'War and Self-Defence: A Critique and a Proposal' (2010) 23 *Diametros* 69.

Montini, M. 'La necessità ambientale e le sue diverse funzioni nel diritto internazionale contemporaneo' in Spinedi, M. et al. (eds), *La codificazione della responsabilità internazionale degli Stati alla prova dei fatti* (Milano: Giuffrè, 2006), 153.

Moore, M. S. 'Torture and the Balance of Evils' (1989) 23 *Israel Law Review* 284.

Morelli, G. *Nozioni di diritto internazionale*, 7th edn (Padova: CEDAM, 1967).

Morgenthau, H. J. 'Théorie des sanctions internationales' (1935) 16 *Revue de droit international et législation comparée* (3rd series) 474.

Moriaud, P. *De la justification du délit par l'état de nécessité* (Geneva: Burkhart, 1889).

Morrison, A. *Places of Refuge for Ships in Distress* (Leiden: Brill, 2012).

Moursi Badr, G. 'The Exculpatory Effect of Self-Defence in State Responsibility' (1980) 10 *Georgia Journal of International & Comparative Law* 1.

Mousourakis, G. 'Distinguishing between Justifications and Excuses in the Criminal Law' (1998) 9 *Stellenbosch Law Review* 165.

'Justification and Excuse' (1998–9) 7 *Tilburg Foreign Law Review* 35.

Murphy, S. D. 'Article 80 of the Rules (Counter-claims)' in Zimmerman, A. et al. (eds), *The Statute of the International Court of Justice: A Commentary* (Oxford: Oxford University Press, 2006), 1000.

Murray, C. F. 'Any Port in a Storm? The Right of Entry for Reasons of *Force Majeure* or Distress in the Wake of the *Erika* and the *Castor*' (2002) 63 *Ohio State Law Journal* 1465.

Neff, S. C. *The Rights and Duties of Neutrals* (Manchester: Manchester University Press, 2000).

*War and the Law of Nations* (Cambridge: Cambridge University Press, 2005).

*Justice among Nations* (Cambridge, MA: Harvard, 2014).

Newcombe, A. and Paradell, L. *Law and Practice of Investment Treaties: Standards of Treatment* (Alphen aan den Rijn: Wolters Kluwer, 2009).

Niemeyer, T. 'International Law in War' (1915) 13 *Michigan Law Review* 175.

Nollkaemper, A. 'Concurrence between Individual Responsibility and State Responsibility in International Law' (2003) 52 *International & Comparative Law Quarterly* 615.

'International Adjudication of Global Public Goods: The Intersection of Substance and Procedure' (2012) 23 *European Journal of International Law* 769.

Nollkaemper, A. and Jacobs, D. 'Shared Responsibility in International Law: A Concept Paper' (2013) 34 *Michigan Journal of International Law* 359.

Nollkaemper, A. and Plakokefalos, I. (eds), *Principles of Shared Responsibility* (Cambridge: Cambridge University Press, 2014).

Noyes, J. E. 'Places of Refuge for Ships' (2008) 37 *Denver Journal of International Law & Policy* 135.

'Ships in Distress' in Wolfrum, R. (ed.), *Max Planck Encyclopedia of Public International Law* (www.mpepil.com, Oxford: Oxford University Press, 2009–).

Nys, E. *Le droit international* (Paris: Fontemoing, 1905) vol. 2.

O'Connell, M. E. 'Evidence of Terror' (2002) 7 *Journal of Conflict & Security Law* 19.

*The Power and Purpose of International Law* (Oxford: Oxford University Press, 2011).

O'Connor, T. 'Free Will' in Zalta, E. N. (ed.), *Stanford Encyclopedia of Philosophy* (2011).

O'Keefe, R. 'Universal Jurisdiction: Clarifying the Basic Concept' (2004) 3 *Journal of International Criminal Justice* 735.

'Proportionality' in Crawford, J. et al. (eds), *The Law of International Responsibility* (Oxford: Oxford University Press, 2010), 1158.

'Jurisdictional Immunities' in Tams, C. and Sloan, J. (eds), *The Development of International Law by the International Court of Justice* (Oxford: Oxford University Press, 2013), 107.

*International Criminal Law* (Oxford: Oxford University Press, 2015).

'Theory and the Doctrinal International Lawyer' (2015) 4 *University College London Journal of Law & Jurisprudence*.

Oberdiek, J. 'Lost in Moral Space: On the Infringing/Violating Distinction and Its Place in the Theory of Rights' (2004) 23 *Law & Philosophy* 325.

'What's Wrong with Infringements (Insofar as Infringements Are Not Wrong): A Reply' (2008) 27 *Law & Philosophy* 293.

Okowa, P. N. 'Defences in the Jurisprudence of International Tribunals' in Goodwin-Gill, G. S. and Talmon, S. (eds), *The Reality of International Law: Essays in Honour of Ian Brownlie* (Oxford: Clarendon Press, 1999), 389.

Omichinski, N. M. 'Applying the Theories of Justifiable Homicide to Conflicts in the Doctrine of Self-Defense' (1986–7) 33 *Wayne Law Review* 1447.

Oppenheim, L. *International Law* (London: Longmans, 1906) vol. 2.

*International Law*, 2nd edn (London: Longmans, 1912) vol. 1.

Orakhelashvili, A. *Peremptory Norms in International Law* (Oxford: Oxford University Press, 2009).

Orrego-Vicuña, F. 'Softening Necessity' in Arsanjani, M. (ed.), *Looking to the Future: Essays on International Law in Honour of W Michael Reisman* (Leiden: Brill, 2010), 741.

Ortiz de Urbino Gimeno, Í. 'De moscas y agresores muertos' (2008) 3 *Revista para el Análisis del Derecho* 2.

Ortolan, T. *Règles internationales et diplomatie de la mer* (Paris: Dumaine, 1845) vols 1–3.

*Règles internationales et diplomatie de la mer*, 4th edn (Paris: Plon, 1864) vol. 1.

Paddeu, F. 'A Genealogy of *Force Majeure* in International Law' (2011) 82 *British Yearbook of International Law* 381.

'Self-Defence as a Circumstance Precluding Wrongfulness: Understanding Article 21 of the Articles on State Responsibility' (2014) 85 *British Yearbook of International Law*.
'Circumstances Precluding Wrongfulness' in Wolfrum, R. (ed.), *Max Planck Encyclopedia of Public International Law* (www.mpepil.com, Oxford: Oxford University Press, 2015–).
'Use of Force Against Non-State Actors and the Circumstance Precluding Wrongfulness of Self-Defence' (2017) 30 *Leiden Journal of International Law* 93.
Padelletti, M. L. *Pluralità di stati nel fatto illecito internazionale* (Milan: Giuffrè, 1990).
Padovani, T. *Diritto penale*, 9th edn (Milano: Giuffrè, 2008).
Palazzo, F. *Corso di diritto penale. Parte generale* (Torino: Giappichelli, 2008).
Palmer, G. 'Settlement of International Disputes: The *Rainbow Warrior* Affair' (1989) 15 *Commonwealth Law Bulletin* 585.
Palmisano, G. 'Sulla decisione arbitrale relativa alla seconda fase del caso *Rainbow Warrior*' (1990) 73 *Rivista di diritto internazionale* 874.
'Colpa dell'organo e colpa dello Stato nella responsabilità internazionale: Spunti critici di teoria e di prassi' (1992) 19–20 *Comunicazioni e Studi* 623.
'Fault' in Wolfrum, R. (ed.), *Max Planck Encyclopedia of Public International Law* (www.mpepil.com, Oxford: Oxford University Press, 2007–).
Paparinskis, M. 'Investment Arbitration and the Law of Countermeasures' (2008) 79 *British Yearbook of International Law* 264.
'Investment Treaty Arbitration and the (New) Law of State Responsibility' (2013) 24 *European Journal of International Law* 617.
Parlett, K. *The Individual in the International Legal System: Continuity and Change in International Law* (Cambridge: Cambridge University Press, 2011).
'The Application of the Rules on Countermeasures in Investment Claims' in Chinkin, C. M. and Baetens, F. (eds), *Sovereignty, Statehood and State Responsibility: Essays in Honour of James Crawford* (Cambridge: Cambridge University Press, 2015), 389.
Passero, L. *Dionisio Anzilotti e la dottrina internazionalistica tra Otto e Novecento* (Milano: Giuffrè, 2010).
Paulsson, J. *Denial of Justice in International Law* (Cambridge: Cambridge University Press, 2005).
Pauwelyn, J. 'Evidence, Proof and Persuasion in WTO Dispute Settlement: Who Bears the Burden?' (1998) 1 *Journal of International Economic Law* 227.
*Conflict of Norms in Public International Law* (Cambridge: Cambridge University Press, 2003).
Pavoni, R. 'Human Rights and the Immunities of Foreign States and International Organizations' in de Wet, E. and Vidmar, J. (eds), *Hierarchy in International Law: The Place of Human Rights* (Oxford: Oxford University Press, 2012), 71.

Pellet, A. 'The Normative Dilemma – Will and Consent in International Law' (1992) 12 *Australian Yearbook of International Law* 22.
  'Remarques sur une Révolution Inachevée: le Projet d'Articles de la Commission du Droit International sur la Responsabilité des Etats' (1996) 42 *Annuaire Français de droit international* 7.
  'La codification du droit de la responsabilité internationale: tatonnements et affrontements' in Boisson de Chazournes, L. and Gowlland-Debbas, V. (eds), *The International Legal System in Quest of Equity and Universality. Liber Amicorum Georges Abi-Saab* (The Hague: Martinus Nijhoff, 2001), 285.
  'Les Articles de la CDI sur la Responsabilité de l'Etat pour fait internationalement illicite. Suite – et fin?' (2002) 48 *Annuaire Français de droit international* 1.
  'Les rapports de Roberto Ago à la CDI sur la responsabilité des Etats' (2002) 4 *Forum du droit international* 222.
  'The Definition of Responsibility in International Law' in Crawford, J. et al. (eds), *The Law of International Responsibility* (Oxford: Oxford University Press, 2010), 3.
  'The ILC's Articles on State Responsibility for Internationally Wrongful Acts and Related Texts' in Crawford, J. et al. (eds), *The Law of International Responsibility* (Oxford: Oxford University Press, 2010), 75.
Penfield, W. 'The Anglo-German Intervention in Venezuela' (1903) 177 *North American Review* 86.
Perassi. 'Necessità e stato di necessità nella teoria dommatica della produzione giuridica' (1917) *Rivista di diritto pubblico* 271.
Perels, M. 'Droit de blocus en temps de paix' (1887–8) 9 *Annuaire de l'Institut de droit international* 275.
Pergola, U. 'Fondamento giustificativo dello stato di necessità' (1909) 70 *Rivista Penale* 405.
Phillimore, R. *Commentaries upon International Law* (Philadelphia: Johnson, 1854) vol. 1.
  *Commentaries upon International Law* (Philadelphia: Johnson, 1855) vol. 2.
  *Commentaries upon International Law* (Philadelphia: Johnson, 1857) vol. 3.
Phillipson, C. *International Law and the Great War* (London: Fisher Unwin, 1915).
  *Wheaton's Elements of International Law*, 5th edn (London: Stevens, 1916).
Picchio Forlati, L. *La sanzione nel diritto internazionale* (Padova: CEDAM, 1974).
Piédelièvre, R. *Précis de droit international public* (Paris: Cotillon, 1894) vol. 1.
Piédelièvre, R. *Précis de droit international public* (Paris: Cotillon, 1895) vol. 2.
Pillet, A. *Recherches sur les droits fondamentaux des Etats* (Paris: Pedone, 1899).
Pillitu, A. P. *Lo stato di necessità nel diritto internazionale* (Perugia: Università di Perugia, 1981).
Pink, T. 'The Will' in Craig, E. (ed.), *Routledge Encyclopedia of Philosophy* (www.rep.routledge.com/article/N086, London: Routledge, 1998).

Pinto, R. 'L'affaire du Rainbow Warrior: à propos de la sentence du 30 avril 1990, Nouvelle-Zélande c/France' (1990) 117 *Journal du droit international* 841.

Pisillo Mazzeschi, R. 'Termination and Suspension of Treaties for Breach in the ILC Works on State Responsibility' in Spinedi, M. and Simma, B. (eds), *United Nations Codification of State Responsibility* (New York: Oceana, 1987), 57.

*Due diligence e responsabilità internazionale degli Stati* (Milano: Giuffrè, 1989).

'Responsabilité de l'état pour violation des obligations positives relatives aux droits de l'homme' (2008) 333 *Recueil des cours de l'Académie de droit international* 175.

Podestá-Costa, L. 'La responsabilidad del Estado por daños irrogados a la persona o a los bienes de extranjeros en luchas civiles' (1939) 34 *Revista de derecho internacional (La Habana)* 5.

Politis, N. 'Les représailles entre Etats membres de la Société des Nations' (1924) 31 *Revue générale de droit international public* 5.

'Le régime des représailles en temps de paix. Rapport et projets de résolution et de règlement' (1934) 38 *Annuaire de l'Institut de droit international* 1.

Politoff, S. et al. 'Chile' in *International Encyclopaedia of Laws (Criminal Law: Suppl. 24)* (The Hague: Kluwer, 2003).

Pradel, J. *Droit pénal comparé*, 2nd edn (Paris: Dalloz, 2002).

Pradier-Fodéré, P. *Traité de droit international: Européen et Américain* (Paris: Pedone, 1885) vol. 1.

Pradier-Fodéré, P. *Traité de droit international: Européen et Américain* (Paris: Pedone, 1894) vol. 6.

Proukaki, E. K. *The Problem of Enforcement in International Law* (London: Routledge, 2011).

Pufendorf, S. *De jure naturae et gentium* (1688, Oldfather trans, Oxford: Clarendon, 1934).

Pugh, M. 'Legal Aspects of the *Rainbow Warrior* Affair' (1987) 36 *International & Comparative Law Quarterly* 655.

Quadri, R. 'Cours général de droit international public' (1964) 113 *Recueil des cours de l'Académie de droit international* 237.

*Diritto internazionale pubblico*, 5th edn (Napoli: Liguori, 1968).

Quigley, J. 'Complicity in International Law: A New Direction in the Law of State Responsibility' (1986) 57 *British Yearbook of International Law* 77.

'The Common Law's Theory of Criminal Liability: A Challenge from Across the Atlantic' (1989-1990) 11 *Whittier Law Review* 479.

Radbruch, G. 'Jurisprudence in the Criminal Law' (1936) 18 *Journal of Comparative Legislation & International Law* 218.

Radouant, J. *Du cas fortuit et de la force majeure* (Paris: Rousseau, 1920).

Randelzhofer, A. 'Article 51' in Simma, B. (ed.), *The Charter of the United Nations*, 2nd edn (Oxford: Oxford University Press, 2002) vol. 1, 788.

Rapisardi-Mirabelli, A. *I limiti d'obbligatorietà delle norme giuridiche internazionali* (Catania: Giannotta, 1922).
  *La ritorsione* (Venezia: Ferrari, 1919).
Ratti, G. B. 'Normative Inconsistency and Logical Theories: A First Critique of Defeasibilism' in Araszkiewicz, M. and Šavelka, J. (eds), *Coherence: Insights from Philosophy, Jurisprudence and Artificial Intelligence* (Dordrecht: Springer, 2013), 123.
Raz, J. 'Legal Principles and the Limits of Law' (1972) 81 *Yale Law Journal* 823.
  *The Concept of a Legal System: An Introduction to the Theory of a Legal System* (Oxford: Clarendon Press, 1980).
Reeves, J. S. 'The Neutralization of Belgium and the Doctrine of *Kriegsraison*' (1915) 13 *Michigan Law Review* 179.
Reinisch, A. 'Necessity in International Investment Arbitration – An Unnecessary Split of Opinions in Recent ICSID Cases?' (2006) 3(5) *Transnational Dispute Management*.
  'Necessity in International Investment Arbitration – An Unnecessary Split of Opinions in Recent ICSID Cases?' (2007) 8 *Journal of World Investment and Trade* 191.
  'Necessity in Investment Arbitration' (2010) 41 *Netherlands Yearbook of International Law* 137.
Reinisch, A. and Binder, C., 'Debts and State of Necessity' in Boholavsky, J. P. and Cernic, J. L. (eds), *Making Sovereign Financing and Human Rights Work* (Oxford: Hart, 2014), 115.
Reinold, T. 'State Weakness, Irregular Warfare, and the Right of Self-Defense Post-9/11' (2011) 105 *American Journal of International Law* 244.
Reisman, M. 'The Supervisory Jurisdiction of the International Court of Justice: International Arbitration and International Adjudication' (1996) 258 *Recueil des cours de l'Académie de droit international* 9.
Renault, L. *First Violations of International Law by Germany: Luxembourg and Belgium* (Frank Carr trans, London: Longmans, 1917).
Reuter, P. 'Principes de droit international public' (1961) 103 *Recueil des cours de l'Académie de droit international* 425.
  *Droit international public*, 6th edn (Paris: PUF, 1983).
Riddell, A. and Plant, B. *Evidence before the International Court of Justice* (London: BIICL, 2009).
Rigaux, F. 'International Responsibility and the Principle of Causality' in Ragazzi, M. (ed.), *International Responsibility Today: Essays in Memory of Oscar Schachter* (Leiden: Martinus Nijhoff, 2005), 81.
Rinaudo. 'Rappresaglia (storia del diritto)' in Azara, A. and Eula, E. (eds), *Novissimo Digesto Italiano* (Torino: Unione Tipografico-Editrice Torinese, 1986).
Ripert, G. 'Les règles de droit civil applicables aux rapports internationaux' (1933) 44 *Recueil des cours de l'Académie de droit international* 569.

Ripinsky, S. 'State of Necessity: Effect on Compensation' (2007) 4(6) *Transnational Dispute Management*.
Rivier, A. *Principes de droit des gens* (Paris: Rousseau, 1896) vols 1 and 2.
Roberts, A. 'Power and Persuasion in Investment Treaty Interpretation: The Dual Role of States' (2010) 104 *American Journal of International Law* 180.
Robinson, P. H. 'A Theory of Justification: Societal Harm as a Prerequisite for Criminal Liability' (1975–6) 23 *University of California in Los Angeles Law Review* 266.
  'Criminal Law Defences: A Systematic Analysis' (1982) 82 *Columbia Law Review* 199.
  *Criminal Law Defences* (Eagan: West Publishing Co, 1984).
  'Rules of Conduct and Principles of Adjudication' (1990) 57 *University of Chicago Law Review* 729.
  'Competing Theories of Justification: Deeds versus Reasons' in Simester, A. and Smith, A. (eds), *Harm and Culpability* (Oxford: Oxford University Press, 1996), 45.
  'The Bomb Thief and the Theory of Justification Defences' (1997) 8 *Criminal Law Forum* 387.
  'Objective Versus Subjective Justification: A Case Study in Function and Form in Constructing a System of Criminal Law Theory' in Robinson, P. H. et al. (eds), *Criminal Law Conversations* (Oxford: Oxford University Press, 2011), 343.
Rodick, B. C. *The Doctrine of Necessity in International Law* (New York: Columbia University Press, 1928).
Rodin, D. *War and Self-Defense* (Oxford: Clarendon Press, 2002).
  'Justifying Harm' (2011) 122 *Ethics* 74.
Rodríguez, J. *The Independence of Spanish South-America* (Cambridge: Cambridge University Press, 1998).
Rolin, A. 'Consultation' in de la Pradelle, A. (ed.), *Causes célèbres du droit des gens: les Suisses et les dommages de guerre* (Paris: Editions Internationales, 1931), 261.
Ronzitti, N. 'Use of Force, *Jus Cogens* and State Consent' in Cassese, A. (ed.), *The Current Legal Regulation of the Use of Force* (Dordrecht: Martinus Nijhoff, 1986), 147.
Root, E. 'The Real Significance of the Declaration of London' (1912) 6 *American Journal of International Law* 583.
  'The "Great War" and International Law' (1921) 83 *Advocate of Peace through Justice* 225.
Rosenne, S. *Committee of Experts for the Progressive Codification of International Law (1925–1928)* (New York: Oceana, 1972).
  *Breach of Treaty* (Cambridge: Grotius, 1985).
Rosenstock, R. 'The ILC and State Responsibility' (2002) 96 *American Journal of International Law* 792.

Ross, A. *A Textbook on International Law* (London: Longmans, 1947).
Rostow, E. V. 'Until What? Enforcement Action or Collective Self-Defense?' (1991) 85 *American Journal of International Law* 506.
Rougier, A. *Les guerres civiles et le droit des gens* (Paris: Larose, 1903).
Roumy, F. 'L'origine et la diffusion de l'adage canonique *Necessitas non habet legem* (VIIIe–XIIIe s.)' in Mueller, W. and Sommar, M. (eds), *Medieval Church Law and the Origins of the Western Legal Tradition: A Tribute to Kenneth Pennington* (Washington: Catholic University of America Press, 2006), 457.
Rousseau, C. *Principes généraux du droit international public* (Paris: Pedone, 1944) vol. 1.
  'Chronique des faits internationaux' (1978) *Revue générale de droit international public* 1125.
  *Droit international public* (Paris: Sirey, 1983) vol. 5.
Roxin, C. *Derecho penal. Parte general* (Madrid: Civitas, 1997) vol. 1.
Ruys, T. *'Armed Attack' and Article 51 of the UN Charter* (Cambridge: Cambridge University Press, 2010).
  'The Meaning of "Force" and the Boundaries of the *Jus ad Bellum*: Are "Minimal" Uses of Force Excluded from UN Charter Article 2(4)?' (2014) 108 *American Journal of International Law* 159.
Ruys, T. and Verhoeven, S. 'Attacks by Private Actors and the Right of Self-Defence' (2005) 10 *Journal of Conflict & Security Law* 289.
Ryngaert, C. 'State Responsibility, Necessity and Human Rights' (2010) 41 *Netherlands Yearbook of International Law* 79.
Salmon, J. 'Les circonstances excluant l'illicéité' in Zemanek, K. and Salmon, J. (eds), *La responsabilité internationale* (Paris: Pedone, 1987), 89.
Salter, J. 'Hugo Grotius: Property and Consent' (2001) 29 *Political Theory* 537.
  'Grotius and Pufendorf on the Right of Necessity' (2005) 26 *History of Political Thought* 285.
Salvioli, G. 'Les règles générales de la paix' (1933) 46 *Recueil des cours de l'Académie de droit international* 1.
Samra, H. 'Five Years Later: The *CMS* Award Placed in the Context of the Argentine Financial Crisis and the ICSID Arbitration Boom' (2007) 38 *University of Miami Inter-American Law Review* 667.
Sánchez de Bustamante y Sirvén, A. *Droit international public* (Paris: Sirey, 1936) vol. 3.
Sánchez de Bustamante y Sirvén, A. *Droit international public* (Paris: Sirey, 1937) vol. 4.
Sander, G. '*Brazilian Loans Case* and *Serbian Loans Case*' in Wolfrum, R. (ed.), *Max Planck Encyclopedia of Public International Law* (www.mpepil.com, Oxford: Oxford University Press, 2008–).
Sandonà, G. *Trattato di diritto internazionale moderno* (Firenze: Pellas, 1870).

Sangero, B. *Self-Defence in Criminal Law* (Oxford: Hart, 2006).
Sawyer, S. '*Rainbow Warrior*: Nuclear War in the Pacific' (1986) 8 *Third World Quarterly* 1325.
Scalese, G. *La rilevanza delle scusanti nella teoria dell'illecito internazionale* (Napoli: Editoriale Scientifica, 2008).
Schachter, O. 'Dispute Settlement and Countermeasures in the International Law Commission' (1994) 88 *American Journal of International Law* 471.
Schauer, F. 'Exceptions' (1991) 58 *University of Chicago Law Review* 871.
  *Playing by the Rules: A Philosophical Examination of Rule-Based Decision-Making in Law and in Life* (New York: Oxford University Press, 1993).
Scheuner, U. 'L'influence du droit interne sur la formation du droit international' (1939) 68 *Recueil des cours de l'Académie de droit international* 95.
Schill, S. 'International Investment Law and the Host State's Power to Handle Economic Crises' (2007) 24 *Journal of International Arbitration* 265.
Schlag, P. 'How to Do Things with Hohfeld' (2015) 78 *Law & Contemporary Problems* 185.
Schreiber, H.-L. 'Problems of Justification and Excuse in the Setting of Accessorial Conduct' (1986) *Brigham Young University Law Review* 611.
Schwarzenberger, G. 'The Inductive Approach to International Law' (1947) 60 *Harvard Law Review* 539.
  'The Fundamental Principles of International Law' (1955) 87 *Recueil des cours de l'Académie de droit international* 191.
Schwarzenberger, G. and Brown, E. *Manual of International Law*, 6th edn (Milton: Professional Books, 1976).
Schwebel, S. 'The Thirty-Second Session of the International Law Commission' (1980) 74 *American Journal of International Law* 961.
Scott, J. B. *The Hague Peace Conferences of 1899 and 1907* (Baltimore: Johns Hopkins Press, 1909) vol. 1.
  'The Declaration of London of February 26, 1909' (1914) 8 *American Journal of International Law* 274.
Sereni, A. *Diritto internazionale* (Milano: Giuffrè, 1962) vol. 3.
Shaw, M. *International Law*, 7th edn (Cambridge: Cambridge University Press, 2014).
Sibert, M. *Traité de droit international public* (Paris: Dalloz, 1951) vol. 1.
Sicilianos, L.-A. *Les réactions décentralisées à l'illicite* (Paris: LGDJ, 1990).
  'The Relationship between Reprisals and Denunciation or Suspension of a Treaty' (1993) 4 *European Journal of International Law* 341.
  'La codification des contre-mesures par la Commission du droit international' (2005) 38 *Revue Belge de droit international* 447.
  'Countermeasures in Response to Grave Violations of Obligations Owed to the International Community' in Crawford, J. et al. (eds), *The Law of International Responsibility* (Oxford: Oxford University Press, 2010), 1137.

Sierra, H. M. and Cantaro, A. S. *Lecciones de derecho penal* (Bahía Blanca: Universidad Nacional del Sur, 2005).
Silingardi, S. *Gli effetti giuridici della guerra sui rapporti economici e commerciali* (Torino: Giappichelli, 2012).
Simester, A. et al. *Criminal Law: Theory and Doctrine*, 4th edn (Oxford: Hart, 2010).
Simester, A. P. 'Necessity, Torture and the Rule of Law' in Ramraj, V. V. (ed.), *Emergencies and the Limits of Legality* (Cambridge: Cambridge University Press, 2008), 289.
Simma, B. 'Reflections on Article 60 of the Vienna Convention on the Law of Treaties and Its Background in General International Law' (1970) 20 *Österreichische Zeitschrift für öffentliches Recht* 5.
  'Counter-Measures and Dispute Settlement: A Plea for a Different Balance' (1994) 5 *European Journal of International Law* 102.
Simma, B. and Spinedi, M. (eds), *United Nations Codification of State Responsibility* (New York: Oceana, 1987).
Simma, B. and Tams, C. 'Article 60 (1969)' in Corten, O. and Klein, P. (eds), *The Vienna Convention on the Law of Treaties: A Commentary* (Oxford: Oxford University Press, 2011), 1351.
  'Reacting against Treaty Breaches' in Hollis, D. (ed.), *The Oxford Guide to Treaties* (Oxford: Oxford University Press, 2012), 576.
Simons, K. 'Exploring the Intricacies of the Lesser Evils Defense' (2005) 24 *Law & Philosophy* 645.
Simpson, A. *Cannibalism and the Common Law* (London: Penguin, 1986).
Sinnott-Armstrong, W. 'Consequentialism' in Zalta, E. N. (ed.), *Stanford Encyclopedia of Philosophy* (2012), http://plato.stanford.edu/archives/win2012/entries/consequentialism/.
Sloane, R. D. 'On the Use and Abuse of Necessity in the Law of State Responsibility' (2012) 106 *American Journal of International Law* 447.
Small, D. H. 'The *Oil Platforms* Case: Jurisdiction through the – Closed – Eye of the Needle' (2004) 3 *Law & Practice of International Courts & Tribunals* 113.
Smith, J. C. *Justification and Excuse in the Criminal Law* (London: Stevens, 1989).
Smit Duijzentkunst, B., *The Concept of Rights in International Law* (PhD thesis, Cambridge University, 2015).
Soler, S. *Derecho penal argentino* (Buenos Aires: La Ley, 1945).
Song, N. 'Between Scylla and Charybdis: Can a Plea of Necessity Offer Safe Passage to States in Responding to an Economic Crisis without Incurring Liability to Foreign Investors?' (2008) 19 *American Review of International Arbitration* 235.
Sørensen, M. 'Principes de droit international public' (1960) 101 *Recueil des cours de l'Académie de droit international* 1.
Sørensen, M. (ed.), *Manual of Public International Law* (London: MacMillan, 1968).
Spencer, J. 'Civil Liability for Crimes' in Dyson, M. (ed.), *Unravelling Tort and Crime* (Cambridge: Cambridge University Press, 2014), 304.

Sperduti, G. 'Introduzione allo studio delle funzioni della necessitá nel diritto internazionale' (1943) 22 *Rivista di diritto internazionale* 19.

Spiermann, O. 'Humanitarian Intervention as a Necessity and the Threat or Use of Jus Cogens' (2002) 71 *Nordic Journal of International Law* 523.

Spinedi, M. 'Problemi di diritto internazionale sollevati dal naufragio della *Torrey Canyon*' (1967) *Rivista di diritto internazionale* 655.

Stapelbroek, K. 'The Progress of Humankind in Galiani's *Dei doveri dei principi neutrali*: Natural Law, Neapolitan Trade and Catherine the Great' (2011) 10 *Helsinki Collegium for Advanced Studies* 161.

Steinhoff, U. 'Self-Defense as Claim Right, Liberty, and Act-Specific Agent-Relative Prerogative' (2016) 35 *Law & Philosophy* 193.

Stephen, J. F. *History of the Criminal Law of England* (London: MacMillan, 1883) vols 1–3.

Stone, J. 'Burden of Proof and the Judicial Process' (1944) 60 *Law Quarterly Review* 262.

*Legal System and Lawyers' Reasoning* (Stanford: Stanford University Press, 1964).

Stowell, E. C. *The Diplomacy of the War of 1914* (Boston: Cambridge University Press, 1915).

*Intervention in International Law* (Washington, DC: John Byrne, 1921).

Stowell, E. C. and Munro, H. F. *International Cases, Arbitrations and Incidents Illustrative of International Law as Practiced by Independent States* (Boston: Houghton Mifflin, 1916) vol. 1.

Strawson, G. 'Free Will' in Craig, E. (ed.), *Routledge Encyclopedia of Philosophy* (London: Routledge, 2011).

Strupp, K. 'L'incident de Janina entre la Grèce et l'Italie' (1924) 31 *Revue générale de droit international public* 255.

*Eléments du droit international public universel, Européen et Américain*, 2nd edn (Paris: Editions Internationales, 1930) vol. 1.

'Règles générales du droit de la paix' (1934) 47 *Recueil des cours de l'Académie de droit international* 259.

Subramanian, S. 'Too Similar or Too Different: State of Necessity as a Defence under Customary International Law and the Bilateral Investment Treaty and Their Relationship' (2012) 9 *Manchester Journal of International Economic Law* 68.

Sucharitkul, S. 'State Responsibility and International Liability under International Law' (1995–6) 18 *Loyola of Los Angeles International & Comparative Law Journal* 821.

Sugarman, S. D. 'The "Necessity" Defense and the Failure of Tort Theory: The Case against Strict Liability for Damages Caused while Exercising Self-Help in an Emergency' (2005) 5 *Issues in Legal Scholarship*, Article 1.

Sussmann, F. B. 'The Defence of Private Necessity and the Problem of Compensation' (1967) 2 *Ottawa Law Review* 184.

Swanson, S. 'The Medieval Foundations of John Locke's Theory of Natural Rights: Rights of Subsistence and the Principle of Extreme Necessity' (1997) 18 *History of Political Thought* 399.
Szurek, S. *La force majeure en droit international* (doctoral thesis, Université Paris II Panthéon-Assas, 1996) vols 1 and 2.
Szurek, S. 'The Notion of Circumstances Precluding Wrongfulness' in Crawford, J. et al. (eds), *The Law of International Responsibility* (Oxford: Oxford University Press, 2010), 427.
　'Force Majeure' in Crawford, J. et al. (eds), *The Law of International Responsibility* (Oxford: Oxford University Press, 2010), 475.
　'Distress' in Crawford, J. et al. (eds), *The Law of International Responsibility* (Oxford: Oxford University Press, 2010), 481.
Taft, W. H. 'Self-Defense and the *Oil Platforms* Decision' (2004) 29 *Yale Journal of International Law* 295.
Talmon, S. '*Jus Cogens* after *Germany v Italy*: Substantive and Procedural Rules Distinguished' (2012) 25 *Leiden Journal of International Law* 979.
　'Determining Customary International Law: The ICJ's Methodology between Induction, Deduction and Assertion' (2015) 26 *European Journal of International Law* 417.
Tams, C. 'All's Well That Ends Well? Comments on the ILC's Articles on State Responsibility' (2002) 62 *Zeitschrift für ausländisches öffentliches Recht und Völkerrecht* 759.
　'Unity and Diversity in the Law of State Responsibility' in Zimmerman, A. and Hofmann, R. (eds), *Unity and Diversity in International Law* (Berlin: Duncker & Humblot, 2005), 435.
　*Enforcing Obligations Erga Omnes in International Law* (Cambridge: Cambridge University Press, 2005).
　'Waiver, Acquiescence and Extinctive Prescription' in Crawford, J. et al. (eds), *The Law of International Responsibility* (Oxford: Oxford University Press, 2010), 1035.
　'Treaty Breaches and Responses' in Tams, C. et al. (eds), *Research Handbook on the Law of Treaties* (Cheltenham: Edward Elgar, 2014), 476.
Tenekides, G. 'Les effets de la contrainte sur les traités à la lumière de la Convention de Vienne du 23 mai 1969' (1974) 20 *Annuaire Français de droit international* 79.
Thakur, R. 'A Dispute of Many Colours: France, New Zealand and the "*Rainbow Warrior*" Affair' (1986) 42 *The World Today* 209.
Thirlway, H. 'Counterclaims before the International Court of Justice: The *Genocide Convention* and *Oil Platforms* Decisions' (1999) 12 *Leiden Journal of International Law* 197.
　*The Sources of International Law* (Oxford: Oxford University Press, 2014).
Thomson, J. J. *Self-Defense and Rights* (Lindley Lecture, University of Kansas, 1976).

'Killing, Letting Die, and the Trolley Problem' (1976) 59 *Monist* 204.
'Rights and Compensation' (1980) 14 *Noûs* 3.
'Self-Defense' (1991) 20 *Philosophy & Public Affairs* 283.
Thorburn, M. 'Justifications, Powers and Authority' (2008) 117 *Yale Law Journal* 1070.
Thouvenin, J. M. 'Self-Defence' in Crawford, J. et al. (eds), *The Law of International Responsibility* (Oxford: Oxford University Press, 2010), 455.
Tierney, B. *The Idea of Natural Rights* (Cambridge: W. B. Eerdmans, 1997).
Tomuschat, C. 'Are Counter-Measures Subject to Prior Recourse to Dispute Settlement Procedures?' (1994) 5 *European Journal of International Law* 77.
'International Law: Ensuring the Survival of Mankind on the Eve of a New Century' (1999) 281 *Recueil des cours de l'Académie de droit international* 9.
'Article 36' in Zimmerman, A. et al. (eds), *The Statute of the International Court of Justice: A Commentary* (Oxford: Oxford University Press, 2006), 633.
Tsagourias, N. 'Necessity and the Use of Force: A Special Regime' (2010) 41 *Netherlands Yearbook of International Law* 11.
'Self-Defence against Non-State Actors: The Interaction between Self-Defence as a Primary Rule and Self-Defence as a Secondary Rule' (2016) 29 *Leiden Journal of International Law*.
Twiss, T. *The Law of Nations* (Oxford: Oxford University Press, 1861).
*The Law of Nations*, 2nd edn (Oxford: Clarendon, 1875).
'The Doctrine of Continuous Voyages, as Applied to Contraband of War and Blockade' (1877-8) 3 *Law Magazine & Review* 1.
Tzanakopoulos, A. and Lekkas, S.-I. '*Pacta Sunt Servanda* versus Flexibility in the Suspension and Termination of Treaties' in Tams, C. J. et al. (eds), *Research Handbook on the Law of Treaties* (London: Edward Elgar, 2014), 312.
Ullmann, E. *Völkerrecht* (Tübingen: Siebeck, 1908).
Uniacke, S. *Permissible Killing: The Self-Defence Justification of Homicide* (Cambridge: Cambridge University Press, 1994).
'In Defense of *Permissible Killing*: A Response to Two Critics' (2000) 19 *Law & Philosophy* 627.
Unterhalter, D. 'Allocating the Burden of Proof in WTO Dispute Settlement Proceedings' (2009) 42 *Cornell International Law Journal* 209.
Upton, F. *The Law of Nations Affecting Commerce during War* (New York: Voorhies, 1863).
Valenti, M. 'Lo stato di necessità nei procedimenti arbitrali ICSID contro l'Argentina' (2008) 91 *Rivista di diritto internazionale* 114.
van Hamel, J. 'Les principes du droit d'extradition et leur application dans l'affaire Savarkar' (1911) 13 *Revue de droit international et de législation comparée* 370.
van Schaack, B. 'The Crime of Political Genocide: Repairing the Genocide Convention's Blind Spot' (1997) 106 *Yale Law Journal* 2259.

van Steenberghe, R. *La légitime défense en droit international public* (Bruxelles: Larcier, 2012).
  'State Practice and the Evolution of the Law of Self-Defence: Clarifying the Methodological Debate' (2015) 2 *Journal of the Use of Force in International Law* 81.
  'The Law of Self-Defence and the New Argumentative Landscape on the Expansionists' Side' (2016) 29 *Leiden Journal of International Law* 43.
Vattel, E. *Droit des gens ou principes de la loi naturelle* (Fenwick trans., Washington, DC: Carnegie Institution, 1916).
  *The Law of Nations* (1797, Indianapolis: Liberty Fund, 2008).
Velásquez, F. 'La culpabilidad y el principio de culpabilidad' (1993) 50 *Revista de derecho y ciencias políticas* 283.
Venezia, J.-C. 'La notion de répresailles en droit international public' (1960) 64 *Revue générale de droit international public* 465.
Venturini, G. 'La portée et les effets juridiques des attitudes et des actes unilatéraux des Etats' (1964) 112 *Recueil des cours de l'Académie de droit international* 363.
  *Necessità e proporzionalità nell'uso della forza militare in diritto internazionale* (Milano: Giuffrè, 1988).
Verdross, A. 'Règles générales du droit de la paix' (1929) 30 *Recueil des cours de l'Académie de droit international* 271.
  'Les principes généraux du droit dans la jurisprudence internationale' (1935) 52 *Recueil des cours de l'Académie de droit international* 191.
Vereshchetin, V. S. 'Some Observations on the New Proposal on Dispute Settlement' (1994) 5 *European Journal of International Law* 54.
Vidmar, J. 'Rethinking *Jus Cogens* after *Germany v Italy*: Back to Article 53?' (2013) 60 *Netherlands International Law Review* 1.
Viganò, F. *Stato di necessità e conflitti di doveri: Contributo alla teoria delle cause di giustificazione e delle scusanti* (Milano: Giuffrè, 2000).
Villalpando, S. *L'émergence de la communauté internationale dans la responsabilité des Etats* (Paris: PUF, 2005).
  'On the International Court of Justice and the Determination of Rules of Law' (2013) 26 *Leiden Journal of International Law* 243.
Viñuales, J. E. 'State of Necessity and Peremptory Norms in International Investment Law' (2008) 14 *Law & Business Review of the Americas* 79.
Viñuales, J. E. *Foreign Investment and the Environment in International Law* (Cambridge: Cambridge University Press, 2012).
Volterra, E. *Istituzioni di Diritto Privato Romano* (Roma: Edizioni Ricerche, 1961).
von Bernstorff, J. *The Public International Law Theory of Hans Kelsen – Believing in Universal Law* (Cambridge: Cambridge University Press, 2010).
von Liszt, F. *Das Völkerrecht: systematisch Dargestellt* (Berlin: Verlag von O Häring, 1898).

*Le droit international: Exposé systématique* (translation of 1913 9th edn, Paris: Pedone, 1927).
Vranes, E. 'The Definition of "Norm Conflict" in International Law and Legal Theory' (2006) 17 *European Journal of International Law* 395.
Waibel, M. 'Two Worlds of Necessity in ICSID Arbitration: *CMS* and *LG&E*' (2007) 20 *Leiden Journal of International Law* 637.
 *Sovereign Defaults before International Courts and Tribunals* (Cambridge: Cambridge University Press, 2011).
Waldock, H. 'The Regulation of the Use of Force by Individual States in International Law' (1952) 81 *Recueil des cours de l'Académie de droit international* 451.
Waldron, J. '"Transcendental Nonsense" and System in the Law' (2000) 100 *Columbia Law Review* 16.
Walker, T. A. *The Science of International Law* (London: Clay and Sons, 1893).
Wallerstein, S. 'Justifying the Right to Self-Defense: A Theory of Forced Consequences' (2005) 91 *Virginia Law Review* 999.
Washburn, A. H. 'The Legality of the Pacific Blockade – I' (1921) 21 *Columbia Law Review* 55.
 'The Legality of the Pacific Blockade – II' (1921) 21 *Columbia Law Review* 227.
 'The Legality of the Pacific Blockade – III' (1922) 21 *Columbia Law Review* 442.
Webb, P. 'Human Rights and the Immunities of State Officials' in de Wet, E. and Vidmar, J. (eds), *Hierarchy in International Law: The Place of Human Rights* (Oxford: Oxford University Press, 2012), 114.
Weidenbaum, P. 'Necessity in International Law' (1938) 14 *Transactions of the Grotian Society* 105.
Weil, P. 'Le droit international en quête de son identité: cours général de droit international public' (1992) 237 *Recueil des cours de l'Académie de droit international* 11.
Weil, P. and Richemond-Barak, D. 'The *Oil Platforms* Case before the International Court of Justice: A Non-Case of International Responsibility' in Ragazzi, M. (ed.), *International Responsibility Today: Essays in Memory of Oscar Schachter* (The Hague: Martinus Nijhoff, 2005), 329.
Wellman, C. H. 'The Rights Forfeiture Theory of Punishment' (2012) 122 *Ethics* 371.
Westen, P. K. 'Comment on Montague's "Rights and Duties of Compensation"' (1985) 14 *Philosophy & Public Affairs* 385.
Westlake, J. *Chapters on the Principles of International Law* (Cambridge: Cambridge University Press, 1894).
 *International Law* (Cambridge: Cambridge University Press, 1907) vol. 2.
 'Pacific Blockade' (1909) 25 *Law Quarterly Review* 13.
 *International Law*, 2nd edn (Cambridge: Cambridge University Press, 1910) vol. 1.
 *International Law*, 2nd edn (Cambridge: Cambridge University Press, 1913) vol. 2.

Wexler, J. 'The *Rainbow Warrior* Affair: State and Agent Responsibility for Authorized Violations of International Law' (1987) 5 *Boston University International Law Journal* 389.

Wharton, F. *A Digest of the International Law of the United States*, 2nd edn (Washington, DC: Government Printing Office, 1887) vol. 2.

Wheaton, H. *Elements of International Law* (Philadelphia: Carey, Lea & Blanchard, 1836).

*Elements of International Law*, 8th edn (updated by R. H. Dana, Boston: Little, Brown & Co, 1866).

Whitehead, L. 'No Port in a Storm: A Review of Recent History and Legal Concepts Resulting in the Extinction of Ports of Refuge' (2009) 58 *Naval Law Review* 65.

Whitman, J. Q. *The Verdict of Battle: The Law of Victory and the Making of Modern War* (Cambridge, MA: Harvard, 2012).

Whitten, D. J. 'The Don Pacifico Affair' (1986) 48 *Historian* 255.

Wiesse, C. *Le droit international appliqué aux guerres civiles* (de Blonay trans., Lausanne: Benda, 1898).

*Reglas de derecho internacional aplicables a las guerras civiles*, 2nd edn (Lima: Torres-Aguirre, 1905).

Wigley, S. 'Disappearing Without a Moral Trace? Rights and Compensation during Times of Emergency' (2009) 28 *Law & Philosophy* 617.

Williams, G. L. 'The Concept of Legal Liberty' (1956) 56 *Columbia Law Review* 1129.

'Offences and Defences' (1982) 2 *Legal Studies* 233.

'The Logic of "Exceptions"' (1988) 47 *Cambridge Law Journal* 261.

Williams, J. F. 'Le droit international et les obligations financières internationales qui naissent d'un contrat' (1923) 1 *Recueil des cours de l'Académie de droit international* 289.

Wilson, G. G. *International Law*, 8th edn (New York: Silver, 1922).

Winfield, P. H. 'The History of Intervention in International Law' (1922–3) 3 *British Yearbook of International Law* 130.

'Grounds of Intervention in International Law' (1924) 5 *British Yearbook of International Law* 149.

Wittich, S. 'The International Law Commission's Articles on the Responsibility of States for Internationally Wrongful Acts Adopted on Second Reading' (2002) 15 *Leiden Journal of International Law* 891.

Wolff, C. *Jus gentium methodo scientifica pertractatum* (1764, Drake trans., Oxford: Clarendon Press, 1934).

Wolff, K. 'Les principes généraux du droit applicables dans les rapports internationaux' (1931) 36 *Recueil des cours de l'Académie de droit international* 479.

Woolsey, T. D. *Introduction to the Study of International Law* (Boston: James Munroe, 1860).

*Introduction to the Study of International Law*, 5th edn (New York: Charles Scribner's Sons, 1886).

Wright, Q. 'Opinion of Jurists on the Janina-Courfou Affair' (1924) 18 *American Journal of International Law* 536.

'When Does War Exist?' (1932) 26 *American Journal of International Law* 362.

'Review: *The Corfu Incident of 1923: Mussolini and the League of Nations* by James Barros' (1966) 60 *American Journal of International Law* 870.

Yamada, C. 'Revisiting the International Law Commission's Draft Articles on State Responsibility' in Ragazzi, M. (ed.), *International Responsibility Today: Essays in Memory of Oscar Schachter* (Leiden: Martinus Nijhoff, 2005), 117.

Yamada, T. 'State of Necessity in International Law: A Study of International Judicial Cases' (2005) 34 *Kobe Gakuin Law Journal* 107.

Yang, X. *State Immunity in International Law* (Cambridge: Cambridge University Press, 2012).

Zegveld, L. *Accountability of Armed Opposition Groups in International Law* (Cambridge: Cambridge University Press, 2002).

Zemanek, K. 'The Unilateral Enforcement of International Obligations' (1987) 47 *Zeitschrift für ausländisches öffentliches Recht und Völkerrecht* 32.

'The Legal Foundations of the International System' (1997) 266 *Recueil des cours de l'Académie de droit international* 9.

Zoller, E. *Peacetime Unilateral Remedies: An Analysis of Countermeasures* (Dobbs Ferry: Transnational Publishers, 1984).

Zollmann, J. 'L'affaire *Naulilaa* entre le Portugal et l'Allemagne, 1914–1933. Réflexions sur l'histoire politique d'une sentence arbitrale internationale' (2013) 15 *J Hist IL* 201.

Zolo, D. 'Hans Kelsen: International Peace through International Law' (1998) 9 *European Journal of International Law* 306.

Zuckerman, L. *The Rape of Belgium: The Untold Story of World War I* (New York: New York University Press, 2004).

# INDEX

Aberdeen, Lord, *Caroline incident* and, 352–53
absent interest theory
  consent and, 115–17
  duty of compensation and, 86–92
  renunciation and, 172–74
  as theory of justification, 115–17
absolute impossibility of performance. *see also* impossibility of performance
  distress defence and, 443–46
  epistemological impossibility of performance, 309–10
  exclusion of fault and, 313–14
  *force majeure* and, 307
  ILC debate concerning, 310–13, 321–22
  material impossibility of performance, 307
  *Rainbow Warrior* case in, 317–18
  relative impossibility of performance and, 309–10, 322–23, 446–47
absolute obligations
  consent and, 163–65
  dispositive obligations and, 163–65, 170–72
abuse of rights. *see also* human rights and fundamental freedoms
  countermeasures and protection of, 263–64, 277–79
  duty of compensation and, 89–90
  self-defence and, 187–88, 191
  state of necessity and, 87–88, 339–43
  total restraint in, 181n34
accessorial responsibility
  aid and assistance and, 66–70, 97
  coercion and, 66–70

derivative responsibility, 66–70
justification and excuse, 101
accessories, responsibility of, 66–70
accidental occurrence of damages, *force majeure* and, 303–06
act-consequentialism
  countermeasures and, 270–72
  self-defence and, 206–10, 270–72
  theory of justification as, 102–06, 469–70
*actori incumbit probatio*, consent and, 194
*actus reus*, justification and excuse and, 29
Aggressor State, rights of
  balance of interests principle and, 206–10
  compensation for material loss and, 222–23
  countermeasures and, 262–64, 276–77, 280
  deontic theory and collateral impairment and, 210–15
  duty of toleration or non-interference and, 210–15
  forfeiture theory and, 218–22, 276–77, 280
  prohibition of force and, 197–98
  self-defence and, 197–98
Ago, Roberto, 4, 24–25
  consent, 132n5, 133–34, 135–36, 138, 144–45, 146–49, 170–72
  countermeasures, 251–52, 254–55, 256–58
  on countermeasures, 267–83
  on countermeasures as sanctions, 251–52, 256–58

525

Ago, Roberto (*cont.*)
  on delictual and criminal responsibility, 258n180
  distress and, 443–46, 447
  on excuse, 40–47, 118, 122–25, 468–69
  on fault, 122–26
  fault-based rationale for *force majeure* and, 308–13
  on *force majeure*, 304–06
  on free-will theory, 331–32
  on Kelsen, 267–70
  *le délit international* and, 41–42, 138
  on necessity, 362n174, 364–65, 367–68, 370, 382–83, 386–87
  primary/secondary rule distinction and, 53–57
  on prohibition of force, 185–89
  relative impossibility concept of, 302–03, 443–46
  *Russian Indemnity* case, consent and, 144
  on self-defence, 185
  as Special Rapporteur, 38, 97
  on state of necessity, 388–89, 393–94
  on States as organs of community, 267–70
  on theory of responsibility, 40–44
Agreement on Prevention of Airspace Violations and for Permitting Over Flights and Landings by Military Aircraft, 183n41
aid or assistance for wrongful acts by state
  complicity, 468–69
  derivative responsibility, 66–70
  responsibility of accessories, 66–70
aircraft in distress
  distress and, 430–32
  epistemological impossibility standard, 314–15
  relative impossibility of performance and, 444–45
*Air Service Agreement* dispute, 113–14
  countermeasures and, 225–28, 271n272
Akehurst, Michael, 424–25
aliens
  damages during internal struggles and, 289, 348–49
  expulsion of in *Savarkar* case, 139–43
  *force majeure* defence in damage claims of, 289–94, 304–06
  injury during internal conflict, 289, 348–49
  treatment of, 289–94
American Civil War, as *force majeure*, 292–94
*Amoco Cadiz* incident, 401n456
angary, right of, necessity and, 362
Anglo-French Extradition Treaty, *Savarkar Arbitration* case and, 140–43
*animus belligerandi*
  *Corfu* incident and, 239–42
  positive reprisals and, 233–34
anticipatory self-defence. *see also* self-defence
  *Caroline* incident and, 355n135
Anzilotti, Dionisio
  on protection of states, 364–65, 367–68, 370–71
  on State responsibility, 53, 137n39
  on wrongful acts, 41–42, 118
Arangio-Ruiz, Gaetano, 254–55, 258, 277–79, 279n304
arbitral tribunals
  countermeasures and investors rights and, 279n303
  *force majeure* in, 294–300, 316–20
  *Fur Seals* arbitration, 357–62, 410n511, 410
  investment arbitration, financial necessity in, 404–09
  *Rainbow Warrior* incident, 2–3
  sequential order of reasoning in, 478n26
Argentina
  justified conduct in, 110–13
  state of necessity, 78–79, 87–88, 95–96, 404–09
armed conflict
  environmental law and, 217–18
  *force majeure* and, 294–303
  positive reprisals and, 232–34
  self-defence and, 180–83, 193–99
Articles on Responsibility of States (ARS)
  Article 16 (complicity), 468–69

INDEX

Article 18 (on coercion), 329
Article 19 (draft on international crimes of States), 258n180, 260–61
Article 20 adoption on consent, 150–54
Article 21 on self-defence, 175–80, 184, 192–99, 203–05, 217–18
Article 22 (countermeasures), 225–28, 253–55
Article 23 (*force majeure*), 286–87, 308–15, 320–23, 324–27
Article 24 (distress), 430–32, 453–55
Article 25 (necessity), 334–39, 394–96, 397, 404–09, 418
Article 26, 408–09
Article 27, 423–25
Article 29, drafting of, 146–50
Article 30 on non-interference, 210–15, 253–55, 273, 274–76
Article 31 (impossibility), 310–15, 317–18
Article 32 (*force majeure*), 310–13, 446–48, 450–51
Article 33 (state of necessity), 390–96, 410–11
Article 34 draft, ILC discussion of, 187–88
Article 35, 423–25
Article 51 (proportionality), 199–202, 262–64
Article 52(3) (countermeasures), 264–66
Article 55, 279–80
cessation and reparations in, 118
circumstances precluding wrongfulness and self-defence in, 192–205
compensation for material loss, 222–23
consent defence in, 131–34, 145–54
countermeasures regime in, 250–51, 261–66
deeds *vs.* reasons concepts of justification and, 113–14
defences included in, 9–11, 15, 83–86, 97
distress defence in, 430–32
duty of compensation in, 77–86

instrumental function countermeasures in, 260–61
involuntary/voluntary conduct discussed in, 83–86
justification and excuse in, 11–12, 24–25, 37–36, 52n142, 467–68
material impossibility of performance in, 307
necessity plea in, 87–88, 337–38
preclusion of wrongfulness and, 48–51
primary/secondary rule distinction and, 53–57, 60–61, 157–58
reaction of States to necessity provisions in, 398–401
reparations in, 63–66
self-defence provisions in, 175–80, 187–88, 189
state of necessity provisions, 388–97, 426–29
systemic excuse-justification distinction in, 61–62
theorisation of justification and, 117
tribunals' reliance on, 4–6
Articles on the Effect of Armed Treaties, 223–24
Ashburton, Lord, necessity self-defence and, 352–53, 355–56, 361
assistance
  consent and, 131–34
  responsibility of accessories and role of, 66–70
asylum, right of, *Savarkar Arbitration* case and, 139–43
Aust, Helmut, 118
Austin, John L., 29–31, 466
Austria, defences in, 153–54, 315–16, 447–48
aviation agreements
  *force majeure* and, 325–26
  self-defence and, 182–83

Bannelier, Karine, 158–59
Barboza, Julio, 79n80
  act-consequentialism and, 270–72
  on countermeasures, 226
  on essential interests, 390–91
  on justification, 390–94
Barsotti, Roberto, 246–47

# INDEX

Basdevant, Charles, 375
Baxter, Richard, 467–68
Belgian Insurrection, 290–92
Belgium
  German invasion of, 341–42, 371–74
  intervention in Serbia, 411–12, 416–17
  neutrality of, 136–38, 170–72
  *Société Commerciale de Belgique* case and, 299–300, 381–82
*Belgium's Case: A Juridical Inquiry* (de Visscher), 373–74
belligerents, right of, blockade violations and, 435–40. *see also* blockade violations
Bentham, Jeremy, 120–22
bilateral negotiations
  duty of compensation, 92–93
  material breach and, 72–77
  reparations as satisfaction and, 66
  right of refuge in, 433–35
  satisfaction, excuse and, 66, 279n302
  self-defence and, 182–83, 189
Bin Cheng, 360n162
blockade
  *Don Pacifico* incident, 232–34, 246–47, 263n219
  effectiveness requirement, 435–40
  *Forte* incident, 234–36, 246–47
  pacific blockade, 237–38
  *Prince of Wales* incident, 232–34
  as reprisals, 232–34, 237–38
blockade violations
  cargo seizure, 435–40
  distress and, 432–42
  humanitarian considerations and, 440–42
  necessity pleas and, 410–11
  nineteenth-century history of, 435–40
  urgent necessity and, 435–40
Bluntschli, Johann, 439–42
Bonfils, Henri, 136n27, 347, 350
Borchard, Edwin, 291n28
Brazil
  on countermeasures, 259–60
  *Forte* incident and, 234–36, 246–47

French loans dispute with, 298–99, 302n96, 304–06
breach of obligations. *see also* Articles on Responsibility of States (ARS), Article 12; material breach
  defences, 304–06, 324–27, 449–53
  involuntary/voluntary conduct and, 83–86
  state reparations tribunals and establishment of, 65–66
  State responsibility and, 70–77, 467–68
Brierly, James, 375–76
Briggs, Herbert (Sir), 53–54
Brownlie, Ian
  on circumstances precluding wrongfulness, 4–6
  on consent, 152–53
  on countermeasures, 260n203
  on free-will theory, 330–33
  on necessity, 361–62
  on prohibition of force, 43n103
  on State responsibility, 11–12, 65–66, 70–77, 467–68
*Brownlie's Principles*, 330–33
Brusa, Emilio, 292–94
Bry, Georges, 441
Bulgaria, *Forests of Central Rhodope* dispute and, 385–86
burden of proof, defences and, 166–69
Burlamaqui, J. J., 440–42
Burundi, 318

Calvo, Carlos, 292–94, 303–04, 349–50, 439–40
Campbell, Angus, 351–57
Canada
  *Caroline* incident and, 351–57
  *Fur Seals* arbitration and, 357–59
Caracas-La Guaira highway system, 319–20
cargo seizure. *see* blockade violations
Carneades's plank, 476n22
*Caroline* incident
  *Fur Seals* arbitration and, 359–63
  self-defence, 410n511
  State of necessity and, 345, 351–57
Caron, David, 50–52

# INDEX

causation
  excuse and, 120–22
  *force majeure* and, 287–88, 303–04
  state of necessity and, 334–39
Cavaglieri, Arrigo, 249–50, 364–65, 369, 374–77, 382–83
Cavarretta, G., 364–65
cessation
  ARS on obligation of, 118, 210–15, 253–55, 273
  countermeasures as tool for, 256–58, 260–61
  effect of excuse on, 77–81
  justification and excuse and, 63–66
  obligations concerning, 76–77, 81–86
  of wrongdoing state toward injured state, 61–62
character theory, excuse and, 120–22
Chicago Convention on Civil Aviation, self-defence and, 182–83
Chile
  on consent, 149–50
  on distress, 447–48
China. *see* People's Republic of China
Christakis, Théodore, 158–59
circumstances precluding responsibility. *see also* excuse
  justification and excuse and, 16–17, 42–44, 97
circumstances precluding wrongfulness
  compensation for material losses, effect on, 77–81
  consent defence and, 150–53
  countermeasures and, 253–55
  distress defence and, 450–51
  ILC classification of, 50–52
  international law definition of justification and, 102
  justification and excuse and, 11–12, 16–17
  law of responsibility and, 3–4
  prohibition of force and, 189
  self-defence and, 179–80, 185–89, 192–205
  state of necessity and, 392–93, 426–29
civil law. *see* domestic law

claim rights (Hohfeld)
  deontic theories and, 210–23
  self-defence as, 185–89, 210–15
  terminology for, 185n56
  waiver of, 273, 277n296
*clasula rebus sic stantibus*, state of necessity and, 390
coastal states
  distress and, 453–55
  right of refuge and, 433–35
coercion. *see also* accessorial responsibility
  of another state, responsibility of accessories and, 66–70
  distress and, 446–47, 456–59
  *force majeure* and, 292–94, 324–27, 328–30
  Kelsen's characterisation of law as, 257–58
  state of necessity and, 426–29
Cohen, Felix, 11
collateral impairment of obligations
  Article 21, 175–80, 184, 192–99, 203–05, 217–18
  peremptory rights and, 217–18
  self defence, justification for, 205–24
  total restraint obligations and, 198–99
collective interests
  consent and, 136–38
  consequentialist theory and, 270–72
  countermeasures and, 250–52, 277–79
  state of necessity and, 394–96
Colombia, countermeasures perspective of, 259–60
Committee of Experts (Hague Codification Conference), 184–85
common law. *see also* domestic law
  crime and, 25–26, 27–31
  holistic and flat conceptions of crime and, 29
  justification and excuse in, 29–31, 33
community interests, necessity plea and. *see* collective interests
community of goods theory
  Grotius and, 339–43
  *Neptune* case and, 343–44
  property rights and, 105, 421–22

compensation. *see also* duty of
    compensation
  countermeasures and, 282–83
  effect of excuse on, 77–81
  exclusion of, 86–92
  justification and excuse and, 469–70
  self-defence and, 222–23
  state of necessity and, 421–25
complicity. *see* accessorial
    responsibility; aid and assistance
conduct rules
  decision rules *vs.*, 58–59
  justification as, 94–97, 102,
    110–13, 328–29
  primary/secondary rule distinction
    and, 58–59
  temporal logic of consent and,
    158–59
Conference of Ambassadors, *Corfu*
    incident and, 239–42
conflict of interests. *see also* superior-
    interests rationale
  consequentialist theory and, 270–72
  state of necessity as, 366–68,
    411–13, 415–18
consent as defence
  absent interest theory and, 115–17
  absolute obligations and, 163–65
  ad hoc consent, 131–34, 135–36
  Ago's report concerning, 146–49
  as agreement, 132n5, 149–50
  ambiguity in practice of, 144–45
  ARS Article 20, 150–54
  Crawford's report and ILC debate
    over, 150–53
  debate over validity of, 154–69
  development of plea of, 134–54
  in domestic law, 131–34,
    155n137, 166–69
  draft Article 29, 146–50
  duty of compensation and, 86–92
  extraterritorial enforcement in
    *Savarkar* and, 140–43
  history from 1898 to 1979 of, 135–45
  ILC codification of, 131–34, 145–54
  in international law, 131–34
  as justification, 133, 170–74, 471–72
  legal scholarship on, 136–38
  as middle case, 147–48,
    150–53, 154–69
  as primary rule, 156–58
  renunciation and justification,
    115–17, 172–74, 419–22
  renunciation of legal protection and,
    170–72
  in *Russian Indemnity* case, 143–44
  in *Savarkar Arbitration* case, 139–43
  State practice and, 139–44,
    149–50, 153–54
  superior-interests rationale and,
    418–21
  support for, 165–69
  temporal logic and, 158–63
  UN General Assembly
    Sixth Committee view of,
    149–50, 153–54
consequentialist theory. *see also*
    conflict of interests
  absent interest theory, 172–74
  compensation and, 222–23,
    282–83, 469–70
  conflict of interest and, 270–72,
    388–89, 414–29, 459–60
  consent as, 172–74
  countermeasures and, 270–72
  distress and, 459–60
  duty of, 206–10
  justification and, 102–06,
    115–17, 469–70
  public benefit theory, 115–17
  state of necessity as, 87–88,
    388–89, 414–29
Consolato del Mare, 433–35
Convention Relating to Intervention
    on the High Seas in Cases of Oil
    Pollution Casualties, 401n456
Corrado, Michael, 474
Corten, Olivier, 410n511
countermeasures. *see also* reprisals
  ARS 2, 261–66
  Article 22, 225–28, 253–55
  breach of obligation, 70–77, 261–62
  consent defence and, 157–58
  consequentialist rationales for, 270–72
  in contemporary international law,
    250–66

deontic rationales for, 272–82
dual role in law of responsibility of, 252–61
duty of compensation and, 86–92, 282–83
excuse and, 77–81, 118–19
existence of wrongful act, response to, 261–62
forfeiture theory and, 276–82
as Hohfeldian liberties, 273–76, 277n296
humanitarian rights and, 263–64, 277–79
implementation of state responsibility through, 255–61
incidental effect of, 253–55, 256–57
inequality of states and, 259–61
injured party's imposition of, 76–77
instrumentality of countermeasures, 259–61
intentionally wrongful acts and, 70–77, 261–62
International Law Commission (ILC) and, 225–28
investor rights and, 278n297, 279n303
as justification, 254–55, 266–84, 328–29, 471–72
against justified conduct or excused actors, 71–72, 328–29
Kelsen on, 251–52, 257–58, 267
legal theory concerning, 225–28, 267–83, 476
as liberty rights, 274–76
obligations, 263–64
origins of, 228–50
procedural conditions, 264–66
proportionality, 242–44, 262–64, 270–72
as reaction against wrongfulness, 70–77
regime in Articles on Responsibility of States of, 261–66
reversibility of, 262–64
right to, 102–06
as sanctions, 256–58
self-defence and, 178–79
States as organs of community and, 267–70

substantive requirements for, 262–64
superior-interests rationale and, 419–22
temporal aspects of, 159–63, 280–81
as treaty violation, justification and, 117
Covenant of the League of Nations, 238–42
Crawford, James, 24–25
on absent obligations and consent, 163–65
*Caroline* incident discussed by, 353–54
on consent, 133, 147–48, 150–53
on countermeasures, 178n19, 255–56, 263–66, 277–79, 282
on distress, 453–55, 456
on duty of compensation, 83
on *force majeure*, 80–81, 313–15, 321–22
free-will theory and, 330–33
instrumental function of countermeasures in, 260–61
on justification and excuse, 47–51, 52n142
on legality of justified conduct, 110–13
primary/secondary rule distinction and, 55–56, 156–58
on prohibition of force and self-defence, 189
on responsibility of accessories, 66–70
on self-defence, 185, 194–95
as Special Rapporteur, 38
on state of necessity, 361, 387–88, 394–96
on State responsibility, 76–77
on temporal logic of consent, 158–63
Crespo revolution (Venezuela), 294–95, 304–06
criminal law
duty of compensation in, 78–79
excuse theory in, 120–22
fault in, 124
in Germany, 27–31
identification doctrines, 331n238

criminal law (*cont.*)
    justification and excuse in,
        25–26, 27–31
    law of State responsibility and, 18–19
    normative consequences of
        justification and excuse and,
        94–97
    objectivity of, 99–100
    state of necessity in, 375–76, 383
criminal responsibility
    aggression and, 208n155
    flat or holistic conceptions of, 29
    structured conception of, 27–31
*culpa*. *see also* fault
    excuse and, 76–77
    *force majeure* and, 304–06
Czechoslovakia, on consent, 149–50
Czech Republic
    on countermeasures, 259–60
    on *force majeure*, 315–16

damages
    duty of compensation, 282–83
    *force majeure* in revolutions and,
        289–94
    to foreigners during internal
        struggles, 289, 348–49
    in *French Company of Venezuelan
        Railroads* case, 294–95, 378–79
    interest-damages, 143–44, 295–97
    justification and excuse and, 9–11
    quantum of, 95–96
    state responsibility for, 291–92
    withholding of, for reprisals,
        234–36
Dan-Cohen, Meir, 58–59
Danish fleet, British seizure of, 345–46
Deane, Bargrave, 439–40
Deane, Henry, 439–40
debt payments
    financial necessity and, 404–09
    in *force majeure*, 294–97
    in *Serbian* and *Brazilian Loans* cases,
        298–99
    in *Société Commerciale de Belgique*
        case, 299–300, 381–82
    withholding of, as negative reprisal,
        234–36

decision rules
    conduct rules *vs.*, 58–59
    excuse and, 94–97
    primary/secondary rule distinction
        and, 58–59
Declaration on Pacific Blockades
    (1887), 237–38
Declaration on the Rights and Duties
    of Man and Citizen, 346–49
Declaration on the Rights and Duties
    of Nations, 346–49
defaulting states. *see also* debt
    payments
    financial necessity and, 404–09
    *force majeure* and, 295–97
    in *Serbian* and *Brazilian Loans* cases,
        298–99
    *Société Commerciale de Belgique*
        case, 299–300, 381–82
defeasibility of legal rules, 6
defence. *see also* excuse; justification
    absence of practice concerning, 8–9
    burden of proof and, 166–69
    circumstances precluding
        wrongfulness defence, 3–4
    classification based on justification
        and excuse, 98–128, 466
    consent defence, 134–54
    Crawford's discussion of, 47–51
    defence and, 150–53, 450–51
    definition and theory and taxonomy
        of, 126–28
    domestic law and, 27–28
    duty of compensation and,
        79–81, 92–93
    ILC on, 38
    international law and, 100, 465
    justification and excuse in, 9–11,
        12–14, 15–16, 27–28, 61–62,
        98–128
    legal theory and, 6, 474–76
    Lowe's characterisation as excuse,
        95–96
    obligations distinguished as, 7n26
    primary/secondary rules and, 52–61
    structure of, 15
    systemic excuse-justification
        distinction and, 61–62

taxonomy of justification *vs.* excuse, 27–28
temporal logic of, 159–63
terminology for, 15–17
third parties and duty of compensation, 92–93
defence of the rights of the State, self-defence codification and, 184–85
defences
sequential order of reasoning in, 478n26
*Definition and Theory in Jurisprudence* (Hart), 100
*De jure belli* (Grotius), 341–42, 344
*de lege ferenda* principle, countermeasures and, 277–79
Democratic Republic of Congo (DRC), territorial sovereignty issue in, 200–02
Denmark, on necessity, 377–78
deontological theory. *see also* justification; rights forfeiture
collateral impairment and, 210–23
countermeasures and, 272–82
justification and, 115–17, 471–72
self-defence and, 210–23
derivative responsibility
coercion as, 329
responsibility of accessories as, 66–70
Despagnet, Frantz, 290n24, 439–40
de Visscher, Charles, 230–31, 373–74
Dickson J., 99–100
diplomatic inviolability
forfeiture theory of countermeasures and, 279–80
primary/secondary rule distinction and, 56
dispositive obligations, consent and, 163–65, 170–72
dispute settlement
countermeasures and, 264–66, 279–80, 281–82
forcible reprisals, outlawing of, 239–42
forfeiture theory of countermeasures and, 279–80
non-forcible reprisals and, 242–44
reprisals and, 238–39
state of necessity in, 375–76, 401–13
distress, 446–47, 455
absolute impossibility of performance, 443–46
Article 24, 430–32, 453–55
definitions and terminology, 4, 17–18, 430–32
as discrete defence, 446–47
duty of compensation and, 83–86
as excuse, 456–59, 472–74
excuse theorisation and, 121–22
fault-based responsibility and, 124–25
historical antecedents, 432–42
human dimension of, 446–47
ILC provisions concerning *force majeure* and, 310–13
in international law, 443–53
as justification, 459–60
law of the sea and right of entry, 433–35
nineteenth-century blockade violations, 435–40
non-wrongful conduct as response to, 112–13
progressive development concerning, 453–55
relative impossibility of performance and, 443–46
state of necessity and, 362
state reactions to, 447–53
state responsibility and, 456
*Torrey Canyon* incident and, 401n456
distress defence
ILC and, 432–42, 443–53
doctrines of identification, 331n238
domestic law. *see also* criminal law
classification of defences in, 27–28
conduct and decision rules in, 58–59
consent in, 131–34, 155n137, 166–69
countermeasures and, 250–52
duty of compensation in, 78–79, 87–88
fault-based responsibility in, 124
forfeiture theory and, 218–22, 474–76

534    INDEX

domestic law (*cont.*)
  justification as permission in, 102–06
  justification and excuse in, 12–14, 25–26, 34, 102–06, 115–17, 476n22
  Kelsen's discussion of, 257–58
  lawful conduct as justified conduct in, 110–13
  law of State responsibility and, 18–19
  state of necessity in, 363–64, 426–29
  states as organs of, 267–70
  temporal aspects of countermeasures in, 280–81
  theorisation of justification in, 115–17
dominion, right of, right of necessity and, 339–43
*Don Pacifico* incident, 232–34, 246–47, 263n219
Draft Articles on the Responsiblity of State for the Internationally Wrongful Acts
  adoption of, 3–6
  distinction in international law, 61–62
  on *force majeure*, 47–51
  on state responsibility, 153–54, 202–03
Drago, Luis María, 237–38
Drago-Porter Convention of 1907, 237–38
Dressler, Joshua, 29–31
Duarte d'Almeida, Luis, 7
due diligence
  *force majeure* and, 166–69, 304–06
  obligation, 124–25
Dugard, John, 56, 152, 165–66
Dupuis, Charles, 276–77
duress, defence of, justification and excuse and, 31–34
duty of compensation. *see also* compensation for material loss
  consent as defence and, 86–92
  countermeasures and, 282–83
  defences based on, 79–81
  distress and, 83–86
  excuse and, 81–86

*force majeure* and, 78–79, 80–81, 83–86
  future theoretical challenges concerning, 93–94
  justification and, 86–92
  legal basis for, 89–90
  state of necessity and, 87–88, 421–25
  strict liability and, 89–90
  third parties and, 92–93

ecological necessity. *see also* state of necessity
  environmental interests and, 401–04
  *Gabčíkovo-Nagymaros* case and, 401–04
Economides, Constantin, 395
Elagab, Omer, 227
enforcement
  jurisdiction in *M/V Saiga* case, 410–11
  regulation of reprisals and, 247–49
environmental law
  distress and, 444–45
  ecological necessity and, 401–04
  in *Fur Seals* arbitration and, 357–59
  peremptory rules and, 217–18
  right of refuge and, 433–35
  total restraint in, 181n34
  total restraint obligations and, 217–18
epistemological impossibility of performance, 314–15. *see also* absolute impossibility of performance; impossibility of performance; relative impossibility of performance
  *force majeure* and, 309–10
  fortuitous event and, 309–10
*erga omnes* obligations, state of necessity and, 394–96
Eser, Albin, 28–29, 477–78
essential interests. *see also* collective interests, consequentialist theory; hierarchy of interests; interest-balancing theory
  balancing of, 391–92
  collective interests and, 394–96
  financial necessity and, 404–09

*force majeure* and, 377, 378–82
ILC deliberations concerning, 390–91, 397
international community interests and, 394–96
reaction of States, 398–401
rule of necessity and, 383–84
state of necessity and, 388–89, 392–393
superiority-of-interest rationale and, 415–18
Eustathiades, Constantin, 54–55, 57–58
exception, defence as, 16n58
exclusive economic zones (EEZ), in *M/V Saiga* case, 410–11
excuse. *see also* justification
accessory responsibility, 66–70
in Articles on Responsibility of States, 11–12, 24–25, 37–36
classification of defences as, 98–128
in common law, 29–31
compensation for material loss and, 77–81, 469–70
consequences of excuse/justification distinction, 31–34, 63–97
countermeasures and, 71–72, 328–29
in criminal law, 27–31
defences in law of responsibility and, 9–11, 12–14
definition and theory of, 9–11, 118–26, 466–67
distress as, 456–59, 461–64, 472–74
duty of compensation and, 81–86, 469–70
evolution of concept of, 27–34
excused actors, 71–72, 74–75, 328–29
fault and, 122–26
*force majeure* as, 328–30, 472–74
free-will theory and, 330–33, 472–74
in international law, 61–62, 23–27, 118–19
in law of state responsibility, 35
material breach in treaty law and, 72–77
necessity plea as, 91–92, 349–50, 364–65, 426–29
neutrality violations on basis of necessity, 371–74

normative considerations in, 94–97
overview in international law of, 23–27
policy-based grounds for, 99–100
practical relevance of, 31–34
primary/secondary rule distinction in, 26–27, 57–61
reactions against wrongfulness as, 70–77
reparations and effect of, 63–66
self-defence as, 189
self-preservation as, 364–66
state of necessity as, 91–92, 349–50, 364–65, 396, 414–29
States' views on, 35–36
systemic distinction in international law of, 60–62
taxonomy of defences and, 126
theorisation of, 120–22, 474
third parties and duty of compensation and, 92–93
total and partial excuse distinguished, 38–39
*ex injuria jus nonoritur* principle, duty of compensation and, 86–92
exonerating circumstances
consent defence and, 136–38
*force majeure* and, 287–88, 303–06
reparations and, 63–66
rule of necessity and, 368–71
self-defence and, 189, 205–06
state responsibility and, 38–39
expropriation, compensation for, 89–90
expulsion of aliens, *Savarkar Arbitration* case and, 139–43
extenuating circumstances. *see also* defence
state responsibility and, 38–39
external event. *see* supervening event
extradition, *Savarkar Arbitration* case and, 139–43
extra-legality principle, state of necessity, suspension of international law and, 370
extraterritorial jurisdiction
consent and, 131–34
in *Fur Seals* arbitration, 357–62
*Savarkar Arbitration* case and, 140–43

536                                     INDEX

*fait du prince. see also force majeure*
   in *Serbian* and *Brazilian Loans* cases,
      298–99, 302n96
Fauchille, Paul, 136–38, 144, 331–32,
   376–77, 439–40
fault
   exclusion and, 122–26
   excuse and, 122–26
   *force majeure* and, 308–13
   involuntary conduct as absence of,
      304–06
   *suitas* and, 124–25
Favre, Antoine, 136–38
Fifth Coalition, war of, 234–36
financial necessity
   Hague Codification conference
      discussion of, 377–78, 384, 385–86
   investment arbitration and, 404–09
Fiore, Pasquale, 347, 364–65
Fitzmaurice, Gerald (Sir), 191n83
Fletcher, George, 29–31, 121–22
force. *see* use of force
*force majeure*
   absence of free choice and, 324–27
   absolute impossibility of
      performance and, 307
   Ago on, 304–06
   Article 23 codification of, 286–87,
      308–15, 320–23, 324–27
   *Aucoven v Venezuela* case, 319–20
   blockade violations and, 435–40
   causation and, 287–88, 303–04
   changing conceptions of, 300–03
   coercion and, 324–27, 328–30,
      427n606
   concepts of, 300–03
   in contemporary international law,
      306–23
   Crawford on, 80–81, 313–15, 321–22
   *de facto* conditions and, 185–89
   definitions and terminology, 285–88
   *De Wytenhove* case (France/Italy),
      316–17
   distress and, 446–47, 456–59
   duty of compensation and, 78–79,
      80–81, 83–86
   essential interests and, 360n162, 377
   exclusion of fault, 122–26, 314–15

   as excuse, 121–22, 328–30, 472–74
   fault and, 122–26, 308–14
   fault-based rationale for,
      122–26, 308–14
   *French Company of Venezuelan
      Railroads* case, 294–95, 378–79
   *Gabčíkovo-Nagymaros* case and,
      318–19
   historical development of,
      288–300, 387–88
   ILC work on, 306–07, 315–16
   impossibility of performance and,
      166–69
   interwar period use of, 387–88
   involuntary/voluntary conduct and,
      83–86, 304–06, 324–27
   judicial and arbitral practice,
      294–300
   as justification, 323–24, 328–30
   *LAFICO v Burundi* case, 318
   material impossibility of
      performance and, 320–23, 476n21
   material impossibility standard and,
      320–23, 476n21
   practice of States and, 315–20
   *Rainbow Warrior* award and, 2–3,
      4, 317–18
   rationales for, 303–06, 324–27
   relative impossibility of performance
      and, 309–10, 322–23
   responsibility of accessories and
      defence of, 69–70
   revolutions in nineteenth century
      and, 289–94
   *Rights of US Nationals in Morocco*
      case, 317
   *Russian Indemnity* case and,
      295–97, 379–80
   in *Serbian* and *Brazilian Loans* cases,
      298–99, 380
   Sixth Committee States' views on,
      315–16
   *Société Commerciale de Belgique* case
      and, 299–300, 381–82
   *SS Wimbledon* case and, 297–98, 380
   state of necessity and,
      334–39, 382–86
   *suitas vs.* fault and, 124–25

temporal logic of defences, 159–63
*Torrey Canyon* incident and,
  401n456
wrongfulness and, 47–51
forcible reprisals
  blockade as, 232–34, 237–38
  negative reprisals, 234–36
  non-forcible reprisals *vs.*,
    242–44, 250–52
  outlawing of, 239–42
  positive reprisals, 232–34
foreigners. *see* aliens
foreign military occupation, consent
  and, 135–36, 154
*Forests of Central Rhodope* dispute,
  385–86
forfeiture theory
  countermeasures and, 276–82, 284,
    471–72, 474–76
  deontological theories of justification
    and, 115–17
  duty of compensation and, 86–92,
    282–83, 469–70
  legal protection of interests and,
    102–06, 218–22
  self-defence and, 223–24,
    471–72, 474–76
*Forte* incident, 234–36, 246–47
fortuitous event. *see also* distress; *force majeure*
  *De Wytenhove* case (France/Italy),
    316–17
  epistemological impossibility of
    performance and, 309–10
  fault and, 308–14, 314–15
  ILC discussion of *force majeure* and,
    310–13, 321–22
Foster, David, 96–97
Fox, Gregory H., 351–57, 361
fragmentation of international law,
  41n93
  conflicts between self-defence and
    use of force prohibition and,
    195–96
France
  *Air Services Agreement* dispute and,
    113–14, 225–28, 271n272
  on countermeasures, 254

*De Wytenhove* case (France/Italy),
  316–17
on *force majeure*, 285n5, 315–16,
  323–24, 378–79
indemnities for revolution of 1848
  in, 78n71
*Rainbow Warrior* incident and, 1–8,
  317–18, 449–53, 472–74
*Rights of US Nationals in Morocco*
  case and, 317
Saida Incident of 1881 and,
  291n27, 303–04
*Savarkar Arbitration* case and,
  139–43
*Serbian* and *Brazilian Loans* cases
  and, 298–99, 380
Francis, Laurel, 276–77
Franck, Thomas, 11–12, 24–25
François, Jean Pierre Adiren,
  364–65, 367–68
Franco-Venezuelan mixed commission,
  294–95
freedom, commerce and navigation
  (FCN) agreements, 202–03
free trade obligations, in *Rights of US
  Nationals in Morocco* case, 317
free-will theory of excuse
  distress and, 447, 458, 472–74
  duty of compensation and, 83–86
  excuse and, 121–22
  *force majeure* and, 323–27,
    330–33, 472–74
  involuntary/voluntary conduct and,
    310–13
French Revolution, fundamental rights
  of States and, 346–49
fundamental rights of States, necessity
  and, 346–49, 363–64

Gaja, Giorgio, 46n118, 60–61, 157–58
  on excuse/justification distinction,
    52n142
García-Amador, F., 38
  on total and partial excuse, 38–39
Garden, Guillaume, Comte de,
  349–50, 360
Gattini, Andrea, 123
Gemma, Scipione, 364–65, 367–68

General Act of Geneva (1928), 238–39
General Agreement on Tariffs and Trade (GATT), *Rainbow Warrior* incident and, 2n5
General Assembly. *see* United Nations General Assembly
*General Company of the Orinoco* case, 422–23
Germany
 accessorial responsibility in law of, 67n18
 on consent, 153–54, 165–69
 invasion of Belgium by, 341–42, 371–74
 *SS Wimbledon* case and, 297–98, 332, 380
 structured concept of criminal law in, 27–31
 Versailles Treaty and, 373
 views on *force majeure* in, 315–16
Goebel, Julius, 292–94
Greece
 *Corfu* incident and, 239–42
 *Don Pacifico* incident and, 263n219
 *Forests of Central Rhodope* dispute and, 385–86
 *Interim Accord* case and, 261–62
 *Ottoman Lighthouses* case, 316–17
 *Société Commerciale de Belgique* case and, 299–300, 381–82
Greenpeace, protest against Mururoa nuclear testing by, 1–8
Grégroire (Abbé), 346–49
Gross, Leo, 269–70
Gross, Oren, 350
Grotius, Hugo, 79n79, 339–43, 421–22, 440–42
guarantee of non-repetition, 63–66
Guerrero, José Gustavo, 184–85
Guggenheim, Paul, 138
Guinea, *M/V Saiga* case and, 410–11

Hague Codification Conference (1930), 43
 non-forcible reprisals and, 242–44
 reprisals and, 249–50
 self-defence development and, 184–85
 state of necessity and, 377–78, 384
Hague Peace Conferences (1899), 238–39
Hall, William, 347, 439–40
Halleck, Henry, 347, 441
Hart, Herbert Lionel Adolphus, 29–31, 100, 120–22
Hautefeuille, Laurent, 441
Heathcote, Sarah, 336, 385–86, 419–22, 443
Heffter, August Wilhelm, 347
Heilborn, Paul, 364–65, 369–70
hierarchy of interests. *see also* essential interests; interest-balancing theory; state of necessity
 collateral impairment of obligations and, 206–10
 countermeasures and, 270–72
 *force majeure* in international disputes and, 378–82
 investment arbitration, financial necessity in, 404–09
 protection of essential interests, necessity and, 377–82
 self-defence and, 206–10
 state of necessity and, 366–68, 371, 375–76, 388–89, 414–29
 States' reactions to ILC deliberations on, 398–401
Higgins, Rosalyn, 123
Hindmarsh, Albert, 248–49
Hohfeld, Wesley, 211–12
Hohfeldian analysis
 countermeasures legality and, 273–76
 deontic theories and, 210–23
 justification and, 102–06
 self-defence as, 210–15
 self-defence exclusion from, 185–89
 superior-interests rationale and, 418–21
Holtzendorff, Franz von, 364–65, 370
Horder, Jeremy, 331n238
Huber, Max, 291–94
humanitarian law
 countermeasures and protection of, 263–64, 277–79
 distress defence and, 430–32, 440–42

necessity of intervention and, 411–12
*Rainbow Warrior* Tribunal and, 450–51, 452–53
right of refuge for vessels and, 433–35
self-defence and, 187–88, 191
human rights and fundamental freedoms. *see also* international humanitarian law
countermeasures and protection of, 263–64, 277–79
self-defence and, 187–88, 191
state of necessity and, 339–43
total restraint in, 181n34
Hungary, *Gabčíkovo-Nagymaros* case and, 318–19, 401–04
Husak, Douglas, 10, 29–31
excuse defined by, 118
justification defined by, 102

ILC. *see* International Law Commission (ILC)
Immigration Treaty of 1880 (China–US), 234–36, 247
implementation of responsibility. *see* claims; countermeasures
impossibility of performance, standard of. *see also* absolute impossibility of performance; material impossibility of performance; relative impossibility of performance
*Aucoven v Venezuela* in, 319–20
debate in legal scholarship over, 320–23
in dispute settlement, 300–03
exclusion of fault and, 313–15
fault-based rationale and, 308–13
*force majeure* and, 300–03, 307
ILC on, 307, 310–13, 321–22
in *Rainbow Warrior* case, 317–18
relative impossibility of performance, 309–10, 443–46
supervening events and, 289, 300–03, 443–46
temporary impossibility principle, 310–13

independent responsibility, 66–70, 76–77
India
on distress, 447–48, 455
*force majeure* and responsibility in, 323–24
individuals
distress and threat to, 445–46
personality principle, countermeasures and, 277–79
responsibility, justification and excuse in, 26–27
*Indus Waters Kishengaga* Tribunal, 334–39
infringement of rights *vs.* violations of rights, 90–91
Institut de Droit International (IDI)
*Corfu* incident and, 239–42
Declaration on Pacific Blockades, 237–38
*force majeure* and State responsibility, 292–94
Resolution of 1934, 242–45, 264–66
Resolution on Maritime Prizes (1882), 437–38
instrumental countermeasures, 259–61
instrumentality, *force majeure* defence and, 300–03
interest-balancing theory. *see also* essential interests; hierarchy of interests
absent interest and renunciation, 172–74
conflict of interests in rule of necessity and, 366–68, 371
consequentialist theory, 270–72, 388–89, 414–29, 459–60
financial necessity in investment arbitration and, 404–09
*force majeure* in international disputes and, 378–82
protection of essential interests, necessity and, 377–82
state of necessity and, 375–76, 388–89, 391–92
States' reactions to ILC deliberations on, 398–401
superiority-of-interest rationale and, 415–18

540                                      INDEX

interest damages, in *Russian Indemnity* case, 143–44, 295–97, 379–80
internal defence
  *force majeure* proceedings and, 289, 294–303
  rights of self preservation and, 348–49
international community
  interests of, 404–09
  investment arbitration and, 404–09
  state of necessity and, 394–96
  States as organs of (Kelsen theory), 267–70
International Court of Justice (ICJ)
  consent, 166–69
  defences in law of responsibility and, 3–4
  *force majeure*, 6
  impossibility of performance standard and, 320–23
  self-defence and, 177–78
  state of necessity and, 386–87, 394–96
  state of necessity plea and, 87–88
  treaty law violations considered by, 117
international humanitarian law. *see* humanitarian law
international law
  accessory responsibility in, 69–70
  Ago's system of responsibility in, 40–44
  coherence and compatibility assumptions concerning, 216–17
  consent in, 131–34
  consequences of excuse/justification distinction in, 63–97
  countermeasures in contemporary law, 250–66
  deeds *vs.* reasons concepts of justification in, 113–14
  defences in, 100, 465
  defining justification in, 102
  distress defence in contemporary law, 443–53
  early modern era of, 339–43
  excuse defined in, 118–19
  *force majeure* defence, contemporary interpretations of, 306–23
  forfeiture theory of countermeasures and, 284
  independent responsibility principle in, 66–70, 76–77
  interest-damages in, 295–97
  justification and excuse in, 13–14, 23–27
  Kelsen's discussion of, 257–58, 267–70
  law of state responsibility and, 18–19
  legality of force under, 193–97
  necessity defence in, 363–82
  primary/secondary rule distinction and, 53–57
  reprisals and enforcement of, 247–49
  right of necessity in, 359–63
  rule of necessity in, 374–77, 382–86
  self-defence in, 179–80
  State capacity constraint in, 326–27, 332–33
  suspension of, in rule of necessity, 370
  systemic justification-excuse distinction in, 61–62, 477–78
  taxonomy of defences, 100
  theorisation of excuse in, 120–22
  theorisation of justification in, 115–17
  use of force in, 165–66, 175–80
International Law Commission (ILC). *see also* Articles on Responsibility of States (ARS)
  absence of meeting records for, 46n118
  Ago's report to, 40–44, 146–49
  Allocation of Loss principles, 89–90
  Article 23 codification and, 308–15
  Article 25 commentary, 397
  circumstances precluding wrongfulness debate and, 3–4
  codification of defences by, 15
  codification of responsibility and, 250–52
  consent defence codification by, 131–34, 145–54
  countermeasures adoption and, 225–28
  debate over consent in, 146–49, 150–53

deeds *vs.* reasons concepts of
  justification and, 113–14
distress defence and, 432–42, 443–53
duty of compensation, 79–81
exclusions from countermeasures
  and, 263–64
excuse, 44–47
*force majeure* defence work of,
  306–07
inconsistency on defence of, 38
justification and excuse in work of,
  11–12
law of responsibility, development
  of, 250–52
material impossibility of
  performance and, 307,
  310–13, 321–22
on off-the-record rejection of excuse
  and, 44–47
primary/secondary rule distinction
  and, 53–57
self-defence, development of Article
  21 on, 184
state of necessity codification, 387–97
States' reactions to codification of
  necessity by, 398–401
theorisation of justification by, 117
third parties in deliberations of,
  92–93, 278n301
on use of force prohibitions and self-
  defence, 195–96
internationally wrongful acts
  accessorial responsibility and, 66–70
  Ago's discussion of, 40–44, 256–58
  breach of obligation and, 61–62
  Crawford's discussion of, 47–51
  duty of compensation and,
    81–86, 89–90
  excuse and, 118–19
  justification and, 26–27
  material breach as element of, 74–75
  responsibility, 41–42, 76–77, 467–68
international relations, reprisals and,
  230–38
inter-state relations, *force majeure*
  defence and, 289–94
intervention, acts of
  consent and, 150–53

justification of, 108–10
necessity and, 360–61, 411–12
self-defence and, 175–80
intrinsic illegality of countermeasures,
  112–13
investor-state arbitration
  countermeasures affecting investors'
    rights, 278n297, 279n303
  state of necessity and, 404–09
involuntary conduct. *see also* voluntary
  conduct
  *force majeure* and, 83–86,
    304–06, 324–27
  free will theory of excuse and, 310–13
  impossibility of performance and,
    309–10, 443–46
Iran–US Treaty of Amity, Economic
  Relations and Consular Rights,
  182n38, 203–05
Israel, on state of necessity, 412–13
Italy
  accessorial responsibility in law of,
    67n16
  civil remedies for criminal behaviour
    in, 78–79
  on consent, 153–54
  *Corfu* incident and, 239–42
  *De Wytenhove* case (France/Italy),
    316–17
  on distress, 447–48
  on *force majeure*, 315–16
ITLOS, *M/V Saiga* case and, 410–11

Japan
  on distress, 447–48
  on *force majeure*, 323–24
Jarvis Thomson, Judith, 280
Jay Treaty, 422–23
  right of refuge in, 433–35
Jennings, Robert (Judge), 199–200
Jèze, Gaston, 381–82
Jhering, Rudolf, 367
Jiménez de Aréchaga, Eduardo,
  136–38, 443, 450–51
Jordan, on distress, 447–48
Jouannet, Emmanuelle, 361–62
judicial economy, operation of
  justification and, 109n33

jural relations, Hohfeld's theory of, 211–12
*jus ad bellum. see also* use of force
   necessity and, 345
   nuclear weapons legality and, 190n79
   self-defence in, 175–76, 179–80
   total restraint obligations and, 191
*jus cogens*
   and consent, 163n164
   necessity of intervention and, 411–12
   prohibition of force/aggression as, 193–97
   self-defence and, 187–88, 195–96
*jus in bello*, necessity and, 345
*jus necessitatis. see also* right of necessity; state of necessity
   right of necessity and, 342–43
   in *SS Wimbledon* case, 380
*justa causa*, positive reprisals and, 233–34
justification. *see also* defence; excuse
   absent interest and renunciation, 172–74
   accessorial responsibility, 66–70
   in Articles on Responsibility of States, 11–12, 24–25, 36–37
   boundaries of, 476
   classification of defences as, 98–128
   for collateral impairment of obligations, 205–24
   in common law, 29–31, 33
   compensation for material loss and, 469–70
   concept of, 27–34
      deeds or reasons, 113–14
      legality of, 110–13
      as permissions, 102–06
   consent as, 133, 170–74
   counterintuitive justification, 419–22
   countermeasures as, 254–55, 266–84
   Crawford's discussion of, 47–51
   in criminal law, 25–26, 27–31
   deeds or reasons concepts of, 113–14
   definition and theory concerning, 9–11, 100–17, 466–67
   distress as, 459–60, 461–64
   in domestic law, 12–14, 25–26, 34, 102–06, 115–17, 476n22
   duty of compensation and, 86–93, 469–70
   effects of, 31–34
   evolution of concept of, 27–34
   excuse/justification distinction, 63–97
   financial necessity plea, 404–09
   *force majeure* as, 323–24, 328–30
   for forcible measures, 192–93
   forfeiture theory of countermeasures and, 284
   ILC work on, 11–12
   in international law, 23–27
   lawful conduct as justified conduct, 110–13
   in law of State responsibility, 11–12, 35
   legality of, 110–13
   material breach in treaty law and, 72–77
   of necessity plea, 12–14, 27–28, 87–88, 95–96, 356, 364–65, 370–71
   normative considerations in, 94–97
   as permissions, 102–06
   policy-based grounds for, 99–100
   practical relevance of, 31–34
   primary/secondary rule distinction in, 26–27, 57–61
   reactions against wrongfulness as, 70–77
   reparations and effect of, 63–66
   responsibility and, 9–11, 12–14
   rights forfeiture and, 223–24
   self-defence as, 189, 223–24
   state of necessity as, 393–94, 396, 414–29
   states' views on, 35–36
   systemic distinction in international law of, 61–62
   taxonomy of defences and, 126
   theorisation of, 115–17, 474
   third parties, 92–93
   weak and strong justification, 105–06
   wrongful acts defences, 41–44

justified conduct, 465
  countermeasures against, 71–72
  lawful conduct as, 110–13
  legal order and, 111–12
  material breach of treaty in Vienna Convention Article 60, 74–75

Kalshoven, Fritz, 266n250
Kamto, Maurice, 395
Kellogg-Briand Pact of 1929, 238–42
Kelsen, Hans
  coercive theory of law and, 257–58
  hypothetical legal norm, 257–58
  on international law, 249
  on reprisals as sanctions, 251–52, 257–58, 267
  on States as organs of the international community, 267–70
  on wrongfulness, 41
Kenya
  on consent, 149–50
  on distress, 447–48
Kessler Ferzan, Kimberley, 13, 126
Kleen, Richard, 439–40
Klüber, Joachim-Ludwig, 349–50, 360
Kohler, Joseph, 376n272
Korea. *see* South Korea
Koskenniemi, Martti, 284

Lapradelle, Albert de, 381–82
law of peace
  armed conflict during, self-defence and, 180–83
  *Fur Seals* arbitration and, 357–59
  positive reprisals and, 233–34
  right of necessity and, 342–43, 357n146
  self-defence and, 180–83, 184–85, 357n146
law of State responsibility
  Ago's discussion of, 40–44
  circumstances precluding wrongfulness and, 3–4
  conflict of interests and rule of necessity and, 368
  countermeasures' dual role in, 252–61
  defences in, 3–4
  distress defence and, 443, 446–47, 449–53, 456

  duty of compensation and, 81–86
  excuse defined in, 118
  fault and, 122–26
  *force majeure* defence and, 289–94, 300–03, 328–29
  implementation of, countermeasures as instrument for, 255–61
  international law and, 18–19
  justification and excuse in, 11–12, 35, 467–68
  necessity plea in, 87–88, 334–39, 363–71
  primary/secondary rule distinction in, 53–57
  rule of necessity and, 364–66
  in *Russian Indemnity* case, 143–44
  State capacity constraint in, 332–33
  third parties and duty of compensation, 92–93
  treaty law separation from, 74–75
  of wrongdoing state toward injured state, 61–62
law of the sea
  British seizure of Danish fleet and, 345–46
  *Caroline* incident and, 351–62
  *force majeure* and, 325–26
  *Fur Seals* arbitration and, 357–59
  right of necessity and, 339–43
  right of refuge of ships in distress and, 433–35
  state of necessity in *M/V Saiga* case, 410–11
law of treaties. *see* treaty law
law of war. *see also* armed conflict
  blockade violations and, 435–40
  *force majeure* and, 294–303, 316–17
  objective and subjective conceptions of war and, 239–42
  right of necessity and, 341–43
  self-defence in armed conflict and, 180–83, 181n29, 189–91
Lawrence, Thomas Joseph, 250–52
League of Nations, 238–39
  *Corfu* incident and, 239–42, 264–66
  in *Société Commerciale de Belgique* case, 299–300

*Le délit international* (Ago), 136–38
legal protection
  consent as renunciation of, 170–72
  forfeiture of, 218–22
Lencker, Theodore, 173–74
Leopold of Belgium (King), 246–47
lesser-evil theory. *see* consequentialist theory
*lex ferenda*
  material impossibility of performance and, 323
  state of necessity and, 377–78
*lex lata*, material impossibility standard and, 323
*lex specialis*
  consent and, 164n167
  countermeasures, 203–05
  diplomatic law and countermeasures and, 279–80
  self-defence in armed conflict and, 181–83, 195–96
liberty rights. *see* Hohfeldian analysis
Libya, *LAFICO v Burundi* case, 318
Lithuania, *Railway Traffic between Lithuania and Poland* case and, 242–44
London Declaration, 437–38
Lowe, Vaughan, 9, 23–24, 465
  on excuse, 95–96
Lushington, Godfrey, 439–40

Macedonia, *Interim Accord* case, 261–62
Macri, G., 349–50
Mafart (Major), 1–8, 449–53, 472–74
material breach of treaty
  compensation for material losses and, 77–81
  countermeasures and, 254–55
  excuse and, 118–19
  justification and excuse distinction, 72–77, 97
  States' reactions against, 70–77
material impossibility of performance. *see also* absolute impossibility of performance; epistemological impossibility of performance; impossibility of performance; relative impossibility of performance
  in contemporary international law, 307
  debate in legal scholarship over, 320–23
  distress and, 443–46
  exclusion of fault and, 313–15
  in *force majeure*, 320–23, 476n21
  ILC debate concerning, 310–13
  involuntariness and, 326–27
  objective elements of, 476n21
  in *Rainbow Warrior* case, 317–18
  state of necessity defence and, 334–39
material loss, duty of compensation for, 81–86
McLeod, Alexander, 352
measures short of war. *see also* countermeasures; forcible reprisals; law of war; reprisals
  *Corfu* incident and, 239–42
  positive reprisals and, 233–34
*mens rea*, justification and excuse and, 29
Mexico
  on countermeasures, 259–60
  on *force majeure*, 320–23
middle case, for consent defence, 147–48, 150–53, 154–69
military necessity, 345
Monaco, Ricardo, 136–38
Mongolia, distress and, 447–48
moral blame, consequentialist theory and, 208n153
Morelli, Gaetano, 136–38
Morocco
  *Rights of US Nationals in Morocco* case and, 317
  views on *force majeure* in, 315–16
Moursi Badr, Gamal, 187
Mousourakis, George, 34

*The Nabby*, 442
NAFTA Tribunals investor–state disputes, countermeasures in, 253n152
Napoleonic wars
  British seizure of Danish fleet during, 345–46
  negative reprisals in, 234–36

National Iranian Oil Corporation, 203–05
natural law
  fundamental rights of States and, 346–49
  right of necessity in, 339–44
  right to refuge and, 440–42
*Naulilaa* award, 242–45, 246–47
navigation agreements
  law of the sea and right of entry in distress, 433–35
  self-defence and, 182–83
*Navigational and Related Rights (Costa Rica v Nicaragua)*, 132–33, 154–56
Nepolitan Insurrection of 1848, 291–92
*necessitas facet legem*, 335
*necessitas non habet legem*, 335
necessitous, early modern concept of, 339–43
necessity, plea of. *see* state of necessity
negative reprisals, 234–36
negative rule-element
  consent and, 157–58, 163–69
  temporal logic of consent and, 158–63
Netherlands, distress and, 447–48
neutrality. *see also* specific countries
  Belgium, 136–38, 170–72, 341–42, 371–74, 411–12, 416–17
  in *Caroline* incident, 351–57
  *force majeure* and, 297–98
  right of necessity and violations of, 341–42, 345–46, 369–70, 371–74
*The New York*, 442
New Zealand
  *Rainbow Warrior* incident and, 1–8, 317–18, 449–53
  self-defence in, 190n79
Ní Aoláin, Fionnuala, 350
non-consent, consent defence and, 165–69
non-forcible reprisals. *see also* forcible reprisals; reprisals
  as countermeasures, renaming of, 250–52
  regulation of, 242–44
non-intervention, right to
  aggressor State's duties concerning, 210–15
  countermeasures and, 273
  in *DRC v Uganda*, 200–02
  in *Nicaragua v US*, 199–200
  self-defence and, 182–83
  territorial sovereignty and, 199–202
non-performance of obligations
  consent to, 132–33, 178–79
  countermeasures as response to, 262–64
  *force majeure* and, 294–300
  *force majeure* proceedings and, 300–03
  involuntary conduct and, 304–06
  as negative reprisal, 234–36
  peremptory rules and, 217n195
  in *Russian Indemnity* case, 295–97
  self-defence and, 191n83, 192–93
  in *SS Wimbledon* case, 297–98
non-precluded measures, state of necessity and, 404–09
non-reciprocity in countermeasures, 262–64, 277–79
non-repetition, obligation of, 63–66, 118–19, 273. *see also* cessation
non-wrongful conduct
  justified conduct as, 110–13
no-rights, justification and, 102–06
Nys, Ernest, 441

obligations
  breach of, 61–62
  of cessation and non-repetition, 81–86
  collateral impairment of, justification for, 205–24
  commercial obligations, 202–05
  consent as negative element of, 131–34, 154–56, 163–65
  countermeasures as suspension of, 254–55
  defences *vs.*, 7n26, 477n24
  due diligence, 124–25, 166–69, 304–06
  duty of compensation, excuse of, 77–81

obligations (*cont.*)
  exemption from violation by way of countermeasures, 263–64
  *force majeure* and breach of, 287–88, 308–13, 324–27
  guarantees of non-repetition as, 63–66
  necessity as limitation on force of, 370–71
  primary/secondary rule distinction, 152–53, 156–58, 170–72
  primary/secondary rules and, 53–57, 152–53
  self-defence and, 175–83, 199–205
  state of necessity and breach of, 390n341, 393–94
  substantive, 262–64
O'Keefe, Roger, 8
Okowa, Phoebe, 166–69
'Opération Satanique,' 2n3
*opinio necessitatis*, 335, 380
Oppenheim, Lassa, 248–49
Organisation for Economic Co-operation and Development (OECD), *Rainbow Warrior* incident and, 2n5
original community of goods
  in *Neptune* case, 343–44
  right of necessity and, 339–43, 349–50
Ottoman Empire, 143–44, 295–97, 379–80
*Ottoman Lighthouses* case, 316–17

pacific blockades. *see also* blockade violations
  nineteenth-century history of, 435–40
  reprisals and, 232–34, 237–38
*pacta sunt servanda* principle, countermeasures and, 254–55
Palmerston (Lord), 230–31
Palmisano, Giuseppe, 124–25
partial excuse
  duty of compensation and, 83
  García-Amador's discussion of, 38–39
Peace Treaty of Constantinople, 295–97

Pellet, Alain, 395
People's Republic of China, on countermeasures, 259–60
Pereira, Fernando, 1–8
peremptory norms. *see also* normative principles
  conflicts between, 196n102
  consent and, 148–49
  consequentialist theory and, 270–72
  countermeasures and, 260–61, 263–64, 277–79
  hierarchy of interests and, 206–10
  self-defence and, 217–18
  state of necessity and, 388–89, 390n341, 408–09, 412–13
Permanent Court of International Justice (PCIJ)
  fault-based responsibility and, 123–24
  non-forcible reprisals and, 242–44, 247
  remedy of satisfaction issued by, 63–66
  reprisals and, 238–39
  *Serbian* and *Brazilian Loans* cases and, 298–99
  *SS Wimbledon* case and, 297–98
permission, justification as, 102–06
personal integrity, distress defence and threat to, 445–46
personhood theory, 120–22
  right of necessity and, 342–43
Phillimore, Robert, 303–04
Phillipson, Coleman, 376–77
physical necessity, *force majeure* defence and, 303–04
Pinto, Christopher, 390–94
Pisillo Mazzeschi, Riccardo, 477–78
' A Plea for Excuses (Lowe)', 95–96
Poland
  on distress, 455
  *Railway Traffic between Lithuania and Poland* case and, 242–44
Politis, Nicolas, 244, 267, 381–82
Portugal, on state of necessity, 377–78
positive reprisals, 232–34. *see also* forcible reprisals; non-forcible reprisals; reprisals

positivism
  conflict of interests in rule of necessity and, 366–68
  fundamental rights of States and, 347–48, 363–64
  international law and influence of, 364–66
  rule of necessity and, 382–86
  self-defence and countermeasures and, 474–76
practical irrelevance critique of justification and excuse, 31–34
practice of states
  on consent, 131–34, 135–36, 139–44, 149–50, 153–54, 471–72
  on distress, 446–47
  on duty of compensation, 423–25
  on excuse, 42–44
  on *force majeure*, 315–20, 328–30
  on free-will theory, 330–33
  on justification, 471–72
  protection of essential interests and, 377–82
  self-defence and, 175–80, 182–83, 471–72
  on state of necessity, 337–38, 375, 377–82, 387–88, 398–413, 471–72
Pradier-Fodéré, Paul, 350
precautionary measures, state of necessity, 354–55, 392–93
preclusion of responsibility. see excuse
preclusion of wrongfulness principle, ARS use of, 24–25. see also justification
prescriptive jurisdiction, in *M/V Saiga* case, 410–11
Prieur, Dominique (Captain), 1–8, 449–53, 472–74
*prima facie* breach
  consent defence and, 150–53
  justification of, 108–10
primary/secondary rule distinction
  Ago's development of, 40–44
  consent and, 152–53, 156–58, 170–72
  defences and, 52–61, 158–59
  ILC and, 53–57

justification and excuse and, 26–27, 57–61
law of responsibility and, 53–57
self-defence and, 189
primitive legal communities, use of force in, 267–70
*Prince of Wales* incident, 232–34
private law
  in *Russian Indemnity* case, 143–44
  state of necessity and, 375–76, 383
private reprisals, history of, 230–31
prize law
  blockade violations and, 435–40
  Continental *vs.* Anglo-American approaches, 435n28, 436–37
  distress as excuse in, 456–59
  humanitarian considerations, 442
procedural respondent, respondent in substance *vs.*, 16n57
property rights
  non-forcible reprisals and, 242–44
  in positive reprisals, 233–34
  right of necessity and, 339–43, 344
proportionality, principle of
  consequentialist theory and, 206–10, 270–72, 459–60
  countermeasures and, 242–44, 262–64, 270–72
  distress defence and threat to, 445–46
  forfeiture theory and, 280, 474–76
  lesser-evils theory and, 459–60
  non-forcible reprisals and, 242–44
  superior-interests rationale and, 418
  total restraint obligations and, 181n34
public benefit theory, justification and, 115–17
public law, state of necessity and, 375–76, 383
Pufendorf, Samuel, 79n79, 340–41, 342–43, 421–22, 440–42
punitive measures, countermeasures as, 258

Quentin-Baxter, Robert, 79n80, 147–48
Questionnaire of the Preparatory Committee (Hague Codification Conference), 242–44, 249–50

548  INDEX

*Rainbow Warrior* incident
  bombing and, 1–8
  classification of defences in, 51
  distress and, 432, 443,
    449–53, 472–74
  fault-based responsibility and, 124–25
  *force majeure* and, 313–14, 317–18
  naming of, 1n2
  state of necessity and, 394
rape, consent as defence to, 165–69
reactive measures, necessity and,
  354–55
reasonable belief criterion, distress and,
  453–55
reasonableness, distress and, 430–32
reasons concept of justification, 113–14
reciprocal taxes, non-forcible reprisals
  and, 242–44
Regime of Peace-Time Reprisals (IDI),
  239–42
relative impossibility of performance.
  *see also* absolute impossibility of
  performance; epistemological
  impossibility of performance
  distress and, 446–47
  *force majeure* and, 309–10, 322–23
rendition, extraterritorial enforcement
  in *Savarkar* and, 140–43
renunciation of legal protection
  absent interest theory and, 172–74
  consent as, 170–72, 471–72
reparations. *see also* responsibility
  Ago on obligations of, 41, 256–58
  ARS Art. 31, 118
  in *Corfu* incident, 239–42
  countermeasures as tool for, 260–61
  duty of compensation for, 81–86
  effect of defences on, 63–66, 77–81
  excuse, 77–81
  extenuating circumstances and,
    38–39
  extraterritorial enforcement in
    *Savarkar* and, 142–43
  justification and, 63–66
  Kelsen's discussion of, 257–58
  non-forcible reprisals and, 242–44
  responsible state's obligations
    concerning, 61–62, 76–77
  victim state's right to, 256–58
reprisals. *see also* countermeasures
  classic age of (1800–1919), 230–38
  countermeasure terminology and,
    225–28, 256–58
  forcible reprisals, 239–42
  illegality of, 246–47
  international law enforcement and,
    247–49
  interwar period (1919–1939), 238–44
  in lawful measures, 249–50
  limits on right to, 237–38
  negative reprisals, 234–36
  non-forcible reprisals, 242–44
  origins of countermeasures and,
    228–50
  positive reprisals, 232–34
  private *vs.* public reprisals, 244–50
  against reprisal, 71–72
reprisals as sanctions
  Kelsen, 251–52, 257–58, 267
repudiation of treaty, material breach
  as, 73
*res judicata*, in *Société Commerciale de
  Belgique* case, 299–300
Resolution on Maritime Prizes (1882),
  437–38
respondent in substance, procedural
  respondent *vs.*, 66.10n57
responsibility. *see also* accessorial
  responsibility; derivative
  responsibility; law of State
  responsibility
  Ago on, 40–44, 185–89
  consent as defence to,
    132–33, 135–38
  countermeasures and law of, 256–58
  delictual and criminal responsibility,
    258n180
  fault and, 122–26
  *force majeure* and, 285n5
  free-will theory and, 330–33
  material breach and, 74–75
  non-forcible reprisals and law of,
    242–44
  primary/secondary rule distinction
    in law of, 53–57
  self-defence and law of, 185–89

structured *vs.* flat systems of, 477–78
of wrongdoing state toward injured
state, 61–62
restitution
extraterritorial enforcement in
*Savarkar* and, 142–43
in *Russian Indemnity* case, 143–44
state of necessity and, 339–43
retaliation, negative reprisals as, 234–36
retorsion, negative reprisals as, 233–34
Reuter, Paul, 326–27, 392–93,
446–47, 458
revolutions, *force majeure* defence and,
289–94
right of necessity
as corollary to right of self-
preservation, 349–50
fundamental rights of States and,
346–49
in international law, 359–63
in natural law, 339–44
nineteenth-century case law and
demise of, 345–63
state of necessity *vs.*, 387–89
right of refuge
aircraft in distress, 314–15,
430–32, 444–45
blockades and, 232–34, 237–38
British seizure of Danish fleet and,
345–46
distress defence and, 430–42, 453–55
*force majeure* and, 325–26
*Fur Seals* arbitration and, 357–62
history of, 351–57
humanitarian considerations and,
440–42
in law of the sea, 433–35
relative impossibility of performance
and, 444–45
state of necessity and, 342–43,
357n146, 410–11
States' limits on, 456
rights
of affected states, 90–91
consent as abrogation of, 132–33,
136–38, 154–69
countermeasures legality and,
272–82

deontological theory of justification
and, 115–17
fundamental rights of States,
346–49, 363–64
justification in context of, 102–06
necessity in early-modern law and,
339–43
self-defence as, 27–28, 179–80
state of necessity and, 339–43
of third parties, duty of
compensation and, 92–93
violation *vs.* infringement of, 90–91
rights-forfeiture. *see* forfeiture theory
Riphagen, Willem, 147–48, 149–50,
187–88, 254–55
on countermeasures, 258, 277–79
on state of necessity, 391–92
Rivier, Alphonse, 347, 349–50, 364–65
Robinson, Paul, 29–31
Rodin, David, 104–05, 220
Rolls of Oleron, 433–35
Romania, on state of necessity, 377–78
Ronzitti, Natalino, 135–36
Ross, Alf, 136–38
rule-consequentialist theory. *see also*
consequentialist theory; justification
countermeasures and, 270–72
hierarchy of interests in, 209–10
self-defence and, 209–10
rules of necessity. *see also* necessity
angary as, 362
*necessitas facet legem* and, 335
state of necessity distinguished, 371–77
Russia
*Caroline* incident and mediation by,
357
on countermeasures, 259–60
Turkish debt obligations to, *force
majeure* proceedings and, 295–97
Russo-Polish War, 297–98

Saida Incident of 1881, 291n27, 303–04
sanctions
countermeasures as, 251–52, 256–58
injured party's imposition of, 76–77
reprisals as, 256–58
responsibility and, 41
states as organs for, 267–70

satisfaction, ARS Article 37 and, 63–66
Savarkar, Vinayak Damodar, 139–43
Scalese, Giancarlo
   on countermeasures, 273, 274–76
   on excuse, 121–22, 123
   on self-defence, 210–15
Schwarzenberger, Georg, 331–32
Schwebel, Stephen, 199–200, 392–93
Scott, William (Sir), 438–39, 442
secondary norm, Kelsen's discussion of, 258n178
secondary rules. *see* primary/secondary rule distinction
security policy, right of refuge and, 433–35
self-defence
   aggressor State rights and, 197–98
   Ago's discussion of, 42–44
   armed conflict during peace and, 180–83
   ARS Article 21 on, 175–80, 184, 192–99, 203–05, 217–18
   in *Caroline* incident, 351–57
   for collateral impairment of obligations, 205–24
   for commercial obligations, 202–05
   consent and, 157–58
   consequentialist theories and, 206–10, 270–72, 419–22
   countermeasures justification and, 71–72, 270–72
   deontic theories and, 210–23
   duty of compensation and, 86–92, 222–23
   exclusion as subjective right of, 185–89
   forfeiture theory and, 218–22
   in *Fur Seals* arbitration, 357–62
   as Hohfeldian privilege, 210–15
   ILC on, 184
   as justification and, 180–83, 185–89, 192–205
   justification and excuse in, 27–28, 471–72
   legal theories of, 175–80
   obligations in practice and, 199–205
   for obligations other than prohibition of force, 189
   peremptory rules, 217–18
   primary/secondary rule distinction and, 57–61
   prohibition of force and, 185–89
   as right, 102–06
   rights forfeiture and justification, 223–24
   right to life and, 273n279
   rule-consequentialist theory and, 209–10
   state of necessity and, 350–59, 360–61, 362–63
   as subjective or claim-right, 185–89
   superior-interests rationale and, 419–22
   temporal logic in, 159–63
   territorial sovereignty and non-intervention and, 199–202
   third parties and, 92–93
   total restraint obligations and, 191, 198–99
   unitary theory concerning, 216–17
self-preservation
   in *Caroline* incident, 351–57
   consent and, 136–38
   fundamental rights of States and, 346–49
   *Fur Seals* arbitration and, 357–62
   Germany's justification of invasion of Belgium based on, 371–74
   intervention and, 364–72, 387–88
   law of State responsibility and, 364–66
   legal scholarship concerning, 359–63
   necessity and right of, 341–43, 345, 346–59, 360–63
   right of necessity as corollary to, 349–50
   state of necessity and, 387–88
   states' right to, 296–97
Serbia
   French loan dispute with, 298–99, 304–06, 302n96, 325, 326–27, 380, 385–86
   NATO intervention in, 411–12, 416–17
Sereni, Angelo, 136–38

## INDEX

*The Shepherdess* case, blockade violations in, 438–39
Sibert, Marcel, 331–32
Simester, Andrew, 331n238
Simma, Bruno, 77–81, 226n7, 279n302
situation of necessity, defined, 337–38, 388–89. *see also* state of necessity
Sixth Committee. *see* United Nations General Assembly Sixth Committee
Slovakia
  on *force majeure*, 315–16
  *Gabčíkovo-Nagymaros* case and, 318–19, 401–04
*Société Commerciale de Belgique* (1939), 299–300, 302–03, 325, 381–82, 385–86
*sommation* principle
  countermeasures and, 264–66, 281–82
  right of reprisal and, 237–38
Sørensen, Max, 450–51
South Africa, on state of necessity, 377–78
*Southern Bluefin Tuna* Tribunal, 216–17
South Korea, countermeasures accepted by, 254
sovereignty. *see also* territorial sovereignty
  in *Caroline* incident, 351–57
  consent and, 136–38
  countermeasures and, 284
  *Savarkar Arbitration* case and issues of, 140–43
  self-defence and, 175–80, 182–83
  state of necessity and, 206–10, 411–12, 416–17
Spain
  on consent, 153–54
  Saida Incident of 1881 and, 291n27, 303–04
Sperduti, Giuseppe, 118
Sri Lanka, on countermeasures, 254
*SS Wimbledon* case, 297–98, 325, 332, 380
statehood, fundamental rights of States and, 346–49

state of necessity
  Ago's development of, 388–89
  ARS Article 25, 17, 334–39, 394–96, 397, 404–09, 418
  autonomous rule of necessity and, 359–63
  British seizure of Danish fleet and, 345–46
  in *Caroline* incident, 351–57
  conflict of interests in, 366–68
  consequentialist theory and, 206–10, 270–72
  as counterintuitive justification, 419–22
  countermeasures and, 281–82
  as customary law, 336–37, 386–87, 414
  deeds *vs.* reasons concepts of justification and, 113–14
  *de facto* conditions and self-defence and, 185–89
  defined, 337–38
  definitions and basic principles concerning, 334–39
  as discrete defence, 359–63
  in dispute settlement, 401–13
  distress defence and, 4, 17–18, 439–40, 443, 456–59
  Draft Article 33, ILC deliberations, 390–94
  duty of compensation and, 78–79, 79n79, 83–86, 87–88, 421–25
  essential interests and *force majeure* in international disputes and, 378–82
  as excuse, 12–14, 27–28, 91–92, 95–96, 121–22, 356, 396, 414–29, 474
  fault-based rationale and, 308–13
  *force majeure* and, 378–86
  foreiture theory and, 280, 474–76
  freedom of choice and, 326–27
  fundamental rights of states and, 346–49, 363–64
  *Fur Seals* arbitration and, 357–62
  in *Gabčíkovo-Nagymaros* case, 401–04
  as general defence, in miscellaneous cases, 410–13

state of necessity (*cont.*)
  Hague Codification Conference and, 377–78
  history in international law, 339–86
  ILC codification of, 387–97
  ILC rehabilitation of, 386–414
  impossibility standard and, 309–10
  including in Draft Articles, 388–97
  interest-damages of States and, 296–97, 371
  international law and state of, 363–82
  in investment arbitration, 404–09
  as justification, 12–14, 27–28, 87–88, 95–96, 356, 364–65, 370–71, 393–94, 396, 414–29, 471–72, 474
  justified conduct as lawful conduct and, 110–13
  law of responsibility and state of, 4, 363–71
  law of state responsibility and, 87–88, 334–39, 363–71
  natural right of necessity, 339–44
  in *Neptune* case, 343–44
  neutrality violations and, 341–42, 345–46, 369–70, 371–74
  new theories on rule of necessity and, 368–71
  in nineteenth-century case law, 345–63
  nuclear weapons deployment and, 190n79
  original community principle and, 339–43
  Palestinian Wall dispute and, 412–13
  policy grounds for, 99–100
  postwar rehabilitation of, 386–414
  practice of States and, 398–413
  precluding circumstances and, 392–93
  primary/secondary rule distinction and, 57–61
  protection of essential interests and, 377–82
  right of affected State and, 90–91
  rights *vs.* no-rights perspective on, 105
  rule of necessity, 364–66
  *Russian Indemnity* case and, 379–80
  self-defence and, 350–59
  self-preservation and, 341–43, 345, 346–59
  States' reactions to ILC work on, 398–401
  subjective elements of, 476n21
  substance and form of, 382–86
  suspension of international law based on, 370
  terminology of, 337–38, 362–63
  *Torrey Canyon* incident and, 401n456
  total restraint and, 181n34
  unitary theory of justification and, 115–17
  use of force, legality of, 411–12
state of war, self-defence and, 180–83
states. *see also* aggressor state, rights of; practice of states; victim state, rights of
  absent interest and renunciation, 172–74
  accessorial responsibility of, 66–70
  anthropomorphisation of, 472–74
  armed conflict and self-defence and, 182–83
  conflict of interests and rule of necessity and, 368
  consent defence and practice of, 131–34, 135–36, 139–44
  countermeasures taken by, 71–72, 225–28
  debtor obligations of, 295–97
  distress defence, perspectives of, 447–53
  excuse as defence to practices of, 42–44
  fault-based rationale for *force majeure* and obligations of, 308–13
  *force majeure* defence and, 294–95, 300–03, 315–20, 324–27
  involuntariness and absence of free choice, *force majeure* defence based on, 324–27
  justification and conduct of, 102

necessity plea and rights of,
  345–49, 414
negative reprisals by, 234–36
obligations to foreigners by, 289–94
as organs of international
  community, 267–70
perspectives on justification vs.
  excuse in, 35–36
reactions against wrongfulness by,
  70–77
reprisals and rights of,
  228–38, 247–49
self-defence and, 175–80, 182–83
self-preservation and right of
  necessity for, 349–50
views on consent from,
  149–50, 153–54
*status necessitatis*, 385
Stephen, James, 33
Stowell, Ellery, 360n164, 367n207
stress of weather, blockade violations
  and, 435–40
strict liability, duty of compensation
  and, 89–90
Strupp, Karl, 364–65, 366–68, 372
St. Vincent and the Grenadines, *M/V
  Saiga* case and, 410–11
*Suez (I)* Tribunal, 96–97
*suitas*, fault vs., 124–25
*summum jus, summa injuria*
  collateral impairment of obligations
    and, 206–10
  counterintuitive justification and,
    419–22
  state of necessity and,
    388–89, 393–94
superior-interests rationale
  as justification, 419–22, 471–72
  quantitative criteria for, 417–18
  state of necessity and, 414–29
supervening event, *force majeure* and,
  289, 300–03, 443–46
Sweden
  on consent, 149–50
  on distress, 447–48
Swiss German Treaty of 1876, 236
Switzerland
  on countermeasures, 259–60

on state of necessity, 377–78
systematisation of defences, law of
  responsibility and, 477–78
systemic integration principle, self-
  defence and use of force and, 205

tacit exceptions, right of necessity and,
  339–43
Tammes, Arnold, 54
temporary impossibility of
  performance, *force majeure* and,
  310–13
*Teoria della responsabilità
  internazionale* (Anzilotti), 53
territorial sovereignty
  *Caroline* incident and, 351–57
  in *DRC v Uganda*, 200–02
  in *Nicaragua v US*, 199–200
  non-intervention and, 199–202
  self-defence and, 175–80, 182–83,
    199–202
  state of necessity and breach of,
    411–12, 416–17
Thailand, on state of necessity defence,
  336
Thiam, Doudou, 45–46
third parties
  consent and, 154–56
  countermeasures and rights of,
    277–79
  duty of compensation and, 92–93
  *force majeure* and claims of, 289–94
  reprisals and rights of,
    233–34, 237–38
  self-defence and role of, 175–80
  state of necessity and, 375–76
threats to life, distress and, 430–32,
  445–46, 453–55
*Torrey Canyon* incident, 401n456
torts
  duty of compensation and, 467–68
total restraint obligations
  in *DRC v Uganda*, 199–202
  environmental law and, 217–18
  human rights and environmental
    law, 181n34
  self-defence and, 175–80,
    191, 198–99

transboundary harm, compensation for, 89–90
treaty law
  consent and, 132–33
  countermeasures and breaches of, 254–55, 262–64
  defences to breaches of, 3–4
  impossibility of performance and, 302–03
  law of State responsibility as separate from, 74–75
  material breach of, justification and excuse in, 72–77
  material impossibility of performance and, 320–23
  negative reprisals involving non-performance and termination, 234–36
  neutrality violations on basis of necessity and, 371–74
  non-performance of obligations in, 191n83
  positive reprisals and, 233–34
  reprisals and, 233–34, 236–37, 242
  rights forfeiture and justification of self-defence and, 223–24
  state of necessity and violations of, 341–42, 404–09
  theorisation of justification and breaches of, 117
  third parties in, 278n301
Treaty of 24 February 1810, 234–36
Treaty of Versailles
  Germany's responsibility in, 373
  SS Wimbledon case and, 297–98, 380
Turco-Russian war of 1877–1878, 143–44, 295–97
Turkey, *force majeure* claims in *Russian Indemnity* case, 143–44, 295–97, 379–80
Twiss, Travers, 441

Ukraine
  on countermeasures, 259–60
  on distress, 447–48
Ullmann, Emanuel, 364–65, 369
ultrahazardous activities, strict liability for, 89–90

unavoidable necessity, *force majeur* and, 334–39
unforeseeability requirement, in *force majeure*, ILC debate on, 310–13
Uniacke, Suzanne, 105–06
United Kingdom
  *Caroline* incident and, 351–57
  on consent, 149–50
  damage claims during Belgian Insurrection by, 290–92
  distress and, 447–48
  *Don Pacifico* incident and, 263n219
  on *force majeure*, 315–16
  *Fur Seals* arbitration and, 357–62
  Neapolitan Insurrection of 1848 and, 291–92
  negative reprisals in Napoleonic wars, 234–36
  *Neptune* case and, 343–44
  *Savarkar Arbitration* case and, 139–43
  *SS Wimbledon* case and, 297–98, 380
  *Torrey Canyon* incident and, 401n456
United Nations General Assembly Sixth Committee
  on consent, 23–24, 149–50, 153–54
  on countermeasures, 225–28
  on *force majeure*, 315–16
  on state of necessity defence, 336
United States
  *Caroline* incident and, 351–57
  damage claims during Belgian Insurrection by, 290–92
  distress and, 447–48
  *Fur Seals* arbitration and, 357–59
  negative reprisals against China by, 234–36
  *Neptune* case and, 343–44
  *Rights of US Nationals in Morocco* case and, 317
  state criminal codes in, 78–79
unity of legal system
  countermeasures and, 276
  deontic theory of justification, 115–17
  of excuse, 120–22
  of justification, 115–17
  self-defence and, 216–17

system of responsibility and, 41, 41n93
universality
  of justification, 31–34
  responsibility of accessories and, 69–70
unlawful armed attack, self-defence and, 192, 197–98
urgent necessity, blockade violations and, 435–40
Uruguay, on countermeasures, 254
US–China immigration dispute, 236, 247
use of force
  aggressor state rights and, 197–98
  consent and, 135–36, 148–49, 165–69
  countermeasures and prohibition of, 263–64
  customary international law prohibition of, 43n103
  justification and excuse in defence of, 27–28
  law of peace and, 184–85
  legality of, 193–97, 411–12
  non-performance of obligations in connection with, 192–93
  peremptory status of prohibition on, 193n92
  as positive reprisal, 232–34
  prohibitions against, evolution of self-defence and, 185–89
  reprisals and, 242, 246–47
  self-defence and, 175–80, 182–83, 189–91
  state of necessity and, 345, 350–51
  temporal logic of consent and, 159–63
  unlawful armed attack as justification for, 192
Ushakov, Nikolai, 147–48, 187, 390–94, 446–47
US–Nicaragua Treaty of Friendship, Commerce and Navigation (FCN Treaty), 182n38, 202–03
utilitarian theory. *see also* consequentialist theory
  of excuse, 120–22
  of justification, 115–17

Vallat, Francis, 148–49, 309–10, 446–47
Vattel, Emer de, 339–43, 440–42
Venezuela
  *Aucoven v Venezuela* case in, 319–20
  on *force majeure*, 315–16, 378–79
  port blockade in, 233–34, 237–38
Verdross, Alfred, 375, 381–82
Verosta, Stephan, 44, 187, 392n365
vessels
  blockades and, 232–34, 237–38
  British seizure of Danish fleet and, 345–46
  *Caroline* incident and, 351–57
  distress and, 430–42
  *force majeure* and, 325–26
  *Fur Seals* arbitration and, 357–62
  law of the sea and refuge in distress, 433–35
  necessity plea in *M/V Saiga* case, 410–11
  prize law and, 435–40
  right of necessity and, 342–43, 357n146
Vienna Conference on the law of treaties, *force majeure* deliberations at, 306–07, 320–23
Vienna Convention on the Law of Treaties (VCLT), 72–77
  countermeasures and, 254–55
  distress and, 446–47, 458
  *Rainbow Warrior* and, 450n155
  systematic integration principle and, 205
Vienna School, countermeasures and theories of, 267
*Vincent v Lake Erie* case, 87–88, 462–62
violations of rights, *vs.* infringement of rights, 90–91
violations of treaties, as material breach, 73
visitation, right of, *Fur Seals* arbitration and, 357–62
*volenti non fit injuria*
  consent and, 134
  duty of compensation and, 86–92
  renunciation of obligations and, 163n164

voluntary conduct
  distress defence and, 456–59
  fault *vs.*, 125–26
  *force majeure* and, 83–86, 304–06, 324–27
  free-will theory and, 330–33
  state of necessity and, 388–89
von Liszt, Franz, 135–38, 144–45, 170–72, 364–65

Waldron, Jeremy, 11
war. *see* armed conflict; law of war
war debts, non-forcible reprisals and, 242–44
Webster, Daniel, 352–53, 355–56, 361
Westlake, John, 350
Wheaton, Henry, 347
Widenbaum, Paul, 331–32
Williams, Glanville, 29–31

will of the state
  absolute impossibility of performance and, 309–10
  *force majeure* and, 300–03, 310–13, 330–33
  state of necessity and, 368–71, 388–89, 426–29
*Wohlgemuth* affair (1889), 236, 247
Wolff, Karl, 136–38, 144–45, 339–43, 364–65, 368
wrongful acts. *see* internationally wrongful acts

Yankov, Alexander, 390–94
Yasseen, Mustafa, 45–46

Zemanek, Karl, 123
Zimbabwe, on state of necessity, 408–09

BOOKS IN THE SERIES

130 *Justification and Excuse in International Law*
Federica Paddeu

129 *Exclusion from Public Space*
Daniel Moeckli

128 *Provisional Measures Before International Courts and Tribunals*
Cameron Miles

127 *Humanity at Sea: Maritime Migration and the Foundations of International Law*
Itamar Mann

126 *Beyond Human Rights: The Legal Status of the Individual in International Law*
Anne Peters

125 *The Doctrine of Odious Debt in International Law: A Restatement*
Jeff King

124 *Static and Evolutive Treaty Interpretation: A Functional Reconstruction*
Christian Djeffal

123 *Civil Liability in Europe for Terrorism-Related Risk*
Lucas Bergkamp, Michael Faure, Monika Hinteregger and Niels Philipsen

122 *Proportionality and Deference in Investor-State Arbitration: Balancing Investment Protection and Regulatory Autonomy*
Caroline Henckels

121 *International Law and Governance of Natural Resources in Conflict and Post-Conflict Situations*
Daniëlla Dam-de Jong

120 *Proof of Causation in Tort Law*
Sandy Steel

119 *The Formation and Identification of Rules of Customary International Law in International Investment Law*
Patrick Dumberry

118 *Religious Hatred and International Law: The Prohibition of Incitement to Violence or Discrimination*
Jeroen Temperman

117 *Taking Economic, Social and Cultural Rights Seriously in International Criminal Law*
Evelyne Schmid

116 *Climate Change Litigation: Regulatory Pathways to Cleaner Energy?*
Jacqueline Peel and Hari Osofsky

115 *Mestizo International Law: A Global Intellectual History 1842–1933*
Arnulf Becker Lorca

114 *Sugar and the Making of International Trade Law*
Michael Fakhri

113 *Strategically-Created Treaty Conflicts and the Politics of International Law*
Surabhi Ranganathan

112 *Investment Treaty Arbitration as Public International Law: Procedural Aspects and Implications*
Eric De Brabandere

111 *The New Entrants Problem in International Fisheries Law*
Andrew Serdy

110 *Substantive Protection Under Investment Treaties: A Legal and Economic Analysis*
Jonathan Bonnitcha

109 *Popular Governance of Post-Conflict Reconstruction: The Role of International Law*
Matthew Saul

108 *Evolution of International Environmental Regimes: The Case of Climate Change*
Simone Schiele

107 *Judges, Law and War: The Judicial Development of International Humanitarian Law*
Shane Darcy

106 *Religious Offence and Human Rights: The Implications of Defamation of Religions*
Lorenz Langer

105 *Forum Shopping in International Adjudication: The Role of Preliminary Objections*
Luiz Eduardo Ribeiro Salles

104 *Domestic Politics and International Human Rights Tribunals: The Problem of Compliance*
Courtney Hillebrecht

103 *International Law and the Arctic*
Michael Byers

102 *Cooperation in the Law of Transboundary Water Resources*
Christina Leb

101 *Underwater Cultural Heritage and International Law*
Sarah Dromgoole

100 *State Responsibility: The General Part*
James Crawford

99 *The Origins of International Investment Law*
Kate Miles

98 *The Crime of Aggression Under the Rome Statute of the International Criminal Court*
Carrie McDougall

97 *Crimes Against Peace and International Law*
Kirsten Sellars

96 *The Non-Legal in International Law*
Fleur Johns

95 *Armed Conflict and Displacement: The Protection of Refugees and Displaced Persons Under International Humanitarian Law*
Mélanie Jacques

94 *Foreign Investment and the Environment in International Law*
Jorge Viñuales

93 *The Human Rights Treaty Obligations of Peacekeepers*
Kjetil Larsen

92 *Cyberwarfare and the Laws of War*
Heather Harrison Dinniss

91 *The Right to Reparation in International Law for Victims of Armed Conflict*
Christine Evans

90 *Global Public Interest in International Investment Law*
Andreas Kulick

89 *State Immunity in International Law*
Xiaodong Yang

88 *Reparations and Victim Support in the International Criminal Court*
Conor McCarthy

87 *Reducing Genocide to Law: Definition, Meaning, and the Ultimate Crime*
Payam Akhavan

86 *Decolonizing International Law: Development, Economic Growth and the Politics of Universality*
Sundhya Pahuja

85 *Complicity and the Law of State Responsibility*
Helmut Philipp Aust

84 *State Control Over Private Military and Security Companies in Armed Conflict*
Hannah Tonkin

83 *'Fair and Equitable Treatment' in International Investment Law*
Roland Kläger

82 *The UN and Human Rights: Who Guards the Guardians?*
Guglielmo Verdirame

81 *Sovereign Defaults Before International Courts and Tribunals*
Michael Waibel

80 *Making the Law of the Sea: A Study in the Development of International Law*
James Harrison

79 *Science and the Precautionary Principle in International Courts and Tribunals: Expert Evidence, Burden of Proof and Finality*
Caroline E. Foster

78 *Transition from Illegal Regimes in International Law*
Yaël Ronen

77 *Access to Asylum: International Refugee Law and the Globalisation of Migration Control*
Thomas Gammeltoft-Hansen

76 *Trading Fish, Saving Fish: The Interaction Between Regimes in International Law*
Margaret Young

75 *The Individual in the International Legal System: Continuity and Change in International Law*
Kate Parlett

74 *'Armed Attack' and Article 51 of the UN Charter: Evolutions in Customary Law and Practice*
Tom Ruys

73 *Theatre of the Rule of Law: Transnational Legal Intervention in Theory and Practice*
Stephen Humphreys

72 *Science and Risk Regulation in International Law*
Jacqueline Peel

71 *The Participation of States in International Organisations: The Role of Human Rights and Democracy*
Alison Duxbury

70 *Legal Personality in International Law*
Roland Portmann

69 *Vicarious Liability in Tort: A Comparative Perspective*
Paula Giliker

68 *The Public International Law Theory of Hans Kelsen: Believing in Universal Law*
Jochen von Bernstorff

67 *Legitimacy and Legality in International Law: An Interactional Account*
Jutta Brunnée and Stephen J. Toope

66 *The Concept of Non-International Armed Conflict in International Humanitarian Law*
Anthony Cullen

65 *The Principle of Legality in International and Comparative Criminal Law*
Kenneth S. Gallant

64 *The Challenge of Child Labour in International Law*
Franziska Humbert

63 *Shipping Interdiction and the Law of the Sea*
Douglas Guilfoyle

62 *International Courts and Environmental Protection*
Tim Stephens

61 *Legal Principles in WTO Disputes*
Andrew D. Mitchell

60 *War Crimes in Internal Armed Conflicts*
Eve La Haye

59 *Humanitarian Occupation*
Gregory H. Fox

58 *The International Law of Environmental Impact Assessment: Process, Substance and Integration*
Neil Craik

57 *The Law and Practice of International Territorial Administration: Versailles to Iraq and Beyond*
Carsten Stahn

56 *United Nations Sanctions and the Rule of Law*
Jeremy Farrall

55 *National Law in WTO Law: Effectiveness and Good Governance in the World Trading System*
Sharif Bhuiyan

54 *Cultural Products and the World Trade Organization*
Tania Voon

53 *The Threat of Force in International Law*
Nikolas Stürchler

52 *Indigenous Rights and United Nations Standards*
Alexandra Xanthaki

51 *International Refugee Law and Socio-Economic Rights*
Michelle Foster

50 *The Protection of Cultural Property in Armed Conflict*
Roger O'Keefe

49 *Interpretation and Revision of International Boundary Decisions*
Kaiyan Homi Kaikobad

48 *Multinationals and Corporate Social Responsibility: Limitations and Opportunities in International Law*
Jennifer A. Zerk

47 *Judiciaries Within Europe: A Comparative Review*
John Bell

46 *Law in Times of Crisis: Emergency Powers in Theory and Practice*
Oren Gross and Fionnuala Ní Aoláin

45 *Vessel-Source Marine Pollution: The Law and Politics of International Regulation*
Alan Tan

44 *Enforcing Obligations Erga Omnes in International Law*
Christian J. Tams

43 *Non-Governmental Organisations in International Law*
Anna-Karin Lindblom

42 *Democracy, Minorities and International Law*
Steven Wheatley

41 *Prosecuting International Crimes: Selectivity and the International Law Regime*
Robert Cryer

40 *Compensation for Personal Injury in English, German and Italian Law: A Comparative Outline*
Basil Markesinis, Michael Coester, Guido Alpa and Augustus Ullstein

39 *Dispute Settlement in the UN Convention on the Law of the Sea*
Natalie Klein

38 *The International Protection of Internally Displaced Persons*
Catherine Phuong

37 *Imperialism, Sovereignty and the Making of International Law*
Antony Anghie

35 *Necessity, Proportionality and the Use of Force by States*
Judith Gardam

34 *International Legal Argument in the Permanent Court of International Justice: The Rise of the International Judiciary*
Ole Spiermann

32 *Great Powers and Outlaw States: Unequal Sovereigns in the International Legal Order*
Gerry Simpson

31 *Local Remedies in International Law, Second Edition*
C. F. Amerasinghe

30 *Reading Humanitarian Intervention: Human Rights and the Use of Force in International Law*
Anne Orford

29 *Conflict of Norms in Public International Law: How WTO Law Relates to Other Rules of International Law*
Joost Pauwelyn

27 *Transboundary Damage in International Law*
Hanqin Xue

25 *European Criminal Procedures*
Edited by Mireille Delmas-Marty and John Spencer

24 *The Accountability of Armed Opposition Groups in International Law*
Liesbeth Zegveld

23 *Sharing Transboundary Resources: International Law and Optimal Resource Use*
Eyal Benvenisti

22 *International Human Rights and Humanitarian Law*
René Provost

21 *Remedies Against International Organisations*
Karel Wellens

20 *Diversity and Self-Determination in International Law*
Karen Knop

19 *The Law of Internal Armed Conflict*
Lindsay Moir

18 *International Commercial Arbitration and African States: Practice, Participation and Institutional Development*
Amazu A. Asouzu

17 *The Enforceability of Promises in European Contract Law*
James Gordley

16 *International Law in Antiquity*
David J. Bederman

15 *Money Laundering: A New International Law Enforcement Model*
Guy Stessens

14 *Good Faith in European Contract Law*
Reinhard Zimmermann and Simon Whittaker

13 *On Civil Procedure*
J. A. Jolowicz

12 *Trusts: A Comparative Study*
Maurizio Lupoi

11 *The Right to Property in Commonwealth Constitutions*
Tom Allen

10 *International Organizations Before National Courts*
August Reinisch

9 *The Changing International Law of High Seas Fisheries*
Francisco Orrego Vicuña

8 *Trade and the Environment: A Comparative Study of EC and US Law*
Damien Geradin

7 *Unjust Enrichment: A Study of Private Law and Public Values*
Hanoch Dagan

6 *Religious Liberty and International Law in Europe*
Malcolm D. Evans

5 *Ethics and Authority in International Law*
Alfred P. Rubin

4 *Sovereignty Over Natural Resources: Balancing Rights and Duties*
Nico Schrijver

3 *The Polar Regions and the Development of International Law*
Donald R. Rothwell

2 *Fragmentation and the International Relations of Micro-States: Self-Determination and Statehood*
Jorri Duursma

1 *Principles of the Institutional Law of International Organizations*
C. F. Amerasinghe

For EU product safety concerns, contact us at Calle de José Abascal, 56–1°,
28003 Madrid, Spain or eugpsr@cambridge.org.

www.ingramcontent.com/pod-product-compliance
Ingram Content Group UK Ltd.
Pitfield, Milton Keynes, MK11 3LW, UK
UKHW020347060825
461487UK00008B/565